NARRATIVE AND DRAMATIC SOURCES OF SHAKESPEARE

Volume IV
LATER ENGLISH HISTORY PLAYS:
KING JOHN   HENRY IV   HENRY V
HENRY VIII

Volumes published

NARRATIVE
AND DRAMATIC
SOURCES OF
SHAKESPEARE

Edited by
GEOFFREY BULLOUGH
Professor of English Language and Literature,
King's College, London

Volume IV
LATER ENGLISH HISTORY PLAYS:
KING JOHN HENRY IV HENRY V
HENRY VIII

LONDON: Routledge and Kegan Paul
NEW YORK: Columbia University Press
1962

First published 1962
by Routledge and Kegan Paul Ltd
Broadway House, 68–74 Carter Lane
London, E.C.4
and Columbia University Press
Columbia University, New York
Made and printed in Great Britain
by William Clowes and Sons, Limited
London and Beccles

Library of Congress Catalog Card Number: 57–9969

To
John Dover Wilson
this tribute from his former College

PREFACE

THE major historical source for the plays discussed in this volume was Holinshed, but Shakespeare referred sometimes to Hall, Foxe or Stow. As in Volume III, the excerpts from Holinshed are given here in the same order as in his *Third volume of Chronicles*, so as to provide as far as possible a consecutive story of events and to let the reader see how Shakespeare altered chronological sequence for dramatic purposes.

The chief literary sources and analogues include *The Troublesome Raigne* and *The Famous Victories of Henry the fifth*, both of which are printed here in their entirety from the earliest editions with some modernization of punctuation and spelling. *The Famous Victories*, which is a debased version of a major source for all the Henry V plays, is printed in the material for *Henry IV, Part 2*. Shakespeare's debt to Daniel's *Civile Wars* seems to have diminished after *Richard II*, but several relevant passages are cited. I am indebted to the Council of the Malone Society for permission to base the excerpts from *When You See Me, You Know Me* upon the Malone Society reprint.

Analogues for Falstaff are given mainly from the Interludes in order to suggest how greatly Shakespeare transcended the Vice of the old comedies and also how far English comedy had progressed in the sixteenth century.

My debt to previous scholars who have written books and articles about sources, plots and characters grows apace. It is impossible in these volumes to discuss every theory with which I disagree or even to give full reasons for my own conclusions (e.g., that *King John* came after *The Troublesome Raigne*). I am obliged to state briefly my point of view and leave students to make up their own minds by studying the plays themselves and the authorities I refer to. The Bibliography is cumulative and some reference back to that in the previous volume is necessary to save space. I have extended the list of historical works on the Middle Ages and the Tudor period.

CONTENTS OF VOLUME IV

LIST OF ABBREVIATIONS

1. *Shakespeare's Works and Apocrypha*

Ado	*Much Ado about Nothing*
AFev	*Arden of Feversham*
AShrew	*The Taming of A Shrew*
AYL	*As You Like It*
CE	*Comedy of Errors*
Cor	*Coriolanus*
Cym	*Cymbeline*
Ham	*Hamlet*
1H4	*Henry the Fourth, Part I*
2H4	*Henry the Fourth, Part II*
H5	*Henry the Fifth*
1H6	*Henry the Sixth, Part I*
2H6	*Henry the Sixth, Part II*
3H6	*Henry the Sixth, Part III*
H8	*Henry the Eighth*
KJ	*King John*
LComp	*Lover's Complaint*
Lear	*King Lear*
LLL	*Love's Labour's Lost*
Luc	*The Rape of Lucrece*
Mac	*Macbeth*
MM	*Measure for Measure*
MND	*A Midsummer Night's Dream*
More	*Sir Thomas More*
MV	*The Merchant of Venice*
MWW	*The Merry Wives of Windsor*
NobKin	*Two Noble Kinsmen*
Oth	*Othello*
Per	*Pericles*
PhT	*The Phoenix and the Turtle*
PPil	*The Passionate Pilgrim*

R2	*King Richard the Second*
R3	*King Richard the Third*
RJ	*Romeo and Juliet*
Son	*Sonnets*
TA	*Titus Andronicus*
Tem	*The Tempest*
TGV	*Two Gentlemen of Verona*
Tim	*Timon of Athens*
TN	*Twelfth Night*
TrC	*Troilus and Cressida*
TSh	*The Taming of The Shrew*
VA	*Venus and Adonis*
WT	*The Winter's Tale*

2. *Modern Editions and Other Works*

Arden	The Arden Shakespeare
Boas	*The Taming of A Shrew*, edited F. S. Boas
Camb	The New Cambridge edition, edited by J. Dover Wilson, A. Quiller-Couch, &c.
Coll	*Shakespeare's Library*, edited J. Payne Collier, 2 vols.
ELH	*English Literary History* (Johns Hopkins University, Washington D.C.)
ElSt	E. K. Chambers, *The Elizabethan Stage*, 4 vols.
EngHist Soc	English Historical Society

FV	The Famous Victories of Henry V	SAB	Shakespeare Association Bulletin (U.S.A.)
5ActS	T. W. Baldwin, Shakspere's Five-Act Structure	ShJb	Jahrbuch der deutschen Shakespeare—Gesellschaft
Genetics	T. W. Baldwin, On the Literary Genetics of Shakspere's Poems and Sonnets	ShLib	Shakespeare's Library, 6 vols. 2nd Edn. 1875, edited J. P. Collier and W. C. Hazlitt
Hol.	Holinshed's Chronicles	ShQ	Shakespeare Quarterly
JEGP	The Journal of English and Germanic Philology	Sh.Soc. Trans.	Transactions of the New Shakespeare Society
Jest Books	Shakespeare Jest Books, edited W. C. Hazlitt	SPhil	Studies in Philology
Lee	Sir Sidney Lee, Life of Shakespeare	Texas	University of Texas Studies in English
MalSoc	Malone Society Reprints	TLS	The Times Literary Supplement (London)
MedSt	E. K. Chambers, The Medieval Stage, 2 vols.	TR	The Troublesome Raigne of King John
MLN	Modern Language Notes	Var.	The New Variorum edition, ed. H. H. Furness, &c.
MLR	The Modern Language Review	WSh	E. K. Chambers, William Shakespeare, 2 vols.
MPhil	Modern Philology		
New Arden	The Arden Edition of Shakespeare (revised and reset)		
N&Q	Notes & Queries	**3. Other Abbreviations**	
Oxf.	The Oxford Edition of Shakespeare, text by W. J. Craig; Introductory Studies by E. Dowden	Arg	Argument
		Chor	Chorus
		Prol	Prologue
		Rev.	Review
		F	Folio edition
PhilQ	Philological Quarterly	Q	Quarto edition
PMLA	Publications of the Modern Language Association of America	n.d.	No date
		S.R.	The Stationer's Register
RES	The Review of English Studies	STC	A Short-Title Catalogue of Books printed .. 1475–1640 (1950)

KING JOHN

INTRODUCTION

KING JOHN was not printed before the First Folio of 1623, in which it is the first of the Histories. The text there is reasonably good, but there is some confusion in scene headings and speech prefixes which Sir W. W. Greg ascribed to the carelessness of the author's MS, used as F1 copy and containing some annotations made by the book-keeper in the theatre. J. D. Wilson sees evidence of revision and considers that a play first written in 1590 was revised in 1594.

The date of composition is hard to decide. The play was mentioned by Francis Meres in 1598, and several internal allusions place it between 1590 and 1597. Kyd's *Spanish Tragedy* (1589?) refers at I.2.170-2 to a man in a dead lion's skin and a cowardly hare which plucks a dead lion's beard; cf. *King John*, II.1.137-8. This has been taken to suggest an early date; but Shakespeare's memory was long. The jesting mention of 'Basilisco' at I.1.244 refers to *Soliman and Perseda*, a play written between 1589 and 1592 and possibly played later. Parallels have been drawn between the reigns of John and Elizabeth, and they were probably intentional, but we must beware of making them too close. Queen Elizabeth defied the Pope and was excommunicated; she was attacked by a Romish monarch, Philip II of Spain, who tried to invade England; the enemy Armada was wrecked in a storm and the danger averted by the unity of her subjects. But it is hard to believe that the audience was intended to see much further resemblance between the weakling John, whose own mother called him a usurper, and the Queen who got the throne rightfully as the third heir of her father; or between Mary, Queen of Scots, and Prince Arthur. It would have been highly dangerous to remind the audience that Elizabeth had wished to have her rival quietly assassinated rather than formally executed, especially since the dramatic parallel would have made the Queen a murderess in fact as King John was only in intention.

There were resemblances between the situations of Hubert
de Burgh and Secretary Davison, who had persuaded Elizabeth
to sign Queen Mary's death-warrant and had later been made a
scapegoat, although he had taken no other part in the execution. Imprisoned and heavily fined, he was released through
Essex's efforts in 1589 and retired into poverty for a time. To
have recalled that affair (which reflected no great credit on the
Queen) in 1590, when Essex and others were vainly trying to
obtain for Davison the Secretaryship left vacant by Walsingham's death, would have been most inopportune. The parallel
tells against an early date for the play.

If *King John* was written soon after the Armada and with
topicality in mind, it is strange that more was not made of the
destruction of Lewis's supply-vessels, which is dismissed
in two brief references (V.3.9–12; V.5.12–16). Both repeat
a deviation from Holinshed made in *The Troublesome Raigne*
(Part II, 957–63). The allusion, like other resemblances between
past and present, would have point at any time in the nineties.
The French sieges, topical in 1590–2 (cf. 1 *Henry VI*), were not
forgotten later; and the backsliding, after much inconclusive
fighting, of a French king from his anti-papal fraternity with
England, occurred in 1593 when Henry of Navarre turned
Catholic. The parallel between him and Philip of France goes a
little further. Elizabeth continued to help Henry IV with a
few troops, though with diminished enthusiasm; and in 1595/6
the French monarch was said to be intriguing with Albert of
Austria, Philip of Spain, and Pope Clement. England itself
was in renewed peril in 1595 when Spanish galleys from
Brittany made landings in Cornwall and Penzance was burned.
King John's submission to Rome and the delay before he got
his crown back may have reminded the audience of Navarre's
submission and the two years' delay before he was absolved
(17 September, 1595), and then only on condition that he
restore Catholicism throughout France, observe the decrees of
the Council of Trent, and build a monastery in every province.
These and other parallels with the events of 1594–6 seem more
striking than the parallels peculiar to 1590–2.[1] Disillusionment

---

[1] The poisoning of John would be topical after the Lopez affair in 1594 (possibly
mentioned in *MV*). The bad weather in *KJ* has been referred to the bad seasons of
1594–6 (cf. *MND*); but it is described in the chronicles. Constance's grief for
Arthur reminds some critics that Shakespeare's son Hamnet died in 1596, but did

with the war and with political manœuvres for and against peace was rife in 1596, but Essex's party was all for continuing the struggle against the Catholic powers. This would explain why Shakespeare departed from the order of his Histories to rewrite *The Troublesome Raigne*. On 3 June, 1596, Essex sailed with Raleigh and Howard against Cadiz. That this exploit may be obliquely referred to in *King John* suggests that the play was possibly written after that date (cf. II.1.56–75).

The reputation of King John had undergone some changes before the fifteen-nineties.[1] Most of the medieval chroniclers were churchmen who regarded him with disapproval, even horror, because he opposed the Pope and laid heavy exactions on the monastic orders. The *Chronicle of Radulph of Coggeshall*, built up gradually soon after the events related, illustrates how differently an East Anglican monk would regard Richard Cœur-de-Lion and his brother. Polydore Vergil in the early sixteenth century also took a hostile view. But the Protestant John Foxe in his *Actes and Monuments* (1563) praised John for his opposition to the Pope, and while reproving him for surrendering his crown to a papal legate treated him as a martyr because he was poisoned by a monk. The poisoning episode is given below [Text II] because it influenced Shakespeare either directly or indirectly through *The Troublesome Raigne* or through Richard Grafton's *Chronicle* (1569) which incorporated much of Foxe's narrative.

A friend of Foxe's, Bishop John Bale, after being converted to Protestantism, wrote during the reign of Henry VIII his *King Johan*, a violently anti-Catholic play which he revised under Edward VI and again in 1561, probably so that Queen Elizabeth might see it at Ipswich, where it remained in manuscript until the nineteenth century. It was first printed by J. Payne Collier in 1838.[2] Shakespeare can hardly have

---

he need personal bereavement to write like that? Perhaps the dramatist omitted the story ascribing the poisoning of John to the monk's fear that he intended to raise the price of bread, because bread was at famine prices in 1596 and there were riots. Shakespeare would not wish to cast any shadow of blame on the Queen.

[1] Cf. R. Wallerstein, *King John in Fact and Fiction*, University of Pennsylvania [1918].

[2] *Kynge Johan. A Play in Two Parts*, by John Bale, ed. J. P. Collier, Camden Society, 1838. Summarized here from this and the Malone Society Reprint, ed. J. H. P. Pafford, 1931.

known this work, but a summary is given below [Text V] because it started the dramatic tradition to which *King John* belongs. One of the first plays to show 'the history play emerging from the morality'[1] *Kynge Johan* describes the King's campaign against the political and religious abuses caused by bad churchmen, and contains passages of chronicle material, with characters such as Stephen Langton, the Pope, Pandulphus (a Cardinal as in later plays), the monkish poisoner. But all the historical figures except John are aliases or incarnations of clerical vices, Sedition, Usurped Power, Private Wealth, Dissimulation, etc., so the reign of John becomes an illustration of moral dangers facing Henry VIII or Elizabeth. There are many statements of the Tudor attitude to kingship and some topical references.

The year 1591 saw the publication of an anonymous play, *The Troublesome Raigne of John King of England*, which was printed in two parts,[2] quite unnecessarily, for it was obviously written as one piece. The two parts were printed together in 1611 by Valentine Simmes for John Helme, as 'Written by W.Sh.'. A third edition in 1622, printed by Aug. Mathewes for Thomas Dewe, asserted that the play was 'Written by W. Shakespeare'. It has often been suggested since that the play was Shakespeare's in whole or in part. Pope attributed it to Rowley and Shakespeare; Fleay thought that Marlowe had made the plot and Greene, Peele and Lodge wrote the scenes. On the other hand Malone ascribed it to Marlowe alone, and Dugdale Sykes has argued more cogently that it may have been by Peele.[3] Most critics have regarded it as Shakespeare's source-play, and Boswell Stone declared that he relied entirely on *The Raigne* 'without making any independent use of historical sources'.

    [1] Irving Ribner, *The English History Play in the Age of Shakespeare*, Princeton U.P., 1957, pp. 37–40.
    [2] *The Troublesome Raigne of John King of England, with the discoverie of King Richard Cordelions Base Sonne (vulgarly named, The Bastard Fawconbridge): also the death of King John at Swinstead Abbey. As it was (sundry times) publikely acted by the Queenes Majesties Players, in the honourable Citie of London. Imprinted at London for Sampson Clarke, and are to be solde at his shop, on the backeside of the Royall Exchange. 1591.*

    The Second part of the troublesome Raigne of King John, conteining the death of Arthur Plantaginet, the landing of Lewes, and the poysning of King John at Swinstead Abbey. As it was (sundry times) publikely acted by the Queenes Majesties Players, in the honourable citie of London. . . . 1591.

    [3] H. Dugdale Sykes, *Sidelights on Shakespeare*, Stratford, 1919, pp. 99–125.

P. Alexander and E. A. J. Honigmann have taken another
position, and the latter, suggesting 'that three early Shakespearian plays—*John*, *The Shrew* and *Richard III*—may have been
re-written for one company, the Queen's, in the early nineties,
has argued that the two King John plays were written within a
few months of each other in 1590 or 1591, and that *The Raigne*
was written second.[1]

Our views about the date of *King John* and about
Shakespeare's approach to the historical material must depend
on the relationship between his play and *The Raigne*. The
problem, as Mr Honigmann states in his excellent edition, is
'obscure and elusive', and I cannot go into detail here. My
own view (reached after some vacillation) is that *The Raigne*
came first in 1590–1, and that Shakespeare rewrote it in 1596,
using the original plot but changing the emphasis, and above
all the style, adding features to give it new topicality, reducing
its length from 3081 lines to 2715, but expanding the first part
of *The Raigne* (from 1840 lines to 1987) at the expense of the
second part (from 1196 lines to 728). As Sir E. K. Chambers
thought, he probably kept the book of *The Raigne* before him
and consulted it frequently, so although not many lines are
kept in their entirety, 'in some 150 places a few words from
The Raigne are picked up and used, by no means always in the
same context'.[2] Shakespeare worked rapidly, and it may well
be that some of the surprising omissions he made, particularly
towards the end of the piece, were to prevent the play's becoming too long. Others were caused by the shift in emphasis
already mentioned. To help readers make up their own minds
about the relationship between the two plays and the major
historical sources I give the relevant passages from Holinshed
[Text I], and Hall [Text III], something of Foxe [Text II],
two passages from Radulph of Coggeshall [Text IV] and the
whole of *The Raigne* [Text VI].

The text of *The Raigne* as it has come down to us is greatly
marred, but the outlines of story and character are clear
enough, and the play as a whole is more satisfactory than *The
Famous Victories of Henry V* on which Shakespeare drew for
his later trilogy. It seems to have been built on Holinshed
and on Foxe's *Actes and Monuments* (though most of the latter's

[1] E. A. J. Honigmann, *New Arden*, 1954, Introduction, lvi.   [2] *WSh* I.367.

material was taken over by Grafton in his *Chronicle at Large* (1569)). John Elson, who examined the sources of *The Raigne*,[1] believed that Bale's *Kyng Johan* was known to the author. But perhaps he knew Matthew Paris's *Historia Majora* (1571), which was more accessible, and found there the comparison of John with King David which appears in Bale (1104–7; 1630–3) and *The Raigne* (II.viii.1078–80). Polydore Vergil's chronicle may have inspired the Bastard's account of his escape from the Wash:

> My selfe upon a Galloway right free, well pacde,
> Outstript the flouds . . .   (II.836–7)

For Vergil wrote that John 'ordered one of his men, who had a spirited and active horse, to explore the shallows' and that 'this man got over because he accidentally found the ford whereas the rest of the army plunged in indiscriminately and got into difficulties'.

Obviously the author of *The Raigne* went to some pains to consult several authorities, as did other historical dramatists before Shakespeare.[2] Like Bale he makes John a victim of clerical intrigue and French ambition. The Catholic clergy are his natural enemies, his exactions are excused, his seizure of their goods is made comic, with broad satire on their alleged unchastity; the story of his death by poison is given in detail. On the other hand, perhaps because Holinshed's less favourable account is combined with Bale's, he is made a weak and violent man. He orders the blinding of Arthur, presumably meaning the boy to die of it, and he has little sense of the morality of his actions, though when forced to submit to Rome he says:

> Thy sinnes are farre too great to be the man
> T'abolish Pope and Popery from thy Realme   (II.278–9)

and when dying he sees his life as 'a catalogue of sin/Wrote by a fiend in marble characters'. After he yields to Pandulph nothing goes right for him. Troubles beset him; he fails in war, and falls ill with a fever before he is poisoned by the Monk.

---

[1] 'Studies in the King John plays' (*J. Q. Adams Memorial Studies*, ed. J. G. McManaway, Washington, 1948).

[2] Thus *Jack Straw* was based on Grafton, Holinshed and Stow, according to H. Schütt.

The inconsistencies of his character are not harmonized in any coherent moral view.

The Bastard Faulconbridge is introduced for comic effect but also to show that despite the failure of the erring monarch the spirit of his brother Richard I—that is, the true spirit of England—still survives. Philip has indeed the geniality and dynamic energy of his father. His introduction was probably initially suggested by Holinshed's statement that 'Philip, bastard sonne to king Richard . . . killed the vicount of Limoges, in revenge of his father's death' (*inf.* 28). But why was he called Philip Faulconbridge? Later writers also imagined a connection between Richard I and the Faulconbridge family. In *Looke About You* (1599), a piece related to the Robin Hood plays, Prince Richard assails (in vain) the virtue of Sir Richard Faulconbridge's wife; and in the romance *The Famous History of George, Lord Fauconbridge, Bastard Son to Richard Cordelion* (1616), the hero is the offspring of an affair with Austria's daughter Claribel. These pieces came after Shakespeare and may derive from our plays, but there may have been some tradition behind the connection. The 'discovery' and choice in *The Raigne* probably came, however, from Hall's account of Dunois, the Bastard of Orleans [Text III]. Shakespeare may have given added point to his version of the scene (I.1) by referring back to that source, which he must have read when writing *1 Henry VI*.[1] There is a reference to a bastard of Lord Falconbridge in *3 Henry VI*, I.1.239, as keeping the narrow seas against Edward IV. This man was 'the valyaunt capitayne, a man of no lesse courage than audacitie (who for hys evyll conditions was such an apte person, that a more meeter could not be chosen to set all the world in a broyle . . .)' (Grafton). In making Philip a worshipper of Commodity, Shakespeare may have recalled this celebrated pirate, Thomas Nevill. But Nevill came to an evil end.

It was long ago suggested by W. Lloyd[2] that Faulconbridge may be partly based on 'a man of great stomach and more rashnesse' (Hol.), Faukes de Brent (Falco in Latin), who was held in great estimation by King John and helped him first

---

[1] Peele has been thought by some critics to have had a hand in *1H6*. If so, and if he wrote *The Raigne*, this incident is a link between them.

[2] Watkiss Lloyd, *Essays on Shakespeare*, 1875, p. 196.

in the Marches of Wales and then in the civil war, being rewarded for his ferocious energy by the gift of many castles, including Bedford. Later he rebelled against Henry III and was besieged in Bedford. He was pardoned but exiled in 1224, and died of poison a year later on his way from Rome to England, 'making an end of his unconstant life, which from the time that he came to years of discretion, was never bent to quietnes' (Holinshed). The portrait of this man in Radulph of Coggeshall is translated below [Text IVb]. The parallel with Faulconbridge is remote, though a hint may have been taken from this loyal, bellicose follower of King John.

Faulconbridge has a romantic heroic quality, indicated in his determination to retrieve from Austria the lionskin which Richard I was said to have got when, as a captive, he killed the beast by thrusting his hand down its throat and tearing out its heart.[1] He speaks heroically, encourages John against his clerical and secular enemies, and when John collapses he takes command, pleads his uncle's cause before the nobles, and tries to hearten him with the significant words:

> God cheere my Lord, King *Richards* fortune hangs
> Upon the plume of warlike *Philips* helme . . .   (II.715–6)

The conception is vigorous and rugged, but the Bastard is not the hero of the play, and England's final salvation is brought not by him so much as by Melun's revelation, the sinking of the French supply ships, Pandulph's support and the accession of Henry III. The author of *The Raigne* was willing to embroider historical facts but not to romanticize them so far as to turn Faulconbridge into the complete epic hero. The main purpose is to show the need of unity, and this doctrine is stated at the close by both the Dauphin and the Bastard.

History in *The Raigne* is arbitrarily rearranged to suit the main topics, which are: the treacherous ambitions of France, the Pope's enmity, the falling off of the barons (ascribed to the King's treatment of Arthur), and the consequent shameful invasion of England. Magna Carta is not mentioned. The issues are simplified to a degree not found in *Henry VI* or *Richard II*, yet they are scarcely made clear enough—another reason for believing that Shakespeare did not invent the plot.

[1] Cf. *KJ* I.1.265–7.

The construction is loose but there is a certain coarse vigour in the action and characterization. The author crammed great variety into his play. As John Munro wrote:

> 'he gives us three battles, disputes of monarchs, a coronation, prophecies and marvels, a betrothal, humour in a friary, plots, rebellions, proclamations, the sufferings of innocence, a death-scene, some bombast and satire, and much patriotic feeling'.[1]

The working-out in detail, however, is clumsy; there is much repetition, especially of anti-papal expressions, and the style is usually flat or turgid. There are reminiscences of Marlowe, as the writer of the address 'To the Gentlemen Readers' noted when he asked for courtesy towards a play which gave, instead of 'the Scythian Tamburlaine', 'A warlike Christian and your countryman'. Senecan rhetoric occurs, e.g. when Faulconbridge is moved to regain his father's lionskin (I.556–79), and when he abuses the fleeing Limoges (I.656–69). On the other hand an agreeable energy marks much of his dialogue with his mother (I.315–421), and his ejaculation when he hears Blanche being offered in marriage to Lewes, 'Swounds Madam, take an English Gentleman!', anticipates the blunt wooing of Shakespeare's Henry V. The piece is far more than 'a hotchpotch of a numerous collection of old plays' (Honigmann), but it certainly lacks unity and economy.

The following running comparison may assist readers in considering the close relationship between *The Troublesome Raigne* and *King John*.

In *The Raigne* the author's purpose was to modernize Bale's presentation of John as a pre-Reformation opponent of Church abuses and papal power and to use him as a mirror in which all would see the dangers of domestic dissension and foreign interference. Parallels were also drawn between the reigns—though not the characters—of John, Henry VIII and Elizabeth. In handling history the dramatist brings together conflicts and incidents which were in fact widely separated. Historically the first four years were largely concerned with John's right to rule and with his relations with Arthur of Brittany, son of his

---

[1] *The Troublesome Reign of King John*, ed. F. J. Furnivall and John Munro (The Shakespeare Library), 1913, xxii.

elder brother Geoffrey of Anjou. The first war of 1199 ended
in a peace treaty (May, 1200) which married John's niece, the
Spanish princess Blanche, to the Dauphin Lewis. John gave up
much French territory. In 1202 the peace was broken when King
Philip urged further claims for Arthur. This led to Arthur's
capture, and to his death in 1203. A second phase began in
1205 with the dispute over the Archbishopric of Canterbury,
which came to a head when the Pope highhandedly rejected
the two rival candidates and appointed Stephen Langton,
whom the King rejected because of his French sympathies.
John's excommunication and the interdiction of England
followed (1208), and in 1212 Phillip was invited to dispossess
him. The King's inability to finance his foreign wars, despite the
exactions which increased his unpopularity, forced him at
Ascensiontide, 1213, to surrender his crown to the papal
legate and receive it again as from the Pope. The last phase of
the reign began when the newly absolved monarch alienated
his nobles so thoroughly that they forced him to sign Magna
Carta (1215). When it was obvious that he would not keep his
promises the nobles invited Philip's help, promising to make
Lewis king in John's place. John's sudden death occurred
before the invaders from France had been squarely faced.
War ended two years later (1218) after the Battle of Lincoln
and the destruction of a French supply fleet by Hubert de
Burgh.

These three phases can be traced in both plays, but in both
they are made to overlap. There is justification for this, since
French enmity ran throughout the reign, and John quarrelled
frequently with the monks from the time (1200) when the
Cistercians refused to pay the tax which he levied to pay relief
to King Philip. In 1203 the Pope protested that John had
refused to allow a papal legate to enter his lands, and that he
had interfered in episcopal elections. But the plays make
Arthur's death (1203) the immediate cause of the nobles'
rebellion (1216) and both occur just before John surrenders
his crown (1213).

The Troublesome Raigne begins with Queen Elinor regretting
the death of Richard I and welcoming the accession of John.
King John starts when the new king is at once (unhistorically)
faced with demands brought by Chatillon, on Arthur's behalf,

for 'the Kingdom of England and the lordship of Ireland, Poitiers, Anjou, Touraine and Maine'. (Holinshed (*inf.* 25) suggests that Arthur was already 'received of' the last three.) John refuses, and Elinor asks Arthur to leave France and 'come to me and to his Unkle here'. The unhistorical episode of Philip Faulconbridge's dispute with his brother and his choice of bastardy follows. Already in both plays the King's desire to make the monastic orders pay for the war is adumbrated. It was probably suggested by the quarrel with the Cistercians which soon followed and by the fact that they were heavily fined in 1210.

Next both plays show the meeting of Austria and France before Angiers. In *The Raigne* Arthur is more realistic than his mother, who hopes that John may be willing to surrender something to keep peace. Chatillon, who has crossed to France on the same vessel as John, brings news of imminent war. In both plays Philip is surprised by this speedy invasion. Shakespeare makes more of Austria in this scene (II.1) so as to make his downfall later more complete. He uses one line from *The Raigne*, 'With them a bastard of the King's deceas'd' (65), and describes more fully the volunteers, who, like those of Essex in 1591 and 1596, were come against the Catholic powers. John enters with his forces, and both plays revel in defiance, particularly between Elinor and Constance. There are references to the will of Richard I which made John, not Arthur, King of England. In *King John* Philip states the case against John more fully, for Shakespeare throughout sees John as monarch *de facto* rather than *de jure*; hence his sympathetic attitude to the rebel barons later. Both plays confuse Limoges with Austria, following the example of a medieval verse-romance, *Kynge Rycharde de Cuer du Lyon*, printed by Wynkyn de Worde (1528).[1] In *The Raigne* Faulconbridge utters lengthy Senecan threats when he sees his father's captor wearing the lionskin, and Blanche hints that she will favour him if he wins the trophy. Shakespeare has no such by-play and Faulconbridge addresses Austria briefly but satirically. In *The Raigne* Philip

---

[1] Cf. G. R. Needler, *Richard Cœur de Lion in Literature* (1890), 56–7, and *New Arden*, xx–xxi. Richard I died of wounds while besieging the castle of Widomar, Viscount of Limoges in 1199. Leopold, Duke of Austria, who had imprisoned Richard, died in 1195.

opposes John's claim to Angiers. John expects the townsmen
to offer him allegiance, and is surprised when he is refused
entrance until he can prove himself rightful King. Philip
then claims the city on Arthur's behalf, but is also refused, and
a set battle follows to prove which is right. In *King John* Philip
states his claim to England and its French possessions before
suggesting that they see whose title Angiers will admit. The
two kings interrupt each other. John asserts that he comes
as a saviour and Philip mixes threats with appeals to loyalty.
The citizens are unmoved. Shakespeare's method here is more
sophisticated, though a less chivalric atmosphere is attempted,
and the Bastard appends a burlesque anticlimax to John's
heroics (273–9), thus preparing for his cynical realism in the
'Commodity' speech.

The *Raigne* shows the Bastard chasing Limoges, regaining his
father's lionskin, and soliloquizing turgidly over 'The first
freehold that *Richard* left his sonne'. Our text of Shakespeare
omits this incident, and the lionskin is not mentioned in III.2,
when the Bastard has slain Austria. Here *The Raigne* is more
effective.

When after indecisive battle the heralds of the 'two victorious
princes' demand the town's surrender, the Citizens ask for a
parley, presumably to suggest that Blanche marry Lewes.
Shakespeare has this, but omits a chivalric passage between
Blanche and Faulconbridge, who rants in favour of more
fighting. In Shakespeare the Bastard expands his suggestion
that the two monarchs unite against Angiers; he delights at
the thought that Austria and the French will injure each other
by their opposed fire, and he mocks the Citizen's rhetoric.
There is no suggestion that he ever aspired to Blanche's hand
or was half-promised her by Queen Elinor. But he jeers at the
lovemaking of Lewis, who is not 'so vile a lout' as he says.
Shakespeare adds the fine soliloquy by which the Bastard ends
the Act and shows himself detached from the aspirations of
John and Philip and contemptuous of political manœuvres
which were very topical in the fifteen-nineties.

In *The Raigne* Constance is present during the making of the
Franco-Spanish match. Her protests are more striking in *King
John* where she is kept away until III.1, when she refuses to
attend the wedding. In both plays the wedding party comes to

her. In *King John* her railings against Philip would be apt in 1596 when Henry IV was suspected of drifting towards a league with Philip of Spain (III.1.99–107). Shakespeare omits the Bastard's challenge of Austria to single combat, which the latter refuses even when Faulconbridge is made Duke of Normandy (950). Instead Constance abuses Austria as a coward ('Thou little valiant, great in villainy' (116)), and Faulconbridge tells him repeatedly to 'hang a calfskin on those recreant limbs!' This seems more like Shakespeare taking a hint from *The Raigne* but avoiding direct imitation, than *vice versa*.

Pandulph's demands and John's reply are given in prose in *The Raigne*, in verse in *King John*. The King's assertion that he owes no homage to the Pope but will 'raigne next under God, supreame head both over spirituall and temrall' (*TR* 981–2) may owe something to the account of Alexander the Mason (Cementarius), which precedes in Holinshed (*inf.* 37). Shakespeare may also have remembered Foxe, whose antipapal language is reflected in III.1.163–71. John's description of himself as standing alone against the Pope recalls Bale's and Foxe's view of him.

In *The Raigne* Philip abandons the English alliance with little protest ('I must obey the Pope') but Shakespeare elaborates the discussion of oath-breaking so as to bring out Pandulph's casuistry (III.1.224–97). He also provides symmetrical contrast in the appeals of Blanche and Constance for and against peace.

In the battle which follows, the Bastard kills Austria, glorying in the deed in *The Raigne*, taking it casually in *King John* III.2.3–4. Whereas *The Raigne* moves to the French side and shows Queen Elinor, taken prisoner, brawling with Constance and honourably treated by Arthur, Shakespeare (like Holinshed, *inf.* 30) leaves it uncertain whether she was captured or only 'assailed', and the Bastard briefly says, 'I rescued her', where the other play shows her rescued by John himself. Shakespeare likewise does not show the capture of Arthur, and in paralleling the next scene in *The Raigne* where John orders Faulconbridge to 'Ransack the Abbeys, Cloysters, Priories' (1107), he omits the veto on appeals to Rome 'for justice and for law'.

Neither play shows Arthur making 'a presumptuous answer'

at Falaise when invited 'to forsake his friendship and alliance with the French King' (cf. Holinshed, *inf.* 31). There is thus less excuse than in the Chronicles for the King's command to Hubert, during a long and subtle interview, to remove the boy (*KJ* III.3.19–67). In *The Raigne* John merely explains that Arthur will never give up his claim, and 'I would he livde not to remember it', and instructs Hubert with the cryptic hint:

> 'Hubert keepe him safe,
> For on his life doth hang thy Soveraignes crowne,
> But in his death consists thy Soveraignes blisse' (I.Sc.ix,
> 1119–21),

promising to send further word soon. How inferior to the skilful manner in which Shakespeare's John weaves his way through indirections to the laconic climax: 'Death' . . . 'A grave.'

Next the French are seen mourning their losses. In *The Raigne* Pandulph speaks a funeral epitaph on Austria (not found in Shakespeare), before Constance comes to lament her son's capture. The legate then urges the Dauphin against England, asserting that Arthur is 'safe', i.e. sure to be put out of the way by John. These details are developed at length by Shakespeare, who gives Constance a long 'passion' (III.4.23–105) and Pandulph a 'politic' prophecy of the inevitable removable of Arthur and the opportunity which will be afforded Lewis by John's consequent loss of popularity (*ibid.* 112–83). Shakespeare's Cardinal thinks that the Bastard's spoliation of the monasteries will also raise enemies against the English king (III.4.171–7). Maybe this reference is an allusion to the comic scene in *The Raigne* (1181ff) in which Faulconbridge makes a friar open an Abbot's treasure-chest and finds a nun inside, whereupon she tells of a 'press full of plate and money', which proves to contain Friar Lawrence.[1] The scene in *The Raigne* is written in so archaic a style that one may wonder whether it was transferred from an earlier play, not necessarily about King John, or whether it was written as a parody of the Morality play manner. It is followed by the discovery by Faulconbridge of Peter the Prophet, who is arrested and taken to the King. Shakespeare omits this also.

---

[1] The name is common enough, but did Shakespeare whimsically recall this episode when he had to name the benevolent friend of lovers in *Romeo and Juliet*? The pious herbalist must have turned over a new leaf in the meantime.

In both plays the attempted blinding of Arthur departs from Holinshed, who declared that 'certaine persons' went to Falaise to do the deed (*inf.* 32), that Hubert de Burgh was the prince's keeper, and that when Arthur strongly resisted one of his torturers (the others abandoning their horrid task), Hubert resolved to save him. In *The Raigne* (1314ff) it is evening; Hubert tells the three attendants that he regrets being the executioner, but that he will carry out the King's command once the youth is bound. The attendants do not protest, for he has shown them his warrant to put out Arthur's eyes. His dialogue with the prince is rhetorically constructed, containing lines of stichomythia. When Arthur accepts his fate he begs Hubert to 'Conclude the period with a mortall stab.' Hubert is torn between obedience to John and obedience to God. Virtue triumphs, and he decides to tell John that Arthur died of the 'languor' (a word used by Holinshed, *inf.* 33). In *King John* it is morning. Hubert at first shows no compunction though one executioner hopes that his warrant 'will bear out the deed'. The warrant is not read aloud as in *The Raigne*, but its purport is made clear by Arthur's horror. The dialogue contains much pathos, for Arthur is not a moralizing young man but a small boy crying out in his innocence ('Is it my fault that I was Geoffrey's son?'), referring to his past kindness to Hubert, and terrified of being bound.[1] There is also an indulgence in fancy, a play on words 'eyes', 'tongue', 'fire', which recalls *Richard II*, *Love's Labour's Lost*, etc. Shakespeare's scene is so full of tenderness and intensity that I cannot believe that *The Raigne* would not have taken more from *King John* had it been written second.

Honigman (*New Arden*) thinks that Shakespeare probably knew Coggeshall's *Chronicle*, of which a relevant passage is given below [Text IVa]. There are certain parallels, but nothing that Shakespeare could not have built on *The Raigne* and on Holinshed, who condensed Coggeshall's account of the end of Arthur.[2]

The next scene begins with discussion of John's second Coronation.[3] In *The Raigne* it has not yet occurred, and Pembroke urges the King not to raise doubts of his rights by

[1] Arthur was born in 1187. [2] But see *New Arden*, 163–7.
[3] This took place in October, 1200. John was crowned a third time in March, 1201.

being crowned again. Later John gives a long explanation, and, after Faulconbridge has announced the success of his mission and the bringing of Peter, he is crowned on the stage. The lords appeal for 'The libertie of Ladie Constance Sonne'; the five moons (1200) are seen in the sky. This introduces Peter, who interprets the mysterious omen (nothing of this in Holinshed), and tells the King that he will lose his royal state 'ere Ascension day/Have brought the Sunne unto his usuall height'. He is arrested, and John refuses to release Arthur. Hubert announces the prince's death and Essex and Pembroke leave the King's side. Realizing his danger John reviles Hubert for killing Arthur, but without expatiating on his own passionate impulsiveness. Hubert informs him that Arthur lives and John bids him tell the lords.

In *King John*, IV.2, the Coronation is over and Salisbury and Pembroke regret it. John does not explain its necessity, though he says he has given some reasons and will give others (40–43). He promises to free Arthur, but Hubert enters and announces his death. Salisbury and Pembroke leave in disgust, and the King says, 'I repent' (103). His gloomy thoughts are increased by news of the French landing, of the deaths of Constance and his own mother Elinor (actually she died in April, 1204, Constance in 1201). Now Peter of Pomfret is introduced and arrested. Shakespeare relates the five moons to Arthur's death rather than to Peter's prophecies (182–202). Perhaps with the Davison affair in mind he makes John expatiate on the need of a king's servants to make allowances for the fluctuations of his temper. But Holinshed had much to say about the anger of princes (*inf.* 32, 49).

The next scene follows Holinshed's account in the main, representing Arthur's death in leaping from the walls—not, however, into the Seine but on to English ground. *King John* cuts down *The Raigne*'s account by more than half, and places before the discovery of the body the political talk which follows it in the other play, substitutes Bigot for Essex,[1] and introduces the Bastard to advise loyalty and moderation and to

---

[1] This substitution was probably to avoid connecting one of Essex's name with treason. In *TR* Essex makes a long speech advocating rebellion (II.378–419). The change is less likely to have been made in 1590/1 than in 1596 when Essex's ambition was suspected by his rivals and Shakespeare was one of his admirers.

take part in the questioning of de Burgh. Shakespeare's handling of this scene is so much more exciting, as he shows Salisbury on the point of killing Hubert, the latter attempting to prove his innocence to Faulconbridge, and the Bastard left behind to soliloquize on 'the thorns and dangers of this world', that once more it is hard to believe that *The Raigne*, if written afterwards, would not have retained more of the material.

The Raigne has a scene (II.110ff) between John and the Prophet in which the King asks Peter to unsay his prophecies. The news of Arthur's death convinces John that his fears were groundless, and the prophet has just been hanged when the Bastard comes to announce that, 'The Nobles have elected Lewes King.' On hearing this John's 'motions are as passions of a madman'. He turns against his only loyal follower, Faulconbridge; he describes the effect of the papal interdict, orders the Bastard to spy on the nobles and 'confound their divelish plots and damn'd devices', and promises to amend his life. But immediately he sends a messenger to bring Pandulph, who, refusing to be satisfied with an offer to go on a Crusade, demands the surrender of his 'crown and diadem'. John agrees when he learns that a French fleet 'is descried on the coast of Kent', since he must get the Pope's help if he is to keep his throne.

Shakespeare omits all this, and his play loses clarity thereby. Maybe he wished to make less of the ecclesiastical motif and more of the baronial and French strains in John's reign; and he did not want to emphasize an English monarch's kneeling submission to a papal legate. Likewise he omits the long and interesting scene in *The Raigne* (II.iii) at St Edmundsbury, whither a 'holy troop' of conspirators come 'in pilgrim's habit' to hear Essex, Pembroke and Salisbury give reasons for dethroning John and 'planting Lewes in the Usurper's roome', ignorant that John has submitted to Rome and will have the Pope's support. The Bastard insists that it is a crime

> To wrest such pettie wrongs, in tearmes of right
> Against a King anoynted by the Lord . . .
> [For] subjects may not take in hand revenge,
> And rob the heavens of their proper power. (*TR* II.461–5)

Calling them 'A troop of traitors, food for hellish fiends', he remains true to King John and the (Tudor) principle of

2—N.D.S.S. 4

monarchy. Lewes enters, gives a romantic version of his arrival in London by sea (contrast Holinshed, *inf.* 45), and welcomes 'this religious league / A holy knot of Catholique consent' (terms which would irritate and amuse an English audience in the days of the Catholic League). He and the barons swear fidelity to each other, but, left alone with Melun, he swears treachery to 'the English traitors' once he is enthroned. This is an excellent scene and by omitting most of it Shakespeare lost a dramatic opportunity.

The fifth Act of *King John* opens with the symbolic surrender and re-taking of the crown, omitting the period of five days during which Pandulph held the King in suspense. *The Raigne* (II.632ff) shows only the handing back of the crown. Shakespeare's King recalls Peter of Pomfret's prophecy and weakly pretends that it was untrue because his surrender of the crown 'is but voluntary'. *The Raigne* does not remind us of Peter. There the symbolic coronation is followed by the entrance of the enemy forces, and Pandulph's failure to persuade Lewes to withdraw; he excommunicates the rebel peers; Faulconbridge tries to hearten John and takes over command. Shakespeare moves to the rebel camp (V.2), where, after the oath has been taken, Salisbury laments his need to bring civil war to his country. (The audience might well remember the very different Salisbury of *1 Henry VI*.) The Dauphin commends him with promise of rewards. Pandulph tries vainly to persuade Lewis to withdraw, and Faulconbridge comes and offers defiance. In this scene the patriotic note is sounded more strongly than in *The Raigne*, yet the ambiguous position of the nobles is made clear and their grief is stressed more than their excuses for rebellion.

Battle follows. In *The Raigne* (II.721ff) Melun, who has played an active part in the previous scene in opposing the Cardinal's efforts for peace, enters wounded, and tells Salisbury and Pembroke that Lewes intends to kill them all should he win the throne. He betrays this secret because he wishes to die guiltless and because 'my Grandsire was an Englishman'. He urges them to submit to John, and this the rebel peers decide to do. Shakespeare uses this material in V.4. In *The Raigne* (II.786) King John is carried in bemoaning his life and sick with a fever; Faulconbridge brings evil tidings that their troops, hearing of the King's illness, have fled, and he has had a narrow escape when most of the men were swallowed up by the sea in the Wash. John makes for Swinstead, hoping to get better there. Shakespeare (V.3) shortens and alters this considerably. Hubert says that the day is going badly, but a Messenger brings word that the Dauphin's supply fleet has been wrecked on the Goodwin Sands, and this news is making the French retire. The Wash disaster is deferred until V.6. The object clearly is to balance ill with good news, to give an assurance of ultimate victory. The tension continues in V.4 where Salisbury and Pembroke are already afraid of defeat at the Bastard's hands before Melun tells his grim tale.

The second part of II.vi in *The Raigne* shows John being welcomed to Swinstead by the Abbot and his Monks. One of them, Thomas, resolves to poison the King in revenge for his misdeeds against the Church, and is absolved beforehand by the Abbot. Shakespeare omits this entirely. Reverting to the fortunes of war *The Raigne* (II.930ff) presents Lewes rejoicing in success, grieving over Melun's death and the staunch defence of Dover Castle, and looking forward to the time when 'The poorest peasant of the Realme of *Fraunce* / Shall be a maister ore an English Lord.' He hears that the English Lords have left him, and that his supply fleet has been lost; on the other hand that John has been drowned in the Wash; he is encouraged by the thought that he is now King of England. This corresponds to Shakespeare's V.5, where the knowledge of the loss of Melun and the fleet is compensated for by the fact that the French are 'Last in the field, and almost lords of it', and that John has fled.

The Raigne now (II.983ff) shows the poisoning of John (as he dines with the Abbot and Faulconbridge) by the Monk who tastes the fatal draught first so that he dies before the King. Faulconbridge kills the Abbot at once, and the King in two long speeches admits his shameful life, 'repleat with rage and tyranie', holds himself responsible for the sudden death of Arthur, and declares that since he yielded to Pandulph 'Nor he nor his have prospered on the earth.' In dying he prophesies that his line will produce one

> Whose armes shall reach unto the gates of *Rome*,
> And with his feete treade downe the Strumpets pride

—Henry VIII no doubt. The Bastard comments that his murder is 'the fruite of Poperie'.

Shakespeare (V.6) does not represent the poisoning, but has Hubert tell it, very briefly, to Faulconbridge when the latter approaches the Abbey at night after losing half his army in the Lincoln Washes. Hubert mentions that the heir, Prince Henry, has been brought to his father by the repentant lords. Both plays introduce the Prince in person. In *The Raigne* (II.1106) he brings the revolted barons to his father in time for the King to raise his dying hand in forgiveness and to see Henry crowned his successor. Informed of the Dauphin's approach they arm against him, but Pandulph goes to bring him to parley, and in the final scene (II.1143ff) Lewes agrees to give up his claim on England now that John is dead and 'the Barons cleave unto their King'; for he says, no foreigner will ever 'win this Island, *Albion*, / Unless he have a partie in the Realme' to help him by treason. So the war ends, John will be buried at Worcester, and after the crown is set on Henry's head the Bastard declares

> Let *England* live but true within it selfe,
> And all the world can never wrong her State.

In *King John* (V.7) the Prince inquires about his father's condition and John is brought in, raging in fever. The Bastard arrives just in time to speak to him, but John dies ere hearing of the Wash mishap. The Bastard wishes to take up the fight against Lewis but is told by Salisbury that Pandulph has brought peace offers from the Dauphin. John must be buried at Worcester, and Prince Henry will be crowned. The nobles do him homage, and Faulconbridge ends the play with a short patriotic speech.

Comparison between the two plays shows how much Shakespeare, while preserving the plot with its cumbrous attempt at compressing events extending from 1199 to 1218 into intelligible shape, gained in economy. He made numerous omissions. He cut out the Bastard's hope of winning Blanche, maybe as an improbable excrescence on the political plot, maybe to preserve some notion of the Bastard as an inspired 'outsider'. But, as E. Rose suggested,[1] his mockery of Lewis's lovemaking and his abuse of him as 'so vile a lout', may be a

[1] 'Shakespeare as an Adapter', in *TR* facsimile, Pt. I, ed. C. Praetorius, 1888.

vestige of this element in *The Raigne*. Moreover, Shakespeare did not account for Faulconbridge's hatred of Austria by recalling the latter's ill-treatment of Richard I; but did he need to do so? Everyone knew the story of Richard's imprisonment and ransom. Shakespeare also kept the mother off stage during the bastardy discussion, probably to avoid making her untruthful as well as to make her dialogue with her son more plausible.

The failure to use Faulconbridge's desire to regain his father's lionskin, the ennoblement which proved Austria's cowardice, and his two encounters with Austria in battle, was perhaps due to a desire not to romanticize the story, and to avoid episodes not essential to the main theme. Compression may explain why the capture and release of Queen Elinor and the capture of Prince Arthur are not shown. The searching of the monastery and nunnery has been condemned by critics as vulgar. It is a commonplace but amusing piece of satiric buffoonery. Shakespeare omits it because he rarely satirizes the Church directly, and the scene distracts from the seriousness of the political conflict between John and the Pope.

Less explicable except by assuming hasty condensation of *The Raigne* are some of the later omissions, in particular the discussion between the nobles at St Edmundsbury, which is looked forward to at IV.3.11–13 and assumed to have been held before V.2. This type of scene was used in *Richard II* and *Henry IV*; but Shakespeare here avoided introducing the barons' political resentment at John's inroads on their ancient privileges which in fact led to Magna Carta and its aftermath. For him their revolt must spring from virtuous disgust at John's maltreatment of Arthur, and the scene would therefore repeat ideas already known to the audience. And Shakespeare did not want his Faulconbridge to inveigh too often or weightily against Salisbury, Pembroke, etc. He wished to show them in a terrible dilemma, as good men rebelling against an erring monarch for a righteous reason, yet in so doing putting themselves in the wrong. Note that Shakespeare omits the long didactic passages in *The Raigne* which preach endurance of tyranny. He lets events speak for themselves. Salisbury is aware of the woe he is bringing to his country but he persists until the eleventh hour. The Bastard does not call him and his friends traitors until V.2;

and soon they return to their rightful allegiance and are forgiven. But the lesson has been learned, what great evil follows when even for good reasons disunity in the state is fostered and the foreigner let in.

Nevertheless one may wish that Shakespeare had made more of the meeting at St Edmundsbury and had not scamped John's end by omitting the poisoning scene and alluding to it so briefly. Was it through dislike of anticlerical satire, or a feeling that the method of John's removal did not matter, or just a wish to finish the play quickly? 'Every change from his source that Shakespeare made was for a greater dramatic effect and finer dramatic truth of character.'[1] This is a debatable assertion.

That *The Raigne* includes so many more scenes, incidents and motifs is one reason for thinking that Shakespeare came second; and the nature of his divergences supports the idea. Often *King John* reads like a running commentary on *The Raigne*, as if the reviser had at times deliberately refrained from repeating its effects, or its material, but had taken them for granted and alluded briefly to them while putting the stress in a different place.

There can be no doubt after Honigmann's searching inquiry[2] that Shakespeare consulted Holinshed, though he preferred to follow the unhistorical medley of *The Raigne* rather than make a new plot.[3] Numerous passages in *King John* become clearer by reference to *The Raigne*—e.g. the reasons for the second coronation, the nobles' pilgrimage to St Edmundsbury, the reasons for, as well as the method of, John's poisoning. None the less *King John* is a superior work. It shares with *The Raigne* the inherent disadvantage that without a fuller pyschological analysis than either dramatist can or will afford him, the King cannot be a satisfactory hero. Shakespeare might conceivably have treated him as he treated Richard II, but nothing could make the brutal, selfish John into a poet; his weaknesses could not be made endearing. And Shakespeare turned away from the sectarian propaganda that had unified Bale's play to emphasize more purely political motives, which neither Holinshed nor the author of *The Raigne*—nor he himself—could fully appreciate

[1] R. Wallerstein, *op cit.*, p. 43.   [2] *New Arden*, 1954, xi–xiii.
[3] John Elson, 'Studies on the King John Plays' (*J. Q. Adams Memorial Studies*, 1948), showed that *The Raigne* was based on Holinshed, Foxe, etc.

since the evidence was confused. Hence the remarkable detachment shown by the Bastard in his 'Commodity' speech was the author's also, and, although he did not carry the idea through (whether because of haste or lack of interest), Shakespeare conceived King John as a King of Commodity, governed by short-term views of personal expediency. 'He tries to find everyone's price' (Honigman). He wars against France but will make peace when it suits him. He will plunder the monks and defy the Pope but is not strong enough in principle to stand firm against the Pope-Philip combination. He will submit and turn submission to good use. With regard to Arthur he shows similar vacillation; and when his actions have united the barons and French against him he collapses and leaves the salvation of Widow England to his brother's Bastard.

In contrast Faulconbridge pretends to be an opportunist, but from the first he sacrifices immediate gain to the deeper ties of blood and loyalty. Throughout he represents the patriotic good of his country, opposing foreign claims and striving for national unity. When all seems lost he fights on in simple loyalty and duty. He is the King's true servant, and Shakespeare goes so far, anticipating Kent at the end of *King Lear* ('I have a journey soon to go'), as to make him suggest that he will shortly follow his master to the grave.

In style the play as a whole sustains but in a cooler way the rhetorical formalities of *Richard II* and earlier Histories. The fanciful word-play of Arthur in IV.1 recalls *Richard II* and the 'fulfilment' imagery of II.1.424–40 reminds one of *Romeo and Juliet*, I.3.79–94. Faulconbridge has something of Petruchio, with a foretaste of Henry V. The psychological references seem to link the play with *Richard II* and *The Merchant of Venice*. Moreover, Shakespeare uses the name Faulconbridge in *Love's Labour's Lost* and *The Merchant of Venice*. In the latter (I.2) that is the name of Portia's English suitor, described as 'a proper man's picture' but knowing not 'Latin, French nor Italian'. This use of the name for a typical 'young baron of England', suggests that Shakespeare was thinking of the Bastard's honest insularity. Such points, with the likely topical references, date the play to 1595 or 1596.

King John is only partly successful, but maybe the exercise it gave in assimilating into a serious historical theme a fictitious character at once comic and heroic gave Shakespeare confidence when he came to plan *Henry IV* and *Henry V*. *King John* helped Shakespeare to free himself from the conception of the History play as tragic or rhetorical drama, and to see the possibility of modulating in the same play from the broadly comic to the epic. What he did hesitantly when rewriting *The Raigne*, he did with magisterial freedom when rewriting *The Famous Victories*.

I. Source

From THE THIRD VOLUME OF CHRONICLES
by R. Holinshed (1587 edition)

[King Richard I had made Arthur his heir, but just before his death in 1199 he changed his testament.]

[156/1/1] Unto his brother John he assigned the crowne of England, and all other his lands and dominions, causing the Nobles there present to sweare fealtie unto him.[1] . . .

[157/1/21] John the yoongest son of Henrie the second . . . so soone as his brother Richard was deceassed, sent Hubert archbishop of Canturburie, and William Marshall earle of Striguill (otherwise called Chepstow) into England, both to proclaime him king, and also to see his peace kept, togither with Geffrey Fitz Peter lord cheefe justice, and diverse other barons of the realme, whilest he himself went to Chinon where his brothers treasure laie, which was foorthwith delivered unto him by Robert de Turneham: and therewithall the castell of Chinon and Sawmer and diverse other places, which were in the custodie of the foresaid Robert. But Thomas de Furnes nephue to the said Robert de Turneham delivered the citie and castell of Angiers unto Arthur duke of Britaine. For by generall consent of the nobles and peeres of the countries of Anjou, Maine, and Touraine, Arthur was received as the liege and sovereigne lord of the same countries.[2]

For even at this present, and so soone as it was knowne that king Richard was deceased, diverse cities and townes on that side of the sea belonging to the said Richard whilest he lived, fell at ods among themselves, some of them indevouring to preferre king John, other labouring rather to be under the governance of Arthur duke of Britaine, considering that he seemed by most right to be their cheefe lord, forsomuch as he was sonne to Geffrey elder brother to John. And thus began the broile in those quarters, whereof

---

[1] II.1.191–4. [2] I.1.9–11.

in processe of time insued great inconvenience, and finallie the death of the said Arthur, as shall be shewed hereafter.

Now whilest king John was thus occupied in recovering his brothers treasure, and traveling with his subjects to reduce them to his obedience, queene Elianor his mother . . . travelled as diligentlie to procure the English people to receive their oth of allegiance to be true to king John. . . . [So] those lords whose fidelities were earst suspected, willinglie tooke their oaths of obedience to the new king, & were assured by the same lords on his behalfe, that they should find him a liberall, a noble & a righteous prince, & such a one as would see that everie man should injoy his owne, & such as were knowne to be notorious transgressors, should be sure to receive their condigne punishment. [The King's mother] being bent to prefer hir sonne John, left no stone unturned to establish him in the throne, comparing oftentimes the difference of governement betweene a king that is a man, and a king that is but a child. For as John was 32 yeares old, so Arthur duke of Britaine was but a babe to speake of.[1] In the end, winning all the nobilitie wholie unto hir will, and seeing the coast to be cleare on everie side, without any doubt of tempestuous weather likelie to arise, she signified the whole matter unto K. John, who foorthwith framed all his indevours to the accomplishment of his businesse.

Surelie queen Elianor the kings mother was sore against hir nephue Arthur, rather mooved thereto by envie conceived against his mother, than upon any just occasion given in the behalfe of the child, for that she saw if he were king, how his mother Constance would looke to beare most rule within the realme of England,[2] till hir sonne should come to lawfull age, to governe of himselfe. . . .

[158/1/71] When this dooing of the queene was signified unto the said Constance, she doubting the suertie of hir sonne, committed him to the trust of the French king, who receiving him into his tuition, promised to defend him from all his enimies, and foorthwith furnished the holds in Britaine with French souldiers. Queene Elianor, being advertised hereof, stood in doubt by and by of hir countrie of Guien, and therefore with all possible speed passed over the sea, and came to hir sonne John into Normandie, and shortlie after they went foorth togither into the countrie of Maine and there tooke both the citie and castell of Mauns . . . bicause they had aided Arthur against his uncle John.

[John was invested Duke of Normandy.]

[158/2/25] In the meane time . . . queene Elianor, togither with capteine Marchades entred into Anjou, and wasted the same,

---

[1] In *TR* Arthur is about fourteen, in *KJ* only eight or ten.   [2] I.i.32–4.

bicause they of that countrie had received Arthur for their sovereigne
lord and governour. And amongst other townes and fortresses,
they tooke the citie of Angiers, slue manie of the citizens, and committed the rest to prison. . . . On Ascension eeve, [John] came to
London there to receive the crowne.

[He was crowned on Ascension Day, 1199. The Scots demanded
restitution of Northumberland and Cumberland, and negotiations
were begun.]

[160/1/6] Whilest these things were a dooing in England,
Philip K. of France having levied an armie, brake into Normandie
and tooke . . . diverse places from the English. In an other part, an
armie of Britains . . . tooke the citie of Angiers, which king John
had woon from duke Arthur, in the last yeare passed. These things
being signified to king John, he thought to make provision for the
recoverie of his losses there, with all speed possible. [He made
provision for his absence then] hasted unto the sea side, and sailed
over into Normandie, landing first at Diep, and from thence went to
Rouen . . . the 26 of June. . . .

[During a short truce between England and France, John made a
league with the Earl of Flanders.]

About the same time king Philip made Arthur duke of Britaine
knight, and received of him homage for Anjou, Poictiers, Maine,
Touraine, and Britaine. Also somewhat before the time that the
truce should expire . . . the two kings . . . came togither personallie,
and communed at full of the variance depending betweene them.
But the French king shewed himselfe stiffe and hard in this treatie,
demanding the whole countrie of Veulquessine to be restored unto
him. . . . Moreover he demanded, that Poictiers, Anjou, Maine, and
Touraine, should be delivered and wholie resigned unto Arthur
duke of Britaine. But these and diverse other requests which he made,
king John would not in any wise grant unto.[1]

[160/2/51] All this while was William de Roches busilie occupied
about his practise, to make king John and his nephue Arthur
freends, which thing at length he brought about, and thereupon
delivered into king Johns hands the citie of Mauns which he had in
keeping. . . . But in the night folowing, upon some mistrust and
suspicion gathered in the observation of the covenants on K. Johns
behalfe, both the said Arthur, with his mother Constance, the said
vicount of Tours, and diverse other, fled awaie secretlie from the
king,[2] and got them to the citie of Angiers, where the mother of the

[1] II.1.151–5.
[2] *In margin:* 'The mistrust that duke Arthur had in his uncle king John.'

said Arthur refusing hir former husband the earle of Chester, married hir selfe to the lord Guie de Tours, brother to the said vicount, by the popes dispensation. The same yere, Philip bastard sonne to king Richard, to whome his father had given the castell and honor of Coinacke, killed the vicount of Limoges, in revenge of his fathers death, who was slaine (as yee have heard) in besieging the castell of Chalus Cheverell.[1]

[In 1200 negotiations were reopened between John and Philip.]

[161/1/56] ... finallie they concluded an agreement, with a marriage to be had betwixt Lewes the sonne of king Philip, and the ladie Blanch, daughter to Alfonso king of Castile the 8 of that name, & neece to k. John by his sister Elianor.[2]

In consideration whereof, king John, besides the summe of thirtie thousande markes in silver, as in respect of dowrie assigned to his said neece, resigned his title to the citie of Evreux, and also unto all those townes which the French king had by warre taken from him, the citie of Angiers onelie excepted, which citie he received againe by covenants of the same agreement.[3] The French king restored also to king John (as *Rafe Niger* writeth) the citie of Tours, and all the castels and fortresses which he had taken within Touraine: and moreover, received of king John his homage for all the lands, fees and tenements which at anie time his brother king Richard, or his father king Henrie had holden of him, the said king Lewes or any his predecessors, the quit claims and marriages alwaies excepted. The king of England likewise did homage unto the French king for Britaine, and againe (as after you shall heare) received homage for the same countrie, and for the countie of Richmont of his nephue Arthur.[4] He also gave the earledome of Glocester unto the earle of Evreux, as it were by way of exchange, for that he resigned to the French king all right, title & claime that might be pretended to the countie of Evreux.

By this conclusion of marriage betwixt the said Lewes and Blanch, the right of king John went awaie, which he lawfullie before pretended unto the citie of Evreux, and unto those townes in the confines of Berrie, Chateau, Roux or Raoul, Cressie and Isoldune, and likewise unto the countrie of Veuxin or Veulquessine, which is a part of the territorie of Gisors: the right of all which lands, townes and countries was released to the king of France by K. John, who

---

[1] *In margin:* 'Philip king Richards bastard son slue the vicount of Limoges.' In *TR* and *KJ* Limoges is confused with the Duke of Austria.

[2] *In margin:* 'A peace concluded with a marriage.' II.1.416ff.

[3] Cf. II.1.486–94; 527–30. Apparently France gives nothing in return. At 552–3 John gives Angiers to Arthur.

[4] II.1.551: 'We'll create young Arthur Duke of Britaine and Earl of Richmond.'

supposed that by his affinitie, and resignation of his right to those places, the peace now made would have continued for ever.[1] And in consideration thereof, he procured furthermore, that the foresaid Blanch should be conveied into France to hir husband with all speed.[2] That doone he returned into England.

[161/2/54] King John being now in rest from warres with forren enimies, began to make warre with his subjects pursses at home, emptieng them by taxes and tallages, to fill his coffers, which alienated the minds of a great number of them from his love and obedience. . . . [He divorced his wife Isabell, daughter of Robert, Earl of Gloucester.] After that, he married Isabell the daughter of Amerie earle of Angolesme, by whome he had two sonnes, Henrie and Richard, and three daughters, Isabell, Elianor, and Jane.

[162/1/36] At the same time he gave commandement unto Hugh Nevill high justice of his forrests, that he should award his precepts unto all forresters within the realme, to give warning to all the white moonks, that before the quindene of S. Michaell they should remoove out of his forrests all their horsses of Haraz, and other cattell, under the penaltie to forfeit so manie of them, as after that day chanced to be found within the same forrests.[3] The cause that mooved the king to deale so hardlie with them was, for that they refused to helpe him with monie, when . . . he demanded it of them towards the paiment of the thirtie thousand pounds which he had covenanted to pay the French king, to live in rest and peace, which he coveted to have doone for reliefe of his people, and his owne suertie,[4] knowing what enimies he had that laie in wait to destroie him, and againe, what discommodities had chanced to his father and brethren, by the often and continuall wars.

[163/1/45] About the moneth of December [1200], there were seene in the province of Yorke five moones,[5] one in the east, the second in the west, the third in the north, the fourth in the south, and the fift as it were set in the middest of the other, having manie stars about it, and went five or six times incompassing the other, as it were the space of one houre, and shortlie after vanished awaie. The winter after was extreamelie cold, more than the naturall course had beene aforetime, And in the springtime came a great glutting and continuall raine, causing the rivers to rise with higher flouds than they had beene accustomed.

[164/1/49] In the yeare 1202 king John held his Christmasse at

---

[1] Cf. II.1.562-3.
[2] In *TR* and *KJ* Blanche is present and is married at once.
[3] An instance of John's 'spurning against the Church'. Cf. III.1.140-2.
[4] Cf. III.3.7-11 and *TR* Pt. 1, 308-12; 1022-4.
[5] *In margin:* 'Five moones.' IV.2.182-5.

Argenton in Normandie, and in the Lent following he and the French king met togither, neere unto the castell of Gulleton, and there in talke had betweene them, he commanded king John with no small arrogancie, and contrarie to his former promise, to restore unto his nephue Arthur duke of Britaine, all those lands now in his possession on that side the sea, which king John earnestlie denied to doo,[1] whereupon the French king immediatlie after, began war against him, and tooke Butevant, Augi and the castell of Linos.[2] Moreover, he besieged the castell of Radepont for the space of eight daies, till king John came thither, and forced him to depart with much dishonor. Howbeit after this, the French king wan Gourney, and then returning to Paris, he appointed certeine persons to have the governement of the foresaid Arthur duke of Britaine, and then sent him foorth with 200 men of armes into Poictou, that he might bring the countrie also under his subjection.

[164/2/7] the yoong Arthur . . . first went into Touraine, and after into Anjou, compelling both those countries to submit themselves unto him, and proclaimed himselfe earle of those places, by commission and grant obteined from king Philip.[3]

Queene Elianor that was regent in those parties[4] being put in great feare with the newes of this sudden sturre, got hir into Mirabeau a strong towne, situat in the countrie of Anjou, and foorthwith dispatched a messenger with letters unto king John, requiring him of speedie succour in this hir present danger. In the meane time, Arthur following the victorie, shortlie after followed hir, and woone Mirabeau, where he tooke his grandmother within the same, whom he yet intreated verie honorablie, and with great reverence (as some have reported).[5] But other write far more trulie, that she was not taken, but escaped into a tower, within the which she was straitlie besieged. Thither came also to aid Arthur all the Nobles and men of armes in Poictou, and namelie the foresaid earle of March according to appointment betwixt them: so that by this meanes Arthur had a great armie togither in the field.

King John in the meane time, having received his mothers letters, and understanding thereby in what danger she stood, was marvellouslie troubled with the strangenesse of the newes, and with manie bitter words accused the French king as an untrue prince, and a fraudulent league-breaker: and in all possible hast speedeth

---

[1] This meeting, and King Philip's demands, are transferred to Angiers in II.1.83–154.

[2] *In margin:* 'The French K. beginneth to make war against king John.'

[3] *In margin:* 'Arthur proclaimeth himselfe earle of Anjou, &c.'

[4] *In margin:* 'Queene Elianor.' Hence I.1.150, 'I am a soldier.'

[5] III.2.6–8, where the Bastard rescues her.

him foorth, continuing his journie for the most part both day and night to come to the succour of his people. To be briefe, he used such diligence, that he was upon his enimies necks yer they could understand any thing of his comming, or gesse what the matter meant, when they saw such a companie of souldiers as he brought with him to approch so neere the citie.[1] . . .

[164/2/55] This their feare being apparent to the Englishmen (by their disorder shewed in running up and downe from place to place with great noise and turmoile) they set upon them with great violence, and compassing them round about, they either tooke or slue them in a manner at their pleasure. And having thus put them all to flight, they pursued the chase towards the towne of Mirabeau, into which the enimies made verie great hast to enter: but such speed was used by the English souldiers at that present, that they entred and wan the said towne before their enimies could come neere to get into it. Great slaughter was made within Mirabeau it selfe, and Arthur with the residue of the armie that escaped with life from the first bickering was taken, who being hereupon committed to prison, first at Falais,[2] and after within the citie of Rouen, lived not long after as you shall heare. The other of the prisoners were also committed unto safe keeping, some into castels within Normandie and some were sent into England.

[165/1/35] It is said that king John caused his nephue Arthur to be brought before him at Falais, and there went about to persuade him all that he could to forsake his freendship and aliance with the French king, and to leane and sticke to him being his naturall uncle.[3] But Arthur like one that wanted good counsell, and abounding too much in his owne wilfull opinion, made a presumptuous answer, not onelie denieng so to doo, but also commanding king John to restore unto him the realme of England, with all those other lands and possessions which king Richard had in his hand at the houre of his death. For sith the same apperteined to him by right of inheritance, he assured him, except restitution were made the sooner, he should not long continue quiet.[4] King John being sore mooved with such words thus uttered by his nephue,[5] appointed (as before is said) that he should be straitlie kept in prison, as first in Falais, and after at Roan within the new castell there. Thus by means of this good successe, the countries of Poictou, Touraine, and Anjou were recovered.

Shortlie after king John comming over into England, caused

---

[1] *In margin:* 'K. John commeth upon his enimies not looked for.'
[2] *In margin:* 'Arthur duke of Britaine taken prisoner.' III.2.
[3] II.1.156–9; III.3.2–4.   [4] Contrast II.1.163–5.
[5] Shakespeare's John has no such excuse.

himselfe to be crowned againe at Canturburie by the hands of Hubert the archbishop there, on the fourteenth day of Aprill,[1] and then went backe againe into Normandie, where immediatlie upon his arrivall, a rumour was spred through all France, of the death of his nephue Arthur. True it is that great suit was made to have Arthur set at libertie, as well by the French king, as by William de Riches a valiant baron of Poictou, and diverse other Noble men of the Britains, who when they could not prevaile in their suit, they banded themselves togither, and joining in confederacie with Robert earle of Alanson, the vicount Beaumont, William de Fulgiers, and other, they began to levie sharpe wars against king John in diverse places, insomuch (as it was thought) that so long as Arthur lived, there would be no quiet in those parts:[2] whereupon it was reported, that king John through persuasion of his councellors, appointed certeine persons[3] to go unto Falais,[4] where Arthur was kept in prison, under the charge of Hubert de Burgh, and there to put out the yoong gentlemans eies.

But through such resistance as he made against one of the tormentors that came to execute the kings commandement (for the other rather forsooke their prince and countrie, than they would consent to obeie the kings authoritie heerein)[5] and such lamentable words as he uttered, Hubert de Burgh did preserve him from that injurie, not doubting but rather to have thanks than displeasure at the kings hands, for delivering him of such infamie as would have redounded unto his highnesse, if the yoong gentleman had beene so cruellie dealt withall. For he considered, that king John had resolved upon this point onelie in his heat and furie . . . and that afterwards, upon better advisement, he would both repent himselfe so to have commanded, and give them small thanke that should see it put in execution.[6] Howbeit to satisfie his mind for the time, and to staie the rage of the Britains, he caused it to be bruted abroad through the countrie, that the kings commandement was fulfilled, and that Arthur also through sorrow and greefe was departed out of this life.[7] For the space of fifteene daies this rumour incessantlie ran through both the realmes of England and France,[8] and there was ringing for him through townes and villages, as it had beene for his funerals. It was also bruted, that his bodie was buried in the monasterie of saint Andrewes of the Cisteaux order.

But when the Britains[9] were nothing pacified, but rather kindled

---

[1] *In margin:* 'King John eftsoones crowned.' IV.2.1–46.
[2] Cf. Pandulph at III.4.131–4.   [3] Hubert in III.3.29ff.
[4] IV.1. is set in England, whither Hubert is sent at III.3.71–3.
[5] Cf. the attendant's scruples at IV.1.6 and 86.   [6] IV.2.205–41.
[7] IV.1.128–9.   [8] IV.2.187–202.   [9] Bretons.

more vehementlie to worke all the mischeefe they could devise, in revenge of their sovereignes death, there was no remedie but to signifie abroad againe, that Arthur was as yet living and in health.[1] Now when the king heard the truth of all this matter, he was nothing displeased for that his commandement was not executed, sith there were diverse of his capteins which uttered in plaine words, that he should not find knights to keepe his castels, if he dealt so cruellie with his nephue.[2] For if it chanced any of them to be taken by the king of France or other their adversaries, they should be sure to tast of the like cup.

But now touching the maner in verie deed of the end of this Arthur, writers make sundrie reports. Neverthelesse certeine it is, that in the yeare next insuing, he was remooved from Falais unto the castell or tower of Rouen, out of the which there was not any that would confesse that ever he saw him go alive. Some have written, that as he assaied to have escaped out of prison, and prooving to clime over the wals of the castell,[3] he fell into the river of Saine, and so was drowned.[4] Other write, that through verie greefe and languor he pined awaie, and died of naturall sicknesse.[5] But some affirme, that king John secretlie caused him to be murthered and made awaie, so as it is not throughlie agreed upon, in what sort he finished his daies: but verelie king John was had in great suspicion, whether worthilie or not, the lord knoweth. . . .

[166/1/60] This yeare [1202] manie woonderfull things happened . . . there followed griselie tempests, with thunder, lightning, and stormes of raine, and haile of the bignesse of hens egs. . . . Also spirits (as it was thought) in likenesse of birds and foules were seene in the aire flieng with fire in their beaks, wherewith they set diverse houses on fire: which did import great troubles yer long to insue,[6] and followed in deed, as shall appeare hereafter.

With this entrance of the yeare of our lord 1203, king John held his Christmasse at Caen, where not having (as some writers say) sufficient regard to the necessarie affaires of his wars, he gave his mind to banketting, and passed the time in pleasure with the queene his wife, to the great greefe of his lords, so that they perceiving his retchlesse demeanour (or as some write, the doubtfull minds of the Nobilitie which served on that side, and were readie dailie to revolt from his obedience) withdrew their dutifull hearts

---

[1] Compare IV.2.243–51.   [2] IV.2.86–103; 260–2.

[3] IV.3 has no definite location in F.

[4] The Seine may have suggested the 'ship-boy's' disguise, but he is killed on the stones.

[5] Hence the ironic references in IV.2.86–8.   [6] Cf. Pandulph, III.4.153–9.

from him, and therefore getting licence, returned home into England. . . .[1]

[167/1/20] Wherefore for this and other matters laid to their charges, he did put them to greevous fines. By meanes whereof, and by leavieng a subsidie of his people, he got togither an huge summe of monie. This subsidie was granted him in a parlement holden at Oxenford,[2] and begun there upon the second of Januarie 1204. . . . Neither were the bishops, abbats, nor any other ecclesiasticall persons exempted, by meanes whereof he ran first into the hatred of the clergie, and consequentlie of manie other of his subjects: so that they failed him at his need.

[167/1/69] King Philip understanding that king John remained still in England, rather occupied in gathering of monie amongst his subjects, than in making other provision to bring them into the field (to the great offense of his said people) thought now for his part to lose no time: but assembling a mightie armie, he came with the same into Normandie, and upon his first comming, he wan the towne of Falaise, and shortlie after was Dampfront delivered unto him by surrender.[3] . . . With this swiftnesse of speed, he brought also such a feare into the hearts of most men, that he wan all the countrie of Normandie even to Mount S. Michaell.

[167/2/73] About this time [1204] queene Elianor the mother of king John departed this life, consumed rather through sorow and anguish of mind, than of any other naturall infirmitie.[4]

[In 1205 King Philip captured Chinon despite a gallant defence by de Burgh 'a right valiant man of warre as was any where to be found'. John retaliated in 1206.]

[170/1/27] Finallie he entred into Anjou, and comming to the citie of Angiers, appointed certeine bands of his footmen, & all his light horssemen to compasse the towne about, whilest he, with the residue of the footmen & all the men of armes, did go to assault the gates. Which enterprise with fire and sword he so manfullie executed, that the gates being in a moment broken open, the citie was entered and delivered to the souldiers for a preie.[5] So that of the citizens some were taken, some killed, and the wals of the citie beaten flat to the ground.[6] This doone, he went abroad into the countrie, and put all things that were in his way to the like destruction. Then came

---

[1] Cf. IV.2.86–102. Salisbury and Pembroke leave him (in England), disgusted by Arthur's supposed death.

[2] *In margin:* 'A subsidie granted.'

[3] *In margin:* 'Towns wun by the French king.'

[4] IV.2.120–3. Constance died in 1201, three years before this.

[5] *In margin:* 'King John wan the citie of Angiers by assault.'

[6] Cf. John's threat, II.1.399.

the people of the countries next adjoining, of their owne accord to submit themselves unto him, promising to aid him with men and vittels most plentifullie.

[A truce was agreed at the end of the year.]

[170/2/23]   After this it chanced that king John remembring himselfe of the destruction of the citie of Angiers, which (bicause he was descended from thence) he had before time greatlie loved, began now to repent him, in that he had destroied it, and therefore with all speed he tooke order to have it againe repaired, which was doone in most beautifull wise, to his great cost and expenses, which he might have saved, had not his foolish rashnesse driven him to attempt that, whereof upon sober advisement afterwards he was ashamed. But what will not an ordinarie man doo in the full tide of his furie; much more princes & great men, whose anger is resembled to the roring of a lion, even upon light occasions often-times, to satisfie their unbrideled and brainsicke affections, which carrie them with a swift and full streame into such follies and dotages as are undecent for their degrees.

[170/2/72]   In this meane while, the strife depended still in the court of Rome betwixt the two elected archbishops of Canturburie, Reginald and John. But after the pope was fullie informed of the manner of their elections, he disanulled them both, and procured by his papall authoritie the moonks of Canturburie (of whome manie were then come to Rome about that matter) to choose one Stephan Langton the cardinall of S. Chrysogon an Englishman borne, and of good estimation and learning in the court of Rome to be their archbishop.[1] The moonks at the first were loth to consent thereto, alledging that they might not lawfullie doo it without consent of their king, and of their covent.

[171/1/35]   [The King] herewith wrote his letters unto the pope,[2] giving him to understand for answer, that he would never consent that Stephan which had beene brought up & alwaies conversant with his enimies the Frenchmen, should now enjoy the rule of the bishoprike and dioces of Canturburie. Moreover, he declared in the same letters, that he marvelled not a little what the pope ment, in that he did not consider how necessarie the freendship of the king of England was to the see of Rome, sith there came more gains to the Romane church out of that kingdome, than out of any other realme on this side the mountaines. He added hereto, that for

---

[1] *In margin:* 'Stephan Langton chosen archbishop of Canturburie by the popes appointment.' III.1.142–6.

[2] *In margin:* 'King John writeth to the pope.' Contrast III.1.152–60, 'Tell him this tale', and the Tudor sentiments.

the liberties of his crowne he would stand to the death, if the matter so required. And as for the election of the bishop of Norwich unto the see of Canturburie, sith it was profitable to him and to his realme, he meant not to release it.

Moreover, he declared that if he might not be heard and have his mind, he would suerlie restraine the passages out of this realme, that none should go to Rome, least his land should be so emptied of monie and treasure, that he should want sufficient abilitie to beat backe and expell his enimies that might attempt invasion against the same. . . .

[171/2/67] The pope perceiving that king John continued still in his former mind (which he called obstinacie) sent over his bulles into England, directed to William bishop of London, to Eustace bishop of Elie, and to Mauger bishop of Worcester, commanding them that unlesse king John would suffer peaceablie the archbishop of Canturburie to occupie his see, and his moonks their abbie, they should put both him and his land under the sentence of inter-diction, denouncing him and his land plainelie accurssed.[1] And further he wrote expresse letters unto all the suffragans of the church of Canturburie, that they should by vertue of their obedience, which they owght to the apostolike see, receive and obeie the archbishop Stephan for their father and metropolitane. . . .

[172/1/11] . . . the king in a great rage sware, that if either they or any other presumed to put his land under interdiction, he would incontinentlie thereupon send all the prelats within the realme out of the same unto the pope, and seize all their goods unto his owne use. And further he added, that what Romans[2] soever he found within the precinct of any his dominions, he would put out their eies, and slit their noses, and so send them packing to Rome, that by such marks they might be knowne from all other nations of the world. And herewith he commanded the bishops to packe out of his sight, if they loved their owne health and preservation. . . .

[173/1/22] It was suerlie a rufull thing to consider the estate of this realme at that present [1209/10], when as the king neither trusted his peeres, neither the nobilitie favoured the king; no, there were verie few that trusted one another, but ech one hid & hourded up his wealth, looking dailie when another should come and enter upon the spoile. The communaltie also grew into factions, some favouring, & some cursing the king, as they bare affection. . . .

[173/1/45] King John notwithstanding that the realme was thus wholie interdicted and vexed, so that no preests could be found to

---

[1] *In margin:* '1208. The pope writeth to the bishops.'

[2] *In margin:* 'Romans, that is such chapleines strangers as belonged to the pope.' Cf. III.1.153 'no Italian priest'.

saie service in churches or chapels, made no great account thereof as touching any offense towards God or the pope: but rather mistrusting the hollow hearts of his people, he tooke a new oth of them for their faithfull allegiance,[1] and immediatlie thereupon assembled an armie to go against Alexander king of Scots.[2] . . .

[173/2/58]   There lived in those daies a divine named Alexander Cementarius,[3] surnamed Theologus, who by his preaching incensed the king greatlie unto all crueltie (as the moonks and friers saie) against his subjects, affirming that the generall scourge wherewith the people were afflicted, chanced not through the princes fault, but for the wickednesse of his people, for the king was but the rod of the Lords wrath, and to this end a price was ordeined, that he might rule the people with a rod of iron, and breake them as an earthen vessell, to chaine the mighty in fetters & the noble men in iron manacles. He did see (as it should seeme) the evill disposed humors of the people concerning their dutiful obedience which they ought to have borne to their naturall prince king John, and therefore as a doctrine most necessarie in that dangerous time, he taught the people how they were by Gods lawes bound in dutie to obeie their lawfull prince, and not through any wicked persuasion of busie heads and lewd discoursers, to be carried away to forget their loyall allegiance, and so to fall into the damnable sinke of rebellion.

He went about also to proove with likelie arguments, that it apperteined not to the pope, to have to doo concerning the temporall possessions of any kings or other potentats touching the rule and government of their subjects, sith no power was granted to Peter (the speciall and cheefe of the apostles of the Lord) but onlie touching the church, and matters apperteining thereunto.[4] By such doctrine of him set foorth, he wan in such wise the kings favour, that he obteined manie great preferments at the kings hands, and was abbat of saint Austines in Canturburie: but at length, when his manners were notified to the pope, he tooke such order for him, that he was despoiled of all his goods and benefices, so that afterwards he was driven in great miserie to beg his bread from doore to doore, as some write. This did he procure to himselfe by telling the trueth against that beast, whose hornes were pricking at everie christian prince that he might set himselfe in a seat of supremasie above all principalities . . .

[175/1/7]   In the same yeare [1211], the pope sent two legats into England, the one named Pandulph a lawier, and the other

---

[1] *In margin:* 'A new oth of allegiance.'
[2] *In margin:* 'Alexander K. of Scots.'
[3] *In margin:* 'Cementarius.'   [4] III.1.147–8; 155–63.

Durant a templer,[1] who comming unto king John, exhorted him
with manie terrible words to leave his stubborne disobedience to
the church, and to reforme his misdooings. The king for his part,
quietlie heard them, and bringing them to Northampton, being not
farre distant from the place where he met them upon his returne
foorth of Wales had much conference with them; but at length, when
they perceived that they could not have their purpose, neither for
restitution of the goods belonging to preests which he had seized
upon, neither of those that apperteined to certeine other persons,
which the king had gotten also into his hands, by meanes of the
controversie betwixt him and the pope the legats departed, leaving
him accursed,[2] and the land interdicted, as they found it at their
comming.

[175/2/17]   In the meane time pope Innocent, after the returne
of his legats out of England, perceiving that king John would not be
ordered by him, determined with the consent of his cardinals and
other councellours, and also at the instant suit of the English
bishops and other prelats being there with him, to deprive king
John of his kinglie state, and so first absolved all his subjects and
vassals of their oths of allegiance made unto the same king,[3] and
after deprived him by solemne protestation of his kinglie adminis-
tration and dignitie, and lastlie signified that his deprivation unto
the French king and other christian princes, admonishing them to
pursue king John, being thus deprived, forsaken, and condemned
as a common enimie to God and his church.[4] He ordeined furthermore, that whosoever imploied goods or other aid to vanquish and
overcome that disobedient prince, should remaine in assured peace
of the church, as well as those which went to visit the sepulchre of
our Lord, not onlie in their goods and persons, but also in suffrages
for saving of their soules.[5]

But yet that it might appeare to all men, that nothing could be
more joyfull unto his holinesse, than to have king John to repent his
trespasses committed, and to aske forgivenesse for the same, he
appointed Pandulph, which latelie before was returned to Rome,
with a great number of English exiles, to go into France, togither
with Stephan the archbishop of Canturburie, and the other English
bishops, giving him in commandement, that repairing unto the
French king, he should communicate with him all that which he
had appointed to be doone against King John, and to exhort the
French king to make warre upon him, as a person for his wicked-

---

[1] *In margin:* 'Pandulph & Durant the popes legats.' Only Pandulph appears at
III.1.135 and later.

[2] III.1.173 'curs'd and excommunicate'.   [3] III.1.173–5.

[4] III.1.193–4: 253–63.   [5] III.1.176–9.

nesse excommunicated.[1] Moreover this Pandulph was commanded by the pope, if he saw cause, to go over into England, and to deliver unto king John such letters as the pope had written for his better instruction, and to seeke by all means possible to draw him from his naughtie opinion.

[176/2/18] Ye shall understand, the French king being requested by Pandulph the popes legat, to take the warre in hand against king John, was easilie persuaded[2] thereto of an inward hatred that he bare unto our king, and thereupon with all diligence made his provision of men, ships, munition and vittell, in purpose to passe over into England[3]: and now was his navie readie rigged at the mouth of Saine, and he in greatest forwardnesse, to take his journie. When Pandulph upon good considerations thought first to go eftsoones, or at the least wise to send into England, before the French armie should land there, and to assaie once againe, if he might induce the king to shew himselfe reformable unto the popes pleasure: king John having knowledge of the French kings purpose and ordinance, assembled his people, and lodged with them alongst by the coast towards France, that he might resist his enimies, and keepe them off from landing.

[176/2/53] To conclude, there was esteemed of able men assembled togither in the armie on Barham downe, what of chosen men of armes, and valiant yeomen, and other armed men, the number of sixtie thousand: so that if they had beene all of one mind, and well bent towards the service of their king and defense of their countrie, there had not beene a prince in christendome, but that they might have beene able to have defended the realme of England against him.[4] He had also provided a navie of ships farre stronger than the French kings, readie to fight with them by sea, if the case had so required.

But as he lay thus readie, neere to the coast, to withstand and beat backe his enimies, there arrived at Dover two Templers,[5] who comming before the king, declared unto him that they were sent from Pandulph the popes legat, who for his profit coveted to talke with him. . . .

[Pandulph came to Dover and told John in a 'sawcie speech' that Philip was about to invade England and had 'a charter made by the cheefest lords of England touching their fealtie and obedience assured to him'.]

---

[1] *In margin:* 'Pandulph sent into France to practise with the French king, for king John his destruction.' III.1.191–320.

[2] He is not easily persuaded in III.1, where the circumstances are different.

[3] *In margin:* 'The French king prepared to invade England.' IV.2.110–12.

[4] Did this suggest V.7.115–18?   [5] *In margin:* 'Two knights of the temple.'

[177/1/60] These words being thus spoken by the legat, king John as then utterlie despairing in his matters, when he saw himselfe constreined to obeie, was in a great perplexitie of mind, and as one full of thought, looked about him with a frowning countenance, waieng with himselfe what counsell were best for him to follow. At length, oppressed with the burthen of the imminent danger and ruine, against his will, and verie loth so to have doone, he promised upon his oth to stand to the popes order and decree. Wherefore shortlie after (in like manner as pope Innocent had commanded) he tooke the crowne from his owne head, and delivered the same to Pandulph the legat, neither he, nor his heires at anie time thereafter to receive the same, but at the popes hands.[1] Upon this, he promised to receive Stephan the archbishop of Canturburie into his favour, with all other the bishops and banished men, making unto them sufficient amends for all injuries to them doone, and so to pardon them, that they should not run into any danger, for that they had rebelled against him.

Then Pandulph keeping the crowne with him for the space of five daies in token of possession thereof, at length (as the popes vicar) gave it him againe.[2] By meanes of this act (saith *Polydor*) the fame went abroad, that king John willing to continue the memorie hereof, made himselfe vassall to pope Innocent, with condition, that his successors should likewise from thenceforth acknowledge to have their right to the same kingdome from the pope. But those kings that succeeded king John, have not observed any such lawes of reconciliation. . . .

[178/2/41] [Pandulph] sailed backe into France, & came to Roan, where he declared to king Philip the effect of his travell, and what he had doone in England.[3] But king Philip having in this meane while consumed a great masse of monie, to the summe of sixtie thousand pounds,[4] as he himselfe alledged, about the furniture of his journie, which he intended to have made into England, upon hope to have had no small aid within the realme, by reason of such bishops and other banished men as he had in France with him, was much offended for the reconciliation of king John, and determined not so to breake off his enterprise, least it might be imputed to him for a great reproch to have beene at such charges and great expenses in vaine.[5]

---

[1] *In margin:* 'K. John delivereth his crowne unto Pandulph.' V.i.1–2; Cf. Foxe's account (Text II).

[2] *In margin:* 'Pandulph restoreth the crowne again to the king.' V.i.2–4.

[3] V.2.68–78. [4] *In margin:* 'Fortie thousand marks of silver saith *Matth. West.*'

[5] *In margin:* 'The French K. displeased for the reconciliation of K. John with the pope.' V.2.78–117.

[The English navy crossed to Flanders and attacked the great French fleet when its men were ashore, capturing over three hundred vessels.]

[180/1/28] There was in this season an heremit, whose name was Peter,[1] dwelling about Yorke, a man in great reputation with the common people, bicause that either inspired with some spirit of prophesie as the people beleeved, or else having some notable skill in art magike, he was accustomed to tell what should follow after. And for so much as oftentimes his saiengs prooved true, great credit was given to him as to a verie prophet: which was no good consequence that therefore his predictions comprised undoubted events . . . he was not as he was taken, but rather a deluder of the people, and an instrument of satan raised up for the inlargement of his kingdome; as the sequele of this discourse importeth. This Peter about the first of Januarie last past, had told the king, that at the feast of the Ascension it should come to passe, that he should be cast out of his kingdome.[2] And (whether, to the intent that his words should be the better beleeved, or whether upon too much trust of his owne cunning) he offered himselfe to suffer death for it, if his prophesie prooved not true. Hereupon being committed to prison within the castell of Corf, when the day by him prefixed came, without any other notable damage unto king John, he was by the kings commandement drawne from the said castell, unto the towne of Warham, & there hanged, togither with his sonne.[3]

The people much blamed king John, for this extreame dealing, bicause that the heremit was supposed to be a man of great vertue, and his sonne nothing guiltie of the offense committed by his father (if any were) against the king. Moreover, some thought, that he had much wrong to die, bicause the matter fell out even as he had prophesied: for the day before the Ascension day, king John had resigned the superioritie of his kingdome (as they tooke the matter) unto the pope, and had doone to him homage, so that he was no absolute king indeed, as authors affirme.[4]

[Stephen Langton entered his see and absolved John. After some delay the interdict was released, in June, 1214. When many nobles refused to help the King in his war against the French a truce was made.]

[183/2/25] After this, about the 19 daie of October he returned into England, to appease certeine tumults which began alreadie to

[1] *In margin:* 'An hermit named Peter of Pontfret, or Wakefield as some writers have.'   [2] IV.2.147–54.

[3] *In margin:* 'The heremit and his sonne hanged.' Cf. IV.2.155–7.

[4] Cf. John, V.1.28–9.

shoot out buds of some new civill dissention. And suerlie the same spred abroad their blossoms so freshlie, that the fruit was knit before the growth by anie timelie provision could be hindered. . . .

The Nobles supposing that longer delaie therein was not to be suffered, assembled themselves togither at the abbeie of Burie (under colour of going thither to doo their devotions to the bodie of S. Edmund which laie there inshrined) [1] where they uttered their complaint of the kings tyrannicall maners, alledging how they were oftentimes called foorth to serve in the wars & to fight in defense of the realme, and yet notwithstanding were still oppressed at home by the kings officers, who (upon confidence of the lawes) attempted all things whatsoever they conceived. . . .

And therfore being thus assembled in the queere of the church of S. Edmund, they received a solemne oth upon the altar there, [2] that if the king would not grant to the same liberties, with others which he of his owne accord had promised to confirme to them, they would from thencefoorth make warre upon him, till they had obteined their purpose, and inforced him to grant, not onelie to all these their petitions, but also yeeld to the confirmation of them under his seale, for ever to remaine most stedfast and inviolable.

[The King promised to consider their demands.]

[184/1/74]   Herewith the minds of the Nobilitie being somewhat pacified, returned home to their houses. The king soone after also, to assure himselfe the more effectuallie if the allegiance of his people in time to come, caused everie man to renew his homage, and to take a new oth to be faithfull to him against all other persons. [3] And to provide the more suerlie for himselfe, on Candlemasse day next insuing, he tooke upon him the crosse to go into the holie land, [4] which I thinke he did rather for feare than any devotion, as was also thought by another, to the end that he might (under the protection thereof) remaine the more out of danger of such as were his foes. . . .

The King, when he saw what they demanded (which in effect was a new order in things touching the whole state of the common wealth) sware in a great furie, that he would never condescend unto those petitions.

[The barons broke into open rebellion.   The King was left desolate of friends and 'there was none that would paie anie monie to the

---

[1] *In margin:* 'A cloked pilgrimage.' Cf. IV.3.11, Salisbury, Pembroke, and Bigot. No pilgrimage is mentioned. Cf. *TR* Pt. 2. 98–108; 349–495.

[2] In V.2. the oath has been sworn, and joined by Lewis and Melun.

[3] *In margin:* 'The king demandeth a new oth of allegiance of his subjects.'

[4] *In margin:* 'The king taketh on him the crosse.'

kings use, nor anie that did obeie him, in somuch that there remained with him but onelie seven horssemen of all his traine at one time'. He was forced to accept his nobles' demands and to sign Magna Carta (15 June, 1215).]

[186/2/13] Great rejoising was made for this conclusion of peace betwixt the king and his barons, the people judging that God had touched the kings heart, and mollified it, whereby happie daies were come for the realme of England, as though it had beene delivered out of the bondage of Aegypt: but they were much deceived, for the king having condescended to make such grant of liberties, farre contrarie to his mind, was right sorowfull in his heart,[1] curssed his mother that bare him, the houre that he was borne, and the paps that gave him sucke, wishing that he had received death by violence of sword or knife, in steed of naturall norishment: he whetted his teeth, he did bite now on one staffe, and now on another as he walked, and oft brake the same in peeces when he had doone, and with such disordered behaviour and furious gestures he uttered his greefe, in such sort that the Noble men verie well perceived the inclination of his inward affection concerning these things, before the breaking up of the councell, and therefore sore lamented the state of the realme, gessing what would follow of his impatiencie and displesant taking of the matter.

Hereupon they said among themselves, Wo be to us, yea rather to the whole realme that wanteth a sufficient king, and is governed by a tyrant that seeketh the subversion thereof. Now hath our sovereigne lord made us subject to Rome, and to the Romish court, so that we must hencefoorth obteine our protection from thence. It is verie much to be feared, least we doo feele hereafter some further peece of mischeefe to light upon us suddenlie. We never heard of any king that would not gladlie indevor to withdraw his necke from bondage & captivitie, but ours of his owne accord voluntarilie submitteth himselfe to become vassall to everie stranger. And thus the lords lamenting the case, left the king, and returned to London. . . .

[John brought over troops from France and Flanders and captured Rochester.]

Here is to be remembered, that whilest the siege laie thus at Rochester, Hugh de Boues . . . came downe to Calice with an huge number of men of warre and souldiers to come to the aid of king John. But as he was upon the sea with all his people, meaning to land at Dover, by a sudden tempest which rose at that instant, the

[1] *In margin:* 'The kings impatience to see himselfe brideled by his subjects.'

said Hugh with all his companie was drowned by shipwracke.
Soone after the bodie of the same Hugh, with the carcases of other
innumerable . . . were found not farre from Yermouth, and all
along that coast.[1]

[190/1/43] The barons of the realme . . . sent unto Lewes the
sonne of Philip the French king, offering him the crowne of
England, and sufficient pledges for the performance of the same . . .
requiring him with all speed to come unto their succour. . . . [King
Philip] prepared an armie, and diverse ships to transport his sonne
and his armie over into England. In the meane time, and to put
the barons in comfort, he sent over a certaine number of armed
men . . . the which taking the sea, arrived with one and fortie ships
in the Thames, and so came to London the seaven and twentith of
Februarie, where they were received of the barons with great joy
and gladnesse.[2] Moreover the said Lewes wrote to the barons, that
he purposed by Gods assistance to be at Calice by a day appointed,
with an armie redie to passe over with all speed unto their
succours.

[190/2/69] Somewhat before this time also, when he heard of
the compact made betwixt the barons and his adversaries the
the Frenchmen, [John] dispatched a messenger in all hast to the
pope,[3] signifieng to him what was in hand and practised against
him, requiring furthermore the said pope by his authoritie to cause
Lewes to staie his journie, and to succour those rebels in England
which he had alreadie excommunicated. This he needed not have
doone, had he beene indued with such prudence and prowesse
as is requisit to be planted in one that beareth rule. . . . The pope
desirous to helpe king John all that he might (bicause he was now
his vassall) sent his legat Gualo into France, to disswade king
Philip from taking anie enterprise in hand against the king of
England.[4] But king Philip though he was content to heare what the
legat could saie, yet by no meanes would be turned from the
execution of his purpose, alledging that king John was not the lawfull
king of England,[5] having first usurped and taken it awaie from his
nephue Arthur the lawfull inheritour, and that now sithens as an
enimie to his owne royall dignitie he had given the right of his
kingdome awaie to the pope (which he could not doo without

---

[1] Cf. the loss of *Lewis's* reinforcements, V.3.9–11; V.5.12–16.

[2] Hence *TR* Pt. 2, 627–8: 673.

[3] *In margin:* 'King John once againe sendeth to the pope.' Cf. John and
Pandulph V.1.5–24.

[4] *In margin:* 'Cardinall Gualo.' Pandulph attempts this at V.2.68–77.

[5] *In margin:* 'The French kings allegations to the popes legat Gualo. Cf. the
English nobles in *TR* Pt.2, 420–43.

consent of his nobles) and therefore through his owne fault he was worthilie deprived of all his kinglie honor.

[191/1/47] Lewes on the morrow following, being the 26 of Aprill [1216], by his fathers procurement, came into the councell chamber, and with frowning looke beheld the legat, where by his procurator he defended the cause that moved him to take upon him this journie into England, disproving not onelie the right which king John had to the crowne, but also alledging his owne interest, not onelie by his new election of the barons, but also in the title of his wife, whose mother the queen of Castile remained onelie alive of all the brethren and sisters of Henrie the second late king of England (as before ye have heard.) [1]

[The Dauphin landed at Sandwich, took Rochester, and came to London where he received homage.]

[191/2/60] [Lewis] tooke an oath to mainteine and performe the old lawes and customes of the realme, and to restore to everie man his rightfull heritage and lands; requiring the barons furthermore to continue faithful towards him, assuring them to bring things so to passe, that the realme of England should recover the former dignitie, and they their ancient liberties. Moreover he used them so courteouslie, gave them so faire words, and made such large promises, that they beleeved him with all their harts. . . . [2]

[He was joined by William, Earl of Salisbury, and William Marshall the younger, among others. The papal legate Gualo excommunicated them all. The Tower of London was given up to Lewis, but Dover held out for John through the constancy of Hubert de Burgh.]

[193/2/6] About the same time, or rather in the yeare last past as some hold, it fortuned that the vicount of Melune, a French man, fell sicke at London, and perceiving that death was at hand, he called unto him certeine of the English barons, which remained in the citie, upon safegard thereof, and to them made this protestation[3]: I lament (saith he) your destruction and desolation at hand, bicause ye are ignorant of the perils hanging over your heads. For this understand, that Lewes, and with him 16 earles and barons of France, have secretlie sworne (if it shall fortune him to conquere this realme of England, & to be crowned king) that he will kill, banish and confine all those of the English nobilitie (which now

---

[1] *In margin:* 'Lewes the French kings sonne mainteineth his pretended title to the crowne of England.' Cf. V.2.78–117.

[2] V.2.1–63.

[3] *In margin:* 'The vicount of Melune discovereth the purpose of Lewes.' Cf. V.4.6–48, where he is wounded in battle.

doo serve under him, and persecute their owne king) as traitours
and rebels, and furthermore will dispossesse all their linage of such
inheritances as they now hold in England. And bicause (saith he)
you shall not have doubt hereof, I which lie here at the point of
death, doo now affirme unto you, and take it on the perill of my
soule, that I am one of those sixteen that have sworne to performe
this thing: wherefore I advise you to provide for your owne safeties,
and your realmes which you now destroie, and keepe this thing
secret which I have uttered unto you. After this speech was uttered
he streightwaies died.[1]

When these words of the lord of Melune were opened unto the
barons, they were, and not without cause, in great doubt of themselves, for they saw how Lewes had alredie placed and set Frenchmen in most of such castels and townes as he had gotten, the right
whereof indeed belonged to them. And againe, it greeved them
much to understand, how besides the hatred of their prince, they
were everie sundaie and holie daie openlie accursed in everie
church, so that manie of them inwardlie relented, and could have
bin contented to have returned to king John, if they had thought
that they should thankfullie have beene received.[2]

[The King 'brake forth of Winchester as it had been an hideous
tempest of weather' and marched into Norfolk dealing out destruction as he went.]

[192/1/45]   Thus the countrie being wasted on each hand, the
king hasted forward till he came to Wellestreme sands, where
passing the washes[3] he lost a great part of his armie, with horsses and
carriages, so that it was judged to be a punishment appointed by
God, that the spoile which had beene gotten and taken out of
churches, abbeies, and other religious houses, should perish,
and be lost by such means togither with the spoilers. Yet the king
himselfe, and a few other, escaped the violence of the waters, by
following a good guide. But as some have written, he tooke such
greefe for the losse susteined at this passage, that immediatlie thereupon he fell into an ague, the force and heat whereof, togither with
his immoderate feeding on rawe peaches, and drinking of new sider,
so increased his sicknesse, that he was not able to ride, but was faine
to be carried in a litter presentlie made of twigs, with a couch of
strawe under him,[4] without any bed or pillow, thinking to have
gone to Lincolne, but the disease still so raged and grew upon him,

---

[1] *In margin:* 'The vicount of Melune dieth.' V.4.58–60.

[2] *In margin:* 'The English nobilitie beginneth to mislike of the match which they
had made with Lewes.' Cf. V.4.1–4; 49–57.

[3] *In margin:* 'The losse of the kings carriages.' V.6.39–41. Cf. *TR* Pt. 2, 831–8.

[4] *In margin:* 'King John falleth sicke of an ague.' V.3.3–4.

that he was inforced to staie one night at the castell of Laford, and on the next day with great paine, caused himselfe to be carried unto Newarke, where in the castell through anguish of mind, rather than through force of sicknesse, he departed this life the night before the ninettenth day of October, in the yeare of his age fiftie and one, and after he had reigned seaventeene yeares, six moneths, and seaven and twentie daies.[1]

There be which have written, that after he had lost his armie, he came to the abbeie of Swineshead in Lincolneshire, and there understanding the cheapenesse and plentie of corne, shewed himselfe greatlie displeased therewith, as he that for the hatred which he bare to the English people, that had so traitorouslie revolted from him unto his adversarie Lewes, wished all miserie to light upon them, and thereupon said in his anger, that he would cause all kind of graine to be at a farre higher price, yer manie daies should passe. Whereupon a moonke that heard him speake such words, being mooved with zeale for the oppression of his countrie, gave the king poison in a cup of ale, wherof he first tooke the assaie, to cause the king not to suspect the matter, and so they both died in a manner at one time.[2]

There are that write, how one of his owne servants did conspire with a convert of that abbeie, and that they prepared a dish of peares, which they poisoned, three of the whole number excepted, which dish the said convert presented unto him. And when the king suspected them to be poisoned indeed, by reason that such pretious stones as he had about him, cast foorth a certeine sweat, as it were bewraieng the poison, he compelled the said convert to tast and eat some of them, who knowing the three peares which were not poisoned, tooke and eat those three, which when the king had seene, he could not longer absteine, but fell to, and eating greedilie of the rest, died the same night, no hurt happening to the convert, who thorough helpe of such as bare no good will to the K. found shift to escape, and conveied himselfe awaie from danger of receiving due punishment for so wicked a deed. . . .

The men of warre that served under his ensignes, being for the more part hired souldiers and strangers, came togither, and marching foorth with his bodie, each man with his armour on his backe, in warlike order, conveied it unto Worcester, where he was pompouslie buried in the cathedrall church before the high altar; not for that he had so appointed (as some write)[3] but bicause it was thought to be a place of most suertie for the lords and other of his freends there to

---

[1] *In margin:* 'King John departed this life.'
[2] V.6.23–9.   [3] V.7.99–100.

assemble, and to take order in their businesse now after his decease.

[Henry III was nine years old when he came to the throne.]

[197/1/12]   Immediatlie after the death of his father king John, William Marshall earle of Pembroke, generall of his fathers armie, brought this yoong prince with his brother and sisters unto Glocester, and there called a councell of all such lords as had taken part with king John . . . [Others came too, and heard Pembroke declare Henry the rightful king.] When the barons had heard this earles words, after some silence and conference had, they allowed of his saiengs, and immediatlie with one consent, proclaimed the yoong gentleman king of England.[1]

[Though Henry was crowned, Lewis did not lose all support in England and while negotiations were in train in 1218 'a new supplie' of men was sent from France to aid him.[2]]

[201/1/43]   [These] on saint Bartholomews day set forth from Caleis, in purpose to arrive in the Thames, and so to come up the river to London. Howbeit Hubert de Burgh [and others] having not yet above the number of 40 ships great and small, upon the discovering of the French fleet, which consisted of 80 great ships, besides other lesser vessels well appointed and trimmed, made foorth to the sea. And first coasting aloofe from them, till they had got the wind on their backs, came finallie with their maine force to assaile the Frenchmen, and with helpe of their crossebowes and archers at the first joining, made great slaughter of their enimies, and so grapling togither, in the end the Englishmen bare themselves so manfullie, that they vanquished the whole French fleet, and obteined a famous victorie.

[Despairing of further succour Lewis shortly afterwards made peace.][3]

[Character of King John.]

[196/1/4]   He was comelie of stature, but of looke and countenance displeasant and angrie; somewhat cruell of nature . . . and not so hardie as doubtfull in time of perill and danger. . . . Howbeit some give this witnesse of him . . . that he was a great and mightie prince, but yet not verie fortunate, much like to Marius the noble Romane, tasting of fortune both waies; bountifull and liberall unto strangers, but of his owne people (for their dailie treasons practised towards him) a great oppressour; so that he trusted more

---

[1] V.7.101–7.   [2] Cf. V.5.9–13; the 'supply' is wrecked.
[3] V.7.81–95.

to forreners than to them, and therefore in the end he was of them utterlie forsaken.

Verelie, whosoever shall consider the course of the historie written of this prince, he shall find, that he hath beene little beholden to the writers of that time in which he lived; for scarselie can they afoord him a good word, except when the trueth inforceth them to come out with it as it were against their willes. The occasion whereof (as some thinke) was, for that he was no great freend to the clergie. . . .

Certeinlie it should seeme the man had a princelie heart in him, and wanted nothing but faithful subjects to have assisted him in revenging such wrongs as were doone and offered by the French king and others. Moreover the pride and pretended authoritie of the cleargie he could not well abide, when they went about to wrest out of his hands the prerogative of his princelie rule and governement. True it is, that to mainteine his warres which he was forced to take in hand, as well in France as elsewhere, he was constreined to make all the shift he could devise to recover monie, and, bicause he pinched their pursses, they conceived no small hatred against him; which when he perceived, and wanted peradventure discretion to passe it over, he discovered now and then in his rage his immoderate displeasure, as one not able to bridle his affections (a thing verie hard in a stout stomach) and thereby missed now and then to compasse that which otherwise he might verie well have brought to passe.

II. Possible Source

From ACTES AND MONUMENTS OF MARTYRS

by John Foxe (1583 edition)

Actes and Monuments of matters most speciall and memorable, happenyng in the Church, with an Universall history of the same, wherein is set forth at large the whole race and course of the Church, from the primitive age to these latter tymes of ours, with the bloudy times, horrible troubles, and great persecutions agaynst the true Martyrs of Christ, sought and wrought as well by

Heathen Emperours, and nowe lately practised by Romish Prelates, especially in the Realme of England and Scotland. Nearly revised and recognised, partly also augmented, and now the fourth time agayne published . . . by the Authour . . . John Foxe An. 1583. Mensis Octobr. [Colophon] At London. Printed by John Daye, dwelling over Aldersgate beneath Sainct Martins. Anno 1583.

[Peter the false prophet]

[p. 252] The next yeare,[1] the French king began his attempt in hope of the crowne of England: being well manned wyth the Bishops, Monkes, Prelates, and Priestes, and theyr servauntes to maintaine the same: bragging of the letters which they had received from the great men there. But behold the worke of God: the English nauie tooke 300. of the French kings ships well loden with wheat, wine, meale, flesh, armour, and such other like, meete for the warre: and an 100. they brent within the haven, taking the spoyle with them.[2] In the meane time the priests within Englande, had provided them a certain false counterfait prophet called Peter Wakefield of Poiz: who was an idle gadder about, and a pratling marchant.[3] This Peter, they made to prophecie lies: rumoring his prophesies abroade, to bring the king out of all credite with his people . . .

This counterfeit soothsayer prophesied of king John: that he shoulde raigne no longer then the ascension day, within the yere of our Lord 1213. which was the 14. yere from his coronation, and this (he sayde) he had by revelation. Then was it of him demaunded, whether he shoulde be slaine or be expelled, or should of himself geve over the crown: He answered, that he coulde not tell.[4] But of this he was sure (he sayde) that neither he, nor any of his stock or linage should raign, that day once finished. The K. hearing of this, laughed muche at it, and made but a scoffe thereof. Tush (sayth he) it is but an idiote knave, and such a one as lacketh his right wyts. But when this foolish prophet had so escaped the daunger of the kings displeasure, & that he made no more of it, he gate him abroade and prated thereof at large (as he was a very idle vagabund) and used to tattle and talk more than inough: so that they which loved the king, caused hym anone after to be apprehended as a

[1] *In margin:* 'Anno 1212.'
[2] *In margin:* 'French ships taken by englishmen.'
[3] *In margin:* 'Peter the false Prophet.'
[4] *In margin:* 'The false prophet found a lyar.'

malefactor, & to be throwen in prison, the king not yet knowing therof.

Anone after, the fame of thys phantasticall[1] Prophet went all the realme over, & his name was knowen every where (as foolishness is much regarded of people, where wisdom is not in place) specially because he was then imprisoned for the matter, the rumor was the larger: theyr wonderings were the wantoner: their practising the folisher: their busy talks & other idle occupying the greater. Continually from thence (as the rude maner of people is) old gossips tales went abroad, new tales were invented, fables were added to fables, and lies grew upon lyes.[2] So that every day, new slanders were raised on the king, and not one of them true: rumours arose, blasphemies were spred, the enemies rejoysed, & treasons by the priests were maintained, and what likewise was surmised, or other subtiltie practised, all was then fathered upon this foolishe prophet. As, thus sayeth Peter Wakefielde: thus hath hee prophesied: and thys shall come to passe: yea many times when he thought nothing lesse. When the Ascension day was come which was prophesied of afore: king John commanded his regal Tent to be spred abroad in the open field, passing that day with his noble counsel and men of honor, in the greatest solemnitie that ever hee did afore, solacing himselfe with musicall instruments & songs, most in sight amongst his trusty frends.[3] When that day was past in all prosperity and myrth, his enemies being confused, turned all to an allegorical understanding, to make the prophecy good, and sayd: he is no longer king, for the Pope raigneth & not he, yet raigned he stil, & his sonne after him, to prove that prophet a lier. Then was the king by his counsel perswaded, that this false prophet had troubled al the realme: perverted the hearts of the people, and raised the commons against him. For hys woordes went over the Sea by the helpe of his Prelates, and came to the French kings eare, & gave unto him a great encouragement to invade the land, he had not els done it so sodenly. But hee was most fouly deceived, as all they are & shall be, that put their trust in such darke drousy dreames of hypocrits. The king therfore commanded that he should be drawen & hanged like a traitor.[4]

[The King's Submission]

[p. 253]   Then sent the Pope againe into England his Legate Pandulphe wyth other Embassadours: the king also at Canterb. (by letters as it should seeme certified from hys owne ambassadors)

---

[1] IV.2.144 'strangely fantasied'.   [2] IV.2.145: 'Possess'd with rumours.'
[3] *In margin:* 'The false prophet proved a lyer of K. John.'
[4] Grafton (1569) tells the story mainly in the same words, but adds that Peter's son was hanged with him, 'least any more false prophets should aryse of that race'.

waited their comming. Where the 13. day of May the king receaived them, making unto them an othe, that of and for al things wherin he stode accursed, he would make ample restitution and satisfaction. Unto whom also all the Lords & Barons of England (so many as there were with the king attending the Legates comming) sware in like maner, and that if the king would not accomplish in every thing the othe which he had taken, that then they wold cause him to hold and confirme the same whether that he wold or not (or by strength) to use the authors words.

... Then submitted the king himselfe unto the Court of Rome and to the pope[1]: And resigning gave up his dominions and realmes of Englande & Ireland from him and from his heires for evermore that should come of him. Wyth this condition, that the king and his heirs should take againe these two dominions of the Pope to ferme, paying yearely therfore to the Court of Rome a 1000. Markes of silver. Then tooke the King the crowne from hys heade, kneeling upon his knees in the presence of all his Lordes & Barons of England to Pandulphe the popes chiefe legate, saying in this wise. Here I resigne up the crowne of the realme of England to the Popes hands Innocent the third, & put me wholy in his mercy and ordinance. Then tooke Pandolphe the crowne of king John, and kept it 5. daies as a possession & seazon taking of these two realmes of England and Ireland. Confirming also al things promised by his charter obligatorie. . . .

Upon this obligation, the king was discharged the 2. day of July, from that Tirannicall interdiction, under which he continued 6. yeares and 3. monethes. . . .

[The King murdered]

[p. 256]   And in the selfe same yeare, as king John was come to Swinestead Abbey, not farre from Lincolne, hee rested there two dayes: where (as most writers testifie) he was most traiterously poisoned by a monke of that Abby, of the secte of the Cistercians or S. Bernardes brethren, called Simon of Swinsted. . . .

As concerning the noble personage of this Prince, this witnes geveth *Roger Hoveden* therein: *Princeps quidem magnus erat sed minus fœlix: atque ut Marius utramq; fortunam expertus.* Doubtles (sayth he) king John was a mighty prince, but not so fortunate as many were. Not altogether unlike to Marius the noble Romaine, he tasted of Fortune both wayes: bountifull in mercie: in warres sometime he wanne, sometime againe he lost. *Munificus ac liberalis in exteros fuit, sed proditionis causa suorum deprædator, plus advenis quam suis confidens.*

---

[1] *In margin:* 'K. John submitteth himselfe and resigneth his crowne.'

Hee was also very bounteous & liberal unto strangers, but of his owne people (for their daily treasons sake) hee was a great oppressor, so that he trusted more to foreiners then to them. . . .[1]

It is recorded and founde in the Chronicle of William Caxton, called *fructus temporum*, and in the 7. Booke. The foresayde monke Simon, being much offended with certaine talke that the king had at his table, concernyng Ludovicke the Frenche kings sonne (which then had entred and usurped upon him)[2] did cast in hys wicked heart, howe he most speedely might bring him to his ende. And first of all he counselled with his Abbot, shewing hym the whole matter, and what hee was minded to doe. He alledged for himselfe the Prophecie of Cayphas, John 11. saying: It is better that one man die, then all the people should perish. I am well contented (sayeth he) to loose my life, and so become a Martyr, that I may utterly destroy this tyraunt.[3] With that the Abbot did weepe for gladnes, and much commended hys fervent zeale, as hee tooke it. The Monke then being absolved of his Abbot for doyng this acte (aforehand)[4] went secretely into a garden uppon the backe side, and finding there a most venemous Toad, he so pricked hym, and pressed him with his penknife: that he made him vomit all the poyson that was wythin hym. This done, he conveyed it into a cuppe of wine, and with a smiling and flattering countenance, he sayde thus to the King: If it shall like your Princely majestie, here is such a cuppe of wine, as yee never dronke a better before in all your life time. I trust this Wassall shal make al England glad. And with that he dranke a great draught thereof, the king pledging him. The Monke anone after went to the farmerye, and there died (his guts gushing out of his belly)[5] and had continually from thencefoorth three Monkes to sing Masse for his soule, confirmed by theyr generall chapter. What became after that of king John, yee shall knowe right well in the processe following. I woulde ye did marke well the wholesome proceedings of these holy votaries, howe vertuously they obey their kings, whome God hath appoynted: and how religiously they bestow their confessions, absolutions and masses.

The king within a short space after (feeling great griefe in his body) asked for Symon the monke: and aunswere was made, that he was

---

[1] *In margin: Ex Chronico cui titulus Eulogium.*

[2] Grafton has: 'hearyng the king upon an occasion to talke of breade, should say that if he lived a yere longer he would make that lofe of breade beying then of the value of one halfepeny woorth twelve pence, meaning that he woulde so persecute his rebellious people, that he would not leave one of them to be the owner of a plough'.

[3] *In margin:* 'Woe be to you that call good evill and evill good.'

[4] *In margin:* 'Simon Monke absolved of his Abbot for poysoning his king.'

[5] *In margin:* 'The monke dyeth of his own poison.' V. 6.30.

departed this life. Then god have mercy upon me (sayd he) I suspected as much, after he had sayd, that al England should therof be
glad: he ment now I perceive then of his owne generation. With that
he commanded his chariot to be prepared, for he was not able to
ride. So went he from thence to Slaford Castel, and from thence to
Newerke upon Trent: and there within less then 3. daies he died.[1]

III. Probable Source

From THE UNION OF THE TWO NOBLE AND ILLUSTRE FAMELIES OF LANCASTRE AND YORKE

by Edward Hall (1548)

[Dunois prefers bastardy to mediocrity.][2]

[civ^v] Here must I a litle digresse, and declare to you, what
was this bastard of Orleance, whiche was not onely now capitain of
the citee, but also after, by Charles the sixt made erle of Dunoys, and
in greate authoritie in Fraunce, and extreme enemie to the Englishe
nacion, as by this story you shall apparauntly perceive, of whose line
and stem[m]e dyscend the Dukes of Longuile and the Marques of
Rutylon. Lewes Duke of Orleance murthered in Paris, by John duke
of Burgoyne, as you before have harde, was owner of the Castle of
Concy, on the Frontiers of Fraunce toward Arthoys, wherof he made
Constable the lord of Cauny, a man not so wise as his wife was faire,
and yet she was not so faire, but she was as well beloved of the duke
of Orleance, as of her husband. Betwene the duke and her husbande
(I cannot tell who was father) she conceived a child, and brought
furthe a pretye boye called John, whiche child beyng of the age of
one yere, the duke diseased and not long after the mother, and the
Lorde of Cawny ended their lives. The next of kynne to the lord
Cawny chalenged the enheritaunce, whiche was worth foure thousande crounes a yere, alledgyng that the boye was a bastard: and the
kynred of the mothers side, for to save her honesty, it plainly denied.
In conclusion, this matter was in contencion before the Presidentes
of the parliament of Paris, and there hang in controversie till the
child came to the age of eight yeres old. At whiche tyme it was

[1] *In margin:* 'The death of K. John.'
[2] *TR* probably drew on this for Faulconbridge. Shakespeare would read it for
1H6.

demaunded of hym openly whose sonne he was: his frendes of his mothers side advertised him to require a day, to be advised of so great an answer, whiche he asked, & to hym it was graunted. In the meane season his said frendes persuaded him to claime his inherit-aunce, as sonne to the Lorde of Cawny, which was an honorable livyng, and an auncient patrimony, affirming that if he said con-trary, he not only slaundered his mother, shamed himself, & stained his bloud, but also should have no livyng nor any thing to take to. The scholemaster thinkyng that his disciple had well learned his lesson, and would reherse it accordyng to his instruccion, brought hym before the Judges at the daie assigned, and when the question was repeted to hym again, he boldly answered, my harte geveth me, & my noble corage telleth me, that I am the sonne of the noble Duke of Orleaunce, more glad to be his Bastarde, with a meane livyng, then the lawfull sonne of that coward cuckolde Cauny,[1] with his foure thousande crounes. The Justices much merveiled at his bolde answere, and his mothers cosyns detested him for shamyng of his mother,[2] and his fathers supposed kinne rejoysed in gainyng the patrimony and possessions. Charles duke of Orleance heryng of this judgement, toke hym into his family & gave him great offices & fees, which he well deserved, for (duryng his captivitie) he defended his lands, expulsed thenglishmen, & in conclusion procured his deliveraunce.

IV. Analogues

From THE ENGLISH CHRONICLE OF RADULPH OF COGGESHALL[3]

(a) The Attempt to Blind Prince Arthur

Cernentes autem regis consiliarii quod multas strages et seditiones facerent ubique Britones pro Arturo domino suo, et quod nulla firma pacis concordia posset fieri, Arturo superstite, suggesserunt regi quatinus praeciperet ut nobilis adolescens oculis et genitalibus privaretur, et sic deinceps ad principandum inutilis redderetur, ut vel sic pars adversa ab insania sedulae expugnationis conquiesceret

---

[1] In *TR* he does not mock at his legal father. Shakespeare makes him do so, perhaps remembering Hall.

[2] Both in *TR* and *KJ* an attempt is made to minimize this 'shaming'.

[3] *Radulphi de Coggeshall Chronicon Anglicanum*, ed. J. Stevenson, Rolls Series, 1875.

et regi se subderet. Exacerbatus itaque indefessa congressione adversariorum, et minis eorum et impropriis lacessitus, praecepit tandem in ira et in furore tribus suis servientibus quatinus ad Falesiam quantocius pergerent, atque hoc opus desabile perpetrarent. Duo vero ex servientibus tam execrabile opus in tam nobili adolescente committere detestantes, a curia domini regis diffugerunt; tertius vero ad castellum pervenit in quo puer regius a domino Huberto de Burch, regis camerario, diligenter custodiebatur, triplices annulos circa pedes habens. Cumque mandatum domini regis Huberto detulisset, exortus est fletus et planctus nimius inter milites qui custodiebant illum, utpote nimia miseratione super nobili adolescente permoti. Arturus autem diram avunculi sui sententiam super se datam cognoscens, atque de salute propria omnino diffidens, totus effluxit in lacrymas et in lamentabiles querimonias. At cum astaret ille praesens qui a rege missus fuerat ad hoc opus exsequendum, et persona gementi et flenti puero innotuisset, inter lamenta subito concitus surrexit, et manus suae dejectionis ultrices in personam illam violenter injecit, ad milites circumstantes voce lacrymabili vociferans: 'O domini mei carissimi! pro Dei amore sinite paulisper, ut me de isto facinoroso ulciscar antequam mihi oculos eripiat; nam hic ultimus omnium existet quem in praesenti saeculo conspiciam.' Ad hunc vero tumultum sedandum ocius surrexere milites, et manus utriusque cohibuerunt, atque, ex praecepto domini Huberti, juvenis ille qui advenerat de thalamo illo ejectus est; ex cujus expulsione atque ex assistentium consolatoria collocutione Arturus aliquantulam, sedata cordis moestitia, recepit consolationem.

Hubertus autem regis camerarius, honestati et famae regiae deferre volens, et indemnitati regis prospiciens, puerum regium servavit illaesum, perpendens quod dominus rex super tali edicto statim poeniteret, ac semper postmodum haberet exosum qui ejus tam crudeli imperio obtemperare praesumpisset; quod magis ex subitaneo furore quam ex perpendiculo aequitatis et justitiae emanare credidit. Volens itaque et domini regis iram ad tempus mitigare ac Britonum saevitiam cohibere, fecit per castellum et per totam provinciam divulgari quod sententia regis effectui esset mancipata, et quod dominus Arturus prae cordis tristitia et vulnerum acerbo dolore diem clausisset extremum: quae fama, per xv. dies, per utrumque regnum volitabat incessanter. Denique classicum per vicos et castella, quasi pro anima ejus, pulsatum est; vestes ejus hospitali leprosorum distributae. Divulgatum est etiam quod corpus ejus ad abbatiam de Sancto Andrea, ordinis Cisterciensis, delatum sit, ibique sepultum. Ad tales igitur rumores, Britones non animis sedati sed magis magisque exacerbati, ferocius quam prius, ubi poterant, debacchati sunt; jurantes quod nunquam deinceps ab expugnatione regis Angliae conquiescerent, qui tam detestabile facinus in dominum suum et nepotem proprium exercere praesumpsisset. Sicque factum est quod necesse erat iterum praedicare Arturum adhuc viventem et incolumem, quem ubique diffamaverant mortuum, ut vel sic efferata Britonum ferocitas aliquantulum mitigaretur. Quod cum regi intimatum esset, nequaquam displicuit ei ad praesens quod mandatum ejus exsecutum non esset. Dicebant etiam quidam militum domino regi, nequaquam ulterius milites se inventurum qui castella sua custodirent, si tam infaustum judicium de domino Arturo nepote suo exercere praesumpsisset; nam, si contingeret aliquos deinceps capi milites a rege Franciae, vel ab adversariis suis, similem statim absque miseratione sortirentur vindictam. [pp. 139–41].

English Translation

So the King's counsellors, realizing that the Bretons were making many massacres and revolts everywhere for the sake of their lord Arthur, and that no firm peace-agreement could be made so long as Arthur remained alive, suggested to the King that he should order the noble youth to be deprived of his eyes and genitals, so that he would thereafter be rendered incapable of princely rule, and also the hostile party would be calmed from the insanity of constant conflict, and submit to the King. Provoked then by the tireless coming together of his enemies and irritated by their threats and evil qualities, at length in fury he ordered three of his servants to go to Falaise as quickly as possible and perform this hateful task. Two indeed of the servants, detesting to commit such a hateful deed against so noble a youth, fled from the King's court. The third, however, came to the castle in which the royal youth was carefully guarded by Sir Hubert de Burgh, the King's chamberlain, with triple fetters about his feet. When this man reported the order of their lord the King to Hubert, great weeping and mourning broke out among the soldiers who guarded Arthur, being moved by intense pity for the noble youth. And Arthur, when he knew the cruel judgment given by his uncle upon him, despairing completely of his own safety, broke down into tears and mournful complaints. But when the man who had been sent by the King to perform this work stood in his presence and his identity was made known to the moaning, tearful boy, suddenly he rose up, excited amid his lamenting and laid hands violently on that man to avenge his own destruction, crying with tearful voice to the soldiers standing round: 'My dearest lords! for the love of God grant me a little time so that I may avenge myself on that wicked man ere he pluck out my eyes, for this may be the last of all men that I may behold in this present life.'

To put an end to this disturbance the soldiers quickly rose and restrained their hands, and at the command of lord Hubert the young man who had come [from the King] was ejected from the bedchamber. Through his expulsion and by the consoling conversation of those present Arthur's agony was relieved and he received some little consolation.

But Hubert, the King's chamberlain, wishing to uphold the King's integrity and good fame, and looking forward to the King's forgiveness, preserved the royal boy unharmed, considering that his lord the King would soon repent of such an order, but would ever afterwards have hated exceedingly the man who had presumed to obey his cruel order, which he believed emanated from a sudden fury rather than from an utter falling away from equity and justice.

Wishing therefore to mitigate in time the King's wrath and to restrain the anger of the Bretons, he let it be known in the castle and throughout the province that the King's judgment had been put into effect and that Prince Arthur had ended his last day through grief of heart and the bitter pain of his wounds, which rumour, for fifteen days, flew ceaselessly through the whole kingdom. In short the trumpet blew through streets and castles as if for his soul. His clothing was distributed to a leper hospital. It was made known that his body had been taken to the Cistercian abbey of St. Andrew, and there buried. At such rumours the Bretons were not pacified in mind but still more fiercely excited and where they could they raged more furiously than before, swearing that they would never desist from warring against the King of England, who had presumed to commit so detestable a crime against his own overlord and nephew. So it came about that it was necessary to declare publicly that Arthur whom they had rumoured to be dead was yet alive and unharmed, so that the ferocity of the Bretons might be somewhat reduced. When this was intimated to the King, he was fruitlessly displeased for a time that his orders had not been carried out. Then some of his soldiers told their lord the King that he would find it impossible to get soldiers to guard his castles if he presumed to carry out such an unhappy judgment on his nephew Prince Arthur; for if hereafter it befell any of his soldiers to be captured by the King of France or other enemies, they would at once be allotted without mercy a similar vengeance.

(b) Faukes[1] de Brent, the King's faithful servant

Rex Johannes habebat quendam servum, probum et audacem, (qui Falco cognominatus est a falce qua occiderat militem in prato patris sui in Normannia,) cui primo commiserat quamdam custodiam in confinio Gualliæ inter marchisos, ubi strenue cum sociis sibi associatis rapinas et cædes in marchisos exercuerat; unde ex infimo cito est inclitus effectus et nominatissimus inter servientes regis. Tandem, in illa discordia quæ facta est inter regem Johannem et barones suos, accitus est Falco cum familia sua plurima et pessima, quæ rapinis atque incendiis, et cædibus et cruciatibus hominum quos capiebant, die noctuque sine miseratione invigilabant; nulli ætati aut sexui, aut clericali, sive religiosorum dignitati, parcentes, quin omnia, ubi poterant, caperent et crudeliter diripirent. . . .

Rex Johannes dedit prædicto Falconi, propter suam et suorum severam probitatem, plures custodias castellorum et comitatuum. Contulit etiam ei terram Willelmi de Bello-campo, qui cum aliis baronibus contra regem conspiraverant. Dedit insuper ei castellum de Bedeford pro servitio suo, et charta sua confirmavit. . . . Sic et prospexis successibus undique elevatus, parem in regno habere dedignabatur . . . [pp. 204–8].

English translation

King John had a certain loyal and bold servant, called Faukes, after the sickle [*a falce*] with which he had killed a soldier in his father's meadow in Normandy. This man had been employed as a sort of warden among the Marchmen on the Welsh border, where with his associates he practised rapine and slaughter, whence his fame grew quickly and from base beginnings he became one of the best known of the King's servants. At last in that conflict which broke out between King John and his barons, Faukes was summoned with his numerous and evil following, who with plundering and burning, the slaughter and torturing of those whom they captured, were vigilant and pitiless day and night, sparing neither for age nor sex nor for the dignity of clerics or of religious persons, but rather wherever they could they seized and cruelly plundered everything. . . .

Because of his savage loyalty and that of his men, King John gave the guardianship of several castles and cohorts to the aforesaid Faukes. He also granted him the lands of William de Beauchamp

[1] Foukes *Hol.*

who had conspired against the King with other barons. He gave him moreover for his services the Castle of Bedford, and confirmed it with a charter. . . . Thus elevated by good fortune Faukes disdained to admit any equal in the realm. . . .

[After John's death he refused to surrender the Castle of Bedford to Henry III and was besieged there, but was finally let go free, 'preferring exile to having to trust in the mercy and goodwill of the barons, many of whom he had grievously offended'.]

V. Summary of Analogue

KING JOHAN

by John Bale (1538-60[1])

King John soliloquizes, referring to his ancestors, to his dead brother 'Rychard curdelyon they callyd hym in Fraunce', and to his own victorious reign:

> And now do purpose by practyse and by stodye
> To reforme the lawes and sett men in good order
> That trew Justyce may be had in every border.   (19–21)

To him enters the Widdow England, complaining of the bad clergy

> Whych in ydelnes do lyve by other menns goodes,
> Monkes, chanons, and nones in dyvers coloure and shappe.
> (37–8)

They are interrupted by Sedition, who declares that he will support the Pope 'So long as I have a hole within my breeche', and 'the pope ableth me to subdewe bothe kyng and keyser'. John promises to take up England's case, and will consult his nobles, clerics and lawyers. Sedition, claiming to have been born 'under the Pope in the holy cyte of Rome', reveals his many clerical disguises, his work as Papal legate and as suborner of traitors and rebels:

> That no prince can have his peples obedyence
> Except yt doth stond with the popes prehemynence.   (221–2)

John says that such work shall not go on in England. When Sedition declares that bishops, as 'Gods vicars' can depose a prince, the King says that he will destroy the bad clergy.

[1] Spelling and punctuation somewhat simplified from text in Malone Society Reprint, ed. J. H. P. Pafford, 1931.

John now tells the Nobility and the Clergy that they are wrong-
fully bound to 'the grett captyvyte of blody Babulon ... the
Romysh churche'. Civil Order (the Judge) submits himself to the
King and supports him against the multiplicity of monastic orders.
To the Clergy John says:

> Nowther thou nor the Pope shall do pore Englond wroñge
> I beyng governor and kyng her peple amonge.   (460–1)

He charges them all:

> For the love of God loke to the state of Englond.
> Leate non enemy holde her in myserable bond:
> Se yow defend her as yt becummeth Nobilite;
> Se yow instrutte her acordynge to yowr degre;
> Fournysh her yow with a cyvyle honeste:
> Thus shall she florysh in honor and grett plente.
> With godly wysdom yowr maters so conveye
> That the commynalte the powers maye obeye,
> And ever be ware of that false thefe Sedycyon,
> Whych poysenneth all realmes and bryng them to perdycyon.
>
> (517–27)

The King goes out with Civil Order, and the other two discuss him.
Nobility calls him 'a man of a wonderfull wytt', and when Clergy
disagrees, accuses the latter of defaming the King:

You pristes are the cawse that Chronycles doth defame
So many prynces, and men of notable name,
For you take upon yow to wryght them evermore,
And therfore Kyng Johan ys lyke to rewe yt sore
Whan ye wryte his tyme, for vexyng of the Clargy.

> CL. I mervell ye take his parte so ernestlye.
> NOB. Yt becomyth Nobelyte his prynces fame to preserve.
> CL. Yf he contynew, we are lyke in a whyle to starve.
> He demaundeth of us the tenth parte of owr lyvyng.
> NOB. I thynke yt is then for sum nessessary thyng.
> CL. Mary, to recover that he hath lost in Fraunce,
> As Normandy dewkedom, and his land beyond Orleaunce.
> NOB. And thynke ye not that a matter necessary?
> CL. No, sur, by my trowth, he takyng yt of the Clergy.
> NOB. Ye cowde be content that he shuld take yt of us?
> CL. Yea, so that he wold spare the Clargy, by swet Jesus.
>
> (577–92)

As they go out Sedition re-enters, closely followed by Dissimulation and there is some amusing by-play, with parody of the Litany and description of the hypocritical lewdness of the monks. Dissimulation prays for the removal of King John or for the Church's victory over him.

> SED.   And why of Kyng Johan? doth he vexe yow so sore?
>
> DISS.   Both chyrchys and abbeys he oppressyth more and more,
> And take of the clergye yt is onresonable to tell.
>
> SED.   Owte with the popes bulles than, and cursse hym downe to hell.
>
> DISS.   Tushe, man, we have done so, but all wyll not helpe,
> He regardyth no more the pope than he dothe a whelpe.   (652–57)

However Dissimulation will bring 'a chylde of myn owne bryngyng uppe', namely, Private Wealth:

> DISS.   I made hym a monke, and a perfytt cloysterer,
> And in the abbeye he becam first celerer,
> Then pryor, then abbote of a thowsand pownd land no wors,
> Now he is a bysshoppe and rydth with an hondryd hors,
> And, as I here say, he is lyke to be a Cardynall.
>
> SED.   Ys he so indede, by the masse than have att all.
>
> DISS.   Nay, fyrst Pryvat Welth shall bryng in Usurpyd Power
> With hys autoryte, and than the gam[e] ys ower.
>
> SED.   Tush, Usurpyd Power dothe faver me of all men,
> For in his trobles I ease his hart now and then.
> Whan prynces rebell agenst hys autoryte,
> I make ther commons agenst them for to be.
> Twenty thousand men are but a mornyng breckefast
> To be slayne for hym, he takying his repast.
>
> DISS.   Thow hast I persayve a very suttyll cast.
>
> SED.   I am for the pope, as for the shyppe the mast.   (736–52)

So

> False Dyssymulacyon doth bryng in Privat Welth,
> And Usurpyd Power, which is more ferce than a Turke,
> Cummeth in by hym to decayve all spirtuall helth.   (766–8)

Sedition then declares:

> We four by our crafts Kyng Johan wyll so subdewe,
> That for three hundred yers all Englond shall yt rewe.   (770–1)

It soon appears that Usurped Power is the 'holy father', the Pope in disguise. To him Dissimulation presents an appeal from the

English bishops 'To save and support the Chyrches lyberte' from
John, who 'wyll suffer non to the court of Rome to appele'.

DISS.   No, he contemnyth yowr autortyte and seale,
And sayth in his lond he wyll be lord and kyng,
No prist so hardy to enterpryse any thyng.
For the whych of late with hym were at varyaunce
Fower of the byssopps, and in maner at defyaunce,
Wyllyam of London, and Eustace byssoppe of Hely,
Water of Wynchester, and Gylys of Hartford trewly.
By yowr autoryte they have hym excomunycate.

US. PO.   Than have they done well, for he is a reprobate:
To that I admytt he ys alwayes contrary.
I made this fellow here the archebysshope of Canterbery
And he wyll agree therto in no condycion.
PR. WE.   Than hath he knowlege that his name ys Sedycyon.
DISS.   Dowtles he hath so, and that drowneth his opynyon. . . .
US. PO.   Now, how shall we do for this same wycked kyng?
SED.   Suspend hym, and curse hym, both with yowr word and
        wrytyng.
Yf that wyll not helpe, than interdyght his lond
With extreme cruellnes; and yf that wyll not stond,
Cawse other prynces to revenge the Churches wronge.
Yt wyll profytte yow to sett them aworke amonge,
For clene remyssyon one kyng wyll subdew another,
Yea, the chyld sumtyme wyll sle both father and mother.

(923–99)

Usurped Power goes out and returns dressed as the Pope to issue his
curse against King John. He identifies Private Wealth with Cardinal
Pandulphus, Sedition with Stephen Langton, and Dissimulation
with Raimundus:

POPE   To colour this thyng thow shalte be callyd Pandulphus,
Thow Stevyn Langton; thy name shall be Raymundus.
Fyrst thow Pandulphus shall openly hym suspend
Wyth boke, bell and candle: yff he wyll not so amend,
Interdycte his lande, and the churches all up speare.
PR. WE.   I have my message; to do yt I wyll not feare.
POPE   And thow, Stevyn Langton, cummand the bysshoppes all
So many to curse as are to hym benefycyall,
Dukes, erles, and lords, wherby they may forsake hym.
SED.   Sur, I wyll do yt, and that I trow shall shake hym.
POPE   Raymundus, go thow forth to the Crysten princes all:
Byd them in my name that they uppon hym fall

Bothe with fyre and sword, that the Churche may hym conquarre.
　　DISS.　Your plesur I wyll no longar tyme defarre.
　　POPE　Saye this to them also: Pope Innocent the thred
Remyssyon of synnes to so many men hath granted,
As wyll do ther best to slee hym yf they may.
　　DISS.　Sur, yt shall be done withowt ony lenger delay.　(1057–74)

The Act ends with a speech by The Interpreter who summarizes
events so far and praises the King:

　　This noble Kynge Johan, as a faythfull Moyses,
　　Withstode proude Pharao for hys poore Israel,
　　Myndynge to brynge it owt of the lande of darkenesse,
　　But the Egyptyanes did agaynst hym so rebell,
　　That hys poore people ded styll in the desart dwell,
　　Tyll that duke Josue, whych was our late Kynge Henrye,[1]
　　Clerely brought us into the lande of mylke and honye.
　　As a stronge David, at the voyce of verytie
　　Great Golye the pope, he strake downe with hys slynge.

　　　　　　　　　　　　　　　　　　　　　　　(1097–1105)

In the Second Act, Sedition, pretending to be Good Perfection,
hears the confession of Nobility, promises to eschew 'the new
lernyng' and to abandon the King. As Stephen Langton, Sedition
next subverts Clergy and Civil Order to work against John:

　　SED.　Now, Clargy, my friend, this must thow do for the pope,
And for Holy Chyrch: thow must mennys conscyence grope,
And as thow felyst them so cause them for to wurke:
Leat them show Kyng Johan no more faver than a Turke.
Everywher sture them to make an insurreccyon.
　　CLE.　All that shall I do, and to provoke them more
This interdyccyon I wyll lament very sore
In all my prechyngs, and saye throwgh his occasyon
All we are under the danger of dampnacyon.
And this wyll move peple to helpe to put hym downe,
Or elles compell hym to geve up septur and crowne . . .
And bysydes all this, the chyrch dores I wyll up seale,
And closse up the bells that they ryng never a pele:
I wyll spere up the chalyce, crysmatory, crosse and all,
That masse they shall have non, baptysm nor beryall,
And thys I know well wyll make the peple madde.

---

[1] Henry VIII.

SED.   Mary, that yt wyll; soche sauce he never had.
And what wylte thow do for Holy Chyrche, Cyvyll Order?
CIV. O.   For the clergyes sake I wyl, in every border
Provoke the gret men to take the commonys parte . . .   (1238–59)

The plotters retire as the King enters. He regrets the trouble fallen
upon his country through his desire 'to execute Upon transgressers
acordyng unto justyce.' Private Wealth comes as Cardinal
Pandulphus.

K.J.   Frynd, ye be welcum: what is yowr plesure with me?
PAND.   From the holy father, Pope Innocent the thred,
As a massanger I am to yow dyrectyd,
To reforme the peace betwyn Holy Chyrch and yow,
And in his behalfe I avertyce yow here now
Of the Chyrchys goods to make full restytucyon,
And to accepte also the popes hely constytucyon
For Stevyn Langton, archebysshop of Canturbery,
And so admytt hym to his state and primacy:
The monkes exilyd ye shall restore agayne
To ther placys and londes, and nothyng of thers retayne.
Owr holy fatheres mynde ys that ye shall agayne restore
All that ye have ravyshyd from Holy Chyrche with the more.
                                        (1307–18)
John refuses to accept Langton, for 'he is moche inclyned to
sturdynesse and sedycyon'; he defies Pandulphus and the Pope:

K.J.   Avant, pevysh prist: what, dost thow thretten me?
I defye the worst both of thi pope and the.
The power of princys ys gevyn from God above,
And, as sayth Saloman, ther hartes the Lord doth move.
God spekyth in ther lyppes whan they geve jugement:
The lawys that they make are by the Lordes appoyntment.
Christ wylled not his[1] the princes to correcte,
But to ther precepptes rether to be subjecte.
The offyce of yow ys not to bere the sword,
But to geve counsell accordyng to Gods word . . .   (1341–50)

At this Pandulphus curses John and lays his land under an interdict:

And I cursse all them that geve to yow ther harte,
Dewks, erlls, and lordes so many as take yowr parte:
And I assoyle yowr peple from yowr abedyence,
That they shall owe yow noyther fewte[2] nor reverence.

---

[1] his Apostles.   [2] fealty.
5—N.D.S.S. 4

By the popys awctoryte I charge them yow to fyght
As with a tyrant agenst Holy Chyrshys ryght;
And by the popes auctoryte I geve them absolucyon
A pena et culpa, and also clene remyssyon.

SED.(*extra locum*[1]).   Alarum, Alarum, tro ro ro ro ro, tro ro, ro, ro!
Thomp, thomp, thomp, downe, downe, downe, to go, to go, to go!
K.J.   What a noyse is thys that without the dore is made?
PAND.   Suche enmyes are up as wyll your realme invade.

K.J.   Ye cowde do no more and ye cam from the devyll of hell,
Than ye go abowt here to worke by yowr wyckyd cownsell . . .

(1378–81)

The King appeals to Civil Order and Clergy, but they desert him.
He tries to show Nobility that the excommunication 'ys but a
fantasy in yowr ymagynacyon', and that 'the fathers sprytuall/Were
under the prynces ever contynewally', but Nobility leaves him too.
He seeks help from Communalty, who comes in with England, but
Communalty is poor and blind, because ignorant of the true Word
of God, and is soon scared off by Pandulphus. The Cardinal asserts
that England is about to be invaded from all sides:

PAND.   . . . . we have this howr great navyes upon the see
In every quarter with this Loller[2] here to fyght,

And to conquarre hym for the Holy Chyrchis ryght.
We have on the northe Alexander, the kyng of Scottes,
With an armye of men that for their townes cast lottes.
On the sowth syde we have the French kyng with his power,
Which wyll sle and burne tyll he cum to London Tower.
In the west parts we have kyng Alphonse with the Spanyards,
With sheppes full of gonepowder now cummyng hether towards,
And on the est syde we have Esterlynges, Danes and Norways,
With soch power landynge as can be resystyd nowayes.

(1619–28)

When the King realizes that this is true he asks whether, if he
submits, it will be possible 'to hold these enemyes backe'. Being
assured that this will be so on condition that he give up his crown,
he goes away to consult his Nobility, and soon returns.

K.J.   I have cast in mynde the great displeasures of warre
The daungers, the losses, the decayes both nere and farre,
The burnynge of townes, the throwynge downe of buyldynges,

---

[1] I.e. *offstage*.   [2] Lollard, heretic.

Destructyon of corne, and cattell with other thynges,
Defylynge of maydes, and shedynge of Christen blood,
With such lyke outrages, neyther honest, true nor good.
These thynges consydered, I am compelled thys houre
To resigne up here, bothe crowne and regall powre.

ENG. For the love of God, yet take some better advysement.
SED. Holde your tunge ye whore, or by the messe ye shall
repent
Downe on your mary bones, and make nomore ado.
ENG. If ye love me sir, for Gods sake do never so.
K.J. O Englande, Englande, shewe now thyselfe a mother.
Thy people wyll els be slayne here without nomber.
As God shall judge me, I do not thys of cowardnesse
But of compassyon, in thys extreme heavynesse.
Shall my people shedde their bloude in suche habundaunce?
Naye, I shall rather gyve upp my whole governaunce.
SED. Come of[f] apace, than, and make an ende of it shortly.
ENG. The most pitiefull chaunce, that hath bene hytherto
surely.
K.J. Here I submyt me to pope Innocent the thred,
Dyssyering mercy, of hys holy fatherhed.
CARD. Geve up the crowne than, yt shalbe the better for ye.
He wyll unto yow the more favorable be.

Here the Kyng delevyr the crowne to the Cardynall.

K.J. To hym I resygne here the septer and the crowne
Of Inglond and Yrelond, with the powre and renowne
And put me wholly to his mercifull ordynance.
CARD. I may say, this day the chyrch hath a full gret chaunce,
Thes five days I wyll kepe this crowne in myne owne hande
In the popes behalfe, upseasing Ynglond and Yrelond.
In the meane season ye shall make an oblygacyon
For yow and yowr ayers, in this sygnyficacyon
To resayve yowr crowne of the pope for ever more
In maner of fe farme, and for a tokyn therfor
Ye shall every yere paye hym a thowsand marke
With the peter pens, and not agenst yt barke.
Ye shall also geve, to the bysshoppe of Cantorbery
A thre thowsand marke, for his gret Injury.
To the chyrche besydes, for the great scathe ye have done
Forty thowsand marke ye shall delyver sone. . . .

(1722–42; 1646–65)

The King protests in vain; he promises to readmit the monks, despite England's lament that he has now made her a bondmaid and destroyed himself and his heirs. When John produces the money for his full restitution, the Cardinall lets him be absolved.

> CARD.　Cum hither my lorde, by the popys autoryte
> Assoyll this man here of irregularite

> *Here the bysshop* Stevyn Langton *cum in*

> K.J.　Methynke this bysshope resembleth moch Sedycyon.
> CARD.　I cownsell yow yet, to beware of wrong suspycyon.
> This is Stevyn Langton, yowr Meteropolytan.
> K.J. Than do the offyce of the good Samarytan
> And pore oyle and wyne in my old festerd wownd.
> Releace me of synne, that yt doth not me confownd.

Langton absolves him, and immediately the Cardinal proves his power when he refuses to let the King execute Treason, a priest who has been falsifying the coinage.

> ENGLANDE　I accompt hym no priest, that worke such haynous treason.
> SED. [Langton]　It is a worlde to heare a folysh woman reason.
> CARD.　After thys maner ye used Peter Pomfrete
> A good symple man, and as they saye, a profete.
> K.J.　Sir, I ded prove hym a very supersticyouse wretche
> And blasphemouse lyar, therfor ded the lawe hym upstretche.
> He prophecyed first, I shuld reigne but fourteen years,
> Makynge the people to beleve he could bynde bears,
> And I have reigned a seventene yeares and more.
> And anon after, he grudged at me very sore
> And sayde I shulde be exylded out of my realme
> Before the Ascencyon, whych was turned to a fantastycall dreame,
> Saynge he woulde hange, if hys prophecye were not true.
> Thus hys owne decaye hys folyshnesse did brue.
> CARD.　Ye should not hange hym, whych is a frynde to the churche.　(1833–47)

The interdict on England is raised. Sedition believes that John will soon 'become unto us a common slave' but advises the Cardinal to make sure of it.

> CARD.　Whye what shall we do, to hym els, in the name of Jesus?
> SED.　Marry fetche in Lewes, kynge Phylyppes sonne of Fraunce
> To fall upon hym, with hys menne and ordynaunce,

With wyldefyer, gunpouder, and suche lyke myrye tryckes
To dryve hym to holde, and searche hym to the quyckes.
I wyll not leave hym, tyll I brynge hym to hys yende.
   CARD.   Well, farewel Sedicyon, do as shal lye in thy myende.
   SED.   I marvele greatly, where Dissymulacyon is!
   DISS.   I wyll come anon, if thou tarry tyll I pysse.
   SED.   I beshrewe your hart, where have ye bene so longe?
   DISS.   In the gardene man, the herbes and wedes amonge,
And there have I gote the poyson of a toade.
I hope in a whyle to wurke some feate abroade . . .
Sir, thys is my mynde, I wyll gyve kynge Johan thys poyson,
So makynge hym sure, that he shall never have foyson,
And thys must thu saye, to colour with the thynge,
That a penye lofe he wolde have brought to a shyllynge . . .
   SED.   I am sure than, thu wylt geve it hym in a drynke.
   DISS.   Marry that I wyll, and the one half with hym swynke
To encourage hym, to drynke the botome off.
   SED.   If thy drynke the halfe, thu shalt fynde it no scoff.
Of terryble deathe thy wylt stacker in the plashes.
   DISS.   Tush, though I dye man, there wyll ryse more of my
     ashes.
I am sure the monkes wyll praye for me so bytterlye
That I shall not come in helle nor in purgatorye . . .
   SED.   To kepe the from thens, thu shalt have fyve monkes
     syngynge
In Swynsett abbeye so longe as the worlde is durynge.
They wyll daylye praye for the sowle of father Symon,
A Cisteane monke, whych poysened kynge John . . . (1952–97)

The King enters, grieving that against him he has the lords and commons, the bishops and the lawyers, who 'in their cruell madnesse / Hath brought in hyther the Frenche kynges eldest sonne Lewes'. He is tired of life. England consoles him:

   ENG.   Sir, be of good chere, for the pope hath sent a legate
Whose name is Gualo, your foes to excommunycate,
Not only Lewes, whych hath wonne Rochestre
Wynsore and London, Readynge and Wynchestre
But so manye els, as agaynst ye have rebelled
He hath suspended, and openly accursed. (2020–5)

However, at this moment Dissimulation enters, singing a Wassail song, to carry out his fiendish plan.

   DISS.   I am as gentle a worme as ever ye see.
   K.J.   But what is thy name, good frynde, I praye the tell me?

DISS.   Simon of Swynsett, my very name is per dee.
I am taken of men for monastycall devocyon,
And here have I brought yow, a marvelouse good pocyon
For I hearde ye saye that ye were very drye.
    K.J.   Indede I wolde gladly drynke, I praye the come nye.

                                          (2052–8)

Since the King insists that Simon drink half, he does so and dies.
The King begins to feel unwell.

    K.J.   My bodye me vexeth, I doubt muche of a tympanye.
    ENG.   Now alas alas, your grace is betrayed coawardlye.
    K.J.   Where became the monke that was here with me latelye?
    ENG.   He is poysened, sir, and lyeth adyenge surelye.
    K.J.   It can not be so, for he was here even now.
    ENG.   Doubtlesse sir it is, so true as I have tolde yow.
A false Judas kysse he hath gyven yow and is gone.
The halte, sore and lame, thys pitifull case wyll mone.
Never prynce was there, that made to poor peoples uses
So many masendewes,[1] hospytals, and spyttle houses
As your grace hath done, yet sens the worlde began.
    K.J.   Of priestes and of monkes I am counted a wycked man
For that I never buylte churche nor monasterye,
But my pleasure was, to helpe such as were nedye.
    ENG.   The more grace was yours, for at the daye of judgement
Christe wyll rewarde them, whych hath done hys commaundement.
There is no promyse for voluntarye wurkes
No more than there is, for sacrifyce of the Turkes.
    K.J.   Doubtlesse I do fele muche grevaunce in my bodye.
    ENG.   As the lorde wel knoweth, for that I am full sorye.
    K.J.   There is no malyce, to the malyce of the clergye.
Well, the lorde God of heaven, on me and them have mercye.
For doynge justyce, they have ever hated me.
They caused my lande, to be excommunycate
And me to resygne both crowne and princely dygnyte
From my obedyence assoylinge every estate,
And now last of all, they have me intoxycate.
I perceyve ryght wele, their malyce hath none ende.
I desyre not els, but that they maye sone amende.
I have sore hungered and thirsted ryghteousnesse
For the offyce sake, that God hath me appoynted . . .

                                      (2090–2120)

---

[1] Maisons de Dieu, hospitals.

He dies and England mourns

> that ever so noble a kynge
> Shoulde thus be destroyed and lost for ryghteouse doynge
> By a cruell sort of disguysed bloud suppers. (2139–41)

An Epilogue follows in which Verity discusses John's life.

VER. I assure ye fryndes, lete men wryte what they wyll,
Kynge Johan was a man both valeaunt and godlye.
What though Poydorus[1] reporteth hym very yll

At the suggestyons of the malicyouse clergye.
Thynke yow a Romane with the Romanes can not lye? (2145–9)

Verity assures Nobility that John was a worthy prince, and reminds
Clergy that St Jerome called any man traitor 'that rebelleth agaynst
the crowne'.

CLER. He speaketh not agaynst the crowne but the man per
dee.
VER. Where is the sprete, which ought to reigne in thee?
The crowne of it selfe without the man is nothynge.
Learne of the scriptures to have better understandynge.
The harte of a kynge is in the handes of the lorde
And he directeth it, wyse Salomon to recorde.
They are abhomynable, that use hym wyckedlye. (2185–91)

Imperial Majesty now enters and the three characters who have
misused King John beg forgiveness for their great enormity and
promise never to offend again. Sedition is shown up in his true
colours and condemned, and the play ends with praise of Queen
Elizabeth, who 'maye be a lyghte to other princes all'.

---

[1] Polydore Vergil, the Italian historian whose account of John gives an
ecclesiastical view of his actions.

VI. Source

THE TROUBLESOME RAIGNE OF KING JOHN

Two Parts. Anonymous (1591)

PART ONE

The Troublesome Raigne of *John* King of *England*, with the discoverie of King Richard Cordelions Base sonne (vulgarly named, The Bastard Fawconbridge): also the death of King *John* at *Swinstead Abbey*. *As it was (sundry times) publikely acted by the Queenes Majesties Players, in the honourable Citie of* London. Imprinted at London for *Sampson Clarke*, and are to be solde at his shop, on the backeside of the *Royall Exchange*. 1591.

TO THE GENTLEMEN READERS[1]

> *You that with friendly grace of smoothed brow*
> *Have entertaind the* Scythian Tamburlaine,
> *And given applause unto an Infidel:*
> *Vouchsafe to welcome (with like curtesie)*
> *A warlike Christian and your Countreyman.*
> *For Christs true faith indur'd he many a storme,*
> *And set himselfe against the Man of* Rome,
> *Untill base treason (by a damned wight)*
> *Did all his former triumphs put to flight,*
> *Accept of it (sweete Gentles) in good sort,*
> *And thinke it was preparde for your disport.*

The Troublesome Raigne of King John

[Part 1]

[Scene i]

> Enter K. *John*, Queene Elinor his mother, William Marshal
> Earle of Pembrooke, the Earles of Essex, and of Salisbury.

---

[1] Text based on the facsimile ed. C. Praetorius, 1888, with some emendation of punctuation and abbreviation of speech-headings. *1591* had no scene-divisions.

QUEENE ELIANOR   Barons of *England*, and my noble
   Lords;
Though God and Fortune have bereft from us
Victorious *Richard* scourge of Infidels,
And clad this Land in stole of dismall hieu:
Yet give me leave to joy, and joy you all,
That from this wombe hath sprung a second hope,
A King that may in rule and vertue both
Succeede his brother in his Emperie.
   K. JOHN   My gracious mother Queene, and Barons all;
Though farre unworthie of so high a place,   10
As is the Throne of mightie *Englands* King:
Yet *John* your Lord, contented uncontent,
Will (as he may) sustaine the heavie yoke
Of pressing cares, that hang upon a Crowne.
My Lord of *Pembrooke* and Lord *Salsbury*,
Admit the Lord *Shattilion* to our presence;
That we may know what *Philip* King of *Fraunce*
(By his Ambassadors) requires of us.
   Q. ELINOR   Dare lay my hand that *Elinor* can gesse
Whereto this weightie Embassade doth tend: 20
If of my Nephew *Arthur* and his claime,
Then say my Sonne I have not mist my aime.

Enter Chattilion and the two Earles.[1]

   JOHN   My Lord *Chattilion*, welcome into *England*:
How fares our Brother *Philip* King of *Fraunce*?
   CHATT.   His Highness at my comming was in health,
And wild me to salute your Majestie,
And say the message he hath given in charge.
   JOHN   And spare not man, we are preparde to heare.
   CHATTILION   *Philip* by the grace of God most Christian
K. of *France*, having taken into his guardain and protection   30
Arthur Duke of *Brittaine*, son & heire to *Jeffrey* thine elder
brother, requireth in the behalfe of the said *Arthur*, the King-
dom of *England*, with the Lordship of *Ireland*, *Poitiers*, *Anjow*,
Torain, *Main*[2]: and I attend thine aunswere.

   JOHN   A small request: belike he makes account
That *England*, *Ireland*, *Poiters*, *Anjow*, *Torain*, *Main*,
Are nothing for a King to give at once:
I wonder what he meanes to leave for me.

---

[1] *KJ* begins here.   [2] I.i.7–15.

Tell *Philip*, he may keepe his Lords at home
With greater honour than to send them thus   40
On Embassades that not concerne himselfe,
Or if they did, would yeeld but small returne.

    CHATTILION   Is this thine answere?

    JOHN   It is, and too good an answer for so proud a
    message.

    CHATTILION   Then King of *England*, in my Masters name,
And in Prince *Arthur* Duke of *Britaines* name,
I doo defie thee as an Enemie,
And wish thee to prepare for bloodie warres.[1]

    Q. ELINOR   My Lord (that stands upon defiance thus)
Commend me to my Nephew, tell the boy,   50
That I Queene *Elianor* (his Grandmother)
Upon my blessing charge him leave his Armes,
Whereto his head-strong Mother pricks him so:[2]

Her pride we know, and know her for a Dame
That will not sticke to bring him to his ende,
So she may bring her selfe to rule a Realme.
Next wish him to forsake the King of *Fraunce*,
And come to me and to his Unckle here,
And he shall want for nothing at our hands.

    CHATTILION   This shall I doo, and thus I take my leave.   60

    JOHN   *Pembrooke*, convay him safely to the sea,
But not in hast: for as we are advisde,
We meane to be in *Fraunce* as soone as he,[3]

To fortefie such townes as we possesse
In *Anjou*, *Torain* and in *Normandy*.   [*Exit Chatt.*

Enter the Shrive, & whispers the Earle of Sals. in the eare.

    SALISBURY   Please it your Majestie, heere is the Shrive of
Northhamptonshire,[4] with certaine persons that of late committed a riot, and have appeald to your Majestie beseeching
your Highnes for speciall cause to heare them.

    JOHN   Wil them come neere, and while we heare the
    cause,   70
Goe *Salsbury* and make provision,

---

[1] I.1.16–22.
[3] Cf. I.1.24–5.
[2] I.1.31–4, 'ambitious Constance'.
[4] I.1.44, 51. No riot mentioned.

We meane with speede to passe the sea to *Fraunce*.
Say Shrieve, what are these men, what have they done?
Or wheretoo tends the course of this appeale?

SHRIEVE   Please it your Majestie these two brethren
unnaturally falling at odds about their Fathers living have
broken your Highnes peace, in seeking to right their own
wrongs without cause of Law, or order of Justice, and unlaw-
fully assembled themselves in mutinous manner, having
committed a riot, appealing from triall in their Countrey to
your Highnes: and here I *Thomas Nidigate* Shrieve of *Northhamptonshire*, doo deliver them over to their triall.   82

JOHN   My Lord of *Essex*, will the offenders to stand foorth,
and tell the cause of their quarrell.

ESSEX   Gentlemen, it is the Kings pleasure that you dis-
cover your griefes, & doubt not but you shall have justice.

PHILIP   Please it your Majestie, the wrong is mine; yet
wil I abide all wrongs, before I once open my mouth to un-
rippe the shamefull slaunder of my parents, the dishonour of
myself, & the wicked dealing of my brother in this princely
assembly.   90

ROBERT   Then by my Prince his leave shall *Robert* speake,
And tell your Majestie what right I have
To offer wrong, as he accounteth wrong.[1]
My Father (not unknowen unto your Grace)
Receivd his spurres of Knighthood in the Field,
At Kingly *Richards* hands in *Palestine*,
When as the walls of *Acon*[2] gave him way:
His name Sir *Robert Fauconbridge* of *Mountbery*.
What by succession from his Auncestours,
And warlike service under *Englands* Armes,   100
His living did amount too at his death
Two thousand Markes revenew every yeare[3]:
And this (my Lord) I challenge for my right,
As lawfull heire to *Robert Fauconbridge*.

PHILIP   If first-borne sonne be heire indubitate
By certaine right of *Englands* auncient Lawe,
How should myselfe make any other doubt,
But I am heire to *Robert Fauconbridge*?

JOHN   Fond Youth, to trouble these our Princely eares
Or make a question in so plaine a case:
Speake, is this man thine elder Brother borne?   110

---

[1] *1591* has: To ouer wrong, as he accouncerd wrong.
[2] I.1.51–4. *Acon*, Acre.   [3] Cf. I.1.69.

ROBERT   Please it your Grace with patience for to heare;
I not denie but he mine Elder is,
Mine elder Brother too: yet in such sort,
As he can make no title to the Land.

JOHN   A doubtfull tale as ever I did heare,
Thy Brother and thine elder, and no heire:
Explaine this darke *Ænigma*.

ROBERT   I graunt (my Lord) he is my mothers sonne,
Base borne, and base begot, no *Fauconbridge*.   120
Indeede the world reputes him lawfull heire,
My Father in his life did count him so,
And here my Mother stands to proove him so:
But I (my Lord) can proove, and doo averre
Both to my Mothers shame and his reproach,
He is no heire, nor yet legitimate.
Then (gracious Lord) let *Fauconbridge* enjoy
The living that belongs to *Fauconbridge*,
And let not him possesse anothers right.

JOHN   Prove this, the land is thine by *Englands* law.   130

Q. ELINOR   Ungracious youth, to rip thy mothers shame,
The wombe from whence thou didst thy being take.
All honest eares abhorre thy wickednes,
But gold I see doth beate downe natures law.

MOTHER   My gracious Lord, & you thrice reverend Dame,
That see the teares distilling from mine eyes,
And scalding sighes blowne from a rented heart:
For honour and regard of womanhood,
Let me entreate to be commaunded hence.
Let not these eares receive the hissing sound   140
Of such a viper, who with poysoned words
Doth masserate[1] the bowels of my soule.

JOHN   Ladie, stand up, be patient for a while:
And fellow, say, whose bastard is thy brother.

PHILIP   Not for my selfe, nor for my mother now:
But for the honour of so brave a Man,
Whom he accuseth with adulterie:
Here I beseech your Grace upon my knees,
To count him mad, and so dismisse us hence.

ROBERT   Nor mad, nor mazde, but well advised, I   150
Charge thee before this royall presence here
To be a Bastard to King *Richards* self,
Sonne to your Grace, and Brother to your Majestie.

---

[1] macerate, waste away. In *KJ* she does not enter till 219.

Thus bluntly, and—

ELIANOR   Yong man thou needst not be ashamed of thy
    kin,
Nor of thy Sire. But forward with thy proofe.

ROBERT   The proofe so plaine, the argument so strong,
As that your Highnes and these noble Lords,
And all (save those that have no eyes to see)
Shall sweare him to be Bastard to the King.   160
First when my Father was Embassadour
In *Germanie* unto the Emperour,[1]
The King lay often at my Fathers house;
And all the Realme suspected what befell:
And at my Fathers back returne agen
My Mother was delivered as tis sed,
Sixe weeks before the account my Father made.[2]
But more than this: looke but on *Philips* face,
His features, actions, and his lineaments,
And all this Princely presence shall confesse,   170
He is no other but King *Richards* Sonne.
Then gracious Lord, rest he King *Richards* Sonne,
And let me rest safe in my Fathers right,
That am his rightfull sonne and onely heire.

JOHN   Is this thy proofe, and all thou hast to say?

ROBERT   I have no more, nor neede I greater proofe.[3]

JOHN   First, where thou saidst in absence of thy Sire
My Brother often lodged in his house:
And what of that? base groome to slaunder him,
That honoured his Embassador so much,   180
In absence of the man to cheere the wife?
This will not hold, proceede unto the next.

Q. ELINOR   Thou saist she teemde six weeks before her
    time.
Why good Sir Squire are you so cunning growen
To make account of womens reckonings:
Spit in your hand and to your other proofes:
Many mischaunces hap in such affaires
To make a woman come before her time.

JOHN   And where thou saist he looketh like the King
In action, feature and proportion: 190
Therein I holde with thee, for in my life
I never saw so lively counterfet
Of *Richard Cordelion*, as in him.[4]

---

[1] I.1.95ff.   [2] I.1.113 'Full fourteen weeks,' thus strengthening Robert's case.
[3] I.1.107–11 adds more evidence.   [4] I.1.85–90.

ROBERT   Then good my Lord, be you indifferent Judge,
And let me have my living and my right.

Q. ELINOR   Nay heare you Sir, you runne away too fast:
Know you not, *Omne simile non est idem*?[1]
Or have read in.[2] Harke ye good sir,
Twas thus I warrant, and no otherwise,   199
    She lay with Sir *Robert* your Father, and thought uppon
King *Richard* my Sonne, and so your Brother was formed in
this fashion.

ROBERT   Madame, you wrong me thus to jest it out,
I crave my right: King *John* as thou art King,
So be thou just, and let me have my right.

JOHN   Why (foolish boy) thy proofes are frivolous,
Nor canst thou chalenge any thing thereby.
But thou shalt see how I will helpe thy claime,
This is my doome, and this my doome shall stand
Irrevocable, as I am King of *England*.   210
For thou knowst not, weele aske of them that know,
His mother and himselfe shall ende this strife:
And as they say, so shall thy living passe.[3]

ROBERT   My Lord, herein I chalenge you of wrong,
To give away my right, and put the doome
Unto themselves. Can there be likelihood
That she will loose?
Or he will give the living from himselfe?
It may not be my Lord. Why should it be?

JOHN   Lords keepe him back, and let him heare the   220
doome. *Essex*, first aske the Mother thrice who was his Sire?

ESSEX   Ladie *Margaret* Widow of *Fauconbridge*, Who was
Father to thy Sonne *Philip*?

MOTHER   Please it your Majestie, Sir *Robert Fauconbridge*.

ROBERT   This is right, aske my felow there if I be a thiefe.

JOHN   Aske *Philip* whose Sonne he is.

ESSEX   *Philip*, who was thy Father?

PHILIP   Mas my Lord, and thats a question: and you had
not taken some paines with her before, I should have desired
you to aske my Mother.   230

JOHN   Say who was thy Father?

PHILIP   Faith (my Lord) to answere you sure he is my
father that was neerest my mother when I was gotten, & him
I thinke to be Sir *Robert Fauconbridge*.[4]

---

[1] 'Likeness does not necessarily mean identity.'
[2] A name missing?   Galen?
[3] Cf. John's assertion of F's legitimacy, I.1.116-29.   [4] Cf. I.1.75-83.

JOHN   *Essex*, for fashions sake demaund agen,
And so an ende to this contention.
  ROBERT   Was ever man thus wrongd as *Robert* is?
  ESSEX   *Philip* speake I say, who was thy Father?
  JOHN   Yong man how now, what, art thou in a traunce?
  ELIANOR   *Philip* awake, the man is in a dreame.   240
  PHILIP   *Philippus atauis ædite Regibus.*
What saist thou *Philip*   sprung of auncient Kings?
Quo me rapit tempestas?
What winde of honour blowes this furie forth?
Or whence proceede these fumes of Majestie?
Me thinkes I heare a hollow Eccho sound,
That *Philip* is the Sonne unto a King:
The whistling leaves upon the trembling trees
Whistle in consort I am *Richards* Sonne:
The bubling murmur of the waters fall,   250
Records *Philippus Regius filius:*[1]
Birds in their flight make musicke with their wings,
Filling the ayre with glorie of my birth:
Birds, bubbles, leaves, and mountaines, Eccho, all
Ring in mine eares, that I am *Richards* Sonne.
Fond man, ah whether art thou carried?
How are thy thoughts ywrapt in Honors heaven?
Forgetfull what thou art, and whence thou camst.
Thy Fathers land cannot maintaine these thoughts,
These thoughts are farre unfitting *Fauconbridge*:   260
And well they may; for why this mounting minde[2]
Doth soare too high to stoupe to *Fauconbridge*.
Why how now? knowest thou where thou art?
And knowest thou who expects thine answere here?
Wilt thou upon a frantick madding vaine
Goe loose thy land, and say thy selfe base borne?
No, keepe thy land, though *Richard* were thy Sire,
What ere thou thinkst, say thou art *Fauconbridge*.
  JOHN   Speake man, be sodaine, who thy Father was.
  PHILIP   Please it your Majestie, Sir *Robert*—   270
Philip, that *Fauconbridge* cleaves to thy jawes:
It will not out, I cannot for my life
Say I am Sonne unto a *Fauconbridge*.
Let land and living goe, tis honors fire
That makes me sweare King *Richard* was my Sire.
Base to a King addes title of more State,

---

[1] Philip, Royal son.   [2] I.1.206, 'mounting spirit'.

Than Knights begotten, though legittimate.
Please it your Grace, I am King *Richards* Sonne.

    ROBERT   *Robert* revive thy heart, let sorrow die,   280
His faltring tongue not suffers him to lie.

    MOTHER What head-strong furie doth enchaunt my
    sonne?

    PHILIP *Philip* cannot repent, for he hath done.

    JOHN Then *Philip* blame not me, thy selfe hast lost
By wilfulnesse, thy living and thy land.
Robert, thou art the heire of *Fauconbridge,*
God give thee joy, greater than thy desert.

    Q. ELIANOR Why how now *Philip,* give away thine owne?

    PHILIP Madame, I am bold to make my selfe your
    nephew,
The poorest kinsman that your Highnes hath:
And with this Proverb gin the world anew,   290
Help hands, I have no lands,[1] honour is my desire;
Let *Philip* live to shew himselfe worthie so great a Sire.

    ELINOR *Philip,* I think thou knewst thy Grandams
    minde:
But cheere thee boy, I will not see thee want
As long as *Elinor* hath foote of land;
Henceforth thou shalt be taken for my sonne,[2]
And waite on me and on thine Unckle heere,
Who shall give honour to thy noble minde.

    JOHN *Philip* kneele down, that thou maist throughly know
How much thy resolution pleaseth us,   300
Rise up Sir *Richard Plantaginet* K. *Richards* Sonne.[3]

    PHIL. Graunt heavens that *Philip* once may shew himself
Worthie the honour of *Plantaginet,*
Or basest glorie of a Bastards name.

    JOHN Now Gentlemen, we will away to *France,*
To checke the pride of *Arthur* and his mates:
Essex, thou shalt be Ruler of my Realme,
And toward the maine charges of my warres,
Ile ceaze the lazie Abbey lubbers lands
Into my hands to pay my men of warre.[4]   310
The Pope and Popelings shall not grease themselves
With golde and groates, that are the souldiers due.
Thus forward Lords, let our commaund be done,
And march we forward mightely to *Fraunce.*   [*Exeunt*

---

[1] Cf. I.1.137, 164.   [2] Cf. I.1.168.   [3] I.1.160–2.
[4] I.1.48–9; III.3.7–9.

Mane[n]t Philip and his Mother.

PHILIP   Madame I beseech you deigne me so much
leasure as the hearing of a matter that I long to impart to you.

MOTHER   Whats the matter *Philip*. I thinke your sute in
secret, tends to some money matter, which you suppose burns
in the bottome of my chest.   320

PHIL.   No Madam, it is no such sute as to beg or borrow,
But such a suite, as might some other grant,
I would not now have troubled you withall.

MOTHER   A Gods name let us heare it.

PHILIP   Then Madame thus, your Ladiship sees well,
How that my scandall growes by meanes of you,
In that report hath rumord up and downe,
I am a bastard, and no *Fauconbridge*.
This grose attaint so tilteth in my thoughts,
Maintaining combat to abridge my ease,   330
That field and towne, and company alone,
Whatso I doo, or wheresoere I am,
I cannot chase the slaunder from thy thoughts.
If it be true, resolve me of my Sire,
For pardon Madame, if I thinke amisse.
Be *Philip Philip* and no *Fauconbridge*,
His Father doubtles was as brave a man.
To you on knees as sometime *Phaeton*,
Mistrusting silly *Merop* for his Sire,[1]
Strayning a little bashfull modestie,   340
I beg some instance whence I am extraught.

MOTHER   Yet more adoo to haste me to my grave,
And wilt thou too become a Mothers crosse?
Must I accuse myself to close with you?
Slaunder myself to quiet your affects:
Thou moovst me *Philip* with this idle talke,
Which I remit, in hope this mood will die.

PHILIP   Nay Ladie mother, heare me further yet,
For strong conceipt drives dutie hence awhile:
Your husband *Fauconbridge* was Father to that sonne,   350
That carries marks of Nature like the Sire,[2]
The sonne that blotteth you with wedlocks breach,
And holds my right, as lineall in discent
From him whose forme was figured in his face.
Can Nature so dissemble in her frame,

[1] Phaeton's mother was Clymene, wife of Merops, but his father was Phoebus.
[2] Cf. I.1.138-47.
6—N.D.S.S. 4

To make the one so like as like may be,
And in the other print no character
To chalenge any marke of true discent?
My brothers minde is base, and too too dull,
To mount where *Philip* lodgeth his affects,   360
And his externall graces that you view
(Though I report it) counterpoise not mine:
His constitution['s] plaine debilitie,
Requires the chayre, and mine the seate of steele.
Nay, what is he, or what am I to him?
When any one that knoweth how to carpe,
Will scarcely judge us both one Countrey borne.
This Madame, this, hath drove me from myselfe:
And here by heavens eternall lampes I sweare,
As cursed *Nero* with his mother did,   370
So I with you, if you resolve me not.

    MOTHER   Let mothers teares quench out thy angers fire,
And urge no further what thou doost require.

    PHILIP   Let sonnes entreatie sway the mother now,
Or els she dies: Ile not infringe my vow.

    MOTHER   Unhappy talke: must I recount my shame,
Blab my misdeedes, or by concealing die?
Some power strike me speechlesse for a time,
Or take from him awhile his hearings use.
Why wish I so, unhappy as I am?   380
The fault is mine, and he the faultie frute,
I blush, I faint, oh would I might be mute.

    PHILIP   Mother be briefe, I long to know my name.

    MOTHER   And longing dye to shrowd thy Mothers
       shame.

    PHILIP   Come Madame come, you neede not be so loth,
The shame is shared equall twixt us both.
Ist not a slacknes in me worthie blame,
To be so olde, and cannot write my name?
Good Mother resolve me.   389

    MOTHER   Then *Philip* heare thy fortune and my griefe,
My honours losse by purchase of thy selfe,[1]
My shame, thy name, and husbands secret wrong,
All maimd and staind by youths unruly sway.
And when thou knowest from whence thou art extraught,
Or if thou knewst what sutes,[2] what threates, what feares,
To moove by love, or massacre by death,

---

[1] I.1.257.   [2] I.1.253-5.

To yeeld with love, or end by loves contempt,
The mightines of him that courted me,
Who tempred terror with his wanton talke,
That something may extenuate the guilt.   400
But let it not advantage me so much:
Upbraid me rather with the *Romane* Dame
That shed her blood to wash away her shame.[1]
Why stand I to expostulate the crime
With *pro & contra*, now the deede is don,
When to conclude two words may tell the tale,
That *Philips* Father was a Princes Son,
Rich *Englands* rule, worlds onely terror hee,
For honours losse left me with childe of thee:
Whose Sonne thou art, then pardon me the rather,   410
For faire King *Richard* was thy noble Father.
   PHILIP   Then *Robin Fauconbridge* I wish thee joy,
My Sire a King, and I a landles Boy.[2]
Gods Ladie Mother, the word is in my debt,
There's something owing to *Plantaginet*.
I marrie Sir, let me alone for game,
Ile act some wonders now I know my name.
By blessed *Marie* Ile not sell that pride
For *Englands* wealth, and all the world beside.
Sit fast the proudest of my Fathers foes,   420
Away good Mother, there the comfort goes.   [*Exeunt*

[Scene ii]

> *Enter Philip the French King and Lewes, Limoges,*[3] *Con-*
> *stance, and her sonne Arthur.*

   KING   Now gin we broach the title of thy claime
Yong *Arthur* in the *Albion* Territories,
Scaring proud *Angiers* with a puissant siedge:
Brave *Austria*, cause of *Cordelions* death,
Is also come to aide thee in thy warres;
And all our Forces joyne for *Arthurs* right.
And, but for causes of great consequence,
Pleading delay till newes from *England* come,
Twice should not *Titan* hide him in the West,   430
To coole the fet-locks of his wearie teame,
Till I had with an unresisted shock

---

[1] Lucrece.   [2] I.1.177.
[3] Shakespeare too identifies Limoges with the Duke of Austria, III.1.114.

Controld the mannage of proud *Angiers* walls,
Or made a forfet of my fame to *Chaunce*.

  CONSTANCE May be that *John* in conscience or in feare
To offer wrong where you impugne the ill,
Will send such calme conditions backe to *Fraunce*,
As shall rebate the edge of fearefull warres:
If so, forbearance is a deede well done.[1]

  ARTHUR Ah Mother, possession of a Crowne is much,   440
And *John* as I have heard reported of,
For present vantage would adventure farre.
The world can witnes in his Brothers time,
He tooke upon him rule and almost raigne:
Then must it follow as a doubtfull poynt,
That hee'le resigne the rule unto his Nephew.
I rather thinke the menace of the world
Sounds in his eares as threats of no esteeme,
And sooner would he scorne *Europaes* power,
Than loose the smallest title he enjoyes;   450
For questionles he is an Englishman.

  LEWES Why are the English peereles in compare?
Brave Cavaliers as ere that Iland bred,
Have livde and dyde, and darde and done inough,
Yet never gracde their Countrey for the cause:
England is *England*, yeelding good and bad,
And *John* of *England* is as other *Johns*.
Trust me yong *Arthur*, if thou like my reede,
Praise thou the French that helpe thee in this neede.

  LYMOGES The Englishman hath little cause I trow,   460
To spend good speaches on so proud a foe.
Why *Arthur* heres his spoyle that now is gon,
Who when he livde outroude his Brother *John*:
But hastie curres that lie so long to catch,
Come halting home, and meete their overmatch.
But newes comes now, heres the Embassadour.

Enter Chattilion.

  K. PHILIP And in good time, welcome my Lord *Chattilion*:
    What newes? will *John* accord to our commaund.

  CHATTILION Be I not briefe to tell your Highnes all,
He will approach to interrupt my tale: 470
For one selfe bottome brought us both to *Fraunce*.[2]

---

[1] II.1.44–9.
[2] Cf. II.1.57–9. Line 73 has 'English bottoms', i.e. vessels.

He on his part will try the chaunce of warre,
And if his words inferre assured truth,
Will loose himselfe and all his followers,
Ere yeeld unto the least of your demaunds.
The Mother Queene she taketh on amaine
Gainst Ladie *Constance*, counting her the cause
That doth effect this claime to *Albion*,   480
Conjuring *Arthur* with a Grandames care,
To leave his Mother[1]; willing him submit
His state to *John* and her protection,
Who (as she saith) are studious for his good:
More circumstance the season intercepts:
This is the summe, which briefly I have showne.
   K. PHIL. This bitter winde must nip some bodies spring,
Sodaine and briefe, why so, tis harvest weather.
But say *Chattilion*, what person of accompt are with him?
   CHATTILION Of *England* Earle *Pembrooke* and *Salsbury*,
The onely noted men of any name.
Next them a Bastard of the Kings deceast,[2]   490
A hardy wilde head, tough and venturous,
With many other men of high resolve.
Then is there with them *Elinor* Mother Queene,
And *Blanch* her Neece daughter to the King of *Spaine*[3]:
These are the prime Birds of this hot adventure.

     Enter John & his followers, Queene, Bastard, Earles, &c.

   K. PHILIP Me seemeth *John* an over-daring spirit
Effects some frenzie in thy rash approach,
Treading my Confines with thy armed Troupes.
I rather lookt for some submisse reply
Touching the claime thy Nephew *Arthur* makes   500
To that which thou unjustly dost usurpe.
   K. JOHN For that *Chattilion* can discharge you all,
I list not plead my Title with my tongue.
Nor came I hether with intent of wrong
To *Fraunce* or thee, or any right of thine;
But in defence and purchase of my right,
The Towne of *Angiers*: which thou doost begirt
In the behalfe of Ladie *Constance* Sonne,
Wheretoo nor he nor she can lay just claime.
   CONSTANCE Yes (false intruder) if that just be just,
And headstrong usurpation[4] put apart,   511

---

[1] II.1.159.   [2] Echoed at II.1.65.   [3] II.1.62–4.   [4] II.1.121.

Arthur my Sonne, heire to thy elder Brother,
Without ambiguous shadow of discent,
Is Soveraigne to the substance thou withholdst.
   Q. ELINOR   Misgovernd Gossip, staine to this resort,
Occasion of these undecided jarres,
I say (that know) to check thy vaine suppose,
Thy Sonne hath naught to doo with that he claymes.
For proofe whereof, I can inferre a Will,
That barres the way he urgeth by discent.[1]   520
   CONSTANCE   A Will indeede, a crabbed Womans will,[2]
Wherein the Divell is an overseer,
And proud dame *Elnor* sole Executresse:
More wills than so, on perill of my soule,
Were never made to hinder *Arthurs* right.
   ARTHUR   But say there was, as sure there can be none,
The law intends such testaments as voyd,
Where right discent can no way be impeacht.[3]
   Q. ELINOR   Peace *Arthur* peace, thy mother makes thee
     wings
To soare with perill after *Icarus*,
And trust me yongling, for the Fathers sake,   530
I pitie much the hazard of thy youth.
   CONSTANCE   Beshrew you els how pitifull you are,
Readie to weepe to heare him aske his owne;
Sorrow betide such Grandames and such griefe,
That minister a poyson for pure love.[4]
But who so blinde, as cannot see this beame,
That you forsooth would keepe your cousin downe,
For feare his Mother should be usde too well?
I theres the griefe, confusion catch the braine,   540
That hammers shifts to stop a Princes raigne.
   Q. ELIANOR   Impatient, frantike, common slanderer,
Immodest Dame, unnurtred quarreller,
I tell thee I, not envie to thy Son,
But justice makes me speake as I have don.
   K. PHILIP   But heres no proof that showes your son a King.
   K. JOHN   What wants, my sword shal more at large set
     down.
   LEWES   But that may breake before the truth be knowne.
   BASTARD   Then this may hold till all his right be showne.
   LYMOGES   Good words sir sauce, your betters are in place.
   BASTARD   Not you sir doughtie with your Lions case.   551

---

[1] II.1.191–2.   [2] II.1.193–4.   [3] I.1.130–3.   [4] Cf. II.1.160–4.

BLANCH   Ah joy betide his soule, to whom that spoile
belongd
Ah *Richard* how thy glorie here is wrongd.[1]
LYMOGES   Me thinkes that *Richards* pride, & *Richards* fall,
Should be a president[2] t'affright you all.
BASTARD   What words are these? how doo my sinews
shake?
My Fathers foe clad in my Fathers spoyle,[3]
A thousand furies kindle with revendge,
This hart that choller keepes a consistorie,
Searing my inwards with a brand of hate: 560
How doth *Alecto* whisper in mine eares?
Delay not *Philip*, kill the villaine straight,
Disrobe him of the matchles moniment
Thy Fathers triumph ore the Savages.
Base heardgroome, coward, peasant, worse than a threshing
slave,
What makst thou with the Trophei of a King?
Shamst thou not coystrell, loathsome dunghill swad,
To grace thy carkasse with an ornament
Too precious for a Monarchs coverture?
Scarce can I temper due obedience   570
Unto the presence of my Soveraigne,
From acting outrage on this trunke of hate:
But arme thee traytor, wronger of renowne.
For by his soule I sweare, my Fathers soule,
Twice will I not review the Mornings rise,
Till I have torne that Trophei from thy back,[4]
And split thy heart, for wearing it so long.
Philip hath sworne, and if it be not done,
Let not the world repute me *Richards* Sonne.
LYMOGES   Nay soft sir Bastard, harts are not split so soone,
Let them rejoyce that at the ende doo win: 581
And take this lesson at thy foemans hand,
Pawne not thy life, to get thy Fathers skin.
BLANCH   Well may the world speake of his knightly valor,
That winnes this hide to weare a Ladies favour.
BASTARD   Ill may I thrive, and nothing brooke with mee,
If shortly I present it not to thee.[5]
K. PHILIP   Lordings forbeare, for time is comming fast,
That deedes may trie what words cannot determine,
And to the purpose for the cause you come.   590

[1] II.1.141–2.   [2] precedent.   [3] Cf. II.1.139–46.   [4] II.1.145–6.
[5] In *KJ* he does not woo Blanche.

Me seemes you set right in chaunce of warre,
Yeelding no other reasons for your claime,
But so and so, because it shall be so.
So wrong shalbe subornd by trust of strength:
A Tyrants practize to invest himselfe,
Where weake resistance giveth wrong the way.
To check the which, in holy lawfull Armes,
I in the right of *Arthur Geffreys* Sonne,
Am come before this Citie of *Angiers*,   600
To barre all other false supposed clayme,
From whence or howsoere the error springs.
And in his quarrell on my Princely word,
Ile fight it out unto the latest man.

    JOHN   Know King of *Fraunce*, I will not be commaunded
By any power or Prince in Christendome,
To yeeld an instance how I hold mine owne,
More than to answere, that mine owne is mine.
But wilt thou see me parley with the Towne,
And heare them offer me alleageance,
Fealtie and homage, as true liege men ought.[1]   610

    K. PHILIP   Summon them, I will not beleeve it till I see
it, and when I see it Ile soone change it.

       They summon the Towne, the Citizens appeare upon the walls.

    K. JOHN   You men of *Angiers*, and as I take it my loyall
Subjects, I have summoned you to the walls: to dispute on
my right, were to thinke you doubtfull therein, which I am
perswaded you are not. In few words, our Brothers Sonne,
backt with the King of *Fraunce*, have beleagred your Towne
upon a false pretended title to the same: in defence whereof I
your liege Lord have brought our power to fence you from
the Usurper, to free your intended servitude, and utterly to
supplant the foemen, to my right & your rest.[2] Say then, who
keepe you the Towne for?

    CITIZEN   For our lawfull King.[3]   624

    JOHN   I was no lesse perswaded: then in Gods name open
your gates, and let me enter.

    CITIZEN   And it please your Highnes we comptroll not
your title, neither will we rashly admit your entrance: if you
bee lawfull King, with all obedience we keepe it to your use,
if not King, our rashnes to be impeached for yeelding, with-

---

    [1] Cf. Philip, II.1.198–200.   [2] II.1.206–25.   [3] II.1.267–8.

out more considerate triall: we answere not as men lawles,
but to the behoofe of him that prooves lawfull.

JOHN I shall not come in then? 633

CITIZEN No my Lord, till we know more.[1]

K. PHILIP Then heare me speake in the behalfe of *Arthur*
Sonne of *Geffrey* elder Brother to *John*, his title manifest without contradiction to the Crowne and Kingdome of *England*,
with *Angiers* and divers Townes on this side the sea: will you
acknowledge him your liege Lord, who speaketh in my word
to intertaine you with all favours as beseemeth a King to his 640
subjects, or a friend to his wel-willers: or stand to the perill of
your contempt, when his title is prooved by the sword.

CITIZEN We answere as before: till you have prooved one
right, we acknowledge none right, he that tries himselfe our
Soveraigne, to him will we remaine firme subjects, and for
him, and in his right we hold our Towne as desirous to know
the truth as loath to subscribe before we knowe: More than
this we cannot say, and more than this we dare not doo.

K. PHILIP Then *John* I defie thee in the name and behalfe of *Arthur Plantaginet* thy King and cousin, whose right 650
and patrimonie thou detainest, as I doubt not ere the day
ende in a set battell make thee confesse: whereunto with a
zeale to right I challenge thee.

K. JOHN I accept the challenge, and turne the defiance
to thy throate.

[Scene iii]

> *Excursions. The Bastard chaseth Lymoges the Austrich Duke,*
> *and maketh him leave the Lyons skinne.[2]*

BASTARD And art thou gone, misfortune haunt thy steps,
And chill colde feare assaile thy times of rest.
Morpheus leave here thy silent Eban cave,
Besiedge his thoughts with dismall fantasies,
And ghastly objects of pale threatning *Mors*. 660
Affright him every minute with stearne lookes,
Let shadowe temper terror in his thoughts,
And let the terror make the coward mad,
And in his madnes let him feare pursute,
And so in frenzie let the peasant die.
Here is the ransome that allays his rage,

---

[1] II.1.270-2.   [2] Not used by Shakespeare.

The first freehold that *Richard* left his sonne:
With which I shall surprize his living foes,
As *Hectors* statue did the fainting *Greekes*. 669

[*Exit*

[Scene iv]

Enter the Kings Herolds with Trumpets to the wals of
Angiers: they summon the Towne.

ENG. HEROLD *John* by the grace of God King of *England*,
Lord of *Ireland, Anjou, Toraine, &c.* demaundeth once againe
of you his subjects of *Angiers*, if you will quietly surrender up
the Towne into his hands?

FR. HEROLD *Philip* by the grace of God King of *Fraunce*,
demaundeth in the behalfe of *Arthur* Duke of *Britaine*, if you
will surrender up the Towne into his hands, to the use of the
said *Arthur*.

CITIZENS Herolds goe tell the two victorious Princes,
that we the poore Inhabitants of *Angiers*, require a parle[1] of
their Majesties. 680

HEROLDS We goe.

Enter the Kings, Queene Elianor, Blaunch, Bastard,
Lymoges, Lewes, Castilean, Pembrooke, Salisbury, Constance,
and Arthur Duke of Britaine.

JOHN Herold, what answere doo the Townsmen send?

PHILIP Will *Angiers* yeeld to *Philip* King of *Fraunce*,

EN. HER. The Townsmen on the wals accept your Grace.

FR. HER. And crave a parley of your Majestie.

JOHN You Citizens of *Angiers*, have your eyes
Beheld the slaughter that our English bowes
Have made upon the coward frawdfull French?
And have you wisely pondred therewithall
Your gaine in yeelding to the English King?[2] 690

PHILIP Their losse in yeelding to the English King.
But *John*, they saw from out their highest Towers
The Chevaliers of *Fraunce* and crossebow shot
Make lanes of slaughtred bodies through thine hoast,
And are resolvde to yeelde to *Arthurs* right.[3]

JOHN Why *Philip*, though thou bravest it fore the walls,
Thy conscience knowes that *John* hath wonne the field.

---

[1] Cf. II.1.205, 'gentle parle'.   [2] II.1.312–24.   [3] Cf. II.1.300–11.

PHILIP   What ere my conscience knows, thy Armie feeles
That *Philip* had the better of the day.

BASTARD   *Philip* indeede hath got the Lyons case,   700
Which here he holds to *Lymoges* disgrace.
Base Duke to flye and leave such spoyles behinde:
But this thou knewst of force to make mee stay.
It farde with thee as with the marriner,
Spying the hugie Whale, whose monstrous bulke
Doth beare the waves like mountaines fore the winde,
That throwes out emptie vessells, so to stay
His furie, while the ship doth saile away.
Philip tis thine: and fore this Princely presence,
Madame I humbly lay it at your feete,   710
Being the first adventure I atchievd,
And first exployt your Grace did enjoyne:
Yet many more I long to be enjoynd.

BLAUNCH   *Philip* I take it, and I thee commaund
To weare the same as earst thy Father did:
Therewith receive this favour at my hands,
T'incourage thee to follow *Richards* fame.

ARTHUR   Ye Citizens of *Angiers*, are ye mute?
Arthur or *John*, say which shall be your King?

CITIZEN   We care not which, if once we knew the right,
But till we know we will not yeeld our right.[1]   721

BASTARD   Might *Philip* counsell two so mightie Kings,
As are the Kings of *England* and of *Fraunce*,
He would advise your Graces to unite
And knit your forces gainst these Citizens,
Pulling their battered walls about their eares.
The Town once wonne then strive about the claime,
For they are minded to delude you both.[2]

CITIZEN   Kings, Princes, Lords & Knights assembled
        here,
The Citizens of *Angiers* all by me   731
Entreate your Majestie to heare them speake:
And as you like the motion they shall make,
So to account and follow their advice.

JOHN. PHILIP   Speake on, we give thee leave.

CITIZEN   Then thus[3]: whereas that yong & lustie knight
Incites you on to knit your kingly strengths:
The motion cannot choose but please the good,
And such as love the quiet of the State.

[1] II.1.325–33; 369–72.   [2] II.1.373–415.   [3] II.1.416–22.

But how my Lords, how should your strengths be knit?   740
Not to oppresse your subjects and your friends,
And fill the world with brawles and mutinies:
But unto peace your forces should be knit
To live in Princely league and amitie:
Doo this, the gates of *Angiers* shall give way
And stand wide open to your harts content.
To make this peace a lasting bond of love,
Remains one onely honorable meanes,
Which by your pardon I shall here display.
Lewes the Dolphin and the heire of *Fraunce*,
A man of noted valor through the world,   750
Is yet unmaried: let him take to wife
The beauteous daughter of the King of *Spaine*,
Neece to K. *John*, the lovely Ladie *Blanche*,
Begotten on his Sister *Elianor*.
With her in marriage will her unckle give
Castles and Towers as fitteth such a match.
The Kings thus joynd in league of perfect love,
They may so deale with *Arthur* Duke of *Britaine*,
Who is but yong, and yet unmeete to raigne,
As he shall stand contented everie way.   760
Thus have I boldly (for the common good)
Delivered what the Citie gave in charge.
And as upon conditions you agree,
So shall we stand content to yeeld the Towne.[1]
    ARTHUR A proper peace, if such a motion hold;
These Kings beare armes for me, and for my right,
And they shall share my lands to make them friends.
    Q. ELIANOR Sonne *John*, follow this motion, as thou
      lovest thy mother,
Make league with *Philip*, yeeld to any thing:
Lewes shall have my Neece, and then be sure   770
Arthur shall have small succour out of *Fraunce*.[2]
    JOHN Brother of *Fraunce*, you heare the Citizens:
Then tell me, how you meane to deale herein.
    CONSTANCE Why *John*, what canst thou give unto thy
      Neece,
That hast no foote of land, but *Arthurs* right?
    LEWES Byr Ladie Citizens, I like your choyce,
A lovely Damsell is the Ladie *Blanche*,
Worthie the heire of *Europe* for her pheere.

[1] II.1.423-55.   [2] II.1.468-73.

CONSTANCE What Kings, why stand you gazing in a
trance?
Why how now Lords? accursed Citizens 780
To fill and tickle their ambicious eares,
With hope of gaine, that springs from *Arthurs* losse.
Some dismall Plannet at thy birthday raignd,
For now I see the fall of all thy hopes.
   K. PHILIP Ladie, and Duke of *Britaine*, know you both,
The King of *Fraunce* respects his honor more,
Than to betray his friends and favourers.
Princesse of *Spaine*, could you affect my Sonne,
If we upon conditions could agree?
   BASTARD Swounds Madam, take an English Gentleman: 790
Slave as I was, I thought to have moovde the match.
Grandame you made me halfe a promise once,
That Lady *Blanch* should bring me wealth inough,
And make me heire of store of English land.
   Q. ELIANOR Peace *Philip*, I will looke thee out a wife,
We must with pollicie[1] compound this strife.
   BASTARD If *Lewes* get her, well, I say no more:
But let the frolicke Frenchman take no scorne,
If *Philip* front him with an English horne. 799
   JOHN Ladie, what answere make you to the King of
France?
Can you affect the Dolphin for your Lord?[2]
   BLANCH I thanke the King that likes of me so well,
To make me Bride unto so great a Prince:
But give me leave my Lord to pause on this.
Least being too too forward in the cause,
It may be blemish to my modestie.
   Q. ELINOR Sonne *John*, and worthie *Philip* K. of *Fraunce*,
Doo you confer a while about the Dower,
And I will schoole my modest Neece so well,
That she shall yeeld assoone as you have done. 810
   CONSTANCE I, theres the wretch that broacheth all this ill,
Why flye I not upon the Beldames face,
And with my nayles pull foorth her hatefull eyes.
   ARTHUR Sweete Mother cease these hastie madding fits:
For my sake, let my Grandame have her will.
O would she with her hands pull forth my heart,
I could affoord it to appease these broyles.[3]
But mother let us wisely winke at all:

---

[1] II.1.396.   [2] II.1.521-3.   [3] Cf. II.1.164-5.

Least farther harmes ensue our hastie speach.

    PHILIP   Brother of *England*, what dowrie wilt thou give   820
Unto my Sonne in marriage with thy Neece?

    JOHN   First *Philip* knowes her dowrie out of *Spaine*
To be so great as may content a King:
But more to mend and amplifie the same,
I give in money thirtie thousand markes.
For land I leave it to thine owne demaund.

    PHILIP   Then I demand *Volquesson, Torain, Main,*
Poiters and *Anjou*, these five Provinces,
Which thou as King of *England* holdst in *Fraunce*:
Then shall our peace be soone concluded on.   830

    BASTARD   No lesse than five such Provinces at once?

    JOHN   Mother what shall I doo? my brother got these lands
With much effusion of our English bloud:
And shall I give it all away at once?

    Q. ELINOR   *John* give it him, so shalt thou live in peace,
And keepe the residue sanz jeopardie.

    JOHN   *Philip* bring forth thy Sonne, here is my Neece,
And here in mariage I doo give with her
From my and my Successors English Kings,
Volquesson, Poiters, Anjou, Torain, Main,   840
And thirtie thousand markes of stipend coyne.[1]
Now Citizens, how like you of this match?

    CITIZEN   We joy to see so sweete a peace begun.

    LEWES   *Lewes* with *Blanch* shall ever live content.
But now King *John*, what say you to the Duke?
Father, speake as you may in his behalfe.

    PHILIP   K. *John*, be good unto thy Nephew here,
And give him somewhat that shall please thee best.

    JOHN   *Arthur*, although thou troublest *Englands* peace,
Yet here I give thee *Brittaine* for thine owne,   850
Together with the Earledome of *Richmont*,
And this rich Citie of *Angiers* withall.[2]

    Q. ELIANOR   And if thou seeke to please thine Unckle *John*,
Shalt see my Sonne how I will make of thee.

    JOHN   Now every thing is sorted to this end,
Lets in and there prepare the mariage rytes,
Which in S. *Maries* Chappell presently[3]
Shalbe performed ere this Presence part.   [*Exeunt*

---

[1] II.1.527–32.   [2] II.1.547–53.   [3] II.1.539.

Manent Constance & Arthur.

ARTHUR   Madam good cheere, these drouping languish-
   ments
Adde no redresse to salve our awkward haps.   860
If heavens have concluded these events,
To small availe is bitter pensivenes:
Seasons will change, and so our present griefe
May change with them, and all to our reliefe.
  CONSTANCE   Ah boy, thy yeares I see are farre too greene
To looke into the bottome of these cares.
But I, who see the poyse that weigheth downe
Thy weale, my wish, and all the willing meanes
Wherewith thy fortune and thy fame should mount,
What joy, what ease, what rest can lodge in me,   870
With whom all hope and hap doth disagree?
   ARTHUR   Yet Ladies teares, and cares, and solemne
   shows,
Rather than helpes, heape up more worke for woes.
  CONSTANCE   If any Power will heare a widdowes plaint,
That from a wounded soule implores revenge[1];
Send fell contagion to infect this Clyme,
This cursed Countrey, where the traytors breath,
Whose perjurie as prowd *Briareus*,
Beleaguers all the Skie with misbeliefe.
He promist *Arthur*, and he sware it too,   880
To fence thy right, and check thy foemans pride:
But now black-spotted Perjure as he is,[2]
He takes a truce with *Elnors* damned brat,
And marries *Lewes* to her lovely Neece,[3]
Sharing thy fortune, and thy birth-dayes gift
Betweene these lovers: ill betide the match.
And as they shoulder thee from out thy owne,
And triumph in a widowes tearefull cares:
So heavens crosse them with a thriftles course.
Is all the bloud yspilt on either part,   890
Closing the cranies of the thirstie earth,
Growne to a lovegame and a Bridall feast?
And must thy birthright bid the wedding banes?
Poore helples boy, hopeles and helples too,
To whom misfortune seemes no yoke at all.
Thy stay, thy state, thy imminent mishaps

---

[1] Cf. III.1.12–15.　　　[2] III.1.62, 107.　　　[3] III.1.34.

Woundeth thy mothers thoughts with feeling care,
Why lookst thou pale? the colour flyes thy face,
I trouble now the fountaine of thy youth,
And make it moodie[1] with my doles discourse,   900
Goe in with me, reply not lovely boy,
We must obscure this mone with melodie,[2]
Least worser wrack ensue our malecontent.   [*Exeunt*

[Scene v]

    Enter the King of England, the King of Fraunce, Arthur,
    Bastard, Lewes, Lymoges, Constance, Blanche, Chattilion,
    Pembrooke, Salisburie, and Elianor.

    JOHN   This is the day, the long desired day,[3]
Wherein the Realmes of *England* and of *Fraunce*
Stand highly blessed in a lasting peace.
Thrice happie is the Bridegroome and the Bride,
From whose sweete Bridale such a concord springs,
To make of mortall foes immortall friends.
    CONSTANCE   Ungodly peace made by an others warre.[4]   910
    PHILIP[5]   Unhappie peace, that ties thee from revenge.
Rouse thee *Plantaginet*, live not to see
The butcher of the great *Plantiginet*.
Kings, Princes, and ye Peeres of either Realmes,
Pardon my rashnes, and forgive the zeale
That caries me in furie to a deede
Of high desert, of honour, and of armes.
A boone O Kings, a boone doth *Philip* beg
Prostrate upon his knee: which knee shall cleave
Unto the superficies of the earth,   920
Till *Fraunce* and *England* graunt this glorious boone.
    JOHN   Speake *Philip*, *England* graunts thee thy request.
    PHILIP   And *Fraunce* confirmes what ere is in his power.
    BASTARD   Then Duke sit fast, I levell at thy head,
Too base a ransome for my fathers life.
Princes, I crave the Combat with the Duke
That braves it in dishonor of my Sire.
Your words are past nor can you now reverse
The Princely promise that revives my soule,
Whereat me thinks I see his sinnews shake: 930

----

[1] Pun on 'muddy', 'moody'?
[2] Probably music followed before the next scene.
[3] III.1.75.   [4] Cf. III.1.83ff.   [5] I.e. the Bastard.

This is the boon (dread Lords) which granted once
Or life or death are pleasant to my soule;
Since I shall live and die in *Richards* right.
    LYMOGES Base Bastard, misbegotten of a King.
To interrupt these holy nuptiall rytes
With brawles and tumults to a Dukes disgrace:
Let it suffice, I scorne to joyne in fight,
With one so farre unequall to my selfe.
    BASTARD A fine excuse, Kings if you wilbe Kings,
Then keepe your words, and let us combat it.   940
    JOHN *Philip*, we cannot force the Duke to fight,
Being a subject unto neither Realme:
But tell me *Austria*, if an English Duke
Should dare thee thus, wouldst thou accept the challendge?
    LYMOGES Els let the world account the *Austrich* Duke
The greatest coward living on the Earth.
    JOHN Then cheere thee *Philip*, *John* will keepe his word.
Kneele downe; in sight of *Philip* King of *Fraunce*
And all these Princely Lords assembled here,
I gird thee with the sword of *Normandie*,   950
And of that land I doo invest thee Duke:
So shalt thou be in living and in land
Nothing inferiour unto *Austria*.
    LYMOGES K. *John*, I tell thee flatly to thy face
Thou wrongst mine honour: and that thou maist see
How much I scorne thy new made Duke and thee,
I flatly say, I will not be compeld[1]:
And so farewell Sir Duke of low degree,
Ile find a time to match you for this geere.   [*Exit*
    JOHN Stay *Philip*, let him goe, the honors thine.[2]   960
    BASTARD I cannot live unles his life be mine.
    Q. ELIANOR Thy forwardnes this day hath joyd my
      soule,
And made me thinke my *Richard* lives in thee.
    K. PHILIP Lordings lets in, and spend the wedding day
In maskes and triumphs, letting quarrells cease.

        Enter a Cardynall from Rome.

    CARD. Stay King of *France*, I charge thee joyn not hands
With him that stands accurst of God and men.   967

---

[1] Hence the term 'recreant', III.1.129, etc.
[2] Contrast Shakespeare's handling of the challenge, III.1.129–33; and John's
rebuke, 134.

Know *John*, that I *Pandulph* Cardinall of *Millaine*,[1] and Legate from the Sea of *Rome*, demaund of thee in the name of our holy Father the Pope *Innocent*, why thou dost (contrarie to the lawes of our holy mother the Church, and our holye father the Pope) disturbe the quiet of the Church, and disanull the election of *Stephen Langhton*, whom his Holines hath elected Archbishop of *Canterburie*: this in his Holines name I demaund of thee?[2]

JOHN   And what hast thou or the Pope thy maister to doo to demaund of me, how I employ mine owne? Know sir Priest as I honour the Church and holy Churchmen, so I scorne to be subject to the greatest Prelate in the world. Tell thy Maister so from me, and say, *John* of *England* said it, that never an Italian Priest of them all, shall either have tythe, tole, or poling penie out of *England*, but as I am King, so wil I raigne next under God, supreame head both over spirituall and temrall[3]: and hee that contradicts me in this, Ile make him hoppe headlesse.

K. PHILIP   What King *John*, know you what you say, thus to blaspheme against our holy father the Pope.[4]

JOHN   *Philip*, though thou and all the Princes of Christendome suffer themselves to be abusde by a Prelates slaverie, my minde is not of such base temper.[5] If the Pope will bee King in *England*, let him winne it with the sword, I know no other title he can alleage to mine inheritance.   990

CARD.   *John*, this is thine answere?

JOHN   What then?

CARD.   Then I *Pandulph* of *Padoa*, Legate from the Apostolick See, doo in the name of S. *Peter* and his successor our holy Father Pope *Innocent*, pronounce thee accursed discharging every of thy subjects of all dutie and fealtie that they doo owe to thee, and pardon and forgivenes of sinne to those of them whatsoever, which shall carrie armes against thee, or murder thee: this I pronounce, and charge all good men to abhorre thee as an excommunicate person.[6]   1000

JOHN   So sir, the more the Fox is curst the better a fares: if God blesse me and my Land, let the Pope and his shavelings curse and spare not.

CARD.   Furthermore I charge thee *Philip* King of *France*, and al the Kings and Princes of Christendome, to make war uppon this miscreant[7]: and whereas thou hast made a league

---

[1] Pandulph was not a Cardinal.   [2] III.1.135–46.
[3] Close to III.1.147–60; 'tithe or toll', etc.   [4] III.1.161.
[5] III.1.162–71.   [6] III.1.173–9.   [7] III.1.191–4.

with him, and confirmed it by oath, I doo in the name of our aforesaid father the Pope, acquit thee of that oath as unlawful, being made with an heretike, how saist thou *Philip*, doost thou obey?

JOHN Brother of *Fraunce*, what say you to the Cardinall?[1]

PHILIP I say, I am sorrie for your Majestie, requesting you to submit your selfe to the Church of *Rome*. 1012

JOHN And what say you to our league, if I doo not submit?

PHILIP What should I say? I must obey the Pope.

JOHN Obey the Pope, and breake your oath to God?

PHILIP The Legate hath absolvde me of mine oath:[2]
Then yeeld to *Rome*, or I defie thee heere.

JOHN Why *Philip*, I defie the Pope and thee,
False as thou art, and perjurde K. of *Fraunce*,
Unworthie man to be accompted King. 1020
Giv'st thou thy sword into a Prelates hands?
Pandulph, where I of Abbots, Monkes and Friers
Have taken somewhat to maintaine my warres,
Now will I take no more but all they have.[3]
Ile rowze the lazie lubbers from their Cells,
And in despight Ile send them to the Pope.
Mother, come you with me, and for the rest
That will not follow *John* in this attempt,
Confusion light upon their damned soules. 1029
Come Lords, fight for your King that fighteth for your good![4]

PHILIP And are they gone? *Pandulph* thy selfe shalt see
How *Fraunce* will fight for *Rome* and *Romish* rytes.
Nobles, to armes, let him not passe the seas.
Lets take him captive, and in triumph lead
The K. of *England* to the gates of *Rome*.
Arthur, bestirre thee man, and thou shalt see
What *Philip* K. of *Fraunce* will doo for thee.

BLANCHE And will your Grace upon your wedding day
Forsake your Bride and follow dreadfull drums:
Nay, good my Lord, stay you at home with mee.[5] 1040

LEWES Sweete heart content thee, and we shall agree.[6]

PHILIP Follow me Lords, Lord Cardynall lead the way,
Drums shalbe musique to this wedding day. *[Exeunt*

[1] III.1.202.   [2] Shakespeare bases 224–97 on this.   [3] III.3.7–11.
[4] Here John and his attendants *exeunt*.   [5] III.1.300–9.   [6] Cf. III.1.337–8.

[Scene vi]

Excursions. The Bastard pursues Austria, and kills him.

BASTARD   Thus hath K. *Richards* Sonne performde his
  vowes.
And offered *Austrias* bloud for sacrifice
Unto his fathers everliving soule.
Brave *Cordelion*, now my heart doth say,
I have deservde, though not to be thy heire
Yet as I am, thy base begotten sonne,
A name as pleasing to thy *Philips* heart,   1050
As to be cald the Duke of *Normandie*.
Lie there[1] a pray to every ravening fowle:
And as my Father triumpht in thy spoyles,
And trode thine Ensignes underneath his feete,
So doo I tread upon thy cursed selfe,
And leave thy bodie to the fowles for food.   [*Exit*

[Scene vii]

Excursions. Arthur, Constance, Lewes, having taken
Q. Elianor prisoner.[2]

CONSTANCE   Thus hath the God of Kings with conquer-
  ing arme
Dispearst the foes to true succession.
Proud, and disturber of thy Countreyes peace,
Constance doth live to tame thine insolence,   1060
And on thy head will now avenged be
For all the mischiefes hatched in thy braine.
  Q. ELINOR   Contemptuous dame unrev[er]ent Dutches
  thou,
To brave so great a Queene as *Elianor*.
Base scolde hast thou forgot, that I was wife,
And mother to three mightie English Kings?[3]
I charge thee then, and you forsooth sir Boy,
To set your Grandmother at libertie,
And yeeld to *John* your Unckle and your King.
  CONSTANCE   Tis not thy words proud Queene shal carry
  it.   1070
  ELIANOR   Nor yet thy threates proud Dame shal daunt
  my minde.

---

[1] III.2.3-4.   [2] Cf. III.2.6-7.
[3] Wife to Henry II, mother to Richard I and John.

ARTHUR   Sweete Grandame, and good Mother leave
these brawles.

ELIANOR   Ile finde a time to triumph in thy fall.

CONSTANCE   My time is now to triumph in thy fall,
And thou shalt know that *Constance* will triumph.

ARTHUR   Good Mother weigh it is Queene *Elianor*.
Though she be captive, use her like herselfe.
Sweete Grandame beare with what my Mother sayes,
Your Highnes shalbe used honourably.

Enter a Messenger.

MESS.   *Lewes* my Lord, Duke *Arthur*, and the rest,   1080
To armes in hast, K. *John* relyes[1] his men,
And ginnes the fight afresh: and sweares withall
To lose his life, or set his Mother free.

LEWES   *Arthur* away, tis time to looke about.

ELIANOR   Why how now dame, what is your courage
coold?

CONSTANCE   No *Elianor*, my courage gathers strength,
And hopes to lead both *John* and thee as slaves:
And in that hope, I hale thee to the field.   [*Exeunt*

[Scene viii]

> *Excursions. Elianor is rescued by John,[2] and Arthur is taken
> prisoner. Exeunt. Sound victorie.*

[Scene ix]

> *Enter John, Elianor, and Arthur prisoner, Bastard, Pem-
> brooke, Salisbury, and Hubert de Burgh.*

JOHN   Thus right triumphs, and *John* triumphs in right.
Arthur thou seest, *Fraunce* cannot bolster thee: 1090
Thy Mothers pride hath brought thee to this fall.
But if at last, Nephew thou yeeld thy selfe
Into the gardance of thine Unckle *John*,
Thou shalt be used as becomes a Prince.[3]

ARTHUR   Unckle, my Grandame taught her Nephew this,
To beare captivitie with patience.
Might hath prevayld not right, for I am King
Of *England*, though thou weare the Diadem.

---

[1] rallies.   [2] Cf. the Bastard, III.2.7. 'I rescu'd her.'   [3] III.3.2-4

Q. ELIANOR   Sonne *John*, soone shall we teach him to
forget
These proud presumptions, and to know himselfe.   1100
  JOHN   Mother, he never will forget his claime,
I would he livde not to remember it.
But leaving this, we will to *England* now,
And take some order with our Popelings there,
That swell with pride, and fat of lay mens lands.
Philip I make thee chiefe in this affaire,
Ransack the Abbeys, Cloysters, Priories,
Convert their coyne unto my souldiers use:
And whatsoere he be within my Land,
That goes to *Rome* for justice and for law,   1110
While he may have his right within the Realme,
Let him be judgde a traitor to the State,
And suffer as an enemie to *England*.[1]
Mother, we leave you here beyond the seas,
As Regent of our Provinces in *Fraunce*,
While we to *England* take a speedie course,
And thanke our God that gave us victorie.
Hubert de Burgh take *Arthur* here to thee,
Be he thy prisoner: *Hubert* keepe him safe,
For on his life doth hang thy Soveraignes crowne,   1120
But in his death consists thy Soveraignes blisse:
Then *Hubert*, as thou shortly hearst from me,
So use the prisoner I have given in charge.
  HUBERT   Frolick yong Prince, though I your keeper bee,
Yet shall your keeper live at your commaund.
  ARTHUR   As please my God, so shall become of me.
  Q. ELIANOR   My Sonne to *England*, I will see thee shipt,
And pray to God to send thee safe ashore.
  BASTARD   Now warres are done, I long to be at home
To dive into the Monkes and Abbots bags,   1130
To make some sport among the smooth skin Nunnes,
And keepe some revell with the fanzen[2] Friers.
  JOHN   To *England* Lords, each looke unto your charge,
And arme yourselves against the Romane pride.   [*Exeunt*

[Scene x]

*Enter the K. of Fraunce, Lewes his sonne, Cardinall Pandolph
Legate, and Constance.*

[1] III.3.6–14 omits the veto on appeals to Rome.   [2] Franciscan?

PHILIP   What, every man attacht with this mishap?
Why frowne you so, why droop ye Lords of *Fraunce*?
Me thinkes it differs from a warlike minde
To lowre it for a checke or two of chaunce.
Had *Lymoges* escapt the bastards spight,
A little sorrow might have servde our losse.   1140
Brave *Austria*, heaven joyes to have thee there.
   CARD.   His sowle is safe and free from Purgatorie,
Our holy Father hath dispenst his sinnes,
The blessed Saints have heard our orisons,
And all are Mediators for his soule,
And in the right of these most holy warres,
His holines free pardon doth pronounce
To all that follow you gainst English heretiques,
Who stand accursed in our mother Church.

Enter Constance alone.[1]

   PHILIP   To aggravate the measure of our griefe,   1150
All malcontent comes *Constance* for her Sonne.
Be briefe good Madame, for your face imports
A tragick tale behinde thats yet untolde.
Her passions stop the organ of her voyce,
Deepe sorrow throbbeth misbefalne events.
Out with it Ladie, that our Act may end
A full Catastrophe of sad laments.
   CONST.   My tongue is tunde to storie forth mishap:
When did I breath to tell a pleasing tale?
Must *Constance* speake? let teares prevent her talke: 1160
Must I discourse? let *Dido* sigh and say,
She weepes againe to heare the wrack of *Troy*:
Two words will serve, and then my tale is done[2]:
Elnors proud brat hath robd me of my Sonne.
   LEWES   Have patience Madame, this is chaunce of
         warre[3]:
He may be ransomde, we revenge his wrong.
   CONSTANCE   Be it ner so soone, I shall not live so long.
   PHILIP   Despaire not yet, come *Constance*, goe with me,
These clowdes will fleet, the day will cleare againe.   [*Exeunt*
   CARD.   Now *Lewes*, thy fortune buds with happie spring,   1170
Our holy Fathers prayers effecteth this.

---

[1] III.4.17 s.d.
[2] Contrast III.4.23-105, where 'two words' will not serve.   [3] III.4.22.

Arthur is safe, let *John* alone with him,
Thy title next is fairst to *Englands* Crowne:
Now stirre thy Father to begin with *John*,
The Pope sayes I, and so is *Albion* thine.
    LEWES Thankes my Lord Legate for your good conceipt,
Tis best we follow now the game is faire.
My Father wants to worke him your good words.
    CARD. A few will serve to forward him in this,
Those shal not want: but lets about it then.   1180
                                    [*Exeunt*

[Scene xi]

      Enter Philip leading a Frier, charging him to show where the
                       Abbots golde lay.

    PHILIP Come on you fat Franciscans, dallie no longer,
        but shew me where the Abbots treasure lyes, or die.
    FRIER *Benedicamus Domini*, was ever such an injurie.
Sweete S. *Withold*[1] of thy lenitie, defend us from extremitie,
And heare us for S. Charitie, oppressed with austeritie.
In nomini Domini, make I my homilie,
Gentle Gentilitie grieve not the Cleargie.
    PHILIP Grey gownd good face, conjure ye,
        ner trust me for a groate,
If this wa[i]ste girdle hang thee not   1190
        that girdeth in thy coate.
Now, balde and barefoote *Bungie* birds[2]
        when up the gallowes climing,
Say *Philip* he had words inough
        to put you downe with ryming!
    FRIER A pardon, *O parce*,[3] Saint *Fraunces* for mercie,
Shall shield thee from nightspells and dreaming of divells,
If thou wilt forgive me, and never more grieve me.
With fasting and praying, and *Haile Marie* saying.
From black Purgatorie a penance right sorie,   1200
Frier *Thomas* will warme you,
It shall never harme you.
    PHILIP Come leave off your rabble,
Sirs hang up this lozell.[4]

---

    [1] Wittol, a cuckold or simpleton.
    [2] Perhaps from 'bung', a pickpocket but there seem to have been Franciscans
at Bungay, Suffolk.
    [3] O spare me!   [4] scoundrel.

2. FRIER   For charitie I beg his life,
Saint *Frauncis* chiefest Frier,
   The best in all our Covent Sir,
to keepe a Winters fier.
   O strangle not the good olde man,
my hostesse oldest guest,   1210
   And I will bring you by and by
unto the Priors chest.

   PHILIP   I, saist thou so, & if thou wilt the frier is at
      libertie,
If not, as I am honest man, Ile hang you both for companie.

   FRIER   Come hether, this is the chest though simple to
      behold
That wanteth not a thousand pound in silver and in gold.
Myselfe will warrant full so much, I know the Abbots store,
Ile pawne my life there is no lesse to have what ere is more.

   PHILIP   I take thy word, the overplus unto thy share shall
      come,
But if there want of full so much, thy neck shall pay the sum.
Breake up the Cofer, Frier.[1]   1221

   FRIER   Oh I am undun, faire *Alice* the Nun
Hath tooke up her rest in the Abbots chest,
Sancte benedicite, pardon my simplicitie.
Fie *Alice*, confession will not salve this transgression.

   PHILIP   What have wee here, a holy Nun? So keepe me
      God in health,
A smooth facte Nunne (for ought I know) is all the Abbots
   wealth.
Is this the Nonries chastitie? Beshrewe me but I thinke
They goe as oft to Venery, as niggards to their drinke.
Why paltrey Frier and Pandar too, yee shamelesse shaven
   crowne,   1230
Is this the chest that held a hoord, at least a thousand pound?
And is the hoord a holy whore? Wel be the hangman nimble,
Hee'le take the paine to paye you home, and teach you to
   dissemble.

   NUNNE   O spare the Frier *Anthony*, a better never was
To sing a Dirige solemnly, or read a morning Masse.
If money be the meanes of this, I know an ancient Nunne,
That hath a hoord this seaven yeares, did never see the sunne;
And that is yours, and what is ours, so favour now be shown,
You shall commaund as commonly, as if it were your owne.

   [1] The chest is opened.

FRIER	Your honour excepted.	1240

NUNNE   I *Thomas*, I meane so.

PHILIP   From all save from Friers.

NUNNE   Good Sir, doo not think so.

PHILIP   I thinke and see so: why how camst thou here?

FRIER   To hide her from lay men.

NUNNE   Tis true sir, for feare.

PHILIP   For feare of the laytie: a pitifull dred
When a Nunne flies for succour to a fat Friers bed.
But now for your ransome my Cloyster-bred Conney,
To the chest that you speake of where lyes so much money.   1250
    NUNNE   Faire Sir, within this presse,[1] of plate & money is
The valew of a thousand markes, and other thing by gis.
Let us alone, and take it all, tis yours Sir, now you know it.
    PHILIP   Come on sir Frier, pick the locke, this geere dooth
        cotton hansome,[2]
That covetousness so cunningly must pay the letchers ransom.
What is in the hoord?
    FRIER   Frier *Laurence* my Lord. Now holy water help us,
Some witch, or some divell is sent to delude us:
Haud credo Laurentius, that thou shouldest be pend thus
In the presse of a Nun. We are all undon,   1260
And brought to discredence if thou be Frier *Laurence*,
    FRIER [LAURENCE]   *Amor vincit omnia*, so *Cato*[3] affirmeth,
And therefore a Frier whose fancie soone burneth:
Because he is mortall and made of mould,
He omits what he ought, and doth more than he should.
    PHILIP   How goes this geere? the Friers chest filde with a
        fausen[4] Nunne,
The Nunne again locks Frier up, to keep him from the Sun.
Belike the presse is purgatorie, or penance passing grievous:
The Friers chest a hel for Nuns. How do these dolts deceive us!
Is this the labour of their lives to feede and live at ease,   1270
To revell so lasciviously as often as they please.
Ile mend the fault or fault my ayme, if I do misse amending,
Tis better burn the cloisters down than leave them for
    offending.
But holy you, to you I speake, to you religious divell,
Is this the presse that holdes the summe to quite you for your
    evill.

---

[1] cupboard.   [2] 'This business prospers admirably.'
[3] Not Cato, but Virgil, *Ecl.* X, 69.
[4] eel-like, wriggling, or perhaps just 'false'.

NUNNE   I crie *Peccavi, parce me*, good Sir I was beguild.

FRIER   *Absolve* Sir, for charitie she would be reconcilde.

PHI.   And so I shall, sirs binde them fast, this is their
absolution,

Go hang them up for hurting them, hast them to execution.

FR. LAWRENCE   *O tempus edax rerum*,[1]   1280

Geve children bookes, they teare them.

O vanitas vanitatis, in this waning *ætatis*,

At threescore welneere to goe to this geere,

To my conscience a clog to dye like a dog.

Exaudi me Domine, sivis me parce

Dabo pecuniam, si habeo veniam[2]

To goe and fetch it, I will dispatch it,

A hundred pounds sterling for my lives sparing.

Enter Peter a Prophet, with people.

PETER   Hoe, who is here? S. *Fraunces* be your speed,

Come in my flock, and follow me, your fortunes I will reed   1290

Come hether boy, goe get thee home, and clime not overhie:

For from aloft thy fortunes stands in hazard; thou shalt die.

BOY   God be with you *Peter*, I pray you come to our house
a Sunday.

PETER   My boy show me thy hand, blesse thee my boy,

For in thy palme I see a many troubles are ybent to dwell,

But thou shalt scape them all and doo full well.

BOY   I thanke you *Peter*, theres a cheese for your labor:
my sister prayes ye to come home, & tell her how many husbands she shall have, and shee'l give you a rib of bacon.   1299

PETER   My masters, stay at the towns end for me, Ile
come to you all anon: I must dispatch some busines with a
Frier, and then Ile read your fortunes.

PHILIP   How now, a Prophet? Sir prophet whence are ye?

PETER   I am of the world and in the world, but live not as
others by the world: what I am I know, and what thou wilt
be I know. If thou knowest me now be answered: if not,
enquire no more what I am.

PHIL.   Sir, I know you will be a dissembling knave, that
deludes the people with blinde prophecies: you are him I
looke for, you shall away with me: bring away all the rabble,
and you Frier *Laurence* remember your raunsome—a hundred

---

[1] 'O Time, consumer of all things!'

[2] 'O Lord, hear my prayer. Spare me if you will. I'll give money, if I have per
mission. . . .'

pound, and a pardon for your selfe, and the rest come on.
Sir Prophet, you shall with me, to receive a Prophets
rewarde.[1]   1313

[*Exeunt*

[Scene xii]

Enter Hubert de Burgh with three men.

HUBERT   My masters, I have shewed you what warrant I
have for this attempt[2]; I perceive by your heavie counten-
ances, you had rather be otherwise imployed, and for my
owne part, I would the King had made choyce of some other
executioner: onely this is my comfort, that a King commaunds, whose precepts neglected or omitted, threatneth
torture for the default.[3] Therefore in briefe, leave me, and be
readie to attend the adventure: stay within that entry, and
when you heare me crie, *God save the King*, issue sodainly
foorth, lay handes on *Arthur*, set him in this chayre,[4] wherin
(once fast bound) leave him with me to finish the rest.   1324
ATTENDANTS   We goe, though loath.   [*Exeunt*
HUBERT   My Lord, will it please your Honour to take the
benefice of the faire evening?[5]

Enter Arthur to Hubert de Burgh.

ARTHUR   Gramercie *Hubert* for thy care of me,
In or to whom restraint is newly knowen,
The joy of walking is small benefit,   1330
Yet will I take thy offer with small thankes,
I would not loose the pleasure of the eye.
But tell me curteous keeper if you can,
How long the King will have me tarrie heere.
HUBERT   I know not Prince, but as I gesse not long.
God send you freedome, and *God save the King*,

They issue forth.

ARTHUR   Why how now sirs, what may this outrage
         meane?
O helpe me *Hubert*, gentle keeper helpe:
God send this sodaine mutinous approach
Tend not to reave a wretched guiltles life.   1340

---

[1] Cf. IV.2.147ff.   [2] Cf. IV.1.6.   [3] Cf. IV.1.7.   [4] IV.1.1-5.
[5] Hubert speaks to Arthur, who is on the inner stage. In *KJ* IV.1.9 the time is
early in the day.

HUBERT   So sirs, depart, and leave the rest for me.[1]

ARTHUR   Then *Arthur* yeeld, death frowneth in thy face,
What meaneth this? Good *Hubert* plead the case.

HUBERT   Patience yong Lord, and listen words of woe,
Harmfull and harsh, hells horror to be heard:
A dismall tale fit for a furies tongue.
I faint to tell, deepe sorrow is the sound.

ARTHUR   What, must I die?

HUBERT   No newes of death, but tidings of more hate,
A wrathfull doome, and most unluckie fate: 1350
Deaths dish were daintie at so fell a feast,
Be deafe, heare not, its hell to tell the rest.

ARTHUR   Alas thou wrongst my youth with words of feare,
Tis hell, tis horror, not for one to heare:
What is it man? if it must needes be don,
Act it, and end it, that the paine were gon.

HUBERT   I will not chaunt such dolour with my tongue,
Yet must I act the outrage with my hand.
My heart my head, and all my powers beside,
To aide the office have at once denide.   1360
Peruse this letter, lines of treble woe,
Read ore my charge, and pardon when you know.

> *Hubert* these are to commaund thee, as thou tendrest
> our quiet in minde and the estate of our person, that
> presently upon the receipt of our commaund, thou put
> out the eyes of *Arthur Plantaginet.*

ARTHUR   Ah monstrous damned man, his very breath
   infects the elements,
Contagious venyme dwelleth in his heart,
Effecting meanes to poyson all the world.
Unreverent may I be to blame the heavens   1370
Of great injustice, that the miscreant
Lives to oppresse the innocents with wrong.
Ah *Hubert*, makes he thee his instrument
To sound the tromp that causeth hell triumph?
Heaven weepes, the Saints doo shed celestiall teares,
They feare thy fall, and cyte thee with remorse,
They knock thy conscience, mooving pitie there,
Willing to fence thee from the rage of hell:
Hell, *Hubert*, trust me, all the plagues of hell
Hangs on performance of this damned deede.   1380

---

[1] IV.1.85.

This seale, the warrant of the[1] bodies blisse,
Ensureth Satan chieftaine of thy soule:
Subscribe not *Hubert*, give not Gods part away.
I speake not onely for eyes priviledge,
The chiefe exterior[2] that I would enjoy:
But for thy perill, farre beyond my paine,
Thy sweete soules losse, more than my eyes vaine lack;
A cause internall, and eternall too.
Advise thee *Hubert*, for the case is hard,
To loose salvation for a Kings reward.   1390
    HUBERT   My Lord, a subject dwelling in the land
Is tyed to execute the Kings commaund.
    ARTHUR   Yet God commands, whose power reacheth
    further,
That no commaund should stand in force to murther.
    HUBERT   But that same Essence hath ordaind a law,
A death for guilt, to keepe the world in awe.
    ARTHUR   I plead not guiltie, treasonles and free.
    HUBERT   But that appeale my Lord concernes not me.
    ARTHUR   Why, thou art he that maist omit the perill.
    HUBERT   I, if my Soveraigne would remit his quarrell.   1400
    ARTHUR   His quarrell is unhallowed false and wrong.
    HUBERT   Then be the blame to whom it doth belong.
    ARTHUR   Why thats to thee if thou as they proceede,
Conclude their judgement with so vile a deede.
    HUBERT   Why then no execution can be lawfull,
If Judges doomes must be reputed doubtfull.
    ARTHUR   Yes where in forme of Lawe in place and time,
The offender is convicted of the crime.
    HUBERT   My Lord, my Lord, this long expostulation,
Heapes up more griefe, than promise of redresse;   1410
For this I know, and so resolvde I end,
That subjects lives on Kings commaunds depend.
I must not reason why he is your foe,
But doo his charge since he commaunds it so.
    ARTHUR   Then doo thy charge, and charged be thy soule
With wrongfull persecution done this day.
You rowling eyes,[3] whose superficies[4] yet
I doo behold with eyes that Nature lent:
Send foorth the terror of your Moovers frowne,
To wreake my wrong upon the murtherers   1420
That rob me of your faire reflecting view:

---

  [1] thy?   [2] Exterior part of me, sense.   [3] stars.   [4] surface, outer form.

Let hell to them (as earth they wish to mee)
Be darke and direfull guerdon for their guylt,
And let the black tormenters of deepe *Tartary*
Upbraide them with this damned enterprise,
Inflicting change of tortures on their soules.
Delay not *Hubert,* my orisons are ended,
Begin I pray thee, reave me of my sight:
But to performe a tragedie indeede,
Conclude the period with a mortall stab.   1430
Constance farewell, tormentor come away,
Make my dispatch the Tirants feasting day.
     HUBERT   I faint, I feare, my conscience bids desist:
Faint did I say, feare was it that I named?
My King commaunds, that warrant sets me free:
But God forbids, and he commaundeth Kings.
That great Commaunder counterchecks my charge,
He stayes my hand, he maketh soft my heart.
Goe cursed tooles, your office is exempt,
Cheere thee yong Lord, thou shalt not loose an eye,   1440
Though I should purchase it with losse of life.
Ile to the King, and say his will is done,
And of the langor[1] tell him thou art dead;
Goe in with me, for *Hubert* was not borne
To blinde those lampes that Nature pollisht so,
     ARTHUR   *Hubert,* if ever *Arthur* be in state,
Looke for amends of this received gift
I tooke my eysight by thy curtesie,
Thou lentst them me, I will not be ingrate.
But now procrastination may offend   1450
The issue that thy kindnes undertakes:
Depart we *Hubert* to prevent the worst.   [*Exeunt*

[Scene xiii]

          Enter King John, Essex, Salisbury, Pembrooke.

     JOHN   Now warlike followers resteth ought undon
That may impeach us of fond oversight?
The French have felt the temper of our swords,
Cold terror keepes possession in their sowles,
Checking their overdaring arrogance
For buckling with so great an overmatch.

---

[1] From Holinshed (*supra*, 33).

The Arche proud titled Priest of *Italy*,   1460
That calles himselfe grand Viccar under God
Is busied now with trentall obsequies,[1]
Masse and months minde,[2] dirge and I know not what
To ease their sowles in painefull purgatory,
That have miscaried in these bloudy warres.
Heard you not Lords when first his holines
Had tidings of our small account of him,
How with a taunt vaunting upon his toes
He urgde a reason why the English Asse
Disdaignd the blessed ordinance of *Rome*?   1470
The title (reverently might I inferre)
Became the Kings that earst have borne the load,
The slavish weight of that controlling Priest:
Who at his pleasure temperd them like waxe
To carrie armes on danger of his curse,
Banding their sowles with warrants of his hand.
I grieve to thinke how Kings in ages past
(Simply devoted to the Sea of *Rome*)
Have run into a thousand acts of shame.
But now for confirmation of our State,   1480
Sith we have proynd the more than needfull braunch
That did oppresse the true wel-growing stock,
It resteth we throughout our Territories
Be reproclaimed and invested King.

    PEMBROOKE My Liege, that were to busie men with
      doubts.
Once were you crownd, proclaimd, and with applause
Your Citie streetes have ecchoed to the eare,
God Save the King, God save our Soveraigne *John*.
Pardon my feare, my censure doth infer
Your Highnes not deposde from Regall State,   1490
Would breed a mutinie in peoples mindes,
What it should meane to have you crownd againe.[3]

    JOHN *Pembrooke* performe what I have bid thee doo,
Thou knowst not what induceth me to this.[4]
Essex goe in, and Lordings all be gon
About this taske, I will be crownd anon.

---

   [1] Obsequies involving thirty masses.

   [2] Monthly memorial services. *1591 has* mouths.

   [3] In IV.2. Pembroke and Salisbury, after the Coronation, describe it as 'superfluous'.

   [4] And Shakespeare evades telling us, IV.2.40-3; but see below, ll. 1538-60.

Enter the Bastard.

Philip, what newes, how doo the Abbots chests?
Are Friers fatter than the Nunnes are faire?
What cheere with Churchmen, had they golde or no?
Tell me how hath thy office tooke effect?   1500
   PHILIP   My Lord, I have performd your Highnes charge:
The ease bred Abbots and the bare foote Friers,
The Monkes the Priors and holy cloystred Nunnes,
Are all in health, and were my Lord in wealth,
Till I had tythde and tolde their holy hoords.
I doubt not when your Highnes sees my prize,
You may proportion all their former pride.[1]
   JOHN   Why so, now sorts it *Philip* as it should:
This small intrusion into Abbey trunkes,
Will make the Popelings excommunicate,   1510
Curse, ban, and breath[e] out damned orisons,
As thick as hailestones fore the springs approach:
But yet as harmles and without effect,
As is the eccho of a Cannons crack
Dischargd against the battlements of heaven.
But what newes els befell there *Philip*?
   BASTARD   Strange newes my Lord: within your territories,
Nere *Pomfret* is a Prophet new sprong up,
Whose divination volleys wonders foorth;
To him the Commons throng with Countrey gifts,   1520
He sets a date unto the Beldames death,
Prescribes how long the Virgins state shall last,
Distinguisheth the mooving of the heavens,
Gives limits unto holy nuptiall rytes,
Foretelleth famine, aboundeth plentie forth,
Of fate, of fortune, life and death he chats,
With such assurance, scruples put apart,
As if he knew the certaine doomes of heaven,
Or kept a Register of all the Destinies.
   JOHN   Thou telst me mervailes, would thou hadst brought
     the man,
We might have questiond him of things to come.   1531
   BASTARD   My Lord, I tooke a care of had I wist,
And brought the Prophet with me to the Court,[2]
He stayes my Lord but at the Presence doore:
Pleaseth your Highnes, I will call him in.

---

[1] IV.2.141–2.   [2] IV.2.143–9.
8—N.D.S.S. 4

JOHN   Nay stay awhile, wee'l have him here anon,
A thing of weight is first to be performd.

Enter the Nobles and crowne King John, and then crie God
save the King.

JOHN   Lordings and friends supporters of our state,
Admire not at this unaccustomd course,
Nor in your thoughts blame not this deede of yours.   1540
Once ere this time was I invested King,
Your fealtie sworne as Liegmen to our state:
Once since that time ambicious weedes have sprung
To staine the beautie of our garden plot:
But heavens in our conduct rooting thence
The false intruders, breakers of worlds peace,
Have to our joy, made Sunshine chase the storme.
After the which, to try your constancie
That now I see is worthie of your names,
We cravde once more your helps for to invest us   1550
Into the right that envie sought to wrack.
Once was I not deposde, your former choyce;
Now twice been crowned and applauded King:
Your cheered action to install me so,
Infers assured witnes of your loves,
And binds me over in a Kingly care
To render love with love, rewards of worth
To ballance downe requitall to the full.
But thankes the while, thankes Lordings to you all:
Aske me and use me, try me and finde me yours.[1]   1560
   ESSEX   A boon my Lord, at vauntage of your words
We aske to guerdon all our loyalties.
   PEMBROOKE   We take the time your Highnes bids us aske:
Please it you graunt, you make your promise good,
With lesser losse than one superfluous haire
That not remembred falleth from your head.
   JOHN   My word is past, receive your boone my Lords.
What may it be? Aske it, and it is yours.
   ESSEX   We crave my Lord, to please the Commons with
The libertie of Ladie *Constance* Sonne: 1570
Whose durance darkeneth your Highnes right,
As if you kept him prisoner, to the end
Your selfe were doubtfull of the thing you have.[2]

[1] IV.2.40–6.   [2] IV.2.47–63.

Dismisse him thence, your Highnes needes not feare,
Twice by consent you are proclaimd our King.
   PEMBROOKE   This if you graunt, were all unto your good:
For simple people muse you keepe him close.
   JOHN   Your words have searcht the center of my thoughts,
Confirming warrant of your loyalties,
Dismisse your counsell, sway my state,   1580
Let *John* doo nothing but by your consents.
Why how now *Philip*, what extasie is this?
Why casts thou up thy eyes to heaven so?

There the five Moones appeare.

   BASTARD   See, see my Lord strange apparitions.
Glauncing mine eye to see the Diadem
Placte by the Bishops on your Highnes head,
From foorth a gloomie cloude, which curtaine like
Displaide it selfe, I sodainly espied
Five Moones reflecting, as you see them now:
Even in the moment that the Crowne was placte   1590
Gan they appeare, holding the course you see.[1]
   JOHN   What might portend these apparitions,
Unusuall signes, forerunners of event,
Presagers of strange terror to the world:
Beleeve me Lords the object feares me much.
Philip thou toldst me of [a][2] Wizzard late,
Fetch in the man to descant of this show.
   PEMBROOKE   The heavens frowne upon the sinfull earth,
When with prodigious unaccustomd signes
They spot their superficies with such wonder.   1600
   ESSEX   Before the ruines of *Jerusalem*,
Such Meteors were the Ensignes of his wrath
That hastned to destroy the faultfull Towne.

Enter the Bastard with the Prophet.

   JOHN   Is this the man?
   BASTARD   It is my Lord.
   JOHN   Prophet of *Pomfret*, for so I heare thou art,
That calculatst of many things to come:
Who by a power repleate with heavenly gift
Canst blab the counsell of thy Makers will.
If fame be true, or truth be wrongd by thee,   1610

---

[1] Described but not seen, in IV.2.182–5.   [2] *1591 repeats* me of.

Decide in cyphering what these five Moones
Portend this Clyme, if they presage at all.
Breath out thy gift, and if I live to see
Thy divination take a true effect,
Ile honour thee above all earthly men.
    PETER   The Skie wherein these Moones have residence,
Presenteth *Rome* the great *Metropolis,*
Where sits the Pope in all his holy pompe.
Fowre of the Moones present fowre Provinces,
To wit, *Spaine, Denmarke, Germanie,* and *Fraunce,*   1620
That beare the yoke of proud commaunding *Rome,*
And stand in feare to tempt the Prelates curse.
The smallest Moone that whirles about the rest,
Impatient of the place he holds with them,
Doth figure foorth this Iland *Albion,*
Who gins to scorne the Sea and State of *Rome,*
And seekes to shun the Edicts of the Pope:
This showes the heaven, and this I doo averre
Is figured in these apparitions.[1]
    JOHN   Why then it seemes the heavens smile on us,   1630
Giving applause for leaving of the Pope.
But for they chaunce in our Meridian,
Doo they effect no private growing ill
To be inflicted on us in this Clyme?
    PETER   The Moones effect no more than what I said:
But on some other knowledge that I have
By my prescience, ere Ascension day
Have brought the Sunne unto his usuall height,
Of Crowne, Estate, and Royall dignitie,
Thou shalt be cleane dispoyld and dispossest.[2]   1640
    JOHN   False Dreamer, perish with thy witched newes,
Villaine thou woundst me with thy fallacies:
If it be true, dye for thy tidings price;
If false, for fearing me with vaine suppose:
Hence with the Witch, hells damned secretarie.
Lock him up sure: for by my faith I sweare,
True or not true, the Wizzard shall not live.[3]
Before Ascension day: who should be cause hereof?
Cut off the cause and then the effect will dye.
Tut, tut, my mercie serves to maime my selfe,   1650
The roote doth live, from whence these thornes spring up,

---

[1] Cf. IV.2, where Peter is taken out before the moons are discussed.
[2] IV.2.150–2.   [3] Cf. IV.2.155–7.

I and my promise past for his delivry:
Frowne friends, faile faith, the divell goe withall,
The brat shall dye that terrifies me thus.
Pembrooke and *Essex* I recall my graunt,
I will not buy your favours with my feare:
Nay murmur not, my will is law enough,
I love you well, but if I lovde you better,
I would not buy it with my discontent.

Enter Hubert.

How now, what newes with thee.   1660
    HUBERT   According to your Highnes strickt commaund
Yong *Arthurs* eyes are blinded and extinct.
    JOHN   Why so, then he may feele the crowne, but never
      see it.
    HUBERT   Nor see nor feele, for of the extreame paine,
Within one hower gave he up the Ghost.
    JOHN   What is he dead?
    HUBERT   He is my Lord.
    JOHN   Then with him dye my cares.
    ESSEX   Now joy betide thy soule.
    PEMBROOKE   And heavens revenge thy death.   1670
    ESSEX   What have you done my Lord? Was ever heard
A deede of more inhumane consequence?
Your foes will curse, your friends will crie revenge.
Unkindly rage more rough than Northern winde,
To chip the beautie of so sweete a flower.
What hope in us for mercie on a fault,
When kinsman dyes without impeach of cause,
As you have done, so come to cheere you with,
The guilt shall never be cast me in my teeth.[1]   [*Exeunt*
    JOHN   And are you gone? The divell be your guide: 1680
Proud Rebels as you are to brave me so:
Saucie, uncivill, checkers of my will.
Your tongues give edge unto the fatall knife:
That shall have passage through your traitrous throats.
But husht, breath[e] not buggs[2] words to[o] soone abroad,
Least time prevent the issue of thy reach.
Arthur is dead, I there the corzie[3] growes:
But while he livde, the danger was the more;
His death hath freed me from a thousand feares,

---

[1] Cf. IV.2.67–102.   [2] terrifying.   [3] corrosive, trouble.

But it hath purchast me ten times ten thousand foes.   1690
Why all is one, such luck shall haunt his game,
To whome the divell owes an open shame:
His life a foe that leveld at my crowne,
His death a frame to pull my building downe.
My thoughts harpt still on quiet by his end,
Who living aymed shrowdly at my roome:
But to prevent that plea twice was I crownd,
Twice did my subjects sweare me fealtie,
And in my conscience lovde me as their liege,
In whose defence they would have pawnd their lives.   1700
But now they shun me as a Serpents sting,
A tragick Tyrant sterne and pitiles,
And not a title followes after *John*,
But Butcher, bloudsucker and murtherer.
What Planet governde my nativitie,
To bode me soveraigne types of high estate,
So interlacte with hellish discontent,
Wherein fell furie hath no interest?
Curst be the Crowne, chiefe author of my care,
Nay curst my will that made the Crowne my care: 1710
Curst be my birthday, curst ten times the wombe
That yeelded me alive into the world.
Art thou there villaine, Furies haunt thee still,
For killing him whom all the world laments.[1]
   HUBERT   Why heres my Lord your Highnes hand &
     seale,
Charging on lives regard to doo the deede.
   JOHN   Ah dull conceipted peazant knowst thou not,
It was a damned execrable deede:
Showst me a seale? Oh villaine, both our soules
Have solde their freedome to the thrall of hell,   1720
Under the warrant of that cursed seale.[2]
Hence villaine, hang thy selfe, and say in hell
That I am comming for a kingdome there.
   HUBERT   My Lord attend the happie tale I tell,
For heavens health send Sathan packing hence
That instigates your Highnes to despaire.
If *Arthurs* death be dismall to be heard,
Bandie the newes for rumors of untruth:
He lives my Lord the sweetest youth alive,
In health, with eysight, not a haire amisse.   1730

<hr>

[1] IV.2.204–6.   [2] IV.2.215–18.

This hart tooke vigor from this forward hand,
Making it weake to execute your charge.[1]
  JOHN What lives he? Then sweete hope come home agen.
Chase hence despaire, the purveyer for hell.
Hye *Hubert*, tell these tidings to my Lords
That throb in passions for yong *Arthurs* death[2]:
Hence *Hubert*, stay not till thou has reveald
The wished newes of *Arthurs* happy health.
I goe my selfe, the joyfulst man alive
To storie out this new supposed crime.   1740
                                        [Exeunt

           The ende of the first part.

PART TWO

The Second part of the troublesome Raigne of King *John, conteining the death* of Arthur Plantaginet, the landing of Lewes, and the poysoning of King John at Swinstead *Abbey. As it was (sundry times) publikely acted by the Queenes Majesties Players, in the honourable Citie of* London. (Imprint as for Part I)[3]

TO THE GENTLMEN READERS.

The changeles purpose of determinde Fate
Gives period to our care, or harts content,
When heavens fixt time for this or that hath end:
Nor can earths pomp or pollicie prevent
The doome ordained in their secret will.
   Gentles we left King John *repleate with blisse*
That Arthur *livde, whom he supposed slaine;*
And Hubert *posting to returne those Lords,*
Who deemd him dead, and parted discontent:
Arthur *himselfe begins our latter Act,*
Our Act of outrage, desprate furie, death;
Wherein fond rashnes murdereth first a Prince,
And Monkish falsnes poysneth last a King.
First Scene shews Arthurs *death in infancie,*
And last concludes Johns *fatall tragedie.*

---

[1] IV.2.249–59.   [2] IV.2.260–9.
[3] Text based on the facsimile ed. C. Praetorius, 1888, with some emendation of punctuation and abbreviation of speech-headings. No scene-divisions in *1591*.

THE SECOND PART

[Scene i]

Enter yong Arthur on the walls.

Now helpe good hap to further mine entent,
Crosse not my youth with any more extreames:
I venter life to gaine my libertie,
And if I die, worlds troubles have an end.[1]
Feare gins disswade the strength of my resolve,
My holde will faile, and then alas I fall,
And if I fall, no question death is next:
Better desist, and live in prison still.
Prison said I? nay, rather death than so:
Comfort and courage come againe to me.   10
Ile venter sure: tis but a leape for life.

He leapes, and brusing his bones, after he was[2] from his
traunce, speakes thus:

Hoe, who is nigh? some bodie take me up.
Where is my mother? let me speake with her.
Who hurts me thus? speake hoe, where are you gone?
Ay me poore *Arthur*, I am here alone.
Why cald I mother, how did I forget?
My fall, my fall, hath kilde my Mothers Sonne.
How will she weepe at tidings of my death?
My death indeed, O God my bones are burst.
Sweet Jesu save my soule, forgive my rash attempt,   20
Comfort my Mother, shield her from despaire,
When she shall heare my tragick overthrowe.
My heart controules the office of my toong,
My vitall powers forsake my brused trunck,
I dye I dye, heaven take my fleeting soule,[3]
And Lady Mother all good hap to thee.   [*He dyes*

Enter Pembrooke, Salsburie, Essex.

ESSEX   My Lords of *Pembroke* and of *Salsbury*,
We must be carefull in our pollicie
To undermine the kepers of this place,
Else shall we never find the Princes grave.   30

---

[1] Cf. IV.3.5–7.   [2] wakes?   [3] IV.3.10.

PEMB.   My Lord of *Essex*, take no care for that,
I warrant you it was not closely done.
But who is this? lo Lords the withered flowre
Who in his life shinde like the Mornings blush,
Cast out a doore, denide his buriall right,
A pray for birds and beasts to gorge upon.
    SALS.   O ruthfull spectacle! O damned deede;
My sinewes shake, my very heart doth bleede.
    ESSEX   Leave childish teares brave Lords of *England*,
If waterfloods could fetch his life againe,   40
My eyes should conduit foorth a sea of teares,
If sobbs would helpe, or sorrowes serve the turne,
My heart should volie out deepe piercing plaints.
But bootlesse weret to breath as many sighes
As might eclipse the brightest Sommers sunne,
Heere rests the helpe, a service to his ghost,
Let not the tyrant causer of this dole,
Live to triumph in ruthfull massacres,
Give hand and hart, and Englishmen to armes,
Tis Gods decree to wreake us of these harmes.   50
    PEMB.   The best advise: But who commes posting heere?

Enter Hughbert

[HUGH]   Right noble Lords, I speake unto you all,
The King entreates your soonest speed
To visit him, who on your present want,
Did ban and cursse his birth, himselfe and me,
For executing of his strict commaund.
I saw his passion, and at fittest time,
Assurde him of his cousins being safe,
Whome pittie would not let me doo to death:
He craves your company my Lords in haste,   60
To whome I will conduct young *Arthur* streight,
Who is in health under my custodie.[1]
    ESSEX   In health base villaine, wert not I leave thy crime
To Gods revenge, to whome revenge belongs,
Heere shouldst thou perish on my Rapires point.
Calst thou this health? such health betide thy friends,
And all that are of thy condition.
    HUGH.   My Lords, but heare me speake, & kil me then,
If heere I left not this yong Prince alive,
Maugre the hastie Edict of the King,   70

---

[1] IV.3.74-5.

Who gave me charge to put out both his eyes,
That God that gave me living to this howre,
Thunder revenge upon me in this place:
And as I tendred him with earnest love,
So God love me, and then I shall be well.
    SALS.   Hence traytor hence, thy councel is heerein.

                                                         [Exit Hughbert[1]

Some in this place appoynted by the King,
Have throwne him from this lodging here above,
And sure the murther hath bin newly done,
For yet the body is not fully colde.   80
    ESSEX   How say you Lords, shal we with speed dispatch
Under our hands a packet into *Fraunce*
To bid the Dolphin enter with his force
To claime the Kingdome for his proper right?[2]
His title maketh lawfull strength thereto.
Besides, the Pope, on perill of his cursse,
Hath bard us of obedience unto *John*.
This hatefull murder, *Lewes* his true discent,
The holy charge that wee receivde from *Rome*,
Are weightie reasons, if you like my reede,   90
To make us all persever in this deede.
    PEMB.   My lord of *Essex*, well have you advisde,
I will accord to further you in this.
    SALS.   And *Salsbury* will not gainsay the same,
But aid that course as far foorth as he can.
    ESSEX   Then each of us send straight to his Allyes,
To winne them to this famous enterprise,
And let us all yclad in Palmers weede,
The tenth of April at Saint *Edmonds Bury*
Meete to confer, and on the Altar there   100
Sweare secrecie and aid to this advise.[3]
Meane while let us conveigh this body hence,
And give him buriall, as befits his state,
Keeping his months minde, and his obsequies
With solemne intercession for his soule.
How say you Lordings, are you all agreed?
    PEMB.   The tenth of Aprill at Saint *Edmonds Bury*,
God letting not, I will not faile the time.
    ESSEX   Then let us all convey the body hence.   *[Exeunt*

---

[1] In *KJ* he stays to protest his innocence to Faulconbridge.
[2] In Holinshed Lewes is sent for *after* the meeting at Bury. Shakespeare follows *TR* in bringing him over earlier (IV.2.110–31).
[3] Cf. IV.3.11–20 where the proposed conference is less clearly explained.

[Scene ii]

Enter King John, with two or three and the Prophet.[1]

JOHN   Disturbed thoughts, foredoomers of mine ill,   110
Distracted passions, signes of growing harmes,
Strange Prophecies of imminent mishaps,
Confound my wits, and dull my senses so,
That every object these mine eyes behold
Seeme instruments to bring me to my end.
Ascension day is come, *John* feare not then
The prodigies this pratling Prophet threates.
Tis come indeede: ah were it fully past,
Then were I careles of a thousand feares.
The Diall tells me, it is twelve at noone.   120
Were twelve at midnight past, then might I vaunt,
False seers prophecies of no import.
Could I as well with this right hand of mine
Remove the Sunne from our Meridian,
Unto the moonsted circle of thantipodes,
As turne this steele from twelve to twelve agen,
Then *John* the date of fatall prophecies
Should with the Prophets life together end.
But *Multa cadunt inter calicem supremaque labra.*[2]
Peter, unsay thy foolish doting dreame,   130
And by the Crowne of *England* heere I sweare,
To make thee great, and greatest of thy kin.
   PETER   King *John*, although the time I have prescribed
Be but twelve houres remayning yet behinde,
Yet do I know by inspiration,
Ere that fixt time be fully come about,
King *John* shall not be King as heeretofore.
   JOHN   Vain buzzard, what mischaunce can chaunce so
      soone,
To set a King beside his regall seate?
My heart is good, my body passing strong,   140
My land in peace, my enemies subdewd,
Only my Barons storme at *Arthurs* death,
But *Arthur* lives: I there the challenge growes.
Were he dispatcht unto his longest home,
Then were the King secure of thousand foes.
Hubert, what news with thee, where are my Lords?

---

[1] *KJ* omits this scene with the Prophet.
[2] 'There's many a slip 'twixt the cup and the lip.'

HUB.   Hard newes my Lord, *Arthur* the lovely Prince
Seeking to escape over the Castle walles,
Fell headlong downe, and in the cursed fall
He brake his bones, and there before the gate   150
Your Barons found him dead, and breathlesse quite.[1]
   JOHN   Is *Arthur* dead? then *Hubert* without more words
      hang the Prophet.
Away with *Peter*, villen out of my sight,
I am deafe, be gone, let him not speake a word.
Now *John*, thy feares are vanisht into smoake,
Arthur is dead, thou guiltlesse of his death.
Sweet Youth, but that I strived for a Crowne,
I could have well affoorded to thine age
Long life, and happines to thy content.

Enter the Bastard.

   JOHN   *Philip*, what newes with thee?   160
   BAST.   The newes I heard was *Peters* prayers,
Who wisht like fortune to befall us all:
And with that word, the rope his latest friend,
Kept him from falling headlong to the ground.
   JOHN   There let him hang, and be the Ravens food,
While *John* triumphs in spight of Prophecies.
But whats the tidings from the Popelings now?
What say the Monkes and Priests to our proceedings?
Or wheres the Barons that so sodainly
Did leave the King upon a false surmise?[2]   170
   BAST.   The Prelates storme & thirst for sharpe revenge:
But please your Majestie, were that the worst,
It little skild: a greater danger growes,
Which must be weeded out by carefull speede,
Or all is lost, for all is leveld at.
   JOHN   More frights and feares! what ere thy tidings be,
I am preparde: then *Philip*, quickly say,
Meane they to murder, or imprison me,
To give my crowne away to *Rome* or *Fraunce*;
Or will they each of them become a King?   180
Worse than I thinke it is, it cannot be.
   BAST.   Not worse my Lord, but everie whit as bad.
The Nobles have elected *Lewes* King,
In right of Ladie *Blanche* your Neece, his Wife:
His landing is expected every hower.

---

  [1] Cf. V.1.39-43.   [2] V.1.37-8.

The Nobles, Commons, Clergie, all Estates,
Incited chiefely by the *Cardinall*,
Pandulph that livs here Legate for the Pope,
Thinks long to see their new elected King.
And for undoubted proofe, see here my Liege   190
Letters to me from your Nobilitie,
To be a partie in this action:
Who under shew of fained holines,
Appoynt their meeting at *S. Edmonds Bury*,[1]
There to consult, conspire, and conclude
The overthrow and downfall of your State.
  JOHN   Why so it must be: one hower of content,
Matcht with a month of passionate effects.
Why shines the Sunne to favour this consort?
Why doo the windes not breake their brazen gates,   200
And scatter all these perjurd complices,
With all their counsells and their damned drifts?
But see the welkin rolleth gently on,
Theres not a lowring clowde to frowne on them;
The heaven, the earth, the sunne, the moone and all
Conspire with those confederates my decay.
Then hell for me if any power be there,
Forsake that place, and guide me step by step,
To poyson, strangle, murder in their steps
These traitors: oh that name is too good for them,   210
And death is easie; is there nothing worse,
To wreake me on this proud peace-breaking crew?
What saist thou *Philip*? why assists thou not?
  BAST.   These curses (good my Lord) fit not the season:
Help must descend from heaven against this treason.[2]
  JOHN   Nay thou wilt proove a traitor with the rest,
Goe get thee to them, shame come to you all.
  BAST.   I would be loath to leave your Highnes thus,
Yet you command, and I though grievd will goe.
  JOHN   Ah *Philip* whether goest thou? come againe.   220
  BAST.   My Lord these motions are as passions of a mad
    man.
  JOHN   A mad man *Philip*, I am mad indeed,
My hart is mazd, my senses all foredone,
And *John* of *England* now is quite undone.
Was ever King as I opprest with cares?
Dame *Elianor* my noble Mother Queene,

---

[1] Cf. Salisbury, IV.3.11.   [2] Cf. V.1.44–61.

My onely hope and comfort in distresse,
Is dead,[1] and *England* excommunicate,
And I am interdicted by the Pope,
All Churches curst, their doores are sealed up,   230
And for the pleasure of the Romish Priest,
The service of the Highest is neglected;
The multitude (a beast of many heads)
Doo wish confusion to their Soveraigne;
The Nobles blinded with ambitions fumes,
Assemble powers to beat mine Empire downe,
And more than this, elect a forren King.
O *England*, wert thou ever miserable,
King *John* of *England* sees thee miserable:
John, tis thy sinnes that makes it miserable,   240
Quicquid delirunt Reges, plectuntur Achivi.[2]
Philip, as thou hast ever lovde thy King,
So show it now: post to S. *Edmonds Bury*,
Dissemble with the Nobles, know their drifts,[3]
Confound their divelish plots, and damnd devices.
Though *John* be faultie, yet let subjects beare,
He will amend and right the peoples wrongs.
A Mother though she were unnaturall,
Is better than the kindest Stepdame is:
Let never Englishman trust forraine rule.   250
Then *Philip* shew thy fealtie to thy King,
And mongst the Nobles plead thou for the King.
   BAST.   I goe my lord: see how he is distraught,
This is the cursed Priest of *Italy*
Hath heapt these mischiefes on this haplesse Land.
Now Philip, hadst thou *Tullyes* eloquence,
Then mightst thou hope to plead with good successe.   [*Exit*
   JOHN   And art thou gone? successe may follow thee:
Thus hast thou shewd thy kindnes to thy King.
Sirra, in hast goe greete the Cardinall,   260
Pandulph I meane, the Legate from the Pope.
Say that the King desires to speake with him.
Now *John* bethinke thee how thou maist resolve:
And if thou wilt continue *Englands* King,
Then cast about to keep thy Diadem;
For life and land, and all is leveld at.
The Pope of *Rome*, tis he that is the cause,

---

[1] IV.2.120–1. She died in 1204.
[2] 'The people suffer for the mad acts of their kings' (Horace).
[3] *KJ* omits this explanation of Philip's presence there in V.2.

He curseth thee, he sets thy subjects free
From due obedience to their Soveraigne:
He animates the Nobles in their warres, 270
He gives away the Crowne to *Philips* Sonne,
And pardons all that seeke to murther thee:
And thus blind zeale is still predominant.
Then *John* there is no way to keepe thy Crowne,
But finely to dissemble with the Pope:
That hand that gave the wound must give the salve
To cure the hurt, els quite incurable.
Thy sinnes are farre too great to be the man
T'abolish Pope, and Popery from thy Realme:
But in thy Seate, if I may gesse at all, 280
A King shall raigne that shall suppresse them all.
Peace *John*, here comes the Legate of the Pope,
Dissemble thou, and whatsoere thou saist,
Yet with thy heart wish their confusion.

Enter Pandulph.

PAND. Now *John*, unworthie man to breath on earth,
That dost oppugne against thy Mother Church:
Why am I sent for to thy cursed selfe?
JOHN Thou man of God, Vicegerent for the Pope,
The holy Vicar of S. *Peters* Church,
Upon my knees, I pardon crave of thee, 290
And doo submit me to the See[1] of *Rome*,
And vow for penaunce of my high offence,
To take on me the holy Crosse of Christ,
And cary Armes in holy Christian warres.
PAND. No *John*, thy crowching and dissembling thus
Cannot deceive the Legate of the Pope.
Say what thou wilt, I will not credit thee:
Thy Crowne and Kingdome both are tane away,
And thou art curst without redemption.
JOHN Accurst indeed to kneele to such a drudge, 300
And get no help with thy submission,
Unsheath thy sword, and sley the misprowd Priest,
That thus triumphs ore thee a mighty King:
No *John*, submit againe, dissemble yet,
For Priests and Women must be flattered.
Yet holy Father thou thy selfe dost know,

[1] sea *1591*. Shakespeare omits this scene of submission, going straight to John's retaking of the Crown; V.i.

No time to[o] late for sinners to repent,
Absolve me then, and *John* doth sweare to doo
The uttermost what ever thou demaundst.

 PAND. *John*, now I see thy harty penitence,   310
I rew and pitty thy distrest estate,
One way is left to reconcile thy selfe,
And only one which I shall shew to thee.
Thou must surrender to the see of *Rome*
Thy Crowne and Diademe, then shall the Pope
Defend thee from th'invasion of thy foes.
And where his Holinesse hath kindled *Fraunce*,
And set thy subjects hearts at warre with thee,
Then shall he cursse thy foes, and beate them downe,
That seeke the discontentment of the King.   320

 JOHN From bad to woorse: or I must loose my realme,
Or give my Crowne for pennance unto *Rome*?
A miserie more piercing than the darts
That breake from burning exhalations power.
What? shall I give my Crowne with this right hand?
No: with this hand defend thy Crowne and thee.
What newes with thee?

Enter Messenger.

 Please it your Majestie, there is descried on the Coast of
Kent an hundred Sayle of Ships, which of all men is thought
to be the French Fleete, under the conduct of the Dolphin,
so that it puts the Cuntrie in a mutinie, so they send to your
Grace for succour.   332

 K. JOHN How now Lord Cardinall, whats your best
  advise?
These mutinies must be allayd in time
By pollicy or headstrong rage at least.
O *John*, these troubles tyre thy wearyed soule,
And like to *Luna* in a sad Eclipse,
So are thy thoughts and passions for this newes.
Well may it be, when Kings are grieved so,
The vulgar sort worke Princes overthrow.   340

 CARD. K. *John*, for not effecting of thy plighted vow,
This strange annoyance happens to thy land:
But yet be reconcild unto the Church,
And nothing shall be grievous to thy state.

 JOHN Oh *Pandulph* be it as thou hast decreed,
John will not spurne against thy sound advise,

Come lets away, and with they helpe I trow
My Realme shall florish and my Crowne in peace.

[Scene iii]

 Enter the Nobles, Pembrooke, Essex, Chester, Bewchampe,
   Clare, with others.

PEMB. Now sweet *S. Edmond* holy Saint in heaven,
Whose Shrine is sacred, high esteemd on earth,   350
Infuse a constant zeale in all our hearts
To prosecute this act of mickle waight,
Lord *Bewchampe* say, what friends have your procurde.
 BEWCH. The L. *Fitz Water,* L. *Percy,* and L. *Rosse,*
Vowd meeting heere this day the leventh houre.
 ESSEX Under the cloke of holie Pilgrimage,
By that same houre on warrant of their faith,
Philip Plantagenet, a bird of swiftest wing,
Lord *Eustace, Vesey,* Lord *Cressy,* and Lord *Mowbrey,*
Appointed meeting at S. *Edmonds* Shrine.   360
 PEMB. Untill their presence ile conceale my tale,
Sweete complices in holie Christian acts,
That venture for the purchase of renowne,
Thrice welcome to the league of high resolve,
That pawne their bodies for their soules regard.
 ESSEX Now wanteth but the rest to end this worke,
In Pilgrims habit commes our holie troupe
A furlong hence with swift unwonted pace,
May be they are the persons you expect.
 PEMB. With swift unwonted gate, see what a thing is
  zeale,   370
That spurrs them on with fervence to this Shrine,
Now joy come to them for their true intent
And in good time heere come the warmen all
That sweate in body by the minds disease:
Hap and heartsease brave Lordings be your lot.

   Enter the Bastard Philip, &c.[1]

[BAST.] Amen my Lords, the like betide your lucke,
And all that travaile in a Christian cause.
 ESSEX Cheerely replied brave braunch of kingly stock,

---

[1] In *KJ* V.2 the oath-taking is omitted and Faulconbridge enters after Lewes and Pandulph.

A right *Plantaginet* should reason so.
But silence Lords, attend our commings cause: 380
The servile yoke that payned us with toyle,
On strong instinct hath framd this conventickle,
To ease our necks of servitudes contempt.
Should I not name the foeman of our rest,
Which of you all so barraine in conceipt,
As cannot levell at the man I meane?
But least Enigmas shadow shining truth,
Plainely to paint, as truth requires no arte,
Theffect of this resort importeth this,
To roote and cleane extirpate tirant *John*, 390
Tirant I say, appealing to the man,
If any heere that loves him, and I aske,
What kindship, lenitie, or christian raigne
Rules in the man, to barre this foule impeach?
First I inferre the *Chesters* bannishment,
For reprehending him in most unchristian crimes,[1]
Was speciall notice of a tyrants will.
But were this all, the devill should be savd,
But this the least of many thousand faults,
That circumstance with leisure might display. 400
Our private wrongs, no parcell of my tale
Which now in presence, but for some great cause
Might wish to him as to a mortall foe.
But shall I close the period with an acte
Abhorring in the eares of Christian men,
His Cosens death, that sweet unguilty childe,
Untimely butcherd by the tyrants meanes.
Heere is my proofes, as cleere as gravell brooke,
And on the same I further must inferre,
That who upholds a tyrant in his course, 410
Is culpable of all his damned guilt.
To show the which, is yet to be describd.
My Lord of *Pembrooke*, shew what is behinde,
Only I say, that were there nothing else
To moove us but the Popes most dreadfull cursse,
Whereof we are assured if we fayle,
It were inough to instigate us all
With earnestnesse of sprit[e] to seeke a meane
To dispossess *John* of his regiment.
      PEMB.   Well hath my Lord of *Essex* tolde his tale, 420

---

[1] The Earl of Chester had reproved John's 'cruel dealings' and adulteries (Hol.).

Which I aver for most substanciall truth,
And more to make the matter to our minde,
I say that *Lewes* in chalenge of his wife,
Hath title of an uncontrouled plea
To all that longeth to an English Crowne.
Short tale to make, the See apostolick,
Hath offerd dispensation for the fault,
If any be, as trust me none I know
By planting *Lewes* in the Usurpers roome:
This is the cause of all our presence heere,   430
That on the holie Altar we protest
To ayde the right of *Lewes* with goods and life,
Who on our knowledge is in Armes for *England*.
What say you Lords?
  SALS.   As *Pembrooke* sayth, affirmeth *Salsburie*:
Faire *Lewes* of *Fraunce* that spoused Lady *Blanch*,
Hath title of an uncontrouled strength
To *England*, and what longeth to the Crowne:
In right whereof, as we are true informd,
The Prince is marching hitherward in Armes.   440
Our purpose, to conclude that with a word,
Is to invest him as we may devise,
King of our Countrey in the tyrants stead:
And so the warrant on the Altar sworne,
And so the intent for which we hither came.
  BAST.   My Lord of *Salsbury*, I cannot couch
My speeches with the needfull words of arte,
As doth beseeme in such a waightie worke,
But what my conscience and my dutie will,
I purpose to impart.   450
For *Chesters* exile, blame his busie wit,
That medled where his dutie quite forbade:
For any private causes that you have,
Me thinke they should not mount to such a height,
As to depose a King in their revenge.
For *Arthurs* death, King *John* was innocent,
He desperat was the deathsman to himselfe,
Which[1] you to make a colour to your crime injustly do impute
     to his default,
But where fell traytorisme hath residence,
There wants no words to set despight on worke.   460
I say tis shame, and worthy all reproofe,

[1] With *1591*.

To wrest such pettie wrongs in tearmes of right,
Against a King annoynted by the Lord.
Why *Salsburie*, admit the wrongs are true,
Yet subjects may not take in hand revenge,
And rob the heavens of their proper power,
Where sitteth he to whom revenge belongs.
And doth a Pope, a Priest, a man of pride
Give charters for the lives of lawfull Kings?
What can he blesse, or who regards his cursse,   470
But such as give to man, and takes from God?
  speake it in the sight of God above,
Theres not a man that dyes in your beliefe,
But sels his soule perpetually to payne.
Ayd *Lewes*, leave God, kill *John*, please hell,
Make havock of the welfare of your soules,
For heere I leave you in the sight of heaven,
A troupe of traytors, foode for hellish feends;
If you desist, then follow me as friends,
If not, then doo your worst as hatefull traytors.   480
For *Lewes* his right, alas tis too too lame,
A senselesse clayme, if truth be titles friend.
In briefe, if this be cause of our resort,
Our Pilgrimage is to the Devils Shrine.
I came not Lords to troup as traytors doo,
Nor will I counsaile in so bad a cause:
Please you returne, wee goe againe as friends,
If not, I to my King, and you where traytors please.   [*Exit*
    PERCY A hote yong man, and so my Lords proceed,
I let him go, and better lost then found.   490
    PENB. What say you Lords, will all the rest proceed,
Will you all with me sweare upon the Aulter
That you wil to the death, be ayd to *Lewes* & enemy to *John*?
Every man lay his hand by mine, in witnes of his harts
        accord.
Well then, every man to Armes to meete the King
Who is alreadie before *London*.

                        Messenger Enter.

    PEMB. What newes Harrold?
    [MESS.] The right Christian Prince my Maister, *Lewes* of
Fraunce, is at hand, comming to visit your Honors, directed
hether by the right honorable *Richard* Earle of *Bigot*, to conferre
with your Honors.

PEMB.   How neere is his Highnesse?
MESS.   Ready to enter your presence.

Enter Lewes, Earle Bigot, with his troupe.

LEWES   Faire Lords of *England*, *Lewes* salutes you all
As friends, and firme welwillers of his weale,
At whose request, from plenty flowing *Fraunce*
Crossing the Ocean with a Southern gale,
He is in person come at your commaunds
To undertake and gratifie withall
The fulnesse of your favours proffred him.
But worlds brave men, omitting promises,   510
Till time be minister of more amends,
I must acquaint you with our fortunes course.
The heavens dewing favours on my head,
Have in their conduct safe with victorie
Brought me along your well manured bounds,
With small repulse, and little cross of chaunce.
Your Citie Rochester with great applause
By some devine instinct layd armes aside:
And from the hollow holes of Thamesis,
Eccho apace replide, *Vive la roy.*[1]   520
From thence, along the wanton rowling glade
To *Troynovant*, your fayre *Metropolis*,
With luck came *Lewes* to shew his troupes of *Fraunce*,
Waving our Ensignes with the dallying windes,
The fearefull object of fell frowning warre;
Where after some assault, and small defence,
Heavens may I say, and not my warlike troupe,
Temperd their hearts to take a friendly foe
Within the compasse of their high built walles,
Geving me title, as it seemd they wish.   530
Thus Fortune (Lords) acts to your forwardnes
Meanes of content in lieu of former griefe:
And may I live but to requite you all,
Worlds wish were mine in dying noted yours.
   SALIS.   Welcome the balme that closeth up our wounds,
The soveraigne medcine for our quick recure,
The anchor of our hope, the onely prop,
Whereon depends our lives, our lands, our weale,
Without the which, as sheep without their heard,

[1] Cf. V.2.103–4.

(Except a shepheard winking at the wolfe) 540
We stray, we pine, we run to thousand harmes.
No mervaile then, though with unwonted joy,
We welcome him that beateth woes away.[1]
    LEWES   Thanks to you all of this religious league,
A holy knot of Catholique consent.
I cannot name you Lordings, man by man,
But like a strange unacquainted yet,
In generall I promise faithfull love:
Lord *Bigot* brought me to S. *Edmonds* Shrine,
Giving me warrant of a Christian oath, 550
That this assembly came devoted heere,
To sweare according as your packets showd,
Homage and loyall service to our selfe.
I neede not doubt the suretie of your wills;
Since well I know, for many of your sakes
The townes have yeelded on their owne accords:
Yet for a fashion, not for misbeliefe,
My eyes must witnes, and these eares must heare
Your oath upon the holy Altar sworne,
And after march to end our commings cause. 560
    SALS.   That we intend no other then good truth,
All that are present of this holy League,
For confirmation of our better trust,
In presence of his Highnes sweare with me,
The sequel that my selfe shal utter heere.
    I *Thomas Plantaginet*, Earle of *Salisbury*, sweare upon the
Altar, and by the holy Armie of Saints, homage and
allegeance to the right Christian Prince *Lewes* of *Fraunce*, as
true and rightfull King to *England*, *Cornwall*, and *Wales*, and
to their Territories: in the defence whereof I uppon the holy
Altare sweare all forwardnes.   [*All the Eng. Lords sweare*
    As the noble Earle hath sworne, so sweare we all. 572
    LEWES   I rest assured on your holy oath,
And on this Altar in like sort I sweare
Love to you all, and Princely recompence
To guerdon your good wills unto the full.[2]
And since I am at this religious Shrine,
My good welwillers, give us leave awhile
To use some orisons our selves apart

---

    [1] Cf. Salisbury's grief, V.2.11–39, and the medical imagery.
    [2] *KJ* V.2 begins about here, with Lewis ordering the agreement to be copied
out.

To all the holy companie of heaven, 580
That they will smile upon our purposes,
And bring them to a fortunate event.
    SALS.   We leave your Highnes to your good intent.
                    [Exeunt Lords of England
    LEWES   Now Vicount *Meloun*, what remaines behinde?
Trust me these traitors to their sovereigne State,
Are not to be beleevde in any sort.[1]
    MELOUN   Indeed my Lord, they that infringe their oaths,
And play the rebells gainst their native King,
Will for as little cause revolt from you,
If ever opportunitie incite them so: 590
For once forsworne, and never after sound,
Theres no affiance after perjurie.
    LEWES   Well *Meloun* well, lets smooth with them awhile,
Untill we have asmuch as they can doo:
And when their vertue is exhaled drie,
Ile hang them for the guerdon of their help.
Meane while wee'l use them as a precious poyson
To undertake the issue of our hope.
    FR. LORD   Tis policie (my Lord) to bait our hookes
With merry smiles, and promise of much waight: 600
But when your Highnes needeth them no more,
Tis good make sure work with them, least indeede
They proove to you as to their naturall King.
    MELUN   Trust me my Lord, right well have you advisde,
Venyme for use, but never for a sport
Is to be dallyed with, least it infect.
Were you install, as soone I hope you shall:
Be free from traitors, and dispatch them all.
    LEWES   That so I meane, I sweare before you all
On this same Altar, and by heavens power,[2] 610
Theres not an English traytor of them all,
John once dispatcht, and I faire *Englands* King,
Shall on his shoulders beare his head one day,
But I will crop it for their guilts desert:
Nor shall their heires enjoy their Signories,
But perish by their parents fowle amisse.
This have I sworne, and this will I performe,
If ere I come unto the height I hope.
Lay downe your hands, and sweare the same with me.

---

[1] *KJ* refers to this conversation only in Melun's confession, V.4.10–20.
[2] V. 4.16–20.

The French Lords swear.

Why so, now call them in, and speake them faire.   620
A smile of *France* will feed an English foole.
Beare them in hand as friends, for so they be:
But in the hart like traitors as they are.

Enter the English Lords.

Now famous followers, chieftaines of the world,
Have we solicited with heartie prayer
The heaven in favour of our high attempt.
Leave we this place, and march we with our power
To rowse the Tyrant from his chiefest hold:
And when our labours have a prosprous end,
Each man shall reape the fruite of his desert.   630
And so resolvde, brave followers let us hence.   [*Exeunt*

[Scene iv]

*Enter K. John, Bastard, Pandulph, and a many Priests with
them.*

[PANDULPH]   Thus John, thou art absolvde from all thy
        sinnes,
And freed by order from our Fathers curse.
Receive thy Crowne againe, with this proviso,
That thou remaine true liegeman to the Pope,[1]
And carry armes in right of holy *Rome.*
    JOHN   I holde the same as tenaunt to the Pope,
And thanke your Holines for your kindnes showne.
    PHILIP   A proper jest, when Kings must stoop to Friers,
Neede hath no law, when Frier must be Kings.   640

Enter a Messenger.

    MESS.   Please it your Majestie, the Prince of *Fraunce,*
With all the Nobles of your Graces Land,
Are marching hetherward in good aray.
Where ere they set their foote, all places yeeld:
Thy Land is theirs, and not a foote holds out
But *Dover* Castle, which is hard besiegd.[2]
    PAND.   Feare not King *John,* thy kingdome is the popes,
And they shall know his Holines hath power
To beate them soone from whence he hath to doo.

_____
[1] V.1.2-4.   [2] V.1.30-2.

Drums and Trumpets. Enter Lewes, Melun, Salisbury, Essex, Pembrooke, and all the Nobles from Fraunce, and England.

LEWES *Pandulph*, as gave his Holines in charge,　　　650
So hath the *Dolphin* mustred up his troupes
And wonne the greatest part of all this Land.
But ill becomes your Grace Lord Cardinall,
Thus to converse with *John* that is accurst.[1]

PAND. *Lewes* of *France*, victorious Conqueror,
Whose sword hath made this Iland quake for fear;
Thy forwardnes to fight for holy *Rome*
Shall be remunerated to the full:
But know my Lord, K. *John* is now absolvde,
The Pope is pleasde, the Land is blest agen,　　　660
And thou hast brought each thing to good effect.
It resteth then that thou withdraw thy powers,
And quietly returne to *Fraunce* againe:
For all is done the Pope would wish thee doo.[2]

LEWES But al's not done that *Lewes* came to doo.
Why *Pandulph*, hath K. *Philip* sent his sonne
And been at such excessive charge in warres,
To be dismist with words? K. *John* shall know,
England is mine, and he usurps my right.[3]

PAND. *Lewes*, I charge thee and thy complices　　　670
Upon the paine of *Pandulphs* holy curse,
That thou withdraw thy powers to *Fraunce* againe,
And yeeld up *London* and the neighbour Townes
That thou hast tane in *England* by the sword.

MELUN Lord Cardinall, by *Lewes* princely leave,
It can be nought but usurpation
In thee, the Pope, and all the Church of *Rome*,
Thus to insult on Kings of Christendome,
Now with a word to make them carie armes,
Then with a word to make them leave their armes.[4]　　　680
This must not be: Prince *Lewes* keep thine owne,
Let Pope and Popelings curse their bellyes full.

BAST. My Lord of *Melun*, what title had the Prince
To *England* and the Crowne of *Albion*,
But such a title as the Pope confirmde:
The Prelate now lets fall his fained claime:

---

[1] In *KJ* V.2 Pandulph meets Lewis at Bury.
[2] V.2.68–77.　　　[3] V.2.78–116,　　　[4] Cf. V.2.83–7.

Lewes is but the agent for the Pope,
Then must the *Dolphin* cease, sith he hath ceast:
But cease or no, it greatly matters not,
If you my Lords and Barrons of the Land   690
Will leave the French, and cleave unto your King.
For shame yee Peeres of *England*, suffer not
Your selves, your honours, and your land to fall:
But with resolved thoughts beate backe the French,
And free the Land from yoke of servitude.

    SALIS.   *Philip*, not so, Lord *Lewes* is our King,
And we will follow him unto the death.

    PAND.   Then in the name of *Innocent* the Pope,
I curse the Prince and all that take his part,
And excommunicate the rebell Peeres   700
As traytors to the King, and to the Pope.

    LEWES   *Pandolph*, our swords shall blesse our selves agen:
Prepare thee *John*, Lords follow me your King.   [*Exeunt*

    JOHN   Accursed *John*, the divell owes thee shame,
Resisting *Rome*, or yeelding to the Pope, alls one.
The divell take the Pope, the Peeres, and *Fraunce*:
Shame be my share for yeelding to the Priest.

    PAND.   Comfort thy selfe K. *John*, the Cardnall goes
Upon his curse to make them leave their armes.   [*Exit*
                                       710

    BAST.   Comfort my Lord, and curse the Cardinall,
Betake your self to armes, my troupes are prest
To answere *Lewes* with a lustie shocke:
The English Archers have their quivers full,
Their bowes are bent, the pykes are prest to push:
God cheere my Lord, K. *Richards* fortune hangs
Upon the plume of warlike *Philips* helme.
Then let them know his brother and his sonne
Are leaders of the Englishmen at armes.

    JOHN   *Philip*, I know not how to answere thee:
But let us hence, to answere *Lewes* pride.   720

[Scene v]

        Excursions. Enter Meloun with English Lords.

    MEL.   O I am slaine, Nobles, *Salsbury*, *Pembrooke*,
My soule is charged, heare me: for what I say
Concernes the Peeres of *England*, and their State.[1]
Listen, brave Lords, a fearfull mourning tale

   [1] V.4.7–61.

To be delivered by a man of death.
Behold these scarres, the dole of bloudie *Mars*
Are harbingers from natures common foe,
Cyting this trunke to *Tellus* prison house?
Lifes charter (Lordings) lasteth not an hower:
And fearfull thoughts, forerunners of my end,   730
Bids me give Phisicke to a sickly soule.
O Peeres of *England*, know you what you doo?
Theres but a haire that sunders you from harme,
The hooke is bayted, and the traine is made,
And simply you runne doating to your deaths.
But least I dye, and leave my tale untolde,
With silence slaughtering so brave a crew,
This I averre, if *Lewes* win the day,[1]
Theres not an Englishman that lifts his hand
Against King *John* to plant the heire of *Fraunce*,   740
But is already damnd to cruell death.
I heard it vowd; my selfe amongst the rest
Swore on the Altar aid to this Edict.[2]
Two causes Lords, makes me display this drift,
The greatest for the freedome of my soule,
That longs to leave this mansion free from guilt:
The other on a naturall instinct,
For that my Grandsire was an Englishman.[3]
Misdoubt not Lords the truth of my discourse,
No frenzie, nor no brainsick idle fit,   750
But well advisde, and wotting what I say,
Pronounce I here before the face of heaven,
That nothing is discovered but a truth.
Tis time to flie, submit your selves to *John*,
The smiles of *Fraunce* shade in the frownes of death.
Lift up your swords, turne face against the French,
Expell the yoke thats framed for your necks.
Back warmen, back, imbowell not the clyme,
Your seate, your nurse, your birthdayes breathing place,
That bred you, beares you, brought you up in armes.   760
Ah! be not so ingrate to digge your Mothers grave,[4]
Preserve your lambes and beate away the Wolfe.
My soule hath said, contritions penitence
Layes hold on mans redemption for my sinne.
Farewell my Lords; witnes my faith when wee are met in
    heaven,

---

[1] V.4.30.   [2] V.4.16–20.   [3] V.4.42 echoes this line.   [4] Cf. V.2.151–3.

And for my kindnes give me grave room heere.
My soule doth fleete, worlds vanities farewell.
　　sals.　Now joy betide thy soule wel-meaning man,
How now my Lords, what cooling card is this?
A greater griefe growes now than earst hath been.　　770
What counsell give you, shall we stay and dye?
Or shall we home, and kneele unto the King.
　　pemb.　My hart misgave this sad accursed newes:
What have we done? fie Lords, what frenzie moved
Our hearts to yeeld unto the pride of *Fraunce*?
If we persever, we are sure to dye:
If we desist, small hope againe of life.
　　sals.　Beare hence the bodie of this wretched man,
That made us wretched with his dying tale,
And stand not wayling on our present harmes,　　780
As women wont: but seeke our harmes redresse.
As for my selfe, I will in haste be gon:
And kneele for pardon to our Sovereigne *John*.[1]
　　pemb.　I, theres the way, lets rather kneele to him,
Than to the French that would confound us all.　　[*Exeunt*

[Scene vi]

Enter king John carried betweene 2 Lords.

　　john　Set downe, set downe　the load not worth your
　　　　pain,
For done I am with deadly wounding griefe:
Sickly and succourles, hopeles of any good,[2]
The world hath wearied me, and I have wearied it:
It loaths I live, I live and loath my selfe.　　790
Who pities me? to whom have I been kinde?
But to a few; a few will pitie me.
Why dye I not? Death scornes so vilde a pray.
Why live I not? life hates so sad a prize.
I sue to both to be retaynd of either,
But both are deafe, I can be heard of neither.
Nor death nor life, yet life and neare the neere,
Ymixt with death, biding I wot not where.
　　phil.　How fares my Lord, that he is caryed thus?
Not all the aukward fortunes yet befalne　　800
Made such impression of lament in me.
Nor ever did my eye attaynt my heart

---

[1] Cf. V.4.52–7　　　[2] V.3.3–4.

With any object moving more remorse,
Than now beholding of a mighty King,
Borne by his Lords in such distressed state.
   JOHN   What news with thee? If bad, report it straite:
If good, be mute, it doth but flatter me.
   PHIL.   Such as it is, and heavie though it be
To glut the world with tragick elegies,
Once will I breath to agravate the rest,   810
Another moane to make the measure full.
The bravest bowman had not yet sent forth
Two arrowes from the quiver at his side,
But that a rumor went throughout our Campe,
That *John* was fled, the King had left the field.
At last the rumor scald these eares of mine,
Who rather chose as sacrifice for *Mars*,
Than ignominious scandall by retyre.
I cheerd the troupes as did the Prince of *Troy*
His weery followers gainst the Mirmidons,   820
Crying alowde, *S. George, the day is ours*.
But feare had captivated courage quite,
And like the Lamb before the greedie Wolfe,
So heartlesse fled our warmen from the feeld.
Short tale to make, my selfe amongst the rest,
Was faine to flie before the eager foe.
By this time night had shadowed all the earth,
With sable curteines of the blackest hue,
And fenst[1] us from the fury of the French,
As *Io* from the jealous *Junos* eye,   830
When in the morning our troupes did gather head,
Passing the Washes with our carriages,
The impartiall tyde deadly and inexorable,
Came raging in with billowes threatning death,
And swallowed up the most of all our men.
My selfe upon a Galloway right free, well pacde,
Out stript the flouds that followed wave by wave,
I so escapt to tell this tragick tale.[2]
   JOHN   Griefe upon griefe, yet none so great a griefe
To end this life, and thereby rid my griefe.   840
Was ever any so infortunate,
The right Idea of a curssed man,
As I, poore I, a triumph for despight.
My fever growes, what ague shakes me so?

---

[1] fenc'd.   [2] V.6.39–44.

How farre to Swinsteed, tell me do you know?
Present unto the Abbot word of my repaire.
My sicknesse rages, to tirannize upon me,
I cannot live unlesse this fever leave me.
    PHIL.   Good cheare my Lord, the Abbey is at hand,
Behold my Lord, the Churchmen come to meete you.   850

Enter the Abbot and certayne Monkes.[1]

    ABB.   All health & happines to our soveraigne Lord the
       King.
    JOHN   Nor health nor happines hath *John* at all.
Say Abbot, am I welcome to thy house?
    ABB.   Such welcome as our Abbey can affoord,
Your Majesty shalbe assured of.
    PHIL.   The King thou seest is weake and very faint,
What victuals hast thou to refresh his Grace?
    ABB.   Good store my Lord, of that you neede not feare,
For Lincolneshire, and these our Abbey grounds
Were never fatter, nor in better plight.   860
    JOHN   *Philip*, thou never needst to doubt of cates,
Nor King nor Lord is seated halfe so well,
As are the Abbeys throughout all the land.
If any plot of ground do passe another,
The Friers fasten on it streight:
But let us in to taste of their repast,
It goes against my heart to feed with them,
Or be beholden to such Abbey groomes.   [*Exeunt*

Manet the Monke.

    MONK   Is this the King that never lovd a Frier?
Is this the man that doth contemne the Pope?   870
Is this the man that robd the holy Church
And yet will flye unto a Friory?
Is this the King that aymes at Abbeys lands?
Is this the man whome all the world abhorres,
And yet will flye unto a Friorie?
Accurst be Swinsteed Abbey, Abbot, Friers,
Moncks, Nuns, and Clarks, and all that dwells therein,
If wicked *John* escape alive away.
Now if that thou wilt looke to merit heaven,

[1] *KJ* does not represent the reception or the poisoning of the King.

And be canonizd for a holy Saint:　　　　　　　　　880
To please the world with a deserving worke,
Be thou the man to set thy cuntrey free,
And murder him that seekes to murder thee.

Enter the Abbot.

ABBOT　Why are not you within to cheare the King?
He now begins to mend, and will to meate.
　MONK　What if I say to strangle him in his sleepe?
　ABB.　What, at thy *mumpsimus*?[1] away,
And seeke some meanes for to pastime the King.
　MONK　Ile set a dudgeon[2] dagger at his heart,
And with a mallet knock him on the head.　　　　890
　ABB.　Alas, what meanes this Monke to murther me?
Dare lay my life heel kill me for my place.
　MONK　Ile poyson him, and it shall ne'ere be knowne,
And then shall I be chiefest of my house.
　ABB.　If I were dead, indeed he is the next,
But Ile away, for why the Monke is mad,
And in his madnesse he will murther me.
　MONK　My L. I cry your Lordship mercy, I saw you not.
　ABB.　Alas good *Thomas* doo not murther me, and thou
shalt have my place with thousand thanks.　　　900
　MONK　I murther you! God sheeld from such a thought.
　ABB.　If thou wilt needes, yet let me say my prayers.
　MONK　I will not hurt your Lordship good my Lord: but
if you please, I will impart a thing that shall be beneficiall to
us all.
　ABB.　Wilt thou not hurt me, holy Monke? say on.
　MONK　You know, my Lord, the King is in our house.
　ABB.　True.
　MONK　You know likewise the King abhors a Frier.
　ABB.　True.　　　　910
　MONK　And he that loves not a Frier is our enemy.
　ABB.　Thou sayst true.
　MONK　Then the King is our enemy.
　ABB.　True.
　MONK　Why then should we not kil our enemy, & the
King being our enemy, why then should we not kill the King.
　ABB.　O blessed Monke! I see God moves thy minde to free
　　　this land from tyrants slavery.
But who dares venter for to do this deede?

---

[1] bigoted opposition.　　　　　[2] indignant, angry.

MONK   Who dare? why I my Lord dare do the deede,   920
Ile free my Country and the Church from foes,
And merit heaven by killing of a King.
    ABB.   *Thomas* kneel downe, and if thou art resolvde,
I will absolve thee heere from all thy sinnes,
For why the deede is meritorious.
Forward, and feare not, man, for every month
Our Friers shall sing a Masse for *Thomas* soule.
    MONK   God and S. *Francis* prosper my attempt,
For now my Lord I goe about my worke.   [*Exeunt*

[Scene vii]

Enter Lewes and his armie.

    LEWES   Thus victory in bloudy Lawrell clad,   930
Followes the fortune of young *Lodowicke*,
The Englishmen as daunted at our sight,
Fall as the fowle before the Eagles eyes.
Only two crosses of contrary change
Do nip my heart, and vexe me with unrest.
Lord *Meluns* death, the one part of my soule,[1]
A braver man did never live in *Fraunce*.
The other griefe, I, thats a gall indeede
To thinke that *Dover* Castell should hold out
Gainst all assaults, and rest impregnable.[2]   940
Yee warlike race of *Francus Hectors* sonne,[3]
Triumph in conquest of that tyrant *John*.
The better halfe of *England* is our owne,
And towards the conquest of the other part,
We have the face of all the English lords,
What then remaines but overrun the land?
Be resolute my warlike followers,
And if good fortune serve as she begins,
The poorest peasant of the Realme of *Fraunce*
Shall be a maister ore an English Lord.   950

Enter a Messenger.

    LEWES   Fellow, what newes?
    MESS.   Pleaseth your Grace, the Earle of *Salsbury*, *Pembroke*,
Essex, *Clare*, and *Arundell*, with all the Barons that did fight for

[1] V.5.10, 14–16.   [2] Cf. V.1.30–1.
[3] I.e. the Franci, later called Franks, the French.

thee, are on a suddeine fled with all their powers, to joyne
with *John*, to drive thee back againe.[1]

Enter another Messenger.

MESS.   *Lewes* my Lord, why standst thou in a maze?
Gather thy troups, hope not of help from *Fraunce*,
For all thy forces being fiftie sayle,
Conteyning twenty thousand souldyers,
With victuall and munition for the warre,   960
Putting from *Callis* in unluckie time,
Did crosse the seas, and on the *Goodwin* sands,
The men, munition, and the ships are lost.[2]

Enter another Messenger.

LEWES   More newes? say on.
MESS.   *John* (my Lord) with all his scattered troupes,
Flying the fury of your conquering sword,
As *Pharaoh* earst within the bloody sea,
So he and his environed with the tyde,
On *Lincolne* washes all were overwhelmed,
The Barons fled, our[3] forces cast away.   970
LEWES   Was ever heard such unexpected newes?
MESS.   Yet *Lodowike* revive thy dying heart,
King *John* and all his forces are consumde.
The lesse thou needst the ayd of English Earles,
The lesse thou needst to grieve thy Navies wracke,
And follow tymes advantage with successe.
LEWES   Brave *Frenchmen* armde with magnanimitie,
March after *Lewes* who will leade you on
To chase the Barons power that wants a head,
For *John* is drownd, and I am *Englands* King.   980
Though our munition and our men be lost,
Phillip of *Fraunce* will send us fresh supplyes.   [*Exeunt*

[Scene viii]

Enter two Friers laying a Cloth.[4]

FRIER   Dispatch, dispatch, the King desires to eate,
Would a might eate his last for the love hee beares to Church-
    men.

---

[1] V.5.10–11.   [2] V.5.12–13.
[3] So in *1591*. 'their'? Cf. V.6.38–42.   [4] *KJ* omits this scene.
10—N.D.S.S. 4

FRIER   I am of thy minde too, and so it should be and we might be our owne carvers.

I mervaile why they dine heere in the Orchard.

FRIER   I know not, nor I care not. The King coms.

JOHN   Come on Lord Abbot, shall we sit together?

ABBOT   Pleaseth your Grace sit downe.   990

JOHN   Take your places sirs, no pomp in penury, all beggers and friends may come; where necessitie keepes the house, curtesie is bard the table; sit downe *Phillip*.

BAST.   My Lord, I am loth to allude so much to the proverb, honors change manners: a King is a King, though fortune do her worst, & we as dutifull in despight of her frowne, as if your highnesse were now in the highest type of dignitie.

JOHN   Come, no more ado, and you tell me much of dignitie, youle mar my appetite in a surfet of sorrow. What cheere Lord Abbot? methinks you frowne like an host that knowes his guest hath no money to pay the reckning.   1001

ABB.   No my Liege, if I frowne at all, it is for I feare this cheere too homely to entertaine so mighty a guest as your Majesty.

BAST.   I thinke rather my Lord Abbot, you remember my last being heere, when I went in progresse for powtches, and the rancor of his heart breakes out in his countenance, to shew he hath not forgot me.

ABB.   Not so my Lord, you, and the meanest follower of his majesty, are hartely welcome to me.

MONKE   Wassell my Liege, and as a poore Monke may   1010 say, welcome to Swinsted.

JOHN   Begin Monke, and report hereafter thou wast taster to a King.

MONKE   As much helth to your highnes, as to my own hart.

JOHN   I pledge thee kinde Monke.

MONKE   The meriest draught that ever was dronk in *England*. Am I not too bold with your Highnesse?

JOHN   Not a whit, all friendes and fellowes for a time.

MONK   If the inwards of a Toad be a compound of any proofe: why so it workes.   1020

JOHN   Stay *Phillip*, wheres the Monke?

BAST.   He is dead my Lord.

JOHN   Then drinke not *Phillip* for a world of wealth.

BAST.   What cheere my Liege? your cullor gins to change.

JOHN   So doth my life: O *Phillip*, I am poysond.

The Monke, the Devill, the poyson gins to rage,
It will depose my selfe a King from raigne.
   BAST.   This Abbot hath an interest in this act.
At all adventures take thou that from me.
There lye the Abbot, Abbey, Lubber, Devill. 1030
March with the Monke unto the gates of hell.
How fares my Lord?[1]
   JOHN   *Philip*, some drinke, oh for the frozen Alps,
To tumble on and coole this inward heate,[2]
That rageth as the fornace sevenfold hote,
To burne the holy three[3] in *Babylon*.
Power after power forsake their proper power,
Only the hart impugnes with faint resist
The fierce invade of him that conquers Kings,[4]
Help God, O payne! dye *John*, O plague 1040
Inflicted on thee for thy grievous sinnes.
Philip, a chayre, and by and by a grave,
My leggs disdaine the carriage of a King.
   BAST.   A[h], good my Liege, with patience conquer
     griefe,
And beare this paine with kingly fortitude.
   JOHN   Me thinks I see a cattalogue of sinne,
Wrote by a friend in Marble characters,
The least enough to loose my part in heaven.
Me thinks the Devill whispers in mine eares
And tels me tis in vayne to hope for grace, 1050
I must be damned for *Arthurs* sodaine death.
I see I see a thousand thousand men
Come to accuse me for my wrong on earth,
And there is none so mercifull a God
That will forgive the number of my sinnes.
How have I livd, but by anothers losse?
What have I lovd, but wrack of others weale?
When have I vowd, and not infringd mine oath?
Where have I done a deede deserving well?
How, what, when, and where, have I bestowd a day 1060
That tended not to some notorious ill?
My life repleat with rage and tyranie,
Craves little pittie for so strange a death.
Or who will say that *John* disceasd too soone?
Who will not say he rather livd too long?

---

[1] In *KJ* Hubert informs Faulconbridge of the poisoning, V.6.19–31.
[2] V.7.35–41.   [3] tree *1591*.   [4] V.7.55–8.

Dishonor did attaynt me in my life,
And shame attendeth *John* unto his death.
Why did I scape the fury of the French,
And dyde not by the temper of their swords?
Shamelesse my life, and shamefully it ends,   1070
Scornd by my foes, disdained of my friends.
    BAST.   Forgive the world and all your earthly foes,
And call on Christ, who is your latest friend.
    JOHN   My tongue doth falter: *Philip*, I tell thee man,
Since *John* did yeeld unto the Priest of *Rome*,
Nor he nor his have prospred on the earth:
Curst are his blessings, and his curse is blisse.
But in the spirit I cry unto my God,
As did the Kingly Prophet *David* cry,
(Whose hands, as mine, with murder were attaint)   1080
I am not he shall buyld the Lord a house,
Or roote these Locusts from the face of earth:
But if my dying heart deceave me not,
From out these loynes shall spring a Kingly braunch
Whose armes shall reach unto the gates of *Rome*,
And with his feete treade downe the Strumpets pride,
That sits upon the chaire of *Babylon*.
Philip, my heart strings breake, the poysons flame
Hath overcome in me weake Natures power,
And in the faith of Jesu *John* doth dye.   1090
    BAST.   See how he strives for life, unhappy Lord,
Whose bowells are devided in themselves.[1]
This is the fruite of Poperie, when true Kings
Are slaine and shouldred out by Monkes and Friers.

Enter a Messenger.

    MESS.   Please it your Grace, the Barons of the Land,
Which all this while bare armes against the King,
Conducted by the Legate of the Pope,
Together with the Prince his Highnes Sonne,
Doo crave to be admitted to the presence of the King.
    BAST.   Your Sonne, my Lord, yong *Henry* craves to see   1100
Your Majestie, and brings with him beside
The Barons that revolted from your Grace.[2]
O piercing sight, he fumbleth in the mouth,

[1] In *KJ* as in Hol. the monk's 'bowels suddenly burst out' (V.6.30); cf. V.7.31.
[2] Hubert describes their coming, and the King's pardon of their revolt,
V. 6.33–6.

His speech doth faile: lift up your selfe my Lord,
And see the Prince to comfort you in death.

*Enter Pandulph, yong Henry, the Barons with daggers in
their hands.*

PRINCE   O let me see my Father ere he dye:
O Unckle, were you here, and sufferd him
To be thus poysned by a damned Monke?
Ah he is dead, Father sweet Father speake.
   BAST.   His speach doth faile, he hasteth to his end.   1110
   PAND.   Lords, give me leave to joy the dying King
With sight of these his Nobles kneeling here
With daggers in their hands, who offer up
Their lives for ransome of their fowle offence.
Then good my Lord, if you forgive them all,
Lift up you hand in token you forgive.
   SALIS.   We humbly thanke your royall Majestie,
And vow to fight for *England* and her King:
And in the sight of *John* our soveraigne Lord,
In spight of *Lewes* and the power of *Fraunce*,   1120
Who hetherward are marching in all hast,
We crowne yong *Henry* in his Fathers sted.[1]
   HEN.   Help, help, he dyes, a[h] Father, looke on mee.
   LEGAT.   K. *John* farewell: in token of thy faith,
And signe thou dyest the servant of the Lord,
Lift up thy hand, that we may witnes here
Thou dyedst the servant of our Saviour Christ.
Now joy betide thy soule: what noyse is this?

Enter a Messenger.

MESS.   Help Lords, the Dolphin maketh hetherward
With Ensignes of defiance in the winde,   1130
And all our armie standeth at a gaze,
Expecting what their Leaders will commaund.
   BAST.   Lets arme our selves in yong K. *Henries* right,
And beate the power of *Fraunce* to sea againe.
   LEGAT.   *Philip* not so, but I will to the Prince,
And bring him face to face to parle with you.[2]

---

[1] *KJ* omits this ceremony, and John dies without consolation, V.7.44–66.
[2] In *KJ* Pandulph has already gone to Lewes and returned with peace-offers
(V.7.81–6) and Lewis is not seen again.

BAST.   Lord *Salsbury*, your selfe shall march with me,
So shall we bring these toubles to an ende.
    KING   Sweete Unckle, if thou love thy Soveraigne,
Let not a stone of *Swinsted* Abbey stand,   1140
But pull the house about the Friers eares:
For they have kilde my Father and my King.   [*Exeunt*

[Scene ix]

A parle sounded, Lewes, Pandulph, Salsbury, &c.

    PAN   *Lewes* of *Fraunce*, yong *Henry Englands* King
Requires to know the reason of the claime
That thou canst make to any thing of his.
King *John* that did offend is dead and gone.
See where his breathles trunke in presence lyes,
And he as heire apparant to the crowne
Is now succeeded to his Fathers roome.
    HEN.   *Lewes*, what law of Armes doth lead thee thus,   1150
To keepe possession of my lawfull right?
Answere in fine if thou wilt take a peace,
And make surrender of my right againe,
Or trie thy title with the dint of sword?
I tell thee Dolphin, *Henry* feares thee not,
For now the Barons cleave unto their King,
And what thou hast in *England* they did get.
    LEWES   *Henry* of *England*, now that *John* is dead,
That was the chiefest enemie to *Fraunce*,
I may the rather be inducde to peace.   1160
But *Salsbury*, and you Barons of the Realme,
This strange revolt agrees not with the oath
That you on *Bury* Altare lately sware.
    SALS.   Nor did the oath your Highness there did take
Agree with honour of the Prince of *Fraunce*.
    BAST.   My Lord, what answere make you to the King?
    LEWES[1]   Faith *Philip* this I say: It bootes not me,
Nor any Prince nor power of Christendome,
To seeke to win this Iland *Albion*,
Unles he have a partie in the Realme   1170
By treason for to help him in his warres.[2]
The Peeres which were the partie on my side,
Are fled from me: then bootes not me to fight,

[1] *Dolphin* 1591.   [2] Hence V.7.112–14.

But on conditions, as mine honour wills,
I am contented to depart the Realme.
   HEN.   On what conditions will your Highnes yeeld?
   LEWES   That shall we thinke upon by more advice.
   BAST.   Then Kings & Princes, let these broils have end,
And at more leasure talke upon the League.
Meanewhile to *Worster* let us beare the King,   1180
And there interre his bodie, as beseemes.[1]
But first, in sight of *Lewes*, heire of *Fraunce*,
Lords take the crowne and set it on his head,
That by succession is our lawfull King.

They crowne yong Henry.

Thus *Englands* peace begins in *Henryes* Raigne,
And bloody warres are closde with happie league.
Let *England* live but true within it selfe,[2]
And all the world can never wrong her State.
Lewes, thou shalt be bravely shipt to *France*,
For never Frenchman got of English ground   1190
The twentith part that thou hast conquered.
Dolphin, thy hand: to *Worster* we will march:
Lords all, lay hands to beare your Soveraigne
With obsequies of honor to his grave:
If *Englands* Peeres and people joyne in one,
Nor Pope, nor *Fraunce*, nor *Spaine* can doo them wrong.

FINIS.

[1] V.7.99–100.   [2] V.7.116–18.

HENRY IV

PART 1

INTRODUCTION

ENTERED IN *S.R.* to Andrew Wyse on 25 February, 1598, this play was published in the same year (Q1) with the title: '*The History of Henrie the Fourth; With the battell at Shrewsburie, betweene the King and Lord Henry Percy, surnamed Henrie Hotspur of the North. With the humorous conceits of Sir John Falstaffe*'. Six Quartos were published before the 1623 Folio, but Q1 is 'the sole authority for the text' (Chambers). At first Falstaff's name was 'Sir John Oldcastle', and although the change was made before publication the character was so well known under its first title that for many years allusions were made to it. This suggests that the play had been performed frequently and for some time before it was registered, with Oldcastle in the comic part.

The play contains allusions to conditions in 1596. There is no necessary reference in I.1 to the campaign against Spain and Essex's Cadiz expedition which sailed in June; but early in 1596 there were complaints about the maltreatment of impressed men by army officers, and Sir John Smithe[1] was up before the Star Chamber on 19 June for inciting Essex recruits to mutiny. In September when a hundred men were to be levied in Northamptonshire for service in Ireland the Council's order insisted that they should be serviceable men, not the baser sort, and declared that the Queen had chosen a captain of good family to lead them, to ensure that they should be used well. Falstaff's attitude to his soldiers (IV.2) would be topical in 1596/7.[2] The price of corn rose very high in 1596, and the reference to Robin Ostler's death, 'Poor fellow! never joyed since the price of oats rose' (II.1.12), seems to allude to a fairly recent change. The substitution of 'Falstaff' for 'Oldcastle' has often been ascribed (though without any real evidence) to

---

[1] More about him *infra*, introductions to *2H4* and *H5*.
[2] Noted by J. E. Morris, *TLS*, 28 January, 1926.

complaints by the Cobhams who were Oldcastle's descendants.[1] William Brooke, 7th Lord Cobham, the Lord Chamberlain, died on 5 March, 1597. If he protested, the play must have been written some time before that, but any complaint might have been made by his heir Henry Brooke, who was an enemy of Essex.[2]

The links with *Richard II* make it likely that the play was written soon after that tragedy, perhaps late in 1596 or early in 1597. Part 2 was probably composed immediately after Part 1, for the 1600 Q of *2 Henry IV* contains vestigial mention of Oldcastle. Peto and Bardolph were at first called 'Rossill' (Russell) and 'Harvey' respectively.

There can be little doubt that Shakespeare conceived his Richard II, Henry IV and Henry V plays as a group and that he intended to follow out the fortunes of Bolingbroke and his son even while he was writing *Richard II*. The father–son relationship exercised Shakespeare's mind so strongly in *Richard II* that he gave two scenes (V.2, V.3) to that between Edmund of York and his son Aumerle, who bursts in to Henry IV's presence to confess his treachery just as the King is complaining of his own 'unthrifty son' (V.3). Henry pardons him as he later pardons his own erring heir. The expansion of this theme in *Richard II* probably derives from the dramatist's foreknowledge of what is to come in *Henry IV*. Already in that scene the King compares the Prince with Hotspur and treats them as about the same age, although Percy (1364–1403) was in fact two years older than the King and twenty-three years older than Hal. This initiates a comparison which becomes conscious rivalry in *Henry IV, Part 1*, and culminates in the Prince's slaying of Hotspur at the Battle of Shrewsbury, a climax for which there is no warrant in the chronicles except possibly an ambiguous sentence in Holinshed. Before *Richard II* was finished it was already in Shakespeare's mind to show two sides of the Prince, his youthful escapades and the heroism befitting the future Henry V. Other links with *Richard II* include the relations between Bolingbroke and his early supporters, Northumberland and Worcester. Also specific prophecies and promises are made in the earlier play which reach their full significance only

---

[1] Cf. the letter by Dr. R. James, Cotton's librarian (c. 1625) in *WSh*. ii. 241–2.
[2] Cf. *WSh*. i. 383.

when recalled in the Henry IV plays. On the other hand Shakespeare did not introduce into *Richard II* everything he might need later; thus we do not see Richard, ere he sets forth on his Irish expedition, proclaiming Mortimer, Earl of March, his heir; but this event is important for *1 Henry IV*, where it is referred to at I.3.145–57.

There has been much inconclusive discussion about the relationship of the two Henry IV plays. R. A. Law argued that Part 2 is so different in structure and intention that it must have been conceived independently of Part 1.[1] J. Dover Wilson (*The Fortunes of Falstaff* (1943)) and E. M. W. Tillyard have declared that the two parts make a single ten-act play of which the end was preconceived at the beginning. By itself, writes Tillyard, Part I is 'patently incomplete'[2]; and Dover Wilson regards the two parts as 'a single structure' embodying the 'normal dramatic curve', with the Battle of Shrewsbury as the 'nodal point we expect in a third act'. Harold Jenkins has argued that Shakespeare originally intended to write only one five-act play, ending with the accession of Henry V and the banishment of Falstaff, but that 'in the course of writing Shakespeare changed his mind'; that 'the new pattern can be seen emerging during the fourth act', and that 'Part 2 expands the unfinished story of Falstaff and reduplicates what is already finished in the story of the Prince.'[3]

The theory fits the facts, explains the lack of progression, the repetition apparent in *2 Henry IV*, and may be correct. But is it the most likely explanation? Consideration of the relationship of the two parts with each other, with *Richard II* and with the Chronicles and other literary treatments of history may lead us back to the simpler theory that Shakespeare from the first conceived *Henry IV*, not indeed as one ten-act drama, since it was not intended to be performed at a sitting, but as two closely linked plays on the usurping King's tribulations and his son's growth to kingly quality.

Richard II described the failure of a weak king misled by evil counsellors and unable to keep the respect of his nobles and the affection of his people. His fall and death were the natural result

---

[1] R. A. Law, 'Structural Unity in the two Parts of *Henry IV*', *SPhil*, 1927.
[2] *Shakespeare's History Plays*, 264.
[3] *The Structural Problem in Shakespeare's Henry the Fourth*, 1956.

of his folly and inadequacy, yet the play showed also Henry Bolingbroke changing from a noble young man intent on obtaining his rights to a usurper responsible for overthrowing the rightful king, dispossessing the lawful heir and bringing on himself the envy and hatred of other nobles who helped his rise to power. In following the subsequent history of the new king Shakespeare's attitude was necessarily ambivalent. As a ruler Henry IV might be strong, lenient, efficient and therefore admirable; as a usurper he must not be happy; his reign could not be peaceful; he must suffer for his sins, both in his public and in his private life. This orthodox moral teaching Shakespeare found in his major historical source, Holinshed (*inf.* 188). It was plainly stated in the title of Edward Hall's chapter, 'The Unquiete Tyme of Kyng Henry IV', which he had certainly read.

The domestic political material in the Chronicles contained four main points of opposition to Henry IV: the Abbot's conspiracy; the revolt of the Percys with Glendower and Douglas in 1403; the Archbishop's rising of 1405; and Northumberland's incursion of 1408 which ended in his death at Bramham Moor.

Of these the first was included in *Richard II* to show how immediate was the reaction to Bolingbroke's usurpation. It would certainly have been possible for Shakespeare to compress the remainder of Henry's reign into an episodic play, and to mention in it the gadfly stingings by French friends of Richard, and even something of the Lollards. The dramatist, however, chose to ignore religious controversies, and in Henry IV's time relations with the Continent were tangled, inconclusive and dull. Alternatively Shakespeare might (like Daniel in his *Civile Wars*) have cut out most of the reign after Shrewsbury, moving swiftly to the King's death. But Shakespeare on the one hand did not want to write a loose chronicle and on the other wished to insist on the 'unquiete tyme' of the usurper, which could better be done by presenting the historic recurrence of revolt than by making Shrewsbury into a decisive and permanent victory.

Moreover Shakespeare was interested not only in Henry IV and his struggle with the barons, but in the youth of the future Henry V, who increased his father's unhappiness, seeming at times likely to prove merely another Richard II in his irresponsibility, and at others (according to the Chronicles) to wish his father's death. To make possible what Hall styled 'The Victorious Actes of King Henry the Fifth' the transformation of the Prince must be shown. This had already been done in the theatre in the play or plays (now extant only in the debased text of *Famous Victories of Henry V*) which Shakespeare certainly recalled in shaping his threefold account of the hero-king.

An argument frequently used to suggest that *2 Henry IV* was an afterthought or forced on Shakespeare by the gradual growth of his comic material is that the second play merely repeats less convincingly the substance of the first. It is true that whereas the political material of 1400–3 with its climax in the Battle of Shrewsbury gives a strong backbone to *1 Henry IV*, the less unified and less interesting risings of 1405 and 1408 afforded weaker dramatic material. Repeated blows and disappointments were, however, the main feature of Henry IV's reign; and, despite the gentleness of his latter days (wrote Holinshed), 'by punishing such as (mooved with disdeine to see him usurpe the crowne contrarie to the oth taken at his entring into this land, upon his returne from exile), did at sundrie times rebell against him, he wan himselfe more hatred, than in all his life time (if it had been longer by manie yeares than it was) had beene possible for him to have weeded out and remooved'.

I suggest therefore that a pattern of repetition in political matters was essential to Shakespeare's historical and moral purpose. But repetition was also deliberately chosen by the dramatist in planning the serious and comic material affecting the Prince. It can scarcely be doubted that from the first his intention was to make the Hal-Hotspur antithesis culminate in the physical and moral triumph of the former at the Battle of Shrewsbury. Yet to give this any weight the Prince must be shown in action as a madcap before 1403. The Chronicles, from Thomas Walsingham to Stow, described at least six legendary incidents relating to his misbehaviour, most of them going back directly or indirectly to stories told by the 4th Earl of Ormonde and included by the English translator of Titus Livius's *Life of Henry V*[1]: (1) the robbing of the Receivers; (2) the riot in

---

[1] Cf. *The First English Life of Henry V*, ed. C. L. Kingsford, 1911.

Eastcheap; (3) the striking of the Lord Chief Justice and the com-
mittal of the Prince to prison; (4) the Prince's coming to Court
strangely dressed and carrying a dagger; (5) the Prince's visit to
his dying father during which he took away the Crown; (6) his
dismissal of his former companions after the Coronation. To
these *Famous Victories* added (7) the new King's commendation
of the Lord Chief Justice, based no doubt on a passage cited
below, pp. 288-9. In the Chronicles the first three incidents
took place at indefinite dates, the rest towards the end of Henry
IV's reign when the King was already ill. Shakespeare made
some use of Nos. 1, 3, 5, 6 and 7, omitting for good reasons to
show the striking of the Lord Chief Justice or the dagger incident. To include all this in one play together with all the political
material would surely have been impossible. Yet the madcap
Prince was basic to Shakespeare's conception. Accordingly he
introduced repetition into this side of his play also, and brought
forward the highway robbery into 1400–3 when the Prince was
only a boy of 13–16, leaving the bulk of the legendary material
for Part 2, which he knew would be somewhat defective on the
political side. This division was probably made in a preliminary
blocking out of a two-part scheme. I do not suggest that the
whole of Part 2, or even of Part 1, was in Shakespeare's mind
when he started to write; but the nature of the historical
material and the wish to improve on the *Famous Victories*
source-play(s) led him irresistibly into a double drama, in
which not only the pattern of revolt would recur but the
Prince's conversion must be repeated. Such a plan barred out
any continuous development in the character of the Prince, but
Shakespeare was not as yet interested in stages of growth in
character, and the Chronicles suggested that the Prince's
behaviour was inconsistent and declined after Shrewsbury
(where he 'holpe his father like a lustie yoong gentleman') until
the King feared, 'least his sonne would presume to usurpe the
crowne'—a motive which Shakespeare avoids.

It is highly probable that the large amount of time given to
tavern scenes and the presentation of Falstaff and the fictitious
characters round him was partly due to the two-part scheme,
for if one five-act play would have been episodic and overfull of
incidents incompletely explained, two left room for manœuvre.
But since Hal was to be the Hero-King Henry V, his offences

against princely decorum must be palliated, and another view
of him must be given than his father's. Apparent 'riot and dishonour' must be shown in a pleasanter light, and this could be
done by building, on the suggestions of *Famous Victories*, a picture of scapegrace youth, not incorrigibly bad but temporarily
misled by companions who should have known better. Out of
this need came the tavern scenes and Falstaff, all that wealth of
Elizabethan life transported back nearly two hundred years and
treated with the delight in vigorous language, robust humour
and the delineation of 'typical' individuals which bloomed in
Shakespeare's plays from about 1595 onwards and was not the
least proof of his dramatic originality.

In constructing the dramatic narrative of Henry IV's conflict with the Percies, Shakespeare makes use primarily of
Holinshed [Text I], with some details from Hall perhaps, but
this is not certain. Many happenings he omits, such as the
King's abortive expeditions into Wales in August, 1402, and the
defeat of the Scots at Nesbit, Henry's marriage to Jane, Duchess
of Brittany, the French anger at Richard II's deposition and
death, and their expeditions against the Isle of Wight, etc., the
difficulties with Parliament, the rise of the Lollards.

To get particular effects events are shifted or compressed. At
the close of *Richard II* the new monarch, having quelled the
Abbot's conspiracy, announced his intention to

> 'make a voyage to the Holy Land
> To wash this blood from off my guilty hand.'

When *Henry IV, Part 1*, begins, a year has passed (not over two
years as in fact); it is June, 1402. The King recalls the final
mood of the previous play by saying that he will take advantage
of peace to raise a force against the pagans, but the preparations have been broken off by news of battles in Wales and on
the Scottish Border. Of course the Crusade is never begun, but
the King refers to it more than once (and again in Part 2 (III.
1.107–8)), and he chooses the Jerusalem Chamber to die in,
thus fulfilling an old prophecy (Pt. 2 IV.5.231–9). All this is
based on a passage in Holinshed describing how in the last year
of his reign he made preparations for a Crusade (*inf.* 276).
Shakespeare makes it a recurrent theme to show Henry's piety
and consciousness of guilt. Despite the temporal links with

Richard II, Henry is now a weary old man, who speaks of his unwillingness 'To crush our old limbs in ungentle steel' (V.1.13). He was only 37 when Shrewsbury was fought.

The first scene affords an interesting example of compression. On 22 June, 1402, Glendower captured Mortimer at Pilleth; on the same day the Scottish Earl of March defeated the Scots in a skirmish at Nesbit. Before the Battle of Homildon Hill on 14 September the King made a triple invasion of Wales (himself leading one force, the Prince of Wales (aged 14) another, the Earl of Arundel a third) which was a dismal failure. Shakespeare omits the Welsh fiasco, and makes Homildon Hill occur on or about the same day as Pilleth, thus getting a moment of suspense before news of the Welsh defeat is counterbalanced by news of the northern victory, and also bringing together two motifs which figure largely in the Percies' later speeches—the captivity of Mortimer (whom Shakespeare, like Hall and Holinshed, mistook for his nephew the Earl of March, the rightful heir to the throne),[1] and the Scottish prisoners, whom the King, contrary to chivalric usage, wished not to be released by their captors without his permission, possibly because he wanted to keep them as hostages.

To make Henry the dominant figure Shakespeare depicts him as summoning Henry Percy to answer for his refusal to surrender his prisoners. In this, and in the excuses made by Hotspur, he departs from Holinshed, who asserts that the Percies came of their own free will to Windsor ('upon a purpose to proove him') and demanded the deliverance of Mortimer (who was Hotspur's brother-in-law) (*inf.* 184). Out of the Percies' 'fume' and 'fury' he creates the fine scene (I.3.125ff) in which they and Worcester inveigh against the King's ingratitude. On the references to the Archbishop of York (*inf.* 186), the correspondence between the conspirators, and the failure of many of them to take an active part, he builds two scenes: II.3, where Hotspur reads a letter from 'a shallow cowardly hind'; and IV.4, where the Archbishop, fearing Percy's defeat, tries to 'make strong' against the King before it is too late. This latter scene provides a link with Part 2.

---

[1] But note: 'As the second son of Philippa of Clarence, Sir Edmund [Mortimer] could show a better claim to the throne by descent than Henry himself; a fact which may explain Henry's unwillingness to see him ransomed.' (*Ramsay*, p. 53.)

The premature division of the realm at Bangor (*inf.* 185) is greatly amplified in the great first scene of Act III. Shakespeare omits the King's preparations for another invasion of Wales, and the charges and countercharges made by the adversaries to gain support in the country. Nor does he state that the Scottish Earl of March advised Henry IV to march against his enemies rapidly to gain surprise, though he makes 'Lord Mortimer of Scotland' (March was George Dunbar, not Mortimer) announce the meeting of Douglas and Percy at Shrewsbury before ever the King sets out. Actually the King reached Shrewsbury first, forestalling an attack on the town, the enemy, as Holinshed states, 'lieing in camp neere to Shrewesburie' (*inf.* 188). In the play the enemy are fully aware of the King's approach.[1]

Shakespeare does not show us the King reading the articles sent by the rebels accusing him, but uses material from them in the parleys of Hotspur with Blunt (IV.3) and Worcester with the King (V.1). The royalist account according to which Worcester 'made relation cleane contrarie to that the King had said' (*inf.* 190) is used (V.2.35ff). Douglas's challenge to the King is invented to make the Prince challenge Hotspur to single combat. The battle mainly follows Holinshed, with the Prince wounded and Douglas slaying Blunt, and three others 'apparelld in the kings sute and clothing' (V.3). (But Holinshed gives two accounts of Blunt's death, and it is not certain that he was dressed like the King.) Shakespeare makes the Prince save his father's life when he has been struck down by Douglas, whereas neither Hall nor Holinshed tells how the King was saved. The Prince also slays Hotspur. R. A. Law has argued ingeniously that this incident, at once the climax and *raison d'être* of the Hal-Hotspur rivalry, was suggested by a misunderstanding of Holinshed's words, 'The other on his part, incouraged by his doings, fought valiantlie, and slue the lord Persie, called sir Henrie Hotspurre' (*inf.* 191). Indeed the whole paragraph might be read as dealing first with the Prince and

---

[1] Did Shakespeare invent the timing in III.2.164–78? In fact the King left London on 4 July, ostensibly to help the Percies against the Scots. Then the plotters showed their hand, and the King was at Burton on the 15th, stayed at Lichfield from the 16th to the 20th, in which day and night he marched 45 miles so as to take the enemy by surprise. He reached Shrewsbury on the 21st and Hotspur fell back to a hill 3½ miles towards Whitchurch, where the battle took place.

then with the King, so it is just possible to take 'The other on
his part' as meaning 'the Prince for his part . . .'; but Hall, who
uses these same words in a longer paragraph, leaves no ambiguity. He means, 'The others on the king's side . . .', and it is
unlikely that Shakespeare would be in any doubt of this. He
may have perceived an ambiguity and seized on it, but surely
the Hal-Hotspur antithesis is not dependent on this climax,
though it is a superb end to their rivalry. The names of the
slain on the King's side are taken from Holinshed, not Hall, and
the capture and condemnation of Worcester and Vernon, the
capture and release of Douglas, agree with Holinshed, except
that the Prince is allowed to hand Douglas over to his brother
John of Lancaster as a reward for his gallantry (V.5.17–33).

The play ends with continuing action as the King sends
Prince John and Westmoreland against old Percy and the Archbishop of York, himself going with Prince Henry towards
Wales. No mention is made, either here or in Part 2, of his
journey to York, his meeting with Northumberland, and the
patching up of a peace between them before he visited Wales
and re-took Carmarthen from Glendower.

Shakespeare probably owed a little to *A Mirror for Magistrates*
and to the Third Book of Daniel's *Civil Wars* in this play. The
Mirror contains at least two relevant tragedies, those of Owen
Glendower and Henry, Earl of Northumberland [Texts IIa, b].
The material for these came largely from Hall, and provided
little historical substance to the dramatist.

The discussion of birth and breeding in *1 Henry IV*, III.1, may
have been suggested by Thomas Phaer, the 'Glendower' poet
who insists on gentle behaviour as more important than gentle
birth in terms which might conceivably be applied to Prince
Hal as well as to the Welshman:

> But who so settes his mind to spoyle and rob,
> Although he cum by due discent from Brute,
> He is a Chorle, ungentle, vile, and brute.

The *Mirror* treated Glendower as an 'ill brought up' reiver.
Shakespeare makes him very conscious that he has been
'train'd up in the English Court' and has composed 'Many an
English ditty lovely well' (III.1); Mortimer calls him 'Exceedingly well read' (*ibid.*, 165). Nor does Shakespeare treat him as

an evil liver who deserves his horrible fate on the cold mountains. But the commentary in the *Mirror* includes a warning against the boastfulness characteristic of Welshmen (*inf.* 201); maybe this encouraged Shakespeare to elaborate the braggart and prophetic sides of the man's personality. The prophecies of Merlin appear in the complaint of Clarence (Vol. III, 302). Some of Shakespeare's details appear there, but he probably also drew on the *Historia Regum Britanniae* of Geoffrey of Monmouth, whose Seventh Book, devoted to Merlin's unintelligible allegories, may have amused the poet as Glendower's 'skimbleskamble stuff' amused Hotspur (III.1.147–63).

Other elements of III.1 may owe something to the *Mirror*, if only by contraries. Whereas the *Mirror* declares that in dividing the land between them the three plotters bound themselves, 'To stand contented each man with his part', Shakespeare makes a special point of their inability to agree, as when Hotspur complains that his part is too small, unless the River Trent be turned from its course (as a legend asserted was indeed done). Hotspur's outburst against poetry may even have been suggested by some revulsion in Shakespeare himself against the Glendower poem, which certainly moves 'like the forced gait of a shuffling nag' (III.1.127–34). This is fanciful, but we are on firmer ground in seeing the *Mirror's* description of Hotspur as one of the 'suresby sots whych cast no kinde of doubt' as a foreshadowing of Shakespeare's presentation of the rash but 'right manly' leader.

Shakespeare does not let Prince Henry pursue Glendower into the mountains and bring about his downfall. His Prince is too busy with Falstaff and the Percies for that. In fact Prince Henry had been nominally governor of North Wales and the Marches since 1400, when he was only thirteen, and Henry Hotspur was chief of his Council. Early in 1403 the Prince became Lieutenant of Wales, but even after Shrewsbury he and his father made little headway against the elusive Welshman until 1406, when the Welsh were defeated soon after Northumberland and Bardolph had met Glendower and had probably signed the tripartite agreement at Bangor which Elizabethan historians, the *Mirror* and Shakespeare ascribed to an earlier date. After that Glendower's power gradually waned, and he wandered about the Welsh hills with few followers. But he was alive in 1415, and may have made peace with Henry V soon after that year.

Shakespeare thus diminishes the importance of Glendower and with it the administrative experience of Prince Hal, who during his father's illness acted as head of the King's ministers in 1410 and was so energetic that the poet Hoccleve, who had a post in the Council office, urged him not to hold business meetings on holy-days:

> In the long yere ben werk dayes ynowe,
> If they be wele spent, for to entende
> To Counceiles.[1]

It is unlikely that Shakespeare's portrait of Northumberland owes anything to that in the *Mirror*, where, although he is a leader in the revolt against Richard II, his ghost says nothing of his part in that King's removal to Pomfret and in putting down the Abbot's plot (cf. *Richard II*, V.6).

Likewise the debt to Daniel's *Civil Wars* in this play is not great, though there are important concurrences in detail [Text III]. Shakespeare shared Daniel's view that Henry IV's reign was afflicted by 'wrong-revenging Nemesis' for his usurpation, and there is some similarity in their attitudes to the Glendower–Northumberland conspiracy. Daniel makes Hotspur a young man (St. 109), and it may be that this supplied a hint for the approximation of his age to Prince Henry's. Moreover, Daniel insists on Hotspur's rashness and ends his account by exclaiming:

> And o that this great spirit, this courage bold,
> Had in some good cause bene rightly showne!
> So had we not thus violently then
> Have term'd that rage, which valor should have ben. (114)

Here maybe is the germ of the antithesis between the Prince and Percy which began in *Richard II*. Neither Hall nor Holinshed declares that Hal saved his father's life from Douglas (*inf.* 191); but Daniel does so (111). Shakespeare follows him (V.4.35–57) but uses the incident to prove (as against the suggestion in *Famous Victories*) that the Prince never desired his father's death. Both poets use the young man's heroism in the battle as an

---

[1] Quoted by C. L. Kingsford, *Henry V*, p. 69.

earnest of his future wondrous actions. So Daniel's laborious epic may have played a part in moulding Shakespeare's conceptions of some principal characters.

The Famous Victories of Henry the Fifth was registered on 14 May, 1594, and published by Thomas Creede in 1598, 'As it was plaide by the Queenes Majesties Players'. It may have been performed before 1588, when the comedian Tarlton died, for an anecdote in *Tarlton's Jests*[1] describes the Prince's insult to the Lord Chief Justice, with Tarlton playing both the Judge and the Clown [*inf.* 289]. Nashe in *Pierce Penilesse* (1592) referred to '*Henrie* the fifth represented on the stage'. Henslowe's Diary mentions a new play 'harey the v' as being frequently performed by the Admiral's men in 1595 and 1596. The relationship between these pieces is unknown.[2] So is the authorship of *Famous Victories*, though Dugdale Sykes attributed it to Samuel Rowley. This play is printed below in the section on *2 Henry IV* [Text VIII].

It is a crude, episodic study of the life of Henry V as Prince and King with special reference to his youthful exploits in London, his relations with his father, his conversion on ascending the throne, and his campaign against the French which ended in Agincourt and his marriage to a French princess. The text as published was vilely corrupt, and probably much cut; which leads to speculations. Was it always one play, or has it been made by cutting out most of the political scenes of a two-part drama? Even in its extant debased form *Famous Victories* has good theatrical moments, some of which Shakespeare recalled, probably from the original as performed, and used in all three of his Henry V plays, drawing from it suggestions for their less purely political aspects. For *Henry IV* he took from it even more than from the chronicles his conception of Prince Hal as the boon companion of a group of jolly knaves whom he must

---

[1] Extant only in a 1638 edition but probably collected soon after Tarlton's death. Its mention of the Queen's player Knell lends the anecdote authenticity and links it with Creede's publication.

[2] Several Queen's plays were registered in 1594 when the company declined and became a provincial touring company. *The True Tragedy of Richard III* and *King Leir* and six other of their plays were published in 1594 or 1595. The delay in printing *FV* may have been due to loss of the script, which was botched up in 1598 after Shakespeare's plays had proved popular. If *FV* had been derived from Henslowe's play, Creede would surely have been glad to say so. I agree with J. D. Wilson that the Admiral's 1595 play was a different one.

dismiss when he becomes King, and also the idea of the Prince who learns how to be a monarch yet to preserve the common touch. In *The Troublesome Raigne* and *King John* the heroic Faulconbridge combines epic patriotism with comic energy; but he must stand aside somewhat, being a Bastard and a fictitious character. From *Famous Victories* Shakespeare learned how to fuse comedy and heroism in one of the greatest national figures.

For I *Henry IV* Shakespeare took over the highway robbery, the comedy of the tavern scenes (mentioned but not shown in *Famous Victories*), the anticipations of misrule under a riotous king, the parodying of authority, the mockery of army-conditions. He also used the first reconciliation of the Prince with his father, but changed its occasion and nature. Indeed he changed everything he borrowed, and nothing shows the splendour of his imaginative alchemy better than his handling of this decrepit pot-boiler.

From *Famous Victories* also come Ned (Poins), Gadshill and 'Jockey' 'Oldcastle', who is transformed into Falstaff. It is not easy to see why Sir John Oldcastle became a comic character, for he was a tragic rather than a humorous figure. Historically he was a Herefordshire landowner, probably born in 1378 (so that he was not old when he died in 1417). A useful supporter of Henry IV in the Welsh Marches, he seems to have become a friend of his son, perhaps when the Prince was his father's lieutenant in Wales. After becoming the (fourth) husband of Joan, Lady Cobham, he was given a barony and the title Lord Cobham. A gallant soldier and a good administrator, Oldcastle probably became a Lollard early in life. In 1410 his estates were placed under an interdict because of the heretical preaching there, and a fortnight before Henry IV died Convocation accused him of spreading Wycliffite doctrines. Henry V tried personally to turn him to orthodoxy and delayed further action against him until after August, 1414, when in an angry interview the King rebuked his obstinacy and he left court. Ignoring a summons to appear before the Archbishop of Canterbury, Cobham sent a confession of faith to the King, who refused to accept it. Sir John was then placed in the Tower, whence he was brought on 23 September to answer the charges against him. He defended himself ably, attacking the worship of images, excessive trust in pilgrimages, the necessity of auricular confession, and aspects of the doctrine of Transubstantiation (he believed that the Host was 'Christ's Body in the form of bread'). Arundel finally declared him a heretic, but he was allowed a respite of forty days in which to recant, and during this period he escaped from the Tower. A rising, or at least an armed demonstration, of Lollards was planned, but the King took the conspirators piecemeal ere they could come together, and some of Oldcastle's friends were executed. For three years he lurked in hiding, plotting, it was said, against the King, before he was captured, hanged and burned in December, 1417. (Stow, *inf.* 291–2.) How could such a person become the 'fat Sir John Oldcastle' of comedy?

Most writers in the fourteenth century admitted his sincerity while condemning his contumacy.[1] The author of *Gesta Henrici Quinti* called him 'a man celebrated among the people, proud in heart, strong in his powers, but weak in virtue, who was presumptuous not only against the king but also against the Church universal'. Walsingham and others found fault with him for his heresies and for the rebellion to which they gave rise. Polydore Vergil styled him a 'strong, impious man, who because of his error had been removed from the army'. An anti-Lollard ballad spoke of his obsession with the Bible[2]; another song called him a robber.

In the Reformation Oldcastle became famous as an early Protestant martyr. John Bale wrote a little book in his praise[3] in which the only mention of ordinary sins was as follows:

> 'His youthe was fulle of wanton wildenesse before he knew the Scripture as he reporteth in his answere and for the more part unknowen to me and therfore I wryte it not here.'

This was a reference to Oldcastle's words when kneeling 'with a most cheerful countenance' before the Archbishop:

> 'I shrive me here unto thee, my eternal loving God, that in my frail youth I offended the Lord, most grievously in pride,

[1] Cf. W. Baeske, *Oldcastle-Falstaff in der englischen Literatur bis zu Shakespeare.* Palaestra, 50, 1905.

[2] 'Hit is unkyndly for a kniȝt / That shuld a kynges Castle kepe, / To bable the Bibel day and niȝt, / In restyng tyme when he shuld slepe.' *Political Poems and Songs,* ed. T. Wright, ii.243–47.

[3] *A brefe Chronycle concernynge the Examinacyon and death of the blessed Martyr of Christ Syr Johan Oldecastell the Lorde Cobham / collected togyther by Johan Bale.* [1544.]

wrath and gluttony, in covetousness and in lechery. Many men have I hurt in mine anger, and done many other horrible sins; good Lord I ask thee mercy.'

Bale found no flaw in his Christian hero:

'In all adventurouse actes of worldlye worthe was he ever bolde, stronge, fortunate doughtye noble and valeaunt. But never so worthye a conqueror as in this his present conflyct with the cruell and furyouse frantyck kyngedome of Antichrist. Farre is this Christen more prayse worthye for that he had so noble a stomake in defence of Christes veritie against those Romyshe supersticyons than for anye temporall nobylnesse eyther of bloude byrthe landes or of marcyall feates. For manye thousandes hath had in that great corage, which in the other have bene most faynt harted cowardes and verye desperate dastardes where as he persevered most faythfullye constant to the ende.'

Bale contrasts Cobham with Becket to the latter's disadvantage:

'Whan the Gospell laye dead, gloryouse Thomas Becket was a saynct and Johan Oldecastell a forgotten heretyque. But now that the lyght therof shyneth we are lyke to see yt farre otherwyse. For proude Becket hath alredye hydden his face and poore Oldecastell begynneth now to appere verye notable.'

Foxe took up the praise of Cobham in his *Actes and Monuments* (1563) giving a long account of his life which he augmented later in answering the attacks on his work made by the Roman Catholic Nicholas Harpsfield, who in his *Dialogi Sex* (published as by Alanus Cope)[1] called Oldcastle a 'pseudo-martyr', a heretic and a traitor. Obviously Sir John was a centre of controversy in the sixteenth century, and even his enemies seldom accused him of leading an immoral life after his early youth, but perhaps the Catholic tradition kept the suspicion going. He had been a friend of Henry V, and his fall from favour, occurring at the beginning of the latter's reign, may have caused him to be

---

[1] *Dialogi Sex contra Summi Pontificatus, Monasticae vitae, Sanctorum, Sacrarum Imaginum oppugnatores, et Pseudomartyres ab Alano Cope Londinensi editi auctores nonnullis in locis et castigatiores.* Antwerp, 1573.

confused with the immoral companions of the Prince who were banished from his presence on his accession. So the Bible-babbling heretic traitor became the sensual old knight, the 'old lad of the Castle'.

But why did Shakespeare in entirely re-making the character from what it was in *Famous Victories* take over the old name? Attempts have been made to show that Falstaff was a Lollard—because he quotes Scripture so much—but this is quite incredible. Little more plausible is the suggestion that the name Oldcastle was preserved as a hit at the Cobhams of Shakespeare's own time, who were hostile to Essex (whom the dramatist praises in *Henry V*, Act V, Chorus). But William Brooke, 7th Lord Cobham, was Lord Chamberlain from July, 1596 to March, 1597. Even if the actors had difficulty with him for some reason unknown, they would not be likely to insult him deliberately. On the whole it seems probable that Shakespeare took over the name from *Famous Victories* without *arrière pensée* and without linking his Sir John with the martyr. He must have known the true history of Sir John Oldcastle as set forth in the chronicles; e.g. he would read of his heresies and escape in the same page where Stow described Henry V's dismissal of his former companions. But he ignored the facts and was later driven to make a perfunctory apology in the Epilogue to Part 2 where he admits that Falstaff may already be killed by the audience's 'hard opinions, for Oldcastle died a martyr, and this is not the man'. Apparently the objections were religious.

In changing Oldcastle's name after protests by pious Protestants or the Cobhams, why substitute 'Falstaff'? Again there are puzzles, but it seems likely that in searching for a name for his antithesis of the real Oldcastle, Shakespeare recalled the Sir John Fastolf of his own *1 Henry VI*, III.2.104–9, whose cowardice before Rouen resembles Falstaff's at Shrewsbury, and who, like the latter, on hastening to the King's coronation (IV.1.9–47) was publicly shamed and banished. (He was called Falstaff in Fl.) This Fastolf was thought by Hall and Holinshed to have been a Lollard, and maybe that helped the association of ideas. He cleared himself of the charge of cowardice, but in later life he proved a greedy landlord and avaricious litigant. He built a great castle at Caister in Norfolk and died of a hectic fever aged 80 or more. 'Cruel and vengeful he hath ever been (wrote his servant Windsor) and for the most part without pity or mercy.'[1] Shakespeare would not be put off by the fact that Fastolf was not born until 1415.

It is just possible that Shakespeare had heard also of—maybe confused him with—another Sir John Fastolf, of Nacton, also in Norfolk, who in the fourth year of Henry V's reign was sued by John, Lord Cobham (Oldcastle's father-in-law), for a debt owed by Fastolf's deceased father; during which action there was a brawl in court for which Fastolf was blamed and obliged, before the King at Westminster, to promise that

> 'the same John Fastolf will not do or cause to be done, by himself or others, to the same jurors or any of them or any of the people of the lord King, damage or bodily hurt, by threats, assaults, insults, or any other means which might in any manner tend to a lesion or disturbance of the peace of the lord King.' [Text V.]

But Falstaff cannot be regarded as an amalgam of two Fastolfs and the fictitious Oldcastle. For the greatest humorous character in English literature no source can be offered beyond Shakespeare's creative genius.

It would be possible to accumulate analogues from earlier drama to the various sides of Falstaff's manifold personality, though not to the unity in its diversity. His braggart cowardice belongs to the Plautine tradition of the 'miles gloriosus' found in numerous Tudor plays besides Nicholas Udall's *Ralph Roister Doister* (1566/7) where the swashbuckling lover is worsted by women. An extract is given below from the earlier interlude *Thersites* (1537), a school play translated from the Latin of a French professor of rhetoric [Text VI].

Rather less infantile (though still bearing evidence that it was played by children), and nearer to Falstaff in extravagance of verbal fancy, is the garrulous, foolish Sir Tophas in Lyly's *Endimion*, whose transformation from dedicated warrior to pursuer of the crone Dipsas may have helped to suggest *The Merry Wives of Windsor*. His comic euphuism and real gift of summary phrase occasionally anticipate Falstaff's. In other

---

[1] Cf. J. Gairdner, 'The Historical Element in Shakespeare's Falstaff', in his *Studies in English History*, 1881, 77; and L. W. V. Harcourt, 'The Two Sir John Fastolfs' in *Roy. Hist. Soc. Trans.*, Series 3, IV, 1910.

respects Sir Tophas is more like Pistol [Text VII]. Such boasters, for all their gift of the gab, lack Falstaff's masterful versatility and his power of turning the tables on morality, his rich knowledge of life.

Similarly there is an element of the common Morality-Play pattern in the relationship between the Prince, his father and Falstaff,[1] and the knight is basically the misleader of youth exemplified in many early plays. Thus the tempter to vice appears as the Bad Angel in *The Castell of Perseverance*. In *The Interlude of the Four Elements* he is Sensual Appetite, who makes Humanity turn away from Studious Desire to seek pleasure in a tavern [Text VIII]. Parallels could be drawn between the situations, and the idea of moral development, in *Henry IV* and the interlude *The World and the Child* [Text IX], where the comic Vice, Folly, leads Manhood away from Conscience to loose revels:

> Yea, and we shall be right welcome, I dare well say,
> In Eastcheap for to dine:
> And then we will with Lombards at passage play,[2]
> And at the Pope's Head sweet wine assay;
> We shall be lodg'd well a-fine.

As Dr Tillyard writes, the Prince 'has to choose, Morality-fashion between Sloth or Vanity, to which he is drawn by his bad companions, and Chivalry, to which he is drawn by his father and brothers. He chooses Chivalry. The action is complicated by Hotspur and Falstaff, who stand for the excess and defect of the military spirit, for honour exaggerated and dishonour' (p. 265). That Falstaff was conceived partly in terms of the old Vice several allusions in Part 1, and maybe too his quoting of Scripture to suit his own purposes, make clear; though we must beware of imposing an allegorical interpretation on a character so rich in individuality. But Tillyard's words agree well with the results of a consideration of Shakespeare's treatment of his sources. At the end of Part 1 the Prince was to be victorious in battle, despite his father's forebodings; and

---

[1] Cf. E. M. W. Tillyard, *Shakespeare's History Plays*, pp. 265–6; also J. D. Wilson, *The Fortunes of Falstaff*, 1943.

[2] Play London bankers (Lombards) at a game of dice. (The robbing of Receivers is only a shade worse!)

incidents were changed or invented to make him into a chivalric hero of single combat. The rivalry with Hotspur, foreseen in *Richard II*, made possible by departing from their historical ages and relationship, is insisted on throughout, and Hotspur's character is largely invented so that Hal's growth in self-mastery may contrast with Percy's lack of self-control. According to the chronicles Henry Percy was the admirable warrior Henry IV declares him to be. Though extremely energetic he was not regarded as particularly rash and impulsive although his nickname might suggest that.[1] Shakespeare probably built his conception of the man on Daniel's account of him, on his fury at the King's demand for his prisoners and refusal to free Mortimer, on the premature division of the realm, and on his resolve to proceed with the rebellion even in his father's absence. By developing such aspects and adding others such as his relations with his wife and his impatience with Glendower, the dramatist created a figure worthy to be contrasted in action and speech with the cool, humorous, equable Prince, whose self-knowledge in the soliloquy 'I know you all . . . ' (I.2.196ff) is not meant to be used against him but is to prevent the audience from being shocked by his unprincely behaviour, and to make them watch for evidence of change. Hotspur's qualities, his aspiration to fame and position, his quickly offended *amour propre*, immersion in the code of nobility, love of battle, self-interest—these are all contrasted with the Prince's qualities as they seem to be and are. Hal seems to lack dignity, but can assume it at need; he seems to mock irreverently at good behaviour, and at the code of honour, yet he conforms gloriously in time of need; he wastes his time in brawls and the trivial mock-battle of Gadshill, yet he will slay Hotspur in single combat; he seems to lack all sense of responsibility, yet when the call of duty comes, to father and to country, he obeys it nobly.

Falstaff presents another extreme. Oldcastle in *Famous Victories*, as we have it, plays only a minor part; he is not a coward, and little can be said about his personality. Shakespeare has made him antithetical both to Hotspur and to the Prince. If the

---

[1] Holinshed (*Hist. of Scotland*, 249/1/30) wrote: 'This Henrie . . . was surnamed, for his often pricking, Henrie Hotspur, as one that seldome times rested, if there were anie service to be doone abroad.'

Prince is better, Falstaff is worse, than he makes himself out to be—though his humour disguises the fact and at times his shameless admission of weaknesses brings his base self-knowledge into vivid contrast with the Prince's firm hold on honour.

Yet the ambivalence of Shakespeare's attitude is such that while recognizing that Falstaff is a 'reverend vice', 'grey iniquity' and 'vanity in years', we cover any moral reproof with delight in his irrepressible zest. As D. Traversi writes:

> 'This variety in his traditional and popular derivations, indeed, largely accounts for the unique fascination exercised by Falstaff; it is as though many anonymous figures, consecrated by established custom and related to living popular tradition, were brought together, at once united and transformed, in this great figure of swelling, if unregulated, vitality and comic vigour.'[1]

The writer continues, 'From participation in this wealth of life, the Prince is, by the very responsibilities of his position, largely excluded.' But the Prince participates deeply in the wealth of experience surrounding Falstaff, leading him on, rivalling him in wit and rhetoric, and planning occasions which enable Falstaff to show to the full his richness of sensuality and verbal intelligence, his adroitness in tight corners. The Prince indeed leads a twofold life, and since he engages both in the world of Eastcheap and in the responsible world of court, it can hardly be claimed that he lacks 'wealth of life'. Is wealth of life found only in sensual gusto? The Prince does not reveal in Part 1 merely a 'coldly practical intellect', but he moves towards a sense of moral perspectives which is more necessary to a whole man than Falstaff's utter immersion in the moment. Never in this play—nor indeed in the whole trilogy—is Henry only 'the finished politician'; but he comes to realize his political obligations, which are also obligations to his father. In Part 1 he can reconcile them with his intimacy with Falstaff, even at Shrewsbury, where he permits the fat rogue to claim credit for killing Hotspur

> For my part, if a lie may do thee grace,
> I'll gild it with the happiest terms I have.
>
> (V.4.158-9)

[1] D. Traversi, *Shakespeare from Richard II to Henry V*, 1958, p. 76.

As Prince he can still do this; as King he will have to behave differently; and that Shakespeare knew must be the climax of Part 2.

Around the two major figures Shakespeare invents groups of minor characters on whom he lavishes in varying degrees his imaginative zest in manifold psychological tempers. Thus the rash Hotspur is contrasted with the cold-blooded turncoat and tempter Worcester, and, more subtly, with the tempestuous and superstitious Glendower. Ignoring the latter's upbringing in England, where he became a barrister, Shakespeare develops the legends of his magical birth and powers told by the chroniclers into turgid boasts of his own cosmic importance and prophetic knowledge. Shakespeare was doubtless right in assuming that it was Glendower who used the prophecies of Merlin at Bangor to promise successful revolt; but Hall and Holinshed do not suggest that Hotspur was impatient with such 'skimble-skamble stuff'. Shakespeare, however, makes Hotspur and Glendower two of a kind, yet different; both are unpractical (Hotspur forgets the map; and Glendower in the end fails to appear in battle), but Hotspur cannot endure the pretentious claims and verbosity of a man equally irascible but less civilized in his self-esteem.

Similarly the Prince is surrounded with companions for whom the chronicles and *Famous Victories* gave the merest hint. Shakespeare first gave them the names of important families; then when he changed them, he still used names of some note in history. Both the Poyntzes and the Petos had been well known in Henry VIII's reign. Sir Francis Poyntz of Gloucestershire was Esquire of the Body to that king and Ambassador to Spain; to John Poins was dedicated one of Wyatt's best satires. The priest William Peto (Petowe) had denounced the King's desire to divorce Katherine of Aragon, and later had been made a Cardinal, for which he was jeered at in the London streets. Sir Edward Peyto was Governor of Warwick Castle in Elizabeth's reign.

Shakespeare probably picked these names haphazard, as indicating that the Prince's companions were not low in birth. Peto is a shadow; Ned Poins, however (the 'Ned' comes from *Famous Victories*), is treated more as an equal by Hal, and is chosen by him to mock at Falstaff and the rest. Bardolph was a strange choice to replace the original, since that was the name of a nobleman in Part 2 who fought against Henry IV with Scrope. There is a mystery here. Bardolph shows no sign of gentle breeding, unlike Poins, who has been called 'a Public School type'. He has little to say in the first part of the play, and the Prince scorns him as a coward and drunkard (II.4.318–29). He is obsequious to Falstaff as well as to the Prince, and in *Henry V* he and Pistol and Nym are styled 'formerly servants to Falstaff'. It has been shown that Sir John Fastolf, when Captain of Honfleur in 1428, had a man-at-arms called Johan Bardolf. Bardolph was a family name in Stratford. 'Perhaps Shakespeare's Stratford contemporary George Bardolph boasted an ancestor who had served in the French wars.'[1]

Hal's pranks have been splendidly elaborated on hints mainly supplied by Stow's *Chronicle* and *Famous Victories*. The robbing of the Receivers was no doubt suggested by *Famous Victories*, which does not as it now stands show the robbery but starts immediately afterwards. Shakespeare, however, also recalled Stow's brief account of this escapade, where the Receivers are said to be Hal's own officials, and he afterwards reimburses them, with special rewards for those who resisted bravely and hit him hardest in so doing [Text IVc]. Shakespeare expands this incident, finding in its planning, conduct and aftermath material for four scenes (I.2; II.1–2; II.4); but although he makes the victims the King's men and not the Prince's, he reduces the seriousness of Hal's offence against law and order by making him more intent on tricking Falstaff than on stealing the money. The Prince takes no active part in the hold-up, but robs the robbers, showing his good humour and sense of comedy.

Here and elsewhere occur details which show how Shakespeare's imagination was helped by distant association with works read long before. Before writing *Richard II* he had read *Thomas of Woodstock*, a play of mingled comedy and tragedy in which extravagant young royalty is misled by irresponsible self-seekers of humbler birth (Vol. III, pp. 460–91). The obvious parallel between Richard II and Prince Hal had been drawn by Hall and Holinshed (who mentions the fear that Hal might prove as unprofitable a king as his father's rival). Furthermore the comic parts of *Woodstock* have features in common with

[1] R. A. Newhall, 'An Historical Bardolph', *MLN* 48, 1933, 436–7.

Famous Victories: references to misrule, a mixing of social classes, above all an active Lord Chief Justice (but wicked, not virtuous as in *Henry IV*). And Tressilian has qualities which foreshadow Falstaff. The principal misleader of the young King, he basks in his favour but is finally brought low; he is completely unscrupulous; he lets men escape his 'justice' by ransoming themselves as Falstaff in *Henry IV* lets off recruits from impressment; he has his hangers-on with whom he bandies words in a garrulous way; he is a coward. There the likeness ends, for Tressilian has none of Falstaff's spacious humour, and most of the individual verbal parallels noted by J. J. Elson are probably coincidental (e.g. Tressilian's 'Would all were well' (2337), cf. Falstaff in a similar state of nerves: 'I would it were bedtime, Hal, and all well' (*IH4* V.1.125)).

One passage in *Woodstock*, however, provides not only some likeness of situation but also a scatter of verbal similarities which suggest that when Shakespeare was portraying the ambush of the travellers in II.2 he recalled the scene in *Woodstock* where Tressilian's charter-servers ambush country-folk on their way to Dunstable market. In the terms of abuse used by Falstaff, 'whoreson caterpillars', 'fat chuffs', 'bacon-fed knaves', there is apparent reminiscence of the other scene of humorous villainy (Vol. III, 475–8).

The hue and cry in II.4 comes from *Famous Victories*, but Falstaff, the 'gross fat man', not Gadshill, is the chief person sought by the Sheriff. The Prince does not give him up then and there, but promises to send him later to answer any charges against him, thus showing a due deference to authority. He lets us know, as in Stow, that 'the money shall be paid back again with advantage', and next day we learn that this has been done. The charges against Falstaff seem to be dropped (III.3.181–9).

Stow describes a riot in Eastcheap in which the Prince's[1] men attacked men of the Court [Text IVa]. The first arrest of the Prince in *Famous Victories* and the consequent inquiry made by the King arose from this. Shakespeare did not use the incident in Part 1, probably to minimize the Prince's contravention of public order.

Chroniclers described three main interviews between the King and his son in which the latter's conduct was rebuked. The

---

[1] More probably the retainers of one of his brothers.

first, placed in 1412 at the onset of the King's illness, was caused by the latter's fear that his son might supplant him. This was the interview to which, according to Stow [Text IVb] and Holinshed (*inf.* 216 and 193), the Prince went with a large company of followers, strangely garbed in a blue satin gown trimmed with eyelet holes and needles, wearing a dog-collar and carrying a dagger. The chroniclers do not explain this; *Famous Victories* not unnaturally described it as a piece of arrant insolence which justified the father's fear, since the needles meant that the Prince was on thorns till he obtained the crown (*inf.* 313). But on seeing the King (who was already ill) and hearing his reproaches, the Prince offered himself to be killed with his own dagger, and was reconciled to his father. Shakespeare does not use this incident in either Part, perhaps to avoid following *Famous Victories* in representing the Prince as behaving ambiguously and grotesquely. Unfilial ambition is not one of Prince Hal's faults; all he has to repent of is a madcap irresponsibility.

On a second occasion, taken by Stow from the English translator of the Life of Henry V by 'Titus Livius', the King summoned the Prince to give him good advice. Stow gives a lengthy account of this interview, and the King's sermon on the right use of Justice and Mercy by a monarch. Probably Shakespeare's III.2, where the King instructs the Prince in a kingly behaviour by recalling how Richard II lost his people's hearts and how he himself gained their confidence, owes something to this interview, though the substance of the sermon is not taken over.

The third interview mentioned by the chroniclers occurred after the Prince had taken his dying father's crown. This appears in muddled fashion in *Famous Victories*. Shakespeare held it over for use in Part 2. For the purposes of Part 1 the Prince's promise of reformation in III.2.91–3, 129ff, was enough. Long before the first play is ended, the Prince is already the chivalrous hero, mighty in battle though still humorous and good-natured, warm in affection for his father and brother John, capable of high responsibility when need arises. He is already fit to succeed to the throne; but the division of the reign into two parts will not allow this. We shall see again what problems this set the dramatist and how he tried to solve them.

I. Source

From THE THIRD VOLUME OF CHRONICLES

by R. Holinshed (1587 edition)

[Owen Glendower's rebellion was accompanied by
other troubles.]

[518/2/58] This Owen Glendouer was sonne to an esquier of
Wales, named Griffith Vichan: he dwelled in the parish of Conwaie,
within the countie of Merioneth in Northwales, in a place called
Glindourwie, which is as much to saie in English, as The vallie by the
side of the water of Dee, by occasion whereof he was surnamed
Glindour Dew.[1]

He was first set to studie the lawes of the realme, and became an
utter barrester, or an apprentise of the law (as they terme him) and
served king Richard at Flint castell, when he was taken by Henrie
duke of Lancaster, though other have written that he served this king
Henrie the fourth, before he came to atteine the crowne, in roome of
an esquier,[2] and after by reason of variance that rose betwixt him
and the lord Reginald Greie of Ruthin, about the lands which he
claimed to be his by right of inheritance: when he saw that he might
not prevaile, finding no such favor in his sute as he looked for, he
first made warre against the said lord Greie, wasting his lands and
possessions with fire and sword, cruellie killing his servants and
tenants.[3] The king advertised of such rebellious exploits, enterprised
by the said Owen, and his unrulie complices, determined to chastise
them, as disturbers of his peace, and so with an armie entered into
Wales[4]; but the Welshmen with their capteine withdrew into the
mounteines of Snowdon, so to escape the revenge, which the king
meant towards them. The king therefore did much hurt in the
countries with fire and sword, sleing diverse that with weapon in

[1] *In margin:* 'Owen Glendouer what he was.'   [2] Cf. III.1.121–6.
[3] *In margin:* 'The occasion that mooved him to rebell.'
[4] *In margin:* 'The king entreth into Wales, meaning to chastise the rebels.'

hand came foorth to resist him, and so with a great bootie of beasts and cattell he returned. . . .

[519/2/21]   About the same time [1401], Owen Glendouer and his Welshmen did much hurt to the kings subjects.[1] One night as the king was going to bed, he was in danger to have beene destroied[2]; for some naughtie traitorous persons had conveied into his bed a certeine iron made with smiths craft, like a caltrop, with three long prickes, sharpe and small, standing upright, in such sort, that when he had laid him downe, & that the weight of his bodie should come upon the bed, he should have beene thrust in with those pricks, and per-adventure slaine: but as God would, the king not thinking of any such thing, chanced yet to feele and perceive the instrument before he laid him downe, and so escaped the danger. Howbeit he was not so soone delivered from feare; for he might well have his life in sus-picion, & provide for the preservation of the same; sith perils of death crept into his secret chamber, and laie lurking in the bed of downe where his bodie was to be reposed and to take rest. Oh what a suspected state therefore is that of a king holding his regiment with the hatred of his people, the hartgrudgings of his courtiers, and the peremptorie practises of both togither? Could he confidentlie com-pose or setle himselfe to sleepe for feare of strangling? Durst he boldly eat and drinke without dread of poisoning? Might he adven-ture to shew himselfe in great meetings or solemne assemblies without mistrust of mischeefe against his person intended? What pleasure or what felicitie could he take in his princelie pompe, which he knew by manifest and fearefull experience, to be envied and maligned to the verie death?[3] The state of such a king is noted by the poet in *Dionysius*, as in a mirror, concerning whome it is said,

> Districtus ensis cui super impia
> Ceruice pendet, non Siculae dapes
> Dulcem elaborabunt saporem,
> Non auium cytharaeque cantus.[4]

[520/1/48]   On Corpus Christi daie at evensong time [1402], the divell (as was thought) appeared in a towne of Essex called Dan-burie, entring into the church in likenesse of a greie frier,[5] behaving

---

[1] *In margin:* 'Owen Glendouer'.

[2] *In margin:* 'The danger of the king to have beene destroied.'

[3] Cf. *1H4* I.i.i.

[4] *In margin:* '*Hor. Lib. Ca. 3. Ode 1.*' 'To the man over whose impious neck the sword hangs, no Sicilian feasts will proffer a sweet savour nor songs of birds and of the cythara (will bring repose).' Dionysius, tyrant of Syracuse, lived in constant fear. The suspended sword refers to his flatterer Damocles who was allowed to mount his throne but soon ceased to envy him.

[5] *In margin:* 'The divell appeareth in likenesse of a greie frier.'

himselfe verie outragiouslie, plaieng his parts like a divell indeed, so that the parishioners were put in a marvellous great fright.

At the same instant, there chanced such a tempest of wind, thunder, and lightning, that the highest part of the roofe of that church was blowen downe, and the chancell was all to shaken, rent, and torne in peeces. Within a small while after, eight of those greie friers that had practised treason against the king, were brought to open judgement, and convicted were drawen and headed at London[1]; and two other suffered at Leicester, all which persons had published king Richard to be alive. Owen Glendouer, according to his accustomed manner, robbing and spoiling within the English borders, caused all the forces of the shire of Hereford to assemble togither against them, under the conduct of Edmund Mortimer earle of March. But comming to trie the matter by battell, whether by treason or otherwise, so it fortuned, that the English power was discomfited, the earle taken prisoner,[2] and above a thousand of his people slaine in the place. The shamefull villanie used by the Welsh-women towards the dead carcasses, was such, as honest eares would be ashamed to heare, and continent toongs to speake thereof.[3] The dead bodies might not be buried, without great summes of monie given for libertie to conveie them awaie.

The king was not hastie to purchase the deliverance of the earle March, bicause his title to the crowne was well inough knowen,[4] and therefore suffered him to remaine in miserable prison, wishing both the said earle, and all other of his linage out of this life, with God and his saincts in heaven, so they had beene out of the waie, for then all had beene well inough as he thought. But to let these things passe, the king this yeare sent his eldest daughter Blanch, accompanied with the earle of Summerset, the bishop of Worcester, the lord Clifford, and others, into Almanie, which brought hir to Colin, and there with great triumph she was married to William duke of Bavier, sonne and heire to Lewes the emperour.[5] About mid of August, the king to chastise the presumptuous attempts of the Welshmen, went with a great power of men into Wales, to pursue the capteine of the Welsh rebell Owen Glendouer, but in effect he lost his labor; for Owen conveied himselfe out of the waie, into his knowen lurking places, and (as was thought) through art magike,[6]

---

[1] *In margin:* 'Eight friers executed.'

[2] *In margin:* 'The earle of March taken prisoner in batell by Owen Glendouer.' [It was not the Earl of March but his uncle.]   [3] I.1.36–46.

[4] *In margin:* 'The suspicion of K. Henrie grounded upon a guiltie conscience.' Cf. I.3.130–47.

[5] *In margin:* 'The kings daughter maried into Germanie.' Colin = Cologne.

[6] Cf. Glendower's claim, III.1.41–53.

he caused such foule weather of winds, tempest, raine, snow, and haile to be raised, for the annoiance of the kings armie, that the like had not been heard of[1]; in such sort, that the king was constreined to returne home, having caused his people yet to spoile and burne first a great part of the countrie. The same time, the Lord Edmund of Langlie duke of Yorke departed this life, and was buried at Langlie with his brethren.

The Scots under the leding of Patrike Hepborne, of the Hales the yoonger, entring into England, was overthrowen at Nesbit, in the marches, as in the Scotish chronicle ye may find more at large. This battell was fought the two and twentith of June, in this yeare of our Lord 1402.

Archembald earle Dowgals sore displeased in his mind for this overthrow, procured a commission to invade England, and that to his cost, as ye make likewise read in the Scotish histories. For at a place called Homildon,[2] they were so fiercelie assailed by the Englishmen, under the leding of the lord Persie, surnamed Henrie Hotspur, and George, Earle of March, that with violence of the English shot[3] they were quite vanquished and put to flight, on the Rood daie in harvest, with a great slaughter made by the Englishmen. . . . There were slaine of men of estimation, sir John Swinton, sir Adam Gordon, sir John Leviston, sir Alexander Ramsie of Dalehousie, and three and twentie knights, besides ten thousand of the commons; and of prisoners among other were these, Mordacke earle of Fife, son to the governour Archembald earle Dowglas, which in the fight lost one of his eies, Thomas erle of Murrey, Robert earle of Angus (and as some writers have) the earles of Atholl & Menteith, with five hundred other of meaner degrees.[4] . . .

[521/1/21] Edmund Mortimer earle of March, prisoner with

---

[1] *In margin:* 'Intemperat weather.' Shakespeare omits this expedition.

[2] Cf. I.1.52–70. Hall has: 'When they were entered into England thinkyng no puissance able to encounterwith their force, out of a valey beside a toune called Homeldon issued sodainly the Lorde Henry Percie, whom the Scottes for his haut and valiant corage called sir Henry Hotspur, and in his company the Lord George of Dunbar erle of Marche before banished Scotlande, . . . with all the gentill menne of Northumberland and eight thousande men on horsebacke and on fote. The encounter was sharpe, the fight was daungerous, the long continuaunce was doubtfull, for some were felled and rescued, some in rescuyng other were slaine, other gredy of praye more then of strokes fled to se what baggages were kept emongest the Pages. Thus with pure fightyng of the Englishemen, and faint hertes of the bragging Scottes, the bright beame of victory shone on sainct Georges crosse. . . . (Cf. I.1.59–61, where the first account is 'Uncertain of the issue any way.')

[3] Cf. I.1.55–8; I.3.60–4.

[4] I.1.67–73. Omission of a comma after 'govenour' made Shakespeare regard Mordake as Douglas's son (71–2).

Owen Glendouer, whether for irkesomnesse of cruell captivitie, or
feare of death, or for what other cause, it is uncerteine, agreed to
take part with Owen, against the king of England, and tooke to wife
the daughter of the said Owen.[1]

Strange wonders happened (as men reported) at the nativitie of
this man, for the same night he was borne, all his fathers horsses in
the stable were found to stand in bloud up to the bellies.[2]

[The Percies' dissatisfaction with Henry IV came to a head
towards the end of 1402.]

[521/1/74] Henrie earle of Northumberland, with his brother
Thomas earle of Worcester, and his sonne the lord Henrie Persie,
surnamed Hotspur, which were to king Henrie in the beginning of
his reigne, both faithfull freends, and earnest aiders, began now to
envie his wealth and felicitie; and especiallie they were greeved,
bicause the king demanded of the earle and his sonne such Scotish
prisoners as were taken at Homeldon and Nesbit: for of all the captives which were taken in the conflicts foughten in those two places,
there were delivered to the kings possession onelie Mordake earle of
Fife, the duke of Albanies sonne,[3] though the king did divers and
sundrie times require deliverance of the residue, and that with great
threatnings: wherewith the Persies being sore offended, for that they
claimed them as their owne proper prisoners, and their peculiar
preies,[4] by the counsell of the lord Thomas Persie earle of Worcester,
whose studie was ever (as some write) to procure malice, and set
things in a broile,[5] came to the king unto Windsore (upon a purpose
to proove him) and there required of him, that either by ransome or
otherwise, he would cause to be delivered out of prison Edmund
Mortimer earle of March,[6] their cousine germane, whome (as they
reported) Owen Glendouer kept in filthie prison, shakled with irons,
onelie for that he tooke his part, and was to him faithfull and true.

The king began not a little to muse at this request, and not with-
out cause: for in deed it touched him somewhat neere, sith this
Edmund was sonne to Roger earle of March, sonne to the ladie
Philip, daughter of Lionell duke of Clarence, the third sonne of king
Edward the third; which Edmund at king Richards going into
Ireland, was proclaimed heire apparant to the crowne and realme,
whose aunt called Elianor, the lord Henrie Persie had married; and

---

[1] *In margin:* 'The earle of March marieth the daughter of Owen Glendouer.' The
true Earl was only twelve, and under ward at Berkhampstead Castle.
[2] Cf. III.1.13–40.   [3] I.1.91–5.
[4] Hall and Grafton add, 'and to deliver them utterly denaied'; whence perhaps
I.3.29,77.   [5] Cf. I.1.96–9; I.3.15–19.
[6] *In margin:* 'The request of the Persies.' I.3.77–80.

therefore king Henrie could not well heare, that anie man should be earnest about the advancement of that linage.[1] The king when he had studied on the matter, made answer, that the earle of March was not taken prisoner for his cause, nor in his service, but willinglie suffered himselfe to be taken, bicause he would not withstand the attempts of Owen Glendouer, and his complices, & therefore he would neither ransome him, nor releeve him.[2]

The Persies with this answer and fraudulent excuse were not a little fumed, insomuch that Henrie Hotspur said openlie: Behold, the heire of the relme is robbed of his right, and yet the robber with his owne will not redeeme him.[3] So in this furie the Persies departed, minding nothing more than to depose king Henrie from the high type of his royaltie, and to place in his seat their cousine Edmund earle of March, whom they did not onlie deliver out of captivitie, but also (to the high displeasure of king Henrie) entered in league with the foresaid Owen Glendouer.[4] Heerewith, they by their deputies in the house of the archdeacon of Bangor, divided the realme amongst them, causing a tripartite indenture to be made and sealed with their seales,[5] by the covenants whereof, all England from Severne and Trent, south and eastward, was assigned to the earle of March: all Wales, & the lands beyond Severne westward, were appointed to Owen Glendouer: and all the remnant from Trent northward, to the lord Persie.[6]

This was doone (as some have said) through a foolish credit given to a vaine prophesie,[7] as though king Henrie was the moldwarpe, cursed of Gods owne mouth, and they three were the dragon, the lion, and the woolfe, which should divide this realme betweene them. Such is the deviation (saith *Hall*) and not divination of those blind and fantasticall dreames of the Welsh prophesiers.[8] King Henrie not knowing of this new confederacie, and nothing lesse minding than that which after happened, gathered a great armie to go

[1] 'And therfore the kyng litell forced although that that lignage were clerely subverted and utterly extincte' (Hall).   [2] I.3.81–92; 113–17.

[3] *In margin:* 'The saieng of the L. Persie.' Cf. I.3.93–112.

[4] *In margin:* 'The conspiracies of the Persies with Owen Glendouer.'

[5] *In margin:* 'An indenture tripartite.' III.1.73–83, etc.

[6] *In margin:* 'A division of that which they had not.'

[7] *In margin:* 'A vaine prophesie.' Contrast III.1.148–54.

[8] 'by the deviacion and not devination of that mawmet Merlin' (Hall). Hall attacks Welsh prophecies: 'O ye waveryng Welshmen, call you these prophesies? nay call them unprofitable practises. Name you them devinacions? nay, name them diabolical devises; say you they be prognosticacions? nay they be pestiferous publishinges. For by declaryng and credite geving to their subtil and obscure meanynges, princes have been deceived, many a noble manne hath suffred, and many an honest man hath been begyled and destroyed.' Shakespeare treats the subject humorously, perhaps amused by Hall's vehemence.

againe into Wales, whereof the earle of Northumberland and his sonne were advertised by the earle of Worcester, and with all diligence raised all the power they could make,[1] and sent to the Scots which before were taken prisoners at Homeldon, for aid of men,[2] promising to the earle of Dowglas the towne of Berwike, and a part of Northumberland, and to other Scotish lords, great lordships and seigniories, if they obteined the upper hand. The Scots in hope of gaine, and desirous to be revenged of their old greefes, came to the earle with a great companie well appointed.

The Persies to make their part seeme good, devised certeine articles by the advise of Richard Scroope, archbishop of Yorke, brother to the lord Scroope, whome king Henrie had caused to be beheaded at Bristow.[3] These articles being shewed to diverse noblemen, and other states of the realme, mooved them to favour their purpose, in so much that manie of them did not onelie promise to the Persies aid and succour by words, but also by their writings and seales confirmed the same. Howbeit when the matter came to triall, the most part of the confederates abandoned them, and at the daie of the conflict left them alone.[4] Thus after that the conspirators had discovered themselves, the lord Henrie Persie desirous to proceed in the enterprise, upon trust to be assisted by Owen Glendouer, the earle of March, & other, assembled an armie of men of armes and archers foorth of Cheshire and Wales. Incontinentlie his uncle Thomas Persie earle of Worcester, that had the governement of the prince of Wales, who as then laie at London in secret manner, conveied himselfe out of the princes house,[5] and comming to Stafford (where he met his nephue) they increased their power by all waies and meanes they could devise. The earle of Northumberland himselfe was not with them, but being sicke, had promised upon his amendement to repaire unto them (as some write) with all convenient speed.[6]

These noble men, to make their conspiracie to seeme excusable, besides the articles above mentioned, sent letters abroad, wherein was conteined, that their gathering of an armie tended to none other end, but onlie for the safegard of their owne persons, and to put some better government in the commonwealth.[7] For whereas taxes and tallages were dailie levied, under pretense to be imploied in

[1] *In margin:* 'The Persies raise their powers.'
[2] *In margin:* 'They crave aid of Scots.'
[3] *In margin:* 'The archbish. of Yorke of counsell with the Persies in conspiracie.' I.3.264–76. Wiltshire was not his brother.
[4] Hence II.3.1–37 and III.1.1–2.
[5] *In margin:* 'The earle of Worcester governour to the prince slippeth from him.'
[6] IV.1.14–31.
[7] *In margin:* 'The pretense of the Persies, as they published it abroad.'

defense of the realme, the same were vainlie wasted, and unprofit-
ablie consumed: and where through the slanderous reports of their
enimies, the king had taken a greevous displeasure with them, they
durst not appeare personallie in the kings presence, untill the prelats
and barons of the realme had obteined of the king licence for them
to come and purge themselves before him, by lawfull triall of their
peeres, whose judgement (as they pretended) they would in no wise
refuse. Manie that saw and heard these letters, did commend their
diligence, and highlie praised their assured fidelitie and trustinesse
towards the commonwealth.

But the king understanding their cloaked drift,[1] devised (by what
meanes he might) to quiet and appease the commons, and deface
their contrived forgeries; and therefore he wrote an answer to their
libels, that he marvelled much, sith the earle of Northumberland,
and the lord Henrie Persie his sonne, had received the most part of
the summes of monie granted to him by the cleargie and communaltie, for defense of the marches, as he could evidentlie proove
what should moove them to complaine and raise such manifest
slanders.[2] And whereas he understood, that the earles of Northumberland and Worcester, and the lord Persie had by their letters
signified to their freends abroad, that by reason of the slanderous
reports of their enimies, they durst not appeare in his presence, without the mediation of the prelats and nobles of the realme, so as they
required pledges, whereby they might safelie come afore him, to
declare and alledge what they had to saie in proofe of their inno-
cencie, he protested by letters sent foorth under his seale, that they
might safelie come and go, without all danger, or anie manner of
indamagement to be offered to their persons.

But this could not satisfie those men, but that resolved to go forwards with their enterprise, they marched towards Shrewesburie,[3]
upon hope to be aided (as men thought) by Owen Glendouer, and
his Welshmen, publishing abroad throughout the countries on each
side, that king Richard was alive,[4] whome if they wished to see, they
willed them to repaire in armour unto the castell of Chester, where
(without all doubt) he was at that present, and redie to come forward. This tale being raised, though it were most untrue, yet it bred
variable motions in mens minds, causing them to waver, so as they
knew not to which part they should sticke; and verelie, divers were
well affected towards king Richard, speciallie such as had tasted of
his princelie bountifulness, of which there was no small number.

---

[1] IV.1.39–41.   [2] *In margin:* 'The kings answer to the Persies libell.'
[3] III.1.84–7.
[4] *In margin:* 'Poore K. Richard is still alive with them that wish K. Henries
overthrow.' Shakespeare ignores this tale.

And to speake a truth, no marvell it was, if manie envied the prosperous state of king Henrie, sith it was evident inough to the world,
that he had with wrong usurped the crowne, and not onelie violent-
lie deposed king Richard, but also cruellie procured his death; for
the which undoubtedlie, both he and his posteritie tasted such
troubles, as put them still in danger of their states, till their direct
succeeding line was quite rooted out by the contrarie faction, as in
Henrie the sixt and Edward the fourth it may appeare.

But now to return where we left. King Henrie advertised of the
proceedings of the Persies, foorthwith gathered about him such
power as he might make, and being earnestlie called upon by the
Scot, the earle of March,[1] to make hast and give battell to his
enimies, before their power by delaieng of time should still too much
increase, he passed forward with such speed, that he was in sight of
his enimies, lieng in campe neere to Shrewesburie, before they were
in doubt of anie such thing,[2] for the Persies thought that he would
have staied at Burton upon Trent, till his councell had come thither
to him to give their advise what he were best to doo. But herein the
enimie was deceived of his expectation, sith the king had great
regard of expedition and making speed for the safetie of his owne
person, whereunto the earle of March incited him, considering that
in delaie is danger, & losse in lingering, as the poet in the like case
saith:

> Tolle moras, nocuit semper differre paratis,
> Dum trepidant nullo firmatæ robore partes.

By reason of the kings sudden comming in this sort,[3] they staied
from assaulting the towne of Shrewesburie, which enterprise they
were readie at that instant to have taken in hand, and foorthwith
the lord Persie (as a capteine of high courage) began to exhort the
capteines and souldiers to prepare themselves to battell,[4] sith the
matter was growen to that point, that by no meanes it could be
avoided, so that (said he) this daie shall either bring us all to
advancement & honor, or else if it shall chance us to be overcome,
shall deliver us from the kings spitefull malice and cruell disdaine:
for plaieng the men (as we ought to doo) better it is to die in battell
for the commonwealths cause, than through cowardlike feare to
prolong life, which after shall be taken from us, by sentence of the
enimie.

[1] George Dunbar, Earl of the March of Scotland. No connection with Mortimer.
[2] *In margin:* 'The kings speedie diligence.' III.2.163–80. But in IV.1.87–93
Hotspur hears of his approach.
[3] *In margin:* 'The Persies troubled with the kings sudden comming.'
[4] *In margin:* 'The lord Persie exhorteth his complices to stick to their tackle.'
Cf. IV.1.112–32.

Hereupon, the whole armie being in number about fourteene thousand chosen men,[1] promised to stand with him so long as life lasted. There were with the Persies as chiefteines of this armie, the earle of Dowglas a Scotish man, the baron of Kinderton, sir Hugh Browne, and sir Richard Vernon[2] knights, with diverse other stout and right valiant capteins. Now when the two armies were incamped, the one against the other, the earle of Worcester and the lord Persie with their complices sent the articles[3] (whereof I spake before) by Thomas Caiton, and Thomas Salvain esquiers to king Henrie, under their hands and seales, which articles in effect charged him with manifest perjurie,[4] in that (contrarie to his oth received upon the evangelists at Doncaster, when he first entred the realme after his exile) he had taken upon him the crowne and royall dignitie, imprisoned king Richard, caused him to resigne his title, and finallie to be murthered. Diverse other matters they laid to his charge, as levieng of taxes and tallages, contrarie to his promise, infringing of lawes & customes of the realme, and suffering the earle of March to remaine in prison, without travelling to have him delivered. All which things they as procurors & protectors of the common-wealth,[5] tooke upon them to proove against him, as they protested unto the whole world.

King Henrie after he had read their articles, with the defiance which they annexed to the same, answered the esquiers,[6] that he was readie with dint of sword and fierce battell to proove their quarrell false, and nothing else than a forged matter, not doubting, but that God would aid and assist him in his righteous cause, against the disloyall and false forsworne traitors. The next daie in the morning earlie, being the even of Marie Magdalene, they set their battels in order on both sides, and now whilest the warriors looked when the token of battell should be given, the abbat of Shrewesburie, and one of the clearks of the privie seale, were sent from the king unto the Persies, to offer them pardon, if they would come to any reasonable agreement.[7] By their persuasions, the lord Henrie Persie began to give eare unto the kings offers, & so sent with them his uncle the earle of Worcester, to declare unto the king the causes of those troubles, and to require some effectuall reformation in the same.[8]

[1] *In margin:* 'The number of the Persies armie.'
[2] Vernon appears in IV.1.86ff; IV.3; V.2.
[3] *In margin:* 'The Persies sent their articles to the king.' Hall gives them more fully. IV.3.52–105 and V.1.30–71 allude to them.
[4] *In margin:* 'King Henrie charged with perjurie.' IV.3.101; V.1.55–8.
[5] *In margin:* 'Procurors & protectors of the commonwealth.'
[6] *In margin:* 'The kings answer to the messengers that brought the articles.'
[7] *In margin:* 'The king offereth to pardon his adversaries.' Cf. Blunt, IV.3.30ff.
[8] IV.3.107–13.

[The Battle of Shrewsbury, 21 July, 1403]

It was reported for a truth, that now when the king had condescended unto all that was resonable at his hands to be required,
and seemed to humble himselfe more than was meet for his estate,
the earle of Worcester (upon his returne to his nephue) made relation cleane contrarie to that the king had said,[1] in such sort that he
set his nephues hart more in displeasure towards the king, than ever
it was before, driving him by that meanes to fight whether he would
or not: then suddenlie blew the trumpets, the kings part crieng S.
George upon them, the adversaries cried *Esperance Persie*,[2] and so the
two armies furiouslie joined. The archers on both sides shot for the
best game, laieng on such load with arrowes, that manie died, and
were driven downe that never rose againe.

The Scots (as some write) which had the fore ward on the Persies
side, intending to be revenged of their old displeasures doone to
them by the English nation, set so fiercelie on the kings fore ward,
led by the earle of Stafford, that they made the same draw backe,
and had almost broken their adversaries arraie.[3] The Welshmen also
which before had laine lurking in the woods, mounteines and
marishes, hearing of this battell toward, came to the aid of the
Persies, and refreshed the wearied people with new succours.[4] The
king perceiving that his men were thus put to distresse, what with
the violent impression of the Scots, and the tempestuous stormes of
arrowes, that his adversaries discharged freely against him and his
people, it was no need to will him to stirre: for suddenlie with his
fresh battell, he approched and relieved his men; so that the battell
began more fierce than before. Here the lord Henrie Persie, and the
earle Dowglas, a right stout and hardie capteine, not regarding the
shot of the kings battell, nor the close order of the ranks, pressing
forward togither bent their whole forces towards the kings person,
comming upon him with speares and swords so fiercelie, that the
earle of March the Scot,[5] perceiving their purpose, withdrew the
king from that side of the field (as some write) for his great benefit
and safegard (as it appeared) for they gave such a violent onset upon
them that stood about the kings standard, that slaieng his standard-
bearer sir Walter Blunt, and overthrowing the standard, they made
slaughter of all those that stood about it, as the earle of Stafford,[6]

---

[1] *In margin:* 'The earle of Worcesters double dealing in wrong reporting the kings
words.' V.2.1–40.

[2] Cf. V.2.96; also II.3.73. Percy's war-cry.   [3] *In margin:* 'The Scots.'

[4] *In margin:* 'The Welshmen come to aid the Persies.' Contrast IV.1.124–6.

[5] *In margin:* 'The earle of March.' George Dunbar.

[6] V.3.7–9; V.4.41.

that daie made by the king constable of the realme, and diverse other.

The prince that daie holpe his father like a lustie yoong gentleman: for although he was hurt in the face with an arrow, so that diverse noble men that were about him, would have conveied him foorth of the field, yet he would not suffer them so to doo, least his departure from amongst his men might happilie have striken some feare into their harts: and so without regard of his hurt, he continued with his men, & never ceassed, either to fight where the battell was most hot, or to incourage his men where it seemed most need.[1] This battell lasted three long houres,[2] with indifferent fortune on both parts, till at length, the king crieng saint George victorie, brake the arraie of his enimies, and adventured so farre, that (as some write) the earle Dowglas strake him downe,[3] & at that instant slue sir Walter Blunt, and three other, apparelled in the kings sute and clothing, saieng: I marvell to see so many kings thus suddenlie arise one in the necke of an other.[4] The king in deed was raised, & did that daie manie a noble feat of armes, for as it is written, he slue that daie with his owne hands six and thirtie persons of his enimies.[5] The other on his part incouraged by his doings, fought valiantlie, and slue the lord Persie, called sir Henrie Hotspurre.[6] To conclude, the kings enimies were vanquished, and put to flight, in which flight, the earle of Dowglas, for hast, falling from the crag of an hie mounteine, brake one of his cullions, and was taken, and for his valiantnesse, of the king frankelie and freelie delivered.[7]

There was also taken the earle of Worcester,[8] the procuror and setter foorth of all this mischeefe, sir Richard Vernon, and the baron of Kinderton, with diverse other. There were slaine upon the kings part, beside the earle of Stafford, to the number of ten knights, sir Hugh Shorlie, sir John Clifton, sir John Cokaine, sir Nicholas Gausell, sir Walter Blunt, sir John Calverleie, sir John Massie of Podington, sir Hugh Mortimer, and sir Robert Gausell, all the which received the same morning the order of knighthood[9]: sir

---

[1] *In margin:* 'The valiance of the yoong prince.' Cf. V.4.1–46, where, though bleeding severely, he saves his father.

[2] *In margin:* 'A sore battell & well mainteined.'   [3] V.4.24–38.

[4] *In margin:* 'The valiant dooings of the earle Dowglas.' Cf. V.3.1–28; V.4.25–38.

[5] *In margin:* 'The high manhood of the king.'

[6] *In margin:* 'The lord Persie slaine.' Cf. Stow: 'Henry the Prince was wounded in the face with an arrow. In the meane season Hen. Percy, whilest he went before his men in the battel, preasing upon his enimies, was sodeinley slaine, which being knowne, the Kings enemies fled.' In V.4.59–110 the Prince kills Hotspur.

[7] *In margin:* 'The earle Dowglas taken prisoner.' V.5.17–33. *cullions,* testicles.

[8] *In margin:* 'The earle of Worcester taken.' V.5.1–15.

[9] *In margin:* 'Knights slaine on the kings part.' V.4.41 (Shirley, Stafford, Blunt); 45 (Gawsey); 46 (Clifton).

Thomas Wendesleie was wounded to death, and so passed out of this life shortlie after. There died in all upon the kings side sixteene hundred, and foure thousand were greevouslie wounded. On the contrarie side were slaine, besides the lord Persie, the most part of the knights and esquiers of the countie of Chester,[1] to the number of two hundred, besides yeomen and footmen, in all there died of those that fought on the Persies side, about five thousand. This battell was fought on Marie Magdalene even, being saturdaie. Upon the mondaie folowing, the earle of Worcester, the baron of Kinderton, and sir Richard Vernon knights, were condemned and beheaded.[2] The earles head was sent to London, there to be set on the bridge.

The earle of Northumberland was now marching forward with great power, which he had got thither, either to aid his sonne and brother (as was thought) or at the least towards the king, to procure a peace: but the earle of Westmerland, and sir Robert Waterton knight, had got an armie on foot, and meant to meet him.[3] The earle of Northumberland, taking neither of them to be his freend, turned suddenlie back, and withdrew himselfe into Warkewoorth castell. The king having set a staie in things about Shrewesburie, went straight to Yorke,[4] from whence he wrote to the earle of Northumberland, willing him to dismisse his companies that he had with him, and to come unto him in peaceable wise. The earle upon receipt of the kings letters came unto him the morow after saint Laurence daie,[5] having but a few of his servants to attend him, and so excused himselfe, that the king (bicause the earle had Berwike in his possession, and further, had his castels of Alnewike, Warkewoorth, and other, fortified with Scots) dissembled the matter, gave him faire words, and suffered him (as saith *Hall*) to depart home, although by other it should seeme, that he was committed for a time to safe custodie.

The king returning foorth of Yorkeshire, determined to go into Northwales, to chastise the presumptuous dooings of the unrulie Welshmen, who (after his comming from Shrewesburie, and the marches there) had doone much harme to the English subjects.[6] But now where the king wanted monie to furnish that enterprise, and to wage his souldiers, there were some that counselled him to be bold with the bishops, and supplie his want with their surplusage.

[1] *In margin:* 'The slaughter of Cheshire men at this battell.'

[2] *In margin:* 'The earle of Worcester and others beheaded.' Cf. V.5.14–15.

[3] *In margin:* 'The earle of Westmerland raiseth a power against the earle of Northumberland.' Cf. V.5.35–7.

[4] *In margin:* 'The king goeth to Yorke.' Contrast V.5.39–40, 'towards Wales'.

[5] *In margin:* 'The earle of Northumberland commeth to the king.'

[6] *In margin:* 'The Welshmen molest the English subjects.' Cf. V.5.39–40.

[During the next years differences arose between the Prince and his father as the former's political influence grew. More than once it was suggested that Henry IV might, or should, abdicate in his son's favour. In November, 1411 he removed the Prince and his supporters from the Council.[1]]

[538/2/74]   Whilest these things were a dooing in France, the lord Henrie prince of Wales, eldest sonne to king Henrie, got knowledge that certeine of his fathers servants were busie to give informations against him, whereby discord might arise betwixt him and his father: for they put into the kings head, not onelie what evill rule (according to the course of youth) the prince kept to the offense of manie: but also what great resort of people came to his house, so that the court was nothing furnished with such a traine as dailie followed the prince.[2] These tales brought no small suspicion into the kings head, least his sonne would presume to usurpe the crowne, he being yet alive, through which suspicious gelousie, it was perceived that he favoured not his sonne, as in times past he had doone.[3]

The Prince sore offended with such persons, as by slanderous reports, sought not onelie to spot his good name abrode in the realme, but to sowe discord also betwixt him and his father, wrote his letters into everie part of the realme, to reproove all such slanderous devises of those that sought his discredit. And to cleare himselfe the better, that the world might understand what wrong he had to be slandered in such wise: about the feast of Peter and Paule, to wit, the nine and twentith daie of June, he came to the court with such a number of noble men and other his freends that wished him well, as the like traine had beene sildome seene repairing to the court at any one time in those daies.[4] He was apparelled in a gowne of blew satten, full of small oilet holes, at everie hole the needle hanging by a silke thred with which it was sewed. About his arme he ware an hounds collar set full of SS of gold, and the tirets likewise being of the same metall.[5]

[1] 'The Kyng discharged the Prynce from his Counsaille,
  And set my lord Syr Thomas in his stede,
  Chief of counsayle for the Kynges more avayle:
  For which the Prynce of wrath and wilful hede
  Agayne him made debate and frowardhede
  With whom the Kyng took parte and held the felde
  To time the Prynce unto the Kyng him yelde.'
                    (Hardyng's *Chronicle*.)
      Cf. III.2.32–3.
[2] *In margin:* 'The Prince of Wales accused to his father.' Cf. III.2.11–28.
[3] *In margin:* 'The suspicious gelousie of the king toward his son.' III.2.122–8.
[4] *In margin:* 'The prince goeth to the court with a great traine.' In II.4.286ff Hal is sent for.   [5] *In margin:* 'His strange apparell.' Cf. *FV*, p. 313 which explains it.

The court was then at Westminster, where he being entred into the hall, not one of his companie durst once advance himselfe further than the fire in the same hall, notwithstanding they were earnestlie requested by the lords to come higher: but they regarding what they had in commandement of the prince, would not presume to doo in any thing contrarie thereunto.[1] He himselfe onelie accompanied with those of the kings house, was streight admitted to the presence of the king his father, who being at that time greevouslie diseased, yet caused himselfe in his chaire to be borne into his privie chamber, where in the presence of three or foure persons, in whome he had confidence, he commanded the prince to shew what he had to saie concerning the cause of his comming.[2]

The prince kneeling downe before his father said[3]: Most redoubted and sovereigne lord and father, I am at this time come to your presence as your liege man, and as your naturall sonne, in all things to be at your commandement. And where I understand you have in suspicion my demeanour against your grace, you know verie well, that if I knew any man within this realme, of whome you should stand in feare, my duetie were to punish that person, thereby to remoove that greefe from your heart. Then how much more ought I to suffer death, to ease your grace of that greefe which you have of me, being your naturall sonne and liege man: and to that end I have this daie made my selfe readie by confession and receiving of the sacrament. And therefore I beseech you most redoubted lord and deare father, for the honour of God, to ease your heart of all such suspicion as you have of me, and to dispatch me heere before your knees, with this same dagger, [and withall he delivered unto the king his dagger, in all humble reverence; adding further, that his life was not so deare to him, that he wished to live one daie with his displeasure][4] and therefore in thus ridding me out of life, and your selfe from all suspicion, here in presence of these lords, and before God at the daie of the generall judgement, I faithfullie protest clearlie to forgive you.

The king mooved herewith, cast from him the dagger, and imbracing the prince kissed him, and with shedding teares confessed, that in deed he had him partlie in suspicion, though now (as he perceived) not with just cause, and therefore from thenceforth no misreport

---

[1] Contrast *FV*.

[2] *In margin:* 'The prince commeth to the kings presence.' Shakespeare substitutes III.2. for this scene.

[3] *In margin:* 'His words to his father.' In III.2 he seeks 'pardon on my true submission' (28).

[4] Cf. *FV* 540–73.

should cause him to have him in mistrust, and this he promised of his honour.[1] So by his great wisedome was the wrongfull suspicion which his father had conceived against him remooved, and he restored to his favour. And further, where he could not but greevouslie complaine of them that had slandered him so greatlie, to the defacing not onelie of his honor, but also putting him in danger of his life, he humblie besought the king that they might answer their unjust accusation; and in case they were found to have forged such matters upon a malicious purpose, that then they might suffer some punishment for their faults, though not to the full of that they had deserved.[2] The king seeming to grant his resonable desire, yet told him that he must tarrie a parlement, that such offendors might be punished by judgement of their peeres: and so for that time he was dismissed, with great love and signes of fatherlie affection.

Thus were the father and the sonne reconciled, betwixt whom the said pickthanks[3] had sowne division, insomuch that the sonne upon a vehement conceit of unkindnesse sproong in the father, was in the waie to be worne out of favour. Which was the more likelie to come to passe, by their informations that privilie charged him with riot and other uncivill demeanor unseemelie for a prince.[4] Indeed he was youthfullie given, growne to audacitie, and had chosen him companions agreeable to his age; with whome he spent the time in such recreations, exercises, and delights as he fansied. But yet (it should seeme by the report of some writers) that his behaviour was not offensive or at least tending to the damage of anie bodie; sith he had a care to avoid dooing of wrong,[5] and to tedder his affections within the tract of vertue, whereby he opened unto himselfe a redie passage of good liking among the prudent sort, and was beloved of such as could discerne his disposition, which was in no degree so excessive, as that he deserved in such vehement maner to be suspected. In whose dispraise I find little, but to his praise verie much, parcell whereof I will deliver by the waie as a metyard whereby the residue may be measured. The late poet that versified the warres of the valorous Englishmen, speaking of the issue of Henrie the fourth saith of his prince (among other things) as followeth:

---

[1] *In margin:* 'The kings words to the prince his son.'

[2] *In margin:* 'The princes request to have his accusors to answer their wrongful slanders.'

[3] III.2.25. 'Smiling pick-thanks and base newsmongers.'

[4] In I.1.85 the King speaks of 'riot and dishonour'.

[5] He does not personally rob the Receivers, and 'the money shall be paid back again with advantage'. II.4.558.

—procero qui natu maximus hæres
Corpore, progressus cum pubertatis ad annos
Esset, res gessit multas iuueniliter audax,
Asciscens comites quos par sibi iunxerat ætas,
Nil tamen iniuste commisit, nil tamen vnquam
Extra virtutis normam, sapientibus æque
Ac aliis charus.[1]

II. Possible Source

From A MYRROURE FOR MAGISTRATES

(1559)

(a)   OWEN GLENDOWER

by Thomas Phaer

Whan he had ended this so wofull a tragedy,[2] and to all Princes a ryght wurthy instruction, we paused: having passed through a miserable time full of piteous tragedyes. And seing the reyne of Henry the fourth ensued, a man more ware & prosperous in hys doynges although not untroubled with warres both of outforth and inward enemies, we began to serch what Piers were fallen therin, wherof the number was not small: and yet because their examples were not much to be noted for our purpose, we passed over all the Maskers (of whom King Richardes brother was chiefe) which were all slayne and put to death for theyr trayterous attempt.[3] And finding Owen Glendour next, one of fortunes owne whelpes, and the Percyes his confederates, I thought them unmete to be over passed, and therfore sayde thus to the silent cumpany: what my maysters is every man at once in a browne study, hath no man affection to any of these storeyes? you minde so much sum other belyke, that these do not move you: And to say the troth there is no speciall cause why they should. Howbeit Owen Glendour because he was one of fortunes darlinges, rather than he should be forgotten, I wil tel his tale for him under the privilege of Martine Hundred:

---

[1] *Anglorum Praelia*, by Christopher Ockland, 1580.
[2] The complaint of Richard II.
[3] The Abbot's conspiracy; *R2* V.2 ; V.3.

whych Owen cumming out of the wilde mountaynes like the Image
of death in all poyntes (his dart onely excepted) so sore hath famine
and hunger consumed hym, may lament his folly after thys maner.

> Howe Owen Glendour seduced by false
> prophesies tooke upon him to be prince of
> Wales, and was by Henry then prince
> therof, chased to the mountaynes,
> where he miserably dyed
> for lacke of foode.

I Pray the[e] Baldwin[1] sith thou doest entend
To shewe the fall of such as clymbe to hye,
Remember me, whose miserable ende
May teache a man his vicious life to flye:
Oh Fortune, Fortune, out on her I crye,   5
My body and fame she hath made leane and slender
For I poore wretch am sterved Owen Glendour.

A Welshman borne, and of a gentle blud,
But ill brought up, wherby full wel I find,
That neither birth nor linage make us good   10
Though it be true that Cat wil after kinde:
Fleshe gendreth fleshe, so doeth not soule or minde,
They gender not, but fowly do degender,
When men to vice from vertue them do surrender.

Ech thing by nature tendeth to the same   15
Wherof it came, and is disposed like:
Downe sinkes the mold, up mountes the fiery flame,
With horne the hart, with hoofe the horse doth strike:
The Wulfe doth spoyle, the suttle Fox doth pyke,
And generally no fish, flesh, fowle, or plant   20
Doth any property that their dame had, want.

But as for men, sith severally they have
A mind whose maners are by learning made,
Good bringing up alonly doth them save
In vertuous dedes, which with their parentes fade.   25
So that true gentry standeth in the trade
Of vertuous life, not in the fleshly line:
For blud is Brute, but Gentry is divine.

---

[1] William Baldwin collected the material for the *Mirror*.

Experience doth cause me thus to say,
And that the rather for my countreymen,   30
Which vaunt and boast their selves above the day
If they may strayne their stocke for wurthy men[1]:
Which let be true, are they the better then?
Nay farre the wurse if so they be not good,
For why they steyne the bewty of theyr blood.   35

How would we mocke the burden bearing mule
If he would brag he wer an horses sunne,
To presse his pride (might nothing els him rule,)
His boast to prove, no more but byd him runne:
The horse for swiftenes hath his glory wunne,   40
To which the mule could never the more aspier
Though he should prove that Pegas[2] was his sier.

Ech man may crake of that which is his own,
Our parentes vertues theirs are and not oures:
Who therfore wil of noble kind be knowen   45
Ought shine in vertue like his auncestors,[3]
Gentry consisteth not in lands and towers:
He is a Churle though all the world be his,
Yea[4] Arthurs heyre if that he live amys.

For vertuous lyfe doth make a gentleman   50
Of her possessour, all be he poore as Job,
Yea though no name of elders shewe he can:
For proofe take Merlyn fathered by an Hob.
But who so settes his mind to spoyle and rob,
Although he cum by due discent fro Brute,   55
He is a Chorle, ungentle, vile, and brute.

Well thus dyd I for want of better wyt,
Because my parentes noughtly brought me up[5]:
For gentle men (they sayd) was nought so fyt
As to attaste by bolde attemptes the cup   60
Of conquestes wyne, wherof I thought to sup:
And therfore bent my selfe to rob and ryve,
And whom I could of landes and goodes depryve.

---

[1] Like Glendower in III.1.   [2] Pegasus.
[3] The theme of the Henry V plays, as of *AWW*.
[4] Yea *1563*. He *1559*.   [5] Contrast III.1.122.

For Henry the fourth did then usurpe the crowne,
Despoyled the kyng, with[1] Mortimer the heyre: 65
For whych his subjectes sought to put him downe.
And I, whyle Fortune offred me so fayre,
Dyd what I myght his honour to appeyre:
And toke on me to be the prynce of Wales,
Entiste thereto by many of Merlines tales.[2]   70

For whych, such Idle as wayte upon the spoyle,
From every parte of Wales unto me drew:
For loytring youth untaught in any toyle
Are redy aye all mischiefe to ensue.
Through help of these so great my glory grew,   75
That I defyed my Kyng through lofty hart,
And made sharp warre on all that tooke his part.

See lucke, I tooke lord Reynolde Grey of Rythen,
And him enforst my doughter to espouse,[3]
And so unraunsomed held him still: and sithen   80
In Wygmore land through battayle rygorous
I caught the ryght heyre of the crowned house
The Erle of March syr Edmund Mortymer,[4]
And in a dungeon kept hym prysoner,

Then al the marches longyng unto Wales   85
By Syverne west I did invade and burne:
Destroyed the townes in mountaynes and in vales,
And riche in spoyles did homward safe retourne:
Was none so bold durst once agaynst me spurne.
Thus prosperously doth Fortune forward call   90
Those whom she mindes to geve the sorest fall.

Whan fame had brought these tidinges to the king
(Although the Skots than vexed him ryght sore)
A myghty army agaynst me he dyd bryng[5]:
Whereof the French Kyng beyng warned afore,   95
Who mortall hate agaynst kyng Henry bore,
To greve our foe he quyckely to me sent
Twelve thousand Frenchmen armed to war, & bent.

---

[1] and robbed.
[2] This was in winter 1400. Cf. III.1.148–54, and Vol. III., 302–3.
[3] Glendower captured Grey in 1402. He married his daughter to Edmund Mortimer. I.3.84–5.   [4] Not the Earl, but his uncle.
[5] Shakespeare omits this abortive expedition.

A part of them led by the Erle of Marche
Lord James of Burbon, a valiaunt tryed knyght   100
Withheld by winds to Wales ward forth to marche,
Tooke lande at Plymmouth pryvily on a nyght:
And when he had done al he durst or myght,
After that a mayny of his men were slayne
He stole to shyp, and sayled home agayne.   105

Twelve thousand moe in Mylford dyd aryve,
And came to me, then lying at Denbygh
With armed Welshmen thousandes double five:
With whom we went to Wurcester well nigh,
And there encampte us on a mount on high,   110
To abide the kyng, who shortly after came
And pitched his feild, on a Hyll hard by the same.

Ther eyght dayes long, our hostes lay face to face,
And neyther durst the others power assayle:
But they so stopt the passages the space   115
That vitayles coulde not cum to our avayle,
Wherthrough constrayned our hartes began to fayle
So that the Frenchmen shrancke away by night,
And I with mine to the mountaynes toke our flight:

The king pursued us, greatly to his cost,   120
From Hyls to wuds, fro wuds to valeyes playne:
And by the way his men and stuf he lost.
And whan he see he gayned nought save payne,
He blewe retreat, and got him home agayne:
Then with my power I boldly came abrode   125
Taken in my cuntrey for a very God.

Immediatly after fell a Joly Jarre
Betwene the king, and Percies worthy bluds,
Which grew at last unto a deadly warre:
For like as drops engendre mighty fluds,   130
And little seedes sprut furth great leaves and buds,
Even so small strifes, if they be suffred run
Brede wrath and war, and death or they be don.

The kyng would have the raunsum of such Scots
As these the Percyes had tane in the feeld: 135
But see how strongly Luker knits her knottes,
The king will have, the Percies will not yeeld.

Desire of goodes soone craves, but graunteth seeld:
O cursed goodes desire of you hath wrought
All wyckednes, that hath or can be thought.   140

   The Percies deemed it meter for the king
To have redeemed theyr cosin Mortymer,
Who in his[1] quarel all his power did bryng
To fight with me, that tooke him prisoner,
Than of their pray to rob his Souldier: 145
And therfore willed him see sum mean wer found,
To quit forth him whom I kept vily bound.

   Because the king misliked their request,
They came them selves and did accord with me,
Complayning how the kyngdome was opprest,   150
By Henries rule, wherfore we dyd agre
To put him downe, and part the realme in three:
The North part theirs, Wales wholy to be mine
The rest to rest to therle of Marches line.[2]

   And for to set us hereon more agog   155
A prophet came (a vengeaunce take them all)
Affirming Henry to be Gogmagog
Whom Merlyn doth a Mouldwarp ever call,[3]
Accurst of god, that must be brought in thrall
By a wulf, a Dragon, and a Lyon strong,   160
Which should devide his kingdome them among.

   This crafty dreamer[4] made us thre such beastes
To thinke we were these foresayd beastes in deede:
And for that cause our badges and our creastes
We searched out, whych scarcely wel agreed: 165
Howbeit the Haroldes[5] redy at such a neede,
Drew downe such issues from olde auncestours,
As proved these ensignes to be surely oures.

   Ye crafty Welshemen, wherfore do you mocke
The noble men thus with your fayned rymes?[6]   170
Ye noble men why flye you not the flocke
Of such as have seduced so many times?

---

[1] Supporting Henry IV. I.3.93–112.
[2] III.1.71–81   [3] III.1.148–52.   [4] III.1.149.   [5] Heralds.
[6] Cf. Hotspur. III.1.128–34.

False Prophesies are plages for divers crymes
Whych god doth let the divilish sorte devise
To trouble such as are not godly wyse.   175

    And that appered by us thre beastes in dede,
Through false perswasion highly borne in hand
That in our feat we could not chuse but spede
To kyll the kyng, and to enjoye his land:
For which exployt we bound our selves in band   180
To stand contented ech man with his part,
So fully folly assured our folysh hart.

    But such they say as fysh before the net
Shal seldome surfyt of the pray they take,
Of thinges to cum the haps be so unset   185
That none but fooles may warrant of them make:
The full assured, succes doth oft forsake.
For Fortune findeth none so fyt to flout,
As suresby[1] sots whych cast no kinde of doute.

    How sayest thou Henry Hotspur, do I lye?   190
For thou right manly gavest the king a feeld,
And there was slayn because thou wouldest not fly:
Sir Thomas Percie thine uncle[2] (forst to yeeld)
Did cast his head (a wunder seen but seeld)
From Shrewsbury town to the top of London bridge.   195
Lo thus fond hope did theyr both lives abridge.

    Whan Henry king this victory had wunne,
Destroyed the Percies, put their power to flyght,
He did appoynt prince Henry his eldest sunne
With all his power to meete me if he might[3]:   200
But I discumfit through my partners fight
Had not the hart to mete him face to face,
But fled away, and he pursued the chase.

    Now Baldwin marke, for I, cald prince of Wales,
And made beleve I should be he in dede,   205
Was made to flye among the hilles and dales,[4]
Where al my men forsooke me at my nede.
Who trusteth loyterers seeld hath lucky spede:
And whan the captaynes corage doth him fayle
His souldiers hartes a litle thing may quayle.   210

[1] cocksure, rash.   [2] The Earl of Worcester, condemned in V.5.
[3] V.5.39–40.   [4] After the peace in 1407.

And so Prince Henry chased me, that loe
I found no place wherein I might abide:
For as the dogges purseu the selly[1] doe,
The brach[2] behind the houndes on every side,
So traste they me among the mountaynes wide: 215
Whereby I found I was the hartles hare
And not the beast Colprophete[3] did declare.

And at the last: like as the litle roche[4]
Must eyther be eat, or leape upon the shore
Whan as the hungry pickrel[5] doth approch, 220
And there find death which it eskapte before:
So double death assaulted me so sore
That eyther I must unto my enmy yeeld,
Or starve for hunger in the barayne feeld.[6]

Here shame and payne a whyle were at a strife, 225
Payne prayed me yeeld, shame bade me rather fast:
The one bad spare, the other spend my life,
But shame (shame have it) overcam at last.
Than hunger gnew, that doth the stone wall brast
And made me eat both gravell, durt and mud, 230
And last of all, my dung, my fleshe, and blud.[7]

This was mine ende to horrible to heare,
Yet good ynough for a life that was so yll.
Wherby (O Baldwin) warne all men to beare
Theyr youth such love, to bring them up in skill 235
Byd Princes flye Colprophetes lying byll:
And not presume to clime above their states,
For they be faultes that foyle men, not their fates.

(b)   HENRY PERCY,
              EARL OF NORTHUMBERLAND

          How Henry Percy Earle of Northhum-
            berland, was for his covetous and
               trayterous attempt put to
                    death at Yorke.

---

[1] simple, harmless.　　[2] bitch.　　[3] the wizard.　　[4] roach.
[5] young pike.　　[6] Cf. Henry of Mortimer, I.3.89.
[7] In *2H4* III.1.102-3, Warwick announces his death, but he was alive in 1416.

O Morall Senec true find I thy saying,
That neyther kinsfolke, ryches, strength, or favour
Are free from Fortune, but are ay decaying:
No worldly welth is ought save doubtful labour,
Mans life in earth is like unto a tabour:
Which now to mirth doth mildly men provoke
And strayt to war, with a more sturdy stroke.

All this full true I Percy find by proofe,
Which whilom was erle of Northumberland:
And therefore (Baldwin) for my Piers behoof   10
To note mens falles sith thou hast tane in hand,
I would thou shouldest my state well understand:
For fewe kinges were more then I redouted,
Through double Fortune lyfted up and louted.

As for my kinne their noblenes is knowen,
My valiauntise were folly for to prayse,
Wherthrough the Scottes so oft were overthrowen
That who but I was doubted in my dayes:
And that kyng Rychard found at all assayes,
For never Scottes rebelled in his rayne   20
But through my force were eyther caught or slayne.

A brother I had was Erle of Worcester
Alwayes in favour and office with the king,
And by my wife Dame Elinor Mortimer,
I had a son which so the Scottes did sting,
That being yong, and but a very spring
Syr Henry Hotspur they gave him to name,
And though I say it, he did deserve the same.

We thre tryumphed in king Richards time,
Til Fortune ought both him and us a spite: 30
But chiefly me, whom clere from any crime,
My king did banish from his favour quite,
And openly proclaymed trayterous knight:
Wherethrough false slaunder forced me to be
That which before I did most deadly flee.

Let men beware how they true folke defame,
Or threaten on them the blame of vices nought,
For infamy bredeth wrath, wreke foloweth shame:
Eke open slaunder, oftentimes hath brought

That to effect, that erst was never thought: 40
To be misdemed men suffer in a sort,
But none can beare the griefe of misreport.

  Because my king did shame me wrongfully,
I hated him, and in dede became his foe:
And while he did at war in Ireland lye,
I did conspire to turne his weale to woe[1]:
And through the duke of Yorke and other moe,
All royall power from him we quickely tooke
And gave the same to Henry Boleynbroke.

  Neyther dyd we this alonely for this cause,   50
But to say truth, force drave us to the same:
For he dispising god and all good lawes
Slew whom he would, made sinne a very game.[2]
And seing neither age nor counsayle could him tame,
We thought it wel done for the kingdomes sake,
To leave his rule that did al rule forsake.

  But whan sir Henry had attaynde his place,
He strayt becam in all poyntes wurse than he:
Destroyed the piers, & slewe kyng Rychards grace,
Against his othe made to the lordes and me[3]:   60
And seking quarelles how to disagre,
He shamelesly required me and my sonne
To yeld him Scottes which we in field had wun.[4]

  My Nephew also Edmund Mortymer
The very heyre apparaunt to the Crowne,
Whom Owen Glendour held as prisoner,
Vilely bound, in dungeon depe cast downe,
He would not raunsum: but did felly frowne
Agaynst my brother and me that for him spake,[5]
And him proclaymed traytour for our sake.   70

  This fowle despite did cause us to conspire
To put him downe as we did Richard erst,
And that we might this matter set on fyre

---

[1] *R2* II.1.263ff.   [2] *R2* II.1.243-6.
[3] In *R2* Percy is less favourably treated.   [4] *1H4* I.1.91-4.
[5] Cf. *1H4* I.3, where Hotspur bears the brunt of Henry's anger.

From Owens jayle, our cosin we remerst,
And unto Glendour all our griefes reherst,
Who made a bonde with Mortymer and me
To pryve the king, and part the realme in thre.

But whan king Henry heard of this devise
Toward Owen Glendour he sped him very quyck
Mynding by force to stop our enterprise: 80
And as the devell would, then fell I sick,
Howbeit my brother, & sonne, more politike
Than prosperous, with an oast[1] fro Scotland brought,
Encountred him at Shrewsbury, wher they fought.

The one was tane and kild, the other slayne,
And shortly after was Owen put to flight:
By meanes wherof I forced was to fayne
That I knew nothing of the former fight.
Fraude oft avayles more than doth sturdy might:
For by my fayning I brought him in belief   90
I knew not that wherin my part was chief.[2]

And while the king thus tooke me for his frend
I sought all meanes my former wrong to wreake,
Which that I might bring to the sooner ende
To the bishop of Yorke I did the matter breake,[3]
And to th'erle Marshall[4] likewise did I speake,
Whose father was through Henries cause exyled,
The bishops brother[5] with trayterous death defiled.

These strayt assented to do what they could,
So did lorde Hastinges and lord Fauconbridge: 100
Which altogether promised they would
Set all their power the kinges dayes to abridge.[6]
Be se the spite, before the byrdes wer flidge
The king had woord, and seysoned on the nest
Wherby alas my frendes wer al opprest.

---

[1] a host.   [2] Shakespeare ignores this.
[3] In *1H4* IV.4 the Archbishop, anticipating defeat at Shrewsbury, writes to the 'lord Marshal' & 'my cousin Scroop'.
[4] Lord Mowbray, son of the Norfolk in *R2*.
[5] Wiltshire, slain at Bristol (*R2* III.2). Not his brother.
[6] In *2H4* I.3 the others doubt Percy's assistance.

The bluddy tyrant brought them all to ende
Excepted me, which into Scotland skapte[1]
To George of Dunbar th'erle of March, my frend,
Who in my cause al that he could ey skrapte:
And when I had for greater succour gapte   110
Both at the Frenchman and the Flemminges hand,
And could get none, I toke such as I fand.

And with the helpe of George my very frend,
I did invade Northumberlande ful bold,
Whereas the folke drew to me stil unend,
Bent to the death my party to uphold:
Through helpe of these ful many a fort and hold,
The which the king right manfully had mand,
I easely wunne, and seysed in my hand.

Not so content (for vengeaunce drave me on)   120
I entred Yorkeshire there to waste and spoyle,
But ere I had far in the countrey gon
The shirif therof, Rafe Rekesby did assoyle
My troubled hoost of much part of our toyle,
For he assauting freshly, tooke through power
Me and lord Bardolph both at Bramham more.[2]

And thence conveyed us to the towne of Yorke
Until he knew, what was the kinges entent:
There loe Lord Bardolf kinder than the Storke,
Did lose his head, which was to London sent,   130
With whom for frendshippe mine in like case went.
This was my hap, my fortune, or my fawte,
This life I led, and thus I came to naught.

Wherefore good Baldwin wil the pyers take hede
Of slaunder, malyce, and conspiracy,
Of covetise, whence al the rest procede:
For covetise joynt with contumacy,
Doth cause all mischief in mens hartes to brede.
Ad therfore this to *Esperance*,[3] my wurd.
Who causeth bludshed shall not skape the swurd.   140

---

[1] Cf. *2H4* II.3: IV.1. He flees to Scotland, abandoning his friends.
[2] Briefly mentioned in *2H4* IV.4.97–101.
[3] 'Hope': the Percy motto.

III. Probable Source

From THE FIRST FOWRE BOOKES OF THE CIVILE WARS BETWEEN THE TWO HOUSES OF LANCASTER AND YORKE

by Samuel Daniel (1595)

BOOK III

[Having seized the throne, Henry IV is faced with many difficulties. He fails to conquer either the Scots or the Welsh.]

86

And yet new *Hydraes* lo, new heades appeare[1]
T'afflict that peace reputed then so sure,
And gave him much to do, and much to feare,
And long and daungerous tumults did procure,
And those even of his chiefest followers were
Of whom he might presume him most secure,
Who whether not so grac'd or so prefer'd
As they expected, these new factions stir'd.

87

The *Percyes* were the men, men of great might,
Strong in alliance, and in courage strong
That thus conspire, under pretence to right
The crooked courses they had suffered long:
Whether their conscience urg'd them or despight,
Or that they saw the part they tooke was wrong,
Or that ambition hereto did them call,
Or others envide grace, or rather all.

88

What cause soever were, strong was their plot,
Their parties great, meanes good, th'occasion fit:
Their practice close, their faith suspected not,
Their states far off and they of wary wit:

---

[1] Cf. the same image in a different context, *1H4* V.4.25.

Who with large promises draw in the Scot
To ayde their cause, he likes, and yeeldes to it,
Not for the love of them or for their good,
But glad hereby of meanes to shed our bloud.

89

Then joyne they with the *Welsh,* who fitly train'd
And all in armes under a mightie head
Great *Glendowr,* who long warr'd, and much attain'd,[1]
Sharp conflicts made, and many vanquished:
With whom was *Edmond Earle* of *March*[2] retain'd
Being first his prisoner, now confedered,
A man the king much fear'd, and well he might
Least he should looke whether his Crown stood right.

90

For *Richard,* for the quiet of the state,
Before he tooke those *Irish* warres in hand
About succession doth deliberate,[3]
And finding how the certaine right did stand,
With full consent this man did ordinate
The heyre apparent in the crowne and land:
Then judge if this the king might nerely touch,
Although his might were smal, his right being much.

91

With these the *Percyes* them confederate,
And as three heades they league in one intent,
And instituting a Triumvirate
Do part the land in triple goverment[4]:
Deviding thus among themselves the state,
The *Percyes* should rule all the *North* from *Trent*
And *Glendowr Wales*: the *Earle* of *March* should bee
Lord of the *South* from *Trent*; and thus they gree.

---

[1] *In margin:* 'Owen Glendor.'
[2] An error. Mortimer was not the Earl of March.
[3] *In margin:* 'Rich. 2nd.' Cf. *1H4* I.3.145–58.
[4] III.1.71ff.

14—N.D.S.S. 4

92

Then those two helpes which still such actors find
Pretence of common good, the kings disgrace
Doth fit their course, and draw the vulgar mind
To further them and aide them in this case:
The king they accus'd for cruell, and unkind
That did the state, and crowne, and all deface;
A perjurde man that held all faith in skorne,[1]
Whose trusted othes had others made forsworne.

93

Besides the odious detestable act
Of that late murdered king they aggravate,
Making it his that so had will'd the fact
That he the doers did remunerate:
And then such taxes daily doth exact
That were against the orders of the state,[2]
And with all these or worse they him assail'd
Who late of others with the like prevail'd.

94

Thus doth contentious proud mortality
Afflict each other and itselfe torment:
And thus o thou mind-tortring misery
Restles ambition, borne in discontent,
Turn'st and retossest with iniquity
The unconstant courses frailty did invent:
And fowl'st faire order and defil'st the earth
Fostring up warre, father of bloud and dearth.

95

Great seem'd the cause, and greatly to, did ad
The peoples love thereto these crimes rehearst,
That manie gathered to the troupes they had
And many more do flocke from costs disperst:
But when the king had heard these newes so bad,
Th'unlookt for dangerous toyle more nearly perst;
For bent t'wards *Wales* t'appease those tumults there,
H'is forc't divert his course, and them forbeare.

---

[1] Cf. IV.3.101: 'Broke oath on oath, committed wrong on wrong.'
[2] Cf. IV.3.92: 'task'd the whole state'.

96

Not to give time unto th'increasing rage
And gathering fury, forth he hastes with speed,
Lest more delay or giving longer age
To th'evill growne, it might the cure exceed:
All his best men at armes, and leaders sage
All he prepar'd he could, and all did need;
For to a mighty worke thou goest o king,
To such a field that power to power shall bring.

97

There shall young *Hotespur* with a fury lead
Meete with thy forward sonne as fierce as he[1]:
There warlike *Worster* long experienced
In forraine armes, shall come t'incounter thee:
There *Dowglas* to thy *Stafford* shall make head:
There *Vernon* for thy valiant *Blunt* shalbe:
There shalt thou find a doubtfull bloudy day,
Though sicknesse keepe *Northumberland* away.[2]

98

Who yet reserv'd, though after quit for this,
Another tempest on thy head to raise,
As if still wrong revenging *Nemesis*
Did meane t'afflict all thy continuall dayes[3]:
And yet this field he happely might misse
For thy great good, and therefore well he staies:
What might his force have done being joyn'd thereto
When that already gave so much to do?

99

The swift approch and unexpected speed
The king had made upon this new-rais'd force
In th'unconfirmed troupes much feare did breed,
Untimely hindring their intended course;
The joyning with the *Welsh* they had decreed
Was hereby stopt, which made their part the worse,
Northumberland with forces from the *North*
Expected to be there, was not set forth.[4]

---

[1] *In margin:* 'The son to the Earle of Northumberland.'
[2] IV.1.16–44.   [3] III.2.4–7.
[4] Shakespeare's Hotspur already knows not to expect his father.

100

And yet undaunted *Hotspur* seeing the king
So nere approch'd, leaving the worke in hand
With forward speed his forces marshalling,
Sets forth his farther comming to withstand:
And with a cheerfull voice incouraging
By his great spirit his well imboldened band,
Bringes a strong host of firme resolved might,
And plac'd his troupes before the king in sight.

101

This day (saith he) o faithfull valiaunt frendes,
What ever it doth give, shall glorie give:
This day with honor frees our state, or endes
Our misery with fame, that still shall live,
And do but thinke how well this day he spendes
That spendes his bloud his countrey to relieve[1]:
Our holie cause, our freedome, and our right,
Sufficient are to move good mindes to fight.

102

Besides th'assured hope of victory
That wee may even promise on our side
Against this weake-constrained companie,
Whom force & feare, not will, and love doth guide
Against a prince whose foule impiety
The heavens do hate, the earth cannot abide,
Our number being no lesse, our courage more,
What need we doubt if we but worke therefore.

103

This said, and thus resolv'd even bent to charge
Upon the king, who well their order view'd
And carefull noted all the forme at large
Of their proceeding, and their multitude:
And deeming better if he could discharge
The day with safetie, and some peace conclude,
Great proffers sendes of pardon, and of grace
If they would yeeld, and quietnes imbrace.[2]

---

[1] V.3.91–5.
[2] Cf. Blunt, IV.3.30–51, and the King, V.1.104–14.

104

But this refus'd,[1] the king with wrath incens'd
Rage against fury doth with speed prepare:
And o saith he, though I could have dispens'd
With this daies bloud, which I have sought to spare
That greater glory might have recompens'd
The forward worth of these that so much dare,
That we might honor had by th'overthrown
That th'wounds we make, might not have bin our own.

105

Yet since that other mens iniquity
Calles on the sword of wrath against my will,
And that themselves exact this cruelty,
And I constrained am this bloud to spill:
Then on my maisters, on couragiously
True-harted subjects against traitors ill,
And spare them not who seeke to spoile us all,
Whose fowle confused end soone see you shall.

106

Straight moves with equall motion equall rage
The like incensed armies unto bloud,
One to defend, another side to wage
Foule civill war, both vowes their quarrell good:
Ah too much heate to bloud doth nowe inrage
Both who the deed provokes and who withstood,
That valor here is vice, here manhood sin,
The forward'st hands doth o least honor win.

107

But now begin these fury-moving soundes
The notes of wrath that musicke brought from hell,
The ratling drums which trumpets voice confounds,
The cryes, th'incouragements, the shouting shrell;
That all about the beaten ayre reboundes,
Thundring confused, murmurs horrible,
To rob all sence except the sence to fight,
Well handes may worke, the mind hath lost his sight.

---

[1] Contrast Hotspur's temporising in IV.3.107–13, and Worcester's misrepresentations in V.2.

108

O war! begot in pride and luxury,
The child of wrath and of dissention,
Horrible good; mischiefe necessarie,
The fowle reformer of confusion,
Unjust-just scourge of our iniquitie,
Cruell recurer of corruption:
O that these sin-sicke states in need should stand
To be let bloud with such a boystrous hand!

109

And o how well thou hadst been spar'd this day
Had not wrong counsail'd *Percy* bene pervers,
Whose yong undanger'd hand[1] now rash makes way
Upon the sharpest fronts of the most fierce:
Where now an equall fury thrusts to stay[2]
And rebeat-backe that force and his disperse,
Then these assaile, then those chace backe againe,
Till staid with new-made hils of bodies slaine.

110

There lo that new-appearing glorious starre
Wonder of Armes, the terror of the field
Young *Henrie*, laboring where the stoutest are,
And even the stoutest forces back to yeild,
There is that hand boldned to bloud and warre
That must the sword in woundrous actions weild:
But better hadst thou learn'd with others bloud
A lesse expence to us, to thee more good.

111

Hadst thou not there lent present speedy ayd
To thy indaungerde father nerely tyrde,
Whom fierce incountring *Dowglas* overlaid,
That day had there his troublous life expirde[3]:
Heroycall Couragious *Blunt* araid[4]
In habite like as was the king attirde
And deem'd for him, excus'd that fate with his,
For he had what his Lord did hardly misse.

---

[1] Daniel's Hotspur is young, like the Prince; cf. III.2.103.
[2] *In margin:* 'The Prince of Wales.'
[3] Shakespeare uses this incident in V.4.25–44.
[4] *In margin:* 'Which was sir Walter Blunt.' V.3.1–24.

112

For thought a king he would not now disgrace
The person then suppos'd, but princelike shewes
Glorious effects of worth that fit his place,
And fighting dyes, and dying overthrowes:
Another of that forward name and race
In that hotte worke his valiant life bestowes,
Who bare the standard of the king that day,[1]
Whose colours overthrowne did much dismaie.

113

And deare it cost, and o much bloud is shed
To purchase thee this loosing victory
O travayl'd king: yet hast thou conquered
A doubtfull day, a mightie enemy:
But o what woundes, what famous worth lyes dead!
That makes the winner looke with sorrowing eye,
Magnanimous *Stafford* lost that much had wrought,
And valiant *Shorly* who great glory gote.[2]

114

Such wracke of others bloud thou didst behold
O furious *Hotspur*, ere thou lost thine owne!
Which now once lost that heate in thine waxt cold,
And soone became thy Armie overthrowne;
And o that this great spirit, this courage bold,
Had in some good cause bene rightly showne!
So had not we thus violently then
Have term'd that rage, which valor should have ben.[3]

IV. Probable Source

From THE CHRONICLES OF ENGLAND
by John Stow (1580)

The Chronicles of England, from Brute unto this present yeare of Christ, 1580, Collected by John Stow Citizen

---

[1] *In margin:* 'Another Blunt which was the kings Standard bearer.'
[2] *In margin:* 'Sir Hugh Shorly.' V.4.40–1.
[3] This touches on a main theme of *1H4*, the nature of true honour, or valour.

of London. Printed at London by Ralphe Newberie,
at the assignement of Henrie Bynneman. [1580]

(a)   [An affray in Eastcheap.]

[p. 573]   Upon the even of *Saint John Baptist* the kings sonne[1]
being in *Eastcheap* at supper, after midnight, betwixt two and three
of the clocke, a great debate hapned betweene his men and men of
the Courte, lasting an hourse, til the Mayor and Sherifes with other
Citizens ceased the same: for the which afterward the sayde Mayor,
Sherifes, and Aldermen, were sent for to appeare before the Kyng,
to aunsweare: at whych the King with his sonnes, and diverse other
Lordes, were highly moved againste the Citie, where through
William Gascoigne chiefe Justice, [they] enquired of the Mayor and
Aldermen, for the Citizens, whether they woulde put them in the
King's grace, whereunto they aunswered, they had not offended the
Kyng nor his sonnes, but according to law stanched the debates:
then the King seeing it woulde be none otherwyse, forgave altogither,
and they departed. . . .

(b)   [The Prince visits his father.]

[pp. 576–9]   Kyng Henrie kept his Christmasse [1412] at his
manour of *Eltham*, being so sore sick, that sometime men thought
that he had bin dead: notwithstanding it pleased God that he
recovered his strength againe a little.

After Christmasse he called the Nobles of the realm togither to a
Parliament at *London*, but he lived not to the end thereof, for now
after the great and fortunate chaunces hapned to him,[2] and being
delivered of all Civill division, hee was taken with sicknesse, of the
which he languished til his appointed houre, during which sickenesse, some evil disposed people laboured to make dissention
betweene the King and the Prince his sonne, by reason whereof, and
by the acte of youth, which he exercised more than meanely[3] and for
the great recourse of people unto him, of whom his Court was at all
times more aboundant that the King his father, the King suspected
that he would presume to usurpe the crown, he being alive: which
suspitious jealousie was occasion that he in part withdrewe his affection and singular love from the Prince. But when this noble Prince
was advertised of his fathers jealousie, he disguised himself in a gown

---

[1] Cf. *Two London Chronicles from the Collection of John Stow* (Camden Misc., x
1910, p.1): 'The xi yere of his reygne began the alaye of goulde; and the kyngs sons
betyn in the Chepe.' This would be 1410. Prince Henry may not have been
involved.

[2] *In margin:* 'Titus Livius.'   [3] than is usual, average.

of blew satten, made full of small Eylet holes, and at every Eylet the needle wherwith it was made hanging stil by a threede of silke. And about his arme he ware a dogges coller set ful of *SS* of golde and the Tirets[1] of the same also of fine gold. Thus apparelled, with a great companye of Lordes and other noblemen of his Court, he came to the King his father, who at that time laye at *Westminster*, where at his comming (by his owne commaundment) not one of his companye avaunced himselfe further than the fire in the Hall, notwithstanding that they were greatly and ofte desired to the contrarie, by the Lordes and great estates of the King's Court: and that the Prince had commanded, to give the lesse occasion of mistrust to the King his father, but he himselfe only accompanyed of the King's house, passed forth to the King his Father, to whom (after due salutation) he desired to shewe the intent of his minde in secrete manner. Then the Kyng caused himselfe to be borne in his chayre into his secrete chamber (bycause he was deseased and might not goe) wher in the presence of three or foure persons, in whom the King had most confidence, he commaunded the Prince to shewe the effect of his minde. Then the Prince kneeling down before his Father, saide to him these wordes, 'Most redoubted Lord and Father, I am this time come to your presence, as your liegman, and as your sonne naturall, in all thyngs to obay your grace as my soveraigne Lord and father. And whereas I understand yee have me suspect of my behaviour against your grace, and that yee feare I would usurpe your Crowne against the pleasure of your highnesse, of my conversation youre grace knoweth that if yee were in feare of any man, of what estate soever he were, my duetie were to the endaungering of my life to punishe that person, thereby to race that sore from your hearte. And then howe much rather oughte I to suffer death to bring your grace from the feare that yee have of me that am your naturall sonne, and your liegeman. And to that intente I have thys daye by confession and receyving the Sacramente, prepared my selfe, and therefore moste redoubted Lorde and Father, I beseeche you in the honour of God, for the easing of your harte, heretofore your knees to slea me with this dagger,' And at that worde wyth all reverence he delivered to the King hys dagger, saying, 'My Lorde and Father, my lyfe is not so desirous to mee, that I woulde live one daye that should be to you displeasure, nor I covet not so much my life as I doe your pleasure and welfare, and in your thus doing, here in the presence of these Lordes, and tofore God at the daye of judgemente I clearelye forgive you my death.'

At these wordes of the Prince, the King taken with compassion of

---

[1] rings (for the leash).

hearte, cast from him the dagger and imbracing the Prince kissed him, and with effusion of teares saide unto him, 'My right deare and hartily beloved sonne, it is of trueth that I had you partly suspecte, and as I now perceyve, undeserved on your partie: but seeing this your humilitie and faithfulnesse, I shall neyther slay you, nor from henceforth have you any more in mistrust, for no report that shall be made unto me, and thereof I assure you upon mine honor.' Thus by his great wisedome was the wrongfull imagination of his Fathers hate utterly avoyded, and hymselfe restored to the Kings former grace and favour.

After thys, as was reported by the Earle of *Ormonde* (to the translatour of myne author *Titus Livius*) the King gave to his sonne the Prince, diverse notable doctrines, and insignments, among which eruditions, one is this: the King lying grievously diseased, called before him the Prince his sonne, and sayd unto him: 'My sonne, I feare me sore after my departure from this life, some discord shal grow and arise betweene thee and thy brother Thomas Duke of *Clarence*, whereby the realme may be brought to destruction and miserie, for I knowe you both to be of greate stomacke and courage. Wherefore I feare that he through his high mynde wyll make some enterprise against thee, intending to usurpe upon thee, whiche I knowe thy stomacke maye not abyde easily. And for dreade hereof, as ofte as it is in my remembraunce, I soare repente me, that ever I charged my selfe with the Crowne of this Realme.'

To these wordes of the King the Prince aunsweared thus: 'Righte redoubted Lorde and Father to the pleasure of GOD your grace shall long continue with us, and rule us both: but if God have so provided that ever I shall succeede you in thys Realme, I shall honour and love my brethren above all menne, as long as they be to me true, faythfull and obediente, as to theyr soveraigne Lord, but if anye of them fortune to conspyre or rebell againste mee, I assure you I shall as soone execute justice uppon one of them, as I shall upon the worst and most simplest person within this your Realme.'

The Kyng hearing thys aunsweare, was therewith marvellouslye rejoyced in hys mynde, and sayde: 'My deare and wel beloved Sonne, wyth thys aunswere thou haste deliverd mee of a greate and ponderous agonye: and I beseech thee, and uppon my blessing charge thee, that like as thou haste sayde, so thou minister justice equally, and in no wise suffer not them that be oppressed long to call upon thee for Justice, but redresse oppressions, and indifferently, and without delay, for no perswasion of flatterers, or of them that bee partiall, or suche as use to have their handes replenished wyth gyftes, deferre not Justice untill to morrowe, of that thou mayste doe Justice thys daye, leaste (peradventure) GOD doe Justice on thee in the meane tyme, and take from thee thyne authoritye: remember, that the wealth of thy body and thy soule, and of thy Realme, resteth in the execution of Justice, and doe not thy Justice, so that thou be called a Tyraunte, but use thy selfe meanely betwixte Justice and mercie in those things that belong to thee. . . . And in thy selfe eschew al vaineglorie and elation of heart, following the holesome counsell of the Psalmist, (which sayeth) *Non nobis Domine, non nobis, sed nomini tuo da gloriam* (which Not unto us Lord, not unto us, but to thy holy Name be given laude and praise.[1] These and many other admonishments and doctrines this victorious king gave unto this noble prince his sonne[2]: who with effect followed the same, after the death of his father: whereby he obtained grace of our Lorde to attaine to gret victories and many glories and incredible conquests, through the helpe and succoure of our Lord, whereof he was never destitute.

(c)   [The Prince as highwayman.]

[p. 582] Whilst his father lived, beying accompanyed with some of his yong Lordes and gentlemen, he wold waite in disguised araye for his owne receyvers, and distresse them of theyr money: and sometimes at suche enterprises both he and his company wer surely beaten: and when his receivers made to him their complaints, how they were robbed in their comming unto him, he would give them discharge of so much money as they had lost, and besides that, they should not depart from him without great rewards for their trouble and vexation, especially they should be rewarded that best hadde resisted hym and his company, and of whom he hadde receyved the greatest and most strokes. But after the decease of his father, was never any youth, or wildnes, that might have place in him, but all his actes were sodainely chaunged into gravitie and discreation.

V. Historical Analogue

SIR JOHN FASTOLF OF NACTON[3]

(a) Hugh Fastolf and John Organ, citizens of London, acknowledge that they owe to John de Cobham, lord Cobham, 800 marks, to be paid to him at the feast of Pentecost next; and, unless they do

[1] Recalled in *H5* after Agincourt, IV.8.110–19.
[2] Cf. *1H4* III.2 and *2H4* IV.5.
[3] From 'The Two Sir John Fastolfs', by L. W. V. Harcourt, in *Transactions of the Royal Historical Society*, Series 3, Vol. IV, 1910, pp. 47–62.

so, they concede that the aforesaid moneys shall be raised from their lands and chattels in London, and in the counties of Essex, Norfolk and Suffolk, and elsewhere. Witness the King at Westminster, the 28th day of March.

(*b*) The jury, between John de Cobham, lord Cobham, by his attorney, plaintiff, and John Fastolf, knight, son and heir of Hugh Fastolf late citizen of London, summoned to find, etc., whether the aforesaid John Fastolf, on the 3rd day of December in the first year of the reign of our present lord King, or at any time afterwards, held the manors of Bradwell, Olton and Kyrkele with their appurtenances in the county aforesaid, which belonged to the aforesaid Hugh after the 28th day of March in the 3rd year of the reign of our lord King Richard, late King of England the second after the conquest, on which day the said Hugh Fastolf and John Organ, then citizens of London, now deceased, in the chancery of the same late King, acknowledged that they owed to the aforesaid John de Cobham 800 marks, as it is alleged, or no, is respited before the lord King until fifteen days from Easter day, wherever, etc., owing to the default of jurors because none, etc. Therefore let the sheriff have their bodies etc., and eight such are appointed, etc. The same day is given to the parties aforesaid.

(*c*) (England.) Memorandum that on Thursday next before the quindene of Hilary in this same term before the lord King at Westminster, came Adam Cliston, knight, of the county of Norfolk, William Calthorp, knight, of the same county, John Wilton, knight, of the same county, and John Norwich of the county of Suffolk, in their own persons, and mainperned for John Fastolf, knight, then present in court, that he would thenceforth be of good behaviour towards the lord King and all his people, and especially towards twelve jurors impanelled and on the said quindene sworn before the King [in the suit] between John lord Cobham, plaintiff, and the said John Fastolf, defendant, upon a certain acknowledgement of 800 marks made in the Chancery of the lord King, as more fully appears by the record before the said King, that the same John Fastolf will not do or cause to be done, by himself or others, to the same jurors or any of them or any of the people of the lord King, damage or bodily hurt, by threats, assaults, insults, or any other means which might in any manner tend to a lesion or disturbance of the peace of the lord King, each of the mainpernors under penalty of 200*l.*, and the said John Fastolf, under penalty of 500*l.*, which 200*l.*, each of the said mainpernors by himself, and which 500*l*, the said John Fastolf, acknowledged that they owed to the lord King to be raised out of the lands and chattels of them and each of them to the King's use according to the mainprise aforesaid, if the said John Fastolf should make default in the premises or any of the premises and therefore be lawfully convicted.

VI. Analogue

From A NEW ENTERLUDE CALLED THERSYTES

Anonymous

A new Enterlude called Thersytes. Thys Enterlude Folowynge Dothe Declare howe that the greatest boesters are not the greatest doers. [Colophon] Imprinted at London, by John Tysdale and are to be solde at hys shop in the upper ende of Lombard strete, in Alhallowes churche yarde neare untoo grace church. [n.d. 1560?][1]

Thersites commeth in fyrste havinge a clubbe uppon his necke

Have in a russler[2] foorth of the Greke lande
Called Thersites, if ye wyll me knowe.
Abacke, geve me roume, in my way do ye not stand
For if ye do, I wyll soone laye you lowe.
In Homere of my actes ye have red I trow.
Neyther Agamemnon nor Ulysses, I spared to checke.
They coulde not bringe me to be at theyr becke.
Of late frome the sege of Troye I retourned
Where all my harnes excepte this clubbe I lost
In an olde house where it was quyte burned   10
Whyle I was preparinge vytayles for the hoste.
I must nedes get me newe, what so ever it cost.
I wyll go seke adventures, for I can not be ydle.
I wyll hamper some of the knaves in a brydle.
It greveth me to heare howe the knaves do bragge
But by supreme Jupiter, when I am harnessed well
I shall make the dasters[3] to renne in to a bagge
To hyde them fro me, as from the devyll of hell.

---

[1] Punctuation modernised.   [2] A bustling fellow.   [3] dastards.

I doubte not but hereafter, of me ye shall heare tell
Howe I have made the knaves for to play cowch quaile.[1]   20
But nowe to the shop of Mulciber, to go I wyll not faile.

    Mulciber must have a shop made in the place and Thersites
       commethe before it sayinge a loude

Mulciber, whom the Poetes doth call the god of fyer,
Smith unto Jupiter kinge over all,
Come foorth, of thy office I the desyre
And graunte me my petition, I aske a thinge but small. . . .

[He gets from Mulciber a sallet (helmet), a habergeon, arm-irons
and a sword. All the time he boasts.]

O good lorde howe brode is my brest   143
And stronge with all for hole is my chest.
He that should medle with me shall have shrewde rest.
Beholde you my handes, my legges and my feete,
Every parte is stronge proportionable and mete.
Thinke you that I am not feared in felde and strete?
Yes yes god wote, they gette me the wall
Or elles with my clubbe, I make them to fall.
Backe knaves I saye to them, then for feare they quake
And take me then to the taverne and good chere me make.
The proctoure and his men I made to renne their waies
And some wente to hide them in broken heys.
I tell you at a woorde
I set not a torde
By none of them al.
Early and late I wyll walke
And London stretes stalke
Spyte of them greate and small   160
For I thinke verely
That none in heaven so hye
Nor yet in hell so lowe
Whyle I have this clubbe in my hande
Can be able me to withstande
Or me to overthrowe

[Determined to seek adventures he rebuffs his mother and brags of
what he will do.]

Where is Robin John and Little Hode?   317
Approche hyther quickely if ye thinke it good.

    [1] hide and seek.

I wyll teache suche outlawes wyth Chrystes curses
How they take hereafter awaye abbottes purses.[1]
Whye wyll no adventure appeare in thys place?
where is Hercules with his greate mase?
where is Busyris, that fed hys horses
Full lyke a tyraunte, with dead mens corses?
Come any of you bothe
And I make an othe
That yer I eate anye breade
I wyll dryve a wayne
Ye[a] for neede twayne
Betwene your bodye and your heade.   330
Thus passeth my braynes.
Wyll none take the paynes
To trye wyth me a blowe?
O what a fellowe am I
whome everye man dothe flye
That dothe me but once knowe!

[Thersites encounters a snail and is terrified. Miles, 'a pore souldiour come of late from Calice' watches him with amusement.]

Plucke in thy hornes thou unhappy beast.   438
What, facest thou me? wilte not thou be in reste?
Why? wylte not thou thy hornes in holde?
Thinkest thou that I am a cockolde?
Goddes armes, the monster cometh towarde me styll.
Excepte I fyght manfully, it wyll me surely kyll.

Then he must fyghte against the snayle with his club

Miles.

O Jupiter Lorde doest thou not see and heare
How he feareth the snayle as it were a bere!

Thersites.

Well with my clubbe I have had good lucke.
Nowe with my sworde have at the a plucke.

And he must cast his club awaye.

I wyll make the or I go, for to ducke
And thou were as tal[l]e a man as Frier Tucke.   450

---

[1] As Robin Hood did in the ballad.

I saye yet agayne thy hornes in drawe
Or elles I wyll make the to have woundes rawe.
Arte not thou aferde
To have thy bearde
Pared with my swearde?

*Here he must fighte then with his sworde against the snayle, and the
snayle draweth her hornes in.*

Ah well: nowe no more.
Thou mightest have done so before
I layed at it so sore
That it thoughte it shoulde have be lore[1]
And it had not drawen in his hornes againe   460
Surelye I woulde the monster have slaine.
But now farewell, I wyll worke the no more payne.
Nowe my fume is paste
And dothe no longer laste
That I did to the monster cast.
Now in other countries both farre and neare
Mo dedes of chyvalrye I wyll go inquere.

Miles.

Thou nedes not seke any further for redy I am here.
I wyll debate anone I trowe thy bragginge chere.

Thersites.

Nowe where is any mo that wyll me assayle?   470
I wyll turne him and tosse him bothe toppe and tayle
Yf he be stronger then Sampson was
Who with his bare handes kylde lyons apas.[2]

Miles.

What nedeth this booste? I am here at hande
That with the will fighte, kepe the heade and stande.
Surelye for al thy hye wordes I wyll not feare
To assaye the a towche tyll some bloude apeare.
I wyll geve the somewhat for the gifte of a newe yeare.

[1] lost.   [2] apace, quickly.

And he begynth to fight with him, but Thersites must ren awaye,
and hyde hym behynde hys mothers backe sayinge.

Thersites.

O mother mother, I praye the me hyde,
Throwe some thinge over me and cover me every syde.   480

Mater.

O my sonne what thynge eldyth the?

Thersites.

Mother a thousande horsemen do persecute me.[1]

Mater.

Marye sonne, then it was time to flye.
I blame the not then, thoughe afrayde thou be.
A deadlye wounde thou mightest there sone catche.
One against so manye, is no indyfferente matche.

Thersites.

No mother but if they had bene but ten to one
I woulde not have avoyded but set them uppon,
But seinge they be so many I ran awaye.
Hyde me mother hyde me, I hartely the pray   490
For if they come hyther and here me fynde
To their horses tayles they wyll me bynde
And after that fasshyon hall me and kyll me,
And thoughe I were never so bolde and stoute
To fyghte againste so manye, I shoulde stande in doubte.

Miles.

Thou that doest seke giauntes to conquere
Come foorth if thou dare, and in this place appere.
Fy for shame doest thou so sone take flighte?
Come forth and shewe somewhat of thy myghte.

Thersites.

Hyde me mother, hyde me, and never worde saye.   500

[1] Compare Falstaff's exaggerations, II. 4
15—N.D.S.S. 4

Miles.

Thou old trotte, seyst thou any man come thys waye
Well armed and weaponed and readye to fighte?

Mater.

No forsothe Maister, there came none in my sight.

Miles.

He dyd avoyde in tyme, for withoute doubtes
I woulde have set on his backe some clowtes
Yf I may take him I wyll make all slowches
To beware by him, that they come not in my clowches.

Then he goeth oute, and the mother saith.

Mater.

Come foorth my sonne, youre enemy is gone.
Be not afrayed for hurte thou canst have none.

Then he loketh aboute if he be gone or not, at the last he sayth.

Thersites.

Ywys thou didest wisely who so ever thou be   510
To tarrye no longer to fighte with me,
For with my clubbe I woulde have broken thy skull
Yf thou were as bigge as Hercules bull.
Why thou cowardely knave, no stronger then a ducke
Darest thou trye maystries with me a plucke
Whiche fere nother giauntes nor Jupiters fire bolte
Nor Beelzebub the mayster devyll as ragged as a colte?
I woulde thou wouldest come hyther ones againe.
I thincke thou haddest rather alyve to be slayne.
Come againe and I sweare by my mothers wombe   520
I wyll pull the in peeces no more then my thombe,
And thy braines abrode, I wyll so scatter
That all knaves shall feare, against me to clatter.

[After this in response to a letter from his old enemy Ulysses Thersites
gets his mother to cure Ulysses' son Telemachus of worms. He speaks
ill of her and boasts how he would maltreat Miles.]

Then Miles cometh in sayinge

Miles.

Wylte thou so in deede?
Hye the, make good spede,
I am at hande here prest.   880
But awaye tongue shakynge
And this folysshe crakynge,
Let us trye for the best.
Cowardes make speake apase,
Strypes prove the manne.
Have nowe at thy face,
Keepe of if thou canne.

*And then he muste stryke at hym, and Thersytes muste runne awaye
and leave his clubbe & sworde behynde.*

Miles.

Whye thou lubber, runnest thou awaye
And leavest thy swearde and thy clubbe thee behynde?
Nowe thys is a sure carde, nowe I maye well saye   890
That a coward crakinge here I dyd fynde.
Maysters ye maye see by this playe in sighte
That great barking dogges, do not most byte,
And oft it is sene that the best men in the hoost
Be not suche, that use to bragge moste.
Yf ye wyll avoyde the daunger of confusion
Printe my wordes in harte and marke this conclusion:
Suche gyftes of god that ye excelle in moste
Use them wyth sobernesse and youre selfe never bost.
Seke the laude of God in all that ye doo   900
So shall vertue and honoure come you too.
But if you geve youre myndes: to the sinne of pryde
Vanisshe shall your vertue, your honoure away wil slide,
For pryde is hated of God above
And meekenesse sonest obtaineth his love.
To youre rulers and parentes, be you obediente
Never transgressinge their lawefull commaundemente.
Be ye merye and joyfull at borde and at bedde,
Imagin no traitourye against youre prince and heade,
Love God and feare him and after him youre kinge   910
Whiche is as victorious as anye is lyvinge.
Praye for his grace, with hartes that dothe not fayne

That longe he maye rule us withoute grefe or paine
Beseche ye also that God maye save his quene
Lovely Ladie Jane, & the prince that he hath send them betwen
To augment their joy and the comons felicitie.[1]
Fare ye wel swete audience, god graunt you al prosperite.

Amen.

VII. Analogue

From ENDIMION

by John Lyly

Endimion, The Man in the Moone. Playd before the Queenes Majestie at Greenewich on Candlemas Day at night, by the Chyldren of Paules. Printed by J. Charlewood for the widdow Broome. 1591.

[Sir Tophas the warrior rejects love.]

[In Act II Sc. 2 the pages Dares and Samias are jesting with the maidens Favilla and Scintilla when Sir Tophas comes in with his page Epiton.]

Enter Sir Tophas

DARES   Sir *Tophas*, syr *Tophas* of whom we tolde you: if you bee good wenches make as though you love him, and wonder at him.

FAVIL.   Wee will doo our parts.

DARES   But first let us stand aside, and let him use his garbe, for all consisteth in his gracing.

TOPHAS   *Epi!*

EPI.   At hand syr.

TOP.   How likest thou this Martiall life, where nothing but bloud besprinkleth our bosomes? Let me see, be our enemies fatte?

EPI.   Passing fat: and I would not chaunge this life to be a Lord;

---

[1] Henry VII's Queen Jane Seymour bore a son, later Edward VI, on 12 October, 1537. She died on 24 October. The play must have been finished between those dates. It is a translation from the Latin of a French professor of Rhetoric, Jean Tissier de Travisy (Ravisius Textor) whose *Dialogi* were first printed in 1530 (*Med. St.* ii.456).

and your selfe passeth all comparison, for other Captaines kill and beate, and there is nothing you kill, but you also eate.

TOP. I will drawe out their guttes out of their bellies, and teare the flesh with my teeth, so mortall is my hate, and so eger my unstaunched stomacke.

EPI. [*aside*] My master thinkes himselfe the valiantest man in the world if hee kill a wren: so warlike a thing he accompteth to take away life, though it be from a Larke.

TOP. *Epi*, I finde my thoughts to swell, and my spirite to take winges, in so much that I cannot continue within the compas of so slender combates.

FAVIL. This passeth!

SCINT. Why, is he not madde?

SAM. No, but a little vaine glorious.

TOP. *Epi!*

EPI. Syr.

TOP. I will encounter that blacke and cruell enemie that beareth rough and untewed lockes upon his bodie, whose Syre throweth downe the strongest walles, whose legs are as many as both ours, on whose head are placed most horrible hornes, by nature, as a defence from all harmes.

EPI. What meane you Master, to be so desperate?

TOP. Honour inciteth mee, and very hunger compelleth mee.

EPI. What is that monster?

TOP. The Monster *Ovis*. I have saide; let thy wits worke.

EPI. I cannot imagin it; yet let me see,—a black enemie with rough lockes; it may be a sheep, and *Ovis* is a sheep: his Syre so strong; a Ram is a sheepes Sire, that beeing also an engine of war; hornes he hath, and foure legs,—so hath a sheepe: without doubt this monster is a blacke sheepe. Is it not a sheepe that you meane?

TOP. Thou hast hit it, that Monster will I kill and sup with.

SAM. Come let us take him off. Syr *Tophas* all haile.

TOP. Welcome children, I seldome cast mine eyes so low as to the crownes of your heads, and therfore pardon me that I spake not all this while.

DAR. No harme done; here be faire Ladies come to wonder at your person, your valour, your witte, the report whereof hath made them careles of their owne honours, to glut their eyes and harts upon yours.

TOP. Report cannot but injure mee, for that not knowing fully what I am, I feare shee hath beene a niggard in her praises.

SCINT. No gentle knight, Report hath beene prodigal, for shee hath left you no equall, nor her selfe credite, so much hath she tolde, yet no more than we now see.

DAR. A good wench.

FAVIL. If there remaine as much pittie toward women as there is in you courage against your enemies, then shall we be happie, who hearing of your person, came to see it, and seeing it, are now in love with it.

TOP. Love me Ladies? I easily beleeve it, but my tough heart receiveiveth no impression with sweet words. *Mars* may pearce it, *Venus* shall not paint on it.

FAVIL. A cruell saying.

SAM. Ther's a girle.

DAR. Will you cast these Ladyes away, and all for a little love? doo but speake kindly.

TOP. There commeth no soft syllable within my lips; custome hath made my wordes bloudy, and my hart barbarous: that pelting word love, how watrish it is in my mouth, it carrieth no sound: hate, horror, death, are speaches that nourish my spirits. I like hony, but I care not for the bees: I delight in musicke, but I love not to play on the bagpipes: I can vouchsafe to heare the voice of women, but to touch their bodies I disdaine it, as thing childish, and fit for such men as can disgest nothing but milke.

SCINT. A[h] hard heart, shall wee dye for your love, and finde no remedy?

TOP. I have already taken a surfet.

EPI. Good master pittie them.

TOP. Pittie them *Epi*? no, I do not thinke that this breast shalbe pestred with such a foolish passion. What is that the gentle-woman carrieth in a chaine?

EPI. Why it is a Squirrill.

TOP. A Squirril? O Gods what things are made for money.

DAR. Is not this gentleman overwise?

FAVIL. I could stay all day with him, if I feared not to be shent.

SCINT. Is it not possible to meete againe?

DAR. Yes at any time.

FAVIL. Then let us hasten home.

SCINT. Sir *Tophas*, the God of warre deale better with you, than you doe with the God of love.

FAVIL. Out love we may dissemble, disgest we cannot, but I doubt not but time will hamper you, and helpe us.

TOP. I defie time, who hath no interest in my heart: come *Epi*, let me to the battaile with that hideous beast: love is pappe and hath no relish in my taste, because it is not terrible.

[*Exeunt Sir Tophas and Epiton.*]

DAR. Indeede a blacke sheepe is a perrilous beast. But let us in till another time.

FAVIL. I shall long for that time.

[*Exeunt*

[Unlike Thersites Sir Tophas does not fight the monster.]

[Sir Tophas in love with the old witch Dipsas.]

Actus Quintus, Scæna Secunda

Sir Tophas, Epiton.

TOP. *Epi*, love hath justled my libertie from the wall, and taken the upper hand of my reason.

EPI. Let mee then trippe up the heeles of your affection, and thrust your goodwill into the gutter.

TOP. No *Epi*, Love is a Lorde of misrule, and keepeth Christmas in my corps.

EPI. No doubt there is good cheere: what dishes of delight doth his Lordshippe feast you withal?

TOP. First, with a great platter of plum-porrige of pleasure, wherein is stued the mutton of mistrust.

EPI. Excellent love lappe.

TOP. Then commeth a Pye of patience, a Henne of honnie, a Goose of gall, a Capon of care, and many other Viandes, some sweete and some sowre; which proveth love to bee as it was saide of, in olde yeeres, *Dulce venenum.*

EPI. A brave banquet.

TOP. But *Epi*, I praye thee feele on my chinne, some thing prycketh mee. What doost thou feele or see.

EPI. There are three or foure little haires.

TOP. I pray thee call it my bearde. Howe shall I bee troubled when this younge springe shall growe to a great wood!

EPI. O sir, your chinne is but a quyller yet, you will be most majesticall when it is full fledge. But I marvell that you love *Dipsas*, that old Crone.

TOP. *Agnosco veteris vestigia flammæ*, I love the smoke of an olde fyre.

EPI. Why shee is so colde, that no fyre can thawe her thoughts.

TOP. It is an olde goose, *Epi*, that will eate no oates; olde Kine will kicke, olde Rats gnawe cheese, and olde sackes will have much patching: I preferre an old Cony before a Rabbet sucker, and an ancient henne before a younge chicken peeper.

EPI. *Argumentum ab antiquitate*. My master loveth anticke worke.

TOP. Give mee a pippin that is withered like an olde wife.

EPI.   Good sir.

TOP.   Then, *a contrario sequitur argumentum.* Give me a wife that lookes like an olde pippin.

EPI.   Nothing hath made my master a foole, but flat Schollership.

TOP.   Knowest thou not that olde wine is best?

EPI.   Yes.

TOP.   And thou knowest that like will to like?

EPI.   I.

TOP.   And thou knowest that *Venus* loved the best Wine.

EPI.   So.

TOP.   Then I conclude, that *Venus* was an olde woman in an olde cuppe of wine. For, *est Venus in vinis, ignis in igne fuit.*

EPI.   O *lepidum caput,* O madcap master! You were worthy to winne *Dipsas,* were shee as olde againe, for in your love you have worne the nappe of your witte quite off, and made it thredbare. But soft, who comes heere?

TOP.   My solicitors. [*Enter Samias and Dares.*]

SAM.   All haile sir *Tophas,* how feele you your selfe?

TOP.   Statelie in every joynt, which the common people terme stifnes. Doth *Dipsas* stoope? wyll shee yeeld? will she bende?

DAR.   O sir as much as you would wish, for her chin almost toucheth her knees.

EPI.   Maister, she is bent I warrant you.

TOP.   What conditions doth she aske?

SAM.   Shee hath vowed shee will never love anie that hath not a tooth in his head lesse then she.

TOP.   How manie hath shee?

DAR.   One.

EPI.   That goeth harde Maister, for then you must have none.

TOP.   A small request, and agreeable to the gravitie of her yeares. What shoulde a wise man doe with his mouth full of bones like a charnell[1] house? The Turtle true hath nere a tooth.

SAM.   Thy Maister is in a notable vaine, that will loose his teeth to be like a Turtle.

EPI.   Let him loose his tongue to[o], I care not.

DAR.   Nay you must also have no nayles, for shee long since hath cast hers.

TOP.   That I yeelde to[o]: what a quiet life shal *Dipsas* and I leade, when wee can neither byte nor scratch! you may see youthes, how age provides for peace.

SAM.   How shal we doe to make him leave his love, for we never spake to her?

---

[1] channel *1591.*

DAR. Let me alone. Shee is a notable Witch, and hath turnde her maide *Bagoa* to an Aspen tree, for bewraying her secretes.

TOP. I honor her for her cunning; for now when I am wearie of walking on two legges, what a pleasure may she doe mee to turne me to some goodly Asse, and help mee to foure.

DAR. Nay then I must tell you the troth; her husband *Geron* is come home, who this fifty yeeres hath had her to wife.

TOP. What doe I heare? Hath she an husbande? Goe to the Sexton,[1] and tell him desire is deade, and will him to digge his grave. O heavens, an husbande? What death is agreeable to my fortune?

SAM. Be not desperate, and we will helpe you to find a young Ladie.

TOP. I love no grissels; they are so brittle, they will cracke like glasse, or so dainty, that if they bee touched they are straight of the fashion of waxe: *Animus maioribus instat*. I desire olde Matrons. What a sight would it be to embrace one whose hayre were as orient as the pearle: whose teeth shal be so pure a watchet, that they shall staine the truest Turkis! whose nose shall throwe more beames from it then the fierie Carbuncle: whose eyes shall be environd about with rednesse exceeding the deepest Corall! And whose lippes might compare with silver for the palenesse! Such a one if you can help me to, I will by peece-meale curtoll my affections towardes *Dipsas*, and walke my swelling thoughts till they be cold.

EPI. Wisely provided. How say you, my freendes, will you angle for my Maisters cause?

SAM. Most willingly

DAR. If wee speede him not shortly, I will burne my cappe; we will serve him of the spades, and digge an old wife out of the grave, that shall be answerable to his gravitie.

TOP. Youthes adiew; hee that bringeth mee first newes, shall possesse mine inheritance.

[*Exit Sir Tophas*

---

[1] Sexteene, *1591*.

VIII. Analogue

From THE NATURE OF THE FOUR ELEMENTS

by John Rastell? (1519)

A new interlude and a mery of the nature of the iiii
elements declarynge many proper poyntes of phylosophy
naturall / and of dyvers straunge landys / and of dyvers
straunge effectes & causis / whiche interlude yf ye
hole matter be playde wyl conteyne the space of an
hour and a halfe / but yf ye lyst ye may leve out
muche of the sad mater / as the messengers parte / and
some of naturys parte and some of experyens parte &
yet the matter wyl depend convenyently / and than it
wyll not be paste thre quarters of an hour of length.

[Sensual Appetite tempts Humanity to leave Studious Desire.]

SEN.   Well hyt,[1] quod Hykman, when that he smot   404
Hys wyffe on the buttockes with a bere-pott.
Aha now god evyn fole, god evyn!
It is even the[e] knave that I mene.
Hast thou done thy babelyng?
    STU.   Ye[a] peradventure what than?
    SEN.   Than hold downe thy hede lyke a pretty man and
        take my blyssyng.   410
Benedicite! I graunt to the[e] this pardon,
And gyve the[e] absolucion
For thy soth saws; stande up Jackdaw!
I beshrew thy faders sone,
Make rome syrs, and let us be mery
With huffa galand, synge tyrll on the bery,
And let the wyde worlde wynde.
Synge fryska Joly with hey troly loly
For I se[e] well it is but a foly
For to have a sad mynd.   420
For rather than I wolde use suche foly,

---

[1] hyet *orig.*

To pray, to study, or be pope holy,
I had as lyf be ded.
By goggys body I tell you trew
I speke as I thynke now else I beshrew
Evyn my next felowes hed.
Master Humanyte syr, be your leve
I were ryght loth you to greve
Though I do hym dyspyse;
For yf ye knewe hym as well as I   430
Ye wolde not use his company
Nor love hym in no wyse.
    HU.   Syr, he loketh lyke an honest man,
Therefore I merveyll that ye can
This wyse hym deprave.
    SEN.   Though he loke never so well
I promise you he hath a shrewde smell.
    HU.   Why so, I prey you tell?
    SEN.   For he saveryth lyke a knave.
    STU.   Holde your pease syr, ye mystake me.   440
What, I trowe that ye wolde make me
Lyke to one of your kyn.
    SEN.   Harke syrs, here ye not how boldly
He callyth me knave agayne by polycy?
The devyll pull of[f] his skyn!
I wolde he were hangyd by the throte
For by the messe I love hym not,
We two can never agre[e].
I am content syr with you to tary
And I am for you so necessary   450
Ye can not lyve without me.
    HU.   Why syr, I say what man be ye?
    SEN.   I am callyd Sensuall Apetyte.
All craturs in me delyte;
I comforte the wyttys fyve,
The tastyng, smellyng, and herynge.
I refresh the syght and felynge
To all creaturs alyve.
For whan the body wexith hongry
For lacke of fode or ellys thursty   460
Than with drynkes plesaund
I restore hym out of payne
and oft refreshe nature agayne
With delycate vyand.
With plesaunde sound of armonye

The herynge alwaye I satysfy,
I dare this well reporte.
The smellynge with swete odour
And the syght with pleasante fygour
And colours, I comforte.   470
The felynge that is so plesaunte
Of every member, fote or hande,
What pleasure therin can be
By the towchynge of soft and harde
Of hote or colde nought in regarde
Excepte it come by me.

    HU.   Than I cannot see the contrary,
But ye are for me full necessary,
And ryght convenyent.

    STU.   Ye[a] syr, beware yet what ye do   480
For yf you forsake my company so,
Lorde Nature wyll not be contente.
Of hym ye shall never lerne good thyng,
Nother vertu nor no other connynge,
This dare I well say.

    SEN.   Mary avaunt knave, I the[e] defye.
Dyde Nature forbyde hym my company?
What sayst thou therto? speke openly.

    HU.   As for that I know well nay.

    SEN.   No by god; I am ryght sure,   490
For he knoweth well no creature
Without me can lyve one day.

    HU.   Syr I pray you be contente.
It is not utterly myne intente
Your company to exyle
But only to have communycacyon
And a pastyme of recreacyon
With this man for a whyle.

    STU.   Well, for you pleasure I wyll depart.

                       [Exit Studious Desire

    HU.   Now go knave, go! I beshrew thy hart.   500
The devyll sende the[e] forwarde!

    SEN.   Now by my trouth I mervell gretly
That ever ye wolde use the company
So myche of suche a knave.
For if ye do no nother thynge
But ever study and to be musynge
As he would have you, it wyll you brynge

At the last unto your grave.
Ye shulde ever study pryncypall
For to comfort your lyfe naturall 510
With metis and drynkes dilycate
And other pastymes and pleasures amonge
Daunsynge, laughinge, or plesaunt songe.
This is mete for your estate.

    HU.   Because ye sey so I you promise
That I have musyd and studyed such wyse
Me thynketh my wyttes wery,
My nature desyreth some refresshynge
And also I have ben so longe fastynge
That I am somwhat hongry. 520

    SEN.   Well then, wyll ye go with me
To a taverne where ye shall se[e]
Good pastaunce and at your lyberte
Have what so ever ye wyll?

    HU.   I am content so for to do
Yf that ye wyll not fro me go
But kepe me company styll.

    SEN.   Company quotha? Ye[a] that I shall poynt-devyse,
And also do you good and trew servyce,
And therto I plyght my trouthe. 530
And yf that I ever forsake you
I pray God the devyl take you!

    HU.   Mary, I thanke you for that othe.

    SEN.   A myschyf on it! my tonge, loo
Wyll tryp somtyme what so ever I do.
But ye wot what I mene well.

    HU.   Ye[a] no force! let this matter passe.
But seydest evin now thou knewyst where was
A good taverne to make solas.
Where is that? I prey the[e] tell. 540

    SEN.   Mary! at the dore evyn here by.
Yf we call any thynge on hye
The taverner wyll answere.

    HU.   I pray thee than, call for hym nowe.

    SEN.   Mary I wyll. How taverner, how!
Why doste thou not appere?

                            [Enter Taverner

    TA.   Who is that calleth so hastely?
I shrew thyne herte, speke softely;
I tell the[e] I am not here. 549

SEN.   Than I beshrew thee, page, of thyne age!
Come hyther knave, for thyne avauntage;
Why makest thou hit so tow?[1]

TA.   For mine avauntage, mary, than I come.
Beware syrs, how, let me have rome.
Lo here I am; what seyst thou?
SEN.   Mary thus: here is a gentylman I say
That nother ete nor dranke this day.
Therfor tell me, I the[e] praye
If thou have any good wyne.

TA.   Ye shall have Spaneshe wyne and Gascoyn   560
Rose coloure, whyt, claret, rampyon,
Tyre, Capryck, and Malvesyne
Sak, raspyce, Alicaunt, rumney,
Greke ipocras, new made clary,
Suche as ye never had
For yf ye drynke a draught or too
Yt wyll make you or ye thens go,
By gogges body, starke madde.

SEN.   I wot thou art not without good wyne,
But here is a gentylman hath lyst to dyne.   570
Canst thou get hym any good mete?

TA.   What mete mayster wolde ye have?

HU.   I care not, so god me save,
So that it be holsome to ete.
I wolde we had a good stewyd capon.

SEN.   As for capons ye can gette none,
The kyngys taker toke up eche one.
I wot well there is none to get.

TA.   Though all capons be gone, what than?
Yet I can get you a stewed hen   580
That is redy dyght.

HU.   Yf she be fat yt wyll do well.

TA.   Fat or lene I cannot tell,
But as for this I wot well
She lay at the stewes all nyght.

HU.   Thou art a mad gest, be this lyght.

SEN.   Ye[a] syr, it is a felow that never faylys
But canst get my mayster a dyshe of quales,
Smal byrdes, swalowes or wagtayles?
They be lyght of dygestyon.   590

TA.   Lyght of dygestyon! for what reason?

---

[1] 'Why do you make it difficult (tough)?'

SEN. For physyk puttyth this reason therto,
Bycause those byrdes fle to and fro,
And be contynuall movynge.
 TA. Then know I a lyghter mete than that.
 HU. I pray the[e] tell me what?
 TA. Yf ye will nedys know, at short and longe
It is evyn a womans tounge
For that is ever sterynge.
 HU. Syr I pray the[e] let such fanteses be   600
And come heder nere and harke to me,
And do after my byddynge.
Goo purvey us a dyner evyn of the moste
Of all maner dysshes both sod and roste
That thou canst get: spare for no coste
Yf thou make thre[e] course.[1] . . .
 TA. What than, I se[e] well ye wyll make a feste.
 HU. Ye[a] by the rode, evyn with the gretest.
 SEN. By my trouth then do ye best   630
Evyn after my mynde.
But ye must have more company.
 HU. That is trewe and so wolde I gladly
If I knew any to fynde.
 SEN. Why, wyll ye folowe my counsell?
 HU. Ye[a].
 SEN. Than we wyll have lytell Nell,
A proper wenche, she daunsith well,
And Jane with the blacke lace.
We will have bounsynge Besse also   640
And two or thre[e] proper wenchis mo
Ryght feyr and smotter[2] of face.
 HU. Now be it so! thou art saunce pere.[3]
 TA. Than I perceyve ye wyll make gode chere.
 HU. Why, what shulde I els do?
 TA. If ye thynke so best, than wyll I
Go before and make all thynge redy,
Agayne ye come therto.
 HU. Mary, I prey the[e] do so.
 TA. Than farewell syrs, for I am gone.   650
            [*Exit Taverner*

 HU. And we shall follow the[e] anon
Without any taryyng.

---

[1] 21 lines of jesting about 'course' and 'coarse' omitted.
[2] smooth.   [3] sans peer, without equal.

SEN.   Then it is best syr ye make hast
For ye shall spende here but tyme i[n] wast
And do no nother thynge.
    HU.   Yf ye wyll let us goo by and by.
    SEN.   I pray you be it, for I am redy,
No man better wyllynge.
    Exeat Sensual Appetite and Humanity.

[After a time Humanity is won back to Studious Desire and tires of
Sensual Appetite's trivial jests.]

    HU.   Sensuall Apetyte I prey the[e]   1012
Let passe all such tryfles and vanyte
For a wyle (it shall not longe be)
And departe I the[e] require,
For I wolde talke a worde or two
With this man here or he hens go
For to satysfy my desyre.
    SEN.   Why goggis soule wyll ye so shortly
Breke poyntment with yonder company   1020
Where ye shulde come to supper?
I trust ye wyll not breke promys so.
    HU.   I care not greatly yf I do.
Yt is but a taverne matter.
    SEN.   Than wyll I go shew them what ye sey.
    HU.   Spare not if thou wylt: go thy wey
For I wyll here tary.

[He settles down with Studious Desire to hear a long lecture by
Experience proving that the earth is round. Other adventures
follow, but in the end Nature agrees with Humanity that the senses
are to be used within reason.]

    NATURE   Well Humanyte now I see playnly   1422
That thou hast usyd muche foly
The whyle I have ben absent.
    HU.   Syr I trust I have done nothynge
That shold be contrary to your pleasynge
Nor never was myne intent.
For I have folowed the counsell clere
As ye me bad of Studyouse Desire
And for necessitye amonge   1430
Somtyme Sensuall Appetites counsell
For without hym ye know ryght well
My lyfe can not endure longe.

NATURE   Though it be for the[e] full necessary
For thy comfort somtyme to satysfy
Thy sensuall appetyte
Yet it is not convenyent for the[e]
To put therin thy felycyte
And all thy hole delyte
For if thou wilt lerne no sciens   1440
Nother by study nor experiens
I shall the[e] never avaunce
But in the worlde thou shalt dure than
Dyspysed of every wyse man
Lyke this rude be[a]st ygnoraunce.

[The text ends here.]

IX. Analogue

From THE WORLD AND
THE CHILD

Anonymous (1522)

Here begynneth a propre newe Interlude of the worlde
and the chylde / otherwyse called Mundus et Infans
and it sheweth of the estate of Chyldehode and Manhode. [Colophon] Here endeth the Interlude of Mundus
et Infans. Imprynted at London in Fletestrete at the
sygne of the Sonne by me Wynkyn de worde. The yere
of our Lorde MCCCCC and xxii. The xvii daye of
July.

[Manhood is tempted by Folly to banish Conscience.]

MANHODE   But herke felowe by thy faythe where was
     thou bore?
FOLYE   By my faythe in Englonde have I dwelled yore   564
And all myne auncetters me before.
But syr, in London is my chefe dwellynge.
MANHODE   In London? where, yf a man the[e] sought?

FOLYE   Syr, in Holborne I was forthe brought
And with the courtyers I am betaught,
To Westmynster I used to wende.   570
  MANHODE   Herke felowe why doost thou to Westmynster
    drawe?
FOLYE   For I am a servaunt of the lawe.
Covetous is myne owne felowe
We twayne plete for the kynge
And poore men that come from uplande
We wyll take theyr mater in hande.
Be it ryght or be it wronge
Theyr thryfte with us shall wende.
  MANHODE   Now here felowe I pray thee, whyder wendest
    thou than?
FOLYE   By my feyth syr, into London I ran   580
To the tavernes to drynke the wyne
And than to the Innes I toke the waye
And there I was not welcome to the osteler
But I was welcome to the fayre tapester
And to all the housholde I was ryght dere
For I have dwelled with her many a daye.
  MANHODE   Now I pray thee, whyder toke thou than the
    waye?
FOLYE   In feythe syr, over London brydge I ran
And the streyght waye to the stewes I came
And toke lodgynge for a nyght   590
And there I founde my brother Lechery.
There men and women dyde folye
And every man made of me as worthy
As thoughe I hadde ben a knyght.
  MANHODE   I pray thee yet tell me mo of thyne adventures.
FOLYE   In feythe even streyght to all the freres,
And with them I dwelled many yeres
And they crowned Folye a kynge.
  MANHODE   I praye the[e] felowe whyder wendest thou
    tho?
FOLYE   Syr, all Englande to and fro.   600
Into abbeys and into nonneryes also
And alwaye Folye dothe felowes fynde.
  MANHODE   Now herke felowe I praye the[e] tell me thy
    name.
FOLYE   I wys, I hyght bothe Folye and Shame. . .

[Folly wishes to be Manhood's servant]

MANHODE   Peace, man: I may not have thee for thy name,   636
For thou sayest thy name is bothe Folye and Shame.
FOLYE   Syr, here in this cloute I knyt Shame,
And clype me but propre Folye.
MANHODE   Ye[a] Folye wyll thou be my trewe servaunt?
FOLYE   Ye[a], Syr Manhode, here my hande.
MANHODE   Now let us drynke at this comnaunt [1]
For that is curtesy.
FOLYE   Mary mayster, ye shall have in hast.
A ha syrs, let the catte wyncke.
For all ye wote not what I thynke
I shall drawe hym suche a draught of drynke
That Conscyence he shall awaye cast.
Have, mayster, and drynke well
And let us make revell-revell   650
For I swere by the chyrche of Saynt Myghell
I woulde we were at stewes
For there is nothynge but revell route.
And we were there I had no doubte
I sholde be knowen all aboute
Where Conscyence they wolde refuse.
MANHODE   Peas Folye, my fayre frende
For by Cryste I wolde not that Conscyence sholde me here
    fynde.
FOLYE   Tusshe mayster, therof speke no thynge,
For Conscyence cometh no tyme here.   660
MANHODE   Peace Folye, there is no man that knoweth me.
FOLYE   Syr, here my trouthe I plyght to the[e]
And thou wylte go thyder with me,
For knowlege have thou no care.
MANHODE   Please, but it is hens a grete waye.
FOLYE   Pardè syr, we may be there on a daye
Ye[a] and we shall be ryght welcome I dare well saye
In E[a]stchepe for to dyne
And than we wyll with Lombardes [2] at passage [3] playe
And at the Popes Heed sweet wyne assaye.   670
We shall be lodged well a fyne.
MANHODE   What sayest thou Folye, is this the best?
FOLYE   Syr, all this is Manhode, well thou knowest.
MANHODE   Now Folye, go we hens in hast.
But fayne wolde I chaunge my name:

[1] covenant.   [2] Italian bankers.
[3] a game played with three dice.

For well I wot, yf Conscyence mete me in this tyde
Ryght well I wote he wolde me chyde.

   FOLYE Sir, for fere of you his face he shall hyde:
I shall clepe you Shame.

   MANHODE Now gramercy Folye, my felowe in fere,   680
Go we hens, tary no lenger here.
Tyll we be gone me thynke it seven yere;
I have golde and good to spend.

   FOLYE Aha, mayster that is good chere
And or it be passed halfe a yere
I shall the[e] shere ryght a lewde frere
And hyther agayne the[e] send.

   MANHODE Folye go before and teche me the waye.

   FOLYE Come after, Shame I the[e] praye
And Conscyence clere ye cast awaye.   690
Lo syrs, this Folye techeth aye
For where Conscyence cometh with his cunnynge
Yet Folye full fetely shall make hym blynde.
Folye before, and Shame behynde,
Lo syrs, thus fareth the worlde alwaye.

                                       [Exit Folly

   MANHODE Nowe I wyll folowe Folye for Folye is my man:
Ye[a] Folye is my felowe and hath gyven me a name.
Conscyence called me Manhode, Folye calleth me Shame.
Folye wyll me lede to London to lerne revell,
Ye[a] and Conscyence is but a flateryng brothell,   700
For ever he is carpyng of care.
The worlde and Folye counseylleth me to all gladnes
Ye[a] and Conscyence counselleth me to all sadnes;
Ye[a] too moche sadnes myght brynge me into madnes.
And now have good daye syrs, to London to seke Folye wyll
    I fare.

                                 [Enter Conscience

   CONSCYENCE Saye Manhode, frende, whyder wyll ye go?

   MANHODE Nay syr in faythe my name is not so.
Why frere, what the devyll hast thou to do
Whyder I go or abide?   710

   CONSCYENCE Yes syr, I wyll counsell you for the best.

   MANHODE I wyll none of thy counsell so have I rest:
I wyll go whyder my lest,
For thou canst nought elles but chyde.

                                 [Exit Manhood

CONSCYENCE Lo syrs, a great ensample you may se[e]
The freylnes of mankynde
How oft he falleth in folye
Throughe temptacyon of the fende,
For whan the fende and the flesshe be at one assent,
Than Conscyence clere is clene out cast.   720
Men thynke not on the grete Jugement
That the sely soule shall have at the last,
But wolde God all men wolde have in mynde
Of the grete daye of dome,
How he shall gyve a grete reckenynge
Of evyll dedes that he hathe done.
But nedeles, syth it is so
That Manhode is forthe with Folye wende,
To seche Perseveraunce now wyll I go.
With the grace of God omnypotent   730
His counseylles ben in fere:
Perseveraunce counsell is moost dere.
Nexte to hym is Conscyence clere
From synnynge.
Now into this presence to Cryst I praye
To spede me well in my Journaye.
Fare well lordynges and have good daye.
To seke Perseveraunce wyll I wende. . . .

[When Manhode becomes Age he listens to Perseveraunce and is called Repentaunce.]

HENRY IV
PART 2

INTRODUCTION

THE PLAY was entered in *S.R.* on 23 August, 1600, and the only Quarto version was published as *The Second part of Henrie the fourth, continuing to his death, and coronation of Henrie the fift. With the humours of sir John Fal staffe, and swaggering Pistoll. As it hath been sundrie times publikely acted by the right honourable, the Lord Chamberlaine his servants. Written by William Shakespeare. London. Printed by V. S [Valentine Simmes] for Andrew Wise, and William Aspley, 1600*. The Quarto has 39 lines not in F1 and omits 171 lines found there. The Folio was probably derived from a scribe's copy of a prompt-book. Sir W. W. Greg argues that Q was printed from Shakespeare's own MS, in which cuts had been marked. The fact that an actor is mentioned in Q (Sincklo (V.4)) might suggest a playhouse acting version. III.1 was omitted from Q at first and later inserted. This may have been only a printer's slip or a defect in the copy, but Dover Wilson believed that the omission was due to fear of the censorship, because of the reference in that scene to Richard II's deposition, a ticklish subject in the year of Essex's conspiracy, when Shakespeare's *Richard II* was regarded by the Queen as touching on the political situation. It is as likely that the references to Northumberland here and elsewhere in the play would offend Henry Percy, the ninth Earl, Essex's brother-in-law. He was not involved in the conspiracy but his grandfather, Sir Thomas Percy, was executed in 1537 as a leader in the Pilgrimage of Grace, and his father Henry the eighth Earl was sent to the Tower three times and died there mysteriously in 1585, shot through the heart, while his uncle Thomas the seventh Earl made a rebellion to restore the Catholic religion in 1569 and was executed at York in 1572 after fleeing to Scotland (cf. II.3), and being sold by the Scottish Regent, the Earl of Mar, to Elizabeth's officers.

It is likely that Elizabethan playgoers would recall the family

history of the papist Northumberland,[1] and the ninth Earl may
have been offended. There is no evidence of this, or that pres-
sure was brought to bear on the players, but no other Quarto of
2H4 was printed, though the play was popular. It was probably
written in 1597.

Shakespeare's sources for this play were mainly Holinshed
[Text I] and *The Famous Victories* [Text VIII]. He probably also
glanced at Daniel's *Civile Wars*, Bk. III [Text II] and Hall's
chronicle [Text III]. The historical material afforded by the
reign of Henry IV after Shrewsbury was less interesting and
unified than what went before.

The Battle of Shrewsbury on 21 July, 1403, was a great victory
for Henry IV but it did not remove all danger. The King's
power was weak and he marched north to meet Northumberland in Yorkshire, where the Earl submitted, and at the end of
August Henry returned to face a threat from the Welsh who
were raiding the Marches. He was unable to pursue them into
Wales owing to lack of means, and after his triumphal entry
into London in November, accompanied by Prince Henry,
Welsh attacks on English garrisons persisted through the winter,
and Owen Glendower, calling himself Prince of Wales, made
an alliance with the French King (June, 1404). Prince Henry,
as Lieutenant in the Marches, could do little owing to lack of
money, as his letters show,[2] until 1404/5 when he had three
victories which might have been followed up had not the
rebellion of Northumberland, Bardolph, Mowbray and Archbishop Scrope diverted the King from Wales. The Prince
hastened to meet his father at York but Scrope's rebellion
collapsed at Shipton Moor on 29 May, 1405. Northumberland
and Bardolph fled to Scotland, but joined Glendower in 1406.
'It was probably at this time, if ever, that the famous Tripartite
Convention for the division of England between Glendower,
Percy and Mortimer was concluded in the Dean's house at
Bangor.'[3]

The Welsh were defeated on St George's Day, 1406, whereupon Northumberland and Bardolph fled to Brittany. Nearly

[1] Richard Simpson in *Sh. Soc. Trans.* 1874, 371–441 argued that Shakespeare
deliberately drew parallels between the Northern Rebellion of 1569 and that of
Northumberland in *Henry IV*. Cf. also L. B. Campbell, *Shakespeare's 'Histories'*,
pp. 228–37.

[2] Cited in Kingsford, *Henry V*, pp. 47–9.   [3] *Ibid.*, p. 54.

two years later Northumberland returned to the attack, and was slain at Bramham Moor in February, 1408. After this the Welsh menace declined, for Glendower's wife, daughter (Edmund Mortimer's widow) and four grandchildren were captured at Harlech Castle. Owen held out in the mountains, moving from place to place, and did not die of starvation. He seems to have made peace with Henry V in or after 1415 and probably died years later at Hereford.

The death of Northumberland marked the end of Henry IV's serious dynastic difficulties. But he was ill from 1405 onwards, and this brought Prince Henry into public life, so when Archbishop Arundel resigned from the Chancellorship in 1409 and was succeeded next year by Thomas Beaufort, the Prince headed the Council. He was friendly with Sir John Oldcastle the Lollard leader, but he never shared Oldcastle's heresies. His orthodoxy and his justice were shown when in March, 1410, he stopped the burning of the Lollard tailor John Padly because he thought the man wished to recant; only to have the fire re-lit when the heretic refused to do so. His energy in Council business was remarked by the poet Hoccleve as excessive, since he held meetings on holy days. In 1411 he planned to marry Burgundy's daughter and sent a force under the Earl of Arundel and Sir John Oldcastle against Burgundy's enemies the Armagnacs.

In the same year the Prince, urged on by his uncle Henry Beaufort, seems to have tried to bring about his sick father's abdication. The King reacted strongly, dismissing the Prince from the Council, replacing him by his second son Thomas. The Beauforts were soon driven from office and the new Council made an alliance with the Armagnacs. In an effort to prevent this the Prince came to London in June, 1412, with such a large following 'as had never been seen in our time',[1] but without success. His enemies worked actively against him, and again in September he came to the Council 'with an huge peple'. There was even an attempt to assassinate him, or so it was said, and the Bishop of Winchester was later accused of the plot (Vol. III, 50). The King's illness increased in 1412–13, and he had many fainting fits before he died on 20 March, 1413, of apoplexy according to some chroniclers, of leprosy according to others.

[1] *Ibid.*, pp. 74–5.

The above outline departs somewhat from the story as told in Holinshed, which includes legendary matter and omits most of the events in Wales. The main features of the later reign of Henry IV were the consolidation of the royal position by the defeat of Northumberland and his friends and by the gradual suppression of the Welsh danger; the suppression of the Lollards; the participation in French affairs; and the Prince's part in the politics of 1410–13. The Prince was thirteen when his father seized the crown, sixteen at the Battle of Shrewsbury, and twenty-six when he ascended the throne. As Kingsford writes: 'What strikes us most is that he should have played so great a part at so young an age . . . his strenuous youth had been spent in the battlefield and the council-chamber, and it seems difficult to guess when, if ever, he could have found relaxation in pursuits more natural to his years' (p. 80). Yet relax he must have done, and there may have been truth in the legend of wildness —perhaps between 1405 and 1410 and after his dismissal from the Council.

In considering Shakespeare's organization of this play we must remember that as a sequel to *1 Henry IV* its functions were to show the consolidation of the Lancastrian dynasty and the continued preparation of Prince Hal for his glorious reign to come, to cover the years 1403–13, from the Battle of Shrewsbury to the accession of Henry V, and to carry on the mingling of comedy and history successfully achieved in the previous play. To introduce new themes, such as the rise of the Lollards or the (very minor) expedition to France, was not to Shakespeare's purpose; nor did he wish to darken his portrait of the Prince by showing him as given to intrigue, ambitious or a trouble-maker. The political material thus left was very thin, and in treating the Prince great care would be needed. Shakespeare's handling of his two main problems deserves attention.

By no means could Scrope's rebellion be made as interesting, menacing or many-sided as that of the Percies and Glendower in *1 Henry IV*. Shakespeare did his best by compressing the historical action and shifting events to give an impression of urgency and speed. Scrope's conspiracy took place in 1405, two years after Shrewsbury, but already *1 Henry IV* (IV.3 and V.5) had started a confusion of dates which now continues. As Rumour tells us in the Prologue, the play begins so soon after the

Battle of Shrewsbury that Northumberland hears two opposed hearsay accounts of it before Morton brings authentic news of total defeat. Here we are in the year 1403 and the scene serves several purposes. It provides close links with the previous play; it recapitulates events represented there; it excites tension, irony and an heroic mood, and it presents a vivid portrait of North-umberland, giving him an importance as a dramatic centre which his previous activities might have led us to expect, and explaining, by his grief at Hotspur's defeat and death, the break-down and retreat which soon follow. The 'speedy power' sent out against him at I.1.131–5 was in fact that taken north after Shrewsbury by the King, who thereby forced him temporarily to submit. Here, however, it is made partly responsible for his flight to Scotland (II.3) which really occurred in 1405. The revolt of Scrope and Mowbray is likewise brought forward from that year, mentioned in I.1.189ff and hatched in I.3. Other examples of anticipation occur; Glendower's death, which Holinshed wrongly ascribed to 1409 occurs (III.1.103) before the suppression of that rising, a description of which (IV.4.84–90) comes immediately before news arrives of Percy's defeat and death, which actually took place in 1408.

So five years of Henry IV's reign are telescoped into a few weeks. His later years are even more summarily treated. Holinshed first mentions the King's illness under 1411, but this is referred to in III.1.104–6. After the announcement of Scrope's destruction he is sick to death (IV.4.102–30), and his death soon occurs, between Acts IV and V. Yet in III.1 the King's reference to Northumberland as he was 'not ten years gone', and 'two years after' shows that he is speaking in 1407, which agrees with Holinshed's dating of the events of this scene. Shakespeare deliberately departed from historical time and sequence to give dramatic force, concentration, and unity of tone to a sprawling series of events.

The material offered less opportunity than that of *1 Henry IV* for heroic contrast or national types. Old Percy, 'crafty-sick', heart-broken, is less interesting than his dead son, and the con-trast between them is pointed in II.3, where (unlike Hotspur in the same scene in *1 Henry IV*) Northumberland lets himself be persuaded by his womenfolk not to fight but to flee. The battle in which he perishes is not even described (IV.4.94–101).

Similarly Scrope lacks Glendower's dramatic power, and his rebellion is put down by guile (IV.2) without a battle. The collapse of the King's enemies is a proof of his success, but it inevitably makes the political side of the play less theatrically effective than its predecessor; indeed it is rather dull.

Shakespeare's main interest lay in the relationship between the King and his son, and this might have been made complex and subtle had the dramatist realized that the future Henry V was already an experienced administrator and also an ambitious schemer. Folklore and the Tudor adoration of the Hero-King obscured these facts, but in accepting the cult Shakespeare diminished the ambiguous elements in the Prince Hal legend. Any opposition between the young man and his father must not be political; any suggestion that Hal desired his father's crown must be refuted. So the prince must remain a madcap scapegrace, as in *1 Henry IV*.

The depiction of Henry IV as a sad and conscience-stricken man may be compared with that in Daniel's *Civile Wars*, Bk 3 [Text II], which probably influenced the dramatist both negatively and positively. For Daniel in his 1595 edition the only events of importance after Shrewsbury were the King's sickness, the Prince's taking of the crown, and their last interview. (In later editions, perhaps affected by Shakespeare's play, he summarized Scrope's revolt.) Daniel makes the King unable to rest owing to 'intricate turmoiles, and sorrowes deepe'. Sickness clarifies his soul with a vision of Death and Conscience. The latter shows him in a mirror 'What he was, and what he straight should bee.' Ordering his crown to be set before him Henry IV apostrophizes it as the cause which made him 'passe those boundes, nature and law ordain'd'. When he wakes from the coma during which his son has taken away the crown, believing him dead, Henry wishes to make some redress for his usurpation by giving up the crown 'to whom it seem'd to appertaine', perhaps Richard of Cambridge. But when he urges Hal to 'let it go' (124), the Prince refuses, asserting his resolve to hold firm what has been won, since 'Time will appease them well that now complaine', and 'Yeares makes that right which never was so borne' (125). The King then counsels him to live so as to

'let the goodnes of the managing
Rase out the blot of foule attayning quite,' (126)

and bids him engage his people in some great actions so as to
distract them from domestic strife, telling him that in his situation he cannot afford to 'riot it', but must win goodwill by hard
toil.

Shakespeare in the main agrees with this treatment, though
he never lets the King propose that the hard-won crown should
be given up, and does not let him appear so wretched. His
Henry IV is a worried, 'unquiet' person with no life apart
from his public cares and his anxiety for his family. He refers
little to the shady means by which he got the throne, speaks to
the lords, whether loyal or rebel, like a true king, and urges his
son to behave more as he himself had done in youth than like
Richard II (III.2). Yet his first words in Part 1, 'So shaken as
we are, and wan with care', set the key of his personality, and he
easily believes that Hal's misbehaviour may be a divine
punishment:

> I know not whether God will have it so
> For some displeasing service I have done,
> That, in his secret doom, out of my blood
> He'll breed revengement and a scourge for me.
> (*1H4*, III.2.4–7)

Part 2 develops this idea of care without at first stressing a
bad conscience. We do not see the King in the first two Acts,
whose political scenes are occupied by his enemies, doubtless to
make their plots seem more dangerous than in fact they were
(I.1; I.3; II.3). We first see him using a motif from Daniel
(though it is conventional enough), soliloquizing about his
inability to sleep (III.1.1–31). His cares are here ascribed to the
responsibilities of his rank, not to his particular faults ('Uneasy
lies the head that wears a crown'). But when he goes on to discuss the distempers of the kingdom, how 'changes fill the cup of
alteration With divers liquors', he recalls Richard II's prophecy
(*R2* V.1.55–68) when forced to abdicate. The sickness of body
and mind from which he suffers affects both his own imagery
and that of others, including Scrope's in IV.1.54–66: 'We are all
diseas'd.' Throughout runs the implication that the whole

realm is sick with domestic strife. In IV.4 the King collapses on
the stage in the moment of success, and we hear that these fits
are 'very ordinary' with him. Clarence thinks he will soon die of
'The incessant care and labour of his mind', and portents taken
from Holinshed are cited to support this. After the Prince has
taken the crown his father blames his son's misconduct as well
as his illness for his approaching death. The full depth of his
self-realization appears at the last when he recognizes his guilt:

> 'God knows, my son,
> By what by-paths and indirect crook'd ways
> I met this crown'

but he also gives what is in effect the verdict of history upon his
reign, since through the troubles which have beset the 'honour
snatch'd with boisterous hand' he has succeeded in handing on
to his son a 'better quiet', and

> 'now my death
> Changes the mode: for what in me was purchas'd
> Falls upon thee in a more fairer sort.' (IV.5.182–200)

As in Daniel he recalls his purpose 'To lead out many to the
Holy Land', but the purpose he mentions was political, to allay
unrest at home; and he advises Hal 'to busy giddy minds with
foreign quarrels', before he declares that speech fails him (as
Daniel says it did). We may agree with F. W. Moorman[1] that
Shakespeare 'knew Daniel's poem, kept it closely in mind in the
composition of both parts of *Henry IV*, and availed himself
of many of those variations from, and expansions of, the
chronicler's story which Daniel had introduced into his *Civile
Wars*'. But he wove whatever he took from Daniel into a much
richer pattern of character, motive, and dramatic poetry.

The Prince plays a less prominent part in both the Falstaff
and the political scenes than he did in Part 1. In portraying his
activities the dramatist draws freely on incidents in *Famous
Victories* not used in the previous play. Hal does not appear till
II.2 but we hear in I.1 of his prowess at Shrewsbury where his
'swift wrath beat down The never-daunted Percy to the earth'.
In the second scene we learn that he has recently been com-

---

[1] 'Shakespeare's History-Plays and Daniel's *Civile Wars*', *ShJb* xl, 1904, 69–83.

mitted to prison for striking the Lord Chief Justice 'about Bardolph' (I.2.55–6; 195–8). This refers to the famous incident first told in *The Governour* [Text IV] by Sir Thomas Elyot, who did not describe the Prince as striking the lawyer but made him be quelled by the latter's courageous rebuke. Holinshed (following Hall [Text III]) imagined the newly crowned Henry V 'calling to mind how once to hie offense of the king his father, he had with his fist striken the cheefe justice for sending one of his minions (upon desert) to prison, when the justice stoutlie commanded himselfe also streict to ward, & he (then prince) obeied' (*inf.* 280). Holinshed associated this incident with the King's dismissal of the Prince from the Council and his replacement by the Duke of Clarence (dated previous to the Battle of Shrewsbury in *1H4* III.2.32–3). It was several times referred to by Elizabethan writers, e.g. by Angel Day in his *English Secretarie* (1586) and John Case in *Sphæra Civitatis* (1588)[1] and was commonly accepted as fact. Thus 'Whidden vouches for a case in the time of Gascoigne, Chief Justice of England, who committed the Prince (who had wished to take away a prisoner from the bar of the King's Bench) to prison; and the Prince obeyed humbly him and his order; whereat the King rejoiced greatly that he had a Chief Justice who dared administer justice to his son the Prince.' [R. Crompton, *L'Authorité et Jurisdiction des Courts.* 1594. Trans.]

In *Famous Victories* (Sc. iv) the thief of Gads Hill is being tried for robbing the carrier Dericke with violence when the Prince enters the courtroom with Ned and Tom, and demands his liberation. When the Lord Chief Justice refuses, Hal gives him a box on the ear, for which he is committed to the Fleet.[2] The scene is repeated comically by Dericke and John Cobler.

Shakespeare, strangely enough, does not represent the incident, perhaps to avoid showing such an act of *lèse majesté*, and the arrest of the future Hero-King, perhaps in order not to seem to be following the old play too closely. Instead we have Falstaff's encounter with the Justice, which rivals in comedy the parallel incident in Part I where he hides from the Sheriff (II.4.495ff).

---

[1] Cf. D. T. Starnes, 'More about the Prince Hal legend', *PhilQ* xv, 1936, 358–66; also W. G. Bowling, 'The Wild Prince Hal in Legend and Literature', *Washington University Studies*, 1926, pp. 305–34.

[2] If Tarlton played in the piece [Text V], it must have been written by 1588.

When the Prince enters he is weary, maybe after his journey from Wales, more probably to initiate a contrast with his father and to show Poins's incomprehension of the cares of true royalty. The Prince reveals his awareness of his unorthodox conduct in liking 'small beer' and mixing with needy rascals. Poins has sufficient delicacy to wonder at Hal's idle talk while his father is ill. Now the ambiguity of Hal's attitude to his father was a marked feature of *Famous Victories*, notably in the scene when he leaves for Court, 'for I heare say, my father lies verie sicke', when he declares, 'the breath shal be no sooner out of his mouth, but I will clap the Crowne on my head' (477ff), explains that he wears his cloak full of needles because, 'tis a signe that I stand upon thorns, til the Crowne be on my head', and mocks at those people who say 'the yoong Prince will be a well toward yoong man and all this geare'. Yet in *Famous Victories* the Prince repents when he sees his father's grief. Shakespeare omits this scene which shows the Prince in a bad light, and he transforms Hal's attitude, explaining his apparent indifference and ambition as suited to the cynical company he is with, and as a mask to hide his real grief which they would think hypocritical. ('Marry, I tell thee, it is not meet that I should be sad', etc.)

The tavern humour is not influenced by *Famous Victories*, which has nothing equivalent to Mistress Quickly and Doll Tearsheet, and the quarrel of Dericke with his unwilling hostess John Cobler's wife (Sc. vii) can at best be the germ of Falstaff's quarrel with Mistress Quickly. The scene where the Prince and Poins disguise themselves like drawers and hear no good of themselves (II.4.239–321) is conceived as a parallel to Part 1, II.4, as the Prince indicates at ll. 316–19. Obviously Shakespeare wrote his Second Part with an eye on both the construction and the comic effects of Part 1. But whereas the Prince there went from Eastcheap to bear a manly part against the rebels, here he is absent when his brother John of Lancaster meets Mowbray, Hastings and Scrope (IV.2) and deceives them into dismissing their forces. This act is transferred to Lancaster from Westmoreland, to whom Holinshed ascribed this 'politike dealing'. (The story, from Walsingham, is not in Hall.) Modern critics have regarded it as a proof of moral turpitude, but wrongly. Almost any trickery was justified in dealing with rebels, and John of Lancaster's verbal quibble ('I

promis'd you redress of these same grievances') was a per-
missible if unheroic device.[1] He must not be made heroic lest he
overshadow his brother, but he is brought to our notice as a
clever and promising Prince. Likewise in IV.4 Holinshed's
account of how the King pleaded with Hal to be good to his
brothers is reversed so as to bring Thomas of Clarence into
favourable notice when his father urges him to cherish the
Prince's affection for him and to help turn his 'humorous'
nature to good. The conversation was probably invented
because Shakespeare knew that Clarence had taken Hal's place
on the Council, and did not wish to suggest any enmity between
them. This scene is remarkable also in that, when the King looks
forward sadly to the time when Hal's 'headstrong riot hath no
curb', Warwick foretells the Prince's reformation and shows the
value of his madcap phase:

> The prince but studies his companions
> Like a strange tongue, wherein, to gain the language,
> 'Tis needful that the most immodest word
> Be look'd upon and learn'd; which once attain'd,
> Your highness knows, comes to no further use,
> But to be known and hated.   (IV.4.67–78)

This both clarifies the Prince's meaning in his conversation with
Poins early in the play and reflects back on the 'I know you all'
soliloquy in Part 1, I.2.196ff. The conception of Kingship is very
different either from the careful remoteness advocated by Henry
IV himself or the 'popularity' of Richard II (*1H4* III.2.39–89).
Warwick penetrates below the surface and suggests that the
Prince has not 'lost his princely privilege By vile participation',
but has been studying human nature. In this play his relations
with his cronies are less familiar than before and his attitude to
Falstaff is more scornful, in preparation for the parting soon to
come. We are thus made ready for the great scene (IV.5) based
on Holinshed [*inf.* 277] and *Famous Victories* [Sc. viii] in
which the Prince finds his father dead (as he thinks) and takes
up the crown with a sense of his new responsibility which
becomes explicit when, after his father has summed up all his
disappointment ('Thy life did manifest thou lov'dst me not),

---

[1] Though it does not show the 'justice and honesty' which Sir T. Elyot in *The
Governour* (III.V) desired even between enemies.

alluded to the dagger interview in *Famous Victories* ('Thou had'st a thousand daggers in thy thoughts') and looked forward to the triumph of disorder, the Prince expresses his love, his loyalty and his resolve to wear the crown rightfully.

Although Shakespeare did not show the striking of the Lord Chief Justice he made good use of his later dialogue with Hal in *Famous Victories*. There it takes place after the coronation and the dismissal of the French ambassadors, when the new King is about to invade France and needs a loyal servant to tend the kingdom in his absence. He calls in the Lord Chief Justice, who comes in some fear but is rewarded for his integrity by being made Protector (Sc. ix, 876–96). Out of this short scene Shakespeare creates, in V.2, a picture of the Court mourning Henry IV and fearful of the misrule expected of his heir. The royal brothers anticipate his hostility; Warwick's previous prophecy of his reformation now seems to have been merely intended to console the dying monarch, for he expects the worst; the Lord Chief Justice awaits punishment with fortitude. Their cares are relieved when Henry V greets his brothers kindly and, after hearing the Lord Chief Justice's dignified self-defence, confirms him in his office, and in a long speech expresses his grief for his father and his determination to turn away from vanity and

> To mock the expectation of the world,
> To frustrate prophecies, and to raze out
> Rotten opinion, who hath writ me down
> After my seeming.   (V.2.43ff)

Again Shakespeare follows *Famous Victories* (Sc. ix) in V.5 when we see the King's old companions outside Westminster Abbey awaiting his return from Coronation, sure that their time has come. And so it has, but in a different sense, for the 'Olympian' quality which some critics have seen in Hal throughout is now given free rein, and he banishes them all, though with 'competence of life' and a promise of advancement should they reform. They are sent to the Fleet by the Lord Chief Justice, but John of Lancaster repeats the King's kind intentions towards them, and the play ends looking forward to war with France, but without any reference to the Lollard 'plot' ascribed to the machinations of Sir John Oldcastle (Text VI).

Recognizing the pattern of the whole play in relation to its predecessor, it is clearly wrong to object to Henry's treatment of his boon companions. The purpose of *Henry IV* was dynastic and political, a preparative to the epic theme of *Henry V*; it was to describe the troubles of the hero's father and the conversion of the son from youthful folly (never entire) to regal worth. In this serious purpose it was unlike *Famous Victories* (as we have it), where the first scenes lack all political content and the episodes revolve round the Prince's zestful participation in the low life of London. In using this play's material Shakespeare has fused it with the chronicle stuff of Holinshed and the moral intensity of Hall so that the Prince leads a double life, and from the first his immersion in Eastcheap is regarded as only temporary. This is made the more apparent in Part 2 by his late entry, and by his absence from several of the Falstaff scenes, which are developed at great length and with consummate comedy in a manner which shows Falstaff in a worse light than before. The parallels between the two Parts are contrived to augment this. Whereas in Part 1 Falstaff helps rob the Receivers (who suffer no final harm, and he himself becomes a figure of fun rather than of moral reprobation), in Part 2 he has systematically robbed the Hostess (II.1) and battens on her folly like a leech ('Hook on; hook on', he cries to Bardolph). To the old errors of wine and gluttony is now added lechery in his dallying with Doll Tearsheet (II.4, etc.). His jests now have often a disagreeably venereal turn. In his selfish malice he shows a jealous enmity to Poins. He is still immensely funny, but the humour has a stronger tang, and the element of Riot is more apparent in his own behaviour and that of his entourage. These realistic scenes still lack the crudity of the city scenes in Whetstone's *Promos and Cassandra*,[1] and we must not exaggerate their moral significance; but like their parallels in Part 1 they exemplify in their sordid unruliness a way of life at the opposite extreme from Kingship. Shakespeare has been said to have tried to give a complete picture of England in these plays. That is palpably untrue; he presents the two opposite poles of Court and Tavern. By moving from one to the other the Prince amuses himself and us vastly, but he also imperils his royal position and his realm, and in Part 2, as G. Sarrazin declared, 'Here the poet obviously has

[1] Cf. Vol. II.

more sympathy with older, mature men, than with youth.' Always when Falstaff comes into contact with the Court he is at a disadvantage, and whereas he could amuse us in Part 1 by hiding from the Sheriff, in Part 2 his first appearance brings him into opposition with the Lord Chief Justice, the King's representative, whose true accusations ('You live in great infamy', 'You have misled the youthful prince') he meets with an insolence and flippancy which, if they make us laugh, also prove his incorrigible lightness and indecency. His verbal genius and mental agility are so great that for a moment we share his indecorum, but the faster and more furious the fun, the more we realize that it cannot last.

When Falstaff goes into Gloucestershire (III.2) we have in his recruiting of soldiers an incident based on his description of his 'charge of foot' near Sutton Coldfield in Part 1, IV.2. As Miss L. B. Campbell has shown,[1] methods of recruitment and mustering were a frequent cause of scandal in Elizabethan days. Barnabe Riche among others published pamphlets on the state of the army, in one of which, *Allarme for England* (1579), he complained:

> 'Our maner of appointing of souldiers, is yet more confused than the rest, they be appointed in the countrie as it pleaseth Maister Constable: for ... if Maister Constable be in love and charitie with his neighbours, then some odde fellowe must be picked out that doth least good in the parish, it is no matter for his conditions, they thinke he cannot be too yll to make a souldier of. ...'

In 1604, Miss Campbell points out, Dudley Digges wrote of the 'poore hunger-starved snakes halfe dead ere they go out of England', and deplored the misbehaviour of

> 'such decayed unthriftie gallants as to gett a little money by the sale, spoile, or slaughter of their Companies, make meanes to be favorable sent from the Court to the Camp, as Commanders, before they knowe how to obey' (*Foure Paradoxes, or Politique Discourses*).

Shakespeare probably knew the *Instructions, Observations and Orders Militarie* of Sir John Smithe (1595), of which more will

---

[1] *Shakespeare's Histories*, by L. B. Campbell, San Marino, Cal., 1947, pp. 245–54.

be said later (*inf.* 374). Smithe believed that the Mustermaster of every shire should be a Knight or Esquire of great worship and knowledge of war, whereas commonly they were 'Captaines newlie come uppe and of small account, or else such as have beene souldiers and officers of bandes' who want 'ordinarie and yearely stipendes at the charge of the shires, as also by divers other waies and meanes to make their unlawfull gaine and profits of the subjectes' (p. 205).

About recruits he states:

> 'I would that such as should be elected and inrolled should be of honest parentage, and that their education and course of life had beene such, as there were no notable vice to be noted in them, and chiefly of drunkennesse, theft, blaspheming, common swearing, or brawling. Al which vices are such, as they cause al such as are possessed of them to be disordered, mutinous, and disobedient, which are things most contrary to al true discipline.
>
> 'Also I would if it might be, that al such as should be elected and chosen to be soldiers, should be of themselves of some abilitie and substance either in landes, or goods, or both: or else that from their parentes, they should be in possibilitie after their deceases to enjoye some lands, or goods, or both.'

Falstaff's recruits are wretched fellows, certainly not men of substance, but they are not likely to be mutinous or disobedient! On the other hand the vices to be avoided are just those found among the Eastcheap rascals who are elevated into positions of some authority. Bardolph becomes a corporal and is later executed (in *Henry V*) for sacrilegious theft, and Pistol obtains a captaincy (II.4.140–7), which excites Doll's derision. Peto perhaps merits a more honourable place, by the Prince's side.

The recruiting scene may have been suggested by the short passage in *Famous Victories* (Sc. x) where John Cobler and the thief are pressed by a Captain and go to war unwillingly whereas Dericke the countryman goes gladly. Shakespeare makes it a formal affair before two Justices of the Peace, and we see the arbitrary nature of Falstaff's proceedings, with Bardolph taking bribes to exempt Mouldy and Bullcalf. Sir John is as irresponsible in rural surroundings as he was in the city.

In Shallow we have the portrait of a foolish unjust Justice to contrast with that of the Lord Chief Justice. For besides letting himself be hoodwinked by Falstaff Shallow is persuaded by his steward Davy to 'countenance William Visor of Woncot against Clement Perkes of the hill', despite the fact that Visor is a knave: 'The knave is mine honest friend, sir; therefore I beseech your worship, let him be countenanc'd.'

Falstaff's rightful place is in this slipshod world of urban and rustic corruption, among roisterers, coney-catchers and their victims. His final error is to fancy that, with Henry V's accession, the day of Misrule has arrived: 'Let us take any man's horses; the laws of England are at my commandment' (V.3. 137–40). One is reminded of Phallax in *Promos and Cassandra*, who misused the law under Promos[1]; and of Nimble in *Thomas of Woodstock*, whom the upstart Lord Chief Justice Tressilian promotes, saying 'I rule the lawe: thou by the lawe shalt stand.'[2] But that Falstaff's world is already tottering appears in V.4 when Mistress Quickly and Doll are arrested, 'for the man is dead that you and Pistol beat among you'. Falstaff thinks that he can free Doll from durance vile, but he soon learns that the new King has 'turn'd away his former self', and there is no place near him for 'the tutor and the feeder of my riots' (V.5.49–64). He cannot believe that the King is not merely pretending; for he cannot understand the nature of true Kingship.

The turning-off of Falstaff shows that Shakespeare's—as well as Henry's—sense of values was firmly based. The summary manner of its performance is a fine theatrical stroke, but it has been prepared for. All that is lacking to make us sympathize fully with the new-crowned King's action is some previous indication either of sorrow at a painful duty or of revulsion against all that Falstaff represented. The dramatist sacrifices this to obtain his *coup de théâtre*, which is also, in its public proof of Henry's conversion to a new way of life, a political necessity. We should not sentimentalize over the grasping rogue's affection for the Prince, which was always based on self-interest, tap-room goodfellowship and the expectation of plenty. He will not starve. So the long, ambivalent relationship in which our pleasure in the play of wit and genial rascality has generally,

---

[1] Cf. Vol. II, p. 454, Act 2, Sc. 4.   [2] Cf. Vol. III, p. 467.

though of late with some difficulty, overborne our disapproval of Falstaff's dangerous influence, ends with a thunderclap of moral judgement. For *Henry IV*, Part 2 is, like Part 1, a play about kingly responsibility and justice and the Prince's growth into these for the orderly rule of the realm.

> 'The auncient Civilians [wrote Sir John Eliot] do saye justyce is a wille perpetuall and constaunt, whiche gyveth to every man his right. In that it is named constaunt, it importeth fortitude; in discernynge what is ryght or wronge, prudence is required; and to proporcion the sentence or jugement in an equalitie, it belongeth to temperaunce. All these to gether conglutinate and effectually executed maketh a perfecte definicion of justyce' (*The Governour*, III.1).

It is easy to see how Shakespeare has handled the chief characters of Part 2 with regard to such a conception of justice. The King has fortitude, prudence and temperance, but since he got his throne by wresting it from the rightful monarch, he lacks the 'wille perpetuall and constaunt, whiche gyveth to every man his right'. Falstaff lacks all the qualities which when 'conglutinate' make up justice. The Prince lacks prudence and temperance, but learns to respect them and finally makes them his own. His sins against giving every man his right are more apparent than real and go back to Part 1 where he robs the Receivers in jest but restores their money 'with advantage'. In Part 2 he sins (offstage) against this quality of justice when he insults and strikes the Lord Chief Justice; but he redeems this fault, and he 'gyveth every man his right' when he banishes his former comrades. He showed fortitude at Shrewsbury and will show it again in *Henry V*. The Lord Chief Justice and Shallow represent degrees of justice in its more narrowly legal aspects.

Encircling this theme is the more general topic of social and moral order which, as Dr Tillyard has shown, pervades all the Histories. The curse of disorder through rebellion which Henry IV brought upon himself in *Richard II* continues to work in this play. He cannot find rest, or wash the blood from off his guilty hand by making the voyage to the Holy Land which he there promised. His enemies deliberately propose to wade through blood to a new order, but their motives are unsound. The 'gentle Archbishop' wishes to avenge the blood of Richard, and blinds himself with the false notions that Bolingbroke's rule is bad and that 'The commonwealth is sick with their own choice.' Mowbray wishes to avenge his father's exile, and the treacherous Northumberland after his son's death wants disruption and chaos:

> 'let order die!
> And let this world no longer be a stage
> To feed contention in a lingering act;
> But let one spirit of the first-born Cain
> Reign in all bosoms, that, each heart being set
> On bloody courses, the rude scene may end,
> And darkness be the burier of the dead!'　(I.1.154–60)

In the opinion of the King and the good men around him the Prince is a danger to order even more insidious and fatal than these open plotters. He has relapsed from the heroic promise shown at the end of Part 1 and there seems a strong likelihood that his reign will be worse than Richard II's, that he will bring in the chaos desired by Percy. Hence his father's despairing cry:

> Harry the Fifth is crown'd! Up vanity!
> Down royal state! all you sage counsellors, hence!
> And to the English court assemble now,
> From every region, apes of idleness! . . .
> For the fifth Harry from curb'd license plucks
> The muzzle of restraint, and the wild dog
> Shall feast his tooth in every innocent.　(IV.5.116–36)

Fortunately we know that, owing to the Prince's innate nobility, this and similar previous forebodings are untrue. A pervasive dramatic irony enables us to enter fully into the humorous disorders of Eastcheap because we know that appearances are contradicted by coming realities, and dire expectations will be confounded. The Falstaff scenes are to be regarded therefore not as a little comedy separable from the rest, but as part of the ethical and sociological pattern of the whole. Shakespeare's inability to make the rebels as interesting as those in Part 1, and the exuberant delight he takes in depicting the London under-world of his own time, fail to provide the desirable dramatic counterweight to these comic scenes, and excite a suspicion that Shakespeare 'was of the devil's party without knowing it'.

This is wrong. A passion for justice need not eliminate all appreciation of the pleasures of self-indulgence. Shakespeare knew that human beings were mixed in their nature, compound of good and bad instincts. So Falstaff was not just a Vice, or even a Hick Scorner [Text VII]. He deserves his by no means harsh fate; but he has been a perpetual spring of humour and dexterity; and he has played a great part in liberalizing Kingship, in giving Hal the wide knowledge of men which the dramatist thought essential to the perfect monarch. We have seen the heir to the throne consciously stooping 'from a prince to a prentice! a low transformation' (II.2.176–7). He has without much difficulty regained his princely level. He has touched pitch and not been defiled. Soon we shall see, in *Henry V*, that, given poise and understanding by such experience, he can walk with common men nor lose the kingly touch.

I. Source

From THE THIRD VOLUME OF CHRONICLES

by R. Holinshed (1587 edition)

[An analogy to Prince Henry.]

[313/2/27]   In the three and thirtith yeare of his reigne, king
Edward put his sonne prince Edward in prison, bicause that he had
riotouslie broken the parke of Walter Langton bishop of Chester[1];
and bicause the prince had doone this deed by the procurement of a
lewd and wanton person, one Peers Gavaston, an esquire of Gas-
coine, the king banished him the realme, least the prince, who
delighted much in his companie, might by his evill and wanton
counsell fall to evill and naughtie rule.

[Edward II.]

[318/1/43]   But now concerning the demeanour of this new king,
whose disordered maners brought himselfe and manie others unto
destruction; we find that in the beginning of his governement,
though he was of nature given to lightnesse, yet being restreined
with the prudent advertisements of certeine of his councellors, to the
end he might shew some likelihood of good proofe, he counterfeited
a kind of gravitie, vertue and modestie; but yet he could not throughlie be so bridled, but that foorthwith he began to plaie divers wanton
and light parts, at the first indeed not outragiouslie, but by little and
little, and that covertlie. For having revoked againe into England
his old mate the said Peers de Gaveston,[2] he received him into most
high favour, creating him earle of Cornewall, and lord of Man, his
principall secretarie, and lord chamberlaine of the realme, through
whose companie and societie he was suddenlie so corrupted, that he
burst out into most heinous vices; for then using the said Peers as a

---

[1] *In margin:* 'Prince Edward committed to ward. Caxton. Fabian.' The King
here was Edward I, whose son became Edward II and ruled badly.
[2] *In margin:* 'Peers de Gaveston.'

procurer of his disordred dooings, he began to have his nobles in no regard, to set nothing by their instructions, and to take small heed unto the good governement of the commonwealth, so that within a while, he gave himselfe to wantonnes, passing his time in voluptuous pleasure, and riotous excesse: and to helpe them forward in that kind of life, the foresaid Peers, who (as it may be thought, he had sworne to make the king to forget himselfe, and the state, to the which he was called) furnished his court with companies of jesters, ruffians, flattering parasites, musicians, and other vile and naughtie ribalds, that the king might spend both daies and nights in jesting, plaieng, banketing, and in such oother filthie and dishonorable exercises: and moreover, desirous to advance those that were like to him selfe, he procured for them honorable offices, all which notable preferments and dignities, sith they were ill bestowed, were rather to be accounted dishonorable than otherwise, both to the giver and the receiver.[1]

[The situation after the Battle of Shrewsbury, 1403.]

[524/1/3] The earle of Northumberland was now marching forward with great power, which he had got thither, either to aid his sonne and brother (as was thought) or at the least towards the king, to procure a peace: but the earle of Westmerland, and sir Robert Waterton knight, had got an armie on foot, and meant to meet him.[2] The earle of Northumberland, taking neither of them to be his freend, turned suddenlie backe, and withdrew himselfe into Warkewoorth castell.[3] The king having set a staie in things about Shrewesburie, went straight to Yorke,[4] from whence he wrote to the earle of Northumberland, willing him to dismisse his companies that he had with him, and to come unto him in peaceable wise. The earle upon receipt of the kings letter came unto him the morow after saint Laurence daie,[5] having but a few of his servants to attend him, and so excused himselfe, that the king (bicause the earle had Berwike in his possession, and further, had his castels of Alnewike, Warkewoorth, and other, fortified with Scots) dissembled the matter, gave him faire words, and suffered him (as saith *Hall*) to depart home,

---

[1] Cf. Henry IV's fears, IV.5.116–36.
[2] *In margin:* 'The earle of Westmerland raiseth a power against the earle of Northumberland.' Cf. I.i.131–5. 'Young Lancaster' replaces Waterton as in *1H4* V.5.35.
[3] Shakespeare begins I.1 at Warkworth, whither Northumberland has gone before hearing of his son's defeat and death. He omits the submission and two subsequent years of peace.
[4] *In margin:* 'The king goeth to Yorke.'
[5] *In margin:* 'The earle of Northumberland commeth to the king.'

although by other it should seeme, that he was committed for a time to safe custodie.

[525/1/46] All this summer, Owen Glendouer and his adherents, robbed, burned, and destroied the countries adjoining neere to the places where he hanted,[1] and one while by sleight & guilefull policie, an other while by open force, he tooke and slue manie Englishmen, brake downe certeine castels which he wan, and some he fortified and kept for his owne defense. John Trenor bishop of Assaph, considering with himselfe how things prospered under the hands of this Owen, fled to him, and tooke his part against the king.

[529/1/46] Whilest such dooings were in hand betwixt the English and French, as the besieging of Marke castell by the earle of saint Paule, and the sending foorth of the English fleet, under the governance of the lord Thomas of Lancaster, and the earle of Kent, the king was minded to have gone into Wales against the Welsh rebels, that under their cheefteine Owen Glendouer, ceassed not to doo much mischeefe still against the English subjects.

But at the same time, to his further disquieting, there was a conspiracie[2] put in practise against him at home by the earle of Northumberland, who had conspired with Richard Scroope archbishop of Yorke, Thomas Mowbraie earle marshall, sonne to Thomas duke of Norfolke, who for the quarrell betwixt him and king Henrie had beene banished (as ye have heard) the lords Hastings, Fauconbridge, Berdolfe, and diverse others. It was appointed that they should meet altogither with their whole power, upon Yorkeswold, at a daie assigned, and that the earle of Northumberland should be cheefteine, promising to bring with him a great number of Scots. The archbishop accompanied with the earle marshall, devised certeine articles of such matters, as it was supposed that not onelie the commonaltie of the Realme, but also the nobilitie found themselves greeved with[3]: which articles they shewed first unto such of their adherents as were neere about them, & after sent them abroad to their freends further off, assuring them that for redresse of such oppressions, they would shed the last drop of blood in their bodies, if need were.[4]

The archbishop not meaning to staie after he saw himselfe accompanied with a great number of men, that came flocking to Yorke to take his part in this quarrell, foorthwith discovered his

---

[1] *In margin:* 'Owen Glendouer wasted the English marches.' [1404].

[2] *In margin:* 'A new conspiracie against king Henrie by the earle of Northumberland & others.' Cf. *1H4* V.5.37–8; *2H4* I.1.189. In I.3 there is doubt about Northumberland's participation.

[3] Cf. I.3.34–108. The articles are later given to Westmoreland, IV.1.168ff.

[4] Cf. IV.2.42–3.

enterprise, causing the articles aforsaid to be set up in the publike streets of the citie of Yorke, and upon the gates of the monasteries, that ech man might understand the cause that mooved him to rise in armes against the king, the reforming whereof did not yet apperteine unto him.[1] Hereupon knights, esquiers, gentlemen, yeomen, and other of the commons, as well of the citie, townes and countries about, being allured either for desire of change,[2] or else for desire to see a reformation in such things as were mentioned in the articles, assembled togither in great numbers; and the archbishop comming foorth amongst them clad in armor,[3] incouraged, exhorted, and (by all meanes he could) pricked them foorth to take the enterprise in hand, and manfullie to continue in their begun purpose, promising forgivenesse of sinnes to all them, whose hap it was to die in the quarrell: and thus not onelie all the citizens of Yorke, but all other in the countries about, that were able to beare weapon, came to the archbishop, and the earle marshall. In deed the respect that men had to the archbishop, caused them to like the better of the cause, since the gravitie of his age, his integritie of life, and incomparable learning, with the reverend aspect of his amiable personage, mooved all men to have him in no small estimation.[4]

The king advertised of these matters, meaning to prevent them, left his journie into Wales, and marched with all speed towards the north parts.[5] Also Rafe Nevill earle of Westmerland, that was not farre off, togither with the lord John of Lancaster the kings sonne, being informed of this rebellious attempt, assembled togither such power as they might make,[6] and togither with those which were appointed to attend on the said lord John to defend the borders against the Scots, as the lord Henrie Fitzhugh, the lord Rafe Eevers, the lord Robert Umfrevill, & others, made forward against the rebels, and comming into a plaine within the forrest of Galtree,[7] caused their standards to be pitched downe in like sort as the archbishop had pitched his, over against them, being farre stronger in number of people than the other, for (as some write) there were of the rebels at the least twentie thousand men.

[1] *In margin:* 'The archbishop of Yorke one of the cheefe conspirators.' Cf. IV.i. 98, Westmoreland on redress: 'it not belongs to you'.

[2] Cf. the Archbishop's attack, I.3.87–108.

[3] *In margin:* 'The archbishop in armor.' Lancaster, IV.2.8, calls him 'an iron man'.

[4] *In margin:* 'The estimation which men had of the archbishop of Yorke.' I.1.200–9. Lancaster, IV.2.15–22, has shared this respect.

[5] He thus upsets the conspirators' hopes expressed in I.3.70–85.

[6] *In margin:* 'The earle of Westmerland and the lord John of Lancaster, the kings sonne prepare themselves to resist the kings enimies.' Cf. I.3.82.

[7] *In margin:* 'The forest of Galtree.' The meeting occurred at Shipton Moor on 29 May, 1405. Cf. IV.1.2.

When the earle of Westmerland perceived the force of the adversaries, and that they laie still and attempted not to come forward
upon him, he subtillie devised how to quaile their purpose,[1] and
foorthwith dispatched messengers unto the archbishop to understand
the cause as it were of that great assemblie, and for what cause (contrarie to the kings peace) they came so in a[r]mour. The archbishop
answered, that he tooke nothing in hand against the kings peace,[2]
but that whatsoever he did, tended rather to advance the peace and
quiet of the common-wealth, than otherwise; and where he and his
companie were in armes, it was for feare of the king, to whom he
could have no free accesse, by reason of such a multitude of flatterers
as were about him[3]; and therefore he mainteined that his purpose to
be good & profitable, as well for the king himselfe, as for the realme,
if men were willing to understand a truth: & herewith he shewed
foorth a scroll, in which the articles were written wherof before ye
have heard.

The messengers returning to the earle of Westmerland, shewed
him what they had heard & brought from the archbishop.[4] When
he had read the articles, he shewed in word and countenance out-
wardly that he liked[5] of the archbishops holie and vertuous intent
and purpose, promising that he and his would prosecute the same in
assisting the archbishop, who rejoising hereat, gave credit to the
earle, and persuaded the earle marshall (against his will as it were)
to go with him to a place appointed for them to commune togither.[6]
Here when they were met with like number on either part, the
articles were read over, and without anie more adoo, the earle of
Westmerland and those that were with him agreed to doo their best,
to see that a reformation might be had, according to the same.

The earle of Westmerland using more policie than the rest[7]: Well
(said he) then our travell is come to the wished end: and where our
people have beene long in armour, let them depart home to their
woonted trades and occupations: in the meane time let us drinke
togither in signe of agreement, that the people on both sides maie see
it, and know that it is true, that we be light at a point. They had no
sooner shaken hands togither, but that a knight was sent streight
waies from the archbishop, to bring word to the people that there

[1] In margin: 'The subtill policie of the earle of Westmerland.' He meets them
himself at IV.1.25.

[2] In margin: 'The archbishops protestation why he had on him armes.' Cf.
IV.2.31: 'I am not here against your father's peace.'　　　　[3] Cf. IV.1.78–9.

[4] Scrope gives them to Westmoreland at IV.1.168–77. Lancaster has read them
before the next scene.

[5] 'I like them all', says Prince John, IV.2.54.　　　　[6] IV.1.178–223.

[7] In margin: 'The earle of Westmerlands politike dealing.' Shakespeare gives the
trick to Prince John, IV.2.55–65.

was peace concluded, commanding ech man to laie aside his armes, and to resort home to their houses. The people beholding such tokens of peace, as shaking of hands, and drinking togither of the lords in loving manner they being alreadie wearied with the unaccustomed travell of warre, brake up their field and returned homewards[1]: but in the meane time, whilest the people of the archbishops side withdrew awaie, the number of the contrarie part increased,[2] according to order given by the earle of Westmerland; and yet the archbishop perceived not that he was deceived, untill the earle of Westmerland arrested both him and the earle marshall, with diverse other.[3] Thus saith *Walsingham*.

But others write somwhat otherwise of this matter, affirming that the earle of Westmerland in deed, and the lord Rafe Eevers, procured the archbishop & the earle marshall, to come to a communication with them, upon a ground just in the midwaie betwixt both the armies,[4] where the earle of Westmerland in talke declared to them how perilous an enterprise they had taken in hand, so to raise the people, and to moove warre against the king, advising them therefore to submit themselves without further delaie unto the kings mercie, and his sonne the lord John, who was present there in the field with banners spred, redie to trie the matter by dint of sword, if they refused this counsell: and therefore he willed them to remember themselves well; & if they would not yeeld and crave the kings pardon, he bad them doo their best to defend themselves.

Hereupon as well the archbishop as the earle marshall submitted themselves unto the king, and to his sonne the lord John that was there present, and returned not to their armie. Whereupon their troops scaled and fled their waies: but being pursued, manie were taken, manie slaine, and manie spoiled of that that they had about them, & so permitted to go their waies. Howsoever the matter was handled, true it is that the archbishop, and the earle marshall were brought to Pomfret to the king, who in this meane while was advanced thither with his power, and from thence he went to Yorke, whither the prisoners were also brought, and there beheaded the morrow after Whitsundaie in a place without the citie, that is to understand, the archbishop himselfe, the earle marshall, sir John Lampleie, and sir Robert Plumpton.[5] Unto all which persons though indemnitie were promised, yet was the same to none of them at anie hand performed. By the issue hereof, I meane the death of the

---

[1] IV.2.105.   [2] IV.2.98–101.

[3] *In margin:* 'The archbishop of Yorke and the earle marshall arrested.' IV.2.108.

[4] Shakespeare uses this (IV.1.179), increasing the Prince's part.

[5] *In margin:* 'The archbishop of Yorke, the earle marshall, & others put to death.' IV.2.122; IV.4.84–5.

foresaid, but speciallie of the archbishop, the prophesie of a sickelie
canon of Bridlington in Yorkeshire fell out to be true, who darklie
inough foretold this matter, & the infortunate event thereof in these
words hereafter following, saieng:

Pacem tractabunt, sed fraudem subter arabunt,
Pro nulla marca, saluabitur ille[1] hierarcha.

The archbishop suffered death verie constantlie, insomuch as the
common people tooke it, he died a martyr,[2] affirming that certeine
miracles were wrought as well in the field where he was executed, as
also in the place where he was buried: and immediatlie upon such
bruits, both men and women began to worship his dead carcasse,
whom they loved so much when he was alive, till they were forbidden
by the kings freends, and for feare gave over to visit the place of his
sepulture. The earle marshals bodie by the kings leave was buried in
the cathedrall church, manie lamenting his destinie; but his head
was set on a pole aloft on the wals for a certeine space, till by the
kings permission [after the same had suffered manie a hot sunnie
daie and manie a wet shower of raine] it was taken downe and buried
togither with the bodie.

After the king, accordinglie as seemed to him good, had ransomed and punished by greevous fines the citizens of Yorke (which
had borne armour on their archbishops side against him) he
departed from Yorke with an armie of thirtie and seven thousand
fighting men, furnished with all provision necessarie, marching
northwards against the earle of Northumberland. At his comming to
Durham, the lord Hastings, the lord Fauconbridge, sir John Colle-
vill of the Dale, and sir John Griffith, being convicted of the conspiracie, were there beheaded.[3] [Northumberland and Bardolf fled
to Scotland.]

[534/1/20] The earle of Northumberland, and the lord Bardolfe,
after they had beene in Wales, in France and Flanders, to purchase
aid against king Henrie, were returned backe into Scotland, and had
remained there now for the space of a whole yeare: and, as their
evill fortune would, whilest the king held a councell of the nobilitie
at London, the said earle of Northumberland and lord Bardolfe, in a
dismall houre, with a great power of Scots returned into England,[4]
recovering diverse of the earls castels and seigniories, for the people

---

[1] *In margin:* 'Archiepiscopus.' Trans.: 'They will treat for peace but foster secret
deceit; nor shall that great priest be saved for all his distinction.'

[2] *In margin:* 'The archbishop reputed a martyr.'

[3] *In margin:* 'The lords executed.' In IV.3 Colevile surrenders to Falstaff.

[4] *In margin:* '1408. The earle of Northumb. & the lord Bardolfe returne into
England.' IV.4.98: 'With a great power of English and of Scots.'

in great numbers resorted unto them. Heereupon, incouraged with hope of good successe, they entred into Yorkeshire, & there began to destroie the countrie. At their comming to Threske, they published a proclamation, signifieng that they were come in comfort of the English nation, as to releeve the common-wealth, willing all such as loved the libertie of their countrie, to repaire unto them, with their armor on their backes, and in defensible wise to assist them.

The king advertised hereof, caused a great armie to be assembled, and came forward with the same towards his enimies: but yer the king came to Nottingham, sir Thomas, or (as other copies have) Rafe Rokesbie shiriffe of Yorkeshire,[1] assembled the forces of the countrie to resist the earle and his power, comming to Grimbaut brigs, beside Knaresbourgh, there to stop them the passage; but they returning aside, got to Weatherbie, and so to Tadcaster, and finallie came forward unto Bramham more, neere to Haizelwood, where they chose their ground meet to fight upon. The shiriffe was as readie to give battell as the earle to receive it,[2] and so with a standard of S. George spred, set fiercelie upon the earle, who under a standard of his owne armes incountred his adversaries with great manhood. There was a sore incounter and cruell conflict betwixt the parties but in the end the victorie fell to the shiriffe. The lord Bardolfe was taken, but sore wounded, so that he shortlie after died of the hurts. As for the earle of Northumberland, he was slaine outright[3]: so that now the prophesie was fulfilled, which gave an inkling of this his heavie hap long before; namelie,

Stirps Persitina periet confusa ruina.[4]

For this earle was the stocke and maine root of all that were left alive called by the name of Persie; and of manie more by diverse slaughters dispatched. For whose misfortune the people were not a little sorrie, making report of the gentlemans valiantnesse, renowne, and honour, and applieng unto him certeine lamentable verses out of *Lucane*, saieng:

> *Sed nos nec sanguis, nec tantum vulnera nostri*
> *Affecere senis; quantum gestata per urbem*
> *Ora ducis, quæ transfixo deformia pilo*
> *Vidimus.*[5]

[1] *In margin:* 'The shiriffe of Yorkeshire.'
[2] *In margin:* 'His hardie corage to fight.' IV.4.99.
[3] *In margin:* 'The earle of Northumberland slaine.'
[4] i.e. 'The Percy stock shall perish in disordered ruin.'
[5] *Pharsalia*, Bk ix, 136: 'But neither the blood nor the wounds of our old father moved us so much as when we saw his head—our leader's head—carried through the city, shapeless and transfixed on a pike.' (Spoken by Pompey's son about his father, slain in Egypt.)

For his head, full of silver horie heares, being put upon a stake, was openlie carried through London, and set upon the bridge of the same citie: in like maner was the lord Bardolfes. The bishop of Bangor was taken and pardoned by the king, for that when he was apprehended, he had no armor on his backe. This battell was fought the ninteenth day of Februarie. The king to purge the North parts of all rebellion, and to take order for the punishment of those that were accused to have succoured and assisted the earle of Northumberland, went to Yorke, where when manie were condemned, and diverse put to great fines, and the countrie brought to quietnesse, he caused the abbat of Hailes to be hanged,[1] who had beene in armour against him with the foresaid earle . . .

[536/1/1]   The Welsh rebell Owen Glendouer made an end of his wretched life in this tenth yeare of king Henrie his reigne, being driven now in his latter time (as we find recorded) to such miserie, that in manner despairing of all comfort, he fled into desert places and solitarie caves, where being destitute of all releefe and succour, dreading to shew his face to anie creature, and finallie lacking meat to susteine nature, for meere hunger and lacke of food, miserablie pined awaie and died[2]. . . [1409]

[540/1/45]   In this yeare [1411] and upon the twelfth day of October, were three flouds in the Thames, the one following upon the other, and no ebbing betweene[3]: which thing no man then living could remember the like to be seene.

[The King falls ill and the Prince takes away the Crown.]

[540/2/60]   In this fourteenth and last yeare of king Henries reigne, a councell was holden in the white friers in London, at the which, among other things, order was taken for ships and gallies to be builded and made readie, and all other things necessarie to be provided for a voiage which he meant to make into the holie land, there to recover the citie of Jerusalem from the Infidels.[4] For it greeved him to consider the great malice of christian princes, that were bent upon a mischeefous purpose to destroie one another, to the perill of their owne soules, rather than to make war against the enimies of the christian faith, as in conscience (it seemed to him) they were bound. He held his Christmas this yeare at Eltham, being sore vexed with sicknesse, so that it was thought sometime, that he

---

[1] *In margin:* 'The abbat of Hails hanged.'

[2] *In margin:* 'Owen Glendouer endeth his life in great miserie.' Not true, but cf. III.1.103.

[3] Cf. Clarence, IV.4.125–8.

[4] *In margin:* 'The k. meant to have made a journie against the Infidels.' Cf. *1H4* I.1.18–29; *2H4* IV.5.208–11. He had visited Jerusalem in 1393.

had beene dead[1]: notwithstanding it pleased God that he somwhat recovered his strength againe, and so passed that Christmasse with as much joy as he might.

The morrow after Candlemas daie began a parlement,[2] which he had called at London, but he departed this life before the same parlement was ended: for now that his provisions were readie, and that he was furnished with sufficient treasure, soldiers, capteins, vittels, munitions, tall ships, strong gallies, and all things necessarie for such a royall journie as he pretended to take into the holie land,[3] he was eftsoones taken with a sore sicknesse, which was not a leprosie, striken by the hand of God (saith maister *Hall*) as foolish friers imagined; but a verie apoplexie,[4] of the which he languished till his appointed houre, and had none other greefe nor maladie; so that what man ordeineth, God altereth at his good will and pleasure, not giving place more to the prince, than to the poorest creature living, when he seeth his time to dispose of him this waie or that, as to his omnipotent power and divine providence seemeth expedient. During this his last sicknesse, he caused his crowne (as some write) to be set on a pillow at his beds head,[5] and suddenlie his pangs so sore troubled him, that he laie as though all his vitall spirits had beene from him departed. Such as were about him, thinking verelie that he had been departed, covered his face with a linnen cloth.[6]

The prince his sonne being hereof advertised, entered into the chamber, tooke awaie the crowne, and departed.[7] The father being suddenlie revived out of that trance, quicklie perceived the lacke of his crowne[8]; and having knowledge that the prince his sonne had taken it awaie, caused him to come before his presence, requiring of him what he meant so to misuse himselfe.[9] The prince with a good audacitie answered; Sir, to mine and all mens judgements you seemed dead in this world, wherefore I as your next heire apparant tooke that as mine owne, and not as yours.[10] Well faire sonne (said the

---

[1] *In margin:* 'The king is vexed with sicknesse.'
[2] *In margin:* '1413. A parlement.'   [3] IV.4.5–8.
[4] *In margin:* 'The K. sick of an apoplexie.' Hall, in a marginal note, gives symptoms of apoplexy which may have suggested Falstaff's comic recital in I.2.108–19. 'Apoplexye is a sicknesse ingendered of grose humors whiche fil the vessels of the heade from whence the felyng of the body cometh. And therefore they whiche have this disease are deprived of felyng, speache & movyng' (Hall). Falstaff, however, says, 'It is a kind of deafness.' Cf. also IV.4.110–11.
[5] Cf. IV.5.5.   [6] Shakespeare omits this.
[7] *In margin:* 'The prince taketh awaie the crowne before his father was dead.' Cf. IV.5.20–46.   [8] IV.5.47–56.
[9] *In margin:* 'He is blamed of the king.' IV.5.58–136.
[10] *In margin:* 'His answer.' IV.5.40–6 (soliloquy).

king with a great sigh) what right I had to it, God knoweth.[1] Well
(said the prince) if you die king, I will have the garland, and trust to
keepe it with the sword against all mine enimies, as you have doone.
Then said the king, I commit all to God, and remember you to doo
well. With that he turned himselfe in his bed, and shortlie after
departed to God[2] in a chamber of the abbats of Westminster called
Jerusalem the twentith daie of March, in the yeare 1413, and in the
yeare of his age 46, when he had reigned thirteene yeares, five
moneths and od daies, in great perplexitie and little pleasure [or
foureteene yeares, as some have noted, who name not the disease
whereof he died, but refer it to sicknesse absolutelie, whereby his
time of departure did approach and fetch him out of the world: as
Ch. Okl.[3] saith, whose words may serve as a funerall epigramme in
memoriall of the said king Henrie:

> *Henricus quartus bis septem rexerat annos*
> *Anglorum gentem summa cum laude & amore,*
> *Iamque senescenti fatalis terminus ævi*
> *Ingruerat, morbus fatalem accerserat horam.*][4]

We find, that he was taken with his last sickenesse, while he was
making his praiers at saint Edwards shrine, there as it were to take
his leave, and so to proceed foorth on his journie: he was so suddenlie
and greevouslie taken, that such as were about him, feared least he
would have died presentlie, wherfore to releeve him (if it were
possible) they bare him into a chamber that was next at hand,
belonging to the abbat of Westminster, where they laid him on a
pallet before the fire, and used all remedies to revive him. At
length, he recovered his speech, and understanding and perceiving
himselfe in a strange place which he knew not, he willed to know if
the chamber had anie particular name, whereunto answer was
made, that it was called Jerusalem. Then said the king; Lauds be
given to the father of heaven, for now I know that I shall die heere in
this chamber, according to the prophesie of me declared, that I
should depart this life in Jerusalem.[5]

Whether this was true that so he spake, as one that gave too much
credit to foolish prophesies & vaine tales, or whether it was fained,
as in such cases it commonlie happeneth, we leave it to the advised

---

[1] *In margin:* 'A guiltie conscience in extremitie of sicknesse pincheth sore.'
IV.5. 182–5; 217–18.

[2] *In margin:* The death of Henrie the fourth.

[3] Christopher Ockland, *Anglorum Praelia ab anno 1327 usque ad annum* 1558.
R. Newberie ex assig. H. Bynneman [1580].

[4] 'For twice seven years Henry IV had ruled the English people with praise and
love; and now the destined end of his old age came upon him, and sickness brought
the fatal hour.'   [5] IV.5.231–9.

reader to judge. His bodie with all funerall pompe was conveied unto Canturburie, and there solemnlie buried,[1] leaving behind him by the ladie Marie daughter to the lord Humfrie Bohun earle of Hereford and Northhampton, Henrie prince of Wales, Thomas duke of Clarence, John duke of Bedford, Humfrie duke of Glocester, Blanch duchesse of Bavier, and Philip queene of Denmarke[2]: by his last wife Jane, he had no children. This king was of a meane stature,[3] well proportioned, and formallie compact, quicke and livelie, and of a stout courage. In his latter daies he shewed himselfe so gentle, that he gat more love amongst the nobles and people of this realme, than he had purchased malice and evill will in the beginning.

But yet to speake a truth, by his proceedings, after he had atteined to the crowne, what with such taxes, tallages, subsidies, and exactions he was constreined to charge the people with; and what by punishing such as mooved with disdeine to see him usurpe the crowne (contrarie to the oth taken at his entring into this land, upon his returne from exile) did at sundrie times rebell against him, he wan himselfe more hatred,[4] than in all his life time (if it had beene longer by manie yeares than it was) had beene possible for him to have weeded out[5] & remooved. And yet doubtlesse, woorthie were his subjects to tast of that bitter cup, sithens they were so readie to joine and clappe hands with him, for the deposing of their rightfull and naturall prince king Richard, whose cheefe fault rested onlie in that, that he was too bountifull to his freends, and too mercifull to his foes; speciallie if he had not beene drawne by others, to seeke revenge of those that abused his good and courteous nature.

[The accession of Henry V.]

[543/1/1]   Henrie prince of Wales son and heire to K. Henrie the fourth, borne in Wales at Monmouth on the river of Wie, after his father was departed tooke upon him the regiment of this realme of England, the twentith of March, the morrow after proclaimed king, by the name of Henrie the fift, in the yeare of the world 5375, after the birth of our saviour, by our account 1413, the third of the emperor Sigismund: the three and thirtith of Charles the sixt French king, and in the seventh yeare of governance in Scotland under Robert brother to him that (before entrance into his kingdome 1390) had John to name, which by devise and order of the states was changed into Robert the third, who at Rotsaie (a towne in the Iland of Got, 1406) deceassed. . . .

---

[1] *In margin:* 'He is buried at Canturburie.'
[3] *In margin:* 'His stature.'
[5] Cf. Scrope, IV.1.205.

[2] *In margin:* 'His issue.'
[4] Cf. IV.5.184–5; 191–7.

[543/1/47] Such great hope, and good expectation was had of
this mans fortunate successe to follow, that within three daies after
his fathers deceasse, diverse noble men and honorable personages
did him homage, and sware to him due obedience, which had not
beene seene doone to any of his predecessors kings of this realme, till
they had beene possessed of the crowne.[1] He was crowned the ninth
of Aprill being Passion sundaie, which was a sore, ruggie, and
tempestuous day,[2] with wind, snow and sleet, that men greatlie
marvelled thereat, making diverse interpretations what the same
might signifie. But this king even at first appointing with himselfe,
to shew that in his person princelie honors should change publike
manners, he determined to put on him the shape of a new man.[3] For
whereas aforetime he had made himselfe a companion unto misrulie
mates of dissolute order and life, he now banished them all from his
presence (but not unrewarded, or else unpreferred) inhibiting them
upon a great paine, not once to approch, lodge, or sojourne within
ten miles of his court or presence[4]: and in their places he chose men
of gravitie, wit, and high policie, by whose wise counsell[5] he might
at all times rule to his honour and dignitie; calling to mind how once
to hie offense of the king his father, he had with his fist striken the
cheefe justice for sending one of his minions (upon desert) to prison,
when the justice stoutlie commanded himselfe also streict to ward, &
he (then prince) obeied.[6] The king after expelled him out of his
privie councell, banisht him the court, and made the duke of
Clarence (his yoonger brother) president of councell in his steed.[7]
This reformation in the new king *Christ. Okl.* hath reported, fullie
consenting with this. For saith he,

> *Ille inter iuvenes paulo lascivior ante,*
> *Defuncto genitore gravis constansque repente,*
> *Moribus ablegat corruptis regis ab aula*
> *Assuetos socios, & nugatoribus acrem*
> *Pœnam (siquisquam sua tecta reviserit) addit,*
> *Atque ita mutatus facit omnia principe digna,*
> *Ingenio magno post consultoribus usus, &c.*[8]

---

[1] *In margin:* 'Homage doone to K. Henrie before his coronation.' Contrast the
doubts expressed in V.2.

[2] *In margin:* 'The day of king Henries coronation a verie tempestuous day.'

[3] Cf. V.2.123–33.

[4] *In margin:* 'A notable example of a woorthie prince.' V.5.58–72.

[5] V.2.135, 'And let us choose such limbs of noble counsel.'

[6] Cf. Texts III, IV; and V.2.63–121.

[7] Contrast IV.4.19–48 where Henry IV tries to prevent any breach between the
brothers.

[8] 'Previously he has been somewhat wanton among the young men, but on the
death of his father immediately becoming grave and reliable he sent away from the

But now that the king was once placed in the royall seat of the realme, he vertuouslie considering in his mind, that all goodnesse commeth of God, determined to begin with some thing acceptable to his divine majestie, and therefore commanded the cleargie sincerelie and trulie to preach the word of God, and to live accordinglie, that they might be the lanternes of light to the temporaltie, as their profession required. The laie men he willed to serve God, and obeie their prince, prohibiting them above all things breach of matrimonie, custome in swearing; and namelie, wilfull perjurie. Beside this, he elected the best learned men in the lawes of the realme, to the offices of justice; and men of good living, he preferred to high degrees and authoritie. Immediatlie after Easter he called a parlement,[1] in which diverse good statutes, and wholesome ordinances, for the preservation and advancement of the common-wealth were devised and established. On Trinitie sundaie were the solemne exequies doone at Canturburie for his father, the king himselfe being present thereat.[2]

About the same time, at the speciall instance of the king, in a convocation of the cleargie holden at Paules in London, it was ordeined, that saint George his daie should be celebrate and kept as a double feast.[3] The archbishop of Canturburie meant to have honored saint Dunstanes daie with like reverence, but it tooke not effect. When the king had setled things much to his purpose, he caused the bodie of king Richard to be remooved with all funerall dignitie convenient for his estate, from Langlie to Westminster, where he was honorablie interred with queene Anne his first wife, in a solemne toome erected and set up at the charges of this king.

---

royal court his accustomed companions with their corrupt manners and also laid down bitter punishments for these triflers should they return to his dwellings. And thus changed he does all things worthy of a prince, and with noble mind makes use of wise counsellors.'

[1] *In margin:* 'A parlement.' V.2.134; V.5.106.

[2] *In margin:* 'The funerals of king Henrie the fourth kept at Canturburie.'

[3] *In margin:* 'S. Georges day made a double feast.'

II. Probable Source

From THE FIRST FOWRE BOOKES OF THE CIVILE WARS BETWEEN THE TWO HOUSES OF LANCASTER AND YORKE

by Samuel Daniel (1595)

THE THIRD BOOKE.

115

But now the king retires him to his peace,
A peace much like a feeble sickemans sleepe,
(Wherein his waking paines do never cease
Though seeming rest his closed eyes doth keepe)
For O no peace could ever so release
His intricate turmoiles, and sorrowes deepe,
But that his cares kept waking all his life
Continue on till death conclude the strife.

116

Whose harald sicknes, being sent before
With full commission to denounce his end,
And paine, and griefe, enforcing more and more,
Besiegd the hold that could not long defend,
And so consum'd all that imboldning store
Of hote gaine-striving bloud that did contend,
Wearing the wall so thin that now the mind
Might well looke thorow, and his frailty find.

117

When lo, as if the vapours vanisht were,
Which heate of boyling bloud & health did breed,
(To cloude the sence that nothing might appeare
Unto the thought, that which it was indeed)
The lightned soule began to see more cleere
How much it was abus'd, & notes with heed
The plaine discovered falsehood open laid
Of ill perswading flesh that so betraid.

118

And lying on his last afflicted bed
Where death & conscience both before him stand,
Th'one holding out a booke wherein he red
In bloudie lines the deedes of his owne hand;
The other shewes a glasse, which figured
An ougly forme of fowle corrupted sand:
Both bringing horror in the hyest degree
With what he was, and what he straight should bee.

119

Which seeing all confus'd trembling with feare
He lay a while, as overthrowne in spirite,
At last commaunds some that attending were
To fetch the crowne and set it in his sight,
On which with fixed eye and heavy cheere
Casting a looke, *O God* (saith he) what right
I had to thee my soule doth now conceive;
Thee, which with bloude I gote, with horror leave.

120

Wert thou the cause my climing care was such
To passe those boundes, nature, and law ordaind?
Is this that good which promised so much,
And seemd so glorious ere it was attaind?
Wherein was never joye but gave a touch
To checke my soule to thinke, how thou were gaind,
And now how do I leave thee unto mine,
Which it is dread to keepe, death to resigne.

121

With this the soule rapt wholy with the thought
Of such distresse, did so attentive weigh
Her present horror, whilst as if forgote
The dull consumed body senceles lay,
And now as breathles quite, quite dead is thought,
When lo his sonne comes in, and takes awaie
The fatall crowne from thence, and out he goes
As if unwilling longer time to lose.

122

And whilst that sad confused soule doth cast
Those great accounts of terror and distresse,
Uppon this counsell it doth light at last
How she might make the charge of horror lesse,
And finding no way to acquit that's past
But onely this, to use some quicke redresse
Of acted wrong, with giving up againe
The crowne to whom it seem'd to appertaine.

123

Which found, lightned with some small joy shee hyes,
Rouses her servaunts that dead sleeping lay,
(The members of hir house) to exercise
One feeble dutie more, during her stay:
And opening those darke windowes he espies
The crowne for which he lookt was borne awaie,
And all-agriev'd with the unkind offence
He causd him bring it backe that tooke it thence.

124

To whom (excusing his presumteous deed
By the supposing him departed quite)
He said: O Sonne what needes thee make such speed
Unto that care, where feare exceeds thy right,
And where his sinne whom thou shalt now succeed
Shall still upbraid thy inheritance of might,
And if thou canst live, and live great from wo
Without this carefull travaile; let it go.

125

Nay father, since your fortune did attaine
So hye a stand: I meane not to descend,
Replyes the Prince; as if what you did gaine
I were of spirit unable to defend:
Time will appease them well that now complaine,
And ratefie our interest in the end;
What wrong hath not continuance quite outworne?
Yeares makes that right which never was so borne.

126

If so, God worke his pleasure (said the king)
And O do thou contend with all thy might
Such evidence of vertuous deeds to bring,
That well may prove our wrong to be our right:
And let the goodnes of the managing
Race[1] out the blot of foule attayning quite:
That discontent may all advantage misse
To wish it otherwise then now it is.

127

And since my death my purpose doth prevent
Touching this sacred warre I tooke in hand,
(An action wherewithall my soule had ment
T'appease my God, and reconcile my land)
To thee is left to finish my intent,
Who to be safe must never idly stand;
But some great actions entertaine thou still
To hold their mindes who else will practise ill.

128

Thou hast not that advantage by my raigne
To riot it (as they whom long descent
Hath purchasd love by custome) but with payne
Thou must contend to buy the worlds content:
What their birth gave them, thou hast yet to gaine
By thine owne vertues, and good government,
And that unles they worth confirme the thing
Thou canst not be the father to a king.

129

Nor art thou born in those calme daies, where rest
Hath brought a sleepe sluggish securitie;
But in tumultuous times, where mindes adrest
To factions are inur'd to mutinie,
A mischiefe not by force to be supprest
Where rigor still begets more enmitie,
Hatred must be beguild with some new course,
Where states are strong, & princes doubt their force.

---

[1] Erase.

130

This and much more affliction would have said
Out of th'experience of a troublous raigne,
For which his high desires had dearly paide
Th'interest of an ever-toyling paine
But that this all-subduing powre here staid
His faultring tongue and pain r'inforc'd againe,
And cut off all the passages of breath
To bring him quite under the state of death.

III. Probable Source

From THE UNION OF THE TWO NOBLE AND ILLUSTRE FAMELIES OF LANCASTRE AND YORKE

by Edward Hall (1548)

[The reformation of Henry V.]

THIS kyng, this man was he, whiche (accordyng to the olde Proverbe) declared and shewed that honors ought to change maners, for incontinent after that he was stalled in the siege royall, and had received the croune and scepter of the famous and fortunate region, determined with hymself to put on the shape of a new man, and to use another sorte of livyng, turnyng insolencie and wildnes into gravitie and sobernes, and waveryng vice into constant vertue. And to thentent that he would so continue without goyng backe, & not thereunto bee allured by his familier compaignions, with whom he passed his young age and wanton pastime & riotous misorder (insomuche that for imprisonmente of one of his wanton mates and unthriftie plaifaiers he strake the chiefe Justice with his fiste on the face. For whiche offence he was not onely committed to streight prison, but also of his father put out of the prevy counsaill and banished the courte, and his brother Thomas duke of Clarence elected president of the kynges counsaill to his great displeasure and open reproche) he therfore banished and seperated from hym all his old flatterers and familier compaignions (not unrewarded nor yet unpreferred) inhibityng them upon a greate pain not once to approche ether to his speche or presence, nor yet to lodge or sojourne within ten miles of his courte or mansion. And in their places he elected and chose men of gravitee, men of witte, and men of high policy, by whose wise counsaill and prudente instruccion he mighte at all tymes rule to his honor and governe to his profite. This prince was almost the Arabicall Phenix, and emongest his predecessors a very Paragon: For that he emongest all governors, chiefly did remembre that a kyng ought to bee a ruler with wit, gravitie, circumspeccion, diligence and constancie, and for that cause to have a rule to hym comitted, not for an honor, but for an onorarious charge and daily burden, and not to looke so muche on other mennes livynges, as to consider and remembre his own doynges and propre actes. For whiche cause, he not to muche trustyng to the readinesse of his owne witte, not to the judgementes of his owne waveryng will, called to his counsaill suche prudent and politique personages, the whiche should not onely help to ease his charge & pain in supportyng the burden of his realme and Empire, but also incense and instruct hym with suche good reasons and fruitefull perswasions, that he might shewe hymself a synguler mirror and manifest example of moral vertues and good qualities to his comen people and loving subjectes. For it is daily seen, that a vicious prince doth muche more hurte with his pernicious example to other, then to hymself by his owne peculier offence. For it is not so muche evill as Cicero saieth (although it bee evill in it self) a prince to do evill, as he by his evil doynges to corrupt other, because it is daily seen, that as princes change, the people altereth, and as kynges go, the subjectes folowe. For certainly he that is preferred to high authoritee, is therefore muche exalted and had in honor, that he should rule, overse and correct the maners and condicions of the people, and vigilantly to forsee and daily study how to acquire to hymself laude and glory, and to other profite and comodite, and not to delight in wor[l]dly pleasures whiche are commen emongest the lowest sorte of the vile and rusticall people. And he that will do nothyng nor can do nothyng is more worthy to be called a servant then a ruler, & a subject rather then a governor. For what can bee more shame or reproche to a prince, then he whiche ought to governe and rule other shall by cowardnes, slouth and ignorance as a pupille not of. viii. or. x. yeres of age, but beyng of. xx. or. xxx. yeares and more, shalbe compelled to obey and folowe the willes of other, and be ruled and beare no rule, like a ward and not like a garder, like a servant and not like a Master. Suche a governour was kyng Richarde the seconde, whiche of hymself beeyng not of the most evill disposicion, was not of so symple a minde, nor of suche debilite of witte, nor yet of so litle herte and corage, but he might have demaunded and learned good and profitable counsaill, and after advise taken, kept, retayned

and folowed the same: But howsoever it was, unprofitable coun-
sailers wer his confusion and finall perdicion. Suche another ruler
was kyng Edwarde the seconde, which two before named kynges
fell from the high glory of fortunes whele to exstreme misery and
miserable calamittee. By whose infortunate chance (as I thynke)
this kyng Henry beyng admonished, expulsed from hym his old
plaie felowes, his previe Sicophantes and ungracious gard as
authors and procurers of al mischifes and riot, and assigned into
their places men of gravitee, persons of activitee, and counsaillers
of greate witte and pollicie. (xxxiii–iv).

IV. Possible Source

From THE GOVERNOUR

by Sir Thomas Elyot (1531)

Book II. Chapter VI

[Prince Henry and the Lord Chief Justice.]

The moste renomed prince, kynge Henry the fifte, late kynge
of Englande, durynge the life of his father was noted to be fierce and
of wanton courage.[1] It hapned that one of his servantes whom he
well favored, for felony by hym committed, was arrayned at the
kynges benche; wherof he being advertised, and incensed by light
persones aboute hym, in furious rage came hastily to the barre,
where his servant stode as a prisoner, and commaunded hym to be
ungyved and sette at libertie, where at all men were abasshed,
reserved the chiefe justice, who humbly exhorted the prince to be
contented that his servaunt mought be ordred accordyng to the
auncient lawes of this realme, or if he wolde have hym saved from
the rigour of the lawes, that he shuld optaine, if he moughte, of
the kynge, his father, his gracious pardone; wherby no lawe or
justice shulde be derogate. With whiche answere the prince nothynge
appeased, but rather more inflamed, endevored hym selfe to take
away his servaunt. The juge consideringe the perilous example
and inconvenience that moughte therby ensue, with a valiant spirite
and courage commaunded the prince upon his alegeance to leve the
prisoner and departe his waye. With whiche commandment the
prince, being set all in a fury, all chafed, and in a terrible maner,

---

[1] Cf. IV.4.33–41.

came up to the place of jugement—men thinkyng that he wolde
have slayne the juge, or have done to hym some damage; but the
juge sittyng styll, without movynge, declarynge the majestie of the
kynges place of jugement, and with an assured and bolde countenance, hadde to the prince these words folowyng: Sir, remembre
your selfe; I kepe here the place of the king, your soveraigne lorde
and father, to whom ye owe double obedience, wherfore, eftsones
in his name, I charge you desiste of your wilfulnes and unlaufull
entreprise, and from hensforth gyve good example to those whiche
hereafter shall be your propre subjectes. And nowe for your contempt and disobedience, go you to the prisone of the kynges benche,
where unto I committe you; and remayne ye there prisoner untill
the pleasure of the kyng, your father, be further knowen. With
whiche wordes beinge abasshed,[1] and also wondrynge at the
mervailous gravitie of that worshipful Justice, the noble prince,
layinge his waipon aparte, doinge reverence, departed and wente
to the kynges benche as he was commaunded. Wherat his servants
disdainyng, came and shewed to the kynge all the hole affaire.
Wherat he a whiles studienge, after as a man all ravisshed with
gladness, holdyng his eien and handes up towarde heven, abrayded,
sayinge with a loude voice, O mercifull god, howe moche am I,
above all other men, bounde to your infinite goodnes; specially,
for that ye have gyven me a juge, who feareth nat to ministre
justice, and also a sonne who can suffre semblably and obey justice?

V. Analogue

From TARLTON'S JESTS
(1638)[2]

Tarltons Jests: drawn into these three parts. Printed by
J. H[aviland] for A. Crook, 1638.

An excellent jest of Tarltons suddenly spoken

At the Bull at Bishops-gate, was a play of Henry the fift, wherein
the judge was to take a box on the eare; & because he was absent
that should take the blowe, Tarlton himselfe, ever forward to
please, tooke upon him to play the same judge, besides his owne

---

[1] Note that the Prince does not strike the Justice. Contrast Hall and Holinshed.

[2] Entered in *S.R.* to C. Knight, 21 February, 1609. Richard Tarlton died in
1588.

part of the clowne: and Knel[1] then playing Henry the fift, hit
Tarlton a sounde boxe indeed, which made the people laugh the
more, because it was he. But anon the judge goes in, and immediately Tarlton in his clownes cloathes comes out, and askes
the actors what newes. O, saith one, hadst thou been here, thou
shouldest have seene Prince Henry hit the judge a terrible box on
the eare: What, man, said Tarlton, strike a judge! It is true, yfaith,
said the other. No other like, said Tarlton, and it could not be but
terrible to the judge, when the report so terrifies me, that me thinkes
the blow remaines still on my cheeke, that it burnes againe. The
people laugh at this mightily.

VI. Possible Source

From THE CHRONICLES OF ENGLAND

by John Stow (1580)

[p. 582]   Henrie the fifth began his raigne the xx. day of March
in the yere 1412 [1413]. This Prince exceeded the mean stature of
men, he was beautiful of visage, his necke long, bodye slender and
leane, and hys bones smal: neverthelesse he was of marvellous
greate strength, and passing swifte in running, in so much that he
with two other of his Lords without bow or other engine, would
take a wild Buck or Doe in a large Park; he delighted in songs and
musical instruments, in so moch that in his Chappel amongst other
his private prayers, he used certaine Psalmes of *David* translated
into heroycall *English* meeter, by *John Lydgate*, Monke of *Bury*. . . .[2]
[p. 583]   To this noble Prince (by assent of the Parliamente) all
the estates of the realme, after three dayes offered to do fealtie
before he was crowned, or had solemnized his othe, wel and justly
to govern the common weale, which offer, before was never found
to be made to any Prince of *England*.
The King gave them all generallye thankes, for theyr good
mindes towardes hym, and therewyth exhorted them to the zeale of
the publike prosperitie and honoure of the Realme. If anye man
hadde offended hym, he pardoned theyr trespasse, and desyred
heartily of God, that if hee should rule and doe all things well to the

---

[1] William Knell the actor, one of the Queen's Men.

[2] The passage about the Receivers (*supra* 219) follows before the next excerpt.

honoure of God and the prosperous commoditie of the Realme, that then God would suffer him to be crowned. But if hys fortune shoulde bee to doe otherwyse, that then God shoulde take hym to hys mercye, and suffer hym rather to be buried than to enterprise the charge of the Realme.

The ninth day of April [1413] he was crowned at *Westminster*, by *Thomas Arundel* Archebyshoppe of *Canterburie*, after whyche Coronation, he called unto hym all those young Lords and Gentlemen that were the folowers of his yong actes, to everye one of whome he gave rich and bounteous giftes, and then commanded that as many as would change their maners as he intended to doe, should abide with him in his Courte, and to all that woulde persever in theyr former light conversation, he gave expresse commaundemente upon paine of their heades, never after that day to come in his presence . . .

[p. 584]   A great part of the Citie of *Norwich* was brent, with all the house of the Frier *Preachers*, and also two Friers of that order. *Sir John Oldcastle*, at that time Lorde of *Cobham*, for diverse pointes touching the Sacrament, before the Archebyshoppe of *Canterburie*, the Bishops of *London*, *Winchester*, and other, was convict and committed to the Tower of *London*, out of which he brake over the walles in the night and escaped, about the feast of Simon and Jude. . . .

Richard the second, somtime king of *England*, which was at the first enterred in the church of the preaching Friers of *Langley*, was taken up and royally buried at *Westminster* with no small charges to the King.

The King keeping his Christmasse at his manour of *Eltham* (vii miles from London) was warned that certain had conspired against him, eyther to have taken, or sodainly slain him and his brethren on Twelfth day at night, wherupon the king sent word to the Mayor of *London*, that he should arrest all suspitious persons: whereupon the Mayor forthwith caused every Alderman in his ward to keep great watch, and about tenne of the clocke at nighte wente hymselfe with a strong power, to the signe of the Axe wythoute *Byshoppes Gate*, where they apprehended the man of the house, called *John Burgate* Carpenter and vii other, and sent them to *Eltham*, where they confessed before the Kyng that they were confederate with Sir John Oldcastell to fight against him and his Lords in *Saint Giles* fielde above *Holborne*. On the morrow after the Twelfth day, the King removed privily to *Westminster*, and with a greate armie kept the fielde of *Saint Giles*, for he was warned that Sir *John Oldcastell*, and Sir *Roger Acton*, woulde be in the same field on the next day following with five and twentie thousand people: and the same night were taken more then fourescore men in armour of the same faction.

Also the King being told of an ambushment gathered in *Harengay Parke*, sente thither certayne Lordes, who tooke many, among whome, was one *William Murle*, a rich Maultman or Bruer of *Dunstaple*, who had his two Horsses trapped with Golde following him, and a paire of gilt Spurres in his bosome, for he thought to have bin made Knight on the morrow by the hands of Sir *John Old-castell*.[1] The twelfth of January, threescore and nine of them were condemned of treason at *Westminster*, and on the morrow after seaven and thirtie of them, were drawne from the *Tower* of *London* to *Newgate*, and so to *Saint Giles*, and there in a place called *Fickets fielde*, were all hanged, and seaven of them brent Gallowes and all. The xix of January, were drawne and hanged Sir *John Beverley* Priest, *John Burgate* Carpenter, a Text writer in *Saint Johns* streete, and a Glover on *London Bridge*, and shortly after, Sir *Roger Acton* Knight was taken, who on the tenth of February, was drawne, hanged, and buryed under the Gallowes. . . .

[p. 599, 1417]   Sir John Oldcastell was sent unto *London* by the Lorde Powers out of Wales, which Sir John was convict by Parliament, drawne to *Saint Giles* Field, where he was hanged by the necke in a chayne of iron, and after consumed with fire.

VII. Analogue

From HICKSCORNER

Anonymous[2] (1510?)

[Unregenerate Imagination describes his crimes to his friend Freewill. He knew Hickscorner in Newgate gaol.]

FREWYLL   Ye[a], but where is Hyckscorner now?   296
IMAGYNATION   Some of these yonge men hathe hydde hym in
   theyr bosomes I warraunt you.
Let us make a crye that he maye us he[a]re.
FREWYLL   How now Hyckscorner, appere.
I trowe thou be hydde in some cornere.

[*Enter Hickscorner*

---

[1] This incident, and the thwarted demonstration, are embodied in *The First Part of Sir John Oldcastle* by Drayton, Munday etc., played in Nov. 1599.
[2] Hyckescorner [Colophon] Enprynted by me Wynkyn de Worde, n.d. [1510?].

HYCKSCOR. Ale the helm, ale, vere, shot of[f], vere sayle,
vere-a.
FREWYLL   Cockes body! herke, he is a shyppe on the see.
HYCKSCOR.   God spede, god spede, who called after me?
IMAGY.   What brother, welcome by this precyous body;
I am gladde that I you se[e].
Hyt was tolde me that ye were hanged;
But out of what countre come ye?
   HYCKSCOR.   Syr I have ben in many a countre . . .   309

[He describes how the ship of the Good was wrecked.]

   FREWYLL   Ye[a] but yet herke Hyckescorner,   364
What company was in your shyppe that came over?
   HYCKSCOR.   Syr I will ayd[1] you to understande,
There were good felawes above fyve thousande
And all they ben kynne to us thre:
There was falsehode, favell and sotylte[2]
Ye[a], theves and hores, with other good company,   370
Lyers, bacbyters and flaterers the whyle,
Braulers, lyers, getters, and chyders,
Walkers by nyght, with grete murderers,
Overthwarte gyle and Joly carders,
Oppressers of people, with many swerers.
There was false lawe with [h]oryble vengeaunce,
Frowarde obstynacion with mischevous governaunce,
Wanton wenches, and also mychers,
With many other of the devylles offycers,
And haterede that is so myghty and stronge   380
Hath made avowe for ever to dwell in Englonde.
   IMAGY.   But is that true that thou doste shewe now?
   HYCKSCOR.   Syr every worde as I do tell you.
   FREWYLL   Of whens is your shyppe? of London?
   HYCKSCOR.   Ye[a] ywys frome thens dyde she come
And she is named The Envy.
I tell you a grete vessell and a myghty:
The owner of her is called Yll wyll
Brother to Jacke Poller of Shoters hyll.
   IMAGY.   Syr what offyce in the shyppe bare ye?   390
   HYCKSCOR.   Mary! I kepte a fayr shoppe of baudrye,
I had thre wenches that were full praty,
Jane true, and Thriftles and wanton Sybble—
If you ryde her a Journay she wyll make you wery,

[1] sayd, *orig.*   [2] subtlety.

For she is trusty at nede.
If ye wyll hyre her for your pleasure
I warrant tire[1] her shall ye never,
She is so sure in dede;
Ryde and you wyll ten tymes a daye,
I warrant you she wyll never saye naye,   400
My lyfe I dare laye to wedde.

    IMAGY.   Now plucke up your hertes and make good chere;
These tydyngs lyketh me wonder wele,
Now vertu shall drawe arere arere.
Herk, felous! a good sporte I can you tell,
At the stues we wyll lye to-nyght,
And by my trouth, yf all go ryght
I will begyle some praty wenche
To gette me monaye at a pynche.
How saye you? shall we go thyder?   410
Let us kepe company all togyder
And I wolde that we had goddes curse
If we some where do not get a purse.
Every man bere his dagger naked in his honde
And yf we mete a treue man make hym stonde
Or elles that he bere a strype.
If that he struggle ond make ony werke
Lyghtly stryke him to the herte
And throwe hym into Thames[2] quyte.

    FREWYLL   Naye, thre knaves in a lease is good at nale: 420
But thou lubber Imagynacion,
That cuckolde thy fader, where is he become?
At Newgate dothe he ly styll at gayle?

    IMAGY.   Avaunt horesone, thou shalte bere me a strype.
Sayst thou, that my moder was a hore?

    FREWYLL   Naye syr, but the last nyght
I sawe Syr Johne and she tombled on the flore.

    IMAGY.   Now by kockes herte thou shalte lose an arme.

    HYCKSCOR.   Naye syr, I charge you do hym no harme.

    IMAGY.   And thou make to moche I wyll breke thy
    heed to[o].   430

    HYCKSCOR.   By Saynt Mary, and I wyst that I wolde be ago

    IMAGY.   Aware, aware! the horsone shall aby,
His preest wyll I be by Cockes body.

    HYCKSCOR.   Keep pease lest knaves blode bee shedde.

    FREWYLL   By god yf his was nought myne was as badde.

---

[1] tere, *orig.*   [2] temmes, *orig.*

IMAGY. By kockes herte he shall dye on this dager.

HYCKSCOR. By our lady than wyll ye be straungled in a halter.

IMAGY. The horesone shall ete hym as fer as he shyll wade.

HYCKSCOR. Beshrewe your herte and put up your blade,
Shethe your whytell or by hyz[1] that was never borne   440
I wyll rappe you on the costard with my horne.
What, wyll ye playe all the knave?

IMAGY. By kockes herte and thou a buffet shalte have.

FREWYLL   Lo syres here is a fayre company, god us save! . . .

[They accuse Pity of theft and shackle him.]

PYTE   O syres I se yt can not be amended,   532
You do me wronge for I have not offended:
Remembre god that is our heven kynge
For he wyll rewarde you after your deservynge
Whan deth with his mace dooth you areest;
We all to hym owe fewte[2] and servyce.
From the ladder of lyfe downe he wyll the[e] threste.
Than maystershyp may not helpe nor grete offyce.

FREWYLL   What, dethe and he were here he sholde syt by
          thee;   540
Trowest thou that he be able to stryve with us thre[e]?
Nay nay nay.

IMAGY. Well felowes now let us go our waye
For at Shoters hyll we have a game to playe.

HYCKSCOR. In good fayth I wyll tary no lenger[3] space.

FREWYLL   Byshrewe hym for me, that is last out of this place.
          [*Exit Imagination, Freewill, and Hickscorner*

[Pity mourns over the bad state of morals, when 'now is lechery
called love indede' and 'Youth walketh by nyght with swerdes and
knyves'. He is freed by Contemplation and Perseverance who
finally win over Freewill to forsake Imagination.]

CONTEM. If that thou for thy sins be sory   864
Our Lorde will forgyve the[e] them.

FREWYLL   Now of all my synnes I axe god mercy.
Here I forsake synne and trust to amende.
I beseche Jhesu that is moost myghty
To forgyve all that I have offende.

PERSEVE. Our Lorde, now wyll shewe the[e] his mercy,
A newe name thou nede nowe[4] have
For all that wyll to heven hye[5]   871

---

[1] him?   [2] fealty.   [3] lender *orig.*   [4] none *orig.*   [5] I.e., go.

By his owne frewyll he must forsake folye.
Than is he sure and save.
   CONTEM. Holde here a newe garment
And hereafter lyve devoutly
And for thy synnes do ever repente.
Sorrowe for thy synnes is very remedy:
And frewyll ever to vertue applye.
Also to sadnes gyve ye attendaunce,   880
Let hym never out of remembraunce.
   FREWYLL I wyll never frome you syr Peseveraunce.
With you wyll I abyde bothe daye and nyght,
Of mynde never to be varyable
And Goddes commandementes to kepe them ryght
In deed and worde and ever full stable.
   PERSEVE. Than heven thou shalte have without fable,
But loke that thou be stedfaste
And let thy mynd with good wyll laste.

                             [Enter Imagination

   IMAGY. Huffe, huffe, huffe! who sent after me?   890
I am Imagynacion, full of Jolyte.
Lorde that my herte is lyght,
Whan shall I peryshe? I trowe never.
By Cryst I recke not a feder,
Even now I was dubbed a knyght.
Where? at Tyborn, of the coller,
And of the stewes I am made controller
Of all the houses of lechery.
There shall no man playe doccy[1] there,
At the Bell, Herteshorne ne elleswhere,   900
Without they have leve of me.
But syres wote ye why I am come hyder?
By our lady, to gather[2] good company togyder:
Sawe ye not of my felawe Frewyll?
I am aferde lest he be serchynge on a hyll.
By god, than one of us is begyled!
What felawe is this that in this cote is fyled?
Kockes deth, whome have we here?
What, Frewyll, myn owne fere?
Arte thou out of thy mynde?   910
   FREWYLL God graunte the way to heven that I may fynde,
For I forsake thy company.
   IMAGY. Goddes armes, my company? and why?

---

[1] doxy, sweetheart.   [2] togyder, *orig.*

FREWYLL   For thou lyvest to[o] synfully.

IMAGY.   Alas, tell me how hyt is with the[e].

FREWYLL   Forsake thy synne for the love of me.

IMAGY.   Kockes herte, arte thou waxed made?

FREWYLL   Whan I thynke on my synne it makes me full sade.

IMAGY.   Goddes woundes! who gave the[e] that counsell?

FREWYLL   Perseveraunce and Contemplacyon, I the[e] tell.

IMAGY.   A vengeaunce on them, I wolde they were in hell. 921

FREWYLL   Amende Imagynacion and mercy crye.

IMAGY.   By goddes sydes! I had lever be hanged on hye.
Naye that wolde I not do: I hadde lever dye.
By goddes passyon, and I hadde a longe knyfe
I wolde bereve these two horesones of theyr lyfe.
How, how! twenty pounde for a dagger!

CONTEM.   Peas, peas, good sone and speke softer,
And amende or[1] deth drawe his draught,
For on the[e] he wyl stele full softe.   930
He gyveth never no man warnynge
And ever to the[e] he is comynge.
Therefore remembre the[e] well.

IMAGY.   A[h] horesone yf I were Jayler of hell,
I wys some sorowe sholde thou fele,
For to the devyll I wolde the[e] sell,
Then sholde ye have many a sory mele.
I wyll never gyve you mete ne drynke,
Ye sholde fast, horesones, tyll ye dyde styncke
Even as a roten dogge, ye[a] by Saynt Tyburne of Kent!   940

PERSEVE.   Imagynacion, thynke what God dyd for the[e].
On Good Frydaye he hanged on a tre[e]
And spent all his precyous blode.
A spere dyde ryve his herte asonder,
The gates he brake up with a clappe of thunder,
And Adam and Eve there delyvered he.

IMAGY.   What, devyll, what is that to me?
By goddes fast I was ten yere in Newgate
And many more felawes with me sate
Yet he never came there to helpe me ne my company.   950

CONTEM.   Yes, he holpe the[e] or thou haddest not been here
now.

IMAGY.   By the mass I can not shewe you,
For he and I never dranke togyder
Yet I knowe many an ale stake.

---

[1] ere.

Neyther at the stues I wyste hym never come thyder.
Gooth he arayed in whyte or in blacke?
For and he out of pryson hadde holpe me
I knowe well ones I sholde hym se[e].
What gowne wereth he I praye you?
    PERSEVE.   Syr he halpe you out by his myght.   960
    IMAGY.   I cannot tell you, by this lyght;
But me thought that I laye there to[o] longe
And the horesone fetters were so stronge
That hadde almost brought my necke out of joynt.
    PERSE.   Amende sone and thou shalt knowe him
That delyvered the[e] out of pryson
And yf thou wylt forsake thy mysse¹
Surely thou shalt come to the blysse
And be inherytoure of heven . . .
    FREWYLL   Beware, for whan thou art buryed in the grounde 992
Fewe frendes for the[e] wyll be founde.
Remembre this styll.
    IMAGY.   No thynge drede I so sore as deth,
Therfore to amende I thynke hyt be tyme.
Synne have I used all the dayes of my breth
With pleasure, lechery, and mysusynge
And spent amys my five wyttes: therefore I am sory.
Here of all my synnes I axe God mercy.   1000
    PERSEV.   Holde, here is a better clothynge for the[e]
And loke that thou forsake thy foly.
Be stedfast, loke that thou fall never.
    IMAGY.   Now here I forsake my synne for ever.
    FREWYLL   Syr, wayte thou now on Perseveraunce,
For thy name shall be called Good Remembraunce,
And I wyll dwell with Contemplacyon,
And folowe hym where ever he become.
    CONTEM.   Well, are ye so bothe agrede?
    IMAGY.   Ye[a] syr, so God me spede.   1010
    PERSEVE.   Syr ye shall wete on me soone
And be Goddes servaunt daye and nyght
And in every place where ye become
Gyve good counseyle to every wyght.
And men axe your name, tell you Remembraunce
That goddes law kepeth truly every daye
And loke that ye forget not repentaunce,
Than to heven ye shall go the nexte² waye,

---

¹ misdeeds.   ² nearest.

Where ye shall se in the hevenly quere
The blessyd company of sayntes so holy,   1020
That lyved devou[t]ly whyle they were here.
Unto the whiche blysse I beseche God Almyghty
To brynge there your soules that here be present
And unto vertuous lyvynge that ye maye applye
Truly for to kepe his commaundemente.
Of all our myrthes here we make an ende.
Unto the blysse of heven Jhesu your soules brynge.

AMEN.

VIII. Source

THE FAMOUS VICTORIES OF HENRY THE FIFTH

Anonymous (1598)

The Famous Victories of Henry the fifth: Containing the Honourable Battell of Agin-court: *As it was plaide by the Queenes Majesties Players*. LONDON Printed by Thomas Creede, 1598.[1]

[Scene 1]

Enter the yoong Prince, Ned, and Tom.

HEN. 5[2]   Come away *Ned* and *Tom*.
BOTH   Here my Lord.
HENR. 5   Come away my Lads:
Tell me sirs, how much gold have you got?
NED   Faith my Lord, I have got five hundred pound.
HEN. 5   But tell me *Tom*, how much hast thou got?
TOM   Faith my Lord, some foure hundred pound.
HEN. 5   Foure hundred pounds, bravely spoken Lads.
But tell me sirs, thinke you not that it was a villainous part of
    me to rob my fathers Receivers?   10

[1] Text here from the facsimile by C. Praetorius (*Sh.Q.* Facsimilies, 39), 1887 with punctuation somewhat modernized.
[°] Q has 'Henry the fifth' centred above. The Prince is called *Hen.5* throughout.

NED   Why no my Lord, it was but a tricke of youth.

HEN. 5   Faith *Ned* thou sayest true.

But tell me sirs, whereabouts are we?

TOM   My Lord, we are now about a mile off *London*.

HEN. 5   But sirs, I marvell that sir *John Old-castle*

Comes not away: Sounds, see where he comes.

Enters Jockey.[1]

How now *Jockey*, what newes with thee?

JOCKEY   Faith my Lord, such newes as passeth,

For the Towne of *Detfort*[2] is risen,

With hue and crie after your man,   20

Which parted from us the last night,

And has set upon, and hath robd a poore Carrier.

HEN. 5   Sownes, the vilaine that was wont to spie

Out our booties.

JOCK.   I my Lord, even the very same.

HEN. 5   Now base minded rascal to rob a poore carrier,

Wel it skils not, ile save the base vilaines life:

I, I may: but tel me *Jockey*, wherabout be the Receivers?

JOCK.   Faith my Lord, they are hard by,

But the best is, we are a horse backe and they be a foote,   30

So we may escape them.

HEN. 5   Wel, I[f] the vilaines come, let me alone with them.

But tel me *Jockey*, how much gots thou from the knaves?

For I am sure I got something, for one of the vilaines

So belamd[3] me about the shoulders,

As I shal feele it this moneth.

JOCK.   Faith my Lord, I have got a hundred pound.

HEN. 5   A hundred pound, now bravely spoken *Jockey*:

But come sirs, laie al your money before me.

Now by heaven here is a brave shewe: 40

But as I am true Gentleman, I wil have the halfe

Of this spent to night, but sirs take up your bags,

Here comes the Receivers, let me alone.

Enters two Receivers.[4]

ONE   Alas good fellow, what shal we do?

I dare never go home to the Court, for I shall be hangd.

But looke, here is the yong Prince, what shal we doo?

HEN. 5   How now you vilaines, what are you?

---

[1] I.e., Old-castle.   [2] Deptford, S. of the Thames, near Greenwich.
[3] lammed, beat. The scene suggested *1H4* II.2
[4] Treasury officials. Cf. *1H4* II.2.52-4.

ONE RECEI.   Speake you to him.

OTHER   No I pray, speake you to him.

HEN. 5   Why how now you rascals, why speak you not?   50

ONE   Forsooth we be—Pray speake you to him.

HEN. 5   Sowns, vilains speak, or ile cut off your heads.

OTHER   Forsooth he can tel the tale better then I.

ONE   Forsooth we be your fathers Receivers.

HEN. 5   Are you my fathers Receivers?
Then I hope ye have brought me some money.

ONE   Money, Alas sir we be robd.

HEN. 5   Robd, how many were there of them?

ONE   Marry sir, there were foure of them:
And one of them had sir *John Old-Castles* bay Hobbie,   60
And your blacke Nag.

HEN. 5   Gogs wounds, how like you this, *Jockey*?
Blood, you vilaines: my father robd of his money abroad,
And we robd in our stables!
But tell me, how many were of them?

ONE RECEI.   If it please you, there were foure of them,
And there was one about the bignesse of you:
But I am sure I so belambd him about the shoulders,
That he wil feele it this month.

HEN. 5   Gogs wounds you lamd them faierly,   70
So that they have carried away your money.
But come sirs, what shall we do with the vilaines?

BOTH RECEI.   I beseech your grace, be good to us.

NED   I pray you my Lord forgive them this once.

[HEN. 5][1] Well, stand up and get you gone,
And looke that you speake not a word of it,
For if there be, sownes ile hang you and all your kin.

[*Exeunt Receivers*[2]

HEN. 5   Now sirs, how like you this?
Was not this bravely done?
For now the vilaines dare not speake a word of it,   80
I have so feared them with words.
Now whither shall we goe?

ALL   Why my Lord, you know our old hostes
At *Feversham*.[3]

HEN. 5   Our hostes at *Feversham*, blood what shal we do there?
We have a thousand pound about us,

---

[1] No speech heading in Q.
[2] Q has *Exit Pursevant*, i.e., warrant officer.
[3] Faversham. Seven miles from Canterbury near the main London road.

And we shall go to a pettie Ale-house.
No, no: you know the olde Taverne in Eastcheape,[1]
There is good wine: besides, there is a pretie wench
That can talke well, for I delight as much in their toongs,
As any part about them.   90
    ALL   We are readie to waite upon your grace.
    HEN. 5   Gogs wounds wait, we will go altogither,
We are all fellowes, I tell you sirs, and the King
My father were dead, we would be all Kings,[2]
Therefore come away.
    NED   Gogs wounds, bravely spoken *Harry*.

[Scene ii]

       Enter John Cobler, Robin Pewterer, Lawrence Costermonger.

    JOHN COB.   All is well here, all is well maisters.
    ROBIN   How say you neighbour *John Cobler*?
I thinke it best that my neighbour
Robin Pewterer went to Pudding lane end,   100
And we will watch here at Billinsgate ward,[3]
How say you neighbour *Robin*, how like you this?
    ROBIN   Marry well neighbours:
I care not much if I goe to Pudding lanes end.
But neighbours, and you heare any adoe about me,
Make haste: and if I heare any ado about you,
I will come to you.   [*Exit Robin*
    LAW.   Neighbor, what newes heare you of the young Prince?
    JOHN   Marry neighbor, I heare say, he is a toward yoong Prince,
For if he met any by the hie way,   110
He will not let[4] to talke with him.
I dare not call him theefe, but sure he is one of these taking fellowes.
    LAW.   Indeed neighbour I heare say he is as lively
A young Prince as ever was.
    JOHN   I, and I heare say, if he use it long,
His father will cut him off from the Crowne:
But neighbour, say nothing of that.
    LAW.   No, no, neighbour, I warrant you.
    JOHN   Neighbour, me thinkes you begin to sleepe,
If you will, we will sit down,   120

---

[1] N. of the Thames, in the City near London Bridge. Later legend calls the tavern the Boar's Head. In *2H4* II.2.149 Bardolph calls it 'the old place . . . in Eastcheap'. Cf. *1H4* I.2.129–31.

[2] Cf. Falstaff's hopes, *1H4* I.2.16, 23, 60.

[3] These places are between Eastcheap and the river.   [4] hesitate.

For I thinke it is about midnight.

    LAW.   Marry content neighbour, let us sleepe.

Enter Dericke roving.[1]

DERICKE   Who, who there, who there?

                          [*Exit Dericke*

Enter Robin.

ROBIN   O neighbors, what meane you to sleepe,
And such ado in the streetes?

    AMBO.   How now neighbor, whats the matter?

Enter Dericke againe.

DERICKE   Who there, who there, who there?

    COBLER   Why, what ailst thou? here is no horses.

    DERICKE   O alas man, I am robd, who there, who there?

    ROBIN   Hold him neighbor *Cobler*.   130

    ROBIN   Why I see thou art a plaine Clowne.[2]

    DERICKE   Am I a Clowne? sownes, maisters,
Do Clownes go in silke apparell?
I am sure all we gentlemen Clownes in *Kent* scant go so
Well: Sownes, you know clownes very well:
Heare you, are you maister Constable? and[3] you be, speake,
For I will not take it at his hands.

    JOHN   Faith I am not maister Constable,
But I am one of his bad[4] officers, for he is not here.

    DERICKE   Is not maister Constable here?   140
Well it is no matter, ile have the law at his hands.

    JOHN   Nay I pray you do not take the law of us.

    DER.   Well, you are one of his beastly officers.

    JOHN   I am one of his bad officers.

    DER.   Why then I charge thee looke to him.

    COBLER   Nay but heare ye sir, you seeme to be an honest
Fellow, and we are poore men, and now tis night:
And we would be loth to have any thing adoo,
Therefore I pray thee put it up.

    DER.   First, thou saiest true, I am an honest fellow,   150
And a proper hansome fellow too,
And you seeme to be poore men, therfore I care not greatly,
Nay, I am quickly pacified:

---

[1] wandering aimlessly.   [2] A countryman.   [3] if.
[4] under orders, competent.

But and you chance to spie the theefe,
I pray you laie hold on him.

    ROBIN   Yes that we wil, I warrant you.

    DER.   Tis a wonderful thing to see how glad the knave
Is, now I have forgiven him.

    JOHN   Neighbors do ye looke about you.
How now, who's there?   160

Enter the Theefe

    THEEFE   Here is a good fellow, I pray you which is the
Way to the old Taverne in Eastcheape?

    DER.   Whoope hollo, now Gads Hill,[1] knowest thou me?

    THEEFE   I know thee for an Asse.

    DER.   And I know thee for a taking fellow,
Upon Gads hill[2] in *Kent*:
A bots[3] light upon ye.

    THEEFE   The whorson vilaine would be knockt.

    DER.   Maisters, vilaine, and ye be men stand to him,
And take his weapon from him, let him not passe you.   170

    JOHN   My friend, what make you abroad now?
It is too late to walke now.

    THEEFE   It is not too late for true men to walke.

    LAW.   We know thee not to be a true man.

    THEEFE   Why, what do you meane to do with me?
Sownes, I am one of the kings liege people.

    DER.   Heare you sir, are you one of the kings liege people?

    THEEFE   I marry am I sir, what say you to it?

    DER.   Marry sir, I say you are one of the Kings filching people.

    COB.   Come, come, lets have him away.   180

    THEEFE   Why what have I done?

    ROBIN   Thou has robd a poore fellow,
And taken away his goods from him.

    THEEFE   I never sawe him before.

    DER.   Maisters who comes here?

Enter the Vintners boy.

    BOY   How now good man Cobler?

    COB.   How now *Robin*, what makes thou abroad
At this time of night?

---

[1] Hence the name of the 'setter' in *1H4* I.2.108, etc.
[2] A hill two miles from Rochester on the London–Dover road.
[3] A horse-disease.

BOY   Marrie I have been at the Counter,[1]
I can tell such newes as never you have heard the like.   190
   COBLER   What is that *Robin*, what is the matter?
   BOY   Why this night about two houres ago, there came the
young Prince, and three or foure more of his companions, and
called for wine good store, and then they sent for a noyse of
Musitians, and were very merry for the space of an houre,
then whether their Musicke liked them not, or whether they
had drunke too much Wine or no, I cannot tell, but our pots
flue against the wals, and then they drew their swordes, and
went into the streete and fought, and some tooke one part, &
some tooke another, but for the space of halfe an houre,
there was such a bloodie fray as passeth, and none coulde part   200
them untill such time as the Mayor and Sheriffe were sent for,
and then at the last with much adoo, they tooke them, and so
the yong Prince was carried to the Counter, and then about
one houre after, there came a Messenger from the Court in all
haste from the King, for my Lord Mayor and the Sheriffe,
but for what cause I know not.[2]
   COBLER   Here is newes indeede *Robert*.
   LAW.   Marry neighbour, this newes is strange indeede, I
thinke it best neighbour, to rid our hands of this fellowe first.   210
   THEEFE   What meane you to doe with me?
   COBLER   We mean to carry you to the prison, and there
to remaine till the Sessions day.
   THEEFE   Then I pray you let me go to the prison where my
maister is.
   COB.   Nay thou must go to the country prison, to Newgate,
Therefore come away.
   THEEFE   I prethie be good to me honest fellow.
   DER.   I marry will I, ile be verie charitable to thee,
For I will never leave thee, til I see thee on the Gallowes.   220

[Scene iii]

Enter Henry the fourth, with the Earle of Exeter,
and the Lord of Oxford.

OXF.   And please your Majestie, heere is my Lord Mayor
and the Sheriffe of London, to speak with your Majestie.
   K. HEN. 4   Admit them to our presence.

---

[1] A prison, mainly for debtors.   [2] Cf. *supra*, p. 216.

20—N.D.S.S. 4

Enter the Mayor and the Sheriffe.

Now my good Lord Mayor of London,
The cause of my sending for you at this time, is to tel you of a
matter which I have learned of my Councell: Herein I
understand, that you have committed my sonne to prison
without our leave and license. What althogh he be a rude
youth, and likely to give occasion, yet you might have considered that he is a Prince, and my sonne, and not to be
halled[1] to prison by every subject.   230

MAYOR   May it please your Majestie to give us leave to
tell our tale?

KING HEN. 4   Or else God forbid, otherwise you might
thinke me an unequall Judge, having more affection to my
sonne, then to any rightfull judgement.

MAYOR   Then I do not doubt but we shal rather deserve
commendations at your Majesties hands, then any anger.

K. HEN. 4   Go too, say on.

MAYOR   Then if it please your Majestie, this night betwixt   240
two and three of the clocke in the morning, my Lord the yong
Prince with a very disordred companie, came to the old
Taverne in Eastcheape, and whether it was that their
Musicke liked them not, or whether they were overcome with
wine, I know not, but they drew their swords, and into the
streete they went, and some tooke my Lord the yong Princes
part, and some tooke the other, but betwixt them there was
such a bloodie fray for the space of halfe an houre, that
neither watchmen nor any other could stay them, till my
brother the Sheriffe of London & I were sent for, and at the
last with much adoo we staied them, but it was long first,   250
which was a great disquieting to all your loving subjects
thereabouts: and then my good Lord, we knew not whether
your grace had sent them to trie us, whether we would doo
justice, or whether it were of their owne voluntarie will or not,
we cannot tell: and therefore in such a case we knew not what
to do, but for our own safegard we sent him to ward, where
he wanteth nothing that is fit for his grace, and your Majesties
sonne. And thus most humbly beseeching your Majestie to
thinke of our answere.

HEN. 4   Stand aside untill we have further deliberated on   260
your answere.

[*Exit Mayor*

---

[1] hauled, or haled.

HEN. 4   Ah *Harry, Harry,* now thrice accursed *Harry,*
That hath gotten a sonne, which with greefe
Will end his fathers dayes.[1]
Oh my sonne, a Prince thou art, I a Prince indeed,
And to deserve imprisonment,
And well have they done, and like faithfull subjects:
Discharge them and let them go.

L. EXE.   I beseech your Grace, be good to my Lord the
yong Prince.   270

HEN. 4   Nay, nay, tis no matter, let him alone.

L. OXF.   Perchance the Mayor and the Sheriffe have bene
too precise in this matter.

HEN. 4   No: they have done like faithfull subjects:
I will go my selfe to discharge them, and let them go.

[*Exit omnes*

[Scene iv]

    Enter Lord chiefe Justice, Clarke of the Office, Jayler,
        John Cobler, Dericke,[2] and the Theefe.

JUDGE   Jayler bring the prisoner to the barre.

DER.   Heare you my Lord, I pray you bring the bar to the
prisoner.

JUDGE   Hold thy hand up at the barre.

THEEFE   Here it is my Lord.   280

JUDGE   Clearke of the Office, reade his inditement.

CLEARK   What is thy name?

THEEFE   My name was knowne before I came here,
And shall be when I am gone, I warrant you.

JUDGE   I, I thinke so, but we will know it better before
thou go.

DER.   Sownes and you do but send to the next Jaile,
We are sure to know his name,
For this is not the first prison he hath bene in, ile warrant you.

CLEARK   What is thy name?   290

THEEFE.   What need you to aske, and have it in writing.

CLEARK   Is not thy name *Cutbert Cutter?*

THEEFE   What the Divell need you ask, and know it so
well.

CLEARK   Why then *Cutbert Cutter,* I indite thee by the

---

[1] Cf. *1H4* III.2.4–11.

[2] This was the scene mentioned in the anecdote about Tarlton (*supra* 289), who
cannot have been playing Dericke as well as the Justice, since both appear at once.
Perhaps he played John Cobler, silent till Sc. V when he too gets a box on the ear.

name of *Cutbert Cutter*, for robbing a poore carrier the 20 day of May last past, in the fourteen yeare of the raigne of our soveraigne Lord King *Henry* the fourth, for setting upon a poore Carrier upon Gads hill in *Kent*, and having beaten and wounded the said Carrier, and taken his goods from him.

DER.   Oh maisters stay there, nay lets never belie the man,   300 for he hath not beaten and wounded me also, but he hath beaten and wounded my packe, and hath taken the great rase[1] of Ginger, that bouncing Besse with the jolly buttocks should have had; that greeves me most.

JUDGE   Well, what sayest thou, art thou guiltie, or not guiltie?

THEEFE   Not guiltie, my Lord.

JUDGE   By whom wilt thou be tride?

THEEFE   By my Lord the young Prince, or by my selfe whether you will.   310

Enter the young Prince, with Ned and Tom.

HEN. 5   Come away my lads, Gogs wounds ye villain, what make you heere? I must goe about my businesse my selfe, and you must stand loytering here.

THEEFE   Why my Lord, they have bound me, and will not let me goe.

HEN. 5   Have they bound thee villain? why, how now my Lord?

JUDGE   I am glad to see your grace in good health.

HEN. 5   Why my Lord, this is my man,
Tis marvell you knew him not long before this,
I tell you he is a man of his hands.   320

THEEFE   I Gogs wounds that I am, try me who dare.

JUDGE   Your Grace shal finde small credit by acknowledging him to be your man.

HEN. 5   Why my Lord, what hath he done?

JUD.   And it please your Majestie, he hath robbed a poore Carrier.

DER.   Heare you sir, marry it was one *Dericke*,
Goodman *Hoblings* man of *Kent*.

HEN. 5   What, wast you butten-breech?
Of my word my Lord, he did it but in jest.

DER.   Heare you sir, is it your mans qualitie to rob folks in   330 jest? In faith, he shall be hangd in earnest.

---

[1] raze, root. Cf. *1H4* II.1.26.

HEN. 5   Well my Lord, what do you meane to do with my man?

JUDGE.   And please your grace, the law must passe on him, According to justice, then he must be executed.

DER.[1]   Heare you sir, I pray you, is it your mans quality to rob folkes in jest? In faith he shall be hangd in jest.

HEN. 5   Well my Lord, what meane you to do with my man?

JUDGE.   And please your grace the law must passe on him, According to justice, then he must be executed.

HEN. 5   Why then belike you meane to hang my man?   340

JUDGE   I am sorrie that it falles out so.

HEN. 5   Why my Lord, I pray ye, who am I?

JUD.   And please your Grace, you are my Lord the yong Prince, our King that shall be after the decease of our soveraigne Lord, King *Henry* the fourth, whom God graunt long to raigne.

HEN. 5   You say true my Lord:
And you will hang my man?

JUDGE   And like your grace, I must needs do justice.

HEN. 5   Tell me my Lord, shall I have my man?

JUDGE   I cannot my Lord.   350

HEN. 5   But will you not let him go?

JUD.   I am sorie that his case is so ill.

HEN. 5   Tush, case me no casings; shal I have my man?

JUDGE   I cannot, nor I may not my Lord.

HEN. 5   Nay, and I shal not say, & then I am answered?

JUDGE   No.

HEN. 5   No: then I will have him.

He giveth him a boxe on the eare.

NED   Gogs wounds my Lord, shal I cut off his head?

HEN. 5   No, I charge you draw not your swords,
But get you hence, provide a noyse of Musitians,   360
Away, be gone.

[Exeunt Ned and Tom[2]

JUDGE   Well my Lord, I am content to take it at your hands.[3]

HEN. 5   Nay and you be not, you shall have more.

---

[1] The next five lines in Q (B3r) were probably printed in error. They repeat what has just been said, except that Dericke spoils his own joke.

[2] Q has *Exeunt the Theefe*, but the Thief presumably goes out with the Jayler after 376.

[3] Cf. *2H4* I.2.195–7: 'For the box o' the ear that the prince gave you, he gave it like a rude prince, and you took it like a sensible lord.'

JUDGE   Why I pray you my Lord, who am I?

HEN. 5   You, who knowes not you?
Why man, you are Lord chiefe Justice of England.

JUDGE   Your Grace hath said truth, therfore in striking
me in this place, you greatly abuse me, and not me onely, but
also your father: whose lively person here in this place I doo
represent. And therefore to teach you what prerogatives
meane, I commit you to the Fleete, untill we have spoken   370
with your father.

HEN. 5   Why then belike you meane to send me to the Fleete?

JUDGE   I indeed, and therefore carry him away.

Exeunt Hen. 5 with the Officers.

JUDGE   Jayler, carry the prisoner to Newgate againe,
until the next Sises.

JAY.   At your commandement my Lord, it shalbe done.

[*Exeunt Jayler and Theefe*[1]

[Scene v]

Enter Dericke and John Cobler.

DER.   Sownds maisters, heres adoo,
When Princes must go to prison:
Why *John*, didst ever see the like?

JOHN   O *Dericke*, trust me, I never saw the like.   380

DER.   Why *John* thou maist see what princes be in choller.
A Judge a boxe on the eare, Ile tel thee *John*, O *John*,
I would not have done it for twentie shillings.

JOHN   No nor I, there had bene no way but one with us,
We should have bene hangde.

DER.   Faith *John*, Ile tel thee what, thou shalt be my
Lord chiefe Justice, and thou shalt sit in the chaire,[2]
And ile be the yong prince, and hit thee a boxe on the eare,
And then thou shalt say, to teach you what prerogatives
Meane, I commit you to the Fleete.   390

JOHN   Come on, Ile be your Judge,
But thou shalt not hit me hard.

DER.   No, no.

JOHN   What hath he done?

DER.   Marry he hath robd *Dericke*.

JOHN   Why then I cannot let him go.

DER.   I must needs have my man.

---

[1] Not in Q.

[2] Cf. the similar device in *1H4* II.4.381ff: 'Do thou stand for my father', etc.

JOHN   You shall not have him.

DER.   Shall I not have my man, say no and you dare:
How say you, shall I not have my man?   400

JOHN   No marry shall you not.

DER.   Shall I not, *John*?

JOHN   No *Dericke*.

DER.   Why then take you that till more come,
Sownes, shall I not have him?

JOHN   Well I am content to take this at your hand,
But I pray you, who am I?

DER.   Who art thou, Sownds, doost not know thy self?

JOHN   No.

DER.   Now away simple fellow,   410
Why man, thou art *John* the Cobler.

JOHN   No, I am my Lord chiefe Justice of England.

DER.   Oh *John*, Masse thou saist true, thou art indeed.

JOHN   Why then to teach you what prerogatives mean
I commit you to the Fleete.

DER.   Wel I will go, but yfaith you gray beard knave, Ile course
   you.

Exit. And straight enters again.

Oh *John*, Come, come out of thy chair, why what a clown
weart thou, to let me hit thee a box on the eare, and now
thou seest they will not take me to the Fleete. I thinke that
thou art one of these Worenday[1] Clownes.   420

JOHN   But I marvell what will become of thee?

DER.   Faith ile be no more a Carrier.

JOHN   What wilt thou doo then?

DER.   Ile dwell with thee and be a Cobler.

JOHN   With me? alasse I am not able to keepe thee,
Why, thou wilt eate me out of doores.

DER.   Oh *John*, no *John*, I am none of these great slouching
fellowes, that devoure these great peeces of beefe and brewes,[2]
alasse a trifle serves me, a Woodcocke, a Chicken, or a Capons
legge, or any such little thing serves me.   430

JOHN   A Capon, why man, I cannot get a Capon once a
yeare, except it be at Christmas, at some other mans house,
for we Coblers be glad of a dish of rootes.

DER.   Rootes, why are you so good at rooting?
Nay Cobler, weele have you ringde.[3]

---

[1] workaday, ordinary?   [2] browis, meat broth.

[3] like a pig, through the nose.

JOHN   But *Dericke*, though we be so poore,
Yet wil we have in store a crab in the fire,
With nut-browne Ale, that is full stale,[1]
Which wil a man quaile, and laie in the mire.

DER.   A bots on you, and be —; but for your Ale,   440
Ile dwel with you, come lets away as fast as we can.   [*Exeunt*

[Scene vi]

Enter the yoong Prince, with Ned and Tom.

HEN. 5   Come away sirs, Gogs wounds *Ned*,
Didst thou not see what a boxe on the eare
I tooke my Lord chiefe Justice?

TOM   By gogs blood it did me good to see it,
It made his teeth jarre in his head.

Enter sir John Old-Castle

HEN. 5   How now sir *John Old-Castle*,
What newes with you?

JOH. OLD.   I am glad to see your grace at libertie,
I was come, I, to visit you in prison.   450

HEN. 5   To visit me? didst thou not know that I am a
Princes son, why tis inough for me to looke into a prison,
though I come not in my selfe, but heres such adoo now
adayes, heres prisoning, heres hanging, whipping, and the
divel and all: but I tel you sirs, when I am King, we will have
no such things,[2] but my lads, if the old king my father were
dead, we would be all kings.

JOH. OLD.   Hee is a good olde man, God take him to his
mercy the sooner.

HEN. 5   But *Ned*, so soone as I am King, the first thing
I wil do, shal be to put my Lord chief Justice out of office,   460
And thou shalt be my Lord chiefe Justice of England.

NED   Shall I be Lord chiefe Justice?
By gogs wounds, ile be the bravest Lord chiefe Justice
That ever was in England.

HEN. 5   Then *Ned*, ile turne all these prisons into fence
Schooles, and I will endue thee with them, with landes to
maintaine them withall: then I wil have a bout with my Lord
chiefe Justice: thou shalt hang none but picke purses and
horse stealers, and such base minded villaines, but that fellow

---

[1] old and strong.
[2] Cf. *1H4* I.2.58: 'Shall there be gallows ... in England when thou art King?'

that will stand by the high way side couragiously with his 470
sword and buckler and take a purse, that fellow give him
commendations; beside that, send him to me and I will give
him an anuall pension out of my Exchequer, to maintaine
him all the dayes of his life.

JOH.   Nobly spoken *Harry*, we shall never have a mery
world til the old king be dead.

NED   But whither are ye going now?

HEN. 5   To the Court, for I heare say, my father lies verie
sicke.

TOM   But I doubt he wil not die.

HEN. 5   Yet will I goe thither, for the breath shal be no
sooner out of his mouth, but I wil clap the Crowne on my 480
head.[1]

JOCKEY   Wil you goe to the Courte with that cloake so full
of needles?

HEN. 5   Cloake, ilat-holes,[2] needles, and all was of mine
owne devising, and therefore I wil weare it.

TOM   I pray you my Lord, what may be the meaning
thereof?

HEN. 5   Why man, tis a signe that I stand upon thorns, til
the Crowne be on my head.

JOC.   Or that every needle might be a prick to their harts
that repine at your doings. 490

HEN. 5   Thou saist true *Jockey*, but thers some wil say, the
yoong Prince will be a well toward yoong man and all this
geare,[3] that I had as leeve they would breake my head with a
pot, as to say any such thing. But we stand prating here too
long. I must needs speake with my father, therefore come
away.

PORTER   What a rapping keep you at the Kings Court gate?

HEN. 5   Heres one that must speake with the King.

POR.   The King is verie sick, and none must speak with him.

HEN. 5   No you rascall, do you not know me?

POR.   You are my Lord the yong Prince. 500

HEN. 5   Then goe and tell my father, that I must and will
speake with him.

NED   Shall I cut off his head?

HEN. 5   No, no, though I would helpe you in other places,
yet I have nothing to doo here, what[4] you are in my fathers
Court.

---

[1] Cf. *2H4* II.2.39–40: 'it is not meet that I should be sad, now my father is sick',
but cf. *ibid.*, 47–9; Shakespeare's Prince loves his father.   [2] eyelet-holes.
[3] a promising, docile young man, and such nonsense.   [4] because.

NED   I will write him in my Tables, for so soone as I am
made Lord chiefe Justice, I wil put him out of his Office.

The Trumpet sounds.

HEN. 5   Gogs wounds sirs, the King comes,
Lets all stand aside.

Enter the King, with the Lord of Exeter.

HEN. 4   And is it true my Lord, that my sonne is alreadie
sent to the Fleete? now truly that man is more fitter to rule
the Realme then I, for by no meanes could I rule my sonne,   511
and he by one word hath caused him to be ruled. Oh my
sonne, my sonne, no sooner out of one prison, but into an
other. I had thought once, whiles I had lived to have seene
this noble Realme of England flourish by thee my sonne, but
now I see it goes to ruine and decaie.   [*He wepeth*

Enters Lord of Oxford.

OX.   And please your grace, here is my Lord your sonne,
That commeth to speake with you,
He saith, he must and wil speake with you.   520
HEN. 4   Who? my sonne *Harry*?
OXF.   I and please your Majestie.
HEN. 4   I know wherefore he commeth,
But looke that none come with him.
OXF.   A verie disordered company, and such as make
Verie ill rule in your Majesties house.
HEN. 4   Well, let him come,
But looke that none come with him.   [*He goeth*
OXF.   And please your grace,
My Lord the King sends for you.   530
HEN. 5   Come away sirs, lets go all togither.
OXF.   And please your grace, none must go with you.
HEN. 5   Why I must needs have them with me,
Otherwise I can do my father no countenance,
Therefore come away.
OXF.   The King your father commaunds
There should none come.
HEN. 5   Well sirs then be gone,
And provide me three Noyse of Musitians.   [*Exeunt knights*

Enters the Prince with a dagger in his hand.

HEN. 4   Come my sonne, come on, a Gods name,[1]   540
I know wherefore thy comming is,
Oh my sonne, my sonne, what cause hath ever bene,
That thou shouldst forsake me, and follow this vilde and
Reprobate company, which abuseth youth so manifestly:
Oh my sonne, thou knowest that these thy doings
Wil end thy fathers dayes.   *[He weepes*
I so, so, my sonne, thou fearest not to approach the presence
of thy sick father, in that disguised sort. I tel thee my sonne,
that there is never a needle in thy cloke, but is a prick to my
heart, & never an ilat-hole, but it is a hole to my soule: and   550
wherefore thou bringest that dagger in thy hande I know not,
but by conjecture.   *[He weepes*
HEN. 5   My conscience accuseth me, most soveraign Lord,
and welbeloved father, to answere first to the last point, That
is, whereas you conjecture that this hand and this dagger
shall be armde against your life: no, know my beloved father,
far be the thoughts of your sonne,—sonne said I, an unworthie sonne for so good a father: but farre be the thoughts
of any such pretended mischiefe: and I most humbly render
it to your Majesties hand, and live my Lord and soveraigne   560
for ever: and with your dagger arme show like vengeance
upon the bodie of that—your sonne, I was about say and
dare not, ah woe is me therefore,—that your wilde[2] slave. Tis
not the Crowne that I come for, sweete father, because I am
unworthie, and those vilde & reprobate company I abandon,
& utterly abolish their company for ever. Pardon sweete
father, pardon: the least thing and most desir'd[3]: and this
ruffianly cloake, I here teare from my backe, and sacrifice it
to the divel, which is maister of al mischiefe: Pardon me,
sweet father, pardon me: good my Lord of *Exeter* speak for
me: pardon me, pardon good father. Not a word: ah he wil
not speak one word! A[h] *Harry*, now thrice unhappie *Harry*!   570
But what shal I do? I wil go take me into some solitarie place,
and there lament my sinfull life, and when I have done, I wil
laie me downe and die.   *[Exit*
HEN. 4   Call him againe, call my sonne againe.
              [The Prince returns[4]
HEN. 5   And doth my father call me again? now *Harry*,
Happie be the time that thy father calleth thee againe.

---

[1] This scene suggested *1H4* III.2, though the treatment is very different.
[2] vilde, vile.   [3] desire Q.   [4] Q has no s.d.

HEN. 4   Stand up my son, and do not think thy father,
But at the request of thee my sonne, wil[1] pardon thee,
And God blesse thee, and make thee his servant.

HEN. 5   Thanks good my Lord, & no doubt but this day,   580
Even this day, I am borne new againe.

HEN. 4   Come my son and Lords, take me by the hands.

[*Exeunt omnes*

[Scene vii]

Enter Dericke.

DER.   Thou art a stinking whore, & a whorson stinking whore,
Doest thinke ile take it at thy hands?

Enter John Cobler running.

JOHN   Derick, D.D.[2] Hearesta,
Do D. never while thou livest use that.
Why, what wil my neighbors say, and thou go away so?

DER.   Shees an arrant whore, and Ile have the lawe on you *John.*

JOHN   Why what hath she done?   590

DER.   Marry marke thou *John.*
I wil prove it, that I wil.

JOHN   What wilt thou prove?

DER.   That she cald me in to dinner.
John, marke the tale wel *John*, and when I was set,
She brought me a dish of rootes, and a peece of barrel butter[3]
      therein: and she is a verie knave,
And thou a drab if[4] thou take her part.

JOHN   Hearesta *Dericke*, is this the matter?
Nay, and it be no worse, we will go home againe,   600
And all shall be amended.

DER.   Oh *John*, hearesta *John*, is all well?

JOHN   I, all is wel.

DER.   Then ile go home before, and breake all the glasse win-
      dowes.

[Scene viii]

Enter the King with his Lords.

HEN. 4   Come my Lords, I see it bootes me not to take any
phisick, for all the Phisitians in the world cannot cure me, no

---

[1] I wil, Q.
[2] Probably the author wrote D. meaning Dericke's name to be repeated.
[3] old salt butter.   [4] it, Q.

not one. But good my Lords, remember my last wil and
Testament concerning my sonne, for truly my Lordes, I doo
not thinke but he wil prove as valiant and victorious a King,
as ever raigned in England.   611

    BOTH   Let heaven and earth be witnesse betweene us, if
we accomplish not thy wil to the uttermost.

    HEN. 4   I give you most unfained thanks, good my lords,
Draw the Curtaines and depart my chamber a while,
And cause some Musicke to rocke me a sleepe.[1]   [*Exeunt Lords*

He sleepeth.

Enter the Prince.

    HEN. 5   Ah *Harry*, thrice unhappie, that hath neglect so
long from visiting of thy sicke father, I will goe. Nay but why
doo I not go to the Chamber of my sick father, to comfort the
melancholy soule of his bodie: his soule said I, here is his   620
bodie indeed, but his soule is whereas it needs no bodie. Now
thrice accursed *Harry*, that hath offended thy father so much,
and could not I crave pardon for all. Oh my dying father,
curst be the day wherin I was borne, and accursed be the
houre wherin I was begotten, but what shal I do? if weeping
teares which come too late, may suffice the negligence neglected too soone,[2] I wil weepe day and night until the
fountaine be drie with weeping.[3]   [*Exit*

Enter Lord of Exeter and Oxford.

    EXE.   Come easily my Lord, for waking of the King.
    HEN. 4   Now my Lords.
    OXF.   How doth your Grace feele your selfe?   630
    HEN. 4   Somewhat better after my sleepe,
But good my Lords take off my Crowne,
Remove my chaire a litle backe, and set me right.
    AMBO.   And please your grace, the crown is taken away.
    HEN. 4   The Crowne taken away,
Good my Lord of *Oxford*, go see who hath done this deed:
No doubt tis some vilde traitor that hath done it,
To deprive my sonne, they that would do it now,
Would seeke to scrape and scrawle for it after my death.

---

[1] This scene suggested *2H4* IV.5.
[2] for too long before. to some, Q.
[3] The Prince takes away the crown, as in *2H4* IV.5, 36–42.

Enter Lord of Oxford with the Prince.

OXF.   Here and please your Grace,   640
Is my Lord the yong Prince with the Crowne.
  HEN. 4   Why how now my sonne?
I had thought the last time I had you in schooling,
I had given you a lesson for all,
And do you now begin againe?
Why tel me my sonne,
Doest thou thinke the time so long,
That thou wouldest have it before the
Breath be out of my mouth?[1]
  HEN. 5   Most soveraign Lord, and welbeloved father,   650
I came into your Chamber to comfort the melancholy
Soule of your bodie, and finding you at that time
Past all recoverie, and dead to my thinking,
God is my witnesse: and what should I doo,
But with weeping tears lament the death of you my father,
And after that, seeing the Crowne, I tooke it:
And tel me my father, who might better take it then I,
After your death? but seeing you live,
I most humbly render it into your Majesties hands,
And the happiest man alive, that my father live: 660
And live my Lord and Father, for ever.[2]
  HEN. 4   Stand up my sonne,
Thine answere hath sounded wel in mine eares,[3]
For I must need confesse that I was in a very sound sleep,
And altogither unmindful of thy comming:
But come neare my sonne,
And let me put thee in possession whilst I live,
That none deprive thee of it after my death.
  HEN. 5   Well may I take it at your majesties hands,
But it shal never touch my head, so long as my father lives.   670

He taketh the Crowne.

  HEN. 4   God give thee joy my sonne,
God blesse thee and make thee his servant,
And send thee a prosperous raigne.
For God knowes my sonne, how hardly I came by it,
And how hardly I have maintained it.[4]

---

[1] Cf. the King's reproaches in *2H4* IV.5.91ff.
[2] Cf. *ibid.*, 141–3.   [3] Cf. *ibid.*, 176–9.
[4] *2H4* IV.5.182–218 expands this.

HEN. 5.   Howsoever you came by it, I know not,
But now I have it from you, and from you I wil keepe it:
And he that seekes to take the Crowne from my head,
Let him looke that his armour be thicker then mine,
Or I will pearce him to the heart,   680
Were it harder then brasse or bollion.[1]
   HEN. 4   Nobly spoken, and like a King.
Now trust me my Lords, I feare not but my sonne
Will be as warlike and victorious a Prince,
As ever raigned in England.
   L. AMBO.[2]   His former life shewes no lesse.
   HEN. 4   Wel my lords, I know not whether it be for sleep,
Or drawing neare of drowsie summer of death,
But I am verie much given to sleepe,
Therefore good my Lords and my sonne,   690
Draw the Curtaines, depart my Chamber,
And cause some Musicke to rocke me a sleepe.

Exeunt omnes.

[*The King dieth*

[Scene ix]

Enter the Theefe.

   THEEFE   Ah God, I am now much like to a Bird
Which hath escaped out of the Cage,
For so soone as my Lord chiefe Justice heard
That the old King was dead, he was glad to let me go,
For feare of my Lord the yong Prince:
But here comes some of his companions,
I wil see and I can get any thing of them,
For old acquaintance.   700

Enter Knights raunging.

   TOM   Gogs wounds, the King is dead.[3]
   JOC.   Dead, then gogs blood, we shall be all kings.
   NED   Gogs wounds, I shall be Lord chiefe Justice
Of England.[4]
   TOM   Why how, are you broken out of prison?
   NED   Gogs wounds, how the villaine stinkes.

---

[1] Cf. *ibid.*, 42–5; 221–3. bullion, any metal in the lump.
[2] I.e., *Both Lords.*   [3] Cf. *2H4* V.3.122–9.
[4] Cf. *2H4* V.3.139–40; 'and woe unto my Lord Chief Justice!'.

JOC.   Why what wil become of thee now?
Fie upon him, how the rascall stinkes.

THEEF.   Marry I wil go and serve my maister againe.

TOM   Gogs blood, doost think that he will have any such   710
Scab'd knave as thou art? what man, he is a king now.

NED   Hold thee, heres a couple of Angels[1] for thee,
And get thee gone, for the King wil not be long
Before he come this way:
And hereafter I wil tel the king of thee.   [*Exit Theefe*

JOC.   Oh how it did me good, to see the king
When he was crowned:
Me thought his seate was like the figure of heaven,
And his person like unto a God.

NED   But who would have thought,   720
That the king would have changde his countenance so?

JOC.   Did you not see with what grace
He sent his embassage into *France*? to tel the French king
That *Harry* of England hath sent for the Crowne,
And *Harry* of England wil have it.[2]

TOM   But twas but a litle to make the people beleeve,
That he was sorie for his fathers death.

The Trumpet sounds.

NED   Gogs wounds, the king comes,
Lets all stand aside.

Enter the King with the Archbishop, and the Lord of Oxford.

JOC.   How do you my Lord?   730
NED   How now *Harry*?[3]
Tut my Lord, put away these dumpes,
You are a king, and all the realme is yours:
What man, do you not remember the old sayings?
You know I must be Lord chiefe Justice of England,
Trust me my lord, me thinks you are very much changed,
And tis but with a litle sorrowing, to make folkes beleeve
The death of your father greeves you,
And tis nothing so.

HEN. 5   I prethee *Ned*, mend thy maners,   740
And be more modester in thy tearmes,
For my unfeined greefe is not to be ruled by thy flattering

---

[1] gold coins worth about 10 shillings.
[2] In *H5* I.2.246–8 the ambassadors demanded 'certain dukedoms'.
[3] Cf. *2H4* V.5.41: 'King Hal! my royal Hal!'

And dissembling talke, thou saist I am changed,
So I am indeed, and so must thou be, and that quickly,
Or else I must cause thee to be chaunged.

   JOC.   Gogs wounds how like you this?
Sownds tis not so sweete as Musicke.

   TOM   I trust we have not offended your grace no way.

   HEN. 5   Ah *Tom*, your former life greeves me,
And makes me to abandon & abolish your company for ever   750
And therfore not upon pain of death to approch my presence
By ten miles space; then if I heare wel of you,
It may be I wil do somewhat for you,[1]
Otherwise looke for no more favour at my hands,
Then at any other mans: And therefore be gone,
We have other matters to talke on.   [*Exeunt Knights*
Now my good Lord Archbishop of *Canterbury*,
What say you to our Embassage into *France*?[2]

   ARCHB.   Your right to the French Crowne of *France*,
Came by your great grandmother *Izabel*,   760
Wife to King *Edward* the third,
And sister to *Charles* the French King[3]:
Now if the French king deny it, as likely inough he wil,
Then must you take your sword in hand,
And conquer the right.
Let the usurped Frenchman know,
Although your predecessors have let it passe, you wil not:
For your Country men are willing with purse and men,
To aide you.[4]
Then my good Lord, as it hath bene alwaies knowne,   770
That *Scotland* hath bene in league with *France*,
By a sort of pensions which yearly come from thence,
I thinke it therefore best to conquere *Scotland*,[5]
And then I thinke that you may go more easily into *France*:
And this is all that I can say, My good Lord.

   HEN. 5   I thanke you, my good lord Archibishop of *Canterbury*.
What say you my good Lord of *Oxford*?

   OXF.   And please your Majestie,
I agree to my Lord Archbishop, saving in this:
He that wil *Scotland* win, must first with *France* begin,[6]   780

---

[1] Cf. *2H4* V.5.58–72.

[2] In *H5* I.2 the claims are discussed before the entry of the French Ambassador.

[3] Cf. *HV* I.2.33–95 on the Salic Law.   [4] *Ibid.*, 97–135.

[5] A strange twist in Canterbury's argument, taken from Westmoreland in Hall. Shakespeare's Archibishop is for France at once.

[6] Contrast Westmoreland, *ibid.*, 167–8: 'If that you will France win, Then with Scotland first begin.' *FV* uses Exeter's jingle which follows in Hall.

According to the old saying.
Therefore my good Lord, I thinke it best first to invade *France*,
For in conquering *Scotland*, you conquer but one,
And conquere *France*, and conquere both.[1]

Enter Lord of Exeter.

EXE.   And please your Majestie,
My Lord Embassador is come out of *France*.
HEN. 5   Now trust me my Lord,
He was the last man that we talked of,
I am glad that he is come to resolve us of our answere,
Commit him to our presence.   790

Enter Duke of Yorke.

YORKE.   God save the life of my soveraign Lord the king.
HEN. 5   Now my good Lord the Duke of *Yorke*,
What newes from our brother the French King?
YORKE   And please your Majestie,
I delivered him my Embassage,
Whereof I tooke some deliberation,
But for the answere he hath sent,
My Lord Embassador of *Burges*, the Duke of *Burgony*,
Monsieur le Cole, with two hundred and fiftie horsemen,
To bring the Embassage.   800
HEN. 5   Commit my Lord Archbishop of *Burges*
Into our presence.[2]

Enter Archbishop of Burges.

Now my Lord Archbishop of *Burges*,
We do learne by our Lord Embassador,
That you have our message to do
From our brother the French King:
Here my good Lord, according to our accustomed order,
We give you free libertie and license to speake,[3]
With good audience.
ARCHB.   God save the mightie King of England!   810
My Lord and maister, the most Christian king,
Charles the seventh, the great & mightie king of *France*,
As a most noble and Christian king,

---

[1] *Ibid.*, 136–220.
[2] *Ibid.*, 221 ff. Ambassadors, but not the Archbishop. *FV* combines two embassies;
The 'tennis-balls' were in 1414; Bourges came in 1415.   [3] *H5* I.2.244–5.

Not minding to shed innocent blood, is rather content
To yeeld somewhat to your unreasonable demaunds,
That if fiftie thousand crownes a yeare with his daughter
The said Ladie *Katheren,* in marriage,
And some crownes which he may wel spare,
Not hurting of his kingdome,
He is content to yeeld so far to your unreasonable desire.[1]   820
   HEN. 5   Why then belike your Lord and maister,
Thinks to puffe me up with fifty thousand crowns a yere!
No, tell thy Lord and maister,
That all the crownes in *France* shall not serve me,
Except the Crowne and kingdome it selfe:
And perchance hereafter I wil have his daughter.
   ARCHB.   And it please your Majestie,
My Lord Prince *Dolphin* greets you well,
With this present.

He delivereth a Tunne of Tennis Balles.[2]

   HEN. 5   What a guilded Tunne?   830
I pray you my Lord of *Yorke,* looke what is in it?
   YORKE   And it please your Grace,
Here is a Carpet and a Tunne of Tennis balles.[3]
   HEN. 5   A Tunne of Tennis balles?
I pray you good my Lord Archbishop,
What might the meaning thereof be?
   ARCHB.   And it please you my Lord,
A messenger you know, ought to keepe close his message,
And specially an Embassador.
   HEN. 5   But I know that you may declare your message   840
To a king: the law of Armes allowes no lesse.
   ARCHB.   My Lord hearing of your wildnesse before your
Fathers death, sent you this my good Lord,
Meaning that you are more fitter for a Tennis Court
Then a field, and more fitter for a Carpet then the Camp.
   HEN. 5   My lord prince *Dolphin* is very pleasaunt with me[4]:
But tel him, that in steed of balles of leather,
We wil tosse him balles of brasse and yron,[5]
Yea such balles as never were tost in *France,*

---

[1] Shakespeare mentions the offer in *Chorus* Act III.28–32 but omits the Bourges embassy.   [2] Q gives this s.d. also after 826.
[3] Carpet to suggest that Henry is a carpet-knight, i.e. unwarlike. Tennis balls only in *H5* I.2.254–8.
[4] Echoed in *H5* I.2.259.   [5] *Ibid.*, 282.

The proudest Tennis Court shall rue it,   850
Aye[1] and thou Prince of *Burges* shall rue it.[2]
Therfore get thee hence, and tel him thy message quickly,
Least I be there before thee: Away priest, be gone.

    ARCHB.   I beseech your grace, to deliver me your safe
Conduct under your broad seale manual.[3]

    HEN. 5   Priest of *Burges*, know,
That the hand and seale of a King, and his word is all one,
And instead of my hand and seale,
I will bring him my hand and sword: 859
And tel thy lord & maister, that I *Harry* of England said it,
And I *Harry* of England wil performe it.
My Lord of *Yorke*, deliver him our safe conduct,
Under our broad seale manual.

        Exeunt Archbishop, and the Duke of Yorke.

Now my Lords, to Armes, to Armes,
For I vow by heaven and earth, that the proudest
French man in all *France*, shall rue the time that ever
These Tennis balles were sent into England.
My Lord, I wil that there be provided a great Navy of ships,
With all speed, at *South-Hampton*,
For there I meane to ship my men,   870
For I would be there before him, if[4] it were possible,
Therefore come, but staie,
I had almost forgot the chiefest thing of all, with chafing
With this French Embassador.
Call in my Lord chiefe Justice of England.[5]

        Enters Lord chiefe Justice of England.

    EXE.   Here is the King my Lord.

    JUSTICE   God preserve your Majestie.

    HEN. 5   Why how now my lord, what is the matter?

    JUSTICE   I would it were unknowne to your Majestie.

    HEN. 5   Why what aile[s] you?   880

    JUST.   Your Majestie knoweth my griefe well.

    HEN. 5   Oh my Lord, you remember you sent me to the
Fleete, did you not?

    JUST.   I trust your grace have forgotten that.

---

[1] I. Q.   [2] *H5* I.2.281–8.

[3] Emanuel, Q; also at 863. seal and signature. Shakespeare merely has 'So get
you hence in peace' (294).   [4] it, Q.

[5] Cf. *2H4* V.2.43ff where the incident occurs before the Coronation.

HEN. 5   I truly my Lord, and for revengement,
I have chosen you to be my Protector over my Realme,[1]
Until it shall please God to give me speedie returne
Out of *France*.

JUST.   And if it please your Majestie, I am far unworthie
Of so high a dignitie.   890

HEN. 5   Tut my Lord, you are not unworthie,
Because I thinke you worthie:
For you that would not spare me,
I thinke wil not spare another,
It must needs be so, and therefore come,
Let us be gone, and get our men in a readinesse.

                                                          [*Exeunt* omnes

[Scene x]

                    Enter a Captaine, John Cobler and his wife.

CAP.   Come, come, there's no remedie,
Thou must needs serve the King.[2]

JOHN   Good maister Captaine let me go,
I am not able to go so farre.   900

WIFE   I pray you good maister Captaine,
Be good to my husband.

CAP.   Why I am sure he is not too good to serve the king.

JOHN   Alasse no: but a great deale too bad,
Therefore I pray you let me go.

CAP.   No, no, thou shalt go.

JOHN   Oh sir, I have a great many shooes at home to Cobble.

WIFE   I pray you let him go home againe.

CAP.   Tush I care not, thou shalt go.   910

JOHN   Oh wife, and you had beene a loving wife to me,
This had not bene, for I have said many times,
That I would go away, and now I must go
Against my will.   [*He weepeth*

                    Enters Dericke.

DER.   How now ho, *Basillus Manus*,[3] for an old codpeece.
Maister Captaine shall we away?
Sownds how now *John*, what a crying?
What make you and my dame there?
I marvell whose head you will throw the stooles at,
Now we are gone.   920

---

[1] Shakespeare confirms him in his office. V.2.112–14.
[2] This scene probably suggested *2H4* III.2.
[3] Besa las manos. Kiss hands; goodbye! (Spanish).

WIFE   Ile tell you, come ye cloghead,
What do you with my potlid? heare you,
Will you have it rapt about your pate?

She beateth him with her potlid.

DER.   Oh good dame,   [*Here he shakes her*[1]
And I had my dagger here, I wold worie you al to peeces,
That I would.
WIFE   Would you so, Ile trie that.   [*She beateth him*
DER.   Maister Captaine will ye suffer her?
Go to[2] dame, I will go backe as far as I can,
But and you come againe,   930
Ile clap the law on your backe thats flat:
Ile tell you maister Captaine what you shall do:
Presse her for a souldier. I warrant you,
She will do as much good as her husband and I too.

Enters the Theefe.

Sownes, who comes yonder?
CAP.   How now good fellow, doest thou want a maister?
THEEFE   I truly sir.
CAP.   Hold thee then, I presse thee for a souldier,
To serve the King in *France*.
DER.   How now Gads, what doest know us,[3] thinkest?   940
THEEFE   I, I knew thee long ago.
DER.   Heare you maister Captaine?
CAP.   What saist thou?
DER.   I pray you let me go home againe.
CAP.   Why, what wouldst thou do at home?
DER.   Marry I have brought two shirts with me,
And I would carry one of them home againe,
For I am sure heele steale it from me,
He is such a filching fellow.[4]
CAP.   I warrant thee he wil not steale it from thee,   950
Come lets away.
DER.   Come maister Captaine lets away,
Come follow me.
JOHN   Come wife, lets part lovingly.
WIFE   Farewell good husband.

---

[1] Q makes Dericke say these words.
[2] too, Q.   [3] knowes, Q.
[4] Cf. *H5* III.2.45: 'Nym and Bardolph are sworn brothers in filching.'

DER.   Fie what a kissing and crying is here?
Sownes, do ye thinke he wil never come againe?
Why *John* come away, doest thinke that we are so base
Minded to die among French men?
Sownes, we know not whether they will laie   960
Us in their Church or no: Come M. Captain, lets away,
    CAP.   I cannot staie no longer, therefore come away.

                                   [*Exeunt omnes*

[Scene xi]

Enter the King,[1] *Prince Dolphin, and Lord*
high Constable of France.

    KING   Now my Lord high Constable,
What say you to our Embassage into England?
    CONST.   And it please your Majestie, I can say nothing,
Until my Lords Embassadors be come home,
But yet me thinkes your grace hath done well,
To get your men in so good a readinesse,
For feare of the worst.
    KING   I my Lord we have some in a readinesse,   970
But if the King of England make against us,
We must have thrice so many moe.
    DOLPHIN   Tut my Lord, although the King of England
Be yoong and wilde headed,[2] yet never thinke he will be so
Unwise to make battell against the mightie King of *France.*
    KING   Oh my sonne, although the King of England be
Yoong and wilde headed, yet never thinke but he is rulde
By his wise Councellors.[3]

Enter Archbishop of Burges.

    ARCHB.   God save the life of my soveraign lord the king.   980

    KING   Now my good Lord Archbishop of *Burges,*
What newes from our brother the English King?
    ARCHB.   And please your Majestie,
He is so far from your expectation,
That nothing wil serve him but the Crowne
And kingdome it selfe,[4] besides, he bad me haste quickly,
Least he be there before me, and so far as I heare,
He hath kept promise, for they say, he is alreadie landed
At *Kidcocks* in *Normandie,* upon the River of *Sene,*
And laid his siege to the Garrison Towne of *Harflew.*   990

[1] The King of France.   [2] *H5* II.4.23–9.   [3] *H5* II.4.33.
[4] Cf. *H5* II.4.81–4 where Exeter makes the demand.

KING   You have made great haste in the meane time,
Have you not?

DOLPHIN   I pray you my Lord, how did the King of England
take my presents?[1]

ARCHB.   Truly my Lord, in verie ill part,
For these your balles of leather,
He will tosse you balles of brasse and yron:
Trust me my Lord, I was verie affraide of him,
He is such a hautie and high minded Prince,
He is as fierce as a Lyon.   1000

CON.   Tush, we wil make him as tame as a Lambe,
I warrant you.

Enters a Messenger.

MESSEN.   God save the mightie King of *France.*

KING   Now Messenger, what newes?

MESSEN.   And it please your Majestie,
I come from your poore distressed Towne of *Harflew*,
Which is so beset on every side,
If your Majestie do not send present aide,
The Towne will be yeelded to the English King.[2]

KING   Come my Lords, come, shall we stand still   1010
Till our Country be spoyled under our noses?
My Lords, let the Normanes, Brabants, Pickardies,
And Danes, be sent for with all speede:
And you my Lord high Constable, I make Generall
Over all my whole Armie.
Monsieur le Colle, Maister of the Bows,[3]
Signior Devens,[4] and all the rest, at your appointment.

DOLP.   I trust your Majestie will bestow,
Some part of the battell on me,
I hope not to present any otherwise then well.   1020

KING   I tell thee my sonne,
Although I should get the victory, and thou lose thy life,
I should thinke my selfe quite conquered,
And the English men to have the victorie.

DOL.   Why my Lord and father,
I would have the pettie king of England to know,
That I dare encounter him in any ground of the world.

---

[1] *Ibid.*, 115–16.

[2] Cf. *H5* III.1, and III.3.44–50. Shakespeare shows the attack on and surrender of the town.

[3] Boas, Q. At Agincourt the 'maister of the crossbowes' was 'lord Rambures' (Hol. 552/2/52).   [4] Nevers? (Hol. 553/1/23).

KING   I know well my sonne,
But at this time I will have it thus[1]:
Therefore come away.   1030

                                                          [*Exeunt omnes*

[Scene xii]

Enters Henry the fifth, with his Lords.

HEN. 5   Come my Lords of England,
No doubt this good lucke of winning this Towne,
Is a signe of an honourable victorie to come.
But good my Lord, go and speake to the Captaines
With all speed, to number the hoast of the French men,
And by that meanes we may the better know
How to appoint the battell.
   YORKE   And it please your Majestie,
There are many of your men sicke and diseased,
And many of them die for want of victuals.[2]   1040
   HEN. 5   And why did you not tell me of it before?
If we cannot have it for money,
We will have it by dint of sword,
The lawe of Armes allow no lesse.
   OXF.   I beseech your grace, to graunt me a boone.
   HEN. 5   What is that my good Lord?
   OXF.   That your grace would give me the
Evantgard in the battell.
   HEN. 5   Trust me my Lord of *Oxford*, I cannot:
For I have alreadie given it to my unck[l]e the Duke of *York*,
Yet I thanke you for your good will.   1051

A Trumpet soundes.

How now, what is that?
   YORKE   I thinke it be some Herald of Armes.

Enters a Herald[3]

HERALD   King of England, my Lord high Constable,
And others of the Noble men of *France*,
Sends me to defie thee, as open enemy to God,
Our Countrey, and us, and hereupon,
They presently bid thee battell.

---

[1] Cf. *H5* III.5.64–8. Shakespeare's Dauphin is present at Agincourt (IV.5).
[2] Cf. *H5* III.6.143–8.
[3] Montjoy in Shakespeare III.6.114ff and IV.3.79–127.

HEN. 5   Herald tell them, that I defie them,
As open enemies to God, my Countrey, and me,   1060
And as wron[g]full usurpers of my right:
And whereas thou saist they presently bid me battell,
Tell them that I thinke they know how to please me:
But I pray thee what place hath my lord Prince *Dolphin*
Here in battell.
   HERALD   And it please your grace,
My Lord and King his father,
Will not let him come into the field.
   HEN. 5   Why then he doth me great injurie,
I thought that he & I shuld have plaid at tennis togither,   1070
Therefore I have brought tennis balles for him,
But other maner of ones then he sent me.
And Herald, tell my Lord Prince *Dolphin*,
That I have inured my hands with other kind of weapons
Then tennis balles, ere this time a day,
And that he shall finde it ere it be long,
And so adue my friend:
And tell my Lord, that I am readie when he will.
                                        [*Exit Herald*
Come my Lords, I care not and I go to our Captaines,
And ile see the number of the French army my selfe.   1080
Strike up the Drumme.   [*Exeunt omnes*

[Scene xiii]

Enter French Souldiers.

   1. SOUL.   Come away Jack Drummer, come away all,
And me will tel you what me wil doo,
Me wil tro one chance on the dice,
Who shall have the king of England and his lords.
   2. SOUL.   Come away Jacke Drummer,
And tro your chance, and lay downe your Drumme.

Enter Drummer.

   DRUM.   Oh the brave apparel that the English mans
Hay broth over, I wil tel you what
Me ha donne, me ha provided a hundreth trunkes,   1090
And all to put the fine parel of the English mans in.
   1. SOUL.   What do thou meane by trunkes?
   2. SOUL.   A shest man, a hundred shests.
   1. SOUL.   *Awee, awee, awee,* Me wil tel you what,
Me ha put five shildren out of my house,

And all too litle to put the fine apparel of the
English mans in.
 DRUM. Oh the brave, the brave apparel that we shall
Have anon, but come, and you shall see what me wil tro
At the kings Drummer and Fife,   1100
Ha, me ha no good lucke: tro you.
 3. SOL. Faith me wil tro at the Earle of *Northumberland*
And my Lord a *Willowby*, with his great horse,
Snorting, farting, oh brave horse.[1]
 1. SOL. Ha, bur Ladie you ha reasonable good lucke,
Now I wil tro at the king himselfe,
Ha, me have no good lucke.

Enters a Captaine.

 CAP. How now what make you here,
So farre from the Campe?
 2. SOL. Shal me tel our captain what we have done here? 1110
 DRUM. Awee, awee.

Exeunt Drum, and one Souldier.

 2. SOL. I wil tel you what whe have doune,
We have bene troing our shance on the Dice,
But none can win the king.
 CAP. I thinke so, why he is left behind for me,
And I have set three or foure chaire-makers a worke,
To make a new disguised chaire to set that womanly
King of England in, that all the people may laugh
And scoffe at him.
 2. SOUL. Oh brave Captaine.   1120
 CAP. I am glad, and yet with a kinde of pitie
To see the poore king:
Why who ever saw a more flourishing armie in *France*
In one day, then here is? Are not here all the Peeres of
France? Are not here the Normans with their firie hand-
Gunnes, and slaunching Curtleaxes?[2]
Are not here the Barbarians with their hard horses,
And lanching speares?
Are not here Pickardes with their Crosbowes & piercing
Dartes.   1130

---

[1] Contrast Grandpré, *H5* IV.2.46–52; and the Frenchmen's hopes in III.7.
[2] Cf. *H5* IV.2.21. *FV* takes this speech from the oration of the Constable of
France in Hall (which Shakespeare had read before writing *1H6*).

The Henues with their cutting Glaves[1] and sharpe
Carbuckles.[2]
Are not here the Lance knights of *Burgondie*?
And on the other side, a site[3] of poore English scabs?[4]
Why take an English man out of his warme bed
And his stale drinke,[5] but one moneth,
And alas what wil become of him?
But give the Frenchman a Reddish[6] roote,
And he wil live with it all the dayes of his life.[7]   [*Exit*

    2. SOUL.   Oh the brave apparel that we shall have of the   1140
    English mans.

[Scene xiv]

       Enters the king of England and his Lords.

    HEN. 5.   Come my Lords and fellowes of armes,
What company is there of the French men?
    OXF.   And it please your Majestie,
Our Captaines have numbred them,
And so neare as they can judge,
They are about threescore thousand horsemen,
And fortie thousand footemen.
    HEN. 5   They threescore thousand,
And we but two thousand.   1150
They threescore thousand footemen,
And we twelve thousand.
They are a hundred thousand,
And we fortie thousand, ten to one[8]:
My Lords and loving Countrymen,
Though we be fewe and they many,
Feare not, your quarrel is good, and God will defend you:
Plucke up your hearts, for this day we shall either have
A valiant victorie, or a honourable death.
Now my Lords, I wil that my uncle the Duke of Yorke,   1160
Have the avantgard in the battell.[9]

---

    [1] glaives (Fr.), swords.   [2] escarboucles (Fr.).   [3] sight, display.
    [4] villains, scurvy knaves. Cf. *H5* IV.2.39ff.
    [5] From Hall: 'kepe an Englishman one moneth from hys warme bed, fat befe,
and stale drynke, and let him that season tast colde and suffre hunger, you then
shall se his courage abated, his bodye waxe leane and bare, & ever desirous to
returne into his own countrey' (cf. *1H6* I.2.9–12). Contrast *H5* III.5.18–19 and
III.7.153–9.
    [6] radish.   [7] Contrast *H5* III.5.15–26.
    [8] Strange arithmetic. Cf. *H5* IV.3.3–4: 'three-score thousand . . . five to one.'
    [9] York asks for this in *H5* IV.3.129.

The Earle of *Darby*, the Earle of *Oxford*,
The Earle of *Kent*, the Earle of *Nottingham*,
The Earle of *Huntington*, I wil have beside the army,
That they may come fresh upon them.
And I my selfe with the Duke of *Bedford*,
The Duke of *Clarence* and the Duke of *Gloster*,
Wil be in the midst of the battell.
Furthermore, I wil that my Lord of *Willowby*,
And the Earle of *Northumberland*,   1170
With their troupes of horsmen, be continually running like
Wings on both sides of the army:
My Lord of *Northumberland*, on the left wing.
Then I wil, that every archer provide him a stake of
A tree, and sharpe it at both endes,
And at the first encounter of the horsemen,
To pitch their stakes downe into the ground before them,
That they may gore themselves upon them,
And then to recoyle backe, and shoote wholly altogither,
And so discomfit them.[1]   1180
    OXF. And it please your Majestie,
I wil take that in charge, if your grace be therwith content.
    HEN. With all my heart, my good Lord of *Oxford*:
And go and provide quickly.
    OXF. I thanke your highnesse.   [*Exit*
    HEN. 5 Well my Lords, our battels are ordeined,
And the French making of bonfires, and at their bankets,
But let them looke, for I meane to set upon them.

The Trumpet soundes.

Soft, here[2] comes some other French message.

Enters Herauld.[3]

    HERALD King of England, my Lord high Constable   1190
And other of my Lords, considering the poore estate of thee
And thy poore Countrey men,
Sends me to know what thou wilt give for thy ransome?
Perhaps thou maist agree better cheape[4] now,
Then when thou art conquered.
    HEN. 5 Why then belike your high Constable
Sends to know what I wil give for my ransome?

---

  [1] Shakespeare substitutes rhetoric (IV.3, etc.) for these orders of battle, which
are taken from Holinshed (*inf.* 393).
  [2] heres Q.   [3] *H5* IV.3.79ff (Montjoy).   [4] at a better rate.

Now trust me Herald, not so much as a tun of tennis bals
No, not so much as one poore tennis ball,
Rather shall my bodie lie dead in the field, to feed crowes,   1200
Then ever England shall pay one penny ransome
For my bodie.[1]

    HERALD   A kingly resolution.

    HEN. 5   No Herald, tis a kingly resolution,
And the resolution of a king:
Here take this for thy paines.   [*Exit Herald*
But stay my Lords, what time is it?

    ALL   Prime my Lord.

    HEN. 5   Then is it good time no doubt,
For all England praieth for us: 1210
What my Lords, me thinks you looke cheerfully upon me?
Why then with one voice and like true English hearts,
With me throw up your caps, and for England,
Cry S. *George*, and God and S. *George* helpe us.[2]

          Strike Drummer.   Exeunt omnes.
     The French men crie within, S. Dennis, S. Dennis,
            Mount Joy, S. Dennis.
               The Battell.[3]

[Scene xv]

       Enters King of England, and his Lords.

    HEN. 5   Come my Lords come, by this time our
Swords are almost drunke with French blood,
But my Lords, which of you can tell me how many of our
Army be slaine in the battell?[4]

    OXF.   And it please your Majestie,
There are of the French armie slaine,   1220
Above ten thousand,[5] twentie sixe hundred
Whereof are Princes and Nobles bearing banners[6]:
Besides, all the Nobilitie of *France* are taken prisoners.
Of your Majesties Armie, are slaine none but the good
Duke of *Yorke*, and not above five or six and twentie
Common souldiers.[7]

    HEN. 5.   For the good Duke of *Yorke* my unckle,
I am heartily sorie, and greatly lament his misfortune,[8]

---

[1] Cf. *H5* IV.3.122–5.   [2] Cf. III.1.32–4, before Harfleur.
[3] Incidents of battle are shown on the stage, as in *H5* IV. 4–7.
[4] Cf. *H5* IV.8.76.   [5] *Ibid.*, 90.
[6] Cf. *H5* IV.8.84: 'of princes. . . . And nobles bearing banners. . . . One hundred twenty-six.'
[7] Cf. *H5* IV.8.105–9.   [8] Cf. *H5* IV.6.

Yet the honourable victorie which the Lord hath given us,
Doth make me much rejoyce. But staie,   1230
Here comes another French message.   [*Sound Trumpet*

Enters a Herald and kneeleth.

HER.   God save the life of the most mightie Conqueror,
The honourable king of England.[1]
HEN. 5   Now Herald, me thinks the world is changed
With you now, what I am sure it is a great disgrace for a
Herald to kneele to the king of England,
What is thy message?
HER.   My Lord & maister, the conquered king of *France*,
Sends thee long health, with heartie greeting.
HEN. 5   Herald, his greetings are welcome,   1240
But I thanke God for my health:
Well Herald, say on.
HERALD   He hath sent me to desire your Majestie,
To give him leave to go into the field to view his poore
Country men, that they may all be honourably buried.
HEN. 5   Why Herald, doth thy Lord and maister
Send to me to burie the dead?
Let him bury them, a Gods name.
But I pray thee Herald, where is my Lord hie Constable,
And those that would have had my ransome?   1250
HERALD   And it please your majestie,
He was slaine in the battell.
HEN. 5   Why you may see, you will make your selves
Sure before the victorie be wonne, but Herald,
What Castle is this so neere adjoyning to our Campe?[2]
HERALD   And it please your Majestie,
Tis cald the Castle of *Agincourt*.
HEN. 5   Well then my lords of England,
For the more honour of our English men,
I will that this be for ever cald the battell of *Agincourt*.   1260
HERALD   And it please your Majestie,
I have a further message to deliver to your Majestie.
HEN. 5   What is that Herald? say on.
HER.   And it please your Majestie, my Lord and maister,
Craves to parley with your Majestie.
HEN. 5   With a good will, so some of my Nobles
View the place for feare of trecherie and treason.
HERALD   Your grace needs not to doubt that.
                                            [*Exit Herald*

[1] Montjoy in *H5* IV.7.65ff.   [2] IV.7.87–9.

HEN. 5　Well, tell him then, I will come.
Now my lords, I will go into the field my selfe,　　　　　1270
To view my Country men, and to have them honourably
Buried, for the French King shall never surpasse me in
Curtesie, whiles I am *Harry* King of England.
Come on my lords.　　　　　　　　　[*Exeunt omnes*

[Scene xvi]

　　　　　　Enters John Cobler, and Robbin Pewterer.

ROBIN　Now, *John Cobler*,
Didst thou see how the King did behave himselfe?
　　JOHN　But *Robin*, didst thou see what a pollicie
The King had, to see how the French men were kild
With the stakes of the trees.
　　ROBIN　I *John*, there was a brave pollicie.　　　　　1280

　　　　　　Enters an English souldier, roming.

　　SOUL.　What are you my maisters?
　　BOTH　Why, we be English men.
　　SOUL.　Are you English men? then change your language
For the Kings Tents are set a fire,[1]
And all they that speake English will be kild.
　　JOHN　What shall we do *Robin*? faith ile shift,[2]
For I can speake broken French.
　　ROBIN　Faith so can I, lets heare how thou canst speak?
　　JOHN　Commodevales[3] Monsieur.
　　ROBIN　Thats well, come lets be gone.　　　　　1290

　　　　　　Drum and Trumpet sounds:

[Scene xvii]

　　　　　*Enters Dericke roming, After him a Frenchman,
　　　　　　　　and takes him prisoner.*

DERICKE　O good *Mounser.*
FRENCH MAN　Come, come, you *villeaco.*[4]
DER.　O I will sir, I will.
FRENCHMAN　Come quickly you pesant.
DER.　I will sir, what shall I give you?

---

[1] No mention of the slaying of the prisoners. Cf. *H5* IV.7.7–10.
[2] manage.　　　　[3] Comment tu vas?—How are you?
[4] villanaccio (Ital.), rustic, clown.

FRENCH. Marry thou shalt give me,
One, to, tre, foure, hundred Crownes.

DER. Nay sir, I will give you more,
I will give you as many crowns as wil lie on your sword.

FRENCH. Wilt thou give me as many crowns 1300
As will lie on my sword?

DER. I marrie will I, I but you must lay downe your
Sword, or else they will not lie on your sword.

> *Here the Frenchman laies downe his sword, and*
> *the clowne takes it up, and hurles him downe.*

DER. Thou villaine, darest thou looke up?

FRENCH. O good *Mounsier comparteue.*[1]
Monsieur pardon me.

DER. O you villaine, now you lie at my mercie,
Doest thou remember since thou lambst me in thy short el?[2]
O villaine, now I will strike off thy head.

> *Here whiles he turnes his backe, the French*
> *man runnes his wayes.*

DER. What is he gone, masse I am glad of it, 1310
For if he had staid, I was afraid he wold have sturd again,
And then I should have beene spilt,
But I will away, to kill more Frenchmen.

> *Enters King of France, King of England,*
> *and attendants.*

HEN. 5 Now my good brother of *France*,
My comming into this land was not to shead blood,
But for the right of my Countrey, which if you can deny,
I am content peaceably to leave my siege,
And to depart out of your land.[3]

CHARLES What is it you demand,
My loving brother of *England*?

HEN. 5 My Secretary hath it written; read it.

SECRET. Item, that immediately *Henry* of England
Be crowned King of *France*.

CHARLES A very hard sentence,
My good brother of England.

HEN. 5 No more but right, my good brother of *France*.

---

[1] Compatez vous! — Have compassion!
[2] beat me with thy curtel (i.e. cutlass, curtleace, short sword).
[3] He had left and come back. Cf. *H5* Chorus Act V.6–42. The 'siege' is probably that of Rouen (1418–19).

FRENCH KING   Well, read on.

SECRET.   Item, that after the death of the said *Henry*,
The Crowne remaine to him and his heires for ever.

FRENCH KING   Why then you do not onely meane to   1330
Dispossesse me, but also my sonne.

HEN. 5   Why my good brother of *France*,
You have had it long inough:
And as for Prince *Dolphin*,
It skils not though he sit beside the saddle:
Thus I have set it downe, and thus it shall be.

FRENCH KING   You are very peremptorie,
My good brother of England.

HEN.   And you as perverse, my good brother of *France*.

CHARLES   Why then belike, all that I have here is yours.   1340

HEN. 5   I even as far as the kingdom of *France* reaches

CHARLES   I for by this hote beginning,
We shall scarce bring it to a calme ending.

HEN. 5   It is as you please, here is my resolution.

CHARLES   Well my brother of England,
If you will give me a coppie,
We will meete you againe to morrow.[1]

HEN. 5   With a good will my good brother of *France*.
Secretary deliver him a coppie.

Exit King of France, and all their attendants.[2]

My lords of England go before,   1350
And I will follow you.   [*Exeunt Lords*

Speakes to himselfe.

HEN. 5   Ah *Harry*, thrice unhappie *Harry*.
Hast thou now conquered the French King,
And begins a fresh supply with his daughter,
But with what face canst thou seeke to gaine her love,
Which hath sought to win her fathers Crowne?
Her fathers Crowne, said I: no it is mine owne:
I, but I love her, and must crave her.
Nay I love her and will have her.

Enters Lady Katheren and her Ladies.

But here she comes: 1360
How now faire Ladie *Katheren* of *France*,
What newes?

---

[1] Shakespeare omits details of the terms, but includes the deferment, V.2.68–82.
[2] Q places this s.d. after l. 1347.

KATHREN   And it please your Majestie,
My father sent me to know if you will debate any of these
Unreasonable demands which you require.[1]

HEN. 5   Now trust me *Kate*,
I commend thy fathers wit greatly in this,
For none in the world could sooner have made me debate it
If it were possible:
But tell me sweete *Kate*, canst thou tell how to love?   1370

KATE   I cannot hate, my good Lord,
Therefore far unfit were it for me to love.

HEN. 5   Tush *Kate*, but tell me in plaine termes,
Canst thou love the King of England?
I cannot do as these Countries do,
That spend halfe their time in woing:
Tush wench, I am none such,
But wilt thou go over to England?[2]

KATE   I would to God, that I had your Majestie
As fast in love, as you have my father in warres,   1380
I would not vouchsafe so much as one looke,
Untill you had related[3] all these unreasonable demands.

HEN. 5   Tush *Kate*, I know thou wouldst not use me so
Hardly: But tell me, canst thou love the king of England?

KATE   How should I love him, that hath dealt so hardly
With my father.[4]

HEN. 5   But Ile[5] deale as easily with thee
As thy heart can imagine, or tongue can require.
How saist thou, what will it be?

KATE   If I were of my owne direction,   1390
I could give you answere:
But seeing I stand at my fathers direction,
I must first know his will.[6]

HEN. 5   But shal I have thy good wil in the mean season?

KATE   Whereas I can put your grace in no assurance,
I would be loth to put you in any dispaire.

HEN. 5   Now before God, it is a sweete wench.

She goes aside, and speakes as followeth.

KAT.   I may thinke my selfe the happiest in the world,
That is beloved of the mightie King of England.

HEN. 5   Well *Kate*, are you at hoast[7] with me?   1400

---

[1] Shakespeare's Katharine cannot speak English. III.4; V.2.
[2] This plain speech is developed in *H5* V.2.124–72.
[3] rebated.   [4] Cf. *H5* V.2.173–4.   [5] ile Q, and elsewhere.
[6] *H5* V.2.253–4.   [7] at home, in accord.

Sweete *Kate*, tel thy father from me,
That none in the world could sooner have perswaded me to
It then thou, and so tel thy father from me.
    KAT.   God keepe your Majestie in good health.   [*Exit Kat.*
    HEN. 5   Farwel sweet *Kate*. In faith, it is a sweet wench,
But if I knew I could not have her fathers good wil,
I would so rowse the Towers over his eares,
That I would make him be glad to bring her me,
Upon his hands and knees.   [*Exit King*

[Scene xix]

        Enters Dericke, with his girdle full of shooes.

    DER.   How now? Sownes it did me good to see how   1410
I did triumph over the French men.

      Enter John Cobler roving, with a packe full of apparell.

    JOHN   Whoope *Dericke*, how doest thou?
    DER.   What *John*, *Comedevales*, alive yet.
    JOHN   I promise thee *Dericke*, I scapte hardly,
For I was within halfe a mile when one was kild.
    DER.   Were you so?
    JOHN   I trust me, I had like bene slaine.
    DER.   But once kild, why it is nothing,
I was foure or five times slaine.
    JOHN   Foure or five times slaine?   1420
Why, how couldst thou have been alive now?
    DER.   O *John*, never say so,
For I was cald the bloodie souldier amongst them all.
    JOHN   Why, what didst thou?
    DER.   Why, I will tell thee *John*.
Every day when I went into the field,
I would take a straw and thrust it into my nose,[1]
And make my nose bleed, and then I wold go into the field,
And when the Captaine saw me, he would say,
Peace! a bloodie souldier, and bid me stand aside,   1430
Whereof I was glad:
But marke the chance *John*.
I went and stood behinde a tree, but marke then *John*.
I thought I had beene safe, but on a sodaine,
There steps to me a lustie tall French man,

---

[1] Cf. *1H4* II.4.313-15. Falstaff suggests this device.

Now he drew, and I drew,
Now I lay here, and he lay there,
Now I set this leg before, and turned this backward,
And skipped quite over a hedge,
And he saw me no more there that day,   1440
And was not this well done *John*?
    JOHN   Masse *Dericke*, thou hast a wittie head.
    DER.   I *John*, thou maist see, if thou hadst taken my counsel,
But what hast thou there?
I thinke thou hast bene robbing the French men.
    JOHN   I' faith *Dericke*, I have gotten some reparrell
To carry home to my wife.
    DER.   And I have got some shooes,
    For Ile tel thee what I did, when they were dead,
I would go take off all their shooes.   1450
    JOHN   I but *Dericke*, how shall we get home?
    DER.   Nay sownds, and they take thee,
They wil hang thee.
O *John*, never do so: if it be thy fortune to be hangd,
Be hangd in thy owne language whatsoever thou doest.
    JOHN   Why *Dericke* the warres is done,
We may go home now.
    DER.   I but you may not go before you aske the king leave,
But I know a way to go home, and aske the king no leave.
    JOHN   How is that *Dericke*?   1460
    DER.   Why *John*, thou knowest the Duke of *Yorkes*
Funerall must be carried into England, doest thou not?
    JOHN   I that I do.
    DER.   Why then thou knowest weele go with it.
    JOHN   I but *Dericke*, how shall we do for to meet them?
    DER.   Sownds if I make not shift to meet them, hang me.
Sirra, thou knowst that in every Towne there wil
Be ringing, and there wil be cakes and drinke,
Now I wil go to the Clarke and Sexton
And keepe a talking, and say, O this fellow rings well,   1470
And thou shalt go and take a peece of cake, then Ile ring,
And thou shalt say, oh this fellow keepes a good stint,
And then I will go drinke to thee all the way:
But I marvel what my dame wil say when we come home,
Because we have not a French word to cast at a Dog
By the way?
    JOHN   Why, what shall we do *Dericke*?
    DER.   Why *John*, Ile go before and call my dame whore,
And thou shalt come after and set fire on the house,

We may do it *John*, for Ile prove it,   1480
Because we be souldiers.

The Trumpets sound.

JOHN   *Dericke* helpe me to carry my shooes and bootes.

[*Exeunt*

[Scene xx]

Enters King of England, Lord of Oxford and Exeter, then the
King of France, Prince Dolphin, and the Duke of Burgondie,
and attendants.

HEN. 5   Now my good brother of *France*,
I hope by this time you have deliberated of your answere?
    FR. KING   I my welbeloved brother of England,
We have viewed it over with our learned Councell,
But cannot finde that you should be crowned
King of *France*.
    HEN. 5   What, not King of *France*? then nothing.
I must be King: but my loving brother of *France*,   1490
I can hardly forget the late injuries offered me,
When I came last to parley,
The French men had better a raked
The bowels out of their fathers carkasses,
Then to have fiered my Tentes,
And if I knew thy sonne Prince *Dolphin* for one,
I would so rowse him, as he was never so rowsed.
    FR. KING   I dare sweare for my sonnes innocencie
In this matter.
But if this please you, that immediately you be   1500
Proclaimed and crowned heire and Regent of *France*,
Not King, because I my selfe was once crowned King.
    HEN. 5   Heire and Regent of *France*, that is well,
But that is not all that I must have.
    FR. KING   The rest my Secretary hath in writing.
    SECRET.   Item, that *Henry* King of England,
Be Crowned heire and Regent of *France*,
During the life of King *Charles*, and after his death,
The Crowne with all rights, to remaine to King *Henry*
Of England, and to his heires for ever.[1]   1510
    HEN. 5   Well my good brother of *France*,
There is one thing I must needs desire.
    FR. KING   What is that my good brother of England?
    HEN. 5   That all your Nobles must be sworne to be true to me.
    [1] *H5* V.2.348–59.

FR. KING   Whereas they have not stucke with greater
Matters, I know they wil not sticke with such a trifle.
Begin you my Lord Duke of *Burgondie.*

HEN. 5   Come my Lord of *Burgondie,*
Take your oath upon my sword.   1520

BURGON.   I *Philip* Duke of *Burgondie,*
Sweare to *Henry* King of England,
To be true to him, and to become his league-man,
And that if I *Philip,* heare of any forraigne power
Comming to invade the said *Henry* or his heires,
Then I the said *Philip* to send him word,
And aide him with all the power I can make,
And thereunto I take my oath.   [*He kisseth the sword*

HEN. 5   Come Prince *Dolphin,* you must sweare too.
                                                    [*He kisseth the sword*

HEN. 5   Well my brother of *France,*   1530
There is one thing more I must needs require of you.[1]

FR. KING   Wherein is it that we may satisfie your Majestie?

HEN. 5   A trifle my good brother of *France.*
I meane to make your daughter Queene of England,
If she be willing, and you therewith content:
How saist thou *Kate,* canst thou love the King of England?

KATE   How should I love thee, which is my fathers enemy?

HEN. 5   Tut, stand not upon these points,
Tis you must make us friends:
I know *Kate,* thou are not a litle proud that I love thee: 1540
What, wench, the King of England?

FRENCH KING   Daughter, let nothing stand betwixt the
King of England and thee, agree to it.

KATE   I had best whilst he is willing,
Least when I would, he will not:
I rest at your Majesties commaund.

HEN. 5   Welcome sweet *Kate,* but my brother of *France,*
What say you to it?

FRENCH KING   With all my heart I like it,
But when shall be your wedding day?   1550

HEN. 5   The first Sunday of the next moneth,[2]
God willing.

Sound Trumpets.

                                                    [*Exuent omnes*

FINIS.

[1] Cf. *H5* V.2.96–7; 360.

[2] *H5* V.2.383. Shakespeare delays the oaths of fealty till then (Trinity Sunday,
2 June, 1420).

HENRY V

INTRODUCTION

HENRY THE FIFTH was probably first performed between March and September, 1599, while Essex was in Ireland. It was not mentioned by Francis Meres in *Palladis Tamia* (1598). An entry in *S.R.* on 4 August, 1600, describes the play as one of several 'to be staied', i.e. not to be published without permission from the Lord Chamberlain's Company who owned the right text. However, a pirated version (Q1) was printed by Thomas Creede for Thomas Millington and John Busby in 1600. On 14 August in the same year an entry in *S.R.* notes the right of Thomas Pavyer to the copy, but the second Quarto, which Creede printed for Pavyer in 1602, was set up from Q1, as was Q3, published in 1619 by William Jaggard but with 'Printed for T.P. 1608' on the title-page.

F1 is the most reliable of the texts. The relation of Q1 to it has caused controversy. 'If Q1 is read side by side with F1', (wrote Chambers), 'it is impossible to regard it as anything but a continual perversion of the same text.' On the other hand Pollard and Wilson treated Q1 as based on an old play already existent before 1593, when it was partly revised by Shakespeare, 'transcribed in an abridged form for provincial use in 1593, and finally printed partly from this transcript and partly from an actor's report of a performance of the play as further revised by Shakespeare from the original manuscript' (*WSh* 1.393–4). If this were true, Q1 must in part represent a source-play; but although one must admire the ingenuity of Pollard and Wilson's reasoning, their theory does not make clear what parts of Q1 are 'old play'. Since 'the original play . . . is taken to have been itself a revision of *The Famous Victories*' (Chambers), I have thought it best to confine my attention to that play as printed in 1598, while recognizing that the original *Famous Victories* may have been longer than it is now, and that more than one stage of writing may have come between that and our *Henry V*.[1]

Actually there is more connection between *Henry V* and *Famous Victories* than between the latter and *Henry IV*. There are many significant resemblances, and although much of the common material was inevitable in any play founded on the chronicles, there can be little doubt that Shakespeare recalled both the structure of the last half of *Famous Victories* (Sc. ix-xx; *supra* 321ff) and some of its incidents, historical and unhistorical. Both plays omit the Lollard unrest and other domestic events, and both make a great scene of the English claim to France, and discuss whether France or Scotland should be attacked first. Immediately afterwards the French ambassador delivers the 'tennis-balls' challenge, which Henry takes in almost identical words, not suggested by Hall or Holinshed:

FV 846 My lord prince Dolphin is very pleasant with me.
H5 I.2.259. We are glad the Dauphin is so pleasant with us.

Both plays then shift to the common people of London, showing three different types of army-recruit (*FV* Sc.x; *H5* II.1). Both show the parting of husband and wife as comic (*FV* Sc.x; *H5* II.3). Both then show the French court remarking on the reception of the embassage to England (*FV* Sc. xi; *H5* II.4). *Famous Victories* in its present mutilated state omits the Siege of Harfleur but alludes to it in five lines (Sc. xii) in a way which suggests that originally the Siege was shown (cf. *H5* III.1, 2, 3). In each play fun is derived from the differences between the French and English languages (*FV* in the dicing Scene xiii; *H5* with Katharine learning English in III.4). Inevitably, following the Chronicles, there is much coming and going of Heralds, messengers, etc. (*FV* Sc. xii, xiv; *H5* III.6; IV.3, 7). Both plays show the encounter of an unheroic English clown with a French soldier (*FV* Sc. xvii; *H5* IV,4); both present matter connected with looting (*FV* Sc. xix; *H5* III.2, 6); and discussions of how to live when disbanded (*FV ibid.*; *H5* V.1). Both plays move from Agincourt to the Treaty of Troyes, omitting the second invasion of France. Each has a royal

[1] Cf. E. A. Morgan's suggestion that *FV* and the Shakespeare trilogy were based on an earlier play now lost (*Some Problems of Shakespeare's Henry IV*, 1924).

wooing scene in which the King shows blunt joviality (*FV* xviii; *H5* V.2). The conduct of the peace negotiations is similar in both plays (*FV* Sc. xviii, xx; *H5* V.2).

Some of these parallels are not close or sustained; some were to be expected in any Elizabethan treatment of the theme. Nevertheless it can hardly be doubted that in writing *Henry V* Shakespeare was affected both positively (to accept) and negatively (to reject and replace) material found in the original of *Famous Victories*. But he transmuted almost everything that he touched, and although his Henry V retains some of the bluff, blunt masculinity of the earlier drama, he gives him a high seriousness, a religious sense of responsibility, entirely lacking there, and also infuses the major scenes with a heroic quality unequalled even in his own earlier Histories.

The reign of Henry V had long been regarded as one mainly of 'Victorious Acts' (so Hall headed his chapter), as the King sought peace through war and 'rest with victorie ... by [his] vertue and battaile' (Titus Livius). The sixteenth century regarded his French claims as just, and his actions as altogether admirable both before and during his invasion. He behaved always in the best chivalric tradition, and his youthful escapades seemed all the more endearing when he became, as Holinshed declared, 'a majestie ... that both lived and died a paterne in princehood, a lode-starre in honour, and mirrour of magnificence'.

All tended therefore to encourage Shakespeare to develop in this play the nobler aspects of his Faulconbridge in *King John* so as to present the hero-king in action as the climax of his dramatic sequence on kingship. But *Henry V* goes further than it need in the direction of epic-drama. Indeed Shakespeare seems to have felt that his theatrical technique was inadequate to his subject. Not that his material itself was too episodic for drama. By compressing the reign into what is virtually one campaign (as did *Famous Victories*) and closely following Agincourt with the successful peace negotiations of five years afterwards, he made his play less fragmentary than *King John* or *Henry VI*. But he obviously believed that the subject deserved epic rather than dramatic treatment. No doubt his reading of the Chronicles and the traditional fame of the monarch who had conquered most of France gave him this idea. But it is likely that his fancy gained support from Samuel Daniel, whose *Civile Wars* he had already used to good effect for *Richard II* and for Hal's youth in *Henry IV*. Daniel himself could not tell of Henry V's victories, since he was limited to relating (as he states)

> 'in lamentable verse
> Nothing but bloudshed, treasons, sin and shame'

He could include from this glorious reign only the wretched conspiracy of Richard Earl of Cambridge, and that he treated summarily with incredible feebleness. But recognizing the poetic possibilities of the period Daniel began his Fourth Book [Text V] by raising the King's ghost to lament the lack of an English epic on himself and other English warriors of his age:

> O what eternall matter here is found!
> Whence new immortal *Iliads* might proceed (6)

(cries the ghost, and)

> O that our times had had some sacred wight
> Whose wordes as happie as our swordes had bin
> To have prepar'd for us *Tropheis* aright
> Of undecaying frames t'have rested in. (8)

He hopes that Queen Elizabeth will order her poets ('bright ornaments to us denide') to 'get our ruyn'd deedes re-edifide' in an immortal poem.

Daniel's own panegyric of Henry V follows the portrait in Hall and Holinshed, describes him as 'Mirror of vertue, miracle of worth', and insists on his powers of leadership and discipline (17, 18), his bringing 'distracted discontent' into a unity of warlike action. Only the treacherous attempt of the Earl of Cambridge marred the domestic peace of a reign marked by justice and order. Daniel was not at his best in this part of his poem, but his remarks not only show that Henry V was regarded as a good ruler at home as well as a conqueror abroad but also reflect an unusual awareness of England's shortcomings in heroic poetry—a lack which neither Daniel nor Drayton—with his Agincourt poem—was able to repair.

Writing a few years after Daniel Shakespeare was also conscious of the need for 'a Muse of fire, that would ascend / The brightest heaven of invention'. Since the form imposed upon him was drama he yearned for a theatre with

> A kingdom for a stage, princes to act
> And monarchs to behold the swelling scene.

As it was he must do his best with the Globe or Curtain stage, and the ability of the audience to 'Piece out our imperfections with your thoughts'. Whereas Ben Jonson in the Prologue to *Every Man in His Humour* complained of the sprawling manner of romantic plays and histories, Shakespeare regretted that his play and stage could not include enough, with its 'Turning the accomplishment of many years / Into an hour-glass'. Accordingly he inserted a Chorus before each Act and added an Epilogue, using them to arouse a sublime feeling of patriotic exaltation and urgency in the audience, to apologize for the stage's shortcomings and at the same time to remedy them by linking the episodes (adding also descriptions of places and incidents not to be represented), to excite suspense about future events, and generally to dignify and elevate the action with heroic glamour.[1] In short, Shakespeare was making an experiment in epic-drama in which, while recognizing the limitations of the theatre, he overcame them by employing a compère to supply epic spaciousness, detachment and sublimity. It rose indeed nearer to epic-tone than anything Daniel or Drayton ever wrote.

Shakespeare's main historical source was Holinshed, who followed Hall closely, compressing his account but supplementing his predecessor with material drawn from elsewhere. Where 'the significant words and phrases are in both' (Walter),[2] as in I.2.75–81, the source is probably Holinshed's shortened version; otherwise one might expect to find occasional departures from his details. Sometimes the play agrees with Holinshed in including matter not in Hall. Thus Hall does not say that the countermining of the French at Harfleur 'somewhat disappointed the Englishmen' (cf. III.2.58–65), nor does Hall mention the wish (ascribed by Shakespeare to Westmoreland in IV.3.16–18) that they had ten thousand more men (cf. *inf.* p. 394); he omits the Constable's taking a banner from a

---

[1] Cf. J. Munro, Introduction to *H5*, *The London Shakespeare*, 1958, IV.1018.
[2] *New Arden*, ed. J. H. Walter, 1954.

trumpet and fastening it on his spear (IV.2.61–2), and the King's threat to the French cavalry (IV.7.54–64).

Nevertheless there are clear signs that the dramatist used Hall as well as Holinshed and that he may have had them both open by his side as he wrote some parts of his play. Thus he follows Hall in placing the tennis-balls incident (I.2) after, not before, the proroguing of Parliament, thereby making Henry's determination to invade France depend not on pique but on the Archbishop's reasoned statement of his claims. In writing of a 'tun' of 'tennis balls' he follows Hall, or *Famous Victories* (which used Hall); the phrase 'meeter for your spirit', however, (254) probably comes from Holinshed's phrase 'more meet'; the reference by Henry to his 'wilder days' (267) probably returns to Hall. The allusion to 'gunstones' (282) appears in neither Hall nor Holinshed, but may be a reminiscence of Caxton's version of the Brut Chronicle (1482) where Henry 'lete make tenys balles for the dolphyn in al the hast that they myght be made, and they were harde and grete gunne-stones for the Dolphyn to playe with-alle'.

A few other illustrations may be desirable. An allusion to Hall's description of Henry IV's reign as an 'unquiet time' appears at the beginning of the play (I.1.4). In I.2, although Canterbury's historical detail closely follows Holinshed, the debate owes something to Hall. For instance, in I.2.100–24, the Archbishop's references to Edward III and the Black Prince and the exhortations of Ely and Exeter to 'awake remembrance of these valiant dead' expand Hall's 'diminishe not youre title, which youre noble progenitors so highly have estemed' (not found in Holinshed). From Hall comes Canterbury's assertion that 'they of the marches' will be adequate to defend the north against the Scots (140–3); in *Famous Victories* (773) the Archbishop advises Henry to attack Scotland before France. Exeter's warning about the bereavements of war (II.4.105–9) may also derive from Hall (*inf.* 401n.). Hall made the French leaders discuss English habits of eating and drinking (*sup.* 332). Shakespeare may have recalled this at III.5.18–19 and 7.153–9, though both *Famous Victories* (1135) and *Henry VI Part 1* (I.2.7–12), had used the passage. Henry's reference to the man who sold the lion's skin before killing it (IV.3.90–4) was probably suggested by Hall's reference to the 'phantasticall braggynge' of the French. Minor hints also came from Fabyan and Stow. The discussion about Scotland in I.2 may owe a little to a passage in Hardyng's *Chronicle* where the poet, who served at the Courts of Henry VI and Edward IV is urging the latter to bring back his defeated predecessor from Scotland, by invading and conquering that country, to which he has a rightful claim:

> Considre also, moste earthly soveraigne Lorde
> Of French not Scottes ye get never to your paie
> Any treaty of trewce, or good concorde
> But if it bee under your banner aye
> Whiche maie never bee—by reason any waie
> But if your realme stande well in unitee
> Conserved well, in peace and equitee.
>
> Your Marches kept, and also your sea full clere
> To Fraunce or Spaine, ye maie ride for your right
> To Portyngale and Scotland with your banner
> Whils your rereward in England standeth wight
> Under your banner, your enemies will you hight
> A better treaty, within a litle date
> Then in four yere, to your ambassate. (1543 edn. f.231ᵛ)

Of the fifteenth-century sources for the life of Henry V, most of them unpublished in the sixteenth century, Shakespeare may have known none directly; but interesting parallels have been drawn, especially by J. D. Wilson. Fluellen's statement that the 'pax' stolen by Bardolph was 'of little price' (III.6.46) resembles that by the chaplain in Henry's army who wrote in his *Gesta Henrici Quinti* (soon after Agincourt) of a soldier who 'had stolen a pyx of gilded copper, perhaps he thought it was gold'. Similarly Gower's 'The enemy is loud' (IV.1.76) on the night before Agincourt is anticipated by the chaplain who writes 'we heard the enemy shouting'; this is in Caxton and implied by Hall and Holinshed. The *Gesta* gives the total of the English army as 'not more than 6,000' (cf. IV.3.76, 'five thousand men'), whereas Holinshed gives 15,000.

In the *Vita et Gesta Henrici Quinti* once ascribed to Thomas of Elmham, Scrope's treason is ascribed to 'diabolical suggestion' (cf. II.2.111-2)—but is this unusual? The same work declares that Henry kissed Princess Katharine at their meeting at Melun (cf. V.2.258–86); but a kiss would be the natural climax of the wooing-scene. More striking is the pseudo-Elmham's account of Henry's change of heart as caused by grief and repentance after his father's death, when 'he is converted by a happy miracle'. This agrees with Canterbury's wonder in I.1.24–37 at the suddenness of the Prince's transformation. Shakespeare had already shown the Prince as needing little alteration to become the ideal king. For dramatic effect at the start of his new play he probably based Canterbury's description on Holinshed's assertion that Henry 'determined to put on him the shape of a new man' (*supra* 280 taken from Hall, *supra* 286). Compare Fabyan's account:

> 'This man before the death of his father, applyed him unto all vyce and insolency, and drewe unto him all riottours and wildly disposed persons. But after he was admitted to the rule of the lande, anon and sodainely he became a newe man, and turned all that rage and wildenesse into sobernesse and wise sadnesse, and the vice into constant vertue. And for he would continewe that vertue, and not to be reduced ther unto by the familiaritie of his old nise company, he therfore after rewardes to them geven, charged them upon paine of their lives, that none of them were so hardy as to come within x. mile of suche place as he were lodged in, after a day by him assigned.' (*Chronicle*, 1559, p. 389)

In the additions to his *Chronicles* made in the *Annales* (1592), Stow made Henry confess himself to 'a certaine monke of holie conversation'. Clearly the tradition was, as Hardyng put it, that

> The houre he was crowned and anoynt
> He chaunged was, of al his olde condicion . . .
> A newe man made, by al good regimence.

The *Vita Henrici Quinti* by 'Titus Livius', in the English version augmented by its translator (1513), reveals certain parallels, such as the Frenchmen's boasts about their horses and armour (cf. III.7), and the King's habit of inspecting his army. Holinshed alludes to this characteristic of Henry V, though less vividly. Maybe Shakespeare took the hint from him, and developed it from a classical parallel in Tacitus, as we shall see.[1] The description of the King's arrival in Dover (Act V, Chorus 9–20) has something in common with a passage in the Latin *Life*, but the resemblance seems generic rather than specific. Shakespeare was probably drawing on Stow (who owned a copy of the work) to supplement Hall and Holinshed.

Shakespeare picks his way through Holinshed's numerous detail, limiting himself mainly to the French business, omitting most happenings in England and ignoring the conflict with the Lollards and the execution of Sir John Oldcastle. He divides his material so as to suggest a climax at the end of each act. Thus Act I extends from the statement of the King's claim to the French throne to his resolution to invade France; Act II extends from the Cambridge conspiracy to the French realization that Henry has arrived to avenge their insults; Act III traces events from the landing and investment of Harfleur to the eve before Agincourt; Act IV includes the battle and victory; Act V treats of the peace conference at Troyes, the King's wooing of Princess Katharine, and the preparation for the union of the two crowns. So the whole drama is organized round the heroic strife between England and France, and after the triumph at Agincourt the historical events of 1416–19 are omitted or telescoped in order to hasten the acceptance of the King's claim and his marriage.

As in *Henry IV* two strands, political and social, are interwoven so as to make England as well as its epic representative the subject of his play. We see Henry V as the ideal man of action, reasonable, just, touched with some of his old impetuosity, but now entirely devoted to the service of his country, and aware of his grave responsibilities. But he is not a king *in vacuo* ; he is King of Britain, surrounded by men of all types and classes, churchmen, nobles, an army of common folk, soldiers willing and unwilling, good and bad, grave and gay, Welshmen, Irishmen and Scots, who participate variously in his war; and he has his enemies at home as well as in France. To present this varied picture of a dutiful monarch and a people on the march the dramatist draws not only from Holinshed and other chroniclers but also from the latter part of *Famous*

---

[1] In *The True Tragedie of Richard III* (1594) before the Battle of Bosworth Oxford reproves Richmond for 'these night walkes and scouting abroad in the evenings so disguised'. But Richmond's purpose was different (cf. Vol. III, 336–7).

Victories. Some indications of his method of adapting and interweaving these materials may be helpful.

According to Holinshed the French ambassadors brought tennis-balls from the Dauphin[1] at the commencement of the reign, before the bill of temporal dispossession of the Church was revived in April, 1414. Shakespeare begins his play with this threat by the Commons not so much to suggest that the Archbishop's desire for war was a 'sharp invention' to 'move the King's mood' away from a measure which would have impoverished the clergy, as to bring out the completeness of the King's conversion (I.1.22–69). Henry is now 'a true lover of the holy church'; he is 'rather swaying more upon our part / Than cherishing the exhibiters against us' (as the Archbishop declares). Shakespeare is careful not to present the churchmen in an unfavourable light. The Archbishop's oration on the King's claims against France seems overlong and dull to modern ears, but it should not be burlesqued (as it was in the Olivier film). Shakespeare thought it so important that he followed Holinshed's points as closely as verse allowed, introducing the details of names and dates (I.2.35–95) Calais had been lost only in 1558; and to an audience owing allegiance to a female monarch (as to her predecessor Mary), the Salic law was interesting. Canterbury's quotation from the Book of Numbers:

> When the son dies, let the inheritance
> Descend unto the daughter

had relevance to England after Henry VIII and his short-lived successor Edward VI. The harangue had many contemporary overtones to enliven it. Similarly the discussion of the Scottish danger must have struck a responsive chord in the minds of many who had not forgotten the past. And the Archbishop's disquisition on bees (taken from Lyly's *Euphues*) preaches the social order and degree which it was the function of Elizabeth as well as of Henry V to preserve.

The tennis-ball insult comes all the more forcefully after these statements of hallowed rights and duties. In presenting it Shakespeare recalled *Famous Victories* and maybe the

---

[1] Louis, not Charles (cf. *inf.* 376–7).

anonymous poem *The Batayll of Egyngecourte* (*c.* 1530) [Text III].

But there is nothing in the sources to suggest the dignity of Henry's answer, his insistence on his kingly state, his 'sail of greatness', his majesty, and his appeal to the will of God. Politics become epic at once; the invasion becomes a 'fair action', and the Chorus before Act II sings of arms and the man, 'the mirror of all Christian kings'; it makes a heroic emblem of Expectation[1] less apologetic than the first Chorus; it triumphs whimsically over space and time; and it contrasts the conspiracy of Cambridge, Scrope and Grey (suborned by French gold) with the aspirations of the majority: 'O England! model to thy inward greatness. . . . '

After winging on such high thoughts it is pleasant in II.1 to descend into Eastcheap where the tavern-haunting rapscallions Bardolph, Pistol and Nym are getting ready for France and modelling to their inward greatness with rich language and clatter of iron. And since in the Epilogue to *Henry IV, Pt. 2*, someone rashly promised that 'our humble author will continue the story, with Sir John in it', there are references to Falstaff showing that he will not go far, for 'The king has killed his heart', and that the just ways of monarchs are mysterious to thin-witted amiable rogues like Nym, who says, 'The king is a good king', but 'The king hath run bad humours on the knight.'

This reminder of the royal justice prepares us for II.2 where Cambridge, Scrope and Grey trap themselves into hypocritical censure of a man who railed on the King. Henry harangues Scrope on his disloyalty and condemns them to death. Shakespeare does not explicitly include Hall's and Holinshed's suggestion that Cambridge confessed wrongly that he had been bought by France in order to avoid bringing suspicion on Edmund Earl of March, for whom he was perhaps really plotting. Nor does he therefore admit that his ultimate motive was to set on the throne his own son, Richard, Duke of York (who afterwards claimed it). Baldwin in *A Mirror for Magistrates*

---

[1] Boswell Stone, *Sh. Hol.* 173, believes that Shakespeare may here 'have been thinking of a woodcut portrait of Edward III which appeared in the first edition of Holinshed (1577, iii. 885)'. It represents the King holding the orb in his left hand, in his right a sword with two crowns surrounding it near the point.

[Text IV] had followed this suggestion. It may lurk behind Cambridge's declaration:

> For me, the gold of France did not seduce,
> Although I did admit it as a motive
> The sooner to effect what I intended.   (II.2.155–7)

Our *Famous Victories* omits the conspiracy, but Shakespeare was wise to introduce it, doubtless with recollections of the *Mirror for Magistrates* and the *Civil Wars*. As Daniel asserted, the plot was the only major sign of political unrest during the reign (leaving out of account, as all did, the unrest among the Lollards). Its discovery in the nick of time ere the King left for France was a proof that Providence watched over him. The affair was also an important point in the flow of history; it linked *Henry V* with *Henry VI*; and it proved that although the curse on the usurping line of Henry Bolingbroke might be suspended for a time, it was always imminent.

The death of Falstaff, seriocomic, bitter-sweet in relation, is the mainstay of II.3 in which we see the army moving towards Southampton. This scene, as in *Famous Victories* (Sc. x) where we see the press-gang at work, is followed by one showing the reactions of the French court to the threat from England, and we learn that Henry 'is footed in this land already'. (He landed on 14 August, 1415.) Holinshed asserts that Charles VI, who had been unsound in mind, was ill again, and that the Dauphin took command and ordered great preparations to be made to resist the invasion. Shakespeare follows *Famous Victories* in putting the King in control of affairs, contrasting his prudence with the rash imprudence of the Dauphin in underrating his opponent and England:

> For, my good liege, she is so idly king'd,
> Her sceptre so fantastically borne
> By a vain, giddy, shallow, humorous youth,
> That fear attends her not.   (II.4.26–9. Cf. *FV*, 973–6)

But Shakespeare omits altogether the Archbishop of Bourges (cf. *FV*, 980–1000), who came to Winchester to offer the hand of Katharine (with an inadequate dowry), and instead transfers Exeter's visit to the French court from February to August so as once more to give fair warning of Henry's reluctance to fight but of his determination to claim his rights. Exeter takes the place of the pursuivant-at-arms who heralded Henry's invasion and also bade the French 'in the bowels of Jesu Christ' to render him what was his own (cf. II.4.102). In Act III Chorus Exeter brings back (28–31) the unsatisfactory terms actually offered earlier by Bourges at Winchester, and used in *Famous Victories* (803–26).

The first scene of Act III, with Henry's exhortation to his men, indicating that other attacks on Harfleur have been repelled ('Once more into the breach . . .'), is based on Holinshed's simple statement: 'And dailie was the towne assaulted'; and the comic scene which follows, in which national humours are added to those of Bardolph, Pistol and Nym, is built round the partial failure of the English mines, which were countermined by the enemy (*inf.* 387). The sounding of a parley which ends that scene (139) refers to the truce prayed by the townsmen to test whether any relief could be expected. III.3, which seems to follow at once, relates to several days later, when the Dauphin has replied that 'his powers are yet not ready / To raise so great a siege' (III.2.46–7). Our text of *Famous Victories* (Sc. xi, xii) shows the appeal reaching the French King, who refuses to venture his son in battle; it does not show the battle for the town, or its surrender—though surely the original play must have done so. According to Holinshed Harfleur was then sacked, but Shakespeare makes Henry describe such a sacking so as to hasten the surrender, ending with the order: 'Use mercy to them all!' (54). In the chronicle Sir John Fastolf made his first appearance then, for he was left by Exeter as lieutenant in charge of Harfleur, with fifteen hundred men. Maybe one reason for Falstaff's death earlier in the play was to avoid confusing that hoary iniquity with the brave officer whose name appeared frequently during the next few years of Holinshed's history, though the charge of cowardice later laid against him had suggested Falstaff's name.

Henry V left Harfleur on 8 October, 1415, and marched towards Calais, for his troops were sick and he had no desire for a winter campaign. Hence III.3.54–6 (cf. *inf.* 389).

In preparation for what is to come later a scene is now

introduced showing the Princess Katharine learning English from her lady-in-waiting. For this no direct source has been found, but as M. L. Radoff showed (*MLN* xlviii, 1933, pp. 427–35) it belongs to a comic genre found in medieval French farces. This kind of scene could also be found in the Italian *commedia erudita* where the comic pedagogue is a common type. Thus Lelio (a girl in disguise) in Secchi's *Interesse* discusses points of grammar with the Pedant, and plays on the sexual meaning of the words.[1] Radoff quotes jests extracted from the alphabet in the *Farce nouvelle très bonne et fort joyeuse a troys personnages de Pernet qui va a l'escolle*.[2] In another farce *D'un qui se fait examiner pour estre prestre*[3] the humour, as in *The Merry Wives of Windsor*, IV.1, depends largely 'on the schoolboy's Latin plus the naïve misunderstanding of a motherly old lady'. In *Henry V* the whole lesson is in French except for the English words for parts of the body; and the fun is mainly innocent until Katharine asks for the English of 'le pied et la robe', and Alice's answer, 'De foot, madame, et de coun' excite her modesty since she mistakes the words for obscenities.

With III.5 we are back in the order of events, when the French King, learning that Henry has passed the river Somme, sends Montjoy to defy him. The discussion is based on the council described in Holinshed (*inf.* p. 390) where, however, a small minority were in favour of letting the English depart unfought. The Dauphin was probably not present, but Shakespeare follows Hall and Holinshed in mistaking Louis King of Sicily, Charles VI's cousin, for the Dauphin. The King refuses to let his son fight (64); indeed he was not at Agincourt, but Shakespeare would not let him escape the punishment for his insults, as *Famous Victories* did, which followed Hall more closely. The reference to the 'captive chariot' (53–5) is introduced from slightly later in Holinshed. In *Famous Victories* it is called 'a new disguised chaire' (1117).

Readers of the chronicles would know that the bridge mentioned by Gower and Fluellen in III.6 was the bridge over the Ternoise which was seized and kept until the army had

---

[1] Sanesi, *Commedie*, I.263.

[2] Cf. *Ancien Théatre Francais*, ed. Viollet de Duc, Paris, 1884, II.360–72.

[3] Cf. *Receuil de Farces, Moralités et Sermons Joyeux*, ed. L. de Lincy et F. Michel, Paris, 1837, III, 17th piece.

passed over on 22 October. Shakespeare gives Exeter the glory of its preservation. Exeter too gives the order that Bardolph be executed for stealing a 'pax' (not a 'pyx' as in Holinshed) [1] and Pistol's attempt to win mercy for him fails because Fluellen is a stickler for discipline (cf. III.2) and the King recalls the orders given on first landing in France against ill-treating the people. So perishes another of Prince Hal's former companions. It was a source of pride that even when Henry's troops were starving, 'the poore people of the countrie were not spoiled, nor anie thing taken of them without paiment' (Hol.). Receiving the French emissary Montjoy, Henry admits the weakness of his forces, but as in Holinshed threatens to dye 'your tawny ground with your red blood' (III.6.162).

So the army approaches Agincourt, where the French bestride the Calais road, and, as in Holinshed, are 'verie merie, pleasant and full of game'. In *Famous Victories* (1081ff) the French common soldiers are seen dicing for their future prisoners, and heard boasting (in pidgin English) of the English apparel they will soon possess; also praising their own army. Shakespeare in III.7 prefers to show the French leaders boasting of their horses, with some bitterness arising between the Dauphin and the Constable, who thinks little of his valour; Rambures asks, 'Who will go to hazard with me for twenty prisoners?' (89).

The Chorus to Act IV in his vivid description of the camps on the eve of the battle insists more than the chroniclers on the sad state of 'the poor condemned English'. Steevens aptly compared this with a description in Tacitus, whose *Annals* had been translated by R. Grenewey in 1598. When Germanicus was avenging the defeat of Varus near Paderborn his lieutenant Caecina had to seize a long causeway and repair its bridges while repelling attacks from the enemy who flooded the area. The importance of the bridges, and the unhappy state of Caecina's men in *Annals* I.xiii [Text IIa] probably combined with other points of resemblance to make Shakespeare draw on a book he had recently read. In the subsequent battle for solid ground the Romans were materially helped by the Germans' lust for

---

[1] *Pax*, a tablet bearing a picture of the Crucifixion, etc., kissed by worshippers at Mass. *Pyx*, the vessel in which the consecrated bread of Holy Communion is reserved.

plunder (contrast the attack on the baggage train in *Henry V*
IV.7), and Caecina's personal courage kept his men from
panic on the second night of the engagement. Doubtless the
several minor points of resemblance brought the incident to
Shakespeare's mind when he was contrasting the mood of the
two camps at night before Agincourt. The debt to Tacitus went
further, however.

The King's walk through the camp was probably prompted
by the knowledge that he often made such inspections. Holinshed relates later (566/1/60) how 'the king in going about the
campe, to surveie and view the warders' espied two soldiers
walking out of bounds and had them hanged as an example.
The translator of Titus Livius asserts that

> 'he daylie and nightlie in his owne person visited the watches,
> orders and stacions of everie part of his hoast, and whome
> he found diligent he praised and thanked, and the negligent
> he corrected and chastened.'[1]

The special nature of Henry's visit to his soldiers on the night
before the battle, as described by the Chorus and amplified in
IV.1, was, however, suggested by Tacitus' *Annals*, II.iii [Text
IIb]. During Germanicus's war against Arminius, having
crossed the River Visurgis, he was told that the Germans
meant to storm his camp that night, so walked among his troops
in disguise to listen to their hopes and fears, and hear their
opinion of him and the campaign. Tacitus does not make
Germanicus talk with his men, but he hears the soldiers praise
him and promise to prove their gratitude on the field of battle.
They indignantly repel an enemy soldier who approaches with
promises of reward should they desert. The enemy desist from
their attack on finding the army in readiness. Germanicus
retires to rest, where he has a joyful vision. In the speech made
before the battle next day the general compares the unwieldiness
of the barbarian armour and weapons with the lightness and
adaptability of Roman arms. His hopes are justified. The battle
has something in common with Agincourt, where the archers
played an important part and, as *Famous Victories* put it,
there were 'troops of horsemen continually running like
wings on both sides of the army' (1171–2); and the enemy were

---

[1] *The First English Life of Henry V*, ed. C. L. Kingsford, p. 381.

thrown into confusion, the first attackers being hurled back against their second line. There was great slaughter. In another battle soon afterwards, Germanicus, rushing among the ranks, exhorted them to give no quarter. These resemblances brought the occasion to Shakespeare's mind and made him use the incident of the prince incognito, which, however, he turned to very different ends.[1]

Shakespeare probably introduced this episode for several reasons. The chroniclers described his troops as 'reconciling themselves with God by hoosell and shrift, requiring assistance at his hands that is the onelie giver of victorie' (Hol.) and the King as 'calling his captains and soldiers about him' and making 'a right grave oration, mooving them to plaie the man . . .'. The scene is based on these passages and the conception of Henry V as a pious monarch, considerate of his men. It also affords a parallel and contrast to the popular activities of Prince Hal, who had been over-familiar with commoners. As King he has not lost the common touch, but his incognito preserves the right distance between him and his subjects while enabling him to obtain their views about himself and letting him play an amusing prank on Williams and Fluellen. What he hears is very different from the conventional praise in Tacitus, and this shows that Henry is not just an epic hero but also a modern ruler of a stiff-necked and highly critical nation. Shakespeare wishes to discuss the limits of such a monarch's responsibility for the actions and fates of his warriors. Are their sins and deaths to be laid to his soul's charge? In order that this problem in law and ethics may be considered seriously, new characters are introduced. The conversation with the loyal grumbler Bates proves Henry's recognition that 'the king is but a man', but that the fiction of heroic fearlessness must be kept up, 'lest he . . . dishearten his army'. The debate with Williams turns on the legal and moral extent of a master's responsibility for the deeds of his agent, concluding that 'Every subject's duty is the king's; but every subject's soul is his own' —a principle still argued today (e.g. in War Crime trials).

[1] Miss Mary Renault points out to me resemblances to Xenophon's *Anabasis* (Bk. iii, &c.) in the army's plight, facing great odds far from home. There are verbal parallels. Xenophon was printed in Greek, Latin, French and Italian before 1600.

Thus Shakespeare shows three sides of war, the heroic, in Henry's oration to Westmoreland, the comic in the humorous characterization, and the individual moral issues involved. The meditation and prayer which follow enforce the frequent theme of the monarch's lonely burden: 'What infinite heart's ease / Must Kings neglect that private men enjoy' (241–2). The English King, unlike Germanicus, is made aware of the inevitable gulf between himself and even his loyalest soldiers, culminating in Williams's disbelief that he would keep his oath not to seek ransom if captured. Things are not so simple as Tacitus (and Daniel) suggest; the Christian King must be infinitely scrupulous, as the representative of his people; and the scene ends with the representative King seeking pardon for his father's fault by which he himself derived his Crown, and recounting the ways in which he has tried to reconcile himself with God. At the moment of crisis we are reminded that the line of the usurper is tainted, though God of His grace may suspend the curse. In this scene Shakespeare takes us below the surface glitter (real though that is) of the Agincourt myth, and unifies the two sides of Prince Hal's activities in one purposive, religious self-dedication.

After this Shakespeare does not give details of Henry's battle-tactics, as *Famous Victories* had done; he even omits mention of the famous stakes placed by the archers so that the enemy cavalry foundered in front of them. The complex spirit in which the battle was fought is alone important, the mingling of soaring patriotism with comic gaiety and realism, as English courage brings the French to shame, the victim turning victor and overthrowing the braggart foe. Yet, unlike the earlier play, *Henry V* does not omit the killing of the French prisoners ordered after the illegal attack on the King's camp and baggage-train. That is, Shakespeare does not shirk mention of an episode which might seem to disprove Henry's humanity and mercy; more, he does not defend it in the usual manner.

Modern historians believe that the baggage was plundered before the main battle, and the King's chaplain who watched the battle asserts that the prisoners were killed through fear that they might take part in another attack on their exhausted captors, who were threatened by a large force of enemy cavalry after the day seemed won. The King's right to command such slaughter was rarely questioned. His biographer Elmham writes that he first sent out a herald to warn the French that he would kill the prisoners if he were attacked (*Vita*, 68); and in 1599 the lawyer R. Crompton justified the action as follows:

> 'When King Henry the fift not having above fifteene thousand men, gave a great overthrow to the French King at *Agincourt* in *France*, where he had assembled to the number of forty thousand of the flower of all his countrey, and had taken many prisoners of the French, both Nobles and others, the French, as they are men of great courage and valure, so they assembled themselves againe in battell array, meaning to have given a new battell to king Henry, which king Henry perceiving, gave speciall commaundement by proclamation, that every man should kill his prisoners: whereupon many were presently slaine, whereof the French king having intelligence, dispersed his army, and so departed: whereby you may see the miseries of warre, that though they had yeelded and thought themselves sure of their lives, paying their ransome, according to the lawes of armes, yet uppon such necessary occasion, to kill them was a thing by all reason allowed, for otherwise the king having lost diverse valiant Captaines and souldiers in this battell, and being also but a small number in comparison of the French kings army, and in a strange countrey, where he could not supply his neede upon the sudden, it might have bene much daungerous to have againe joyned with the enemy, and kept his prisoners alive, as in our Chronicles largely appeareth.'
>
> (*The Mansion of Magnanimitie*, 92v.)

In presenting the battle Shakespeare has both followed generally the order of events, and led up to this illustration of 'the miseries of war'. Before the fight begins Montjoy comes again to offer the King ransom, which is indignantly refused in nobler terms than Hall and Holinshed can provide.[1] York is given command of the vanguard. The taking of French prisoners is illustrated in the comic scene IV.4, where Pistol takes a captive; this parallels Falstaff with Colevile in *2H4*

[1] French chronicles assert that Henry tried even now to negotiate a free passage to Calais, offering to give up Harfleur and his prisoners, but the French demanded that he resign all claims on France; so Henry determined to cut his way through. (J. H. Ramsay, *Lancaster and York*, 1892. I.218–19.)

IV.3, and Dericke with his Frenchman (in *FV*). The Boy (whom we have already seen in Eastcheap in II.1 and 3) is introduced to indicate that the baggage is unprotected: 'for there is none to guard it but boys'. Next we pass to the French side where the leaders bewail their catastrophic defeat, and return to the fight either to perish in the heaps of dead (as described by the King's chaplain[1]) or to attempt a counter-attack, for, as Orleans says:

> We are enough yet living in the field
> To smother up the English in our throngs,
> If any order might be thought upon. (IV.5.19–21)[2]

IV.6 shows that the battle is not yet won; the news that York and Suffolk are dead has scarcely been digested when a new alarum sounds, and realizing that 'The French have reinforc'd their scatter'd men', the King orders that 'every soldier kill his prisoners!' This agrees with accounts by the Chaplain[3] and others. Holinshed, however, ascribes the order to the tumult caused by the attack on the baggage train and the King's fear lest the enemy 'should gather togither againe, and begin a new field' (*inf.* 397). In IV.7 the attack on the baggage, with the killing of the helpless boys, is given by Fluellen and Gower as the reason for the order, and the King's anger at this breach of the laws of chivalric war is reflected in the words which preface his new threat (taken from Holinshed) to slay all prisoners unless the French cavalry gathering on the hill 'void the field': 'I was not angry since I came to France / until this instant', he exclaims (54–5).

For Shakespeare the command was in line with the im-petuosity ascribed to Henry in *Henry IV, Pt. 2*:

> being incens'd, he's flint;
> As humorous as winter, and as sudden
> As flaws congealed in the spring of day.
> (*2H4* IV.4.33–5)

---

[1] 'which heaps, higher than a man, our soldiers climbed to cut their throats with swords, bills, etc.'

[2] Actually his body was found in one of the piles of slain.

[3] 'But behold, suddenly, I know not by what stroke of God's anger, a shout went up that a force of enemy cavalry, fresh and vast in numbers, was being drawn up again in line of battle to fall upon our scanty and weary troops. Wherefore (except for the Dukes of Orleans, Bourbon and a few other nobles who were in the

It was an act of justifiable anger, needing no apology, yet that Shakespeare's attitude to it was ambivalent is suggested by Fluellen's disquisition in IV.7.11–52. Henry of Monmouth is the modern Alexander of Macedon, like him not only in his victories but also in 'his rages, and his furies, and his wraths, and his cholers, and his moods, and his displeasures, and his indignations'. And Fluellen reminds the audience (which has heard, and maybe shared, some criticism of the King for turning off his old friend Falstaff) that he was like Alexander also in that, for Alexander killed his friend Cleitus. But whereas Alexander was 'in his ales and his cups', Harry Monmouth did it 'in his right wits and his good judgements'. His action in banishing Falstaff was just; so was his action in killing the prisoners; both were inevitable in the circumstances; yet however necessary, they were both regrettable. The comparison with Alexander shows that the slaughter of the prisoners made Shakespeare reflect on the nature of the Heroic King. Because he is different from ordinary men, 'his affections . . . higher mounted than ours', he must at times flout our ordinary sentiments; and we should gladly put up with it and accept him for what he is. Falstaff's name is already fading from Fluellen's memory, for all his 'jests and gipes, and knaveries, and mocks'; but Harry of Monmouth will always be celebrated as a good man. So once more Shakespeare refuses to let the epic conception of his hero pass without considering other aspects of his nature.

The glove-episode which follows the naming of the battle adds appreciation of the King's humour and comic relief after the combat. The idea of an exchange of gloves to be worn as challenging favours on soldiers' bonnets probably grew out of Shakespeare's insistence on the Welshness of King Henry, which appealed to an audience ruled by an offspring of the Welsh Tudors, and his refusal merely to mock at Fluellen. Was he deliberately trying to make up for his mockery of Hugh Evans in *The Merry Wives*? The long-lived jest about Welshmen being leek-eaters is countered by the King's regarding 'wearing leeks in their Monmouth caps' as an

King's own company, and a few other prisoners already or later taken) the captives were all put to the sword lest they bring disaster on us in the anticipated struggle.' (*Henrici Quinti Gesta*, ed. B. Williams, 1850, pp. 55–6.)

'honourable badge' (IV.7.98). When Henry exchanges gloves with Williams in IV.1 it is in preparation for the gradual revelation of himself as Williams's challenger, and also for the trick by which he makes Fluellen his substitute. The episode reaches its climax when the King reveals himself (IV.8.25ff) and the *lèse majesté* theme of *Henry IV, Pt. 2*. V.2 is repeated. For Williams, like the Lord Chief Justice, has treated the royal personage as a common man, and defends himself similarly:

> 'Your majesty came not like yourself, you appeared to me but as a common man ... and what your highness suffered under that shape, I beseech you take it for your own fault and not mine.' (Cf. *2H4* V.2.76–90)

Honest sincerity and courage are rewarded in both plays. And after the dead have been numbered (in close accord with Holinshed's account) the scene ends with humble piety— *Non nobis* and *Te Deum*.

Famous Victories says nothing of the King's departure from France, the jubilation at home, his return in 1417 and the hard campaigns which preceded the peace negotiations of 1419–20. The earlier play goes straight to the King's demand that he be crowned King of France (which he never asked for) and be made heir (which he did require). The French King retires to consider these articles, and Henry is shown wooing Katharine, without any comedy of linguistic difficulties, but with blunt frankness:

> I cannot do as these Countries do,
> That spend halfe their lives wooing. (1373ff)

After the comic soldiers have passed by laden with trivial booty and the wily Dericke has described his own cowardice and the trick by which they can get home to England with the Duke of York's funeral train (of 1415), we are shown the French accepting Henry's terms save for his demand to be crowned at once; instead he is to be 'crowned heire and Regent of France'. He demands an oath of allegiance then and there from the French nobles including the Dauphin and the Duke of Burgundy, and the wedding is arranged for 'the first Sunday of the next month' (correctly, for it took place on 2 June, 1420)

In general plan Shakespeare followed this scheme, dividing

his final scene into four parts: 1. soldier-comedy; 2. the French reception of the English demands; 3. the King's wooing; and 4. the final agreement. But in the Act V Chorus he describes the triumphant homecoming after Agincourt, and the King's solemn piety, the visit to England of the Emperor Sigismund in May, 1416, in an attempt to make peace and a threefold alliance including France. But he avowedly omits much: the peace mission of the Duke of Burgundy, and his murder by the Dauphin's men in 1419; the French attempts to retake Harfleur, and the preparations for 'Henry's back-return again to France' (41) in August, 1417; the carefully planned attack on Rouen and the terrible siege which lasted from July, 1418, to January, 1419.

The first scene of Act V is intended to bridge the gap between 1415 and 1419. Coming after the Chorus, it must take place in 1417–19, but it carries on the mood of IV.8 and might occur a day or two after that. It recalls Pistol's boast at IV.1.52–63, when he insulted the King as well as Fluellen, and he is forced to eat the leek which he there threatened to knock about the the latter's pate. Moreover, he is obliged to accept a beggar's groat to heal his own pate (contrast the scene where Fluellen gives the worthy Williams a shilling). Left alone he tells us that Nell (or Doll) is dead, and he will return home to live, not like Dericke by old soldiers' tales, but as a bawd and cutpurse. So, old, broken and debased, the last of Falstaff's crew vanishes from the scene.

V.2 compresses into one scene the events of April, 1419–May, 1420. Negotiations begun at Melun were broken off in May, 1419. In December a treaty was drafted, and in the following April the English envoys met the French King and Queen at Troyes. In May King Henry went there to meet Charles VI and the new Duke Philip of Burgundy, their successful deliberations culminating in the signing of a peace and the bethrothal of Henry and Katharine.

Shakespeare combines elements from various stages of the negotiations. Thus the first speeches, and the reference to 'this bar and royal interview', seem to be drawn from the Melun meeting, where Queen Isabel brought the Duke of Burgundy with her because her husband 'was fallen into his old frantike disease' (Hol.) and where King Henry first met and fell in love with the Princess, and kissed her on parting. The dramatist also combines features taken from two Dukes of Burgundy. The King's grave warning (68–73) seems to be based on that described by Holinshed as occurring at the end of the abortive parleys at Melun, where Duke John the Fearless was believed by Henry to be 'the verie let and stop of his desires'. Quarrels between this Duke and the Dauphin had previously made Burgundy seek a league with Henry and the Emperor, and attempts to unify French forces against the invaders collapsed when in 1419 the Duke was treacherously murdered by the Dauphin's orders. So the Duke at Troyes was his young successor, Philip (the Good), who was given full powers by the French Queen and court to come to terms with the English. His moving speech, in which the Garden imagery of *Richard II*, III.4 is transferred to French farms and vineyards, may have been suggested by a passage in which, after relating the murder of his predecessor, Holinshed describes France as

> 'verie sore afflicted; onsomuch that one miserie riding on anothers necke, the whole land was in danger of desolation by civill dissensions and mutuall mutinities . . .' (Hol. 571/2/11–14)

The articles referred to (73) as having been handed to the French are those of Melun or, more simply, those of *Famous Victories* 1345–49. The English King was not at Troyes when negotiations started there with the King and Queen of France. He was at Rouen when he appointed Exeter, Clarence, etc. (83–90), as plenipotentiaries to deliberate with Burgundy. He himself came only after agreement had been reached. He found the French royal family in Saint Peter's Church.

> 'where was a verie joyous meeting betwixt them . . . and there the King of England and the ladie Katharine were affianced'

before the treaty was modified and signed.

Henry's wooing of Katharine is a long expansion of the crude peasant wooing in *Famous Victories*. It recalls Petruchio in *The Shrew* with his Kate, rather than Navarre's wooing of the French Princess in *Love's Labour's Lost*. Henry is here the blunt, matter-of-fact Englishman, scornful of continental courtiers' elegance and rhetoric, proud of his physical prowess (described by Holinshed in his final eulogy) and of his martial exploits, but with a certain humility as he offers Katharine a 'good heart', a 'plain and uncoined constancy' to make up for his 'stubborn outside, with an aspect of iron'. Despite his modesty he is proud of his position and almost as convinced as his prototype in *Famous Victories* that any woman must be delighted to be the wife of the King of England. To some critics this scene seems an anticlimax, or inconsistent with the sensitive, imaginative prince previously depicted. It is an instance of Shakespeare's resolve not to depart from his sources but to transform them as far as might be; and it adds another facet to the many sided view of the King which we have gained in his trilogy.

Shakespeare ends the play with hopes of peace as the French King and Queen look forward to 'neighbourhood and Christian-like accord' between the two peoples, and such a union, 'That English may as French, French Englishmen, / Receive each other!'—a union not anticipated in the peace treaty, but like that long afterwards offered by England to France in the dark days of 1940. Shakespeare puts off the oaths of fealty till later, whereas *Famous Victories* pressed home the English triumph to the limit, making even the Dauphin pay homage. Shakespeare omits some facts. The Dauphin Louis died in 1415; his brother Charles refused peace, and, discredited by the assassination of Burgundy, had no part in the negotiations at Troyes. The Dauphin disappears from our play after Agincourt, though *1 Henry VI* had already proved Charles important. Shakespeare ends at Henry's crowning moment of complete victory, but adds a final Chorus which regrets his short life, glorifies him partly in Holinshed's terms, and looks forward to the unhappy sequel when under his infant son Henry VI, 'Whose state so many had the managing', disaster unmade Henry V's conquests—'Which oft our stage hath shown'. So Shakespeare brings to full circle his great cycle of plays.

The comic scenes in *Henry V*, like the recruiting scenes in *Henry IV* are related to the general themes of war and justice which work through the whole piece; and they are topical. Fluellen indeed has been thought to be drawn from life. J. D. Wilson and others have seen his prototype in Sir Roger Williams (1540?–95), a valiant Welshman of Penrhos in

Monmouthshire, who spent most of his life fighting on the
Continent, first with the Duke of Alva, then in the Low
Countries with Sir John Norris, again at Zutphen when Sidney
was fatally wounded, and lastly with Henry of Navarre.
'Roger Williams is worth his weight in gold', wrote Leicester,
'for he is noe more valiant than he is wise, and of judgement
to governe his doings.' And he earned the highest praise from
Navarre for his soldierly courage. He was a great supporter of
Essex, who was with him during his last illness (caused by a
surfeit), and who 'saved his soule, for none but he could make hym
take a feeling of his end, but he died well, and very repentant'.

A doughty warrior, blunt in speech, somewhat eccentric in
manners and language, Williams admired Spanish army-
methods, which he described in his *A Briefe Discourse of Warre,
Written by Sir Roger Williams, Knight, With his opinion concerning
some parts of the Martiall Discipline* (1590). A great upholder of
experience against mere theory, he asserted there that 'without
triall of government against equall enemies, the perfecte
Captaine cannot bee knowne from the most ignorant' (*To the
Reader*), and

> 'whether it be for pollicie or Armes, it is an error to thinke
> men without triall worthie to be compared unto the others
> tried, in what place soever, great or smal. Divers play
> Alexander on the stage, but fewe or none in the field. Our
> pleasaunt Tarlton would counterfeite many artes, but he was
> no bodie out of his mirths.'

> 'The Warres', he declared, 'consists altogether in good
> Chiefs, and experimented Soldiers, and ever did since the
> world began to this houre. What caused *Alexander* to over-
> throw *Darius*, with few men, considering his number? but
> his valorous person, with the experience of his Captaines and
> Souldiers. . . . Our famous Kings *Henrie* the fift and *Edward*
> the third, gave their Overthrowes with few in respect of
> their Enimies.'   (p. 4)

Like Fluellen Sir Roger regarded war as a science to be
studied:

> 'It is an errour to thinke that experimented Souldiers are
> sodeinlie made, like glasses, in blowing them out with a
> puffe out of an iron instrument.'   (p. 6)

Only those who had been in battle had a right to judge of things military. 'None knowes the worth of honest Souldiers, but such as have been in action with equall Enemies.' And like the soldiers encountered by the King on the eve of Agincourt, he believed that subordinates had a right to judge the worth of their leaders.

'Theeves are tried by God and their countrie; so ought the great Captaines to be tried by the multitude that serves under them, especiallie by their officers in generall.' (p. 3)

'The famous Monsieur de la Noue was wont to say, It was necessary for the greatest Commanders, to give eare often unto al their under Officers, I meane their simplest Captaines, to heare their opinions, concerning their discipline in open audience.'

Which is very much what Henry did, though incognito.

Like Fluellen Williams had experience of sieges. In 1587 he was besieged in Sluys and had to surrender it, and never forgave Leicester for not getting him a reward from the Queen for his service there. In 1591 Essex left him in charge of the English troops besieging Rouen and in 1592 when besieged in Rue he and his small force of men behaved with incredible gallantry, winning high praise from Henry of Navarre:

'The King doth commend him very highly,' wrote the English ambassador in France: 'and doth more than wonder at the valour of our nation. I never heard him give more honour to any service nor to any man.'

Williams's grudge against Leicester led him to make bitter allusions to the ingratitude of absent superiors:

'Wherefore all men of warre ought to pray to hazarde their lives in the sight of their Princes or estates, then likelie they [i.e. the latter] will confesse no traffique so deare as lives, especiallie being in action with equall enemies. It is hard to please the most masters, and impossible to content the rude multitude.' (p. 54)

Underlings suffer for the weakness of their superiors:

'Sometimes fortune frownes on the greatest Captaines, in such sorte, that they cannot, or will not performe that the world lookes they should do; then likelie had they rather burie their instruments and inferiors, rather than bee touched themselves with the least disgrace. Therefore you cannot blame the poore Souldier to desire the eye of his master when he hazardeth his life.'

It seems likely that when Shakespeare wanted a valorous Welshman—of different cast from Glendower—to fight for the King born in Monmouth he remembered the heroic, irascible Monmouth man whom Essex had helped to make a good end and who had fought over some of Henry V's battlefields. Fluellen with his insistence on discipline and experience may owe something to Sir Roger's character and writings. The defence of the lower officers and the assertion of the great Captain's responsibility to his men found in *A Briefe Discourse* may have helped to prompt some of the discussion in IV.2 which follows Fluellen's exit. Maybe the querulous Englishman Williams gets his name by association or in jesting proof that Fluellen was *not* meant to portray a Welshman of that name.

Nor was Fluellen a simple portrait. Discussion of the art of war was frequent in the Elizabethan period and especially in the decade or so when the Spanish menace was greatest and the 1588 muster had revealed grave defects in the army. Miss L. B. Campbell has shown that most of the topics touched on in the play—the procedure in declaring and making war, the need of order and discipline, the King's responsibility for waging war, the soldier's responsibility for his own soul—were discussed by contemporary writers.

The problem of discipline was particularly relevant to the presentation of Henry V, who was cited as a strict disciplinarian not only by Sir Roger Williams but also by Sir John Smithe, whose *Instructions, Observations and Orders Militarie* was published in 1595. Smithe (1534?–1607) was an Essex man who after serving in France, the Low Countries and Hungary lost any chance of preferment by his complaints and hasty temper. In 1588 at Tilbury he astonished Leicester by criticizing the army in 'foolish vainglorious paradoxes'. His *Certain Discourses* (1590) in which he advocated the use of the bow as well as of more modern weapons, was at first called in because it contained a bitter attack on Leicester and other leaders.

In 1597 he quarrelled with Sir Thomas Lucas over the training of the Essex militia, and committed an act of mutiny for which he was kept in the Tower for eighteen months and then placed under house-arrest until the Queen's death. Such a man could not be a model for Fluellen, but his treatise, though mainly a textbook of military drill, contains many observations on discipline, mustering, and the state of the army which are of interest to students of Shakespeare. Some of his notes on Mustermasters and Recruiting have already been cited (*supra* 263). His discussion of discipline in the 'Dedicatorie' [Text VI] probably owes something to Sir Roger Williams. It looks back on the days before the reign of Henry VI as a period of 'excellent orders, exercises and proceedings militarie' the like of which had never returned. It is not necessary to believe that Shakespeare read Smithe's book, but that querulous martinet's writings throw light on what many of Shakespeare's audience must have known about the history of the army and the problems which Shakespeare touches on with so much humour and human understanding in his three plays about Henry the Fifth.

From THE THIRD VOLUME OF CHRONICLES

by R. Holinshed (1587 edition)

[Holinshed begins his account of Henry V's reign with the description of his reformation and his banishment of his old companions (*supra* 280). The new King had the body of Richard II reinterred with all honour.]

[544/1/17]   Also in this first yeere of this kings reigne, sir John Oldcastell,[1] which by his wife was called lord Cobham, a valiant capteine and a hardie gentleman, was accused to the archbishop of Canturburie of certeine points of heresie, who knowing him to be highlie in the kings favour, declared to his highnesse the whole accusation. The king first having compassion of the noble man, required the prelats, that if he were a straied sheepe, rather by gentlenes than by rigor to reduce him to the fold. And after this, he himselfe sent for him, and right earnestlie exhorted him, and lovinglie admonished him to reconcile himselfe to God and to his lawes. The lord Cobham not onelie thanked him for his most favourable clemencie, but also declared first to him by mouth, and afterwards by writing, the foundation of his faith, and the ground of his beliefe, affirming his grace to be his supreme head and competent judge, and none other person, offering an hundred knights and esquiers to come to his purgation, or else to fight in open lists in defense of his just cause.

[Oldcastle was sent to the Tower to await trial, but escaped to Wales. A meeting of his Lollard supporters in London was broken up and several were executed for heresy and treason. Henceforth Oldcastle was an outlaw till captured and executed in 1417.]

[545/1/1]   Whilest in the Lent season [1414] the king laie at Killingworth,[2] there came to him from Charles[3] Dolphin of France

---

[1] See Introduction to *1H4 supra*.   [2] Kenilworth.   [3] Louis.

certeine ambassadors,[1] that brought with them a barrell of Paris balles, which from their maister they presented to him for a token that was taken in verie ill part, as sent in scorne, to signifie, that it was more meet[2] for the king to passe the time with such childish exercise, than to attempt any worthie exploit. Wherfore the K. wrote to him, that yer ought long, he would tosse him some London balles that perchance should shake the walles of the best court in France.[3] . . .

[545/2/6] In the second yeare of his reigne,[4] king Henrie called his high court of parlement, the last daie of Aprill in the towne of Leicester, in which parlement manie profitable lawes were concluded, and manie petitions mooved, were for that time deferred. Amongst which, one was, that a bill exhibited in the parlement holden at Westminster in the eleventh yeare of king Henrie the fourth (which by reason the king was then troubled with civill discord, came to none effect)[5] might now with good deliberation be pondered, and brought to some good conclusion. The effect of which supplication was, that the temporall lands devoutlie given, and disordinatlie spent by religious, and other spirituall persons, should be seized into the kings hands,[6] sith the same might suffice to mainteine, to the honor of the king, and defense of the realme, fifteene earles, fifteene hundred knights, six thousand and two hundred esquiers, and a hundred almesse-houses, for reliefe onelie of the poore, impotent, and needie persons, and the king to have cleerelie to his coffers twentie thousand pounds, with manie other provisions and values of religious houses, which I passe over.

This bill was much noted, and more feared among the religious sort, whom suerlie it touched verie neere, and therefore to find remedie against it, they determined to assaie all waies to put by and overthrow this bill[7]: wherein they thought best to trie if they might moove the kings mood with some sharpe invention, that he should

---

[1] *In margin:* 'A disdainefull ambassage.' Hall, who, like Shakespeare, places this after Parliament was prorogued, has: 'the Dolphin thinkynge Kyng Henry to be geven still to suche plaies and light folies as he exercised and used before the tyme that he was exalted to the croune sente to hym a tunne of tennis balles to plaie with, as who said that he coulde better skil of tennis then of warre, and was more expert in light games then marciall pollicy.' Cf. I.2.255–82. Henry's allusion there to 'gunstones' (282) may come from Caxton's *Chronicle* (1482) where he 'lete make tenys balles for the dolphyn in al the hast that they myȝt be made, and they were grete gunne stones for the Dolphyn to playe with all.'

[2] Cf. I.2.254: 'meeter for your spirit'.

[3] Cf. III.4.132. [4] *In margin:* 'Anno Reg.2. 1414.'

[5] Cf. *H5* I.1.1–5. It was originally moved by the Lollards.

[6] *In margin:* 'A bill exhibited to the parlement against the clergie.' *H5* I.1.7–19 follow closely. Shakespeare makes clear that Henry is no King John, but 'a true lover of the holy church' (23). [7] I.1.20–1; 69–71.

not regard the importunate petitions of the commons.[1] Whereupon, on a daie in the parlement, Henrie Chichelie archbishop of Canturburie made a pithie oration,[2] wherein he declared, how not onelie the duchies of Normandie and Aquitaine, with the counties of Anjou and Maine, and the countrie of Gascoigne, were by undoubted title apperteining to the king, as to the lawfull and onelie heire of the same; but also the whole realme of France, as heire to his great grandfather king Edward the third.

Herein did he much inveie against the surmised and false fained law Salike,[3] which the Frenchmen alledge ever against the kings of England in barre of their just title to the crowne of France. The verie words of that supposed law are these, *In terram Salicam mulieres ne succedant*, that is to saie, Into the Salike land let not women succeed. Which the French glossers expound to be the realme of France, and that this law was made by king Pharamond; whereas yet their owne authors affirme, that the land Salike is in Germanie, betweene the rivers of Elbe and Sala; and that when Charles the great had overcome the Saxons, he placed there certeine Frenchmen, which having in disdeine the dishonest maners of the Germane women, made a law, that the females should not succeed to any inheritance within that land, which at this daie is called Meisen,[4] so that if this be true, this law was not made for the realme of France, nor the Frenchmen possessed the land Salike, till foure hundred and one and twentie yeares after the death of Pharamond,[5] the supposed maker of this Salike law, for this Pharamond deceassed in the yeare 426, and Charles the great subdued the Saxons, and placed the Frenchmen in those parts beyond the river of Sala, in the yeare 805.

Moreover, it appeareth by their owne writers, that king Pepine,[6] which deposed Childerike, claimed the crowne of France, as heire generall, for that he was descended of Blithild daughter to king Clothair the first: Hugh Capet also, who usurped the crowne upon Charles duke of Loraine, the sole heire male of the line and stocke of Charles the great, to make his title seeme true, and appeare good,

---

[1] Shakespeare avoids making the French invasion a clerical red-herring, but Canterbury offers monetary aid (I.1.75–81) unlike the clergy in King John's day.

[2] *In margin:* 'The archbishop of Canturburies oration in the parlement house.' I.2.33ff.

[3] *In margin:* 'The Salike law.' I.2.35–100 closely paraphrase this speech.

[4] *In margin:* 'Mesins.'

[5] Bad arithmetic; 379 years after the death of Pharamond. Shakespeare repeats Holinshed's error.

[6] The order of French kings was: Clothair I (511–61); Childeric III (742–52); Pepin (752–68); Charles the Great (768–814); Lewis I (814–40); Charles II (843–77); Hugh Capet (987–96); Lewis IX (1226–1270).

though in deed it was starke naught, conveied himselfe as heire to the ladie Lingard, daughter to king Charlemaine, sonne to Lewes the emperour, that was son to Charles the great.[1] King Lewes also the tenth otherwise called saint Lewes, being verie heire to the said usurper Hugh Capet, could never be satisfied in his conscience how he might justlie keepe and possesse the crowne of France, till he was persuaded and fullie instructed, that queene Isabell his grand-mother was lineallie descended of the ladie Ermengard daughter and heire to the above named Charles duke of Loraine, by the which marriage, the bloud and line of Charles the great was againe united and restored to the crowne & scepter of France, so that more cleere than the sunne it openlie appeareth, that the title of king Pepin, the claime of Hugh Capet, the possession of Lewes, yea and the French kings to this daie, are derived and conveied from the heire female, though they would under the colour of such a fained law, barre the kings and princes of this realme of England of their right and lawfull inheritance.

The archbishop further alledged out of the booke of Numbers this saieng: When a man dieth without a sonne, let the inheritance descend to his daughter. At length, having said sufficientlie for the proofe of the kings just and lawfull title to the crowne of France, he exhorted him to advance foorth his banner to fight for his right, to conquer his inheritance,[2] to spare neither bloud, sword, nor fire, sith his warre was just, his cause good, and his claime true. And to the intent his loving chapleins and obedient subjects of the spiritualtie might shew themselves willing and desirous to aid his majestie, for the recoverie of his ancient right and true inheritance, the arch-bishop declared that in their spirituall convocation, they had granted to his highnesse such a summe of monie, as never by no spirituall persons was to any prince before those daies given or advanced.[3]

When the archbishop had ended his prepared tale, Rafe Nevill earle of Westmerland, and as then lord Warden of the marches against Scotland, understanding that the king upon a couragious desire to recover his right in France, would suerlie take the wars in hand, thought good to moove the king to begin first with Scotland,[4] and thereupon declared how easie a matter it should be to make a

[1] Shakespeare follows Holinshed in calling Charles I (840–77) Charlemain; also in calling St Louis Louis X instead of Louis IX. Hall has 'Kyng Lewes also the ninth'.
[2] I.2.100–24, and Hall 'diminishe not youre title whiche your noble progenitors so highly have estemed. Wherefore avance forth your banner . . . conquere your inheritaunce.'   [3] Cf. I.1.75–81; I.2.130–5.
[4] *In margin:* 'The earle of Westmerland persuadeth the king to the conquest of Scotland.' Cf. I.2.166–73.

conquest there, and how greatlie the same should further his wished purpose for the subduing of the Frenchmen, concluding the summe of his tale with this old saieng: that *Who so will France win, must with Scotland first begin.* Manie matters he touched, as well to shew how necessarie the conquest of Scotland should be,[1] as also to proove how just a cause the king had to attempt it, trusting to persuade the king and all other to be of his opinion.

But after he had made an end, the duke of Excester, uncle to the king, a man well learned and wise, who had beene sent into Italie by his father, intending that he should have been a preest) replied against the erle of Westmerlands oration, affirming rather that he which would Scotland win, he with France must first begin.[2] For if the king might once compasse the conquest of France, Scotland could not long resist; so that conquere France, and Scotland would soone obeie.[3] For where should the Scots lerne policie and skill to defend themselves, if they had not their bringing up and training in France? If the French pensions mainteined not the Scotish nobilitie, in what case should they be? Then take awaie France, and the Scots will soone be tamed; France being to Scotland the same that the sap is to the tree, which being taken awaie, the tree must needs die and wither.[4]

To be briefe, the duke of Excester used such earnest and pithie persuasions, to induce the king and the whole assemblie of the parlement to credit his words, that immediatlie after he had made an end, all the companie began to crie; Warre, warre; France, France.[5] Hereby the bill for dissolving of religious houses was cleerelie set aside, and nothing thought on but onelie the recovering of France,[6] according as the archbishop had mooved. And upon this

---

[1] Hall gives as one of his arguments: 'None of your progenitors ever passed the sea in just quarrell against the Frenche nacion, but the Scottishe people in their absence entered your realme, spoyled your houses slewe your people and toke great praies innumerable, only to provoke your auncestors for to returne from the invadyng of Fraunce.' Shakespeare makes Henry V note this peril, I.2.143–54.

[2] *In margin:* 'The duke of Excester his wise and pithie answer to the earle of Westmerlands saieng.'

[3] *In margin:* 'A true saieng.' Not used in Shakespeare.

[4] Hall makes Exeter say that 'the Scottes have seldom of their owne mocion invaded or vexed England. . . . And wher they have invaded, . . . what glory or what profite succeded of their enterprise. . . . David le Bruse also entered Englande, your greate graundfather kyng Edward the third lying at the siege of Caleis. Was not Malcolm slain beside Tinmouth and Kyng David taken beside Durrham?' David II was taken at Nevill's Cross in 1346. Cf. Canterbury, I.2.155–65.

[5] In Hall Exeter's exhortations were liked by the King, his brothers, 'and diverse other lordes beynge yonge and lusty, desirous to win honour and profite in the realme of Fraunce. . . . So that now all men cried warre, warre, Fraunce, Fraunce.' Cf. Chorus Act II.1, 'Now all the youth of England are on fire.'   [6] I.2.222–33.

point, after a few acts besides for the wealth of the realme established, the parlement was proroged unto Westminster.

[Ambassadors came from France and the King sent Ambassadors over in return, who were banqueted by the French monarch.]

[546/2/54] When the triumph was ended, the English ambassa-dors,[1] having a time appointed them to declare their message, admitted to the French kings presence, required of him to deliver unto the king of England the realme and crowne of France, with the entier duchies of Aquiteine, Normandie and Anjou, with the countries of Poictiou and Maine. Manie other requests they made: and this offered withall, that if the French king would without warre and effusion of christian bloud, render to the king their maister his verie right & lawfull inheritance, that he would be con-tent to take in mariage the ladie Katharine, daughter to the French king, and to indow hir with all the duchies and countries before rehearsed: and if he would not so doo, then the king of England did expresse and signifie to him, that with the aid of God, and helpe of his people, he would recover his right and inheritance wrongfullie withholden from him, with mortall warre, and dint of sword. This in effect dooth our English poet comprise in his report of the occa-sion, which Henrie the fift tooke to arrere battell against the French king: putting into the mouthes of the said king of Englands ambassa-dors an imagined speech, the conclusion whereof he maketh to be either restitution of that which the French had taken and deteined from the English, or else fier and sword. His words are these,

> *raptum nobis aut redde Britannis,*
> *Aut ferrum expectes, ultrices insuper ignes.*[2]

The Frenchmen being not a little abashed at these demands, thought not to make anie absolute answer in so weightie a cause, till they had further breathed; and therefore praied the English ambassadors to saie to the king their maister, that they now having no opportunitie to conclude in so high a matter, would shortlie send ambassadors into England, which should certifie & declare to the king their whole mind, purpose, and intent. The English ambassa-dors returned with this answer, making relation of everie thing that was said or doone. King Henrie after the returne of his ambassadors, determined fullie to make warre in France, conceiving a good and perfect hope to have fortunate successe, sith victorie for the most

---

[1] Referred to by the First French Ambassador at I.2.246–48, where only 'certain dukedoms' are mentioned. Katharine is not referred to.

[2] C. Ockland, *Anglorum Prælia*, 1580.

part followeth where right leadeth, being advanced forward by justice, and set foorth by equitie.

[Delegates were sent to the Council of Constance. Money and transports were obtained for the invasion.]

[547/2/7] The Frenchmen having knowledge hereof, the Dolphin, who had the governance of the realme, bicause his father was fallen into his old disease of frensie, sent for the dukes of Berrie and Alanson, and all the other lords of the councell of France: by whose advise it was determined, that they should not onelie prepare a sufficient armie to resist the king of England, when so ever he arrived to invade France, but also to stuffe and furnish the townes on the frontiers and sea coasts with convenient garrisons of men[1]: and further to send to the king of England a solemne ambbasage, to make to him some offers according to the demands before rehearsed. The charge of this ambassage was committed to the earle of Vandosme, to maister William Bouratier archbishop of Burges, and to maister Peter Fremell bishop of Liseux, to the lords of Yvry and Braquemont, and to maister Gaultier Cole the kings secretarie, and diverse others.

These ambassadors[2] accompanied with 350 horsses, passed the sea at Calis, and landed at Dover,[3] before whose arrivall the king was departed from Windsore to Winchester, intending to have gone to Hampton, there to have surveied his navie: but hearing of the ambassadors approching, he tarried still at Winchester, where the said French lords shewed themselves verie honorablie before the king and his nobilitie. At time prefixed, before the kings presence, sitting in his throne imperiall, the archbishop of Burges made an eloquent and a long oration, dissuading warre, and praising peace; offering to the king of England a great summe of monie, with diverse countries, being in verie deed but base and poore, as a dowrie with the ladie Catharine in mariage, so that he would dissolve his armie, and dismisse his soldiers, which he had gathered and put in a readinesse.[4]

When his oration was ended, the king caused the ambassadors to be highlie feasted, and set them at his owne table. And after a daie assigned in the foresaid hall, the archbishop of Canturburie to their oration made a notable answer, the effect whereof was, that if the

---

[1] Cf. II.4.1–14. But Shakespeare's French king is able to command; the Dauphin is complacent in face of English threats (*ibid.* 15–29).

[2] *In margin:* 'Anno Reg.3.' [1415.]

[3] *In margin:* 'Ambassadors out of France.'

[4] Cf. Act III. Chorus, 29–31, where the message is brought by Exeter (ambassador in II.4.76ff) to Harfleur.

French king would not give with his daughter in mariage the duches of Aquiteine, Anjou, and all other seigniories and dominions sometimes apperteining to the noble progenitors of the king of England, he would in no wise retire his armie, nor breake his journie; but would with all diligence enter into France, and destroie the people, waste the countrie, and subvert the townes with blood, sword, and fire, and never cesse till he had recovered his ancient right and lawfull patrimonie. The king avowed the archbishops saieng, and in the word of a prince promised to performe it to the uttermost.[1]

The archbishop of Burges[2] much greeved, that his ambassage was no more regarded, after certeine brags blustered out with impatience, as more presuming upon his prelasie, than respecting his dutie of considerance to whom he spake and what became him to saie, he praied safe conduct to depart. Which the king gentlie granted, and added withall to this effect[3]: I little esteeme your French brags, & lesse set by your power and strength; I know perfectlie my right to my region, which you usurpe; & except you denie the apparant truth, so doo your selves also: if you neither doo nor will know it, yet God and the world knoweth it. The power of your master you see, but my puissance ye have not yet tasted. If he have loving subjects, I am (I thanke God) not unstored of the same: and I saie this unto you, that before one yeare passe, I trust to make the highest crowne of your countrie to stoope, and the proudest miter to learne his humiliatedo. In the meane time tell this to the usurper your master, that within three moneths, I will enter into France, as into mine owne true and lawfull patrimonie, appointing to acquire the same, not with brag of words, but with deeds of men, and dint of sword, by the aid of God, in whome is my whole trust and confidence. Further matter at this present I impart not unto you, saving that with warrant you maie depart suerlie and safelie into your countrie, where I trust sooner to visit you, than you shall have cause to bid me welcome. With this answer the ambassadors sore displeased in their minds (although they were highlie interteined and liberallie rewarded) departed into their countrie, reporting to the Dolphin how they had sped. . . .

[Arrangements were made to defend the north against the Scots.]

[548/1/40] When the king had all provisions readie, and ordered all things for the defense of his realme, he leaving behind him for

---

[1] The territorial claims and threats are used by Exeter as ambassador in II.4.77–126, when Henry is already in France (143).

[2] *In margin:* 'A proud presumptuous prelat.'

[3] *In margin:* 'The wise answer of the K. to the bishop.'

governour of the realme, the queene his moother in law, departed to Southampton, to take ship into France. And first princelie appointing to advertise the French king of his comming, therefore dispatched Antelope his pursevant at armes[1] with letters to him for restitution of that which he wrongfully withheld, contrarie to the lawes of God and man: the king further declaring how sorie he was that he should be thus compelled for repeating of his right and just title of inheritance, to make warre to the destruction of christian people, but sithens he had offered peace which could not be received, now for fault of justice, he was forced to take armes. Neverthelesse exhorted the French king in the bowels of Jesu Christ,[2] to render him that which was his owne, whereby effusion of Christian bloud might be avoided. These letters cheeflie to this effect and purpose were written and dated from Hampton the fift of August. When the same were presented to the French king, and by his councell well perused, answer was made, that he would take advise, and provide therein as time and place should be convenient, so the messenger licenced to depart at his pleasure.

When king Henrie had fullie furnished his navie with men, munition, & other provisions, perceiving that his capteines misliked nothing so much as delaie, determined his souldiors to go a shipboord and awaie. But see the hap, the night before the daie appointed for their departure, he was crediblie informed, that Richard earle of Cambridge brother to Edward duke of Yorke, and Henrie lord Scroope of Masham lord treasuror, with Thomas Graie a knight of Northumberland, being confederat togither, had conspired his death[3]: wherefore he caused them to be apprehended.[4] The said lord Scroope was in such favour with the king, that he admitted him sometime to be his bedfellow,[5] in whose fidelitie the king reposed such trust, that when anie privat or publike councell was in hand, this lord had much in the determination of it.[6] For he represented so great gravitie in his countenance, such modestie in behaviour, and so vertuous zeale to all godlinesse in his talke,[7] that whatsoever he said was thought for the most part necessarie to be doone and followed. Also the said sir Thomas Graie (as some write) was of the kings privie councell.

These prisoners upon their examination,[8] confessed, that for a

---

[1] Cf. Exeter's mission, II.4. In Hall too Exeter goes.

[2] II.4.102–5.   [3] Cf. Act II Chorus, 20–30; II.2.1–7.

[4] *In margin:* 'The earle of Cambridge & other lords apprehended for treason.'

[5] II.2.8 'that was his bedfellow'.

[6] Cf. II.2.96 'didst beare the key of all my counsels'.

[7] II.2.127–36 expands this.

[8] *In margin:* 'King Henries words to the traitours.' What follows suggested II.2.167–81. Contrast the way they are tricked in II.2.

great summe of monie[1] which they had received of the French king, they intended verelie either to have delivered the king alive into the hands of his enimies, or else to have murthered him before he should arrive in the duchie of Normandie.[2] When king Henrie had heard all things opened, which he desired to know, he caused all his nobilitie to come before his presence, before whome he caused to be brought the offendors also, and to them said. Having thus conspired the death and destruction of me, which am the head of the realme and governour of the people, it maie be (no doubt) but that you likewise have sworne the confusion of all that are here with me, and also the desolation of your owne countrie. To what horror (O lord) for any true English hart to consider, that such an execrable iniquitie should ever so bewrap you, as for pleasing of a forren enimie to imbrue your hands in your bloud, and to ruine your owne native soile. Revenge herein touching my person, though I seeke not; yet for the safegard of you my deere freends, & for due preservation of all sorts, I am by office to cause example to be shewed.[3] Get ye hence therefore ye poore miserable wretches to the receiving of your just reward, wherein Gods majestie give you grace of his mercie and repentance of your heinous offenses. And so immediatlie they were had to execution.[4]

This doone, the king calling his lords againe afore him, said in words few and with good grace.[5] Of his enterprises he recounted the honor and glorie, whereof they with him were to be partakers, the great confidence he had in their noble minds, which could not but remember them of the famous feats that their ancestors aforetime in France had atchived, whereof the due report for ever recorded remained yet in register. The great mercie of God that had so gratiouslie revealed unto him the treason at hand, whereby the true harts of those afore him made so eminent & apparant in his eie, as they might be right sure he would never forget it. The doubt of danger to be nothing in respect of the certeintie of honor that they should acquire, wherein himselfe (as they saw) in person would be lord and leader through Gods grace. To whose majestie as cheeflie was knowne the equitie of his demand: even so to his mercie did he onelie recommend the successe of his travels. When the king had said, all the noble men kneeled downe, & promised faithfullie to serve him, dulie to obeie him, and rather to die than to suffer him to fall into the hands of his enimies.

This doone, the king thought that suerlie all treason and

---

[1] II.2.89 'for a few light crowns'.
[2] Cf. II.2.91: 'To kill us here in Hampton.'   [3] II.2.170-7.
[4] *In margin:* 'The earle of Cambridge and the other traitors executed.'
[5] Cf. his address in II.2.182-93.

conspiracie had beene utterlie extinct[1]: not suspecting the fire which was newlie kindled, and ceassed not to increase, till at length it burst out into such a flame, that catching the beames of his house and familie, his line and stocke was cleane consumed to ashes.[2] Diverse write that Richard earle of Cambridge did not conspire with the lord Scroope & Thomas Graie for the murthering of king Henrie to please the French king withall,[3] but onelie to the intent to exalt to the crowne his brother in law Edmund earle of March as heire to Lionell duke of Clarence: after the death of which earle of March, for diverse secret impediments, not able to have issue, the earle of Cambridge was sure that the crowne should come to him by his wife, and to his children, of hir begotten. And therefore (as was thought) he rather confessed himselfe for need of monie to be corrupted by the French king, than he would declare his inward mind, and open his verie intent and secret purpose, which if it were espied, he saw plainlie that the earle of March should have tasted of the same cuppe that he had drunken, and what should have come to his owne children he much doubted.[4] Therefore destitute of comfort & in despaire of life to save his children, he feined that tale, desiring rather to save his succession than himselfe, which he did in deed: for his sonne Richard duke of Yorke not privilie but openlie claimed the crowne,[5] and Edward his sonne both claimed it, & gained it, as after it shall appeare.[6] Which thing if king Henrie had at this time either doubted, or foreseene, had never beene like to have come to passe, as Hall saith. . . . [The disclosure of the plot thwarted a foray by Lord Cobham.]

[549/2/20] But now to proceed with king Henries dooings. After this, when the wind came about prosperous to his purpose, he caused the mariners to weie up anchors, and hoise up sailes, and to set forward with a thousand ships, on the vigill of our ladie daie the Assumption, and tooke land at Caur, commonlie called Kidcaux, where the river of Saine runneth into the sea, without resistance.[7] At his first comming on land, he caused proclamation to be made,[8] that no person should be so hardie on paine of death, either to take anie thing out of anie church that belonged to the same,[9] or to hurt

---

[1] II.2.187–8.   [2] Shakespeare ignores this irony of prophecy.
[3] Hence II.2.155–7.
[4] *A Myrroure for Magistrates* uses this motive. Shakespeare does not, explicitly.
[5] Cf. *2H6* II.2 and *3H6* I.1.   [6] Cf. *3H6* II.2.87; II.6.87ff.
[7] *In margin:* 'Titus Livius. The king saileth over into France with his host.' Cf. Act III Chorus.
[8] *In margin:* 'Titus Livius. A charitable proclamation.'
[9] Cf. *infra* 389 and Bardolph's crime, III.6.100ff.

or doo anie violence either to priests, women, or anie such as should be found without weapon or armor, and not readie to make resistance: also that no man should renew anie quarell or strife, whereby anie fraie might arise to the disquieting of the armie.[1]

The next daie after his landing, he marched toward the towne of Harflue, standing on the river of Saine betweene two hils; he besieged it on everie side,[2] raising bulwarks and a bastell, in which the two earles of Kent & Huntington were placed, with Cornwall, Graie, Steward, and Porter. On that side towards the sea, the king lodged with his field, and the duke of Clarence on the further side towards Rone. There were within the towne the lords de Touteuill and Gaucourt, with diverse other that valiantlie defended the siege, dooing what damage they could to their adversaries; and damming up the river that hath his course through the towne, the water rose so high betwixt the kings campe, and the duke of Clarence campe (divided by the same river) that the Englishmen were constreined to withdraw their artillerie from one side, where they had planted the same.

The French king being advertised, that king Henrie was arrived on that coast, sent in all hast the lord de la Breth constable of France, the seneshall of France, the lord Bouciqualt marshall of France, the seneshall of Henault, the lord Lignie with other, which fortified townes with men, victuals, and artillerie on all those frontiers towards the sea.[3] And hearing that Harflue was besieged,[4] they came to the castell of Candebecke, being not farre from Harflue, to the intent they might succor their freends which were besieged, by some policie or meanes: but the Englishmen, notwithstanding all the damage that the Frenchmen could worke against them, forraied the countrie, spoiled the villages, bringing manie a rich preie to the campe before Harflue.[5] And dailie was the towne assaulted: for the duke of Glocecester, to whome the order of the siege was committed,[6] made three mines under the ground, and approching to the wals with his engins and ordinance, would not suffer them within to take anie rest.[7]

---

[1] *In margin:* 'Princelie and wiselie.' [2] *In margin:* 'Harding.'

[3] Cf. the preparations ordered in II.4.

[4] *In margin:* 'The king besieged Harflue.' Cf. Act III Chorus, 25–7.

[5] Cf. III.2.42–6.

[6] Cf. III.2.66–7: 'The Duke of Gloucester, to whom the order of the siege is given.'

[7] Cf. III.2.55–65, which alludes also to the next lines in Hol. 'For although they with their countermining somwhat disappointed the Englishmen, and came to fight with them hand to hand within the mines, so that they went no further forward with that worke; yet they were so inclosed on ech side, as well by water as land that succour they saw could none come to them. . . .'

[Knowing their walls were undermined the French asked for a truce, promising to surrender if no relief came within a fortnight.]

[550/1/38] The king advertised hereof, sent them word, that except they would surrender the towne to him the morow next insuing, without anie condition, they should spend no more time in talke about the matter. But yet at length through the earnest sute of the French lords, the king was contented to grant them truce untill nine of the clocke the next sundaie, being the two and twentith of September[1]; with condition, that if in the meane time no rescue came, they should yeeld the towne at that houre, with their bodies and goods to stand at the kings pleasure. And for assurance thereof, they delivered into the kings hands thirtie of their best capteins and merchants within that towne as pledges. But other write, that it was covenanted, that they should deliver but onelie twelve pledges, and that if the siege were not raised by the French kings power within six daies next following, then should they deliver the towne into the king of England hands, and thirtie of the cheefest personages within the same, to stand for life or death at his will and pleasure: and as for the residue of the men of warre and townesmen, they should depart whether they would, without carieng foorth either armour, weapon, or goods.

The king neverthelesse was after content to grant a respit upon certeine conditions, that the capteins within might have time to send to the French king for succour (as before ye have heard) least he intending greater exploits, might lose time in such small matters. When this composition was agreed upon, the lord Bacqueuill was sent unto the French king, to declare in what point the towne stood. To whome the Dolphin answered, that the kings power was not yet assembled, in such number as was convenient to raise so great a siege.[2] This answer being brought unto the capteins within the towne, they rendered it up to the king of England,[3] after that the third daie was expired, which was on the daie of saint Maurice being the seven and thirtith daie after the siege was first laid. The souldiors were ransomed, and the towne sacked, to the great gaine of the Englishmen.[4] . . .

[550/2/30] All this doone, the king ordeined capteine to the towne his uncle the duke of Excester,[5] who established his lieutenant there, one sir John Fastolfe,[6] with fifteene hundred men, or (as some

---

[1] *In margin:* 'A five daies respit.' The French prayed 'parlee' on 17 Sept., and the truce was ratified next day. III.2.139 refers to 17 September. III.3 starts on 22 September when the truce ended.

[2] Cf. III.3.44–50.   [3] *In margin:* 'Harflue yeelded and sacked.'

[4] Cf. III.3.54: 'Use mercy to them all.'   [5] Cf. III.3.51–3.

[6] The first mention of Fastolf in Holinshed.

have) two thousand and thirtie six knights, whereof the baron of Carew, and sir Hugh Lutterell, were two councellors. . . .

King Henrie, after the winning of Harflue, determined to have proceeded further in the winning of other townes and fortresses: but bicause the dead time of the winter approched, it was determined by advise of his councell, that he should in all convenient speed set forward, and march through the countrie towards Calis by land, least his returne as then homewards should of slanderous toongs be named a running awaie: and yet that journie was adjudged perillous, by reason that the number of his people was much minished by the flix and other fevers, which sore vexed and brought to death above fifteene hundred persons of the armie[1]: and this was the cause that his returne was the sooner appointed and concluded.

[552/1/15] and therewith [he] determined to make haste towards Calis, and not to seeke for battell, except he were thereto constrained, bicause that his armie by sicknesse was sore diminished, in so much that he had but onelie two thousand horssemen and thirteene thousand archers, bilmen, and of all sorts of other footmen.[2]

The Englishmen were brought into some distresse in this jornie,[3] by reason of their vittels in maner spent, and no hope to get more: for the enimies had destroied all the corne before they came. . . . Yet in this great necessitie, the poore people of the countrie were not spoiled, nor anie thing taken of them without paiment,[4] nor anie outrage or offense doone by the Englishmen, except one, which was, that a souldiour took a pix out of a church, for which he was apprehended, & the king not once remooved till the box was restored, and the offendor strangled.[5] The people of the countries thereabout, hearing of such zeale in him, to the maintenance of justice, ministred to his armie victuals, and other necessaries, although by open proclamation so to doo they were prohibited.[6]

The French king being at Rone, and hearing that king Henrie was passed the river of Some, was much displeased therewith, and assembling his councell to the number of five and thirtie, asked their advise what was to be doone.[7] There was amongst these five and thirtie, his sonne the Dolphin, calling himself king of Sicill[8]; the

---

[1] *In margin:* 'Great death in the host by the flix.' III.3.54–6.

[2] *In margin:* 'The kings armie but of 15000.'

[3] *In margin:* 'The English armie sore afflicted.'

[4] Cf. III.6.107–13, the King's orders.

[5] *In margin:* 'Justice in warre.' Cf. Bardolph, III.6.40–113. J. D. Wilson notes in *Henrici Quinti Gesta*: 'he had stolen a pix of gilded copper which maybe he believed to be of gold'; cf. 46, 'For pax of little price.'

[6] *In margin:* 'Note the force of justice.' 'Hall.'

[7] *In margin:* 'The French king consulteth how to deale with the Englishmen.' Cf. III.5.   [8] *In margin:* 'Dolphin king of Sicill.'

dukes of Berrie and Britaine, the earle of Pontieu the kings yoongest
sonne, and other high estates. At length thirtie of them agreed, that
the Englishmen should not depart unfought withall,[1] and five were
of a contrarie opinion, but the greater number ruled the matter: and
so Montjoy king at armes was sent to the king of England to defie
him as the enimie of France, and to tell him that he should shortlie
have battell.[2] King Henrie advisedlie answered[3]: Mine intent is to
doo as it pleaseth God, I will not seeke your maister at this time[4]; but
if he or his seeke me, I will meet with them God willing. If anie of
your nation attempt once to stop me in my journie now towards
Calis, at their jeopardie be it: and yet wish I not anie of you so un-
advised, as to be the occasion that I die your tawnie ground with
your red bloud.[5]

When he had thus answered the herald, he gave him a princelie
reward, and licence to depart.[6] . . . The Dolphin sore desired to have
beene at the battell, but he was prohibited by his father[7]: likewise
Philip earle of Charolois would gladlie have beene there, if his father
the duke of Burgognie would have suffered him: manie of his men
stale awaie, and went to the Frenchmen. The king of England hearing that the Frenchmen approched, and that there was an other
river for him to passe with his armie by a bridge, and doubting least
if the same bridge should be broken, it would be greatlie to his
hinderance, appointed certeine capteins with their bands, to go
thither with all speed before him, and to take possession thereof, and
so to keepe it, till his comming thither.[8]

Those that were sent, finding the Frenchmen busie to breake
downe their bridge, assailed them so vigorouslie, that they discomfited them, and tooke and slue them; and so the bridge was preserved till the king came, and passed the river by the same with his
whole armie.[9] This was on the two and twentith day of October.

[The Duke of York, who led the vanguard, learned that a great
army of Frenchmen was at hand.]

[552/2/24] The duke declared to the king what he had heard,
and the king thereupon, without all feare or trouble of mind, caused
the battell which he led himselfe to staie, and incontinentlie rode

---

[1] Cf. III.5–12: 'Unfought withal.'
[2] *In margin:* 'The French K. sendeth defiance to king Henrie.' Cf. III.5.36–7 and
III.6.118–37.
[3] *In margin:* 'K. Henries answer to the defiance.' Cf. III.6.140–67.
[4] Cf. III.6.140–1.   [5] Cf. III.6.160–3. Verbal borrowing.
[6] Cf. III.5.159, 168.
[7] Cf. III.5.64. But the Dauphin is at Agincourt (III.7.&c).
[8] Exeter 'keeps the bridge' over the Ternoise (III.6.6–12).
[9] Cf. III.6.171–2.

foorth to view his adversaries,[1] and that doone, returned to his people, and with cheerefull countenance caused them to be put in order of battell, assigning to everie capteine such roome and place, as he thought convenient, and so kept them still in that order till night was come, and then determined to seeke a place to incampe & lodge his armie in for that night.

There was not one amongst them that knew any certeine place whither to go, in that unknowne countrie: but by chance they happened upon a beaten waie, white in sight; by the which they were brought unto a little village, where they were refreshed with meat and drinke somewhat more plentiouslie than they had beene diverse daies before. Order was taken by commandement from the king after the armie was first set in battell arraie, that no noise or clamor should be made in the host; so that in marching foorth to this village, everie man kept himselfe quiet: but at their comming into the village, fiers were made to give light on everie side, as there likewise were in the French host,[2] which was incamped not past two hundred and fiftie pases[3] distant from the English. The cheefe leaders of the French host were these: the constable of France, the marshall, the admerall, the lord Rambures maister of the cros- bowes,[4] and other of the French nobilitie, which came and pitched downe their standards and banners in the countie of saint Paule, within the territorie of Agincourt, having in their armie (as some write) to the number of threescore thousand horssemen,[5] besides footmen, wagoners and other.

They were lodged even in the waie by the which the Englishmen must needs passe towards Calis, and all that night after their com- ming thither, made great cheare and were verie merie, pleasant, and full of game.[6] The Englishmen also for their parts were of good comfort, and nothing abashed of the matter, and yet they were both hungrie, wearie, sore travelled, and vexed with manie cold diseases.[7] Howbeit reconciling themselves with God by hoossell and shrift,[8]

---

[1] *In margin:* 'King Henrie rideth foorth to take view of the French armie.'
[2] Cf. the quietness and the fires in Act IV Chorus.
[3] 'Fifteen hundred paces' in III.7.130.
[4] Cf. the speakers in III.7; Constable, Rambures, etc.
[5] *In margin:* 'The number of the French men three score thousand.'
[6] Cf. III.7 and Act IV Chorus 17–22. J. D. Wilson derives IV.1.76, 'the enemy is loud' from *Henrici Quinti Gesta*, 'audivimus adversariam hospitatam, et ... vociferantem (shouting).' Caxton, however, also mentions their 'many grete fyres and moche revel with houting and shouting.'
[7] Cf. IV Chorus, 22–43, and the King's part.
[8] Housel (reception of the Holy Communion) and Confession. Cf. IV.1.179–87, and the King's prayer, 294ff. Fabyan has 'upon the morowe beynge the xxv daye of Octobre, and the daye of the holy marters Crispyne and Crispinian, the kynge

requiring assistance at his hands that is the onelie giver of victorie, they determined rather to die, than to yeeld, or flee. The daie following was the five and twentith of October in the yeare 1415, being then fridaie, and the feast of Crispine and Crispinian,[1] a day faire and fortunate to the English, but most sorrowfull and unluckie to the French.[2]

[The French order of battle is described.]

[553/1/29] Thus the Frenchmen being ordered under their standards and banners, made a great shew: for suerlie they were esteemed in number six times as manie or more, than was the whole companie of the Englishmen, with wagoners, pages and all.[3] They rested themselves, waiting for the bloudie blast of the terrible trumpet, till the houre betweene nine and ten of the clocke of the same daie, during which season, the constable made unto the capteins and other men of warre a pithie oration, exhorting and incouraging them to doo valiantlie, with manie comfortable words and sensible reasons.[4] King Henrie also like a leader, and not as one led; like a sovereigne, and not an inferior, perceiving a plot of ground verie strong & meet for his purpose, which on the backe halfe was fensed with the village, wherein he had lodged the night before, and on both sides defended with hedges and bushes, thought good there to imbattell his host, and so ordered his men in the same place, as he saw occasion, and as stood for his most advantage.

First, he sent privilie two hundred archers into a lowe medow, which was neere to the vauntgard of his enimies[5]; but separated with a great ditch, commanding them there to keepe themselves close till they had a token to them given, to let drive at their adversaries: beside this, he appointed a vaward, of the which he made

---

caused dyvers masses to be songyn. And wher the nyghte before the Englysshe hoost was occupyed in prayer and confession, he than caused the bysshoppes and other spirituall men to gyve unto them general absolucion' (579).

[1] Cf. IV.3.57: 'Crispin Crispian'.

[2] *In margin:* 'The battell of Agincourt, the 25 of October 1415.'

[3] *In margin:* 'The French esteemed six to one English.' Cf. IV.3.4, 'five to one'.

[4] Holinshed refers to the long speech in Hall, on which *FV* drew, and in which the multifarious French army is contrasted with the 'smal handfull of pore Englishmen . . . whiche by reason that their vitaill is consumed and spent, are by daily famin sore wekened, consumed and almost without spirites . . . so that or the battailes shall joyne they shalbe for very feblenes vanquished and overcom, and in stede of men ye shal fight with shadowes. . . . Therefore nowe it is no mastery to vanquishe and over throwe them, beyng both wery and weake, for by reason of feblenes and faintnes their weapons shal fal out of their handes when they profer to strike, so that ye may no easilier kyll a poore shepe then destroye them beyng alredy sicke and hungerstarven.' Hence *H5* IV.2.15-55.

[5] *In margin:* 'The order of the English armie and archers.'

capteine Edward duke of Yorke, who of an haultie courage had desired that office, and with him were the lords Beaumont, Willoughbie, and Fanhope, and this battell was all of archers.[1] The middle ward was governed by the king himselfe, with his brother the duke of Glocester, and the earles of Marshall, Oxenford, and Suffolke, in the which were all the strong bilmen. The duke of Excester uncle to the king led the rereward, which was mixed both with bilmen and archers. The horssemen like wings went on everie side of the battell.

Thus the king having ordered his battels, feared not the puissance of his enimies, but yet to provide that they should not with the multitude of horssemen breake the order of his archers, in whome the force of his armie consisted.[2] For in those daies the yeomen had their lims at libertie, sith their hosen were then fastened with one point, and their jackes long and easie to shoot in; so that they might draw bowes of great strength, and shoot arrowes of a yard long beside the head; he caused stakes bound with iron sharpe at both ends, of the length of five or six foot to be pitched before the archers,[3] and of ech side the footmen like an hedge, to the intent that if the barded horsses ran rashlie upon them, they might shortlie be gored and destroied. Certeine persons also were appointed to remoove the stakes, as by the mooveing of the archers occasion and time should require, so that the footmen were hedged about with stakes, and the horssemen stood like a bulwarke betweene them and their enimies, without the stakes. . . .

[553/2/21]   King Henrie, by reason of his small number of people to fill up his battels, placed his vauntgard so on the right hand of the maine battell, which himselfe led, that the distance betwixt them might scarse be perceived, and so in like case was the rereward joined on the left hand, that the one might the more readilie succour an other in time of need. When he had thus ordered his battels, he left a small companie to keepe his campe and cariage, which remained still in the village, and then calling his capteins and soldiers about him,[4] he made to them a right grave oration,[5] mooving them to plaie the men, whereby to obteine a glorious victorie, as there was hope certeine they should, the rather if they would but remember the just cause for which they fought, and whome they

---

[1] *In margin:* 'The vaward all of archers.' Cf. Fabyan: 'And [at] the proper request of the duke of Yorke he ordeyned hym to have the vawewarde of that felde.' IV.3. 129–31.

[2] *In margin:* 'Archers the greatest force of the English armie.'

[3] *In margin:* 'A politike invention. Not in Shakespeare.

[4] Cf. IV.1.292.   [5] *In margin:* 'K. Henries oration to his men.'

should incounter, such faint-harted people as their ancestors had so often overcome. To conclude, manie words of courage he uttered, to stirre them to doo manfullie, assuring them that England should never be charged with his ransome, nor anie Frenchman triumph over him as a captive; for either by famous death or glorious victorie would he (by Gods grace) win honour and fame.

It is said, that as he heard one of the host utter his wish to another thus: I would to God there were with us now so manie good soldiers as are at this houre within England![1] the king answered: I would not wish a man more here than I have, we are indeed in comparison to the enimies but a few, but if God of his clemencie doo favour us, and our just cause (as I trust he will) we shall speed well inough.[2] But let no man ascribe victorie to our owne strength and might, but onelie to Gods assistance, to whome I have no doubt we shall worthilie have cause to give thanks therefore. And if so be that for our offenses sakes we shall be delivered into the hands of our enimies, the lesse number we be, the lesse damage shall the realme of England susteine: but if we should fight in trust of multitude of men, and so get the victorie (our minds being prone to pride) we should therupon peradventure ascribe the victorie not so much to the gift of God, as to our owne puissance, and thereby provoke his high indignation and displeasure against us: and if the enimie get the upper hand, then should our realme and countrie suffer more damage and stand in further danger. But be you of good comfort, and shew your selves valiant, God and our just quarrell shall defend us, and deliver these our proud adversaries with all the multitude of them which you see (or at the least the most of them) into our hands. Whilest the king was yet thus in speech, either armie so maligned[3] the other, being as then in open sight, that everie man cried; Forward, forward. The dukes of Clarence, Glocester, and Yorke, were of the same opinion, yet the king staied a while, least anie jeopardie were not foreseene, or anie hazard not prevented. The Frenchmen in the meane while, as though they had beene sure of victorie, made great triumph, for the capteins had determined before, how to divide the spoile, and the soldiers the night before had plaid the Englishmen at dice.[4] The noble men had devised a chariot, wherein they might triumphantlie conveie the king captive to the citie of Paris,[5] crieng to their soldiers; Haste you to the spoile, glorie and honor; little weening (God wot) how soone their brags should be blowne awaie.

---

[1] *In margin:* 'A wish.' Cf. Westmoreland's exclamation and Henry's reply, IV.3.16–67.
[2] *In margin:* 'A noble courage of a valiant prince.'
[3] menaced, insulted.   [4] Cf. III.7.89ff; Act IV Chorus, 17–19.
[5] Cf. III.5.53–5.

Here we may not forget how the French thus in their jolitie, sent an herald to king Henrie, to inquire what ransome he would offer.[1] Whereunto he answered, that within two or three houres he hoped it would so happen, that the Frenchmen should be glad to common rather with the Englishmen for their ransoms, than the English to take thought for their deliverance, promising for his owne part, that his dead carcasse should rather be a prize to the Frenchmen, than that his living bodie should paie anie ransome.[2] When the messenger was come backe to the French host, the men of warre put on their helmets, and caused their trumpets to blow to the battell. They thought themselves so sure of victorie, that diverse of the noble men made such hast towards the battell, that they left manie of their servants and men of warre behind them, and some of them would not once staie for their standards: as amongst other the duke of Brabant, when his standard was not come, caused a baner to be taken from a trumpet and fastened to a speare, the which he commanded to be borne before him in steed of his standard.[3]

But when both these armies comming within danger either of other, set in full order of battell on both sides, they stood still at the first, beholding either others demeanor, being not distant in sunder past three bow shoots. And when they had on both parts thus staied a good while without dooing anie thing, (except that certeine of the French horsemen advancing forwards, betwixt both the hosts, were by the English archers constreined to returne backe) advise was taken amongst the Englishmen, what was best for them to doo. Thereupon all things considered, it was determined, that sith the Frenchmen would not come forward, the king with his armie imbattelled (as yee have hard) should march towards them, and so leaving their trusse and baggage in the village where they lodged the night before, onelie with their weapons, armour, and stakes prepared for the purpose, as yee have heard.

These made somewhat forward, before whome there went an old knight sir Thomas Erpingham (a man of great experience in the warre)[4] with a warder in his hand; and when he cast up his warder, all the armie shouted, but that was a signe to the archers in the medow, which therwith shot wholie altogither at the vanward of the Frenchmen,[5] who when they perceived the archers in the medow, and saw they could not come at them for a ditch that was betwixt

---

[1] *In margin:* 'Hall', who comments on the French brags 'Of thys doynge you may gather, that it is . . . muche madnes to make a determinate judgement of thinges to come.' Cf. IV.3.93–4. Mountjoy comes at IV.3.79.

[2] Cf. IV.3.90–125.   [3] The Constable does this, IV.2.61–2.

[4] Cf. IV.1.13 'old Sir Thomas Erpingham'.

[5] *In margin:* 'The English gave the onset.'

them, with all hast set upon the fore ward of king Henrie,[1] but yer they could joine, the archers in the forefront, and the archers on that side which stood in the medow, so wounded the footmen, galled the horsses, and combred the men of armes, that the footmen durst not go forward, the horssemen ran togither upon plumps without order, some overthrew such as were next them, and the horsses overthrew their masters, and so at the first joining, the Frenchmen were foulie discomforted, and the Englishmen highlie incouraged.

When the French vanward was thus brought to confusion, the English archers cast awaie their bowes, & tooke into their hands, axes, malls, swords, bils, and other hand-weapons, and with the same slue the Frenchmen, untill they came to the middle ward.[2] Then approched the king, and so incouraged his people, that shortlie the second battell of the Frenchmen was overthrowne, and dispersed, not without great slaughter of men[3]; howbeit, diverse were releeved by their varlets, and conveied out of the field. The Englishmen were so busied in fighting, and taking of the prisoners at hand, that they followed not in chase of their enimies, nor would once breake out of their arraie of battell. Yet sundrie of the Frenchmen stronglie withstood the fiercenesse of the English, when they came to handie strokes, so that the fight sometime was doubtfull and perillous. Yet as part of the French horssemen set their course to have entred upon the kings battell, with the stakes overthrowne, they were either taken or slaine. Thus this battell continued three long houres.

The king that daie shewed himselfe a valiant knight,[4] albeit almost felled by the duke of Alanson; yet with plaine strength he slue two of the dukes companie, and felled the duke himselfe[5]; whome when he would have yelded, the kings gard (contrarie to his mind) slue out of hand. In conclusion, the king minding to make an end of that daies jornie, caused his horssemen to fetch a compasse about, and to joine with him against the rereward of the Frenchmen, in the which was the greatest number of people. When the Frenchmen perceived his intent, they were suddenlie amazed and ran awaie like sheepe, without order or arraie.[6] Which when the king perceived, he incouraged his men, and followed so quickelie upon the enimies, that they ran hither and thither, casting awaie their armour: manie on their knees desired to have their lives saved.[7]

---

[1] *In margin:* 'The two armies joine battell.'
[2] *In margin:* 'The vanward of the French discomfited.'
[3] *In margin:* 'Their battell beaten.'
[4] *In margin:* 'A valiant king.   [5] Referred to at IV.7.152–4.
[6] *In margin:* 'The French rereward discomfited.' Cf. IV.5.6 'all our ranks are broke'.   [7] Cf. Pistol's captive, IV.4.13–62.

In the meane season, while the battell thus continued, and that the Englishmen had taken a great number of prisoners, certeine Frenchmen on horssebacke, whereof were capteins Robinet of Bornevill, Rifflart of Clamas, Isambert of Agincourt, and other men of armes, to the number of six hundred horssemen, which were the first that fled, hearing that the English tents & pavilions were a good waie distant from the armie, without anie sufficient gard to defend the same, either upon a covetous meaning to gaine by the spoile, or upon a desire to be revenged, entred upon the kings campe, and there spoiled the hails, robbed the tents, brake up chests, and caried awaie caskets, and slue such servants as they found to make anie resistance.[1] For which treason and haskardie in thus leaving their campe at the verie point of fight, for winning of spoile where none to defend it, verie manie were after committed to prison, and had lost their lives, if the Dolphin had longer lived.

But when the outcrie of the lackies and boies, which ran awaie for feare of the Frenchmen thus spoiling the campe, came to the kings eares, he doubting least his enimies should gather together againe, and begin a new field; and mistrusting further that the prisoners would be an aid to his enimies, or the verie enimies to their takers in deed if they were suffered to live, contrarie to his accustomed gentlenes, commanded by sound of trumpet, that everie man (upon paine of death) should incontinentlie slaie his prisoner. When this dolorous decree, and pitifull proclamation was pronounced, pitie it was to see how some Frenchmen were suddenlie sticked with daggers, some were brained with pollaxes, some slaine with malls, other had their throats cut, and some their bellies panched, so that in effect, having respect to the great number, few prisoners were saved.[2]

When this lamentable slaughter was ended, the Englishmen disposed themselves in order of battell, readie to abide a new field, and also to invade, and newlie set on their enimies, with great force they assailed the earles of Marle and Fauconbridge, and the lords of Louraie, and of Thine, with six hundred men of armes, who had all that daie kept together, but now slaine and beaten downe out of hand.[3] Some write, that the king perceiving his enimies in one part to assemble together, as though they meant to give a new battell for preservation of the prisoners, sent to them an herald, commanding them either to depart out of his sight, or else to come forward at once, and give battell: promising herewith, that if they did offer to fight againe, not onelie those prisoners which his people alreadie had taken; but also so manie of them as in this new conflict, which they

[1] *In margin:* 'The kings campe robbed.' Cf. IV.7.1–8.
[2] *In margin:* 'All the prisoners slaine.' This follows Hall closely. Cf. IV.6.35–8; IV.7.8–10.   [3] *In margin:* 'A fresh onset.'

thus attempted should fall into his hands, should die the death
without redemption.[1]

The Frenchmen fearing the sentence of so terrible a decree, without further delaie parted out of the field. And so about foure of the
clocke in the after noone, the king when he saw no apperance of
enimies, caused the retreit to be blowen; and gathering his armie
togither, gave thanks to almightie God for so happie a victorie,[2]
causing his prelats and chapleins to sing this psalme: *In exitu Israel de
Aegypto*, and commanded everie man to kneele downe on the ground
at this verse: *Non nobis Domine, non nobis, sed nomini tuo da gloriam*.
Which doone, he caused *Te Deum*, with certeine anthems to be
soong, giving laud and praise to God, without boasting of his owne
force or anie humane power.[3] That night he and his people tooke
rest, and refreshed themselves with such victuals as they found in the
French campe, but lodged in the same village where he laie the
night before.[4]

In the morning, Montjoie king at armes and foure other French
heralds came to the K, to know the number of prisoners, and to
desire buriall for the dead. Before he made them answer (to understand what they would saie) he demanded of them whie they made
to him that request, considering that he knew not whether the
victorie was his or theirs?[5] When Montjoie by true and just confession had cleered that doubt to the high praise of the king, he
desired of Montjoie to understand the name of the castell neere
adjoining: when they had told him that it was called Agincourt, he
said, Then shall this conflict be called the battell of Agincourt.[6] He
feasted the French officers of armes that daie, and granted them
their request, which busilie sought through the field for such as were

---

[1] *In margin:* 'A right wise and valiant challenge of the king.' Cf. IV.7.54–64.
The incident is from Titus Livius. Fabyan runs the two incidents together, leaving
it uncertain whether the prisoners were in fact killed: 'When the kinge by grace and
power of God, more than by force of man, had thus gotten this triumphant victory,
and returned his people from the chase of their enemies tidings were brought unto
him that a newe host of Frenchemen were comminge towarde him. Wherefore,
he anon commaunded his people to be embatayled, and that dooen, made
proclamacions through his host, that every man should slee his prisoner. By
reason of whiche proclamacion, the duke of Orleaunce and the other lordes of
Fraunce, were in suche feare, that thei anon by licence of the king sent suche
word unto the said hoste, that thei withdrew them' (1559, 393–4).
  Stow in *Annales* (1592) omits the attack on the camp but relates that the
English killed their prisoners at threat of a new attack. The King did not order
any prisoners to be slain; his threat to do so was enough to make the enemy
depart forthwith (p. 595).

[2] *In margin:* 'Thanks given to God for the victorie.'
[3] *In margin:* 'A woorthie example of a godlie prince.' IV.8.109–26.
[4] *In margin:* 'Titus Livius.'   [5] Cf. IV.7.65–85.
[6] *In margin:* 'The battell of Agincourt.' Cf. IV.7.86–90.

slaine. But the Englishmen suffered them not to go alone, for they searched with them, & found manie hurt, but not in jeopardie of their lives, whom they tooke prisoners, and brought them to their tents. When the king of England had well refreshed himselfe, and his souldiers, that had taken the spoile of such as were slaine, he with his prisoners in good order returned to his towne of Calis.

When tidings of this great victorie, was blowne into England, solemne processions and other praisings to almightie God with boune-fires and joyfull triumphes, were ordeined in everie towne, citie, and burrow, and the mayor & citizens of London went the morow after the daie of saint Simon and Jude from the church of saint Paule to the church of saint Peter at Westminster in devout maner, rendring to God hartie thanks for such fortunate lucke sent to the king and his armie.[1] . . .

[The French buried 5,800 corpses in three graves.]

[555/2/26] It was no marvell though this battell was lamentable to the French nation, for in it were taken and slaine the flower of all the nobilitie of France.

There were taken prisoners,[2] Charles duke of Orleance nephue to the French king, John duke of Burbon, the lord Bouciqualt one of the marshals of France (he after died in England) with a number of other lords, knights, and esquiers, at the least fifteene hundred, besides the common people. There were slaine in all of the French part to the number of ten thousand men,[3] whereof were princes and noble men bearing baners one hundred twentie and six; to these, of knights, esquiers, and gentlemen, so manie as made up the number of eight thousand and foure hundred (of the which five hundred were dubbed knights the night before the battell) so as of the meaner sort, not past sixteene hundred. Amongst those of the nobilitie that were slaine, these were the cheefest, Charles lord de la Breth high constable of France, Jaques of Chatilon lord of Dampier admerall of France, the lord Rambures master of the crossebowes, sir Guischard Dolphin great master of France, John duke of Alanson, Anthonie duke of Brabant brother to the duke of Burgognie, Edward duke of Bar, the earle of Nevers an other brother to the duke of Burgognie, with the erles of Marle, Vaudemont, Beaumont, Grandprée, Roussie, Fauconberge, Fois and Lestrake, beside a great number of lords and barons of name.

---

[1] *In margin:* 'The same day that the new mayor went to Westminster to receive his oth, the advertisement of this noble victorie came to the citie in the morning betimes yer men were up from their beds. (Register of mayors.)'

[2] *In margin:* 'Noble men prisoners.' IV.8.78–82 follow this.

[3] *In margin:* 'The number slaine on the French part.' IV.8.83–104.

Of Englishmen, there died at this battell, Edward duke [of]
Yorke, the earle of Suffolke, sir Richard Kikelie, and Davie Gamme
esquier, and of all other not above five and twentie persons, as some
doo report; but other writers of greater credit affirme, that there
were slaine above five or six hundred persons.[1] *Titus Livius* saith,
that there were slaine of Englishmen, beside the duke of Yorke, and
the earle of Suffolke, an hundred persons at the first incounter. The
duke of Glocester the kings brother was sore wounded about the
hips, and borne downe to the ground, so that he fell backwards, with
his feet towards his enimies, whom the king bestrid, and like a
brother valiantlie rescued from his enimies, & so saving his life,
caused him to be conveied out of the fight, into a place of more
safetie. The whole order of this conflict which cost manie a mans
life, and procured great bloudshed before it was ended, is livelie
described in *Anglorum præliis*.[2] . . .

[556/1/16] After that the king of England had refreshed himselfe, and his people at Calis, and that such prisoners as he had left
at Harflue (as ye have heard) were come to Calis unto him, the sixt
daie of November, he with all his prisoners tooke shipping, and the
same daie landed at Dover,[3] having with him the dead bodies of the
duke of Yorke, and the earle of Suffolke, and caused the duke to be
buried at his colledge of Fodringhey, and the earle at new Elme. In
this passage, the seas were so rough and troublous,[4] that two ships
belonging to sir John Cornewall, lord Fanhope, were driven into
Zeland; howbeit, nothing was lost, nor any person perisht. The
mayor of London, and the aldermen, apparelled in orient grained
scarlet, and foure hundred commoners clad in beautifull murrie,
well mounted, and trimlie horssed, with rich collars, & great chaines,
met the king on Blackheath,[5] rejoising at his returne: and the clergie
of London, with rich crosses, sumptuous copes, and massie censers,
received him at saint Thomas of Waterings with solemne procession.[6]

---

[1] *In margin:* 'Englishmen slaine.' Cf. IV.8.105–9. Shakespeare gives the smallest
number. See also IV.6 on York and Suffolk.

[2] *In margin:* 'Abr. Fl. out of *Anglorum præliis sub Henr.5*.'

[3] Cf. Act V Chorus, 1–14.   [4] *Ibid.*, 'like a mighty whiffler'.

[5] *Ibid.*, 16; 22–28. Stow tells how, at Dover, 'innumerable people of religion,
priests, and Noble-men, and of the Commons came running to meete the King in
every way'.

[6] Stow has: 'The gates and streetes of the Citie were garnished and apparrelled
with precious clothes, of Arras, containing the victories, triumphs and princely
Acts of the Kings of England his progenitors, which was done to the end that the
King might understand, what remembrance his people would to their posterity of
these his great victories and triumphes. The Conduits through the City ranne none
other but good sweete wines, and that abundantly. There were also made in the
streetes many Towers and stages, adorned richly, and upon the height of them sate

The king like a grave and sober personage, and as one remembring from whom all victories are sent, seemed little to regard such vaine pompe and shewes as were in triumphant sort devised for his welcomming home from so prosperous a journie, in so much that he would not suffer his helmet to be caried with him, whereby might have appeared to the people the blowes and dints that were to be seene in the same[1]; neither would he suffer any ditties to be made and soong by minstrels of his glorious victorie, for that he would wholie have the praise and thanks altogither given to God. The news of this bloudie battell being reported to the French king as then sojourning at Rone, filled the court full of sorrow.[2]

[The events of 1416 included further inroads by the English, a league between Henry V and the Emperor Sigismund, a truce with the Duke of Burgundy. In 1417 the King invaded France again and captured Caen. At home Sir John Oldcastle was taken and executed. In 1418 Rouen was besieged in July and the Irish soldiers did good service there, so 'that no men were more praised, nor did more damage to their enimies than they did.']

[566/1/60] Now as it chanced, the king in going about the campe, to surveie and view the warders, he espied two souldiers that were walking abroad without the limits assigned, whom he caused straightwaies to be apprehended and hanged upon a tree of great height, for a terrour to others, that none should be so hardie to breake such orders as he commanded them to observe.[3]

[Extreme famine raged in Rouen.]

[566/2/25] If I should rehearse . . . how deerelie dogs, rats, mise, and cats were sold within the towne, and how greedilie they were by

---

small children apparelled in semblance of Angels, with sweete tuned voyces singing prayses and laudes unto God: for the victorious King would not suffer any Ditties to bee made and sung of his victory, for that hee would wholly have the praise given to God: neither would he suffer to be carried before him, nor shewed unto the people his helmet, wherupon his Crowne of gold was broke, and deposed in the fields by the violence of the enemie, and great strokes that hee had received, nor his other armour that in that cruell battaile was so sore broken, but as the faithfull constant Champion of God, hee eschewed all occasions of vaine glory, and refused the vaine praises of the people.' (*Annales*, 1592; text from 1631 reprint.)

[1] *In margin*: 'The great modestie of the king.' Cf. Act V Chorus, 17–22.

[2] Hall added: 'And yet the dolor was not onely hys, for the ladyes swouned for the deaths of theyr husebandes, the Orphalines wepte, and rent their heares for the losse of their parentes, the fayre damoselles deyed that daye in whiche they had lost their paramors, the servantes waxed mad for the destruccion of their masters. . . . Cf. Exeter's use of this conventional catalogue, II.4.105–9.

[3] *In margin*: 'King Henrie his justice.'

the poore people eaten and devoured, and how the people dailie died
for fault of food, and yoong infants laie sucking in the streets on their
mothers breasts, lieng dead, starved for hunger; the reader might
lament their extreme miseries. A great number of poore sillie
creatures were put out at the gates, which were by the Englishmen
that kept the trenches beaten and driven back againe to the same
gates, which they found closed and shut against them. And so they
laie betweene the wals of the citie and the trenches of the enimie,
still crieng for helpe and releefe, for lacke whereof great numbers of
them dailie died.

Howbeit, King Henrie mooved with pitie, upon Christmasse daie,
in the honor of Christes Nativitie,[1] refreshed all the poore people
with vittels, to their great comfort and his high praise. . . .

[At New Year the inhabitants requested a parley, and messengers
were brought to the King.]

One of them seene in the civill lawes, . . . shewing himself more
rash than wise, more arrogant than learned,[2] first tooke upon him to
shew wherin the glorie of victorie consisted, advising the king not to
shew his manhood in famishing a multitude of poore, simple, and
innocent people, but rather to suffer such miserable wretches as laie
betwixt the wals of the citie, and the trenches of his siege, to passe
through the campe, and then if he durst manfullie assault the citie
and by force subdue it, he should win both worldlie fame, and merit
great meed at the hands of almightie God, for having compassion of
the poore, needie and indigent people.'

[Henry V was furious at this.]

With a fierce countenance, and bold spirit he reprooved them,[3]
both for their subtill dealing with him, and their malapert presumption, in that they should seeme to go about to teach him what
belonged to the dutie of a conquerour. And therefore since it
appeared that the same was unknowne unto them, he declared that
the goddesse of battell called *Bellona*, had three handmaidens, ever
of necessitie attending up on hir, as blood, fire, and famine. And
wheareas it laie in his choise to use them all three; yea, two, or one of
them at his pleasure, he had appointed onelie the meekest maid of
those three damsels to punish them of that citie, till they were
brought to reason.[4]

And whereas the gaine of a captaine atteined by anie of the said
three handmaidens, was both glorious, honourable, and worthie of

---

[1] *In margin:* 'A vertuous and charitable prince.'

[2] *In margin:* 'A presumptuous orator.'

[3] *In margin:* 'The king's answer to this proud message.'

[4] Cf. Prologue, 6–8. Shakespeare had used the image in *1H6* IV.2.10–14.

triumph: yet of all the three, the yoongest maid, which he meant to use at that time was most profitable and commodious . . . And as to assault the towne, he told them that he would they should know, he was both able and willing thereto, as he should see occasion: but the choise was in his hand, to tame them either with blood, fire, or famine, or with them all, whereof he would take the choise at his pleasure, and not at theirs.

This answer put the French ambassadors in a great studie, musing much at his excellent wit and hawtinesse of courage.

[Rouen yielded in January, 1419. The Duke of Burgundy sought peace talks, and Henry sent the Earl of Warwick as his representative. The King of France went to Pontoise, and Henry kept Pentecost at Mantes.]

[569/1/64]   After this solemne feast ended, the place of enterview and meeting was appointed to be beside Meulan on the river of Seine, where in a faire place everie part was by commissioners appointed to their ground.[1] When the daie of appointment approched, which was the last daie of Maie, the king of England accompanied with the dukes of Clarence, and Glocester, his brethren, the duke of Excester his uncle, and Henrie Beauford clerke his other uncle, which after was bishop of Winchester and cardinall, with the earles of March, Salisburie, and others, to the number of a thousand men of warre, entered into his ground, which was barred about and ported, wherin his tents were pight in a princelie maner.[2]

Likewise for the French part[3] came Isabell the French queene, bicause hir husband was fallen into his old frantike disease, having in hir companie the duke of Burgognie, and the earle of saint Paule, and she had attending upon hir the faire ladie Katharine hir daughter, with six and twentie ladies and damosels; and had also for hir furniture a thousand men of warre. The said ladie Katharine was brought by hir mother, onelie to the intent that the king of England beholding hir excellent beautie, should be so inflamed and rapt in hir love, that he to obteine hir to his wife, should the sooner agree to a gentle peace and loving concord. But though manie words were spent in this treatie, and that they met at eight severall times,[4] yet no effect insued, nor any conclusion was taken by this freendlie

---

[1] *In margin:* 'Either part was appointed to bring with them not past two thousand and five hundred men of warre as *Tit. Liv.* saith.'

[2] Cf. V.2.27: 'this bar and royal interview'; but the occasion there is the 1420 conference at Troyes.

[3] *In margin:* 'A treatie of peace' (i.e. conference); not shown in *H5*, but referred to at V.2.76.

[4] *In margin:* 'Seven times, the last being on the last day of June. *Titus Livius.*'

consultation, so that both parties after a princelie fashion tooke leave ech of other, and departed; the Englishmen to Mante, and the Frenchmen to Pontoise. . . . By reason wherof no conclusion sorted to effect of all this communication, save onlie that a certaine sparke of burning love was kindled in the kings heart by the sight of the ladie Katharine.

The king without doubt was highlie displeased in his mind, that this communication came to no better passe. Wherefore he mistrusting that the duke of Burgognie was the verie let[1] and stop of his desires, said unto him before his departure: Coosine, we will have your kings daughter, and all things that we demand with hir, or we will drive your king and you out of his realme.[2] Well (said the duke of Burgognie) before you drive the king and me out of his realme, you shall be well wearied, and therof we doubt little.

[Henry sent men secretly out of Mantes to take Pontoise by surprise ('And to the intent that no inkling of the enterprise should come to the enimies eare, he kept the gates himselfe as porter.'). Pontoise fell, and Gisors, and the whole Duchy of Normandy, 'which had been wrongfullie deteined from the Kings of England ever since the daies of king John, who lost it about the yeare 1207.' The Duke of Burgundy, John the Fearless, was murdered by the Dauphin's men, and his son Duke Philip wanted peace.]

[572/1/15]   Whilest these victorious exploits were thus happilie atchived by the Englishmen, and that the king laie still at Rone, in giving thanks to almightie God for the same, there came to him eftsoones ambassadours from the French king and the duke of Burgognie to moove him to peace.[3] The king minding not to be reputed for a destroier of the countrie, which he coveted to preserve, or for a causer of christian bloud still to be spilt in his quarell, began so to incline and give eare unto their sute and humble request, that at length (after often sending to and fro) and that the bishop of Arras, and other men of honor had beene with him, and likewise the earle of Warwike, and the bishop of Rochester had beene with the duke of Burgognie, they both finallie agreed upon certeine articles, so that the French king and his commons would thereto assent.

Now was the French king and the queene with their daughter Katharine at Trois in Champaigne governed and ordered by them, which so much favoured the duke of Burgognie, that they would not for anie earthlie good, once hinder or pull backe one jot of such articles as the same duke should seeke to preferre. And therefore

---

[1] At V.2.65 the Duke asks what the 'let' (obstacle) is.

[2] *Ibid.*, 71, Henry reiterates 'all our just demands'.

[3] *In margin:* 'King Henrie condescendeth to a treatie of peace.'

what needeth manie words, a truce tripartite was accorded betweene the two kings and the duke, and their countries,[1] and order
taken that the king of England should send in the companie of the
duke of Burgognie his ambassadours unto Trois in Champaigne
sufficientlie authorised to treat and conclude of so great matter. The
king of England, being in good hope that all his affaires should take
good successe as he could wish or desire, sent to the duke of Burgognie, his uncle the duke of Excester, the earle of Salisburie, the
bishop of Elie, the lord Fanhope, the lord Fitz Hugh, sir John
Robsert, and sir Philip Hall, with diverse doctors, to the number of
five hundred horsse, which in the companie of the duke of Burgognie
came to the citie of Trois the eleventh of March.[2] The king, the
queene, and the ladie Katharine them received, and hartilie welcomed, shewing great signes and tokens of love and amitie.[3]

After a few daies they fell to councell, in which at length it was
concluded, that king Henrie of England should come to Trois, and
marie the ladie Katharine; and the king hir father after his death
should make him heire of his realme, crowne and dignitie.[4] It was
also agreed, that king Henrie, during his father in lawes life, should
in his steed have the whole governement of the realme of France, as
regent thereof, with manie other covenants and articles, as after
shall appeere. To the performance whereof, it was accorded, that all
the nobles and estates of the realme of France, as well spirituall as
temporall, and also the cities and commonalties, citizens and bur-
gesses of townes, that were obeisant at that time to the French king,
should take a corporall oth.[5] These articles were not at the first in all
points brought to a perfect conclusion.[6] But after the effect and
meaning of them was agreed upon by the commissioners, the
Englishmen departed towards the king their maister, and left sir
John Robsert behind, to give his attendance on the ladie Katharine.

King Henrie being informed by them of that which they had done,
was well content with the agreement and with all diligence prepared
to go to Trois. . . . The duke of Burgognie accompanied with manie
noble men, received him two leagues without the towne, and conveied him to his lodging. . . . And after that he had reposed himselfe a little, he went to visit the French king, the queene, and the
ladie Katharine, whome he found in saint Peters church, where was
a very joyous meeting betwixt them (and this was on the twentith
daie of Maie) and there the king of England, and the ladie Katharine

---

[1] *In margin:* 'A truce tripartite.'
[2] *In margin:* 'Ambassadors from K. Henrie to the French king.'
[3] Cf. Queen Isabel's friendly manner in V.2.12–20, etc.
[4] *In margin:* 'The articles of the peace concluded betweene king Henrie and the
French king.'   [5] Cf. V.2.384–5.   [6] Cf. V.2.342–47.

were affianced. After this, the two kings and their councell assembled togither diverse daies, wherein the first concluded agreement was in diverse points altered and brought to a certeinetie, according to the effect above mentioned.

[The articles of peace included the following:]

1 First, it is accorded betweene our father and us, that forsomuch as by the bond of matrimonie made for the good of the peace betweene us and our most deere beloved Katharine, daughter of our said father, & of our most deere moother Isabell his wife; the same Charles and Isabell beene made our father and mother: therefore them as our father and moother we shall have and worship, as it fitteth and seemeth so worthie a prince and princesse to be worshipped, principallie before all other temporall persons of the world.

25 Also that our said father, during his life, shall name, call, and write us in French in this maner: *Nostre treschier filz Henry roy d'Engleterre heretere de France*. And in Latine in this maner: *Praeclarissimus filius noster Henricus rex Angliae & haeres Franciae*.[1]

28 Also that henceforward, perpetuallie, shall be still rest, and that in all maner of wise, dissentions, hates, rancors, envies and wars, betweene the same realmes of France and England, and the people of the same realmes, drawing to accord of the same peace, may ceasse and be broken.[2]

[Henry and Katharine were married on 2 June, 1420. But the Dauphin, robbed of his inheritance, held the south and resisted strongly. During the campaign of 1422 Henry V fell ill, and died at Bois de Vincennes, outside Paris, on the last day of August in that year.]

[Character of Henry V.]

[583/1/59] This Henrie was a king, of life without spot, a prince whome all men loved, and of none disdained, a capteine against whome fortune never frowned, nor mischance once spurned, whose people him so severe a justicer both loved and obeied (and so humane withall) that he left no offense unpunished, nor freendship unrewarded; a terrour to rebels, and suppressour of sedition, his vertues notable, his qualities most praise-worthie.[3]

In strength and nimbleness of bodie from his youth few to him comparable, for in wrestling, leaping, and running, no man well able to compare.[4] In casting of great iron barres and heavie stones he excelled commonlie all men, never shrinking at cold, nor slothfull

---

[1] Cf. V.2.348–60.   [2] V.2.362–81.

[3] *In margin:* 'The commendation of king Henrie the fift as is expressed by maist. *Hall.*'   [4] Cf. Henry's boast to Katharine, V.2.138–44.

for heat; and when he most laboured, his head commonlie un-covered; no more wearie of harnesse than a light cloake, verie valiant-lie abiding at needs both hunger and thirst; so manfull of mind as never seene to quinch at a wound, or to smart at the paine; not to turne his nose from evill favour, nor close his eies from smoke or dust; no man more moderate in eating and drinking, with diet not delicate, but rather more meet for men of warre, than for princes or tender stomachs. Everie honest person was permitted to come to him, sitting at meale, where either secretlie or openlie to declare his mind. High and weightie causes as well betweene men of warre and other he would gladlie heare, and either determined them himselfe, or else for end committed them to others. He slept verie little, but that verie soundlie, in so much that when his soldiers soong at nights, or minstrels plaied, he then slept fastest; of courage invincible, of purpose unmutable, so wisehardie alwaies, as feare was banisht from him; at everie alarum he first in armor, and formost in order-ing. In time of warre such was his providence, bountie and hap, as he had true intelligence, not onelie what his enimies did, but what they said and intended: of his devises and purposes few, before the thing was at the point to be done, should be made privie.

He had such knowledge in ordering and guiding an armie, with such a gift to incourage his people, that the Frenchmen had con-stant opinion he could never be vanquished in battell. Such wit, such prudence, and such policie withall, that he never enterprised any thing, before he had fullie debated and forecast all the maine chances that might happen, which doone with all diligence and courage he set his purpose forward. What policie he had in finding present remedies for sudden mischeeves, and what engines in saving himselfe and his people in sharpe distresses: were it not that by his acts they did plainlie appeare, hard were it by words to make them credible. Wantonnesse of life and thirst in avarice had he quite quenched in him; vertues in deed in such an estate of sovereigntie, youth, and power, as verie rare, so right commendable in the highest degree. So staied of mind and countenance beside, that never jolie or triumphant for victorie, nor sad or damped for losse or mis-fortune. For bountifulnesse and liberalitie, no man more free, gentle, and franke, in bestowing rewards to all persons, according to their deserts: for his saieng was, that he never desired monie to keepe, but to give and spend.

Although that storie properlie serves not for theme of praise or dispraise, yet what in brevitie may well be remembred, in truth would not be forgotten by sloth, were it but onlie to remaine as a spectacle for magnanimitie to have alwaies in eie, and for incourage-ment to nobles in honourable enterprises. Knowen be it therefore, of person and forme was this prince rightlie representing his heroicall affects, of stature and proportion tall and manlie, rather leane than grose, somewhat long necked and blacke haired, of countenance amiable, eloquent and grave was his speech, and of great grace and power to persuade: for conclusion, a majestie was he that both lived & died a paterne in princehood, a lode-starre in honour,[1] and mirrour of magnificence: the more highlie exalted in his life, the more deepelie lamented at his death, and famous to the world alwaie.

II. Source

From THE ANNALS OF CORNELIUS TACITUS. THE DESCRIPTION OF GERMANIE

translated by R. Grenewey (1598)[2]

(*a*) BOOK I, CHAPTER XIII

[Cæcina in difficulties]

Cæcina, who conducted another companie, although he was skilfull in the wayes, yet was charged to returne with all diligence by the long bridges; which was a narrow causey betwixt wide marishes, throwne up in times past by *L. Domitius*. The rest of the countrey was miry, and full of fast binding clay, with some doubtfull brookes. Round about were woods, ascending little and little, which *Arminius* had filled by a nearer way, and light armie, preventing the Romans, loden with armour and carriages. *Cæcina* doubting how he should at once repaire those bridges, alreadie decayed with age, and drive back the enimie; thought it best to encamp in the same place: that whilest some were fortifying, others might skirmish with the enimie. The barbarians used all force to breake the wardes,

---

[1] 'This star of England.' V.2.393.
[2] Printed at London by Arn. Hatfield, for Bonham & John Norton.

and make way to the trench-makers: set on them, compassed them in; ranne from place to place; leaving nothing undone to disturb them. The labourers and the fighters made one confuse cry: nothing prospering on the Romans side. . . .

CHAPTER XIV

Cæcina had then in qualitie of a soldier of commande fortie yeere received pay: and therefore being acquainted as well with the changeable events of fortune as prosperous successes, fell nothing at all in courage: but pondering in his mind what might follow, found nothing more expedient then to inclose the enimie in the wood, untill the wounded, and the cariages were gotten before. For betwixt the hills and the marshes, there stretched out a plaine, capable of a small armie. . . The night was unquiet for divers respects: the barbarous enimie, in feasting and banketting, songs of joie, and hideous outcries filled the valleies and woods, which redoubled the sounde againe. The Romans had small fires, broken voices, laie neere the trenches, went from tent to tent, rather disquieted, and not able to sleepe, then watchfull. The general had that night a heavie dreame, which drove him into a feare. . . At day breaking, the legions appointed for the flankes, either for feare, or contempt, abandoned their standings; and seased on the fielde adjoininge beyond the marshes. *Arminius* although hee might safely have assaulted them, yet forbare a time. But he no sooner perceived their bag and baggage to stick in the mire and ditches, and the souldiers troubled about it, disbanded and out of order . . . but he encharged the Germanes to breake in. . . .

[The Romans, hampered by the bogs, were confined to their trenches, which the enemy now tried to storm.]

The enimies imagining it but an easie conquest, and that there were but fewe to resist, and those but halfe armed; hearing the sound of the trumpets, and seeing the glittering of the armour, which seemed so much the greater, by how much the lesse they were esteemed: on a sudden were beaten downe and slaine, as men in prosperitie greedy and in adversitie, uncircumspect. *Arminius* and *Inguiomerus* fled th'one not hurt, and the other greevously wounded. The common sort were slaine as long as the daie and anger lasted: the legions returned at night to their forte. And although there were more wounded then the day before, and no lesse want of victuales: yet with the victorie they thought they had recovered strength, courage, health, and all other necessaries.

(*b*) BOOK II, CHAPTER III

[Germanicus walks through his Camp.]

. . . When *Cæsar* [Germanicus] had passed the river Visurgis, he understoode by a fugitive from the enemie campe, what place *Arminius* had chosen to give battell: and that other nations were assembled in a wood consecrated to *Hercules*, with intention to assaile the camp by night. The runnagate was beleeved: lights were seene: and the espiales getting neerer, reported they heard a great confuse noise of men and horses. Being therefore at a jumpe to hazard all, thinking it convenient to sounde the souldiers minde, he bethought himselfe what was the fittest expedient to trie the truth. The Tribunes and Centurions brought him oftener pleasing then true newes: the freed men were of a servile disposition: in friends there was flatterie: if he should call an assembly, that which a few should begin, the rest would applaud. That their minds would be best knowen, when they were by themselves; not overlooked: in eating and drinking they would utter their fear or hope. As soone as it was night, going out at the Augural gate, accompanied with one alone, in secret and unknowen places to the watch: casting a savage beasts skin on his backe, he went from one place to another: stoode listning at the tents: and joyeth in the praise of himselfe: some extolling the nobilitie of their Captaine: others his comely personage: many his patience, and courtesie: that in sports and serious matters, he was still one man: confessing therefore that they thought it their parts, to make him some requitall in this battell, and sacrifice the traitors and peace-breakers to revenge and glory.

CHAPTER IV

[Arminius overthrown.]

Amidst these things, one of the enimie campe, skilfull in the Latine toong: riding close to the trench: promiseth alowd in *Arminius* name, wives, and lands, and a hundred sesterses[1] a day, as long as the war continued, if any would flee from the Romans, and come to his side. That bravado did greatly exasperate the legions: wishing among themselves: O that the day were come, that we might once come to joine battell with them: saying, that they would take possession of the Germans lands, and bring away their wives by force. . . About the third watch the enimie assailed the campe, but threw no dart: bicause he perceived many in a readines to defend their fortes: and no man remisse in his charge.

---

[1] *In margin:* 'About fifteene shillings seven pence.'

The same night *Germanicus* in a pleasant dreame, thought he had beene offering of sacrifice, and that his pretext or robes of his infancie, had beene sprinkled with holy blood, and that he received another at the hands of *Augusta* his grandmother. Emboldened with that dreame, and the Augures foretelling lucky successe, concurring with it: he called the soldiers to an assembly: and declared unto them what things by wisedome he had foreseene: and what he thought expedient for the imminent danger of the battell. That not onely the open fields were commodious for the Romans to fight in, but the woods also and forests; if they proceeded by discretion. Neither were the barbarous huge targets, and long pikes so handsome, among trees and low shrubs; as darts and swords; and armour close to the bodie. . . . And although they [the Germans] were grim in countenance, and of some courage for a short fit: yet being once wounded they would flee and be gone without shame of discredit, or care of their Captaine: in adversitie faint harted and timorous: but in prosperitie, unmindfull both of divine and humane lawes. . . . Behinde them [the Germans] was a wood of high trees: and betweene those trees a plaine and even ground, which the Barbarians had possessed with the entrance of the wood: the Cherusci put themselves on the tops of the hills, to fall furiously upon the Romans in the heat of the fight. . . .

[When defeated] some cowardly fleeing away, sought to clamber the tops of trees, and there hiding themselves in the boughes, were shot through by the archers in a mockerie: and others brused by the overturning of the trees. The victory was great, and unto us not bloudie. From five of the clock, untill night, the enemies were slaine, which filled ten miles of ground with dead carcasses, and armour. Some chaines were found among their spoiles; brought to emprison the Romans: as not doubting a prosperous successe. The souldiers saluted Tiberius by the name of Emperour in the same place where the battell was fought: and erected a mount of earth, as a token of victory: and put on it the armour of the enemie: and underneath the names of the nations which they had conquered.

CHAPTER V

[In a second battle the light armed Romans slaughtered the heavier Germans.]

And *Germanicus* to be the better knowne, unlaced his helmet, and besought them to continue the slaughter: captives there was no neede of: only the generall butchery of the nation would make an ende of the warre.

III. Possible Source

From THE BATTLE OF AGINCOURT
Anonymous (printed c. 1530)

Here after foloweth yᵉ Batayll of Egyngecourte, and the Great sege of Rone. . . . Imprynted at London, in Foster lane in saynt Leonardes parysshe, by me John Skot. [n.d.][1]

[The poem begins by praising Henry V.]

Of Henry the fyfthe, noble man of warre,
Thy dedes may never forgoten be.
Of knyghthod thou wert the very lodestarre;   10
In thy tyme Englande flowred in prosperyte.
Thou mortall myrour of all chevalry,
Though thou be not set amonge the worthyes nyne,
Yet wast thou a conqueroure in thy tyme.
Our kynge sende in to Fraunce full rathe,
His harraude that was good and sure;
He desyred his herytage for to have,
That is, Gascoyne and Gyen and Normandye;
He bad the Dolphyne delyver it shulde be his,
All that belongyd to the furst Edwarde,   20
And yf he sayd me nay I wys,
I wyll get it with dent of swerde.
But than answered the Dolphyne bolde
By our inbassatours sendynge agayne,
Me thynke that your kynge is not so olde
Warres great for to mayntayne.
Gre[e]te well, he sayd, your comely kynge,
That is bothe gentyll and small,
A tun full of tenys balles I wyll hym send,
For to play hym therwithall.   30
Than bethought our lordes all
In Fraunce they wolde no lenger abyde,
They toke theyr leve bothe great and small,

---

[1] Text from *Remains of the Early Popular Poetry of England*, ed. W. C. Hazlitt, 1866, ii.88ff.

And home to Englande gan they ryde.
To our kynge they tolde theyr tale to the ende,
What that the Dolphyne dyde to them saye.
I wyll hym thanke, than sayd the kynge,
By the grace of God, yf I may.
Yet by his owne mynde this Dolphyne bolde
To our kynge he sent agaynne hastely,   40
And prayed him trews for to holde,
For Jesus love that dyed on a tree.
Nay, than sayd our comely kynge,
For in Fraunce wyll I wynde,
The Dolphyne angre I trust I shall,
And suche a tenys ball I shall hym sende
That shall bere downe the hye rofe of his hall. . . .

[The King asked his lord's advice and the Duke of Clarence replied,
favouring an expedition.]

Great ordynance of gunnes the kynge let make,   70
And shypte them at London all at ones,
Bowes and arowes in chestes were take,
Speres and bylles with yren gunstones,[1]
And armynge dagars made for the nones
With swerdes and bucklers that were full sure,
And harneys bryght that strokes wolde endure.
The kynge to Southampton than dyde ryde
With his lordes, for no longer wolde he dwell.

. . . .

Bytwene Hampton and the Yle of Wyght
These goodly shyppes lay there at rode,
With mastyardes a crosse full semely of syght,
Over all the haven speade a brode;
On every paves[2] a crosse rede,
The wastes decked with serpentynes stronge,   90
Saynt Georges stremers sprede over hede,[3]
With the armes of Englande hangynge all alonge.
Our kynge full hastely to his shyppe yede,
And all other lordes of every degree;
Every shyp wayed his anker in dede,
With the tyde to hast them to the see,
They hoysed theyr sayles sayled alofte;

---

[1] I.2.282.   [2] pavis, protective shield on ship's side.
[3] Note the resemblance to Act III Prologue.

A goodly syght it was to see.
The wynde was good and blew, but softe,
And forth they wente in the name of the Trynyte. . . .

[Soon they laid siege to Harfleur.]

Our kynge his banner there did splay
With standerdes bryght and many penowne,
And there he pyght his tente adowne,
Full well broydered with armory gaye; . . .   120
My brother Clarence, the kynge did say,
The toures of the towne wyll I kepe,
With her doughters and her maydens gay,
To wake the Frenchemen of theyr slepe;
London,[1] he sayd, shall with hym mete,
And my gunnes that lyeth fayre upon the grene,
For they shall play with Harfflete
A game at tennys, as I wene;   130
Goo we to game, for goddes grace;
My chyldren, be redy everychone:
For every great gunne that there was
In his mouthe he had a stone. . . .
        Than sayde the greate gunne,
Bolde felowes, we go to game:
Thanked be Mary, and Jesu her sone,
They dyde the Frenchemen moche shame.   150
    Fyftene afore, sayd London: tho
Her balles fully fayre she gan out throwe;
    Thyrty, sayd the seconde gun, I wyll wyn and I may.
There as the wall was moost sure
They bare it downe without nay. . . .
The Normandes sayd, let ys not abyde,   160
But go we in haste by one assent
Where so ever the gunstones do glyde;
Our houses in Harfflete is all to rent,
The Englysshemen our bulwarkes have brent;
And women cryed, Alas! that ever they were borne.

[Harfleur was finally surrendered on a Sunday by the Captain of
the place.]

And whan he to our kynge dyde come,
Lowly he set hym on his kne;
Hayle! comely prynce, than dyde he say,

---

[1] A large gun.

The grace of God is with the;
Here have I brought the keys all
Of Harfflete, that is so royall a cytye,
All is yours, both chambr[e] and hall,
And at your wyll for to be.
Thanked be Jesu, sayd our kynge,   220
And Mary his mother truely;
Myne oncle Dorset without lettynge
Captaine of Herfflete shall he be; . . .

[The army was reduced by sickness, and the French threw down the bridge over the River Seine. The French nobles boasted of their approaching victory.]

The Frencemen our kynge about becaste
With batayles stronge on every side;
The duke of Orlyaunce sayd in haste,
The kynge of Englande shal abyde.
Who gave hym leve this waye to passe?
I trust that I shall hym begyle,
Full longe or he come to Calays.
The duke of Burbone answeryd sone,
And I swere by god and by Saynt Denys,   280
We will play them everchone,
These lordes of Englande, at the tenys;
Theyr Gentylmen, I swere by saynt Jhon,
And archers we wyll sell them greate plentye,
And so wyll we ryd them sone,
Sir, for a peny of our monye.
Than answered the duke of Bare,
Wordes that were of greate pryde;
By god he sayd, I will not spare
Over all the Englysshemen for to ryde,   290
If that they dare us abyde,
We wyll overthrowe them in fere,
And take them prysoners in this tyde,
Than come home agayne to our dynere.

[Henry prepared for battle—ordering stakes to be cut &c.]

Our kynge wente up upon an hyll hye,
And loked downe to the valyes lowe;
He sawe where the Frenchemen came hastely,
As thycke as ever dyde hayle or snowe;
Than kneled our kynge downe in that stounde,

And all his men on every syde.
Every man made a crosse, and kyssed the grounde,
And on theyr fete fast ganne abyde.   310
Our kynge said, Syrs, what tyme of the day?
My lege, they sayd, it nye pryme.
Than go we to our journey:
By the grace of Jesu, it is good tyme;
For sayntes that lye in theyr shryne
To god for us they be prayenge;
All the relygyouse of Englande in this tyme
Ora pro nobis for us they synge.
Saynt George was sene over our hoste,
Of very trouthe this syght men dyde se;   320
Downe was he sent by the holy goste
To gyve our kynge the vyctory.
Than blewe the trompetes merily;
These two batayles togyther yede. . . .

[The battle is very briefly described. After the victory]

   He toke his presoners, bothe olde and yonge,
And towarde Calayes fourth he went;
He shypped there with good entent.
To Cauntorbury full fayre he passed,   350
And offered to Saynt Thomas shryne,
And through Kent he rode in haste;
To Eltam he cam all in good tyme,
And over Blackeheth, as he was rydynge,
Of the Cytye of London he was ware.
   Hayle! ryall Cytye, sayd our kynge,
Cryste kepe the ever from sorowe and care!
And whan he gave that noble Cyte his blessynge,
He prayed Jesu it myght well fare.
To Westmynster dyde he ryde,   360
And the Frenche prysoners with hym also;
He raunsommed them in that tyde,
And agayne to theyr contrye he let them goo.
Thus of this matter I make an ende,
To theffecte of the battayll have I gone;
For in this boke I cannot comprehende
The greatest batayll of all, called the sege of Rone,
For that sege lasted iii yere and more. . . .

IV. Analogue

From A MYRROURE FOR MAGISTRATES

(1559)

[After the ghost of Henry Percy, Earl of Northumberland has told his tragedy, Baldwin, the editor of the *Myrroure* continues:]

By that this was ended, I had found out the storie of Richard earle of Cambridge: and because it conteyned matter in it, though not very notable, yet for the better understanding of the rest, I thought it mete to touche it, and therfore sayd as foloweth, You have sayd wel of the Percies and favourably. For in dede as it should appere, the chyefe cause of theyr conspiracie agaynst kyng Henry, was for Edmund Mortimer theyr cosins sake, whom the king very maliciously proclaymed to have yelded hym selfe to Owen colourably, whan as in deede he was taken forcibly against his wil, & very cruelly ordered in prison. And seing we are in hand with Mortimers matter, I wyll take uppon me the person of Richard Plantagenet Earle of Cambridge, who for his sake likewise died. . . . In the beginning of . . . Henry the fyfts rayne, dyed this Rychard, and with him Henry the lord Scrope & others, in whose behalfe this may be sayd.

> How Richard erle of Cambridge en-
> tending the kinges destruction
> was put to death at
> Southhampton.

Hast maketh wast, hath commonly ben sayd,
And secrete mischiefe seeld hath lucky spede:
A murdering mind with proper peyze is wayd,
Al this is true, I find it in my Crede.
And therfore Baldwin warne all states take hede,   5
How they conspire any other to betrappe,
Least mischiefe meant light in the miners lappe.

    For I lord Richard, heyre Plantagenet
Was Erle of Cambridge, and right fortunate,
If I had had the grace my wit to set   10

To have content me with mine owne estate:
But o false honours, breders of debate,
The love of you our lewde hartes doth allure
To lese our selves by seking you unsure.

Because my brother Edmund Mortimer,   15
Whose eldest sister was my wedded wife,
I meane that Edmund that was prisoner
In Wales so long, through Owens busy strife,
Because I say, that after Edmundes life,
His rightes and titles must by law be mine,   20
(For he ne had, nor could encrease his line)

Because the right of realme & crowne was ours,
I serched means to helpe him therunto.
And where the Henries held it by their powers
I sought a shift their tenures to undo,   25
Which being force, sith force or sleyt must do,
I voyde of might, because their power was strong
Set privy sleyte agaynst theyr open wrong.

But sith the deathes of most part of my kinne
Did dash my hope, throughout the fathers dayes   30
I let it slip, and thought it best beginne
Whan as the sonne shuld dred lest such assayes:
For force through spede, sleyght spedeth through delayes
And seeld doth treason time so fitly find
As whan al dangers most be out of minde.   35

Wherfore while Henry of that name the fifte,
Prepared his army to go conquer Fraunce,
Lord Skrope and I thought to attempt a drifte
To put him downe my brother to avaunce:
But were it gods wil, my luck, or his good chaunce,   40
The king wist wholy wherabout we went,
The night before the king to shipward bent.

Then were we strayt as traytours apprehended,
Our purpose spied, the cause therof was hid,
And therfore loe a false cause we pretended
Wherthrough my brother was fro daunger ryd:[1]

[1] Cf. the Complaint of Richard, Duke of York:

For whan king Henry of that name the fift,
Had tane my father in this conspiracy,
He from Sir Edmund all the blame to shift,

We sayd for hier of the French kinges coyne, we did
Behight to kil the king: and thus with shame
We stayned our selves, to save our frend fro blame.

   Whan we had thus confest so foule a treason,   50
That we deserved, we suffred by the lawe.
Se Baldwin see, and note (as it is reason)
How wicked dedes to wofull endes do drawe.
All force doth fayle, no crafte is wurth a straw,
To attayne thinges lost, and therfore let them go,   55
For might ruleth right, and wil though God say no.

Whan stout Richarde had stoutly sayd his mind, belike quoth one, this Rychard was but a litle man, or els litle favoured of wryters, for our Cronicles speake very litle of him. But seyng we be cum now to king Henries viage into Fraunce, we can not lack valyant men to speake of: for among so many as were led and sent by the Kyng out of thys realme thyther, it can not be chosen but sum, and that a great summe, were slayne among theym: wherfore to speake of them all, I thynke not nedefull. And therfore to let passe Edwarde Duke of Yorke, and the Earle of Suffolke slayne both at the battayle of Aginecourte, as were also many other, Let us ende the time of Henry the fyfth, and cum to hys sunne Henry the syxt: whose nonage brought Fraunce and Normandy out of bondage, and was cause that fewe of our noble men died aged.

Was fayne to say the French king, his ally,
Had hyred him this trayterous act to trye,
For which condemned, shortly he was slayne.
In helping right this was my fathers gayne.   (50–56).

V. Possible Source

From THE FIRST FOWRE BOOKES OF THE CIVILE WARS BETWEEN THE TWO HOUSES OF LANCASTER AND YORKE

by Samuel Daniel (1595 edition)[1]

THE ARGUMENT OF THE FOURTH BOOKE

> *Henry the fifth cuts off his enemy*
> *The earle of* Cambridge *that conspir'd his death:*
> *Henry the sixt maryed unluckily*
> *He and his countryes glory ruineth:*
> Suffolke *that made the match prefer'd too hie*
> *Going to exile a pirat murthereth:*
> *What meanes the Duke of Yorke observ'd to gaine*
> *The worlds goodwill, seeking the crowne t'attaine.*

I

Close smothered lay the low depressed fire,
Whose after-issuing flames confounded all[2]
Whilst thou victorious Henry didst conspire
The wracke of Fraunce, that at thy feete did fall:
Whilst joyes of gotten spoiles, and new desire
Of greater gaine to greater deedes did call
Thy conquering troupes, that could no thoughts retaine
But thoughts of glorie all that working raigne.

2

What do I feele O now in passing by
These blessed times that I am forst to leave?
What trembling sad remorse doth terrefie
M'amazed thought with what I do conceive?
What? doth my pen commit impietie

---

[1] 'At London. Printed by P. Short for Simon Waterson.'
[2] I.e. the conflicts caused by Henry IV's usurpation.

To passe those sacred *tropheis* without leave?
And do I sin not to salute your ghostes
Great worthies, so renown'd in forraine coasts?

3

Who do I see out of the darke appeare,
Covered almost with clowdes as with the night,
That here presents him with a martiall cheere
Seeming of dreadfull, and yet lovely sight?
Whose eye gives courage, & whose brow hath feare
Both representing terror and delight,
And staies my course, and off my purpose breakes,
And in obraiding wordes thus fiersly speakes.

4

Ungratefull times that impiously neglect
That worth that never times againe shall shew,
What, merites all our toile no more respect?
Or else standes idlenes asham'd to know
Those wondrous Actions that do so object
Blame to the wanton, sin unto the slow?
Can *England* see the best that shee can boast
Ly thus ungrac'd, undeckt, and almost lost?

5

Why do you seeke for fained *Palladins*
Out of the smoke of idle vanitie
That maie give glorie to the true dissignes
Of *Bourchier, Talbot, Nevile, Willoughby*?
Why should not you strive to fill up your lives
With wonders of your owne, with veritie?
T'inflame their ofspring with the love of Good
And glorious true examples of their bloud.

6

O what eternall matter here is found!
Whence new immortal *Iliads* might proceed,
That those whose happie graces do abound
In blessed accents here maie have to feed
Good thoughts, on no imaginary ground
Of hungrie shadowes which no profit breed:
Whence musicke like, instant delight may grow,
But when men all do know they nothing know.

7

And why dost thou in lamentable verse
Nothing but bloudshed, treasons, sin and shame,
The worst of times, the'extreame of ils rehears,
To raise old staines, and to renew dead blame?
As if the minds of th'evill, and perverse
Were not far sooner trained from the same
By good example of faire vertuous acts,
Then by the shew of foule ungodly facts.

8

O that our times had had some sacred wight,
Whose wordes as happie as our swordes had bin
To have prepar'd for us *Tropheis* aright
Of undecaying frames t'have rested in:
Triumphant Arkes of perdurable might.
O holy lives; that such advauntage win
Upon the Sieth[1] of time in spite of yeares,
How blessed they that gaine what never weares.

9

What is it O to do, if what we do
Shall perish nere as soone as it is donne?
What is that glorie we attaine unto
With all our toile, if lost as soone as wonne?
O small requitall for so great a doo
Is this poore present breath a smoake soone gone;
Or these dombe stones erected for our sake,
Which formles heapes few stormie chaunges make.

10

Tell great ELIZA since her daies are grac'd
With those bright ornaments to us denide,
That she repaire what darknes hath defac'd,
And get our ruyn'd deeds reedifide:
She in whose all directing eye is plac'd
A powre the highest powers of wit to guide,
She may commaund the worke and oversee
The holy frame that might eternall bee.

---

[1] Scythe.

11

O would she be content that time should make
A ravenous pray upon her glorious raigne;
That darknes and the night should overtake
So cleere a brightnes, shining without staine?
Ah no, she fosters some no doubt that wake
For her eternity, with pleasing paine:
And if she for her selfe prepare this good,
O let her not neglect those of her bloud.

12

This that great *Monarch Henry* seemed to crave[1];
When (weighing what a holy motive here
Vertue propos'd, and fit for him to have,
Whom all times ought of dutie hold most deare)
I sigh'd, and wish'd that some would take t'ingrave
With curious hand so proud a worke to reare,
To grace the present, and to blesse times past,
That might for ever to our glorie last.

13

So should our well taught times have learn'd alike
How faire shin'd vertue, and how foule vice stood,
When now my selfe have driven to mislike
Those deedes of worth I dare not vow for good:
I cannot mone who lose, nor praise who seeke
By mightie Actions to advaunce their bloud;
I must saie who wrought most, least honor had:
How ever good the cause, the deedes were bad.

14

And onely tell the worst of every raine
And not the intermedled good report,
I leave what glorye vertue did attaine
At th'evermemorable Agincorte:
I leave to tell what wit, what powre did gaine
Th'assieged, *Roan, Caen, Dreux,* or in what sort:
How majestie with terror did advaunce
Her conquering foote on all subdued *Fraunce.*

[1] In margin: '*Hen. 5*'.

15

All this I passe, and that magnanimous King
Mirror of vertue, miracle of worth,
Whose mightie Actions with wise managing
Forst prouder bosting climes to serve the North:
The best of all the best the earth can bring
Skarse equals him in what his raigne brought forth,
Being of a mind as forward to aspire
As fit to governe what he did desire.

16

His comely body was a goodly seate
Where vertue dwelt most faire as lodg'd most pure,
A bodie strong where use of strength did get
A stronger state to do and to endure[1]:
Making his life th'example to beget
Like spirit in those he did to good in ure,
Most glorying to advaunce true vertuous bloud,
As if he greatnes sought but to do good.

17

Who as the chiefe, and all-directing head,
Did with his subjects as his members live,
And them to goodnes forced not, but lead
Winning not much to have, but much to give:
Deeming the powre of his, his powre did spread
As borne to blesse the world & not to griev:
Adorn'd with other spoiles not subjects store,
No king exacting lesse, none winning more.

18

He after that corrupted faith had bred
An ill inur'd obedience for commaund,
And languishing luxuriousnes had spred
Feeble unaptnes over all the land,
Yet he those long unordered troupes so led
Under such formall discipline to stand,
That even his soule seem'd only to direct
So great a bodie such exploys t'effect.

[1] Cf. Holinshed, *supra*, 407.

19

He bringes abrode distracted discontent,
Disperst ill humours into actions hie,
And to unite them all in one consent
Plac'd the faire marke of glorie in their eye,
That malice had no leasure to dissent,
Nor envie time to practise treachery,
The present actions do divert the thought
Of madnes past, while mindes were so well wrought.

20

Here now were pride, oppression, usury,
The canker-eating mischeifes of the state,
Cal'd forth to praie uppon the enemie,
Whilst the home-burthned better lightned sate:
Ease was not suffered with a gredie eye
T'examine states or private wealthes to rate,
The silent Courtes warr'd not with busie wordes,
Nor wrested law gave the contentious swordes.

21

Now nothing entertaines th'attentive eare
But stratagems, assaults, surprises, fights;
How to give lawes to them that conquered were,
How to articulate with yeelding wights:
The weake with mercie, and the proud with feare
How to retaine, to give desarts their right,
Were now the Arts, and nothing else was thought
But how to win and maintaine what was gote.

22

Here O were none that privately possest
And held alone imprisoned majestie,
Proudly debarring entraunce from the rest
As if the praie were theirs by victorie:
Here no detractor woundes who merits best,
Nor shameles brow cheeres on impietie,
Vertue who all her toyle with zeale had spent
Not here all unrewarded, sighing went.

23

But here the equally respecting eye
Of powre, looking alike on like desarts,
Blessing the good made others good thereby,
More mightie by the multitude of harts:
The field of glorie unto all doth lie
Open alike, honor to all imparts;
So that the only fashion in request
Was to bee good or good-like as the rest.

24

So much O thou example dost effect
Being far a better maister than commaund,
That how to do by doing doth direct
And teachest others action by thy hand,
Who followes not the course that kings elect?
When Princes worke, who then will idle stand?
And when that dooing good is onely thought
Worthy reward; who will be bad for nought?

25

And had not th'earle of *Cambridge* with vaine speed
Untimely practiz'd for anothers right,
With hope t'advaunce those of his proper seed,
(On whom yet rule seem'd destined to light)
The land had seene none of her owne to bleed
During this raigne, nor no aggrieved sight:
None the least blacknes interclouded had
So faire a day, nor any eye looke sad.

26

But now when *Fraunce* perceiving from afar
The gathering tempest growing on from hence
Readie to fall, threatning their state to marre,
They labor all meanes to provide defence:
And practising how to prevent this warre,
And shut out such calamities from thence,
Do foster here some discord lately growne
To hold Ambition busied with her owne.

27

Finding those humors which they saw were fit
Soone to be wrought and easie to be fed,
Swolne full with envie that the crowne should sit
There where it did, as if established:
And whom it toucht in bloud to grieve at it
They with such hopes and helps sollicited,
That this great Earle was drawne t'attempt the thing
And practises how to depose the king.

28

For being of mightie meanes to do the deed
And yet of mightier hopes then meanes to do,
And yet of spirit that did his hopes exceed,
And then of bloud as great to ad thereto:
All which, with what the gold of *Fraunce* could breed
Being powers inough a climing mind to woo,
He so imploid, that many he had wonne
Even of the chiefe the king relide uppon.

29

The wel-known right of the Earle of *March* alur'd
A leaning love, whose cause he did pretend;
Whereby he knew that so himselfe procur'd
The Crowne for his owne children in the end:
For the Earle being (as he was assur'd)
Unapt for issue, it must needes descend
On those of his being next of *Clarence* race,
As who by course of right should hold the place.

30

It was the time when as the forward Prince
Had all prepar'd for his great enterprize[1],
And readie stand his troupes to part from hence
And all in stately forme and order lyes:
When open fame gives out intelligence
Of these bad complots of his enemies:
Or else this time of purpose chosen is
Though knowne before, yet let run on till this.

---

[1] In margin: '*At Southhamton*'.

31

That this might yeeld the more to aggravate
Upon so foule a deed so vilely sought,
Now at this time t'attempt to ruinate
So glorious great disseignes so forward brought:
Whilst carefull vertue seekes t'advaunce the state
And for her everlasting honour fought
That though the cause were right, and title strong
The time of dooing it, yet makes it wrong.

32

And straight an unlamented death he had,
And straight were joyfully the Anchors weigh'd
And all flocke fast aboord, with visage glad,
As if the sacrifize had now beene pay'd
For their good speed; that made their stay so sad
Lothing the least occasion that delay'd.
And now new thoughts, great hopes, calme seas, fair windes
With present action intertaines their mindes.

33

No other crosse O *Henry* saw thy daies
But this that toucht thy now possessed hold;
Nor after long, till this mans sonne[1] assaies
To get of thine the right that he controwl'd:
For which contending long, his life he paies;
So that it fatall seem'd the father should
Thy winning seeke to staie, and then his sonne
Should be the cause to loose, when thou hadst won.

34

Yet now in this so happie a meane while
And interlightning times they vertues wrought,
That discord had no leasure to defile
So faire attempts with a tumultuous thought:
And even thy selfe, thy selfe didst so beguile
With such attention uppon what was sought,
That time affoordes not now with care or hate
Others to seeke, thee to secure thy state.

---

[1] *In margin:* 'Richard Duke of Yorke.'

35

Else O how easie had it beene for thee
All the pretendant race t'have laid full low
If thou proceeded hadst with crueltie
Not suffering anie fatall branch to grow:
But unsuspicious magnanimitie
Shames such effects of feare, and force to show:
Busied in free, and open Actions still
Being great; for being good, hates to be ill.

.   .   .   .

39

Yet how hath fate dispos'd of all this good?
What have these vertues after times avail'd?
In what steed hath hy-raised valor stood,
When this continuing cause of greatnes fail'd?
Then when proud-growne the irritated bloud
Enduring not itselfe it selfe assail'd,
As though that *Prowesse* had but learnt to spill
Much bloud abrode to cut her throte with skill.

40

O doth th'Eternall in the course of thinges
So mixe the causes both of good and ill,
That thus the one effects of th'other bringes,
As what seemes made to blisse, is borne to spill?
What from the best of vertues glorie springes
That which the world with miserie doth fill?
Is th'end of happines but wretchednesse,
Hath sin his plague, and vertue no successe?

41

Either that is not good, the world holds good,
Or else is so confus'd with ill, that we
Abused with th'appearing likelihood
Run to offend, whilst we thinke good to be:
Or else the heavens made man, in furious bloud
To torture man: And that no course is free
From mischiefe long. And that faire daies do breed
But storms, to make more foule, times that succeed.

42

Who would have thought but so great victories,
Such conquests, riches, land, and kingdome gain'd,
Could not but have establish't in such wise
This powreful state, in state to have remain'd?
Who would have thought that mischief could devise
A way so soone to loose what was attain'd?
As greatnes were but shew'd to grieve not grace,
And to reduce us into far worse case.

[When Henry V died, Fortune abandoned England.]

45

An infant king doth in the state succeed
Skarse one yeare old, left unto others guide,
Whose carefull trust, though such as shew'd indeed
They waigh'd their charge more than the world beside;
And did with dutie, zeale and love proceed:
Yet for all what their travaile could provide
Could not woo fortune to remaine with us
When this her Minion was departed thus. . . .

VI. Possible Source

From
INSTRUCTIONS, OBSERVATIONS AND ORDERS MILITARIE

by Sir John Smithe (1595)

Instructions, Observations and Orders Militarie, Requisite for all Chieftaines, Captaines and higher and lower men of charge, and Officers to understand, knowe and observe. Composed by Sir John Smithe, Knight. And now Imprinted. Richard Johnes, 1595.

Dedicatorie to the Knightes, Esquiers, and Gentlemen of England that are honorablie delighted in the Arte and Science Militarie.

. . . . the Exercise of Armes and Discipline Military, is the maintainer of peace, and Bulwarke of securitie . . . By that Arte and Discipline also great *Alexander* with small Armies of disciplinde and exercised souldiers, did vanquish infinite and most great and huge Armies of his enemies, and did conquer a great part of the world, and beyond the hope and expectation of all men did march unto the utmost partes of the earth then known.

[After asserting that neglect of military science brings civil confusion and decay, and that 'Civill warre is the subverting of al orders and discipline Militarie', Smithe discusses the 'Wonderful victories atchived by our Ancestors through their orders and exercises militarie.']

. . . . the Kings and Chieftaines with verie small Armies did atchieve manie wonderfull victories against exceeding great and huge hostes of forren Nations. And those excellent orders, exercises and proceedings militarie did continue in great perfection, in the raines of divers Kings, untill that by the civill warres betwixt the two houses of *Yorke* and *Lancaster*, they were greatlie blemished and decayed: And yet after againe, by the wisedome and vallour of King Edward the fourth, when he came to the quiet enjoying of the Crowne, were restored againe to the auncient perfection: and so continued the rest of his time, untill his brother *Richarde* the third, by his cruell destroying of his Nephewes, came to the Crowne, who for his injustice and crueltie comming to be hated both of God and man, did in the smal time that he raigned (partly forced by necessitie) subvert all orderly proceedings both in warre and peace. Since whose time, the auncient orders and proceedings in the composing and forming of Armies, and divers other matters militarie was never againe restored to that excellence that it was before his time . . .

[Something has been regained under the Tudors, but] not in manie things comparable to the Militia and discipline of King *Edward* the third, *Henrie* the fifth and such other most martiall and valiant Kinges . . . [In those days] it was never seene that English souldiers, were they in health, sicke or hurt, did go a begging, or become any waies rogues, under pretence that they had bene souldiers, as now most commonly they doe . . . But now within these very fewe yeares, since our Nation hath haunted and served in the civill warres of *Fraunce* and the *Lowe Countries*, divers of our men of

warre have so affected the infinit disorders and lack of Discipline
of those civill warres, in respect of unlawfull gaine, that in these
dayes the discipline Militarie of our auncestors and of all other
warlike Nations is so forgotten and neglected amongst us . . . that
. . . all is turned from the orders, exercises and Discipline of our
most valiant and worthie Auncestors, to disorders and confusion.

HENRY VIII

INTRODUCTION

HENRY VIII was first printed in the First Folio as 'The Famous History of the Life of King Henry the Eight'. The text there is good, with act- and scene-divisions and some full stage-directions for ceremonial purposes of the kind found in earlier plays such as *Richardus Tertius* and *Thomas of Woodstock*, in which the Chroniclers were drawn on for descriptions of pageantry. The Folio text was set up from a scribal copy, probably made from the author's own MS.[1]

The play was published as by Shakespeare, and was long generally regarded as his, but the abnormality of the versification (e.g. frequency of double-endings and of caesura near the end of the lines) was noted by Richard Roderick in 1758. In the nineteenth century Browning, Tennyson and Emerson felt the presence of another hand, and many critics have suggested that this was John Fletcher's and that the play was a work of collaboration between Shakespeare and John Fletcher, in which Shakespeare wrote Act I, 1 and 2; Act II, 3 and 4; Act III, 2.1–203; Act V, 1. A few writers have argued for Massinger's participation.[2] On the other hand Swinburne, while admitting resemblances to Fletcher's style, thought the play too good for him, and suggested that the exceptional qualities of the play 'might perhaps be explicable as a tentative essay in a new line by one who tried so many styles before settling into his latest'. More recently Peter Alexander and others have argued cogently for Shakespeare's sole authorship.[3]

The play was probably written early in 1613. A letter from Sir Henry Wotton to Sir Edmund Bacon on 2 July of that year

---

[1] See W. W. Greg, *The Editorial Problem in Shakespeare*, 1942, 152; E. K. Chambers, *WSh* I.495–8; A. Walker, *Textual Problems of the First Folio*, 1953, 8ff.

[2] There is a useful summary of diverse opinions in *The London Shakespeare*, ed. J. Munro, 1958, IV.1144–50.

[3] P. Alexander in *Essays and Studies*, xvi, 1930, 85–120. Cf. B. Maxwell, *Studies in Beaumont, Fletcher and Massinger*, 1939, 54–73; H. Craig, *An Interpretation of Shakespeare*, 1948, 368; R. A. Foakes, *New Arden*, 1957, Introduction.

relates how the Globe Theatre was burned down during a play on the same theme:

> 'The Kings Players had a new Play called *All is True*, representing some principal pieces of the Reign of Henry 8, which was set forth with many extraordinary circumstances of Pomp and Majesty, even to the matting of the stage; the Knights of the Order, with their Georges and Garter, the Guards with their embroidered Coats, and the like: sufficient in truth within a while to make greatness very familiar, if not ridiculous. Now, King *Henry* making a Masque at Cardinal *Wolsey's* House, and certain Canons being shot off at his entry, some of the Paper, or other stuff wherewith one of them was stopped, did light on the Thatch, where being thought at first but an idle smoak, and their eyes more attentive to the show, it kindled inwardly, and ran round like a train, consuming within less then an hour the whole House to the very grounds.
>
> This was the fatal period of that vertuous Fabrique; wherein yet nothing did perish, but a few forsaken Cloaks; only one man had his Breeches set on fire, that would perhaps have broyled him, if he had not by the benefit of a provident wit put it out with bottle ale.' [1]

On the day after the fire Thomas Lorkin wrote to Sir Thomas Puckering that it occurred 'while Bourbege his companie were acting at the Globe the play of Hen: 8'. Much later Edmund Howes, in his continuation of Stow's *Annals* for the 1618 edition, wrote that the house was 'filled with people, to behold the play, *viz.* of Henry the eight'. There can be little doubt that the 'new play' was *Henry VIII*, in which at 1.4.49 the stage direction 'Drum and trumpet: chambers discharged' heralds the arrival of the masquers at Wolsey's banquet.

The play may well have been written in connection with the marriage of the Princess Elizabeth, James I's daughter, to the Elector Palatine in February, 1613. A piece which scorned Roman Catholic pretensions and included both the birth of a Princess Elizabeth to a fair Queen Anne [2] and the prophecy of a

---

[1] *The Life and Letters of Sir H. Wotton*, ed. L. P. Smith, 1907, II.32. The allusions appear in full in *New Arden*, App. I.
[2] James I's Queen was Anne of Denmark.

glorious future for her would be topical when London was *en fête* for the Protestant Crusader and his bride. At least six of Shakespeare's plays were performed for the happy pair. *Henry VIII* is not listed among them, but it may well have been played only in the public theatre, and it may even have been the piece which someone wrote of as being cancelled in favour of a Masque on 16 February:

> 'Much expectation was made of a stage play to be acted in the Great Hall by the King's players, where many hundred of people stood attending the same; but it lapsed contrarie, for greater pleasures were attending.'[1]

The Elector and his wife left for Germany on 10 April. So the play was probably composed during the first four or five months of 1613.

Wotton's assertion that the play was called *All is True* probably refers to a sub-title of *Henry VIII*. A ballad not now extant in its original format but printed in *The Gentleman's Magazine* for February, 1816,[2] from a seventeenth-century MS then extant and apparently composed soon after the burning of the Globe, contains many topical references and has the refrain, 'all this is true', e.g.:

> All yow that please to understand
> Come listen to my storye;
> To see Death with his rakeing brande,
> Mongst such an auditorye:
> Regarding neither Cardinall's might,
> Nor yet the rugged face of Henry the eight.
> Oh sorrow, pittifull sorrow, and yett all this is true.

Important in this connection is the existence of another Henry VIII play, Samuel Rowley's *When You See Me You Know Me*, published in 1605 and reprinted in 1613, probably after a revival by the Elector Palatine's Men, who had been Prince Henry's players until his death in 1612. This piece was very unhistorical; it contained much clowning by the court jesters Will Summers and Patch, and showed Henry VIII walking the streets at night in disguise and being put in prison

---

[1] *The Magnificent Marriage of the Two Great Princes* (1613), given in *WSh* II.342.
[2] Cf. *ElSt* II.420–2.

for fighting. Shakespeare's Prologue seems to refer to these ingredients when it warns the audience not to expect

> a merry, bawdy play,
> A noise of targets, or to see a fellow
> In a long motley coat guarded with yellow,

and disclaims any intention

> To rank our chosen truth with such a show
> As fool and fight. . . .

The nature of *When You See Me* and its relation to *Henry VIII* are therefore worthy of further inquiry. Plays on the reign were undoubtedly popular. Henslowe had one in 1598 in which the King's jester appeared. In June/July, 1601, he paid Chettle for a play about Wolsey which included Summers and was so successful that between August and December of the same year Chettle, Drayton, Munday and Smith were paid for a 'first Part' on the Cardinal's early life, to be inserted before its predecessor, which thus became *Part 2*. These plays are now unknown. Rowley's piece was probably written in 1603 or 1604 and performed when the Fortune Theatre reopened on Easter Monday, 1604, and the Admiral's company had become Prince Henry's men.[1]

The unusual treatment of history in this play and the prominence given in it to Henry VIII's son Edward (later Edward VI) indicates that the piece was intended to honour James I's heir, then a boy of ten. Maybe an effort was made not to duplicate the material of the previous plays on Wolsey, for though the Cardinal's machinations are described and his fall is briefly shown, he is not the main figure, and the divorce of Katherine of Aragon and the marriages with Anne Boleyn and Katherine Howard are ignored. To include Prince Edward the play is set later in the reign, but Wolsey still lives (though he really died in 1530) and his personal and political intrigues are intermingled with those of Bonner and Gardiner. His fall is ascribed to his enmity towards the Emperor, his arrogance as the Pope's representative, and his accumulation of wealth whereby to bribe his way to the papal throne.

---

[1] *ElSt* II.186. Excerpts are given below [Text III].

When You See Me sprawls over the years 1514–44. It begins when Ambassadors from France come seeking to marry Henry's sister Mary to the aged French King Louis XII. This occurred in 1514, but is made to coincide with the lying-in of Jane Seymour in October, 1537. Her pains come upon her when waiting to greet the visitors. The King is told that he must choose between the child's life and hers. He wishes to save hers, but she persuades him otherwise and dies in giving birth to Prince Edward (Sc. ii).

By Scene iv some time has elapsed. The King's grief for his wife has made him solitary and savage. He is offended when Wolsey intrudes into his presence, but he is solaced by the jests of the fools Will Summers and Patch. He is rewarded by the Pope for defending the faith against Luther and is asked to join a crusade against the Turks (1518). He resolves to inspect the efficiency of the London watch.

Scene v presents the comic Constable and Watch, who fall asleep on duty and let the King through without challenging him. He meets Black Will, a robber armed with sword and buckler, who first invites Henry to join him and then fights with him. They are both arrested and put in the Counter, where the King hears complaints against one of his own servants and one of the Cardinal's. He enjoys himself hugely before being released by Brandon, whom he sends to France to bring Mary home on learning that the French King has died (January, 1515). Apparently he is now married to Ann of Cleves, for he announces that she is to be sent home (1540), and that he will wed Lady Katherine Parr (1543). The marriage with Katherine Howard (1540–42) is ignored.

Scene viii shows Wolsey hindered in his ambitions by the King of France's death and the coolness of the Emperor ('But we shall crosse him for't, I doubt it not'). He hates the King's union with Katherine Parr, for 'she is the hope of *Luthers* heresie'.

Henry gives justice to those whose complaints he heard in prison. Learning that Brandon has married his sister Mary he pretends ferocity but soon forgives them (Sc. ix).

The material in Scene x indicates that the play was for performance before the boy Prince Henry. Here we see Cranmer as Prince Edward's tutor exercised about his charge's love of tennis, and there is some good fun with the Prince's whipping boy, who is knighted for his pains. The Prince has a lesson on the difference between men and animals and another by Dr Tye on the value of music (2032–61).

Bishops Bonner and Gardiner (Sc. xi) hate Cranmer and the Queen as Protestants: "There must be no Queen or the Abbies fall." The Queen debates with the Catholic Bishops the question of their divided allegiance (2219ff) and various Romish practices, and she is accused by Gardiner of treason. Incensed by this suspicion and by Luther's attacks on him, Henry orders Katherine's arrest.

The religious divisions among the King's children appear in Scene xii when the Prince reads characteristic letters from Princess Mary and Princess Elizabeth. Cranmer is forbidden the Court; the Queen tells the Prince that twelve articles have been brought against her. Urged to plead her innocence to the King she does so in Scene xiv; and in winning back his love for her the Prince plays a prominent part. Henry sends his ring to Cranmer in token of his esteem. When Bonner and Gardiner come to arrest the Queen they are in turn accused, but Katherine pleads for them and they are allowed to go free.

Meanwhile the two Fools, while Wolsey has been on the Continent trying to make peace between France and the Emperor, have been feasting in his cellar and there found barrels filled with treasure—which he has extorted from the people to use as bribes on his way to the Papacy. The King pretends not to believe anything against the Cardinal, but when the Emperor arrives and accuses Wolsey of having made an English herald defy him as an enemy (Sc. xv; this happened at Burgos in 1528), the King inveighs against Wolsey's arrogance and is enraged when the Cardinal says that he obeys the Pope. Wolsey is immediately removed from his offices, and the play ends with a rhyming match between Will Summers and the rest, and a promise of festivities to come when the Emperor will be made a Knight of the Garter.

The play takes much from Hall or Holinshed. From Foxe come the assertion that Gardiner plotted Katherine's death, the story of her interview with him, and the King's anger at those who wish to arrest her in a garden at Hampton Court.

This is a play of Protestant propaganda, with its discussions of religion and its presentation of Bonner and Gardiner as evil plotters; but Henry VIII is presented as the enemy of Luther, and he deplores sectarian divisions (as in fact he did in his last Parliament (24 December, 1545)).

In all probability *Henry VIII* was intended not only to honour the Elector and his bride but also to present a truer picture of the first Protestant monarch and his chief servants than Samuel Rowley had done. *When You See Me* provided a spring-board for the dramatist's imagination as he sought for a fitting veracity and regal solemnity.

The features common to the two plays were listed in detail by Karl Elze in his edition of *When You See Me*.[1] Many of them were unavoidable in plays drawing on the same source-material. Others prove that the later and better dramatist took suggestions from his predecessor. The compression of history to bring Wolsey's fall and Cranmer's narrow escape into the same piece while omitting the tragedies of Thomas Cromwell and Sir Thomas More may come from Rowley, who, however, treats both subjects very inadequately. Shakespeare makes of the juxtaposition a notable contrast in character, setting against the arrogant Wolsey the humble scholar of whom it was commonly said, 'Doe unto my lord of Canterbury displeasure, or a shrewd turne, and then you may be sure to have him your friend whiles he liveth.'[2]

Henry VIII also follows *When You See Me* in giving prominence to the birth of a royal baby, but Shakespeare makes this a climax very suitable for a dramatic epithalamion in honour of a Princess Elizabeth. There is a strong resemblance between the announcements of the birth, the rewarding of the messenger and the allusions to the child's likeness to his father.

As Elze pointed out:

'King Henry ... with both poets makes frequent use of his favourite ejaculation, Ha! ... By both poets he is exhibited leaning on the shoulder of some one of his intimate courtiers, by both walking in the gallery as was his custom "always of the afternoon". Both poets show the king's angry impatience when interrupted in his privacy; the only

---

[1] 1874. Cf. also W. Zeitlin in *Anglia*, 1881, iv.73ff.
[2] Foxe. Cf. *H8* V.2.210–13.

difference is that with Rowley it is Wolsey who provokes the king's rage by his impertinence, whereas with Shakespeare the dukes of Norfolk and Suffolk have to 'endure the storm' on such an occasion. . . . The fatal influence which the cardinal exercises over the king is by both poets ascribed to his wonderful eloquence. . . . Both poets derive the cardinal's downfall almost in the self-same words from the same causes . . . [Holinshed] was certainly the common source of both poets, but why did they select from among the long list of charges the very same items for introduction into their plays? . . . '[1]

Some of Elze's points of influence are more cogent than others. I omit the less likely. Nichol Smith has added to the list, showing that Gardiner's allusion at V.3.29–31 to disturbances in Germany is clarified by Rowley (2201ff); the letter to the Chamberlain (II.2.1–8) may have been suggested by Rowley's 1266ff; Wolsey's criticism of Anne Boleyn (III.2.99) may be taken from his criticism of Katherine Parr in the earlier play (1489ff); and 'the remarks on Latimer and Ridley [Rowley 1499ff] correspond with Gardiner's taunt at Cranmer and Cromwell' (V.3.80ff).

There is enough here to prove positive influence; and it may well be that the great part given to ceremonial in *Henry VIII* was in imitation of *When You See Me* and an attempt to outdo its court pageantry. It was to be, as Coleridge saw, 'a sort of historical masque or show-play', not a mixture of polemics, historical portraiture and low-comedy. The reduction in controversial discussion is doubtless due as much to Shakespeare's disinclination for sectarian dispute as because of James I's known dislike of poets who dabbled in state affairs. The jesters Will and Patch also disappear, for *Henry VIII* is conducted throughout on a higher level than their crude japes would allow; moreover, the handling of political material, the development of character through action and rhetoric are so extensive as not to require padding out with buffoonery. Similarly, whereas Rowley had imitated Shakespeare's Henry V plays in the King's night-walk through the city, his brawl and imprisonment, Shakespeare does not return the compliment.

[1] Elze, cited by D. Nichol Smith, Warwick edn., pp. xv–xvi.

For the new play belongs to a different kind of drama from *Henry IV* or *Henry V*. It is 'chronicle-pageant' rather than 'chronicle-and-comedy' or 'epic-and-comedy'.

The main source of *Henry VIII* was Holinshed's *Chronicles*, which were followed very closely in some parts of the play, with occasional verbal echoes [Text I and notes]. Hall was referred to, and the recently published *History of Great Britain*, by John Speed (1611),[1] was probably drawn on for two images in Wolsey's acknowledgement of his decline where in III.2 he speaks of having passed 'the full meridian of my glory' (222–7) and being like boys 'that swim on bladders' that break and let them drown (359–62). For the intrigue against Cranmer Foxe's *Actes and Monuments* was used.

Incidents from the *Chronicles* have been selected with care to subserve a dramatic purpose which seems to be fourfold: to show the evil ambitions of papist churchmen, first Wolsey and then Gardiner, and their varying influence on King and people; to portray the King's own self-willed nature and its bad and good effects; to present some major people and incidents involved in these two themes; to suggest the alternation of tragic and joyous motifs in the King's reign, culminating in the happy birth of the future Queen Elizabeth.

These themes are worked out with special reference to six main historical situations: the conflict between Buckingham and Wolsey in which the Cardinal triumphs; the tragedy of Katherine of Aragon; Wolsey's fall; the marriage with Anne Boleyn; Gardiner's plot against Cranmer; the birth of Princess Elizabeth.

To concentrate the events of some twenty years into the play, chronology is upset and the order of Holinshed freely varied, usually by anticipating time. The Field of the Cloth of Gold meeting was held in 1520. Buckingham was executed in 1521. Henry did not marry Anne Boleyn until 1532, but his fateful meeting with her is placed before Buckingham's condemnation, and his marriage before Wolsey's fall and death (1530). Katherine of Aragon died in 1536, but this is made to occur before Princess Elizabeth is born (1533), as is the plot against Cranmer, which may have occurred in 1540. The main reasons for such changes were, to give some illusion of

[1] Cf. *inf.* 472.

enchainment or interconnection to the incidents, and to suggest dramatic parallels or contrasts emergent in a survey of the whole reign.

In Act I, Sc. 1 the description of the famous meeting of the English and French Kings [1520] is used to show the dislike of some courtiers for needless and futile extravagance and for Wolsey's double dealing. Buckingham was at the meeting, but in the play he was absent ill, 'a prisoner in my chamber'. This enables him to be told about it by the hostile observer Norfolk, and also affords a touch of irony when he becomes a prisoner in earnest. The hatred between him and Wolsey is shown. Once he is arrested he knows that 'It will help me nothing To plead mine innocence.' The King's gratitude to Wolsey (I.2) is countered by Queen Katherine's plea for those who suffer under a tax of one-sixth which he has imposed, and his wiliness appears when the King countermands his orders (I.2.88–108). The Surveyor runs through the major charges against Buckingham—and there is a link with the Buckingham of *Richard III* in the accusation that he would assassinate the King as his father intended to do (I.2.193–209).

By now the audience knows something of Wolsey's murderous intrigues, his political double dealing, his exactions from the people (actually to pay for the King's war against France). His regal magnificence is presently to be shown in the feast at York Place. The first mention of this occurs in the slight scene I.3, which is introduced also to show the evil effects of French travels, French fashions and French extravagance ('fights and fireworks', 'tennis and silk stockings'—all vanities much condemned by Jacobean moralists (e.g. Joseph Hall), and as topical when the play was written as when the Council intervened in Henry's reign to get rid of his undesirable friends). After this there is a delicate irony in the courtiers' praise of Wolsey's liberality. The feast, inserted here from Holinshed's illustration of Wolsey's splendour [*inf.* 478], shows another side of the man, and of the King, and is used by the dramatist to introduce a new feminine interest, the first hint of danger to the Queen whose noble generosity we have just seen. After the Masque of Shepherds Wolsey guesses the King's identity rightly (not wrongly as in Holinshed) and the royal Romeo meets Anne Boleyn (I.4.75–6) some years before the fact.

Act II begins with a report of Buckingham's trial and condemnation; he makes three speeches full of dignity and goes out to die. Immediately we hear 'A buzzing of a separation, Between the King and Katherine' (II.1.148–9), and the suspicion that Wolsey is thus trying to avenge himself on the Emperor Charles V, Katherine's nephew. Both here and in the next scene (II.2) we see how in all things great and small (e.g. the post horses) the Cardinal's will is law and how 'the bold bad man' is hated. The King's impatience at being interrupted when pondering on his marriage may be suggested by the scene in *When You See Me* where the King is grieving for Jane Seymour's death, at affairs in Ireland and at Luther's book attacking him. But whereas in *When You See Me* the Cardinal is rebuked in a frenzy of rage

> Presumptuous priest, proud prelate as thou art,
> How comes it you are growne so saucie sir,
> Thus to presume upon our patience,
> And crosse our royall thoughts disturb'd and vext,
> By all your negligence in our estate,
> Of us and of our countries happinesse? . . .   (640–5)

in *Henry VIII* Norfolk is rebuked, and the Cardinal is greeted as 'a cure fit for a king' when he brings Campeius to join the enquiry into the royal marriage. Gardiner too is introduced here as the 'new Secretary'. The tenderness of the King's conscience in this scene is paralleled in II.3 by a tenderness in Anne Boleyn's. She is depicted not as the scapegrace she seems to have been but as an innocent, gentle girl, pitiful for the Queen, ignorant of the honours about to descend on her, and certainly guiltless as yet of any amour with the King. The Old Woman with her innuendoes sees further, and knows that ambition grows with having, though the girl is scared. So the dramatist shows the 'beauty and honour' of Queen Elizabeth's mother. Such youthful perturbation is contrasted with the mature dignity of Katherine's public self-defence in II.4, where she protests her wifely obedience, confronts Wolsey, and appeals to the Pope. She sweeps out, leaving the King to praise her virtues and to absolve Wolsey from taint of pressing the divorce. In terms drawn from Holinshed he explains how his conscience was awakened, but is displeased when the Cardinals delay a decision ('These Cardinals trifle with me'). He turns from Wolsey to Cranmer with words which recall those previously used to Wolsey ('with thy approach I know My comfort comes along' (II.4.237–8).

Holinshed's account of the interview between the Cardinals and the Queen is elaborated in III.1, when her suspicion of Wolsey is deeper and her grief mingled more with anger. Here as in the trial scene the strength of mind indicated by the chroniclers only in her refusal to attend the court is developed into the portrait of a noble, long-suffering, indignant and determined woman ('nothing but death / Shall e'er divorce my dignities'). At the close of the interview she is more ready to believe them to be 'those we profess, peace-makers, friends and servants', though Wolsey's sincerity is not made clear. In III.2, after the lords have plotted to complain against him, we learn that 'The Cardinal's letter to the Pope miscarried', that the King knows that he tried 'to stay the judgement o' the divorce', and (following Hall's account) Campeius has stolen away to Rome, while Cranmer has returned after satisfying foreign authorities with his legal reasons for the divorce. The Cardinal is turning over plans against Cranmer and Anne ('virtuous and well deserving' but 'a spleeny Lutheran'), and hoping to marry Henry to the French King's sister (as he in fact planned in 1528).

Another accident not unlike that of his errant letter is now introduced to reveal to the King the vastness of Wolsey's private wealth. In *When You See Me* the clowns, revelling in Wolsey's cellar while he was absent abroad, found barrels full of treasure. In *Henry VIII* an inventory is accidentally included among papers of state sent to the King. A similar mishap is said to have happened to the Bishop of Durham, whom Wolsey wished to ruin, earlier in the reign (*c.* 1522) [*inf.* 452–3], and Shakespeare (who liked resemblant effects) has transferred it to Wolsey himself, so that the King may play cat and mouse with him before giving him both letter and inventory to read and dismissing him from his offices. The courage and defiance with which he meets his enemies' taunts, their recital of charges from the articles drawn up by the Lords and brought down to the Commons [*inf.* 474] closely follow Holinshed. Wolsey's reformation in the last months of his life, his discovery of humility, are swiftly summarized in the great speeches at the end of III.2 when time is telescoped so that he learns of Sir Thomas More's appointment as Chancellor (1529), Cranmer's as Archbishop of Canterbury (1532) and, most crushing blow, Anne Boleyn's marriage to the King (1532), and thinks of his servant Cromwell's future. The last speech to Cromwell contains matter spoken (in Holinshed) to Kingston at Leicester just before his death [*inf.* 476].

In Act IV.1 Katherine's divorce after long sustained contumacy (1529) is made to precede only shortly the Coronation of Anne, the order of which ceremony is based on Holinshed, with necessary diminution of attendants. The chronicle's account is summarized, with many signs of popular joy, but the dramatist prepares us for what is to come by noting the enmity of Gardiner, Bishop of Winchester, towards Cranmer, who has a stout ally in the rising Cromwell. From this glad scene we turn to the sadness of the sick Katherine, who is told by her usher, Griffith, of Wolsey's death. Seeking to give a fair picture of the dead Cardinal, the dramatist makes Katherine describe his bad points and Griffith correct her one-sided view by describing the good he did and his good end. The garland-dance which she sees in her Vision indicates her saintliness—a remarkable thing for a Jacobean dramatist to admit in a Spanish Catholic.[1] Her anger at the insolence of the Messenger (IV.2.100–8) is as Foakes suggests based on Holinshed's statement that when she was deprived of her servants except those who swore 'to serve hir not as queene, but as princesse Dowager', she refused the service of those who took that oath. Her reception of the Emperor's ambassador Caputius, her petitions and the simplicity of her last words keep close to the sources, but are raised to tragic dignity.

The fifth Act might have been an anticlimax but the play does not sag, passing rapidly by some months to the time when

---

[1] A historical parallel has been found by Mrs. E. E. Duncan-Jones. The funeral oration (1550) for the evangelical Queen Marguerite of Navarre describes her as seeing shortly before death 'a very beautiful woman holding in her hand a crown which she showed her, saying that soon the Queen would be crowned with it'. (*Notes and Queries*, April 1961, pp. 142-3), Wolsey had hoped that Henry VIII would marry Marguerite after his divorce. (Cf. II.2.38–41; III.2.85–88.) Shakespeare's source is not yet known. His transference of the protestant's vision to the orthodox Katherine is itself remarkable.

the new Queen is in labour (1533), and, unlike Katherine Parr in *When You See Me*, unable to speak for herself or her friends against the attacks of Bishop Gardiner. Shakespeare combines the birth of the Princess Elizabeth (always remembered joyfully) with the intrigues of Gardiner against Cranmer, which show the bad side of the old religion. Here Foxe is called in to amplify Holinshed [Text II]. Whether this would have been included but for the attack on Cranmer in *When You See Me* is uncertain, but Shakespeare makes good use of it. For although the plot of *Henry VIII* is not formally satisfying, it is carefully arranged to show various facets of the King's nature. A sincere husband to the regal Katherine, he divorces her to marry the sweet and winsome Anne; he is misled by Wolsey and overthrows him; he defends Cranmer, showing a certain development in knowledge of life from what he was at first. From being *Defensor Fidei* he becomes the Defender, not perhaps of Protestantism, but of the rights of the private conscience; and the enemy of divisions in Church and State. King Henry in this play is not the violent, frenzied man of moods depicted (and rather well too) in *When You See Me*. He is vigorous in pleasure and in anger, mingles courtliness with bluntness, is generous and trusting until he realizes he has been deceived or that villainy is intended. The ambiguity of his attitude to Katherine is made up for by his youthful love for Anne, and his benevolence to his loyal Cranmer and Cromwell. Politically the portrait of him here is in some respects truer than that in *When You See Me*, where the divorce is ignored altogether.

The importance of the cult of Queen Elizabeth is denoted by the time given in the play to her baptism. Mention of it by the King in V.2 is followed by long accounts of the multitude crowding to the service (not in Holinshed) and of the baptismal procession and ceremony.

The long controversy about the extent of Shakespeare's part in the composition of *Henry VIII* will never be decided, for external evidence is wanting (except the important fact that the play was printed as Shakespeare's in the First Folio), and the internal evidence is largely dependent on the critic's taste and other subjective factors. Some readers have 'felt' that the loose flowing style in much of the play with its frequent addition of unstressed syllables both within and at the end of lines, its unstopt lines with light or weak endings and its extra feet cannot be Shakespeare's, but could be Fletcher's. Other critics cannot believe that after the great tragedies and *The Tempest* Shakespeare would return to a laxer form of structure. A discussion of style is not possible here, but I agree with those writers who, perceiving more than one style in the play, believe that the differences are functional and that there is nothing there which could not have been written by the poet of the last comedies. To accuse *Henry VIII* of unShakespearian slackness in construction is to ignore the poet's flexibility, the looseness of *The Winter's Tale* and *Cymbeline,* and (above all) the circumstances of its composition and its relation to *When You See Me.*

The use made of sources points to Shakespeare's total authorship rather than to collaboration. To take another play as a point of departure was nothing new for him; and the historical authorities, Holinshed, Foxe and Hall, were his favourites. Shakespeare was by no means the only Elizabethan dramatist to consult more than one source for a play, but as R. A. Foakes writes: 'if two authors wrote the play, they read the same parts of these authorities with a strangely similar attention to detail'.[1] Fletcher never showed such patience. The play shows a more frequent and extended use of close paraphrase from Holinshed than do most of the other Histories. This may well be due to a wish for authenticity, to make All as True as possible. The liberties taken with chronology—not arbitrarily, but for dramatic purposes, are like Shakespeare's practice elsewhere. Shakespearian too are the use of parallel situations, repetition, contrast, thematic material of ethical significance, the linking and cross-references, the absence of polemical rancour and the air of generosity and sincerity with which actions not easily condoned are glossed over.

The structure of the play recalls that of Shakespeare's earliest Histories. In *Henry VI* we saw a series of major figures portrayed in their successive clashes with each other and as they affected and were affected by their relations to the King. Here the play is built up on a series of portraits of six people of

---

[1] *New Arden,* xxiii.

importance in their day—Buckingham, Katherine, Wolsey, Ann Boleyn, Cranmer and Gardiner—with the King as the pivot round whom they revolve. It has been called 'an anthology of falls' in the manner of *A Mirror for Magistrates*.[1] This also reminds one of *Henry VI*.

But if the technique is somewhat similar the tone is very different, not only because Shakespeare's mind and poetry have been enriched by twenty years of experience in life and the theatre but also because his historical material is different. *Henry VIII* deals not with civil or foreign wars but with court politics in peacetime. It contains no rebellion, invasion or usurpation, and if it contains the falls of three great personages, a nobleman, a Cardinal and a Queen, it portrays also a happy bridal, a birth and the salvation of a good man, and it prophesies happier days to come. An editor has asserted that the play 'cannot be fitted into the scheme of the earlier histories'[2]; but surely it depicts the end of the struggle towards which (for supporters of the Tudor compromise) the agonies of Richard II, Henry IV and Henry VI all tended, namely, the end of the bad old order when the King's peace could be destroyed by the barons, and churchmen took too prominent a part in secular affairs. It sets forth a King who is no Prospero controlling all men and events in justice but a man of sensual lust and self-will who can be misled by self-seekers but who nevertheless does good in the main, is master of his house, defies the Pope and puts down a Cardinal's pride as neither Henry VI nor King John could do, growing (unhistorically) in wisdom and benevolence as the drama proceeds.

If in the symphonic pattern of English history as Shakespeare saw it *Henry V* was a heroic movement glowing between the sombre and anguished moods of other reigns, *Henry VIII* is a resplendent Finale, ritualistically expanding through conflict into grace and happy augury. It is also a fitting end to the dramatist's great cycle, which has shown all the English monarchs from the doleful tragedy of Richard II to what Hall styled 'The Triumphant Reigne of Kyng Henry the VIII'.

The play has in common with the last comedies an air of detachment, an ability to view bad deeds without falling into

---

[1] F. Kermode, 'What is Shakespeare's Henry VIII about?', *Durham Un. Journal*, March, 1948.   [2] *New Arden*, xlii.

Senecan horror or tragic gloom, to incorporate the mixed
motives of this world into the charitable pattern of the Christian
life; and there appears throughout a tendency to see 'a soul
of goodness in things evil'. Wolsey dies a better man than
he has lived. Katherine, his accuser, is led to forgive him
and see his better side. Though Buckingham is wrongfully
accused and executed, Cranmer, also wrongfully accused, is
sustained by his grateful master. There is suffering in the play,
but the movement on the whole is towards the triumph of
goodness, not through physical battle, as in *Richard III* and
Henry V, but by dignified acceptance, by the strength of its
own nature.[1]

[1] I had written this before reading Professor Wilson Knight's essay on *Henry
VIII* in *The Crown of Life* (1947). The truth and wisdom of this superb interpreta-
tion of the play decided me to add no more. Readers should study Professor
Knight's panegyric, and his convincing argument that the play is entirely by
Shakespeare.

I. Source

From THE THIRD VOLUME OF CHRONICLES

by R. Holinshed (1587 edition)

[A wealthy Bishop destroyed by his own mistake.]

[796/1/72]   This yeare [1508] was Thomas Ruthall made bishop of Durham. . . . To whome (remaining then at the court) the king gave in charge to write a booke of the whole estate of the kingdome, bicause he was knowne to the king to be a man of sufficiencie for the discharge thereof, which he did accordinglie.[1]

Afterwards, the king commanded cardinall Woolseie to go to this bishop, and to bring the booke awaie with him to deliver to his majestie. But see the mishap! that a man in all other things so provident, should now be so negligent: and at that time most forget himselfe, when (as it after fell out) he had most need to have remembred himselfe. For this bishop having written two bookes (the one to answer the kings command, and the other intreating of his owne private affaires) did bind them both after one sort in vellame, just of one length, bredth, and thicknesse, and in all points in such like proportion answering one an other, as the one could not by anie especiall note be discerned from the other: both which he also laid up togither in one place of his studie.

Now when the cardinall came to demand the booke due to the king: the bishop unadvisedlie commanded his servant to bring him the booke bound in white vellame lieng in his studie in such a place. The servant dooing accordinglie, brought foorth one of those bookes so bound, being the booke intreating of the state of the bishop, and delivered the same unto his maister, who receiving it (without further consideration or looking on) gave it to the cardinall to beare unto the king. The cardinall having the booke, went from the bishop, and after (in his studie by himselfe) understanding the con-

---

[1] *In margin:* 'The king commandeth him to write a booke of the whole estate of the kingdom.' The anecdote which follows was used of Wolsey in III.2.120ff.

tents thereof, he greatlie rejoised, having now occasion (which he long sought for) offered unto him to bring the bishop into the kings disgrace.[1]

Wherefore he went foorthwith to the king, delivered the booke into his hands, and breefelie informed the king of the contents thereof; putting further into the kings head, that if at anie time he were destitute of a masse of monie, he should not need to seeke further therefore than to the cofers of the bishop, who by the tenor of his owne booke had accompted his proper riches and substance to the value of a hundred thousand pounds.[2] Of all which when the bishop had intelligence (what he had doon, how the cardinall used him, what the king said, and what the world reported of him) he was striken with such greefe of the same, that he shortlie through extreame sorrow ended his life at London, in the yeare of Christ 1523.[3]

[French fashions, 1520.]

[850/1/11] During this time remained in the French court diverse yoong gentlemen of England, and they with the French king rode dailie disguised through Paris, throwing egges, stones, and other foolish trifles at the people, which light demeanour of a king was much discommended and jeasted at.[4] And when these yoong gentlemen came againe into England, they were all French, in eating, drinking, and apparell, yea, and in French vices and brags, so that all the estates of England were by them laughed at: the ladies and gentlewomen were dispraised, so that nothing by them was praised, but if it were after the French turne, which after turned them to displesure, as you shall heare. . . .

[852/1/66] After this feast[5] ended, the king came to Richmond, and so to Greenewich, and there laie all Maie. In which moneth the kings councell secretlie communed togither of the kings gentlenesse and liberalitie to all persons: by the which they perceived that certeine yoong men in his privie chamber, not regarding his estate or degree, were so familiar and homelie with him, that they forgat themselves. Which things although the king of his gentle nature suffered, and not rebuked nor reprooved it: yet the kings councell thought it not meet to be suffered for the kings honour, and

---

[1] *In margin:* 'The bishops booke of his privat affaires unadvisedlie delivered in steed of the kings.'

[2] *In margin:* 'The bishops owne booke disadvantageable to himselfe.' III.2.125–9.

[3] *In margin:* 'The bishop dieth of a sorowfull and pensive conceipt.'

[4] *In margin:* 'The light and misliked demeanour of diverse yoong gentlemen of England & the French king.' I.3.1–41.

[5] To celebrate the election of Charles V as Emperor.

therefore they all togither came to the king, beseeching him to have more regard to his royaltie.[1]

To whome the king answered, that he had chosen them of his councell, both for the maintenance of his honour, and for the defense of all things that might blemish the same: wherefore if they saw anie about him misuse themselves, he committed it unto their reformation. Then the kings councell caused the lord chamberleine to call before them diverse of the privie chamber, which had beene in the French court, and banished them the court for diverse considerations, laieng nothing particularlie to their charges, & they that had offices were commanded to go to their offices. Which discharge out of court greeved sore the hearts of these yoong men, which were called the kings minions.

[852/2/66] In the moneth of November [1520] the king came from Lambeth to Westminster hall, and so to the Starchamber,[2] and there were brought before him the lord Ogle, the lord Howard, sir Matthew Browne, sir William Bulmer, and John Scot of Camerwell, for diverse riots, misdemeanors, & offenses by them committed: but the king speciallie rebuked sir William Bulmer knight, bicause he being his servant sworne, refused the kings service, and became servant to the duke of Buckingham[3]: yet at length upon his humble craving of mercie, still kneeling on his knees before his grace, the king pardoned him his offense: and likewise he pardoned the lord Howard, and sir Matthew Browne, their offenses: but bicause the lord Ogles matter concerned murther, he remitted him to the common law. . . .

[A meeting arranged between Henry and Frances I.]

[853/1/11] The French king desirous to continue the friendship latelie begun betwixt him and the king of England, made meanes unto the cardinall, that they might in some convenient place come to an interview togither, that he might have further knowledge of king Henrie, and likewise king Henrie of him. But the fame went that the cardinall desired greatlie, of himselfe, that the two kings might meet, who mesuring by his will what was convenient, thought it should make much with his glorie, if in France also at some high assemblie of noble men, he should be seene in his vaine pompe and shew of dignitie[4]: hee therefore breaketh with the king of that matter, declaring how honourable, necessarie, and convenient

---

[1] *In margin:* 'The kings affablenesse & familiaritie with the inferior sort of people grudged at of the councell.' I.3.42–3.

[2] *In margin:* 'The king sitteth in the Starchamber in judgement.'

[3] I.2.188–92. *F.* Blumer.

[4] *In margin:* 'Note the ambicious humor of the cardinal of Yorke.'

it should be for him to gratifie his friend therein, and thus with his persuasions the K. began to conceive an earnest desire to see the French king, and thereupon appointed to go over to Calis, and so in the marches of Guisnes to meet with him. . . .

[853/1/35] Herewith were letters written to all such lords, ladies, gentlemen, and gentlewomen, which should give their attendance on the king and queene, which incontinentlie put themselves in a readinesse after the most sumptuous sort. Also it was appointed that the king of England, & the French king, in a campe betweene Ard and Guisnes,[1] with eighteene aides, should in June next insuing abide all commers being gentlemen, at the tilt, at tourneie, and at barriers. . . .

[853/2/10] Moreover, now that it was concluded, that the kings of England and France should meet (as yee have heard) then both the kings committed the order and manner of their meeting, and how manie daies the same should continue, & what preheminence each should give to other, unto the cardinall of Yorke, which to set all things in a certeintie, made an instrument, conteining an order and direction concerning the premisses by him devised and appointed.[2] . . .

[855/2/1] The peeres of the realme receiving letters to prepare themselves to attend the king in this journie, and no apparant necessarie cause expressed, why nor wherefore; seemed to grudge, that such a costlie journie should be taken in hand to their importunate charges and expenses, without consent of the whole boord of the councell. But namelie the duke of Buckingham, being a man of a loftie courage, but not most liberall, sore repined that he should be at so great charges for his furniture foorth at this time, saieng: that he knew not for what cause so much monie should be spent about the sight of a vaine talke to be had, and communication to be ministred of things of no importance.[3] Wherefore he sticked not to saie, that it was an intollerable matter to obeie such a vile and importunate person.[4] The duke indeed could not abide the cardinall . . .

[855/2/21] Now such greevous words as the duke thus uttered against him, came to the cardinals eare; where upon he cast before hand all waies possible to have him in a trip, that he might cause him to leape headlesse. But bicause he doubted his freends, kinnesmen, and alies, and cheeflie the earle of Surrie lord admerall, which had married the dukes daughter, he thought good first to send him some whither out of the waie, least he might cast a trumpe in his

---

[1] I.1.6–7.   [2] I.1.45–51.   [3] I.1.83–7.
[4] I.1.52–7. Buckingham was present at the meeting. The play makes him absent, ill.

waie. There was great enimitie betwixt the cardinall and the earle, for that on a time, when the cardinall tooke upon him to checke the earle, he had like to have thrust his dagger into the cardinall.

At length there was occasion offered to him to compasse his purpose, by occasion of the earle of Kildare his comming out of Ireland. . . . Such accusations were framed against him . . . that he was committed to prison, and then by the cardinals good preferment the earle of Surrie was sent into Ireland as the kings deputie, in lieu of the said earle of Kildare, there to remaine rather as an exile, than as lieutenant to the king, even at the cardinals pleasure, as he himselfe well perceived.[1]

[855/2/73] Now in this meane while, the cardinall ceassed not to bring the duke out of the kings favour, by such forged tales, and contrived surmises, as he dailie put into the kings head: insomuch that (through the infelicitie of his fate) diverse accidents fell out to the advantage of the cardinall; which he not omitting, atchived the thing whereat he so studiouslie (for the satisfieng of his canckered & malicious stomach) laid full aime. Now it chanced that the duke comming to London with his traine of men, to attend the king into France, went before into Kent unto a manor place which he had there. And whilest he staid in that countrie till the king set forward, greevous complaints were exhibited to him by his farmars and tenants against Charles Knevet his surveiour, for such bribing as he had used there amongst them. Whereupon the duke tooke such displeasure against him, that he deprived him of his office, not knowing how that in so dooing he procured his owne destruction, as after appeared.[2]

[The Emperor visited England]

[856/1/58] Thus the emperour and his retinue, both of lords and ladies, kept their Whitsuntide with the king and queene of England, in the citie of Canturburie with all joy and solace. . . . The chiefe cause that mooved the emperour to come thus on land at this time, was to persuade that by word of mouth, which he had before done most earnestlie by letters; which was, that the king should not meet with the French king at anie interview: for he doubted least if the king of England & the French king should grow into some great friendship and faithfull bond of amitie, it might turne him to displeasure.[3]

But now that he perceived how the king was forward on his journie, he did what he could to procure, that no trust should be

[1] II.1.40-6; III,2.260-5.   [2] I.2.171-6.   [3] I.1.176-83.

committed to the faire words of the Frenchmen[1]: and that if it were possible, the great friendship that was now in breeding betwixt the two kings, might be dissolved. And forsomuch as he knew the lord cardinall to be woone with rewards, as a fish with a bait: he bestowed on him great gifts, and promised him much more, so that hee would be his friend, and helpe to bring his purpose to passe. The cardinall not able to susteine the least assault by force of such rewards as he presentlie received, and of such large promises as on the emperours behalfe were made to him, promised to the emperour, that he would so use the matter, as his purpose should be sped.[2] . . .

[The Field of the Cloth of Gold.]

[858/1/23]   The king of England had given unto the said cardinall full authoritie, power, and libertie, to affirme and confirme, bind and unbind, whatsoever should be in question betweene him and the French king: and the like authoritie, power, and libertie, did the French king by his sufficient letters patents, grant to the same cardinall, which was accepted to be a signe of great love, that he should commit so great a trust unto the king of Englands subject.[3] The daie of the meeting was appointed to be on the thursdaie the seaventh of June, upon which daie the two kings met in the vale of Andren,[4] accompanied with such a number of the nobilitie of both realmes, so richlie appointed in apparell, and costlie jewels, as chaines, collars of SS, & other the like ornaments to set foorth their degrees and estates, that a woonder it was to behold and view them in their order and roomes, which everie man kept according to his appointment.

The two kings meeting in the field, either saluted other in most loving wise, first on horssebacke, and after alighting on foot eftsoones imbraced with courteous words, to the great rejoising of the beholders[5]: and after they had thus saluted ech other, they went both togither into a rich tent of cloath of gold, there set up for the purpose, in the which they passed the time in pleasant talke, banketting, and loving devises, till it drew toward the evening, and then departed for that night, the one to Guisnes, the other to Ard. At this meeting of the two kings in open sight, I then well perceived (saith *Hall*) the habillements royall of the French king. . . .

[859/1/7]   Thus with honour and noble courage these two noble kings with their companies entered into the field, and them

---

[1] *In margin:* 'The emperor laboureth to hinder the purposed interview.'
[2] I.1.183–90.
[3] *In margin:* 'Great credit committed to the cardinall by both the kings.'
[4] *In margin:* 'The interview of the two kings in the Vale of Andren.' I.1.7.
[5] *In margin:* 'The two kings enter into the field.' I.1.8–12.

presented unto the queenes. After reverence doone, they rode
round about the tilt, and so tooke their places appointed, abiding
the answers. . . . [The tilting is described at length.]

[859/2/31]   Thus course after course ech with other, his counter
partie did right valiantlie: but the two kings surmounted all the rest
in prowesse and valiantnesse.[1] . . .

[860/2/74]   On mondaie, the eighteenth of June, was such an
hideous storme of wind and weather, that manie conjectured it did
prognosticate trouble and hatred shortlie after to follow betweene
princes.[2] [Henry afterwards met the Emperor at Calais.]

[862/2/52] [1521] the cardinall boiling in hatred against the duke
of Buckingham, & thirsting for his bloud, devised to make Charles
Knevet, that had beene the dukes surveior, and put from him (as ye
have heard) an instrument to bring the duke to destruction.[3] This
Knevet being had in examination before the cardinall, disclosed all
the dukes life. And first he uttered, that the duke was accustomed by
waie of talke, to saie, how he meant so to use the matter, that he
would atteine to the crowne, if king Henrie chanced to die without
issue: & that he had talke and conference of that matter on a time
with George Nevill, lord of Aburgavennie, unto whome he had
given his daughter in marriage; and also that he threatned to punish
the cardinall for his manifold misdooings, being without cause his
mortall enimie.[4]

The cardinall having gotten that which he sought for, incouraged,
comforted, and procured Knevet, with manie comfortable words and
great promises, that he should with a bold spirit and countenance
object and laie these things to the dukes charge, with more if he
knew it when time required.[5] Then Knevet partlie provoked with
desire to be revenged, and partlie mooved with hope of reward,
openlie confessed, that the duke had once fullie determined to devise
meanes how to make the king away, being brought into a full hope
that he should be king, by a vaine prophesie which one Nicholas
Hopkins, a monke of an house of the Chartreux order beside
Bristow, called Henton,[6] sometime his confessor had opened unto
him.

The cardinall having thus taken the examination of Knevet, went
unto the king, and declared unto him, that his person was in danger

---

[1] I.1.33–6.

[2] *In margin:* 'A great and tempestuous wind prognosticating trouble.' I.1.89–94.

[3] *In margin:* 'The cardinall deviseth the destruction of the duke of Buckingham.'

[4] I.2.132–8.

[5] *In margin:* 'The cardinall imboldeneth Knevet against the duke.'

[6] I.2.146–50. *F. has* Nicholas Henton *here,* Hopkins *at* II.1.22. Henton was the
priory.

by such traitorous purpose, as the duke of Buckingham had conceived in his heart, and shewed how that now there is manifest tokens of his wicked pretense: wherefore, he exhorted the king to provide for his owne suertie with speed.[1] The king hearing the accusation, inforced to the uttermost by the cardinall, made this answer; If the duke have deserved to be punished, let him have according to his deserts. The duke herupon was sent for up to London, & at his comming thither, was streightwaies attached, and brought to the Tower by sir Henrie Marneie, capteine of the gard, the sixteenth of Aprill.[2] There was also attached the foresaid Chartreux monke, maister John de la Car *alias* de la Court, the dukes confessor, and sir Gilbert Perke priest, the dukes chancellor.[3]

After the apprehension of the duke, inquisitions were taken in diverse shires of England of him; so that by the knights and gentlemen, he was indicted of high treason, for certeine words spoken (as before ye have heard) by the same duke at Blechinglie, to the lord of Aburgavennie[4]: and therewith was the same lord attached for concelement,[5] and so likewise was the lord Montacute, and both led to the Tower.

[The Duke was accused of preparing revolt, of taking notice of Hopkins's prophecy 'that before Christmas next there should be a change, and that the duke should have the rule and governement of all England.'[6] Other charges follow.]

[864/1/43] He said further at the same time to the said Gilbert,[7] that what so ever was doone by the kings father, was doone by wrong. And still he murmured against all that the king then presentlie reigning did.

[864/1/64] And furthermore, the same duke on the fourth of November, in the eleventh yere of the kings reigne, at east Greenwich in the countie of Kent, said unto one Charles Knevet esquier, after that the king had reprooved the duke for reteining William Bulmer knight into his service, that if he had perceived that he should have beene committed to the Tower (as he doubted hee should have beene) hee would have so wrought, that the principall dooers therein should not have had cause of great rejoising: for he would have plaied the part which his father intended to have put in practice against king Richard the third at Salisburie, who made earnest sute to have come unto the presence of the same king

---

[1] *In margin:* 'The cardinall accuseth the duke of Buckingham to the king.' As in I.2.140-2.   [2] I.1.198-209.   [3] I.1.216-19. *F has* Pecke.

[4] *In margin:* 'The duke of Buckingham indicted of treason.'

[5] I.1.211-16.   [6] I.2.169-71.

[7] This was 'his chancellor Robert Gilbert chapleine'. Hol. may confuse him with Gilbert Perke.

Richard[1]: which sute if he might have obteined, he having a knife secretlie about him, would have thrust it into the bodie of king Richard, as he had made semblance to kneele down before him. And in speaking these words, he maliciouslie laid his hand upon his dagger, and said, that if he were so evill used, he would doo his best to accomplish his pretensed purpose, swearing to confirme his word by the bloud of our Lord.[2]

Beside all this, the same duke the tenth of Maie, in the twelfe yeare of the kings reigne, at London in a place called the Rose, within the parish of saint Laurence Poultnie in Canwike street ward, demanded of the said Charles Knevet esquier, what was the talke amongest the Londoners concerning the kings journeie beyond the seas? And the said Charles told him, that manie stood in doubt of that journeie, least the Frenchmen meant some deceit towards the king. Whereto the duke answered, that it was to be feared, least it would come to passe, according to the words of a certeine holie moonke.[3] For there is (saith he) a Chartreux moonke, that diverse times hath sent to me, willing me to send unto him my chancellor: and I did send unto him John de la Court my chapleine, unto whome he would not declare anie thing, till de la Court had sworne unto him to keepe all things secret, and to tell no creature living what hee should heare of him, except it were to me.[4]

And then the said moonke told de la Court, that neither the king nor his heires should prosper, and that I should indevour my selfe to purchase the good wils of the communaltie of England; for I the same duke and my bloud should prosper, and have the rule of the realme of England.[5] Then said Charles Knevet; The moonke maie be deceived through the divels illusion: and that it was evill to meddle with such matters. Well (said the duke) it cannot hurt me, and so (saith the indictment) the duke seemed to rejoise in the moonks woords.[6] And further, at the same time, the duke told the said Charles, that if the king had miscaried now in his last sicknesse, he would have chopped off the heads of the cardinall, of sir Thomas Lovell knight, and of others; and also said, that he had rather die for it, than to be used as he had beene.[7]

Moreover, on the tenth daie of September, in the said eleventh yere of this kings reigne, at Blechinglie, in the countie of Surrie, walking in the gallerie there with George Nevill knight, lord

---

[1] *In margin:* 'See the historie of Richard the third, pag. 744.' Cf. Hall, *supra*, Vol. III, 284. *R3* V.1.1–2.   [2] I.2.193–209.

[3] *In margin:* 'The duke discovereth the secrecie of all the matter to his owne undooing.' I.2.151–60, 'Spoke by a holy monk.'

[4] I.2.160–7.   [5] I.2.168–71.

[6] *In margin:* 'But the end of that joy was heavinesse.'   [7] I.2.177–86.

Aburgavennie, the duke murmuring against the kings councellors, and there governement, said unto the said George; that if the king died, he would have the rule of the realme in spite of who so ever said the contrarie; and withall said, that if the said lord Aburgavennie would say, that the duke had spoken such words, he would fight with him, and lay his sword upon his pate: & this he bound up with manie great oths. These were the speciall articles & points comprised in the indictment, and laid to his charge: but how trulie, or in what sort prooved, I have not further to say, either in accusing or excusing him, other than as I find in *Hall* and *Polydor*, whose words in effect, I have thought to impart to the reader, and without anie parciall wresting of the same either to or fro.

Saving that (I trust) I maie without offense saie, that (as the rumour then went) the cardinall chieflie procured the death of this noble man, no lesse favoured and beloved of the people of this realme in that season, than the cardinall himselfe was hated and envied.[1] Which thing caused the dukes fall the more to be pitied and lamented, sith he was the man of all other, that chieflie went about to crosse the cardinall in his lordlie demeanor, & headie proceedings. But to the purpose. Shortlie after that the duke had beene indicted (as before ye have heard) he was arreigned in Westminster hall,[2] before the duke of Norffolke, being made by the kings letters patents high steward of England, to accomplish the high cause of appeale of the peere or peeres of the realme, and to discerne and judge the cause of the peeres.

[865/1/20] When the lords had taken their place, the duke was brought to the barre, and upon his arreignement pleaded not guiltie, and put himselfe upon his peeres. Then was his indictment read, which the duke denied to be true, and (as he was an eloquent man) alledged reasons to falsifie the indictment; pleading the matter for his owne justification verie pithilie and earnestlie. The kings attourneie against the dukes reasons alledged the examinations, confessions, and proofes of witnesses.[3]

The duke desired that the witnesses might bee brought foorth. And then came before him Charles Knevet, Perke, de la Court, & Hopkins the monke of the priorie of the Charterhouse beside Bath, which like a false hypocrite had induced the duke to the treason with his false forged prophesies.[4] Diverse presumptions and accusations were laid unto him by Charles Knevet, which he would faine have covered. The depositions were read, & the deponents delivered as

---

[1] II.1.50-3.
[2] *In margin:* 'The duke of Buckingham arreigned at Westminster.' II.1.11-14.
[3] II.1.15-18. [4] II.1.19-23.

prisoners to the officers of the Tower. [The peers and judges conferred.]

[865/1/47] Then said the duke of Norffolke to the duke of Suffolke; What say you of sir Edward duke of Buckingham touching the high treasons? The duke of Suffolke answered; He is giltie: & so said the marques and all the other earls and lords. Thus was this prince duke of Buckingham found giltie of high treason, by a duke, a marques, seven earles, & twelve barons.[1] The duke was brought to the barre sore chafing, and swet marvellouslie; & after he had made his reverence, he paused a while.[2] The duke of Norffolke as judge said; Sir Edward, you have heard how you be indicted of high treason, you pleaded thereto not giltie, putting your selfe to the peeres of the realme, which have found you giltie. Then the duke of Norffolke wept and said; You shall be led to the kings prison, and there laid on a hardle, and so drawne to the place of execution, and there be hanged, cut downe alive, your members cut off and cast into the fire, your bowels burnt before you, your head smitten off, and your bodie quartered and divided at the kings will, and God have mercie on your soule, Amen.[3]

The duke of Buckingham said, My lord of Norffolke, you have said as a traitor should be said unto, but I was never anie: but my lords I nothing maligne for that you have doone to me, but the eternall God forgive you my death, and I doo: I shall never sue to the king for life, howbeit he is a gratious prince, and more grace may come from him than I desire. I desire you my lords and all my fellowes to pray for me. Then was the edge of the axe turned towards him, and he led into a barge. Sir Thomas Lovell desired him to sit on the cushins and carpet ordeined for him. He said nay; for when I went to Westminster I was duke of Buckingham, now I am but Edward Bohune the most caitife of the world.[4] Thus they landed at the Temple, where received him sir Nicholas Vawse[5] & sir William Sands baronets, and led him through the citie, who desired ever the people to pray for him, of whome some wept and lamented, and said: This is the end of evill life, God forgive him, he was a proud prince, it is pitie that hee behaved him so against his king and liege lord, whome God preserve. Thus about foure of the clocke he was brought as a cast man to the Tower.

On fridaie the seventeenth daie of Maie, about eleven of the clocke, this duke of Buckingham, earle of Hereford, Stafford, and Northampton, with a great power was delivered to John Keime &

---

[1] *In margin:* 'The duke of Buckingham convinced of high treason.' II.1.26–7.
[2] II.1.31–6.
[3] *In margin:* 'The duke of Buckinghams judgement pronounced by the duke of Norffolke.'   [4] Cf. II.1.97–106   [5] Vaux. II.1.54 *s.d.* and 96.

John Skevington shiriffes, who led him to the scaffold on Tower hill, where he said he had offended the kings grace through negligence and lacke of grace, and desired all noble men to beware by him, and all men to pray for him, and that he trusted to die the kings true man.[1] Thus meekelie with an axe he tooke his death.[2] Then the Augustine friers tooke his bodie, and head, and buried them. Alas that ever the grace of truth was withdrawne from so noble a man, that he was not to his king in allegiance as he ought to have beene! Such is the end of ambition, the end of false prophesies, the end of evill life, and evill counsell; but speciallie the end of malice, which grew to so huge and monstruous a fire in the hautie hart of the proud cardinall, that nothing could asswage it, but the bloud of this noble duke, against whome he had procured this processe in judgement ended with the execution of death: the torments whereof were (as it seemeth by the sentence of the judge) much diminished through the mercie of the king. . . .

[A note on Buckingham's father, and himself, as high
constables of England.]

[869/2/66]   Henrie Stafford,[3] whome our chronicles doo in manie places corruptlie terme Edward, was sonne to Humfrie earle Stafford, & was high constable of England, and duke of Buckingham. This man raising warre against Richard the third usurping the crowne, was in the first yeare of the reigne of the said Richard, being the yeare of Christ 1483, betraied by his man Humfrie Banaster (to whome being in distresse he fled for succour) and brought to Richard the third then lieng at Salisburie, where the said duke confessing all the conspiracie, was beheaded without arreignement or judgement, upon the second of November, in the said yere of our redemption 1483. . . .

[870/1/13]   Edward Stafford sonne to Henrie duke of Buckingham, being also duke of Buckingham after the death of his father was constable of England, earle of Hereford, Stafford, and Northhampton, being in the first yeare of Henrie the seventh, in the yeare of our redemption 1485, restored to his fathers dignities and possessions. He is tearmed in the books of the law in the said thirteenth yeare of Henrie the eight (where his arreignement is liberallie set downe) to be the floure & mirror of all courtesie.[4] This man (as before is touched) was by Henrie the seventh restored to his fathers

---

[1] Cf. II.1.55–91.
[2] *In margin:* 'The duke of Buckingham beheaded on a scaffold at Tower hill.'
[3] *In margin:* 'Henrie Stafford.' The Buckingham of *R3*.
[4] II.1.53. 'The mirror of all courtesy.'

inheritance, in recompense of the losse of his fathers life, taken awaie (as before is said) by the usurping king Richard the third.

[Holinshed describes the capture of the French king by the Emperor in 1525, his imprisonment in Spain, and the terms of his release. Henry VIII had intended to invade France in support of the Emperor, who had promised to marry the Princess Mary, but in fact wished to marry Isabella of Portugal.]

[891/1/31] The king being determined thus to make wars in France, & to passe the sea himselfe in person, his councell considered that above all things great treasure and plentie of monie must needes be provided. Wherfore, by the cardinall there was devised strange commissions, and sent in the end of March into everie shire, and commissioners appointed, and privie instructions sent to them how they should proceed in their sittings, and order the people to bring them to their purpose: which was, that the sixt part of everie mans substance should be paid in monie or plate to the king without delaie, for the furniture of his war.[1] Hereof followed such cursing, weeping, and exclamation against both king & cardinall, that pitie it was to heare. And to be breefe, notwithstanding all that could be said or doone, forged or devised by the commissioners to persuade the people to this contribution, the same would not be granted. . . .

[891/2/4] In Essex the people would not assemble before the commissioners in no houses, but in open places, and in Huntington-shire diverse resisted the commisioners, and would not suffer them to sit, which were apprehended and sent to the Fleet.[2] The duke of Suffolke sitting in commission about this subsidie in Suffolke, per-suaded by courteous meanes the rich clothiers to assent therto: but when they came home, and went about to discharge and put from them their spinners, carders, fullers, weavers, and other artificers, which they kept in worke afore time, the people began to assemble in companies. Whereof when the duke was advertised, he com-manded the constables that everie mans harnes should be taken from him. But when that was knowne, then the rage of the people increased, railing openlie on the duke, and sir Robert Drurie, and threatned them with death, and the cardinall also.[3] And herewith there assembled togither after the maner of rebels foure thousand men of Lanam, Sudberie, Hadleie, and other townes thereabouts, which put themselves in harnesse, and rang the bels alarme, and began still to assemble in great number. . . .

[1] *In margin:* 'The sixt part of everie mans substance demanded.' I.2.18–108.

[2] *In margin:* 'The commissioners for the tax resisted.'

[3] *In margin:* 'A rebellion in Suffolke by the grievousnesse of the subsidie.' I.2.29–37.

[The King called a Council to inquire into the unrest.]

[891/2/68] ... he willed to know by whose meanes the commissions were so streictlie given foorth, to demand the sixt part of everie mans goods.

The cardinall excused himselfe, and said, that when it was mooved in councell how to levie monie to the kings use; the kings councell, and namelie the judges, said, that he might lawfullie demand anie summe by commission, and that by the consent of the whole councell it was doone,[1] and tooke God to witnes that he never desired the hinderance of the commons, but like a true councellor devised how to inrich the king. The king indeed was much offended that his commons were thus intreated, & thought it touched his honor, that his councell should attempt such a doubtfull matter in his name, and to be denied both of the spiritualtie and temporaltie. Therefore he would no more of that trouble, but caused letters to be sent into all shires, that the matter should no further be talked of: & he pardoned all them that had denied the demand openlie or secretlie.[2] The cardinall, to deliver himselfe of the evill will of the commons, purchased by procuring & advancing of this demand, affirmed, and caused it to be bruted abrode, that through his intercession the king had pardoned and released all things.[3]

[The King's marriage brought in question, 1527.]

[897/1/65] There rose a secret brute in London that the kings confessor doctor Longland, and diverse other great clerks had told the king that the marriage betweene him and the ladie Katharine, late wife to his brother prince Arthur was not lawfull[4]: whereupon the king should sue a divorse, and marrie the duchesse of Alanson sister to the French king at the towne of Calis this summer: and that the vicount Rochford had brought with him the picture of the said ladie. The king was offended with those tales, and sent for sir Thomas Seimor mayor of the citie of London, secretlie charging him to see that the people ceassed from such talke.[5] ...

[906/2/28] The truth is, that whether this doubt was first mooved by the cardinall, or by the said Longland, being the kings confessor, the king was not onelie brought in doubt, whether it was a lawfull marriage or no; but also determined to have the case examined, cleered, and adjudged by learning, law, and sufficient

---

[1] *In margin:* 'The cardinall of Yorke excuseth himselfe touching the streict commission for the tax.' I.2.68–88.

[2] I.2.98–102.   [3] I.2.103–8.

[4] *In margin:* 'The kings marriage brought in question.' II.1.147–9.

[5] II.1.150–3.

authoritie. The cardinall verelie was put in most blame for this scruple now cast into the kings conscience, for the hate he bare to the emperor, bicause he would not grant to him the archbishoprike of Toledo, for the which he was a suter.[1] And therefore he did not onlie procure the king of England to joine in freendship with the French king, but also sought a divorse betwixt the king and the queene, that the king might have had in marriage the duchesse of Alanson, sister unto the French king: and (as some have thought) he travelled in that matter with the French king at Amiens, but the duchesse would not give eare thereunto.

But howsoever it came about, that the king was thus troubled in conscience concerning his mariage, this followed, that like a wise & sage prince, to have the doubt cleerelie remooved, he called togither the best learned of the realme, which were of severall opinions. Wherfore he thought to know the truth by indifferent judges, least peradventure the Spaniards, and other also in favour of the queene would saie, that his owne subjects were not indifferent judges in this behalfe.[2] And therefore he wrote his cause to Rome, and also sent to all the universities in Italie and France, and to the great clearkes of all christendome, to know their opinions, and desired the court of Rome to send into his realme a legat, which should be indifferent, and of a great and profound judgement, to heare the cause debated. At whose request the whole consistorie of the college of Rome sent thither Laurence Campeius, a preest cardinall, a man of great wit and experience,[3] which was sent hither before in the tenth yeare of this king, as yee have heard, and with him was joined in commission the cardinall of Yorke and legat of England.

[907/1/27] The place where the cardinals should sit to heare the cause of matrimonie betwixt the king and the queene, was ordeined to be at the Blacke friers in London,[4] where in the great hall was preparation made of seats, tables, and other furniture, according to such a solemne session and royall apparance. The court was platted in tables and benches in manner of a consistorie, one seat raised higher for the judges to sit in.[5] Then as it were in the midst of the said judges aloft above them three degrees high, was a cloth of estate hanged, with a chaire royall under the same, wherein sat the

---

[1] *In margin:* 'Why the cardinall was suspected to be against the marriage.' II.1. 153-67. Katharine was the Emperor Charles V's aunt.

[2] *In margin:* 'The king is desirous to be resolved by the opinions of the learned touching his marriage.'

[3] *In margin:* 'Cardinall Campeius sent into England.' II.1.159-61.

[4] II.3.137-8.

[5] *In margin:* 'The maner of the session, everie personage of account in his place.' Cf. II.4. *s.d.* which is supplemented from Hol. 921 &c; *inf.* 478.

king; and besides him, some distance from him sat the queene, and under the judges feet sat the scribes and other officers: the cheefe scribe was doctor Steevens, and the caller of the court was one Cooke of Winchester.

Then before the king and the judges within the court sat the archbishop of Canturburie Warham, and all the other bishops. Then stood at both ends within the counsellors learned in the spirituall laws, as well the kings as the queenes. The doctors of law for the king (whose names yee have heard before) had their convenient roomes. Thus was the court furnished. The judges commanded silence whilest their commission was read, both to the court and to the people assembled. That doone the scribes commanded the crier to call the king by the name of king Henrie of England, come into the court, &c.[1] With that the king answered and said, Heere. Then called he the queene by the name of Katharine queene of England come into the court, &c. Who made no answer, but rose out of hir chaire.[2]

And bicause shee could not come to the king directlie, for the distance severed betweene them, shee went about by the court, and came to the king, kneeling downe at his feet, to whome she said in effect as followeth[3]: Sir (quoth she) I desire you to doo me justice and right, and take some pitie upon me, for I am a poore woman, and a stranger, borne out of your dominion, having heere no indifferent counsell, & lesse assurance of freendship. Alas sir, what have I offended you, or what occasion of displeasure have I shewed you, intending thus to put me from you after this sort? I take God to my judge, I have beene to you a true & humble wife, ever conformable to your will and pleasure, that never contraried or gainesaid any thing thereof, and being alwaies contented with all things wherein you had any delight, whether little or much, without grudge or displeasure, I loved for your sake all them whome you loved, whether they were my freends or enimies.

I have beene your wife these twentie yeares and more, & you have had by me diverse children. If there be anie just cause that you can alleage against me, either of dishonestie, or matter lawfull to put me from you; I am content to depart to my shame and rebuke: and if there be none, then I praie you to let me have justice at your hand. The king your father was in his time of excellent wit,[4] and the king of Spaine my father Ferdinando was reckoned one of the wisest

---

[1] *In margin:* 'The king and queene called into the court.'

[2] II.4.10 s.d.

[3] *In margin:* 'Queene Katharines lamentable and pithie speech in presence of the court.' II.4.11–55 follows Hol. closely.

[4] *In margin:* 'The queene justifieth the mariage.'

princes that reigned in Spaine manie yeares before. It is not to be doubted, but that they had gathered as wise counsellors unto them of everie realme, as to their wisedoms they thought meet, who deemed the marriage betweene you and me good and lawfull, &c. Wherefore, I humblie desire you to spare me, untill I may know what counsell my freends in Spaine will advertise me to take, and if you will not, then your pleasure be fulfilled. With that she arose up, making a lowe curtesie to the king, and departed from thence.

The king being advertised that shee was readie to go out of the house, commanded the crier to call hir againe, who called hir by these words; Katharine queene of England, come into the court. With that (quoth maister Griffith) Madame, you be called againe.[1] On on (quoth she) it maketh no matter, I will not tarrie, go on your waies. And thus she departed,[2] without anie further answer at that time, or anie other, and never would appeare after in anie court. The king perceiving she was departed, said these words in effect: For as much (quoth he) as the queene is gone, I will in hir absence declare to you all, that shee hath beene to me as true, as obedient, and as conformable a wife, as I would wish or desire. She hath all the vertuous qualities that ought to be in a woman of hir dignitie, or in anie other of a baser estate, she is also surelie a noble woman borne, hir conditions will well declare the same.[3]

With that quoth Wolseie the cardinall: Sir, I most humblie require your highnesse, to declare before all this audience, whether I have beene the cheefe and first moover of this matter unto your majestie or no, for I am greatlie suspected heerein.[4] My lord cardinall (quoth the king) I can well excuse you in this matter, marrie (quoth he) you have beene rather against me in the tempting heereof, than a setter forward or moover of the same. The speciall cause that mooved me unto this matter, was a certeine scrupulositie that pricked my conscience, upon certeine words spoken at a time when it was, by the bishop of Baion the French ambassador, who had beene hither sent, upon the debating of a marriage to be concluded betweene our daughter the ladie Marie, and the duke of Orleance, second son to the king of France.

Upon the resolution and determination whereof, he desired respit to advertise the king his maister thereof, whether our daughter Marie should be legitimate in respect of this my marriage with this woman, being sometimes my brothers wife. Which words once con-

---

[1] *In margin:* 'The queene departing out of the court is called againe.' In *H8* she bandies words with Wolsey, II.4.67–119; cf. *inf.* 469.

[2] II.4.122–31.   [3] II.4.131–41.

[4] *In margin:* 'The cardinall requireth to have that declared which was well enough known.' II.4.142–53.

ceived within the secret bottome of my conscience, ingendered such a scrupulous doubt, that my conscience was incontinentlie accombred, vexed, and disquieted[1]; whereby I thought my selfe to be greatlie in danger of Gods indignation. Which appeared to be (as me seemed) the rather, for that he sent us no issue male: and all such issues male as my said wife had by me, died incontinent after they came into the world, so that I doubted the great displeasure of God in that behalfe.

Thus my conscience being tossed in the waves of a scrupulous mind, and partlie in despaire to have anie other issue than I had alredie by this ladie now my wife, it behooved me further to consider the state of this realme, and the danger it stood in for lacke of a prince to succeed me, I thought it good in release of the weightie burthen of my weake conscience, & also the quiet estate of this worthie relme, to attempt the law therin, whether I may lawfullie take another wife more lawfullie,[2] by whome God may send me more issue, in case this my first copulation was not good, without anie carnall concupiscence, and not for anie displeasure or misliking of the queenes person and age, with whome I would be as well contented to continue, if our mariage may stand with the laws of God, as with anie woman alive.

In this point consisteth all this doubt that we go about now to trie, by the learning, wisedome, and judgement of you our prelats and pastors of all this our realme and dominions now heere assembled for that purpose; to whose conscience & learning I have committed the charge and judgement: according to the which I will (God willing) be right well content to submit my selfe, and for my part obeie the same.[3] Wherein, after that I perceived my conscience so doubtfull, I mooved it in confession to you my lord of Lincolne then ghostlie father. And for so much as then you your selfe were in some doubt, you mooved me to aske the counsell of all these my lords: whereupon I mooved you my lord of Canturburie, first to have your licence, in as much as you were metropolitane, to put this matter in question, and so I did of all you my lords: to which you granted under your seales, heere to be shewed. That is truth, quoth the archbishop of Canturburie. After that the king rose up, and the court was adjorned untill another daie.

Heere is to be noted, that the queene in presence of the whole court most greevouslie accused the cardinall of untruth, deceit,

---

[1] *In margin:* 'The king confesseth that the sting of conscience made him mislike this mariage.' II.4.153–84.

[2] *In margin:* 'The state of the question.' II.4.184–99.

[3] *In margin:* 'The king submitteth himselfe to the censures of the learned in this case of divorse.' II.4.200–20.

wickednesse, & malice, which had sowne dissention betwixt hir and
the king hir husband[1]; and therefore openlie protested, that she did
utterlie abhorre, refuse, and forsake such a judge, as was not onelie a
most malicious enimie to hir, but also a manifest adversarie to all
right and justice, and there with did she appeale unto the pope,
committing hir whole cause to be judged of him.[2]

[The Council alleged that the King's marriage was unlawful
because the Queen's marriage with his brother had been consum-
mated. She denied this, so 'no man knew the truth'.]

[908/1/67] And thus this court passed from sessions to sessions,
and daie to daie, till at certeine of their sessions the king sent the two
cardinals to the queene (who was then in Bridewell) to persuade
with hir by their wisdoms, and to advise hir to surrender the whole
matter into the kings hands by hir owne consent & will, which should
be much better to hir honour, than to stand to the triall of law, and
thereby to be condemned, which should seeme much to hir dishonour.[3]

The cardinals being in the queenes chamber of presence, the
gentleman usher advertised the queene that the cardinals were come
to speake with hir.[4] With that she rose up, & with a skeine of white
thred about hir necke, came into hir chamber of presence, where the
cardinals were attending. At whose comming, quoth she, What is
your plesure with me? If it please your grace (quoth cardinall
Wolseie) to go into your privie chamber, we will shew you the cause
of our comming. My lord (quoth she) if yee have anie thing to saie,
speake it openlie before all these folke, for I feare nothing that yee
can saie against me, but that I would all the world should heare and
see it, and therefore speake your mind. Then began the cardinall to
speake to hir in Latine. Naie good my lord (quoth she) speake to me
in English.[5]

Forsooth (quoth the cardinall) good madame, if it please you, we
come both to know your mind how you are disposed to doo in this
matter betweene the king and you, and also to declare secretlie our
opinions and counsell unto you: which we doo onelie for verie zeale
and obedience we beare unto your grace. My lord (quoth she) I
thanke you for your good will, but to make you answer in your
request I cannot so suddenlie,[6] for I was set among my maids at

---

[1] *In margin:* 'The queene accuseth cardinall Wolsie.' II.4.66–116.

[2] *In margin:* 'She appeleth to the pope.' II.4.116–19.   [3] III.1.92–6.

[4] *In margin:* 'Queene Katharine and the cardinals have communication in hir
privie chamber.' This sets the scene for III.1.   [5] III.1.23–49.

[6] *In margin:* 'The queene refuseth to make sudden answer to so weightie a matter
as the divorse.' III.1.49–78.

worke, thinking full little of anie such matter, wherein there needeth
a longer deliberation, and a better head than mine to make answer:
for I need counsell in this case which toucheth me so neere, & for
anie counsell or freendship that I can find in England, they are not
for my profit. What thinke you my lords, will anie Englishman counsell me, or be freend to me against the K. pleasure that is his subject?
Naie forsooth. And as for my counsell in whom I will put my trust,
they be not here, they be in Spaine in my owne countrie.

And my lords, I am a poore woman, lacking wit, to answer to anie
such noble persons of wisedome as you be, in so weightie a matter,
therefore I praie you be good to me poore woman, destitute of
freends here in a forren region,[1] and your counsell also I will be
glad to heare.[2] And therewith she tooke the cardinall by the hand and
led him into hir privie chamber with the other cardinall, where they
tarried a season talking with the queene. Which communication
ended, they departed to the king, making to him relation of hir
talke. Thus this case went forward from court to court, till it came to
judgement, so that everie man expected that judgment would be
given the next day.[3] At which daie the king came thither, and set
him downe in a chaire within a doore, in the end of the gallerie
(which opened directlie against the judgement seat) to heare the
judgement given, at which time all their proceedings were red in
Latine.

That doone, the kings councell at the barre called for judgement.
With that (quoth cardinall *Campeius*) I will not give judgement till I
have made relation to the pope of all our proceedings,[4] whose counsell and commandement in this case I will observe: the case is verie
doubtfull, and also the partie defendant will make no answer here,
but dooth rather appeale from us, supposing that we be not indifferent. Wherfore I will adjourne this court for this time, according
to the order of the court of Rome. And with that the court was
dissolved, and no more doone. This protracting of the conclusion of
the matter, king Henrie tooke verie displeasantlie. Then cardinall
Campeius tooke his leave[5] of the king and nobilitie, and returned
towards Rome.[6]

---

[1] Her speeches in III.1.82–180 enlarge on this.   [2] III.1.181–4.

[3] *In margin:* 'The king & queenes matter commeth to judgement.'

[4] *In margin:* 'Cardinall Campeius refuseth to give judgement.' The play omits
this scene.   [5] III.2.56–8: 'hath ta'en no leave'.

[6] Here the dramatist probably consulted John Speed's *History of Great Britaine*,
1611: 'But whatsoever the cause was, that *Campius* denied his sentence for the
Divorce, certaine it was that Cardinal *Wolsey* fell likewise in great displeasure of the
King though he sought to excuse himselfe with want of sufficient authority: but
now his Sunne having passed the Meridian of his greatnesse, began by degrees
againe to decline, till lastly it set under the cloud of his fatall eclipse.

[The Fall of Wolsey.]

[908/2/70]   Whilest these things were thus in hand, the cardinall
of Yorke was advised that the king had set his affection upon a yoong
gentlewoman named Anne, the daughter of sir Thomas Bullen
vicount Rochford, which did wait upon the queene.[1] This was a
great griefe unto the cardinall, as he that perceived aforehand, that
the king would marie the said gentlewoman, if the divorse tooke
place. Wherfore he began with all diligence to disappoint that
match, which by reason of the misliking that he had to the woman,
he judged ought to be avoided more than present death. While the
matter stood in this state, and that the cause of the queene was to be
heard and judged at Rome, by reason of the appeale which by hir
was put in: the cardinall required the pope by letters and secret
messengers, that in anie wise he should defer the judgement of the
divorse, till he might frame the kings mind to his purpose.[2]

Howbeit he went about nothing so secretlie, but that the same
came to the kings knowledge,[3] who tooke so high displeasure with
such his cloked dissimulation, that he determined to abase his
degree, sith as an unthankefull person he forgot himselfe and his
dutie towards him that had so highlie advanced him to all honor
and dignitie. When the nobles of the realme perceived the cardinall
to be in displeasure, they began to accuse him of such offenses as they
knew might be proved against him, and thereof they made a booke
conteining certeine articles, to which diverse of the kings councell
set their hands.[4] The king understanding more plainlie by those
articles, the great pride, presumption, and covetousnesse of the
cardinall, was sore mooved against him; but yet kept his purpose
secret for a while. Shortlie after, a parlement was called to begin at
Westminster the third of November next insuing.

In the meane time the king, being informed that all those things
that the cardinall had doone by his power legantine within this
realme, were in the case of the premunire and provision, caused his
atturneie Christopher Hales to sue out a writ of premunire against

---

Formerly we have spoken of the rising of this man, who now being swoln so bigge
by the blasts of promotion, as the bladder not able to containe more greatnesse,
suddenly burst, and vented forth the winde of all former favours. Vaine-glorious he
was, in state, in dyet, and in rich furniture for house, and in prodigall intertaine-
ments, more like to a Prince then a Prelate. . . .' Cf. III.2.233–8 and 359–65.

[1] *In margin:* 'The kings affection and goodwill to the ladie Anne Bullen.'

[2] *In margin:* 'The secret working and dissimulation of cardinall Wolseie.'
III.2.30–7.

[3] *In margin:* 'The king conceiveth displeasure against the cardinall.' III.2.30–
7; 52–4.

[4] *In margin:* 'Articles exhibited against the cardinall.' Hence III.2.1–9.

him, in the which he licenced him to make his atturneie.[1] And further, the seventeenth of November the king sent the two dukes of Norffolke and Suffolke[2] to the cardinals place at Westminster, who went as they were commanded, and finding the cardinall there, they declared that the kings pleasure was that he should surrender up the great seale into their hands, and to depart simplie unto Asher, which was an house situat nigh unto Hampton court, belonging to the bishoprike of Winchester. The cardinall demanded of them their commission that gave them such authoritie, who answered againe, that they were sufficient commissioners, and had authoritie to doo no lesse by the kings mouth. Notwithstanding, he would in no wise agree in that behalfe, without further knowledge of their authoritie, saieng; that the great seale was delivered him by the kings person, to injoy the ministration thereof, with the roome of the chancellor for the terme of his life, whereof for his suertie he had the kings letters patents.[3]

This matter was greatlie debated betweene them with manie great words, in so much that the dukes were faine to depart againe without their purpose, and rode to Windsore to the king, and made report accordinglie; but the next daie they returned againe, bringing with them the kings letters. Then the cardinall delivered unto them the great seale,[4] and was content to depart simplie, taking with him nothing but onelie certeine provision for his house: and after long talke betweene him and the dukes, they departed with the great seale of England, and brought the same to the king. Then the cardinall called all his officers before him, and tooke accompt of them for all such stuffe, whereof they had charge.[5] And in his gallerie were set diverse tables, whereupon laie a great number of goodlie rich stuffe, as whole peeces of silke of all colours, velvet, sattin, damaske, taffata, grograine, and other things. Also, there laie a thousand peeces of fine Holland cloth.

There was laid on everie table, bookes reporting the contents of the same, and so was there inventaries of all things in order against the kings comming. He caused to be hanged the walles of the gallerie on the one side with cloth of gold, cloth of tissue, cloth of silver, and rich cloth of bodken of diverse colours. On the other side were hanged the richest sute of coapes of his owne provision made

---

[1] *In margin:* 'The cardinall sued in a premunire.' III.2.338–45.

[2] Shakespeare adds the Earl of Surrey, forgetting that the Thomas Howard sent to Ireland (III.2.261) had become Duke of Norfolk in 1524. The Surrey of this date (1529) was Henry Howard his son, the poet, beheaded for treason in 1547.

[3] *In margin:* 'The cardinall is loth to part from the great seale.' III.2.229–52.

[4] *In margin:* 'The cardinall discharged of the great seale.'

[5] *In margin:* 'The cardinall calleth all his officers to accounts.'

for his colleges of Oxford and Ipswich, that ever were seene in England. Then had he two chambers adjoining to the gallerie, the one most commonlie called the gilt chamber, and the other the councell chamber, wherein were set up two broad and long tables upon trestles, wherupon was set such a number of plate of all sorts, as was almost incredible. . . .

[912/2/15] During this parlement was brought downe to the commons the booke of articles, which the lords had put to the king against the cardinall, the chiefe wherof were these.[1]

1 First, that he without the kings assent had procured to be a legat, by reason whereof he tooke awaie the right of all bishops and spirituall persons.[2]

2 Item, in all writings which he wrote to Rome, or anie other forren prince, he wrote *Ego & rex meus*, I and my king: as who would saie, that the king were his servant.[3]

3 Item, that he hath slandered the church of England in the court of Rome. For his suggestion to be legat was to reforme the church of England, which (as he wrote) was *Facta in reprobum sensum*.

4 Item, he without the kings assent carried the kings great seale with him into Flanders, when he was sent ambassador to the emperour.[4]

5 Item, he without the kings assent, sent a commission to sir Gregorie de Cassado, knight, to conclude a league betweene the king & the duke of Ferrar, without the kings knowledge.[5]

6 Item, that he having the French pockes presumed to come and breath on the king.

7 Item, that he caused the cardinals hat to be put on the kings coine.[6]

8 Item, that he would not suffer the kings clerke of the market to sit at saint Albons.

9 Item, that he had sent innumerable substance to Rome, for the obteining of his dignities, to the great impoverishment of the realme.[7]

These articles, with manie more, read in the common house, and signed with the cardinals hand, was confessed by him. And also there was shewed a writing sealed with his seale, by the which he gave to the king all his mooveables and unmooveables.[8]

[Wolsey was allowed to go to his diocese of York, but delayed on his journey, staying at Richmond and Southwell. He was arrested at Cawood for treason by Northumberland, 1530.]

---

[1] *In margin:* 'Articles exhibited against the cardinall of Yorke.' III.2.294ff.
[2] III.2.311–13.   [3] III.2.314–17.   [4] III.2.317–20.
[5] III.2.321–4.   [6] III.2.325–6.   [7] III.2.327–31.
[8] Cf. III.2.342–5.

[915/2/67]   Then the cardinall tooke the earle by the hand, and had him up into the chamber, whome followed all the number of the earles servants. From thence he led him into his bed-chamber, and they being there all alone, the earle said unto the cardinall with a soft voice, laieng his hand upon his arme: My lord I arrest you of high treason.[1] With which words the cardinall being marvellouslie astonied, standing both still a good space. At last (quoth the cardin-all) What authoritie have you to arrest me? Forsooth my lord (quoth the erle) I have a commission so to doo. Where is your commission (quoth he) that I may see it? Naie sir that you may not (said the erle.) Well then (quoth the cardinall) I will not obeie your rest. But as they were debating this matter betweene them in the chamber, as busie was maister Walsh in arresting doctor Augustine at the doore of the palace, saieng unto him, Go in traitor or I shall make thee.

At the last maister Walsh being entred into the cardinals cham-ber, began to plucke off his hood, and after kneeled downe to the cardinall. Unto whom the cardinall said, Come hither gentleman & let me speake with you: Sir, heere my lord of Northumberland hath arrested me, but by whose authoritie he sheweth not; if yee be joined with him I praie you shew me. Indeed my lord (quoth maister Walsh) he sheweth you the truth. Well then (quoth the cardinall) I praie you let me see it.[2] Sir I beseech you (quoth maister Walsh) hold us excused: there is annexed to our commission certeine instructions, which you may not see. Well (quoth the cardinall) I trow yee are one of the kings privie chamber, your name is Walsh, I am content to yeeld to you, but not to my lord of Northumberland without I see his commission: the worst in the kings privie chamber is sufficient to arrest the greatest peere of the realme by the kings commandement, without anie commission, therefore put your commission and authoritie in execution, spare not, I will obeie the kings will; I take God to judge, I never offended the king in word nor deed. [On the way south he fell ill at Sheffield Parck.]

[916/2/74]   When night came, the cardinall waxed verie sicke with the laske,[3] the which caused him continuallie to go to the stoole all that night, in so much that he had that night fiftie stooles: there-fore in consideration of his infirmitie, they caused him to tarrie all that day: and the next daie he tooke his journie with master King-ston, and them of the gard, till he came to an house of the earle of Shrewesburies called Hardwike hall, where he laie all night verie evill at ease. The next daie he rode to Notingham, and there lodged that

---

[1] *In margin:* 'The action of arrest which the cardinall taketh in ill part.' Referred to, IV.2.12–14.

[2] *In margin:* 'The cardinall desireth to see the commission of the arest.'

[3] *In margin:* 'The cardinall extremelie' [sic!]. *laske,* diarrhoea.

night more sicke: and the next daie he rode to Leicester abbeie, and by the waie waxed so sicke that he was almost fallen from his mule[1]; so that it was night before he came to the abbeie of Leicester, where at his comming in at the gates, the abbat with all his convent met him with diverse torches light, whom they honorablie received and welcomed.

To whom the cardinall said: Father abbat, I am come hither to lay my bones among you; riding so still untill he came to the staires of the chamber, where he allighted from his mule, and master Kingston led him up the staires, and as soone as he was in his chamber he went to bed. This was on the saturdaie at night, and then increased he sicker and sicker, untill mondaie, that all men thought he would have died: so on tuesdaie saint Andrewes even, master Kingston came to him and bad him good morrow, for it was about six of the clocke, and asked him how he did? Sir (quoth he) I tarrie but the pleasure of God, to render up my poore soule into his hands. Not so sir (quoth master Kingston) with the grace of God, yee shall live and doo verie well, if yee will be of good cheere. Nay in good sooth master Kingston, my disease is such, that I can not live: for I have had some experience in physicke.[2] . . .

[917/1/42] Sir (quoth maister Kingston) you be in much pensivenes, doubting the thing, that in good faith yee need not. Well, well, master Kingston (quoth the cardinall) I see the matter how it is framed: but if I had served God as diligentlie as I have doone the king, he would not have given me over in my greie haires: but it is the just reward that I must receive for the diligent paines and studie that I have had to doo him service, not regarding my service to God, but onelie to satisfie his pleasure.[3]

I praie you have me most humblie commended unto his royall majestie, & beseech him in my behalfe to call to his princelie remembrance all matters proceeding betweene him & me from the beginning of the world, and the progresse of the same, &c. Master Kingston farewell, I can no more saie, but I wish all things to have good successe, my time draweth on fast. And even with that he began to draw his speech at length, & his toong to faile, his eies being set, whose sight failed him.[4] Then they did put him in remembrance of Christ his passion, & caused the yeomen of the gard to stand by to see him die, and to witnesse of his words at his departure: & incontinent the clocke stroke eight,[5] and then he gave up the ghost, and departed this present life: which caused some to call to remembrance

---

[1] IV.2.15, 16.   [2] IV.2.17–27.

[3] *In margin:* 'The cardinall ascribeth his fall to the just judgement of God.' III.2.455–9.

[4] *In margin:* 'Manifest indication of death in the cardinall.'   [5] IV.2.26–7.

how he said the daie before, that at eight of the clocke they should loose their master.

Here is the end and fall of pride and arrogancie of men exalted by fortune to dignitie: for in his time he was the hautiest man in all his proceedings alive, having more respect to the honor of his person, than he had to his spirituall profession, wherin should be shewed all meekenes, humilitie, and charitie.[1]

[917/2/20] This cardinall (as *Edmund Campian* in his historie of Ireland describeth him) was a man undoubtedly borne to honor[2]: I thinke (saith he) some princes bastard, no butchers sonne, exceeding wise, faire spoken, high minded, full of revenge, vitious of his bodie, loftie to his enimies, were they never so big, to those that accepted and sought his freendship woonderfull courteous,[3] a ripe schooleman, thrall to affections, brought a bed with flatterie, insatiable to get, and more princelie in bestowing, as appeareth by his two colleges at Ipswich and Oxenford, the one overthrowne with his fall, the other unfinished, and yet as it lieth for an house of students, considering all the appurtenances incomparable thorough Christendome,[4] whereof Henrie the eight is now called founder, bicause he let it stand. He held and injoied at once the bishopriks of Yorke, Duresme, & Winchester, the dignities of lord cardinall, legat, & chancellor, the abbeie of saint Albons, diverse priories, sundrie fat benefices *In commendam*, a great preferrer of his servants, an advancer of learning, stout in everie quarell, never happie till this his overthrow. Wherein he shewed such moderation, and ended so perfectlie, that the houre of his death did him more honor, than all the pompe of his life passed.[5] Thus far *Campian*.

[917/2/52] This Thomas Wolseie[6] was a poore mans sonne of Ipswich, in the countie of Suffolke, & there borne, and being but a child, verie apt to be learned, by the meanes of his parents he was conveied to the universitie of Oxenford, where he shortlie prospered so in learning, as he was made bachellor of art, when he passed not fifteene yeares of age,[7] and was called most commonlie thorough the universitie the boie bachellor. Thus prospering in learning, he was made fellow of Mawdeline college, and afterward appointed to be schoolemaster of Mawdelin schoole. . . .

[His pomp as Cardinal.]

[921/1/63] Before him was borne first the broad seale of England, and his cardinals hat, by a lord, or some gentleman of worship

---

[1] *In margin:* 'Example of pride and arrogancie.'

[2] *In margin:* 'The description of cardinall Wolseie, set doone by *Edmund Campian*.' IV.2.48–50.   [3] IV.2.52–4.   [4] IV.2.55–63.   [5] IV.2.64–8.

[6] *In margin:* 'The ascending of Thomas Wolseie.' This comes from Stow.

[7] *In margin:* 'Bachellor of art at fifteene yeares old.' IV.2.50–1.

right solemnlie[1]: & as soone as he was once entered into his chamber of presence, his two great crosses were there attending to be borne before him: then cried the gentlemen ushers, going before him bare headed, and said: On before my lords and maisters, on before, make waie for my lords grace. Thus went he downe through the hall with a sergeant of armes before him, bearing a great mace of silver, and two gentlemen carieng two great pillers of silver.[2] . . .

[921/2/42] Thus in great honour, triumph, and glorie, he reigned a long season, ruling all things within the realme apperteining unto the king. His house was resorted to with noblemen and gentlemen, feasting and banketting ambassadors diverse times, and all other right noblie.[3] And when it pleased the king for his recreation to repaire to the cardinals house (as he did diverse times in the yeare) there wanted no preparations or furniture: bankets were set foorth with maskes and mummeries, in so gorgeous a sort and costlie maner, that it was an heaven to behold. There wanted no dames or damosels meet or apt to danse with the maskers, or to garnish the place for the time: then was there all kind of musike and harmonie, with fine voices both of men and children.

On a time[4] the king came suddenlie thither in a maske with a dozen maskers all in garments like sheepheards, made of fine cloth of gold, and crimosin sattin paned, & caps of the same, with visards of good physnomie, their haires & beards either of fine goldwire silke, or blacke silke, having sixteene torch-bearers, besides their drums and other persons with visards, all clothed in sattin of the same color. And before his entring into the hall, he came by water to the water gate without anie noise, where were laid diverse chambers and guns charged with shot, and at his landing they were shot off,[5] which made such a rumble in the aire, that it was like thunder: it made all the noblemen, gentlemen, ladies, and gentlewomen, to muse what it should meane,[6] comming so suddenlie, they sitting quiet at a solemne banket, after this sort.

First yee shall understand, that the tables were set in the chamber of presence just covered, & the lord cardinall sitting under the cloth

---

[1] *In margin:* 'The tokens and marks of his dignities borne before him.'

[2] Cf. II.4.*s.d.*9–10.

[3] *In margin:* 'The cardinals house like a princes court for all kind of braverie & sumptuousnesse.'

[4] *In margin:* 'A maske and banket, the king in person present at the cardinals house.' Used in I.4.63*s.d.*, etc.—to bring Henry and Anne Boleyn together.

[5] I.4.49*s.d.* These 'chambers' (small cannon) set fire to the Globe in 1613.

[6] I.4.50: 'What's that?'

of estate, there having all his service alone[1]: and then was there set a ladie with a noble man, or a gentleman and a gentlewoman throughout all the tables in the chamber on the one side,[2] which were made and joined as it were but one table, all which order and devise was doone by the lord Sandes then lord chamberleine to the king[3] and by sir Henrie Gilford comptrollor of the kings majesties house. Then immediatlie after the great chamberleine, and the said comptroller,[4] sent to looke what it should meane (as though they knew nothing of the matter) who looking out of the windowes into the Thames, returned againe and shewed him, that it seemed they were noblemen and strangers that arrived at his bridge, comming as ambassadours from some forren prince.[5]

With that (quoth the cardinall) I desire you, bicause you can speake French, to take the paines to go into the hall, there to receive them according to their estates, and to conduct them into this chamber, where they shall see us, and all these noble personages being merie at our banket, desiring them to sit downe with us, and to take part of our fare.[6] Then went he incontinent downe into the hall, whereas they received them with twentie new torches, and conveied them up into the chamber, with such a noise of drums and flutes, as seldome had beene heard the like. At their entring into the chamber two and two togither, they went directlie before the cardinall, where he sate and saluted him reverentlie.[7]

To whom the lord chamberleine for them said: Sir, for as much as they be strangers, and can not speake English, they have desired me to declare unto you, that they having understanding of this your triumphant banket, where was assembled such a number of excellent dames, they could doo no lesse under support of your grace, but to repaire hither, to view as well their incomparable beautie, as for to accompanie them at mum-chance, and then to danse with them: and sir, they require of your grace licence to accomplish the said cause of their comming. To whom the cardinall said he was verie well content they should so doo.[8] Then went the maskers, and first saluted all the dames, and returned to the most worthie, and there opened their great cup of gold filled with crownes and other peeces of gold, to whome they set certeine peeces of gold to cast at.

Thus perusing all the ladies and gentlewomen, to some they lost, and of some they woone: and marking after this maner all the ladies,

---

[1] *In margin:* 'The cardinals statelie sitting at table like a prince.'   [2] I.4.21–5.
[3] Cf. I.4.7s.d.; and I.3 where Sands and the Lord Chamberlain are different people.   [4] I.3.66–7.   [5] I.4.50–6.
[6] *In margin:* 'The cardinall knew not that the king was in the number.' I.4.56–60.
[7] *In margin:* 'The cardinall reverentlie saluted of the maskers.' I.4.63s.d.
[8] I.4.64–74.

they returned to the cardinall with great reverence, powring downe all their gold so left in their cup, which was above two hundred crownes: At all (quoth the cardinall) and so cast the dice and wan them, whereat was made a great noise and joy.[1] Then quoth the cardinall to the lord chamberleine, I praie you (quoth he) that you would shew them, that me seemeth there should be a nobleman amongst them, who is more meet to occupie this seat and place than I am, to whome I would most gladlie surrender the same according to my dutie, if I knew him.[2]

Then spake the lord chamberleine to them in French, and they rounding him in the eare, the lord chamberlein said to my lord cardinall: Sir (quoth he) they confesse, that among them there is such a noble personage, whome, if your grace can appoint him out from the rest, he is content to disclose himselfe, and to accept your place. With that the cardinall taking good advisement among them, at the last (quoth he) me seemeth the gentleman with the blacke beard, should be even he: and with that he arose out of his chaire, and offered the same to the gentleman in the blacke beard with his cap in his hand. The person to whom he offered the chaire was sir Edward Nevill, a comelie knight, that much more resembled the kings person in that maske than anie other.[3]

The king perceiving the cardinall so deceived, could not forbeare laughing, but pulled downe his visar and master Nevels also, and dashed out such a pleasant countenance and cheere, that all the noble estates there assembled, perceiving the king to be there among them, rejoised verie much.[4] The cardinall eftsoons desired his highnesse to take the place of estate. To whom the king answered, that he would go first and shift his apparell, and so departed into my lord cardinals chamber, and there new apparelled him: in which time the dishes of the banquet were cleane taken up, and the tables spred againe with new cleane perfumed cloths, everie man and woman sitting still, untill the king with all his maskers came among them againe all new apparelled.

Then the king tooke his seat under the cloth of estate, commanding everie person to sit still as they did before: in came a new banket before the king and to all the rest throughout all the tables, wherein were served two hundred diverse dishes, of costlie devises and subtilties.[5] Thus passed they foorth the night with banketting, dansing, and

[1] *In margin:* 'The cardinall plaieth at dice.'

[2] *In margin:* 'He suspecteth that the king is present and abateth his estate.' I.4.76–81.

[3] *In margin:* 'He taketh his marks amisse and is deceived.' In the play he guesses right, I.4.82–7.

[4] *In margin:* 'The king disvisardeth his face and is verie pleasant.'

[5] *In margin:* 'A new banket upon the sudden of 200 dishes.'

other triumphs, to the great comfort of the king, and pleasant regard of the nobilitie there assembled.

[Holinshed's editors quote Hall's description of Wolsey[1]:]

[922/2/48] This cardinall (as you may perceive in this storie) was of a great stomach,[2] for he compted himselfe equall with princes, & by craftie suggestion gat into his hands innumerable treasure: he forced little on[3] simonie, and was not pittifull, and stood affectionate in his owne opinion: in open presence he would lie and saie untruth, and was double both in speach and meaning: he would promise much & performe little: he was vicious of his bodie, & gave the clergie evill example: he hated sore the citie of London & feared it: it was told him that he should die in the waie toward London, wherefore he feared least the commons of the citie would arise in riotous maner and so slaie him, yet for all that he died in the waie toward London, carrieng more with him out of the world than he brought into it: namelie a winding sheete, besides other necessaries thought meet for a dead man, as christian comelinesse required.

[928/1/67] The king having purchased of the cardinall after his attendure in the premunire his house at Westminster, called Yorke place,[4] and got a confirmation of the cardinals feoffement thereof, made of the chapter of the cathedrall church of Yorke, purchased this yeare also all the medows about saint James,[5] and there made a faire mansion and a parke for his greater commoditie & pleasure. And bicause he had a great affection for the said house at Westminster, he bestowed great cost in going forward with the building thereof, and changed the name, so that it was after called the kings palace of Westminster. . . .

[928/2/29] On the first of September [1532] being Sundaie, the K. being come to Windsor, created the ladie Anne Bullongne marchionesse of Penbroke, and gave to hir one thousand pounds land by the yeare.[6]

[Henry visited France and persuaded King Francis to urge the Pope to allow the divorce.]

[929/1/58] [The king] taking his ship, landed at Dover the next daie about five of the clocke in the morning.[7] And herewith upon his returne, he married privilie the ladie Anne Bullongne the same daie,[8]

---

[1] *In margin:* 'The description of the cardinall. *Ab. Fl[eming] ex. Edw. Hal.*'
[2] IV.2.33–44.   [3] 'he had few scruples about'. Cf. IV.2.36.
[4] *In margin:* 'Yorke place or white Hall now the palace of Westminster.' Cf. IV.1.94–9.   [5] *In margin:* 'S. James.'   [6] II.3.58–65.
[7] *In margin:* 'The king returneth into England.'
[8] *In margin:* 'He marrieth the lady Anne Bullongne.' [Actually in Jan. 1533.]

being the fourteenth daie of November, and the feast daie of saint
Erkenwald; which marriage was kept so secret, that verie few knew
it till Easter next insuing, when it was perceived that she was with
child.

[929/2/28] It was also enacted the same time, that queene
Katharine should no more be called queene, but princesse Dowager,
as the widow of prince Arthur.[1] In the season of the last summer died
William Warham archbishop of Canturburie, and then was named
to that sea Thomas Cranmer the kings chapleine, a man of good
learning, and of a vertuous life, which latelie before had beene
ambassador from the king to the pope.[2]

After that the king perceived his new wife to be with child, he
caused all officers necessarie to be appointed to hir, and so on Easter
even she went to hir closet openlie as queene; and then the king
appointed the daie of hir coronation to be kept on Whitsundaie next
following: and writings were sent to all shiriffs, to certifie the names
of men of fortie pounds to receive the order of knighthood, or else
to make fine.[3] The assesment of the fine was appointed to Thomas
Cromwell, maister of the kings jewell house, & councellor to the
king, a man newlie received into high favour. He so used the matter,
that a great summe of monie was raised to the kings use by those
fines. The matter of the queenes appeale whereunto she still sticked,
and by no means could be remooved from it, was communed of,
both in the parlement house, and also in the convocation house,
where it was so handled, that manie were of opinion, that not onelie
hir appeale, but also all other appeales made to Rome were void and
of none effect: for that in ancient councels it had beene determined,
that a cause rising in one province should be determined in the
same.

This matter was opened with all the circumstances to the ladie
Katharine Dowager (for so was she then called) the which persisted
still in hir former opinion, and would revoke by no meanes hir
appeale to the court of Rome. Whereupon the archbishop of Canturburie accompanied with the bishops of London, Winchester, Bath,
Lincolne, and divers other learned men in great number, rode to
Dunstable, which is six miles from Ampthill, where the princesse
Dowager laie, and there by one doctor Lee she was cited to appeare
before the said archbishop in cause of matrimonie in the said towne
of Dunstable, and at the daie of appearance she appeared not, but
made default, and so she was called peremptorie everie daie fifteene
daies togither, and at the last, for lacke of appearance, by the assent

---

[1] *In margin:* 'Queene Katharine to be named princesse Dowager.' [1533.]

[2] III.2.62–74; 401–3.　　[3] *In margin:* 'Queene Anne.' III.2.67–9; 403–7.

of all the learned men there present, she was divorsed from the king, and the mariage declared to be void and of none effect.[1]

[The comelie order and araie kept on the coronation daie of everie attendant in his degree.[2]]

[933/1/1] First went gentlemen, then esquiers, then knights, then the aldermen ... after them the judges in their mantels of scarlet and coiffes. Then followed the knights of the Bath being no lords. ... After them came the lord chancellor in a robe of scarlet open before ... after him came the kings chapell and the moonks solemnelie singing with procession, then came abbats and bishops mitered ... then after them went the mayor of London with his mace and garter in his cote of armes, then went the marquesse Dorset in a robe of estate which bare the scepter of gold, and the earle of Arundell which bare the rod of ivorie with the dove both togither.

Then went alone the earle of Oxford ... which bare the crowne, after him went the duke of Suffolke in his robe of estate, also for that daie being high steward of England, having a long white rod in his hand, and the lord William Howard [Norfolke] with the rod of the marshalship, and everie knight of the garter had on his collar of the order. Then proceeded foorth the queene in a circot and robe of purple velvet furred with ermine, in hir here coiffe and circlet ..., and over hir was borne the canopie by foure of the five ports, all crimsin with points of blue and red hanging on their sleeves, and the bishops of London and Winchester bare up the laps of the queenes robe. The queenes traine which was verie long was borne by the old duches of Norffolke: after hir folowed ladies being lords wives, which had circots of scarlet. ...

[933/1/47] When she was thus brought to the high place made in the middest of the church, betweene the queere and the high altar, she was set in a rich chaire.[3] And after that she had rested a while, she descended downe to the high altar and there prostrate hir selfe while the archbishop of Canturburie said certeine collects: then she rose, and the bishop annointed hir on the head and on the brest, and then she was led up againe, where after diverse orisons said, the archbishop set the crowne of saint Edward on hir head, and then delivered hir the scepter of gold in hir right hand, and the rod of ivorie with the dove in the left hand, and then all the queere soong *Te Deum, &c.* Which doone, the bishop tooke off the crowne of saint Edward being heavie and set on the crowne made for hir. Then

---

[1] *In margin:* 'The ladie Katharine Dowager called peremptorilie.' IV.i.22–33.

[2] *In margin.* Cf. IV.i.36*s.d.*

[3] *In margin:* 'The maner of the coronation as it was then used.'

went she to saint Edwards shrine and there offered, after which offering doone she withdrew hir into a little place made for the nones on the one side of the queere.

Now in the meane season everie duches had put on their bonets a coronall of gold wrought with flowers, and everie marquesse put on a demie coronall of gold, everie countesse a plaine circlet of gold without flowers, and everie king of armes put on a crowne of coper and guilt, all which were worne till night. When the queene had a little reposed hir, the companie returned in the same order that they set foorth, and the queene went crowned and so did the ladies aforesaid.[1]

[The birth of the Princess Elizabeth, 1533.]

[934/2/1] The seventh of September being sundaie, betweene three & foure of the clocke in the afternoone, the queene was delivered of a faire yoong ladie,[2] on which daie the duke of Norffolke came home to the christening, which was appointed on the wednesdaie next following, and was accordinglie accomplished on the same daie, with all such solemne ceremonies as were thought convenient. The godfather at the font, was the lord archbishop of Canturburie, the godmothers, the old dutches of Norffolke, & the old marchionesse Dorset widow; and at the confirmation the ladie marchionesse of Excester was godmother: the child was named Elizabeth.[3]

[The Baptismal procession is described, as in V.5 *Entry*.]

[934/2/64] When the ceremonies and christening were ended, Garter cheefe king of armes cried alowd, God of his infinite goodnesse send prosperous life & long to the high and mightie princesse of England Elizabeth: & then the trumpets blew.[4] Then the archbishop of Canterburie gave to the princesse a standing cup of gold: the dutches of Norffolke gave to hir a standing cup of gold, fretted with pearle: the marchionesse of Dorset gave three gilt bolles, pounced with a cover: and the marchionesse of Excester gave three standing bolles graven, all gilt with a cover.[5] Then was brought in wafers, comfets, & ipocrasse in such plentie, that everie man had as much as he would desire. Then they set forwards, the trumpets going before in the same order towards the kings palace, as they did when they came thitherwards. . . .

[The death of ex-Queen Katherine, 1536.]

[939/2/13] The princesse Dowager lieng at Kimbalton, fell into hir last sicknesse,[6] whereof the king being advertised, appointed the

---

[1] *In margin:* 'The queene and the ladies in their pompe.' IV.1.62–70; 81–94.
[2] V.1.158–70.   [3] V.5 *Entry*; 1–11.   [4] V.5.1–3.
[5] *In margin:* 'Rich gifts given to the princesse.'
[6] *In margin:* 'The ladie Katharine Dowager deceaseth.' IV.2.1–3.

Emperors ambassador that was legier here with him named Eusta-
chius Caputius, to go to visit hir, and to doo his commendations to
hir, and will hir to be of good comfort.[1] The ambassador with all
diligence did his duetie therein, comforting hir the best he might:
but she within six daies after, perceiving hir selfe to wax verie weake
and feeble, and to feele death approching at hand, caused one of hir
gentlewomen to write a letter to the king,[2] commending to him hir
daughter and his, beseeching him to stand good father unto hir: and
further desired him to have some consideration of hir gentlewomen
that had served hir, and to see them bestowed in marriage. Further,
that it would please him to appoint that hir servants might have their
due wages, and a yeeres wages beside. This in effect was all that she
requested,[3] and so immediatlie hereupon she departed this life the
eight of Januarie at Kimbalton aforesaid, and was buried at
Peterborow. The nine and twentith of Januarie queene Anne was
delivered of a child before hir time, which was borne dead.[4]

II. Source

From ACTES AND MONUMENTS OF MARTYRS

by John Foxe (1583 edition)

[p. 1866] Notwithstanding, not long after that, certayne of the
Counsaile, whose names neede not to be repeated, by the entisement
and provocation of his auncient enemye the Byshoppe of Winchester,[5] and other of the same secte, attempted the Kyng agaynst
him, declaring plainely, that the Realme was so enfected with
heresies and heretickes,[6] that it was daungerous for his highnesse,
farther to permit it unreformed, least peradventure by long suffering,
such contention should arise, and ensue in the realme among his
subjectes, that thereby might spring horrible commotions, and
uprores, like as in some partes of Germanie, it did not long agoe:
The enormitie whereof they coulde not impute to any so much, as
to the Archbishop of Canterbury, who by his owne preaching, and
his Chapleins, had defiled the whole realme full of divers pernicious

---

[1] IV.2.105–28.   [2] IV.2.128–31.   [3] IV.2.132–60.
[4] This perhaps suggested her difficult labour in V.1.18–20; 61–78.
[5] Stephen Gardiner.
[6] Cf. V.1.42–6: 'a pestilence That does infect the land'.

heresies. The Kyng would needes knowe his accusers. They aunswered that forasmuch as he was a Counceller no man durst take upon him to accuse him: but if it would please his highnesse, to committe him to the Tower for a tyme, there would be accusations, and proofes enough against him . . .

The king perceiving their importunate sute against the Archbishop (but yet meaning not to have him wronged . . .) graunted unto them that they should the next day, committe him to the Tower for his triall. When night came, the Kyng sent Sir Anthonie Denie about midnight, to Lambeth to the Archbishop, willing him forthwith to resorte unto him at the Court.[1] The message done, the Archbishop spedely addressed himselfe to the Court, and comming into the Galerie where the king walked, and taried for him, his highnesse sayd: Ah my Lorde of Caunterburie, I can tell you newes. For divers waightie considerations it is determined by me, and the Counsaile, that you to morrowe at nine of the clocke shall be committed to the Tower, for that you and your Chaplains . . . have taught and preached, and thereby sowen within the realme such a number of execrable heresies, that it is feared, the whole realme being infected with them no smale contention, and commotions will rise thereby amongst my subjectes, as of late dayes the like was in divers parts of Germanie, and therfore the Counsaile have requested me, for the triall of the matter, to suffer them to commit you to the Tower, or els no man dare come forth, as witnesse in these matters, you being a Counsellour.[2]

When the king had sayde his minde, the Archbishop kneeled downe and sayd: I am content if it please your grace, with all my heart, to goe thither at your highnesse commandement, and I most humbly thanke your majesty that I may come to my triall, for there be that have many wayes slandered me, and nowe this way I hope to trie my selfe not worthy of such report.

The king perceivyng the mans uprightnesse, joyned with such simplicitie, sayd: Oh Lorde, what maner a man be you? What simplicitie is in you? I had thought that you would rather have sued to us to have taken the paynes to have heard you, and your accusers together for your triall, without any such indurance. Do not you know, what state you be in with the whole world, and how many great enemies you have? Do you not consider what an easy thing it is, to procure three or foure false knaves to witnesse agaynst you? Thinke you to have better lucke that way, then your maister Christ had? I see by it, you will run hedlong to your undoyng, if I would suffer you.[3] Your enemies shall not so prevayle

[1] V.1.79–82. [2] V.1.92–109. [3] V.1.110–41.

against you, for I have otherwyse devised with my selfe to keepe
you out of their handes. Yet notwithstanding to morrow when the
Counsaile shal sit, and send for you, resort unto them, and if in
chargyng you with this matter, they do commit you to the Tower,
require of them, because you are one of them, a Counsailor, that
you may have your accusers brought before them without any
further indurance, and use for your selfe as good perswasions that
way as you may devise, and if no intreatie or reasonable request will
serve, then deliver unto them this my ring . . . and say unto them,
if there be no remedie my Lordes, but that I must needes go to the
Tower, then I revoke my cause from you, and appeale to the kings
owne person by this his token unto you all, for (sayd the King then
unto the Archbishop) so soone as they shall see this my ryng, they
know it so well that they shall understande that I have resumed
the whole cause into myne owne handes[1] and determination, and
that I have discharged them thereof.

The Archbishop perceivyng the Kinges benignitie so muche to
hym wardes, had much adoe to forbeare teares. Well, sayd the Kyng,
go your waies my Lorde, and doe as I have bidden you.[2] My Lord
humblyng himselfe with thankes, tooke hys leave of the Kynges
highnesse for that nyght.

On the morrow about 9. of the clocke before noone, the Counsaile
sent a gentleman Usher for the Archbishop, who when he came to
the Counsaile chamber dore, could not be let in, but of purpose
(as it seemed) was compelled there to waite among the Pages,
Lackies, and servyng men all alone.[3] Dr. Buts the Kings phisition
resortyng that way, and espying how my Lord of Cant. was handled,
went to the Kings highnesse and sayd: My Lord of Cant. if it please
your grace is well promoted: for nowe he is become a Lackey or a
servyng man, for yonder he standeth this halfe hower at the
Counsaile chamber dore amongest them. It is not so (quoth the
Kyng) I trowe, not the Counsail hath not so little discretion as to
use the Metropolitane of the Realme in that sort, specially beyng
one of their own number. But let them alone (said the King) and
wee shal heare more soone.[4]

Anone the Archbishop was called into the Counsaile chamber,
to whome was alledged, as before is rehearsed. The Archb. aunswered
in like sort, as the king had advised him: and in the end when he
perceived that no maner of perswasion or intreatie could serve, he
delivered them the Kings ring, revoking his cause into the Kings

---

[1] V.1.143–53.   [2] V.1.153–8.
[3] *In margin:* 'The archbishop being one of the Counsel, made to stand at the
Counsel chamber doore waiting.' V.2.1–6.   [4] V.2.6–34.

hands.[1] The whole Counsaile being thereat somewhat amazed, the Earle of Bedford with a loude voyce confirmyng his wordes with a solemne othe, sayde: when you first began the matter my Lordes, I told you what would come of it. Do you thinke that the King will suffer this mans finger to ake? Much more (I warrant you) will hee defend hys life against brabling varlets. You doe but comber your selves to heare tales and fables agaynst hym.[2] And so incontinently upon the receipt of the Kyngs token, they all rose, and caried to the K. his ryng, surrenderyng that matter as the order and use was, into hys owne hands.[3]

When they were all come to the kynges presence, hys highnes with a severe countenaunce, sayd unto them: Ah my Lordes, I thought I had had wiser men of my counsaile then now I finde you. What discretion was this in you, thus to make the Primate of the realme, & one of you in office, to waite at the counsaile chamber dore amongst servyng men? You might have considered that hee was a counsellor as wel as you, and you had no such commission of me so to handle hym. I was content that you should trie hym as a Counseller, and not as a meane subject. But now I well perceive that thynges bee done agaynst him maliciously, and if some of you might have had your minds, you would have tried him to the uttermost. But I do you all to wit, and protest, that if a Prince may bee beholdyng unto hys subject (and so solemnely laying his hand uppon his brest) sayde: by the fayth I owe to God, I take this man here, my L. of Canterbury, to bee of all other a most faythfull subject unto us, and one to whome wee are much beholding, gevyng him great commendations otherwise. And with that one or two of the chiefest of the Counsaile, makyng their excuse, declared, that in requesting his indurance, it was rather ment for hys triall, and his purgation agaynst the common fame, and slaunder of the world, then for any malice conceyved agaynst hym. Well, well my Lordes, quoth the king, take hym and well use hym, as he is worthy to be, and make no more adoe. And with that every man caught hym by the hand,[4] and made fayre weather of altogethers, which might easilie bee done with that man.[5]

And it was much to be mervailed, that they would go so far with him, thus to seeke his undoyng, this well understanding before, that the king most entirely loved him and alwaies would stand in

---

[1] *In margin:* 'The Counsaile being set against the Archb. he sheweth the kinges ring and appealeth from them.' V.3.1–101.

[2] V.3.102–13 divide Bedford's words among Suffolk, Norfolk and Cromwell.

[3] The King comes to them at V.3.113.

[4] *In margin:* 'The Lordes of the Counsaile glad to be friendes agayne with the Archbishop.'   [5] V.3.114–73.

hys defence whosoever spake against hym: as many other times the Kinges pacience was by sinister informations agaynst him tried.[1]

III. Probable Source

From WHEN YOU SEE ME, YOU KNOW ME

by Samuel Rowley (1605)[2]

When you see me, You know me. Or the famous Chronicle Historie *of king Henry the eight, with the* birth and vertuous life of Edward *Prince of Wales.* As it was playd by the high and mightie Prince *of Wales his servants.* By Samuell Rowly, servant to the Prince. LONDON, Imprinted for *Nathaniell Butter,* and are to be sold in Paules Church-yeard neare Saint *Austines* gate. 1605.

[From Scene iv]

Enter Brandon, Dudley, Gray, Seymer, Compton

BR.　How now Sir *William Cumpton,* where is the king?

CUM.　His grace is walking in the gallery,   550
As sad and passionate as ere he was.

DUD.　Twere good your grace went in to comfort him.

BRAN.　Not I Lord *Dudley,* by my George I sweare,
Unlesse his Highnesse first had sent for me,
I will not put my head in such a hazzard,
I know his anger, and his spleene too well.

GRAY　Tis strange, this humor hath his highnesse held,
Ever since the death of good Queen *Jane,*
That none dares venture to conferre with him.

---

[1] *In margin:* 'The king a great supporter of Cranmer.'
[2] Text based on the Malone Society Reprint, ed. F. P. Wilson, 1952.

Enter Cardinall, Sommers, and Patch.   560

DUD. Here comes the Cardinall.

BRAN. I, and two fooles after him, his Lordship is well
attended still.

SEM. Lets win this prelate to salute the king.
It may perhaps worke his disgrace with him.

WOOL. How now *William*, what? are you here to[o].

WILL. I my Lord, all the fooles follow you. I come to
bid my cosin *Patch* welcome to the court, and when I
come to Yorke house, hele do as much for me, will yee
not *Patch*?   570

PAT. Yes cosin, hey, da, tere, dedell, dey, day.   [*sing*

WOOL. What, are you singing sirra.

WILL. Ile make him cry as fast, anon I hold a peny.

DUD. God morrow to your grace my good Lord Cardinall.

WOOL. We thanke your honour.

                    [*Enter king within*

KYNG What *Cumpton, Carew.*   [*Call within*

BRAND. Harke, the king cals.

KING Mother of God, how are we attended on: who
waights without?   580

BRAND. Go in Sir *William*, and if you find his grace
In any milder temper then he was last night,
Let us have word, and we will visit him.

CUMP. I will my Lord.   [*Exit*

WOOL. What is the occasion, that the kings so mov'd?

BRAND. His grace hath taken such an inward greefe,
With sad remembrance of the Queene that's dead,
That much his highnesse wrongs his state and person,
Besides in Ireland, do the Burkes rebell,
And stout *Pearsie* that disclo[s]d the plot,   590
Was by the Earle of *Kildare* late put to death.
And *Martin Luther* out of Germanie,
Has writ a booke against his Majestie,
For taking part with proud Pope *Julius*,
Which being spred by him through Christendome,
Hath thus incenst his royall majestie.

WOOL. Tush, I have newes, my Lord, to salve that sore,
And make the king more fear'd through christendome,
Then ever was his famous auncestors:
Nor can base *Luther* with his heresies,   600
Backt by the proudest germaine potentate,
Heretically blurre king *Henries* fame:

For honour that he did Pope *Julius*,
Who in high favour of his Majestie,
Hath sent *Campeus* with a bull from Rome,
To adde unto his title this high stile:
That he and his faire posteritie,
Proclaim'd defenders of the faith shall be:
For which intent the holy Cardinals come,
As Legats from the Emperiall court of Rome.   610

GR.   This newes, my Lord, may somthing ease his mind,
Twere good your grace would go and visit him.

WOOL.   I will, and doubt not but to please him well.

SEYM.   So, I am glad he's in, and the king be no better
pleased then he was at our last parting, hele make him repent
his saucinesse.

BRAND.   How now old *William*, how chance you go not to
the king, and comfort him.

WILL.   No birlady, my Lord, I was with him too lately already, his fist is too heavie for a foole to stand under, I went
to him last night, after you had left him, seeing him chafe so   620
at *Charles*, here to make him merry: and he gave me such a
boxe on the eare, that stroke me cleane through three
chambers, downe foure paire of staires, fell ore five barrels,
into the bottome of the seller, and if I had not well lickard my
selfe there, I had never liv'd after it.

BRAN.   Faith *Will*, ile give thee a velvet coate, and thou
canst but make him merry.

WILL.   Will ye my Lord, and ile venter another boxe on
the eare but ile do it.

[*Enter Cumpton*

CUM.   Cleare the presence there, the king is comming,   630
Gods me, my Lords, what meant the Cardinall,
So unexpected thus to trouble him.

GRAY   Is the king mov'd at it?

Enter the king and Woolsie.

CUMPT.   Judge by his countenance, see he comes.

BRAN.   Ile not indure the storme.

DUD.   Nor I.

WIL.   Runne foole your maister will be feld else.

KING   Did we not charge that none should trouble us?
Presumptuous priest, proud prelate as thou art,   640
How comes it you are growne so saucie sir,
Thus to presume upon our patience,

And crosse our royall thought disturb'd and vext,
By all your negligence in our estate,
Of us and of our countries happinesse.

   WOOL. My gracious Lord.

   KING Fawning beast stand backe:
Or by my crowne, ile foote thee to the earth,
Wheres *Brandon, Surrey, Seymer, Gray,*
Where is your counsell now, O now ye crooch,   650
And stand like pictures at our presence doore.
Call in our guard, and beare them to the Tower.
Mother of God, ile have the traitors heads,
Go hale them to the blocke, up, up, stand up,
Ile make you know your duties to our state.
Am I a cypher, is my sight growne stale,
Am I not *Hary,* am I not Englands king, Ha?

   WILL. So la, now the watchwords given, nay and hee
once cry ha, neare a man in the court dare for his head
speake againe; lye close cosin *Patch.*   660

   PATCH Ile not come neare him cosin, has almost kil'd
me with his countenance.

   KING We have bene too familiar, now I see,
And you may dally with our majestie:
Where are my pages there?

   PAGE My Lord.   *[Enter pages*

   KIN. Trusse sirra, none to put my garter on,
Give me some wine, here stuffe a the tother side,
Proud Cardinall who follow'd our affaires in Italy,
That we that honor'd so Pope *Julius,*   670
By dedicating bookes at thy request,
Against that upstart sect of Lutherans,
Should by that hereticke be banded thus,
But by my *George,* I sweare, if *Henry* live,
Ile hunt base *Luther* through all Germany,
And pull those seven electors on their knees:
If they but backe him against our dignities.
Bace slave tie soft, thou hurtst my legge,
And now in Ireland the Burkes rebell,
And with his stubborne kernes makes hourely rodes,   680
To burne the borders of the English pale,
And which of all your counsels helpes us now?

Enter Cumpton with wine.

   CUMPT. Heres wine, my Lord.

   KIN. Drinke, and be damb'd. I cry thee mercy *Cumpton,*

What the divell mentst thou to come behind me so,
I did mistake, ile make thee amends for it,
By holy *Paule*, I am so crost and vext,
I knew not what I did, and here at home,
Such carefull statesmen to attend us,   690
And lookes so wisely to our common weale,
That we have ill May-dayes, and riots made:
For lawlesse rebels do disturbe our state.
Twelve times this terme, have we in person sate,
Both in the starre chamber, and Chauncery courts,
To heare our subjects sutes determined:
Yet tis your office *Woolsie*, but all of you
May make a packehorse of king *Henry* now:
Well, what would ye say?

    WOOL.   Nothing that might displease your majesty,   700
I have a message from the Pope to you.

    KING   Then keepe it still, we will not heare it yet,
Get all of you away, avoid our presence.
We cannot yet commaund our patience,
Reach me a chaire. . . .

[Sc. xii]

       Enter the Prince, Cranm: Tye, and the young Lords.

    PRIN.   *Cranmer.*
    CRAN.   My Lord.   2370
    PRIN.   Where is *Franciscoe* our Italian Tutor?
    CRAN.   He does attend your Grace without my Lord.
    PRIN.   Tell him anon we will conferre with him,
Weele plie our learning *Browne* least you be beaten,
We will not have your Knighthood so disgrast.

    BROW.   I thanke yee good my Lord,
And your Grace would but a little plie your learning,
I warrant yee Ile keepe my Knighthood from breeching.

    PRIN.   Faith *Ned* I will: how now what letter's that?
    I SER.   From your Graces sister the Lady *Mary*.   2380
    PRIN.   Come give it me, we gesse at the contents.
Cranmer, my sister oft hath writ to me,
That you and Bishop *Bonner* might conferre,
About these points of new Religion,
Tell me Tutor will yee dispute with him.

    CRAN.   With all my hart my Lord, and wish the king
Would daine to here our disputation.

    PRIN.   What hast thou there?

2 SER.   A Letter from your royall sister, young *Elizabeth*.

PRIN.   Another Letter ere we open this,   2390
Well we will view them both immediatly,
I pray yee attend us in the next Chamber,
And Tutors if I call yee not before,
Give me some notice, if the king my Father
Be walkt abroade, I must goe visite him.

TYE   We will faire Prince.

PRIN.   What sayes my sister *Mary*? she is eldest,
And by due course must first be answered,

> *The blessed Mother of thy redeemer, with all the Angels &*
> *holy Saints be intermissers to preserve thee of Idolatrie,*   2400
> *to invocate the Saints for helpe.*

Alas good sister, still in this opinion!
These are thy blinded Tutors, *Bonner, Gardner,*
That wrong thy thoughts with foolish herisies,
Ile read no farther: to him will *Edward* pray
For preservation, that can himselfe preserve me,
Without the helpe of Saint or cerimonie.
What writes *Elizabeth*, sweete sister thou hast my hart,
And of Prince Edwards love hast greatest part.

> *Sweete Prince I salute thee with a Sisters love,*   2410
> *Be stedfast in thy faith, and let thy prayers*
> *Be dedicate to God onely, for tis he alone*
> *Can strengthen thee, and confound thine enimies,*
> *Give a setled assurance of thy hopes in heaven.*
> *God strengthen thee in all temptations,*
> *And give thee grace to shun Idolatrie,*
> *Heaven send thee life to inherite thy election,*
> *To God I commend thee, who still I pray preserve thee.*
>   Thy loving Sister *Elizabeth.*

Loving thou art, and of me best beloved.   2420
Thy lines shalbe my contemplations cures,
And in thy vertues will I meditate.
To Christ Ile onely pray for me and thee: [*Enter Cranmer*
This I imbrace, away Idolatrie,
How now *Cranmer*, where's the King?

CRAN.   Conferring with his counsell gratious Prince,
There is some earnest businesse troubles him:
The Guardes are doubled, and commandment given,
That none be suffered to come neere the presence,
God keepe his Majestie from traitors hands.   2430

PRI.   Amen good *Cranmer*, what should disturbe him thus?
Is Cardinall *Wolsey* yet return'd from *France*?
  TYE   I my good Lord, and this day comes to court.
  PRIN.   Perhaps this hastie businesse of the King,
Is touching *Wolsey* and his Embassage.
  CRAN.   Pray God it be no worse my Lord.   [*Ent. Compt.*
  TYE   Here comes sir *William Compton* from his highnesse.
  COMP.   Health to your excellencie.
  PRIN.   What newes sir *William*?
  COMP.   The King expects your Graces companie,   2440
And wils your Highnesse come and speake with him,
And doctor *Cranmer*, from his Majestie,
I charge yee speedily to leave the Court,
And come not neere the Prince on paine of death,
Without direction from the King and Peeres.
  CRAN.   Sir I obey yee, God so deale with me,
As I have wisht unto his Majestie.
  PRIN.   *Cranmer* banisht the Court, for what I pray?
  COMP.   I know not gratious Lord, pray pardon me,
Tis the Kings pleasure; and trust me I am sorry   2450
It was my hap to bring this heavie message.
  CRAN.   Nay good sir *William*, your message moves not me,
My service to his royall Majestie
Was always true and just, so helpe me heaven:
Onely I pray your Grace to move the King,
That I may come to tryall speedily,
And if in ought I have deserved death,
Let me not draw another minutes breath.[1]   [*Exit Cranmer*
  COMPT.   Will yee goe my Lord?
  PRIN.   Not yet, we are not your prisoner, are we sir?   2460
  COMPT.   No my deere Lord.
  PRIN.   Then goe before, and we will follow yee,
Your worship will forget your selfe I see.   [*Enter Tye*
My tutor thrust from court so sodainly, this is strange.
  TYE   The Queene my Lord is come to speake with you.

                Enter Queene.

  PRIN.   Avoyde the presence then, and conduct her in,
Ile speake with her, and after see the King,
  QUEE.   Leave us alone I pray yee.
  PRIN.   Your grace is welcome, how fares your Majestie?   2470
  QUEE.   Never so ill deare Prince, for now I feare,
Even as a wretched caitiffe kil'd with care,

---

[1] Cf. V.3.42–8.

I am accusde of treason, and the king
Is now in counsell to dispose of me,
I know his frowne is death, and I shall dye.
    PRIN. Who are your accusers?
    QUEE. I know not.
    PRIN. How know yee then his Grace is so incenst?
    QUEE. One of my Gentlemen passing by the presence,
Tooke up this bill of accusations,   2480
Wherein twelve Articles are drawne against me,
It seems my false accusers lost it there.
Here they accuse me of conspiracie,
That I with *Cranmer*, *Latimer*, and *Ridley*,
Doo seeke to raise rebellion in the state,
Alter religion, and bring *Luther* in,
And to new government inforce the king,
    PRIN. Then thats the cause that *Cranmer* was remooved,
But did your Highnesse ere conferre with them.
As they have here accusde yee to the king?   2490
    QUEE. Never nor ever had I one such thought,
As I have hope in him my soule hath bought.
    PRIN. Then feare not gratious Maddam, Ile to the king,
And doubt not but Ile make your peace with him.
    QUEE. O pleade for me, tell him my soule is cleare,
Never did thought of treason harbor heere,
As I intended to his sacred life,
So be it to my soule or joy or greefe.
    PRIN. Stay here till I returne, Ile move his majestie,
That you may answer your accusers presently. [*Exit Prince* 2500
    QUEE. O I shall never come to speake with him,
The Lion in his rage is not so sterne,
As Royal *Henry* in his wrathfull spleene,
And they that have accus'd me to his grace,
Will worke such meanes I neare shall see his face.
Wretched Queene *Katherin*, would thou hadst beene
Kate Parre still, and not great Englands Queene.   [*Ent. Comp.*
    COMP. Health to your Majestie.
    QUEE. Wish me good *Compton* woe and miserie,
This giddie flattering world I hate and scoffe,   2510
Ere long I know Queene *Katherins* head must off.
Came ye from the King?
    COMP. I did fayre Queene, and much sad tidings bring.
His grace in secret hath reveil'd to me
What is intended to your Majesty,
Which I in love and duty to your highnesse,

Am come to tell ye and to counsell ye
The best I can in this extremitie.
Then on my knees I dare intreat your grace,
Not to revaile what I shall say to you,   2520
For then I am assurde that deaths my due.
   QUEE. I will not on my faith, good *Comptton* speake,
That with thy sad reports my heart may breake.
   COMP. Thus then at your fayre feete my life I lay,
In hope to drive your highnes cares away:
You are accusde of high conspiracy
And treason gainst his royall majesty.
So much they have insenst his excellency,
That he hath granted firme comm[i]ssion
To attach your person and convay ye hence,   2530
Close prisoner to the Towre. Articles are drawne,
And time appoynted for arrainement there.
Good maddame be advis'd, by this I know,
The officers are sent to arest your person:
Prevent their malice, hast ye to the King.
Ile use such meanes that you shall speake with him,
There plead your Innocency, I know his grace
Will heare ye mildly therfore delay not,
If you be taken ere you see the king,
I feare ye never more shall speake to him.   2540
   QUE. Oh *Compton* twixt thy love and my sage feare,
I feele ten thousand sad vexations here,
Leade on I pray, Ile be advis'd by thee,
The King is angry and the Queene must dye.   [*Exit*

[*Sc. xiii.*]

       Enter Boner & Gardner *with the commission.*

   GARD. Come *Boner* now strike sure; the yrons hott.
Urge all thou canst, let nothing be forgot.
We have the Kings hand here to warrant us,
Twas well the Cardinall came and so luckely,
Who urg'd, the state would quite be ruined,   2550
If that religion thus were altered.
Which made his highnes with a firy spleene,
Direct out warrants to attache the Queene.
   BON. Twas excellent; that Ceder once orethrowne,
To crop the lower shrubs let us alone.
   GARD. Those Articles of accusations,
We fram'd against her being lost by you

32—N.D.S S. 4.

Had like to overthrow our pollicy,
Had we not stoutly urg'd his majesty.

    BON. Well well, what's now to be done.   2560

    GARD. A gard must be provided speedely,
To beare her prisoner unto London Towre,
And watch convenient place to arest her person.

    BON. Tush any place shall serve, for who dare contradict
His highnesse hand; even from his side wele hale her,
And beare her quickly to her longest home,
Lest we and ours by her to ruine come.

    GARD. About it then, let them untimely dye,
That scorne the Pope and *Romes* supremacie.   [*Exeunt*

[*Sc. xiv.*]

        Enter the King & Prince, *the* Guarde *before them.*

    KING Guarde, watch the dores and let none come nere
        us,   2571
But such as are attendant on our person:
Mother a God, tis time to sturre, I see,
When traitors creeps so nere our majesty:
Must English *Harry* walke with armed Gards,
Now in his old age, must I feare my life,
By hatefull treason of my Queene and wife?

    PRIN. I do beseech your royall majesty,
To here her speake ere ye condemne her thus.

    KING Go to *Ned*, I charge ye speake not for her,   2580
Shes a dangerous traytor, how now, who knockes so loud there?

    GARD. Tis Cardinall *Wolsye* my Lord.

    KIN. And it be the Devill, tell him he comes not here.
Byd him attend us till our better leasure:
Come hither *Ned*, let me conferre with you.
Didst ever heare the disputation
Twixt *Cranmer* and the Queene about Religion?

    PRIN. Never my Lord, I thinke they never yet
At any time had speech concerning it.

    KING O thou art deceaved *Ned*, it is too certaine.   2590
                                            [*knocks*

Hoyday, more knocking, knock yrons on his heeles,
And beare him hence what ere he be disturbe us, who ist?

    GARD. S. *William Compton* my Leedge.

    KIN. Ist he, well let him in, Gods holy mother, heere's a
stur indeed. *Compton* ye knock too lowde for entrance here.

You care not though the king be neere so neere, say ye sir,
haw?

 COMP. I do beseech you pardon for my bouldnesse.

 KING Well, what's your busines?

 COMP. The Queene my Lord intreats to speake with you, 2600

 KIN. Body a me, is she not rested yet?
Why doe they not convay her to the Towre,
We gave commission to attach her presently.
Where is she?

 COMP. At the dore my Soveraigne.

 KIN. So nere our presence, keepe her out I charge ye.
Bend all your Holbeards points against the dore,
If she presume to enter strike her through.
Dare she presume againe to looke on us?

 PRI. Upon my knees, I do beseech your highnes 2610
To heare her speake.

 KIN. Up *Ned*, stand up. I will not looke on her,
Mother a god, stand close and gard it sure,
If she come in, ile hang ye all I sweare.

 PRIN. I doe beseech your Grace.

 KIN. Sir boye no more, ile here no more of her,
Proud slut, bold traitresse, and forgetfull beast,
Yet dare she further move our patience?

 PRIN. Ile pawne my princely word, right royall father,
She shall not speake a word to anger ye. 2620

 KIN. Will you pawne your word for her? mother a god
The Prince of *Wales* his word is warrant for a king,
And we will take it *Ned*, go call her in, [*Enter Queene*
Sir *William* let the gard attend without.
Reach me a chaire, all but the prince depart.
How now, what doe you weepe and kneele,
D[o]us your black soule the gylte of conscience feele?
Out, out, your a traytor.

 QUE. A traytor, O you all seeing powres,
Here witnesse to my Lord my loyalty. 2630
A traytor. O then you are too mercifull.
If I have treason in me, why rip ye not
My ugly hart out with your weapons poynt?
O my good Lord, If it have traytors blood,
It will be black, deform'd, and tenibrous,
If not, from it will spring a scarlet fountaine,
And spit defiance in their perjurde throates
That have accusde me to your majesty,
Making my state thus full of misery.

KIN.   Canst thou deny it?   2640
QUEE.   Else should I wrongfully accuse my selfe.
O my deare Lord I do beseech your highnesse
To satisfie your wronged Queene in this,
Upon what ground growes this suspicion,
Or who thus wrongfully accuseth me
Of cursed treason gainst your majesty.
KIN.   Some probable effects my selfe can witnesse,
Others our faithfull subjects can testifie:
Have you not oft maintained arguments,
Even to our face against religion: 2650
Which joyn'd with other complots show it selfe,
As it is gathered by our loyall subjects,
For treason Cappitall against our person?
Gods holy mother, youle remove us quickly,
And turne me out, old *Harry* must away,
Now in mine age, lame and halfe bed-rid,
Or else youle keepe me fast inough in prison.
Haw, mistris, these are no hatefull treasons these.
QUEEN   Heaven on my fore-head write my worst intent,
And let your hate against my life be bent,   2660
If ever thought of ill against your majestie,
Was harbor'd here refuse me gratious God,
To your face, my ledge, if to your face I speake it.
It manifestes no complot, nor no treason,
Nor are they loyall that so injure me;
What I did speake, was as my womans wit,
To hold out Argument could compasse it,
My puny schollership is helde too weake
To maintaine proofes about religion.
Alas I did it but to wast the time,   2670
Knowing as then your grace was weake and sickly,
So to expell parte of your paine and griefe:
And for my good intent they seeke my life,
O God, how am I wrong'd.
KIN.   Ha, saist thou so, was it no otherwise?
QUE.   What should I say, that you might credit me,
If I am false, heaven strike me sodainly.
KING   Body a me, what everlasting knaves are these that
wrong thee thus, alas poore *Kate*, come stand up, stand up,
wipe thine eyes, wipe thine eyes, fore god twas told me that   2680
thou wert a traytor: I could hardly thinke it, but that it
was applide so hard to me. Godsmother *Kate* I feare my life
I tell ye, King *Harry* would be loath to die by treason now,

that has bid so many brunts unblemished, yet I confesse
that now I growe stiffe, my legges faile me first, but they
stand furthiest from my hart, and thats still sound, I thanke
my God. Give me thy hand, come kisse me *Kate*, so now ime
friends againe. Hurson knaves, crafty varlets, make thee a
traytor to oulde *Harries* life, well, well, ile meete with some on
them. Sfoute come sit on my knee *Kate*. Mother a god he that 2690
says th'art false to me, by Englands crowne ile hang him
presently.

    QUE. When I have thought of ill against your state,
Let me be made the vildest reprobate.

    KIN. Thats my good *Kate*, but byth mary God, Queene
Katherne you must thanke prince *Edward* here.
For but for him th'adst gone toth towre I swere.

    QUE. I shalbe ever thankfull to his highnesse,
And pray for him and for your majesty,

    KI. Come *Kate* weell walke a while eth garden heere; who 2700
keepes the dore there?

    COMP. My Lord.

    KING Sir *William Compton*, here, take my ring,
Bid Doctor *Cranmer* haste to Court againe,
Give him that token of king *Henries* love,
Discharge our guards, we feare no traytors hand,
Our State beloved of all doth firmely stand:
Go *Compton*.

    COMP. I go my Lord.

    KING Bid *Wolsey* haste him to our royall presence. 2710
Great *Charles* the mighty Romane Emperour,
Our Nephew, and the hope of Christendome
Is landed in our faire Dominion,
To see his Unckle and the English Court;
Wee'le entertaine him with imperiall port:
Come hither *Ned*.

Enter Bonner *and* Gardner *with the guard.*

    GAR. Felows, stay there, and when I cal, come forward,
The service you pursue, is for the king;
Therefore I charge you to performe it boldly, 2720
We have his hand and seale to warrant it.

    GUARD Wee'le fellow you with resolution sir,
The Church is on our side, what should we feare?

    GARD. See yonder, shees talking with his Majesty,
Thinke you we may attempt to take her heere?

BON.   Why should we not, have we not firme commission
To attach hir any where? be bold, and feare not:
Fellowes come forward.

KING   How now, whats heere to do?

QU.   The Bishops it seemes my Lord would speake   2730
with you.

KING   With bills and holberds, well, tarry there *Kate*,
Ile go my selfe; Now wherefore come you?

GARD.   As loyall subjects to your state and person,
We come to apprehend that trayterous woman.

KING   Y'are a couple of drunken knaves and varlets.
Gods holy mother, shee is more true and just,
Then any Prelate that Subornes the Pope
Thus to usurpe upon our government?
Call you her traytor? y'are lying beastes and false   2740
conspiratours.

BON.   Your Majesty hath seene what proofes we had.

KING   Here you *Bonner*, you are a whorson coxcomb.
What proofes had ye, but treasons of your owne inven-
tions?

QUEENE   O my deare Lorde, respect the reverend
Bishoppes.
Bonner and *Gardner* loves your Majestie.

KING   Alas poore *Kate*, thou think'st full little what
they come for;   2750
Thou hast small reason to commend their loves,
That falsly have accusde thy harmelesse life.

QUEENE   O God, are these mine enemies?

GARD.   We have your highnesse hand to warrant it.

KING   Lets see it then.

GARD.   Tis heere my Liege.

KING   So, nowe yee have both my hand[s] to contradict
what one hand did: and now our word againe shal serve
as warrant to beare you both as prisoners to the Fleete,
Where you shall answer this conspiracie.   2760
You fellows that came to attach the Queene,
Lay hands on them, and beare them to the Fleete.

QUEENE   O I beseech your highnesse on my knees,
Remit the doome of their imprisonment.

KING   Stand up good *Kate*, thou wrongst thy Majesty,
To plead for them that thus have injurde thee.

QUEENE   I have forgotten it, and do still intreate
Their humble pardons at your gratious feet.

KING   Mother of God, what a foolish woman's this,
Well, for her sake we rovoke our doome,   2770
But come not neere us as you love your lives:
Away and leave us, you are knaves and miscreants,
Whorson Caitifes, come to attach my Queene!
    QUEENE   Vex not my Lord, it will distemper you.

Enter Branden

KING   Mother a God, Ile temper some on them for't
How now *Branden*?
    BRAN.   The Emperour my Lord.
    KING   Get a traine readie there, *Charles Branden*, come,
Weel'e meete the Monarke of imperiall *Rome*:   2780
Go *Ned*, prepare your selfe to meete the Emperour,
Weele send you further notice of our pleasure.

Enter Cardinall and Wil.

Attend the Prince there: Welcome Lord Cardinall,
Hath not your tedious jorney into *France*,
Disturbed your Graces health and reverent person?
    WIL.   No, no, ne're feare him *Harry*, he haz got
More by the journey, heele be Pope shortly.
    KING   What, *William*, how chance I have not seene 2790
you to day? I thought you would not have bin the hind-
most man to salute me.
    WIL.   No more I am not *Harry*, for yonder is Patch
behinde me, I could never get him before me; since thou
conjurst him i'th great chamber, all the horse i'th towne
cannot hawle him into thy presence I warrant thee.
    KING   Will hee not come in?
    WIL.   Not for the world, he stands watching at the dore.
Hee'le not stirre while the Cardinal come;
Then the foole will follow him every where.
    WOOL.   I thank you *William*, I am beholding to you stil. 2800
    WIL.   Na my Lord, I am more beholding unto you, I
thanke your foole for it, we have ransakled your wine-
sellers since you went into *France*: Doe you blush my Lord?
na, thats nothing, you have wine there, is able to set a colour
in any mans face I warrant it.
    KING   Why *William*, is the Cardinalls wine so good?
    WIL.   Better then thine Ile be sworne, Ile take but
two handfulls of his wine, and it shall fill foure hogges-
heads of thine (looke here else).

wool.   *Mor[t] dieu.*   2810

wil.   Mor divell, ist not? for without conjuring, you could
never do it: But I pray you my Lord call uppon Mor dieu
no longer, but speake plaine English, you have deceived
the king in French and Latine long enough a conscience.

king   Is his wine turned into gold, *Wil*?

wool.   The foole mistakes, my gratious Soveraigne.

wil.   I, I my Lord, ne're set your wit to the fooles, *Wil
Summers* will be secret now, and say nothing; if I would
be a blabbe of my tongue, I could tell the King how many   2820
barrells full of gold and silver there was sixe times filled
with plate and jewells, twentie great truncks with Crosses,
Crosiers, Copes, Miters, Maces, golden Crucifixes, besides
the foure hundreth and twelve thousand pound that poore
Chimneys paid for Peeter pence. But this is nothing, for
when you are Pope, you may pardon your selfe for more
knavery then this comes to.

king   Go too foole, you wrong the Cardinall,
But grieve not *Woolsey, William* will be bold:
I pray you set on to meete the Emperour,   2830
The Mayor and Cittizens are gone before,
The Prince of *Wales* shall follow presently,
And with our George and coller of estate,
Present him with the order of the Garter:
Great *Maximilian* his progenitour,
Upon his breast did weare the English Crosse,
And underneath our Standerd marcht in armes,
Receiving pay for all his warlike hoste;
And *Charles* with knighthood shall be honored:
Beginne Lord Cardinall, greete his Majestie,   2840
And we our selfe will follow presently.

wol.   I go my Soveraigne.

wil.   Faire weather after yee:
Well, and ere he come to be Pope, I shall bee plung'd
for this.

queene   *William*, you have angred the Cardinall I can
tell you.

king   T'is no matter *Kate*, Ile anger him worse ere long,
Though for a while I smooth it to his face:
I did suspect what heere the foole hath found.   2850
He keepes forsooth, a high Court Legantine,
Taxing our subjects, gathering summes of gold,
Which he belike hath hid to make him Pope;
A Gods name let him, that shall be our owne.

But to our businesse, come Queene *Katherin*,
You shall with us to meete the Emperour.
Let all your Ladies be in readinesse:
Go, let our guard attend the Prince of *Wales*;
Upon our selfe, the Lords and Pentioners
Shall give attendance in their best array,   [*Sound*   2860
Let all estates be ready; come faire *Kate*,
The Emperour shall see our English state.

[*Sc. xv.*]   [*Sound*

Enter Emperour, Cardinall, Mayor,
and Gentlemen.

 WOOL.   Your Majesty is welcome into *England*,
The king our Master, will rejoyce to see
Great *Charles* the royall Emperours Majesty.
 EMPE.   We thank your paines my good L. Cardinall,
And much our longing eyes desires to see   2870
Our kingly unckle and his princely sonne,
And therefore, when you please I pray set on.
 WOOL.   On gentlemen, and meete the Prince of *Wales*,
That comes forerunner to his royall father,
To entertaine the Christian Emperour:
Meane while, your Majesty may heere behold
This warlike kingdome faire *Metropolis*,
The Citty *London*, and the river *Thames*,
And note the scituation of the place.
 EMPE.   We do my Lord, and count it admirable: 2880
But see Lord Admirall, the Prince is comming.

                  [*Sound*

Enter the Prince with a Herald before him, bearing the
Coller and garter, the guard and Lords attending.

 EMP.   Well met yong coosen.
 PRIN.   I kisse your highnesse hand,
And bid you welcome to my fathers land;
I shall not neede inferre comparisons,
Welcome beyond compare, for so your excellencie
Hath honoured England, in containing you,   2890
As with all princely pompe and state we can,
Weele entertaine great *Charles* the Austrian:
And first, in signe of honour to your grace,
I heere present this collar of estate,
This golden garter of the knighthoods order,

An honour to renowne the Emperour:
Thus as my father hath commanded me,
I entertaine your royall Majestie.

    EMP. True honoured off-spring of a famous King,
Thou dost amaze me, and doost make me wish   2900
I were a second sonne to *Englands* Lord,
In interchange of my imperiall seate;
To live with thee faire hope of Majestie,
So well our welcome we accept of thee,
And with such princely spirit pronounce the word,
Thy fathers state can no more state afford.

    PRINCE Yes my good Lord, in him theres Majesty,
In me theres love with tender infancie.   [*Sound trum.*

    WOOL. The trumpets sound my Lord, the King is
comming.   2910

    PRINCE Go all of you attend his royall person,
Whilst we observe the Emperours Majesty.

                [*Sound*

Enter the Heralds first, then the Trumpets next the guard, then
    Mace-bearer and swords, then the Cardinall, then Branden,
    then the King, after him the Queene, Lady Mary, *and Ladies*
    attending.

    KING Hold, stand I say.
    BRAN. Stand gentlemen.
    WOOL. Cease those trumpets there.   2920
    KING Is the Emperour yet come in sight of us?
    WOOL. His Majestie is hard at hand my Lord.
    KING Then *Branden*, sheathe our Sword, and beare our
    Maces downe,
In honour of my Lord, the Emperour:
Forward againe.

    BRAN. On Gentlemen afore, sound trumpets and
set forwards.

    PRINCE Behold my father, gratious Emperour.
    EMPE. Weele meete him Coosen: 2930
Unckle of *England*, King of *France* and *Ireland*, defender
of the antient Christian faith;
With greater joy I do embrace thy breast,
Then when the seaven Electors crowned me,
Great Emperour of the Christian Monarchy.

    KING Great *Charles*, the first Emperour of *Almayne*,
King of the Romans, *Semper Augustus*, warlike king of *Spaine*
and *Cicily*, both *Naples*, *Navar* and *Arragon*, king of *Creete*

and great *Jerusalem*, Arch-duke of *Austria*, Duke of *Millaine*,
Brabant, Burgundy, Tyrrell and *Flanders*, with this great title   2940
I embrace thy breast,
And how thy sight doth please, suppose the rest.
Sound trumpets, while my faire Queene *Katerine*
Gives entertainment to the Emperour.   [*Sound*
Welcome againe to England princely Coosen,
We dwell heere, but in an outward continent,
Where winters ice-cickles hangs on our beards,
Bordring upon the frozen Orcades,
Our northern-point, compast with the Artike sea,
Where raging *Boreas* styes from winters mouth,   2950
Yet are our bloods as hote, as where the Sun doth rise.
We have no golden mines to leade you to,
But hearts of proofe, and what we speake, weele do.
    EMP.   We thanke you Unckle, & now must chide you;
If we be welcome to your Country,
Why is the antient league now broke betwixt us?
Why have your Heralds in the French kings cause,
Breathed defiance gainst our dignity,
When face to face, we met at *Landersey?*
    KING   My Heroalds to defie your Majestie?   2960
Your grace mistakes, we sent Ambassadors
To treate a peace betweene the French and you,
Not to defie you as an enemy.
    EMP.   Yet Unckle in king *Henries* name he came,
And boldly to our face did give the same.
    CARD.   Hell stop that fatall boding Emperors throte,
That sings against us this dismall Ravens note.
    KING   Mother of God, if this be true, we see
There are more kings in *England* now then wee:
Wheres Cardinall *Woolsey?*   2970
Heard you this newes in *France?*
    WOOL.   I did my Liege, and by my meanes twas done,
Ile not deny it; I had Commission
To joyne a league between the French and him,
Which he withstanding as an enemie,
I did defie him from your Majestie.
    KING   Durst thou presume so, base-borne Cardinall,
Without our knowledge to abuse our name;
Presumptuous traitor, under what pretence
Didst thou attempt to brave the Emperour?   2980
Belike thou meantst to levell at a crowne,
But thy ambitious crowne shall hurle thee downe.

WOOL. With reverence to your Majesty, I did no more
Then I can answer to the holy sea.

KING Vilaine, thou canst not answer it to me,
Nor shadow thy insulting trechery:
How durst ye sirra, in your ambassage,
Unknowne to us, stampe in our royall coyne
The base impression of your Cardinall hat,
As if you were copartner in the Crowne?   2990
Ego & Rex meus: you and your king must be
In equal state, and pompe, and Majestie:
Out of my presence hatefull impudencie.

WOOL. Remember my Liege, that I am Cardinall
And deputie unto his holinesse.

KING Be the divells Deputie, I care not I,
Ile not be baffeld by your trechery;
Y'are false abusers of religion,
You can corrupt it and forbid the King,
Upon the penaltie of the Popes blacke curse,   3000
If he should pawne his Crowne for souldiers pay,
Not to suppresse an old religious Abbey,
Yet you at pleasure have subverted foure,
Seizing their lands, tunning up heapes of gold,
Secret convaiance of our royall Seale,
To raise Collections to inrich thy state,
For which sir, we command you leave the Court.
We heere discharge you of your offices:
You that are *Caiphas*, or great Cardinall,
Haste ye with speede unto your Bishopricke,   3010
There keepe you, till you heare further from us:
Away and speake not.

WOOL. Yet will I prowdly passe as Cardinall,
Although this day define my heavy fall.   [*Exit*

EMP. I feare king *Henry*, and my royall Unckle,
The Cardinall will curse my progresse hether.

KING No matter coosen, beshrew his trecherous hart,
Haz moov'd my blood to much impatience.

Enter Will Summers.

Wheres *Wil Summers*? come on wise *William*,   3020
We must use your little wits, to chase this
Anger from our blood againe:
What art thou doing?

WIL. I am looking round about the Emperour, mee

thinks tis a strange sight, for though he have seene more
fooles then I, yet I never saw no more Emperours but
him.

    EMP.   Is this *Wil Summers*? I have heard of him in all
the Princes Courts in Christendome.

    WIL.   Law ye my lord, you have a famous foole of mee,   3030
I can tell yee,
Wil Summers is knowne farre and neere yee see.

    KING   I, are you ryming *William*, na, then I am for yee,
I have not rymed with yee a great while, and now Ile
challenge yee, and the Emperour shall bee judge beetweene
us.

    WIL.   Content my Lord, I am for ye all, come but one
at once and I care not.

    KING   Say yee so sir, come *Kate*, stand by mee,
Weele put you to an unplus presentlie.   3040

    QUEENE   To him *Wil*.

    WIL.   I warrant you Madam.

    KING   Answer this sir,
The bud is spread, the Rose is red, the leafe is greene,

    WIL.   A wench t'is sed, was found in your bed, besides
the Queene.

    QUEENE   Godamarcy for that *Wil*,
Theres two angells for thee:
Ifaith my Lord I am glad I know it.

    KING   Gods mother *Kate*, wilt thou beleeve the foole?   3050
he lies, he lies! a sirra *William*, I perceive and't had beene
so, you would have shamed me before the Emperour,
yet *William* have at you once more,
In yonder Tower, theres a flower, that hath my hart.

    WIL.   Within this houre, she pist full sower, & let a fart.

    EMP.   Hees too hard for you my Lord, i'le try him
one venye my selfe, what say you to this, *William*?
An Emperour is greate, high is his seate, who is his foe?

    WIL.   The wormes that shall eate, his carkas for meate,
whether he will or no.   3060

    EMP.   Well answer'd *Wil*, yet once more I am for ye,
A ruddy lip, with a cherry tip, is fit for a King.

    WIL.   I, so he may dip, about her hip, i'th tother thing.

    EMP.   Haz put me downe my Lord.

    WIL.   Who comes next then?

    KING   The Queene *William*, looke to your selfe;
To him *Kate*.

    QUEENE   Come on William, answer to this,

What could I take, my head doth ake, what phisick's
    good?   3070
    WIL. Heeres one will make, the cold to breake, and
    warme your blood.
    QUEENE I am not repulst at first *William*, againe sir,
Women and their wills, are dangerous ills, as some men
    suppose.
    WIL. She that pudding fills, when snow lies o'th hills,
    must keepe cleane her nose.
    KING Inough good *William*, y'are too hard for all:
My Lord the Emperour, we delay too long,
Your promised welcome to the English Court.   3080
The honourable order of the garter
Your Majestie shall take immediately,
And sit instalde therewith in *Windsor* Castle.
I tell ye there are lads girt with that order,
That wil ungirt the prowdest Champion:
Set forwards there, regard the Emperours state,
First in our Court weele banquet merrily,
Then mount on steedes, and girt in complete steele,
Weele tugge at Barriers, Tilt and turnament:
Then shall yee see the Yeomen of my guard   3090
Wrestle, shoote, throw the sledge, or pitch the barre,
Or any other active exercise:
Those triumphs past, weele forthwith haste to *Windsor*,
S. *Gorges* knight shall be the Christian Emperour.

                                        [*Exeunt Omnes*

F I N I S

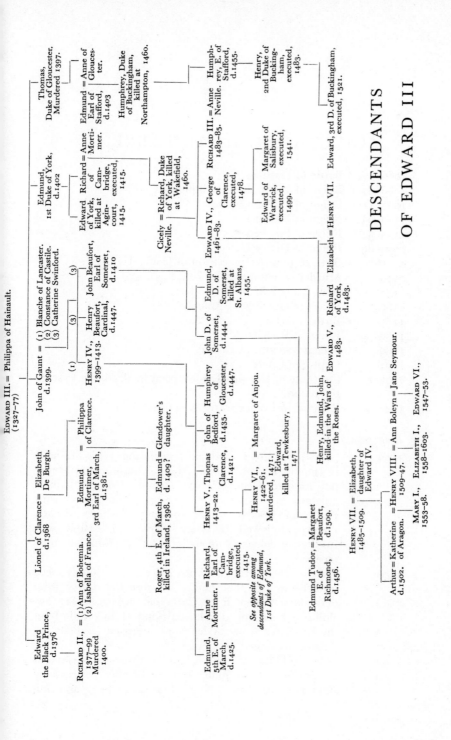

DESCENDANTS OF EDWARD III

CHRONOLOGICAL TABLE

1066   Battle of Hastings.
1066–87   Reign of William the Conqueror.
1087–1100   Reign of William Rufus.
1100–35   Reign of Henry I.
1135–54   Reign of Stephen.
1154–89   Reign of Henry II.
c. 1167   Birth of John, youngest son of Henry II.
1170   Murder of Thomas à Becket.
1177   John made King of Ireland.
1186   Death of Geoffrey of Anjou.
1187   Birth of Arthur, Duke of Anjou.
1189–99   Reign of Richard I.
1189   Richard went on Crusade.
1191   Capture of Acre.
1193–4   Captivity of Richard I. John tried ineffectually to seize the realm.
1194–9   Richard in France warring against Philip.

King John

1199   (April) Richard I died after declaring John his heir. Normandy accepted John; Anjou, Touraine and Maine put forward Geoffrey's son Arthur. (May 27) John crowned at Westminster. (Aug.) Conference with Philip of France (who supported Arthur's French claims), followed by war. (Sept. 22) Arthur and Constance delivered up to John at Le Mans, but they escaped.

1200   (Jan.) Truce arranged, with marriage of John's niece Blanche to Dauphin Louis. To raise the dowry John demanded money from Cistercian abbots. (May 22) Philip acknowledged John as King of England. John divorced his wife Avice and married Isabella of Angoulême (aged 12).

1202   (March) Philip demanded John's continental possessions for Arthur. (July) John's mother Eleanor besieged by Arthur in Mirebeau. (Aug.) John freed her, capturing

Arthur and his sister Eleanor. Arthur refused to abandon French alliance.

1203	(April?) Arthur died, probably murdered.
1204	Normandy lost by John's inaction.
1205	John interfered in election of new Archbishop of Canterbury.
1206	Inconclusive war in France. (Oct. 26) John accepted truce for two years, surrendering claim to dominions north of Loire.
1207	(June) Pope consecrated Stephen Langton as Archbishop. (July) John drove out the monks of Canterbury.
1208	(March) Pope laid interdict on England.
1208-9	Negotiations about interdict failed. Threatened with excommunication, John pillaged the clergy, especially Cistercians.
1210	Expedition to Ireland. Arrest and fine of all Jews in England.
1211	Welsh expedition. (Aug.) Abortive meeting with Pandulf and Durand, papal legates.
1212	A papal bull excommunicated John and asked Philip to depose him. (Aug.) Plots against him revealed. Prophecy of Peter of Pomfret.
1213	(May) Lords invited Philip to invade England. John submitted to Pandulf. (June) French fleet destroyed by Earl of Salisbury. Peter of Pomfret hanged on Ascension Day. (July) Archbishop Langton absolved John, who promised to observe laws of Henry I.
1214	Northern barons refused help, but John and Otho of Saxony invaded France. (July 27) Otho crushed at Bouvines; Salisbury captured; John driven home discredited. (Nov.) Northern lords met at Bury St. Edmunds, demanding a charter of liberties.
1215	John gave way, temporarily, at Runnymede. (June 15) Magna Carta signed. King gathered mercenaries; Pope freed him from his oath and excommunicated his enemies. (Oct.) John took Rochester. Legate Gualo forbade Louis to invade England.
1216	(May) Louis landed; (June 14) took Winchester; was joined by Earl of Salisbury and others. John retreated into East Anglia, wasting the country. (Oct.) Lost his baggage in the Wash. Fell ill at Cistercian Abbey of Swinstead. (Oct. 19) Died at Newark. William, Earl of Pembroke crowned John's elder son (aged 9) at Gloucester, and raised siege of Lincoln.

1217 (May) Louis's army defeated at Lincoln, and Hubert de Burgh destroyed the French fleet. (Sept.) Louis made peace at Lambeth and left England.

1216–72 Reign of Henry III.

1272–1307 Reign of Edward I.

1307–27 Reign of Edward II.

1327–77 Reign of Edward III.

1377–99 Reign of Richard II.

Henry IV

1367 Henry son of John of Gaunt born at Bolingbroke, Lincolnshire.

c. 1380 Henry married to Mary Bohun.

1387 Henry joined Gloucester, Arundel, Warwick and Mowbray (the Appellants) against Richard II. (Aug.) Son Henry born.

1389 Richard dismissed the Appellants, but restored Henry to favour.

1390 Henry promised to join a crusade against Barbary (N. Africa), but instead joined one into Lithuania, and besieged Vilna.

1392 (July) Went on Crusade in Prussia. (Sept. 23) Started from Danzig on pilgrimage to Jerusalem, which he reached early in 1393. (July 5) Arrived home.

1395 Henry's wife died.

1397 (Sept.) Henry made Duke of Hereford.

1398 (Sept.) The abortive duel at Coventry: Hereford exiled; his son Henry treated kindly by Richard II.

1399 (July) Henry landed at Ravenspur. (Sept. 30) Claimed throne. (Oct. 13) Coronation.

1399–1413 Reign of Henry IV.

1400 (Aug.) Henry invaded Scotland but with forces too weak to proceed. (Sept.) Owen Glendower's rising, after a feud with Lord Grey of Ruthin. King invaded N. Wales but could not find Glendower. Prince Henry left in authority at Chester. (Dec.) Visit of Greek Emperor, Manuel Palaiologos, but Henry too poor to give him aid against Turks.

1401 Prince of Wales ordered to attack Glendower. (Sept. 8) Attempt to murder King in his bed. (Oct.) Short expedition to N. Wales.

1402 Negotiations to wed Prince Henry to Scandinavian princess Catharine. A false 'Richard II' appeared in

	Scotland. (June) Owen Glendower captured Lord Grey and Edmund Mortimer. (Sept.) Bad weather foiled King's retaliatory invasion, but (Sept. 14) the Percies defeated the Scots at Homildon Hill. (Oct.) Northumberland brought chief prisoners to White Hall.
1403	(Feb.) Henry IV married Joan of Brittany. (March) Quarrel with the Percies. (July 21) Battle of Shrewsbury; death of Hotspur. (Aug.) Northumberland surrendered his castles. Henry made a short Welsh campaign.
1404	French invaders captured at Dartmouth. King unwell; at Eltham for Christmas, when a plot to murder him was discovered.
1405	Bardolph joined Northumberland in revolt, suggesting tripartite division of the land between Percy, Glendower and Edmund Mortimer. Archbishop Scrope of York and Thomas Mowbray, Earl of Nottingham, also rebelled, but surrendered to Westmoreland on May 29, and were hastily executed. Henry drove Percy into Scotland. (Aug.) An expedition into Wales failed but the Welsh menace declined.
1406	Prince of Wales's influence grew as King's health failed. Struggle between the Beauforts and Arundel to dominate the Council. Prince under Beauforts' influence.
1407	Prince in Wales (captured Aberystwyth), and Scotland (forced Scots to a truce).
1408	(Feb. 19) Defeat and death of Northumberland and Bardolph at Bramham Moor.
1410	Parliament suggested confiscation of all Church property, but King and Prince prevented it.
1411–12	Beauforts tried to force ailing King to abdicate in favour of Prince Henry. King refused; Prince dismissed from Council and retired into private life. They were reconciled after Prince was wrongly accused of embezzlement. King planning a crusade.
1413	(March 20) Death of Henry IV, some said from leprosy.

Henry V

1413	King granted a general pardon. Richard II's remains re-buried in Westminster Abbey. Sir John Oldcastle arrested, but escaped from Tower. Lollard plot to seize Henry at Christmas frustrated.

1414 (Jan.) Lollard gathering prevented; many punished. Churchmen advocated war with France. (May 31) Embassy to France, bearing large demands, including hand of Charles VI's daughter Katherine. Other embassies followed French refusal.

1415 Embassies continued, but Henry prepared for war. (July) Conspiracy of Cambridge, Scrope and Grey discovered. (Aug. 7) King embarked for France. (Aug. 17–Sept. 22) Siege of Harfleur. Army weakened by disease; King marched towards Calais but the enemy had broken bridges. (Oct. 25) Battle of Agincourt. (Nov. 16) Henry crossed to Dover; (Nov. 23) entered London in simple attire.

1416 Heirs of Mortimer, Percy and Holland restored to their estates. Attempt to pacify Wales and Scotland. Visits of Emperor Sigismund, William of Holland and envoy from Burgundy to make peace. French refused. Sigismund became Henry's ally.

1417 (July 23) Henry V's second French expedition set sail. Sir John Oldcastle captured in Wales and executed in
1418 London. (July 29) Siege of Rouen began.

1419 (Jan. 13) Rouen capitulated. Burgundy and Dauphin Charles began negotiations (in bad faith). English victories continued. (Sept. 11) Burgundy murdered by Dauphin's men; the new Duke (Philip) recognized Henry V as heir to France. (Dec. 24) General truce, excluding Dauphin.

1420 Conference at Troyes. (May 20) Henry arrived and was betrothed to Katherine. Treaty of Troyes. (June 2) Marriage of Henry and Katherine.

1421 (Feb. 24) Katherine crowned at Westminster. War against Dauphin continued. (June 10) Henry left for Calais. (Dec. 6) Katherine bore a son (Henry VI).

1422 (Aug. 31) Henry V died at Bois de Vincennes, of dysentery or pleurisy. (Nov. 11) Buried in Westminster Abbey.

1422–61 Reign of Henry VI.
1461–83 Reign of Edward IV.
1483 Edward V.
1483–85 Reign of Richard III.
1485–1509 Reign of Henry VII.
1486 Queen Elizabeth bore a son, Arthur.
1491 Birth of Henry VIII.
1501 Prince Arthur married to Katherine of Aragon.

1502	Death of Prince Arthur.
1503	Death of Queen Elizabeth. Henry VII proposed to marry Katherine in order to keep her dowry. Prince Henry contracted to her.
1509	(April 21) Death of Henry VII.

Henry VIII

1509	(June 24) Henry crowned, after marrying Katherine.
1511	Birth of a son, who died.
1513	Defeat and death of James IV of Scotland at Flodden.
1514	(Oct.) King's sister Mary married to Louis XII.
1515	(Jan. 1) Louis XII died; succeeded by Francis I. Henry's envoy, Charles Brandon, Duke of Suffolk, married Mary secretly. Wolsey made a Cardinal and Lord Chancellor.
1516	Birth of Princess Mary (later Queen).
1517	'Evil May-Day' riot against foreigners in London.
1519	Henry dismissed his favourites. Rebuked Sir William Bulmer for leaving his service for Buckingham's.
1520	(June) Henry met Francis I of France at the Field of the Cloth of Gold.
1521	(May 11) Execution of Duke of Buckingham. (Dec. 2) Pope Leo X died; succeeded by Adrian VI; Wolsey disappointed. Wolsey arranged alliance with the Emperor Charles V.
1523	On Adrian VI's death, Clement VII made Pope.
1525	Francis I invaded Italy; captured by Emperor at Pavia. King's demands for money to finance an invasion of France caused riots in East Anglia and opposition in London. Contributions made voluntary.
1526	(Aug.) English alliance with France.
1527	(May) Imperial troops sacked Rome. (July) Wolsey sent to France to fortify alliance. Divorce from Katherine first proposed.
1528	(Jan.) An English and a French herald formally defied the Emperor at Burgos. Interruption of trade with Spain and Netherlands caused new unrest among East-Anglian cloth-makers. Stephen Gardiner and Edward Foxe got Pope's commission for Wolsey and legate Campeggio to hear divorce cause in England.
1529	Campeggio delayed his arrival and then the divorce-hearing. Clement VII fell ill and Wolsey hoped to succeed him, but the Pope recovered and revoked the

trial to Rome. (Oct.) Fall of Wolsey caused by Anne Boleyn and her friends. Sir Thomas More made Chancellor. Favourable opinions about the divorce sought from continental Universities.

1530   (Nov. 4) Wolsey arrested for treason. (Nov. 29) Died at Leicester Abbey.

1531   (May) Lords visited Queen at Greenwich and begged her to allow settlement by arbitration. She refused. (July) Henry parted finally from Katherine.

1532   Church submitted to King. More resigned Great Seal. Cranmer became Archbishop of Canterbury. Pope demanded restitution of Katherine's rights as wife.

1533   (Jan. 25) Henry married Anne Boleyn. (May 23) Cranmer declared the marriage to Katherine invalid. (June 1) Anne Boleyn crowned. (July 11) Pope excommunicated Henry. (Sept.) Anne Boleyn gave birth to a daughter (Elizabeth I). King treated Mary as a bastard.

1534   Act of Succession entailing crown on Anne Boleyn's descendants. More and Bishop Fisher refused to swear.

1535   More and Fisher beheaded. Pope urged European princes to dispossess Henry. Royal visitation of monasteries began under Thomas Cromwell as King's vicegerent.

1536   Spoliation of smaller monasteries. (Jan. 8) Katherine died. (May) Anne Boleyn arrested, accused of incest, etc., and beheaded (19th). (May 20) King betrothed to Jane Seymour. (Oct.) Revolt in north, 'Pilgrimage of Grace'.

1537   (Oct. 12) Queen Jane bore a son (Edward VI). (Oct. 24) She died.

1538   Pope arranged ten years' truce between Charles V and Francis I.

1540   (Jan.) Political Marriage with German Protestant Anne of Cleves. (July) Divorce. Thomas Cromwell executed. (Aug.) Henry married Katherine Howard.

1542   Execution of Katherine Howard for unchastity.

1543   (July) King married Katherine Parr.

1547   (Jan. 21) Execution of Norfolk's son, Surrey the poet. (Jan. 28) Death of Henry VIII.

1547–53 Reign of Edward VI.

1553–58 Reign of Queen Mary.

1558–1603 Reign of Elizabeth I.

1603–25 Reign of James I (James VI of Scotland).

BIBLIOGRAPHY

I. Modern Historical Works
[To supplement the list in Vol. III. 499.]

(*a*) GENERAL

ABRAM, A. *Social Life in the Fifteenth Century*. 1909.

BINDOFF, S. T. *Tudor England*. 1950.

BROWNING, A. *The Age of Elizabeth*. 1935.

CALMETTE, J. AND DEPREZ, E. *La France et L'Angleterre en Conflit*. [Vol. vii, Pt. i of 'Histoire du Moyen Age', in *Histoire Genérale*, ed. G. Glotz, Paris, 1937.]

GROSS, C. *Sources and Literature of English History from the Earliest Times to about 1485*. 1915 edn.

LEE, S. 'The Last Years of Elizabeth', in *Camb. Mod. History*, iii. 1905.

MCKISACK, M. *The Fourteenth Century (1307–1399)*. 1959.

MACKIE, J. D. *The Earlier Tudors*. 1952.

MAITLAND, F. W. 'The Anglican Settlement and the Scottish Reformation', in *Camb. Mod. History*, ii. 1903.

MCFARLANE, K. B. 'England: the Lancastrian Kings, 1399–1461', in *Camb. Medieval History*, viii, Ch. xl. 1936.

MYERS, A. R. *The Late Middle Ages*. 1952.

NEALE, J. E. *Queen Elizabeth*. 1934.

NEWHALL, R. A. *The English Conquest of Normandy, 1416–24*. 1924.

OMAN, C. *The Political History of England (1377–1485)*. 1906.

PETIT-DUTAILLIS, C. *The Feudal Monarchy in France and England*. 1936.

POOLE, A. L. *Medieval England*. 2 vols. 1958 edn.

POOLE, R. L. *Wyclif and Movements for Reformation*. 1889.

READ, CONYERS. *The Bibliography of British History: Tudor Period*. 1933.

TREVELYAN, G. M. *England in the Age of Wycliffe*. 1899.

WILLIAMS, C. H. *The Making of the Tudor Despotism*. 1935 edn.

(*b*) PARTICULAR REIGNS

King John

DAVIS, H. W. C. *England under the Normans and Angevins (1066–1272)*. 1949 edn.

NEEDLER, G. H. *Richard Cœur de Lion in Literature*. 1890.

NORGATE, KATE. *John Lackland*. 1902.

PAINTER, S. *The Reign of King John*. Baltimore. 1949.
POOLE, A. L. *From Domesday Book to Magna Carta (1087–1216)*. 1951.
WARREN, W. L. *King John*. 1961.

Henry IV

BRADLEY, A. G. *Owen Glyndwr and the Last Struggle for Welsh Independence*. N.Y., 1901.
[HAYWARD, SIR JOHN] *The First Part of the Life and Raigne of King Henrie the IIII. extending to the end of the first yeare of his raigne. Written by I. H.* John Wolfe. 1599.
LUDERS, A. *An Essay on the Character of Henry V when Prince of Wales*. 1813.
WYLIE, J. H. *History of England under Henry IV*. 4 vols. 1884–98.

Henry V

BROUGHAM, HENRY. *History of England under the House of Lancaster*. 1852; 1861.
GOODWIN, T. *History of the Reign of Henry V*. 1704.
KINGSFORD, C. L. *Henry V*. (Heroes of the Nations.) 1910; 1923.
MOWAT, R. B. *Henry V*. 1919.
TYLER, J. E. *Henry of Monmouth, or the Life of Henry V*. 2 vols. 1838.
WYLIE, J. H. *The Reign of Henry the Fifth*. 3 vols. 1914–29.

Henry VIII

ACTON, LORD. 'Wolsey and the divorce of Henry VIII', in *Historical Essays and Studies*. 1907.
CREIGHTON, M. *Cardinal Wolsey*. 1888.
FROUDE, J. A. *The Divorce of Catherine of Aragon*. 1891; 1897.
GAIRDNER, J. 'Henry VIII' in *Dictionary of National Biography*.
—— 'The Early Tudors', in *Camb. Mod. History*, i. 1902.
——'Henry VIII' in *Camb. Mod. History*, ii. 1903.
—— ed. *The Reign of Henry VIII from his accession to the death of Wolsey*. 2 vols. 1884.
HACKETT, F. *Henry the Eighth*. 1929.
MERRIMAN, R. B. *The Life and Letters of Thomas Cromwell*. 2 vols. 1902.
POLLARD, A. F. *Henry VIII*. 1905 edn.
—— *Wolsey*. 1929; 1953.
STUBBS, BISHOP. *Lectures on Medieval and Modern History*. 1887.
WILLIAMS, C. H. *England under the Early Tudors*. 1925.

II. Chronicles, Biographies and Historical Poems before Shakespeare

[To supplement the list in Vol. III. 500–1.]

[Anon.] *Gesta Henrici Quinti, Regis Angliae*. Trans. B. Williams. Eng. Hist. Soc. 1850.

COGGESHALL, R. DE. *Radulphi de Coggeshall Chronicon Anglicanum.* Ed. J. Stevenson. Rolls Series, 66, 1875.

ELMHAM, T. *Liber Metricus de Henrico Quinto.* Ed. C. A. Cole (*Memorials of Henry V*). 1858.

ELMHAM, T. (Pseudo-Elmham). *Vita et Gesta Henrici Quinti.* Ed. T. Hearne. 1727.

LE FEVRE, J. *Chronique (1408–35).* Ed. F. Morand. 2 vols. Paris, 1876–81.

MONSTRELET, F. DE. *Chronique (1400–44).* Trans. T. Johnes, 1810. Vol. iv.

NICHOLAS, N. H. ed. *The Battle of Agincourt* (contemporary accounts). 1827.

STRECCHE, J. *Chronicle for the reign of Henry V (1414–22).* Ed. F. Taylor, *John Rylands Library Bulletin*, xvi, 1932.

TITUS LIVIUS. *Titi Livii Foro-Juliensis Vita Henrici Quinti.* Ed. T. Hearne. 1716.

TITUS LIVIUS [Translator of]. *The First English Life of Henry the Fifth* (1513). Ed. C. L. Kingsford. 1911.

WALSINGHAM, T. *The St. Albans Chronicle (1406–20).* Ed. V. H. Galbraith. 1937.

WARNER, W. *Albions England, or historicall map of the same Island. In verse and prose.* G. Robinson for T. Cadman. 1586, 1589, 1592, 1596, 1601.

WAURIN, J. DE. *Recueil des croniques et anchiennes istories de la Grant Bretagne.* Ed. W. Hardy and E. L. C. P. Hardy. 5 vols. Rolls Series, 1864–91.

III. History and Politics in Shakespeare, etc.

[See the list in Vol. III. 501–2.]

ARMSTRONG, W. A. 'The Elizabethan Conception of the Tyrant', *RES* xxii. July, 1946, 161–81.

BAILEY, J. 'Shakespeare's Histories' in *The Continuity of Letters.* 1923.

CHARLTON, H. B. *Shakespearian Tragedy.* Chs. II and III. 1948.

CHAPMAN, R. 'The Wheel of Fortune in Shakespeare's Historical Plays'. *RES* n.s. i. Jan., 1950, 1–7.

KNIGHT, G. W. *The Olive and the Sword.* 1944.

LAIRD, J. 'Shakespeare on the Wars of England', in *Philosophical Incursions into English Literature.* 1947.

REED, H. *English History and Tragic Poetry, as Illustrated by Shakespeare.* 1859.

SIMPSON, R. 'The Politics of Shakespeare's Historical Plays', in *Sh. Soc. Trans.* 1874.

WARNER, B. E. *English History in Shakespeare's Plays.* N.Y., 1894.

ZEEVELD, W. G. 'The Influence of Hall on Shakespeare's English Historical Plays'. *ELH* 3. 1936, 317–53.

IV. Editions and Criticism of Individual Plays

King John

1. Editions of (*a*) the Play, (*b*) Sources and Analogues

(*a*) Fɪ 1623. Modern edns.: F. G. Fleay, 1878; G. C. Moore Smith, *Warwick*, 1900; I. B. John, *Arden*, 1907; H. H. Furness, *Variorum*, 1919; S. T. Williams, *Yale*, 1927; M. R. Ridley, *New Temple*, 1933; J. D. Wilson, *Camb*, 1936; E. A. J. Honigmann, *New Arden*, 1954.

(*b*) FOXE, JOHN. *The Actes and Monuments of Martyrs* . . . 1563.

HALL, EDWARD. *The union of the two noble and illustre famelies* . . . 1548.

HOLINSHED, RAPHAEL. *The Third volume of Chronicles* . . . 1587.

For further details of these see Vol. III, 500–1.

BALE, JOHN. *Kynge Johan*. Ed. J. P. Collier, Camden Soc., 1838; J. S. Farmer (in *The Dramatic Writings of J. B.*) 1907; J. M. Manly, *Specimens of Pre-Shakespearian Drama*, i. 1897–8; W. Bang, *Materialen*, xxv, 1909; J. H. P. Pafford, *MalSoc*, 1931.

COGGESHALL, R. DE. *Chronicon Anglicanum*. Ed. J. Stevenson. Rolls Series, 66, 1875.

[Anon.] *The Troublesome Raigne of John King of England, with the discoverie of King Richard Cordelions Base Sonne (vulgarly named, The Bastard Fawconbridge): also the death of King John at Swinstead Abbey. As it was (sundry times) publikely acted by the Queenes Majesties Players, in the honourable Citie of London.* Imprinted at London for Sampson Clarke . . . 1591.

The Second part of the troublesome Raigne of King John, conteining the death of Arthur Plantaginet, the landing of Lewes, and the poysning of King John at Swinstead Abbey . . . Imprinted at London for Sampson Clarke . . . 1591. Parts 1 and 2 republished as by Shakespeare, V. Simmes for J. Helme, 1611; A. Mathewes for T. Dewe, 1622. Modern edns.: Facsimiles, C. Praetorius, *Sh. Quartos*, xl, xli (Pts. 1, 2), 1888; J. S. Farmer, *Tudor Facsim. Texts*, 1911. W. C. Hazlitt, *ShLib* v, 1875; F. G. Fleay (with *KJ*), 1878; A. Morgan, *Bankside* (with *KJ*), 1892; F. J. Furnivall and J. Munro, *Sh. Classics*, 1913; H. H. Furness, *New Variorum* (with *KJ*), 1919.

2. Critical Studies of Sources, etc.

BONJOUR, A. 'The Road to Swinstead Abbey', *ELH*, xviii, 1951, 253–6.

BOSWELL-STONE, W. G. *Shakspere's Holinshed, The Chronicle and the History Plays Compared*. 1896; 1907.

ELSON, J. 'Studies in the *King John* Plays', in *J. Q. Adams Memorial Studies*. 1948.

GREENEWALD, G. M. *Shakespeare's Attitude to the Catholic Church in King John*. 1938.

KOPPLOW, G. H. E. *Shakespeare's 'King John' und seine Quellen*. Kiel, 1900.

LIEBERMANN, F. 'Shakespeare als Bearbeiter des *King John*', in *Archiv*, 1921–2, cxlii, 177; cxliii, 17, 190.

MOORE SMITH, G. C. 'Shakespeare's *King John* and the *Troublesome Reign*', in *Furnivall Misc.* 1901.

NEEDLER, G. H. *Richard Cœur de Lion in Literature*. 1890.

NICOLL, A. AND J. *Holinshed's Chronicle as Used in Shakespeare's Plays*. 1927.

ROSE, E. 'Shakespeare as an Adapter', in *Macmillan's Mag*. 1878.

SALTER, F. M. 'Shakespeare's King John', in *Trans. of Royal Soc. of Canada*, xliii. 1949, 115–36.

SIMPSON, R. 'The Politics of Shakespeare's Historical Plays', in *Sh. Soc. Trans*. 1874.

SYKES, H. DUGDALE. 'The Troublesome Reign of King John', in *Sidelights on Shakespeare*. 1919.

VAN DE WATER, J. C. 'The Bastard in *King John*', in *ShQ*, xi. 1960, 137–46.

Henry IV, Pts. 1 and 2

1. Editions of (*a*) the Plays, (*b*) Sources and Analogues

(*a*) the Plays

Part 1

Q1 1598. *The History of Henrie the Fourth; With the battell at Shrews-burie, betweene the King and Lord Henry Percy, surnamed Henrie Hotspur of the North. With the humorous conceits of Sir John Falstalffe* ... P(eter) S(hort) for Andrew Wise ... 1598.

Q2 1599. *Newly corrected by W. Shake-speare.* S(imon) S(tafford) for Andrew Wise. Q3 1604. Valentine Simmes, for Mathew Law. Q4 1608. Q5 1613. Q6 1622. F1 1623.

Modern edns.: Q1 facsimile ed. W. Griggs, *Sh. Quartos*, viii, 1881; W. H. Fleming, *Bankside* (parallel text), 1890. R. P. Cowl and A. E. Morgan, *Arden*, 1914; 1923; S. B. Hemingway, *Yale*, 1917, and *New Variorum*, 1936; G. L. Kittredge, Boston, 1940; J. D. Wilson, *Camb.*, 1946; A. R. Humphreys, *New Arden*, 1960.

Part 2

Q 1600 *The Second part of Henrie the fourth, continuing to his death, and coronation of Henrie the fift. With the humours of sir John Falstaffe, and swaggering Pistoll* ... *Written by William Shakespeare.* V(alentine) S(immes) for Andrew Wise.

F1 1623.
Modern edns.: Q facsimile, ed. W. Griggs, *Sh. Quartos*, ix, 1882; W. H. Fleming, *Bankside* (parallel text), 1890; S. B. Hemingway, *Yale*, 1921; R. P. Cowl, *Arden*, 1923; M. A. Shaaber, *New Variorum*, 1940; J. D. Wilson, *Camb.* 1946.

(*b*) Sources and Analogues

(i) For both Parts

BALDWIN, W. ed. *A Myrroure for Magistrates* . . . 1559.
DANIEL, S. *The first fowre bookes of the civile wars* . . . 1595.
HOLINSHED, R. *The Third volume of Chronicles* . . . 1587 edn.
STOW, JOHN. *The Chronicles of England*. 1580; *Annales*, 1592.
[For further details of these see Vol. III, 500–1.]

[Anon.] *The Famous Victories of Henry the fifth: Containing the Honourable Battell of Agin-court* . . . Thomas Creede. 1598. Another issue, 1617. Modern edns.: J. Nichols, *Six Old Plays*, ii, 1779; W. C. Hazlitt, *ShLib* v, 1875. Facsimiles: P. A. Daniel, *Sh. Quartos*, 1887; J. S. Farmer, *Tudor Facsim. Texts*. 1912.

(ii) For Part 1

[Anon.] *A new Enterlude called Thersytes* . . . Imprinted by John Tysdale. n.d. [*c.* 1537]. Modern edns.: J. Haslewood, Roxburghe Club, 1820; Hazlitt's *Dodsley*, i, 1874; J. S. Farmer, *Six Anon. Plays*, 1905. Facsimiles: E. W. Ashbee, 1876; J. S. Farmer, *Tudor Facsim. Texts*. 1912.
[Anon.] *Here begynneth a proper new Interlude of the worlde and the chylde otherwyse called Mundus et Infans and it sheweth of the estate of Chyldehode and Manhode.* Wynkyn de Worde, 1522. Modern edns.: Roxburghe Club, 1817; J. P. Collier, *Dodsley's Old Plays*, xii, 1827; Hazlitt's *Dodsley*, i, 1874; J. M. Manly, *Specimens of Pre-Shakespearian Drama*, i, 1897–8. Facsimile: J. S. Farmer, *Tudor Facsim. Texts*. 1909.
HARCOURT, L. W. V. 'The Two Sir John Fastolfs', in *Trans. of Royal Hist. Soc.* Series 3, iv. 1910.
LYLY, JOHN. *Endimion, The Man in the Moone* . . . 1591. Modern edns.: C. W. Dilke, *Old English Plays*, ii, 1814; G. P. Baker, 1894; F. W. Fairholt, *Dramatic Works*, 2 vols. 1858, 1892; R. W. Bond, *Complete Works*, 3 vols. 1902.
RASTELL, J.? *A new interlude and a mery of the nature of the iiii elements* . . . [1519]. Modern edns.: Percy Society, 1848; Hazlitt's *Dodsley*, i, 1874; T. Fischer, Marburg, 1903; J. S. Farmer, *Six Anonymous Plays*, 1905. Facsimile: J. S. Farmer, *Tudor Facsim. Texts*. 1908.

(iii) For Part 2

[Anon.] *Hyckescorner*. Emprynted by me Wynkyn de Worde [1512?].
   Modern edns.: T. Hawkins, *Origin of English Drama*, i, 1773;
   W. C. Hazlitt's *Dodsley*, i, 1874; J. M. Manly, *Specimens of
   Pre-Shakespearian Drama*, i, 1897–8; J. S. Farmer, *Six Anonymous
   Plays*, 1905. Facsimile: J. S. Farmer, *Tudor Facsim. Texts*. 1908.
[Anon.] *Tarltons Jests*. 1638. Modern edns.: J. O. Halliwell, *Sh. Soc.*
   1844; W. C. Hazlitt, *Sh. Jest-Books*, ii, 1864; Facsimile ed.
   E. W. Ashbee, [1877?]
CROMPTON, R. *L'Authoritie et Jurisdiction des Courts de la Majestie de
   la Roygne* ... 1594.
ELYOT, SIR THOMAS. *The Boke named the Governour*. 1531. 7 other
   editions by 1580. Modern edns.: H. H. S. Croft, 2 vols. 1880;
   F. Watson, 1907.
SMITHE, SIR JOHN. *Instructions, Observations and Orders Militarie* ...
   1595.

2. Critical Studies of Sources, etc.

AX, H. *The Relation of Shakespeare's 'Henry IV' to Holinshed*. Freiburg.
   1912.
BAESKE, W. *Oldcastle-Falstaff in der englischen Literatur bis zu Shakes-
   peare*. Palaestra. l. Berlin. 1905.
BOSWELL-STONE, W. G. *Shakspere's Holinshed, The Chronicle and
   the Historical Plays Compared*. 1896; 1907.
BOWLING, W. G. *The Wild Prince Hal in Legend and Literature*.
   (Washington Univ. Studies, xiii, 1926.)
BRADLEY, A. C. 'The Rejection of Falstaff', in *Oxford Lectures on
   Poetry*. 1909.
CAIN, H. E. 'Further Light on the Relation of *1 and 2 Henry IV*'.
   ShQ iii. 1952, 21–38.
CHARLTON, H. B. 'Shakespeare, Politics and Politicians', in *English
   Assn. Pamph.* 72. 1929.
—— 'Falstaff', in *John Rylands Lib. Bull.*, xix. 1935.
CUNLIFFE, J. W. 'The Character of Henry V as Prince and King',
   in *Columbia Univ. Shakesp. Studies*. N.Y., 1916.
DAWTREY, J. *The Falstaff Saga*. 1927.
DRAPER, J. W. 'Sir John Falstaff'. *RES* viii. 1932, 414–24.
DUTHIE, D. W. *The Case of Sir John Fastolf*. 1907.
GAIRDNER, J. 'Historical Elements in Shakespeare's Falstaff', in
   Fortnightly Review. 1873. (Reprint in Gairdner and Spedding,
   Studies in English History. 1881.)
HART, A. *Shakespeare and the Homilies*. 1934.
HOTSON, L. *Shakespeare versus Shallow*. 1931.
JENKINS, H. *The Structural Problem in Shakespeare's Henry IV*. 1956.
LAW, R. A. 'Structural Unity in the two Parts of Henry IV'. *SPhil.*
   xxiv. 1927, 223.
LEECH, C. 'The Unity of 2 *Henry IV*'. *Sh. Survey*. 1953.

MAXWELL, BALDWIN, 'The Original of Sir John Falstaff—Believe it or not'. *SPhil.* xxvii. 1930.

MONAGHAN, J. 'Falstaff and his Forebears'. *SPhil.* xviii. 1921, 353.

MOORMAN, F. W. 'Shakespeare's History Plays and Daniel's *Civil Wars*'. *ShJb.* xl. 1904.

MORGAN, A. E. 'Some Problems of Shakespeare's *Henry IV*'. *Sh. Assoc.* 1924.

MORGANN, M. *An Essay on the Dramatic Character of Sir John Falstaff.* 1777. Modern edns.: W. A. Gill, 1912; D. Nichol Smith, in *Eighteenth Century Essays on Shakespeare.* 1903.

MOULTON, R. G. 'On Character Development in Shakespeare as illustrated by Macbeth and King Henry V'. *Sh.Soc.Trans.* xxv. 1880–6.

NICOLL, A. AND J. *Holinshed's Chronicle as Used in Shakespeare's Plays.* 1927.

SARRAZIN, G. 'Falstaff, Pistol, Nym und ihre Urbilder', in *Kleine Sh. Studien.* 1902.

SHAABER, M. A. 'The Unity of *Henry IV*', in *J. Q. Adams Memorial Studies.* 1948, 217–27.

STARNES, D. T. 'Shakespeare and Elyot's *Governour*', in *U. of Texas Studies in English,* vii. 1927, 112–32.

——— 'More about the Prince Hal Legend'. *PhilQ.,* xv. 1936. 358–66.

SOLLY-FLOOD, F. 'The Story of Prince Henry of Monmouth and Chief Justice Gascoign'. *2 Royal Hist. Soc. Trans.* iii. 1886.

STOLL, E. E. 'Falstaff', in his *Shakespeare Studies.* 1927.

THÜMMEL, J. 'Der Miles gloriosus bei Shakespeare'. *ShJb* xiii. 1878.

TOLMAN, A. H. 'Why did Shakespeare create Falstaff?' *PMLA* n.s. xxvii. 1919.

TRAVERSI, D. A. '*Henry IV, Pt. 1* and *Henry IV, Pt. 2.*' *Scrutiny* xv. 1948, 24–35; 117–27.

WILSON, J. D. *The Fortunes of Falstaff.* 1943.

Henry V

1. Editions of (*a*) the Play, (*b*) Sources and Analogues

(*a*) Q1 1600 [a 'bad' Quarto]. *The Chronicle History of Henry the fift, With his battel fought at Agin Court in France. Togither with Auntient Pistoll* . . . Thomas Creede, for Tho. Millington, and John Busby. 1600.

Q2 1602; Q3 1619 (dated 1608). F1 1623, *The Life of King Henry the Fift.*

Modern edns. Q1: B. Nicholson, 1875; W. A. Wright, *Camb. Sh.* ix, 1893; Facsimile: C. Praetorius, *Sh. Quartos,* xxvii, 1886. Q3: Facsimile: C. Praetorius, *Sh. Quartos,* xxviii, 1886; Q2: W. W. Greg, 1957. F1: Facsimile: J. D. Wilson, 1931. Parallel Texts: B. Nicholson and P. A. Daniel, 1877; H. P. Stokes, *Bankside,* 1892. W. G. [Boswell-] Stone, 1880; G. C. Moore Smith, *Warwick,* 1896; C. H. Herford,

Eversley, 1900; H. A. Evans, *Arden*, 1903; R. D. French, *Yale*, 1918; G. L. Kittredge, N.Y., 1945; J. D. Wilson, *Camb*, 1947; J. H. Walter, *New Arden*, 1954.

(*b*) BALDWIN, W. ed. *A Myrroure for Magistrates* . . . 1559.

[BRUT] *Chronicles of England*. Ed. W. Caxton, 1580.

DANIEL, S. *The first fowre books of the civile wars* . . . 1595.

FABYAN, R. *The new Chronicles of England and of France* . . . 1516, 1559.

HALL, E. *The union of the two noble and illustre famelies* . . . 1548.

HOLINSHED, R. *The Third volume of chronicles* . . . 1587 edn.

STOW, J. *The Chronicles of England* . . . 1580.

—— *The Annales of England* . . . 1592.

WALSINGHAM, T. *Ypodigma Neustriae vel Normanniae* . . . 1574; 1576.

—— *Historia Anglicana* (1272–1422).

[For further details of these see Vol III, 500–1.]

[Anon.] *The Famous Victories of Henry the fifth* . . . Printed by Thomas Creede. 1598 [cf. *supra*].

[Anon.] *Herafter followeth the Batayll of Egynecourte, and the Great sege of Rone* . . . John Skot [1530?].

CROMPTON, R. *The Mansion of Magnanimitie; wherein is shewed the acts of sundrie English kings, princes, etc.* For W. Ponsonby. 1599.

LEDUC, V. ed. *Ancien Théâtre Francais*. 10 vols. Paris, 1884.

LINCY, L. DE, et MICHEL, F., *Receuil de Farces, Moralités, et Sermons Joyeux*, 4 vols. Paris, 1837.

OCKLAND, CHRISTOPHER. *Anglorum Praelia. Ab anno Domini 1327 usque ad annum Domini 1558*. R. Neuberie for H. Bynneman. 1580.

SANESI, I. *Commedie del cinquecento*. 2 vols. Bari. 1912.

SMITHE, SIR J. *Instructions, Observations and Orders Militarie* . . . Composed by Sir John Smithe. Richard Johnes. 1595.

TACITUS, C. *The Annales of Cornelius Tacitus. The Description of Germanie*. Translated by Richard Grenewey. A Hatfield for B. and J. Norton. 1598.

WILLIAMS, SIR R. *A Briefe Discourse of Warre. Written by Sir Roger Williams, Knight, With his opinion Concerning some parts of Martiall Discipline* . . . T. Orwin. 1590.

2. Critical Studies of Sources, etc.

BOSWELL-STONE, W. G. *Shakspere's Holinshed. The Chronicle and the Historical Plays Compared.* 1896; 1907.

HARRIES, F. J. *Shakespeare and the Welsh.* 1919.

KABEL, P. *Die Sage von Heinrich V bis zu Shakespeare.* Palaestra lxix. Berlin, 1908.

MOULTON, R. G. 'On character development in Shakespeare illustrated by *Macbeth* and *Henry V*.' *Sh.Soc.Trans.* xxv. 1880–6.

NEWHALL, R. A. 'An Historical Bardolph.' *MLN* xlviii. 1933, 436–7.
NICOLL, A. AND J. *Holinshed's Chronicle as Used in Shakespeare's Plays.* 1927.
RADOFF, M. L. 'The Influence of French Farce in *Henry V* and *The Merry Wives.*' *MLN* xlviii. 1933, 427–35.
STOLL, E. E. 'Henry V', in *Poets and Playwrights.* Minneapolis, 1930.
SYKES, H. D. *The authorship of 'The Taming of A Shrew', 'The Famous Victories', and the additions to Marlowe's 'Faustus'.* 1920.
WALTER, J. H. 'With Sir John in it.' *MLR* xli. July 1946. 237–45.
WARD, B. M. 'The Famous Victories of *Henry V*, its place in Elizabethan Dramatic Literature.' *RES* iv. 1928, 270–94.
WILSON, J. D. 'Martin Marprelate and Shakespeare's Fluellen', in *The Library*, III. 1912.
—— *The Fortunes of Falstaff.* 1943.

Henry VIII

1. Editions of (*a*) the Play, (*b*) Sources and Analogues

(*a*) F1 1623. 'The Life of King Henry the Eight.'
    Modern edns.: D. Nichol Smith, *Warwick*, 1899; C. K. Pooler, *Arden*, 1915; J. M. Berdan and T. Brooke, *Yale*, 1925; R. A. Foakes, *New Arden*, 1957.
(*b*) FOXE, JOHN. *Actes and Monuments of Martyrs* . . . 1583 edn.
    HOLINSHED, R. *The Third volume of Chronicles* . . . 1587 edn.
    [For further details of these see Vol. III. 500–1.]
    CAVENDISH, GEORGE. *The Life of Cardinal Wolsey.* 1641.
        Modern edns.: S. W. Singer, 2 vols. 1827; H. Morley, 1885.
    ROWLEY, SAMUEL. *When you see me, You know me. Or the famous Chronicle Historie of King Henry the eight, with the birth and vertuous life of Edward Prince of Wales. . . .* By Samuell Rowly . . . For Nathaniel Butter, 1605; 1613; 1621; 1632.
        Modern edns.: K. Elze, 1874; F. P. Wilson, *MalSoc*, 1952 (based on 1605). Facsimile of 1613: J. S. Farmer, *Tudor Facsim. Texts*, 1912.

2. Critical Studies of Sources, etc.

ALEXANDER, P. 'Conjectural History, or, Shakespeare's *Henry VIII*', in *Essays and Studies*, xvi, 1930.
BOSWELL-STONE, W. G. *Shakspere's Holinshed, The Chronicle and the Historical Plays Compared.* 1896; 1907.
BOYLE, R. '*Henry VIII*, An Investigation into the Origin and Authorship of the Play'. *Sh.Soc.Trans.* xxi. 1880–6.
CLARK, CUMBERLAND. *A Study of Shakespeare's 'Henry VIII.'* 1931.
CONRAD, H. '*Henry VIII*, Fletchers Werk, überarbeitet von Shakespeare.' *Eng. Studien*, lii, 1918, 204–64.
KNIGHT, G. W. '*Henry VIII* and the Poetry of Conversion', in *The Crown of Life.* 1947.

MAXWELL, B. 'Fletcher and *Henry VIII*', in *Manly Studies*, 1923.

NICHOLSON, M. H. 'The authorship of *Henry VIII*', *PMLA* xxxvii, 1922. 484–502.

NICOLL, A. AND J. *Holinshed's Chronicle as Used in Shakespeare's Plays.* 1927.

SPEDDING, J. 'On the Several Shares of Shakespeare and Fletcher in the Play of *Henry VIII*'. *Sh.Soc.Trans.* 1874, Appendix.

THORNDIKE, A. H. *The Influence of Beaumont and Fletcher on Shakespeare.* Worcester, U.S.A., 1901.

ZEITLIN, W. 'Shakespeares *Henry VIII* und Rowleys *When You See Me*.' *Anglia*, iv. 1881, 73–96.

INDEX TO THE INTRODUCTIONS

531